Oxford Dictionary of

Humorous Quotations

Ned Sherrin CBE was presenter of BBC Radio 4's *Loose Ends*. Producer and director of the ground-breaking 1960s satire TV show *That Was the Week that Was*, and producer of a number of films, including *The Virgin Soldiers* (1968) and *Up Pompeii* (1971), he also wrote extensively for stage and screen. He directed many theatre productions such as *Side by Side by Sondheim* (London 1976 and New York 1977) and *Jeffrey Bernard is Unwell* (1989). He compiled a number of anthologies, including *Cutting Edge* (1984), *Theatrical Anecdotes* (1991), *Ned Sherrin in His Anecdotage* (1993), and *I Wish I'd Said That* (2004). He has also written a novel, *Scratch an Actor* (1995), and his autobiography *Ned Sherrin: The Autobiography* was published in 2005.

Oxford Paperback Reference

The most authoritative and up-to-date reference books for both students and the general reader.

" Oxford Dictionary of
Humorous Quotations

THIRD EDITION

Edited by **Ned Sherrin**

OXFORD
UNIVERSITY PRESS

OXFORD
UNIVERSITY PRESS

Great Clarendon Street, Oxford OX2 6DP

Oxford University Press is a department of the University of Oxford.
It furthers the University's objective of excellence in research, scholarship,
and education by publishing worldwide in

Oxford New York

Auckland Cape Town Dar es Salaam Hong Kong
Karachi Kuala Lumpur Madrid Melbourne Mexico City Nairobi
New Delhi Shanghai Taipei Toronto

With offices in

Argentina Austria Brazil Chile Czech Republic France Greece
Guatemala Hungary Italy Japan Poland Portugal
Singapore South Korea Switzerland Thailand Turkey Ukraine Vietnam

Oxford is a registered trade mark of Oxford University Press
in the UK and in certain other countries

Published in the United States
by Oxford University Press Inc., New York

First edition published 1995
Second edition published 2001
Third edition published 2005
Third edition published in paperback 2007
Third edition published in Oxford Paperback Reference 2008

British Library Cataloguing in Publication Data
Data available

Library of Congress Cataloging-in-Publication Data
Data available

ISBN 978-0-19-923497-4

10 9 8 7 6 5 4 3 2 1

Designed by Jane Stevenson
Typeset by SPI Publisher Services, Pondicherry, India
Printed in Great Britain
by Clays Ltd, St Ives plc

Contents

Project Team

" Preface to Third Edition

A new edition of this dictionary inspires mixed emotions in the editor's breast. There is the business of welcoming new friends and saying farewell to old ones who have already served through two editions. However, some are waved goodbye with relief, while some new entries are welcomed with apprehension. The editor may love his new babies, but can he be sure that they will find favour with his readers?

Take the very first themes, *Acting* and *Actors*. Five of those severe and perhaps too clever verdicts on Shakespearean performances have gone: Agate on Balliol Holloway's Othello, Tynan on Margaret Leighton's Rosalind, Cardus on Forbes Robertson's Hamlet, and Darlington on Richard Briers's Dane. But newly arrived is Tynan on Yvonne Furneaux in *Ondine*, 'A buxom temptress . . . more impressive in silhouette than in action.' (So much more restrained than John Simon on Diana Rigg as a naked Heloïse, 'built like a brick mausoleum with insufficient flying buttresses'.) And plenty of the harsh old excoriations remain, Alan Brien on Michael Hordern's Macbeth, Noel Coward on Anna Neagle's Queen Victoria ('Albert must have married beneath him'), Nancy Banks Smith on John Hannah's Inspector Rebus ('He could also play John Knox, the teenage years'), and Tynan again on Claire Bloom's Virgilia ('she yearns so hungrily that I longed to throw her a fish').

To Ralph Richardson's splendid summing up of acting, 'the art of keeping a large group of people from coughing', we now add Patrick Troughton's even sharper definition, 'Acting is shouting in the evening', and Katharine Hepburn's dismissive, 'Acting is the most minor of gifts and not a very high-class way to earn a living. Shirley Temple could do it at the age of four.' The late Miss Hepburn is backed up by another new (and contemporary) entry from Johnny Depp, 'There's nothing worse than actors who give the impression that they've taken on the priesthood. Acting is really about lying and, in my case, drinking coffee.' Give the last new word to Joanne Woodward, 'Acting is like sex. You should do it, not talk about it.'

An editor required to find the space for well over 600 new quotations and nearly 30 new themes can luxuriate in a sigh of relief when he spots a candidate for rejection. It may have truth, it may be pertinent, it may be strongly expressed—but why did he ever think it was funny? An example, from Osbert Lancaster, 'The aristocracy and landed gentry, although Nationally Entrusted and sadly Thirkellised, are still thank goodness, for all their constant complainings of extinction, visibly and abundantly there.' This reads as well past its sell-by date, and plenty of Osbert Lancaster's wit survives alongside the newcomers.

Alan Bennett is guaranteed to set the armchair on a roar. Now we have room to add up-to-date Bennett from his latest play, *The History Boys*, 'History is a commentary on the various and continuing incapabilities of men. What is history? History is women following behind with the buckets.' And that wonderful mute, inglorious Mrs or Ms Milton who found her anonymous voice when she queued to see the Prime Minister at the Hutton Enquiry: 'I want to see the hand of history on his collar.' Sadly her wish was not granted.

In choosing new quotations we have leaned towards the contemporary across a variety of fields. Nigella Lawson defended toad-in-the-hole to an American audience: 'This is nothing to do with frogs' legs. No amphibian is harmed in making this dish.' On the football field, Liverpool fans serenaded West Ham supporters to the tune of *La Donna e Mobile*, 'You've got DiCanio, We've nicked your stereo.' From *The Simpsons*, Groundskeeper Willie's opinion of the French was a classic cliché, 'Bonjour, you cheese-eating surrender monkeys.' (Woody Allen had a more liberal comment, 'I don't want to have to refer to my French fry potatoes as freedom fries, and I don't want to have to freedom kiss my wife.') According to Christina Onassis's deadly phrase, Teddy Kennedy arrived at her father's funeral, 'Looking like a priestly hustler peddling indulgences.'

Alastair Campbell's unconsciously hilarious, 'We don't do God', when Tony Blair was asked about his faith, jostles with a line from Monty Python's *Life of Brian*, the more artful, 'He's not the Messiah, he's a very naughty boy!' A book published in 2004 (Bevis Hillier's *The Bonus of Laughter*) reminded us, just in time, of John Betjeman's comment when he saw a commemorative stone engraved, 'Laid by the Poet Laureate' and murmured, 'Every nice girl's ambition.'

Few comments are as succinct as Hugh Dyson's protest at the appearance of yet another elf when he was listening to a reading from Tolkien's *The Lord of the Rings* (Mrs Patrick Campbell might have warned that its strength could 'frighten the horses'). And it was high time that the traditional BBC management cry was included, 'Assistant heads must roll!'

A dictionary of quotations can acquaint a phrase-maker with strange bedfellows. How happy would Baden-Powell be to be crammed between the covers alongside Lord Rochester? How shocked would he have been by the latter Lord's account of precisely how he expressed a fit of rage. Imagine Rochester's contempt for Baden-Powell's mistrust of 'men with waxed moustaches'—'It often means vanity and sometimes drink.'

Lord Melbourne is a world away from Miss Janet Jackson, but both find a place: Melbourne with his reasons for not reading *Oliver Twist*, 'It's all among workhouses and Coffin Makers and Pickpockets . . . I wish to avoid them'; Ms Jackson with the excuse for her sartorial comeuppance while duetting with young Mr Timberlake, 'A wardrobe malfunction.' The globetrotting Peter Ustinov, of whom his Army Selection Board reported 'On no account is this man to be put in charge of others' has little in common with the reluctant traveller Philip Larkin, 'I wouldn't mind seeing China if I could come back the same day.'

Three new women contributors are more in sympathy. Barbara Skelton and Elizabeth Arden would probably both sympathize with Lynn Fontanne, mystified by baseball, 'Finally I realized that the gentleman holding the bat is antagonistic to the man throwing the ball.' Fontanne and Arden would understand Skelton's keenly felt disappointment, 'My birthday. No adequate fuss made.' So would the other two appreciate Arden's reaction to the Wall Street Crash, 'Our clients are coping with the stress of financial loss by soaking in a hot bath scented with my Rose Geranium bath crystals.'

From a different generation Johnny Depp is vivid about his two small children, 'It's like hanging out with two miniature drunks.'

But all my choices remain subjective. For anyone who turns the pages with a long face I can only offer my apologies. Let me rather point you to some felicities. To Sydney Smith on Brighton Pavilion, 'As if St Paul's had come down and littered', I have added Keith Waterhouse's exact verdict on the recently elevated city, 'Brighton looks like a town that is constantly helping the police with their enquiries.'

'Regrets, I've had a few . . . ' as that appalling song puts it; but my regrets for the third time are the quotations which came too late into my ken. They repeated the 1980s *Arena* Profile of Mel Brooks with the funny title *I Thought I Was Taller*, to celebrate the opening of *The Producers* at the end of 2004. It reminded me of his line in the earlier interview, 'What's going on? I have meetings with important gentiles.' Jimmy Carr, suddenly a favourite comedian, vouchsafed his favourite joke—black as they get, 'Throwing acid is wrong—in some people's eyes.' Petronella Wyatt, no stranger to romance in Doughty Street herself, summed up the luncheon at which she introduced Mr David Blunkett to Mrs Kimberly Quinn, 'David and I ate Dover sole, Kimberly ate Mr Blunkett.'

Talking of Doughty Street, it was also too late when I remembered Mrs Leo Hunter's immortal poem in *The Pickwick Papers*:

> . . . Can I unmoved see thee dying
> On a log
> Expiring frog!

'Finely expressed' as Mr Pickwick put it. Perhaps we can have it *all* next time.

Sometimes a new quip arrived too late to be subjected to the strict standard of OUP verification. Sitting in the stalls on the first night of the new, stage, musical version of *Mary Poppins*, I joined in the laughter when the boy child describes the Nasty Nanny who had terrified his father a generation earlier, 'She looks like someone who would eat her own young.' Is that a line from one of P. L. Travers's original books (unlikely) or the screenplay of the 1964 film, or did it spring from Julian Fellowes' fertile mind when he worked on the book of the stage show? Then we must enquire if the writer concerned knew of Harry Champion, the great turn-of-the-century music-hall star (sadly neither 'Boiled beef and carrots' nor 'Any old iron' have found a place in the book). Asked about unfriendly audiences in a Glasgow hall he said, 'They eat their own young.'

Perhaps we can resolve it before a 4th edition. There might even be room for, 'This is my Jerry Springer moment!'

NED SHERRIN

January 2005

Preface to Second Edition

This edition of the *Oxford Dictionary of Humorous Quotations*, like its predecessor, attempts to ensure that 'the liveliest effusions of wit and humour are conveyed to the world in the best chosen language' (Jane Austen, *Northanger Abbey*). In pursuit of this aim, over 800 new quotations have been added, some material has (regretfully but firmly) been cut, and over 30 completely new themes (from **Baseball** to **Secrecy**) have been added.

Canvassing readers' opinions confirmed the importance of contemporary resonance, and underlined (as a critic of the first edition pointed out) that we are now so blest with living humorists. Among welcome new arrivals to the *Dictionary* are Dick Vosburgh ('I'm aghast! if there ever was one') and David Mamet ('They say the definition of ambivalence is watching your mother-in-law drive over a cliff in your new Cadillac'). Some older quotations have had to go, but earlier periods still make fresh contributions, as with Lady Mary Wortley Montagu's view of Queen Caroline and her maids-of honour dressed in pink:

> Superior to her waiting nymphs,
> As lobster to attendant shrimps.

Inadvertent humour can also make an insistent claim, as with the rebuke to Zero Mostel when appearing before the House Un-American Activities Committee: 'If your interpretation of a butterfly at rest brought any money into the coffers of the Communist Party, you contributed directly to the propaganda effort of the Communist Party.'

In reviewing another dictionary, the same critic, Mr Bevis Hillier, took issue with the recycling of quotations: 'As a child I would politely decline the gobstopper that three other kids had already sucked.' The problem here is that a dictionary is a reference book, and if its proud purchaser wishing to check a famous quotation dimly recalled goes to his *Humorous Quotations* and does not find it there, he feels short changed. Again, some wiseacres opening the book will discover that a quotation the editor has rejected is absent, and conclude gleefully that ignorance is the explanation. And what if this Mr Know-All has less self-awareness than the character in Edward Albee's *Who's Afraid of Virginia Woolf*: 'I have a fine sense of the ridiculous but no sense of humour'?

Mr Hillier's advice is to 'buy a large hard-backed notebook, read books and newspapers for ten years, writing down the things that make you smile or laugh, then organize them into a book'. This is very much the method I have employed for both these editions, augmenting my own finds from the Oxford University Press's vast store of quotations. Items which I have been pleased to add range from Gore Vidal's response to his novel *Lincoln* being described as 'meretricious' ('Really? Well, meretricious and a happy New Year to you!') to Lord Runcie's comment after appearing on Loose Ends with Diana Rigg in the last months of his life: 'Being hugged by Diana Rigg is worth three sessions of chemotherapy.' Despite the risk of contagion from a second suck at the gobstopper, I have included those quotations which amused me from lists of omissions in reviews: two welcome additions of this kind are Mary Anne Disraeli's assessment of her husband ('I wish you could only see Dizzy in his bath, then you would know what a white skin is') and Else Mendl on her dislike of soup: 'I do not believe in building a meal on a lake.'

It is not only a fisherman who laments the one that got away. One quotation found just too late was Peter Nichols' comment on Harold Hobson's assessment of Tom Stoppard: 'Last time Hobson compared him favourably with Shakespeare. This time he puts him in the scales with God and finds the older man a bit lightweight.' And only as the Dictionary goes to press have I remembered that Arlington Stringham's jokes were filched (on Clovis's evidence) from Lady Isabel, 'who slept in a hammock and understood Yeats's poems'. Eleanor Stringham took an overdose on discovering this. When the story was first published in a Saki collection in 1912, the *New Age* complained, 'Why, oh why, can we see no humour in these stories?' John Lane published the criticism in the midst of universal raves to advertise the book, but the sole voice of dissent reminds us of the eternal problem of humour— its unassailable subjectivity.

Another wonderful item, which also surfaced just too late, was a couplet by H. F. Ellis, quoted by Miles Kington in his *Guardian* obituary of Ellis in December 2000:

> Mine eyes have missed the glory of the coming of the Lord
> Through searching through my pockets where my optic aids are stored . . .

Here I hope to have included 'the Quip Modest, the Reproof Valiant and the Countercheck Quarelsome' in sufficient measure to satisfy the reader. At least the Quips, Reproofs and Counterchecks are offered without analysis. 'Humour can be dissected in the same way a frog can—but the thing dies in the process' (E. B. White).

As a tiny envoi to this preface, here is a story that does not fit the main text. Sir Michael Gambon told me the other day that he had once played Oscar Wilde. A civilian had asked him, 'Was it hard playing a homosexual?'

'Oh, no,' said the great Gambon, whimsically leading him on. 'You see, I used to be one.'

'Why did you stop?'

'It made my eyes water.'

On reflection, I think 'It made my eyes water' might slip into the literature to do duty for a multitude of excuses.

NED SHERRIN

November 2000

Introduction to the First Edition

Wittgenstein claimed that his ambition to write a philosophical work constructed entirely of jokes was frustrated when he realized that he had no sense of humour. The editor of a dictionary of humorous quotations, looking back on his final selection, must wonder how many of his choices will convince the reader that he shares Wittgenstein's disability. For the philosopher there was comfort in the thought that no-one *completely* devoid of a sense of humour would be so aware of his limitations. There is also the suspicion, supported by diligent research, that many jokes are indeed fashioned by people who have no sense of humour.

These reassurances are denied to an editor. He is accountable for deciding that every one of roughly 5,000 quotations in this collection is likely to set the table on a roar. His paranoia is increased by the spectrum of attitudes to humour. 'Humour's a funny thing,' says a character in Terry Johnson's play *Dead Funny*. But an old lady coming out of one of Victoria Wood's shows complained within earshot of the star, 'I don't find humour funny.'

'The joy of simple laughter' is another of Terry Johnson's deftly deployed clichés. Laughter is not invariably joyous and what produces it is rarely simple. I make this disclaimer because I have been encouraged by the publishers to make a more personal selection than the compilers of the fourth edition of the *Oxford Dictionary of Quotations* and the *Oxford Dictionary of Modern Quotations*. These were assembled in the former case by recruiting 'a team of distinguished advisers, united by scholarship in particular literary periods and subject fields' who picked their way through 'the *embarras de richesses*' offered by earlier editions; and in the latter by reducing 'a collection of more than 200,000 citations assembled by combing books, magazines, and newspapers'. Both books are 'an objective selection of quotations which are most widely known and used'.

It is impossible to be objective about humour. Therefore although I have combed both dictionaries because they contain so many quotations which are humorous as well as well-known, I have also sought to admit many which gain entrance not because they are well-known but because they are amusing and deserve our better acquaintance.

Chronologically the spread is from the earliest quotations; but I have justified the inclusion of antique saws solely on the grounds that they raise a smile today. Paul Johnson recently suggested in the *Spectator* that the first recorded laughter occurred at the end of the Early Bronze Age, about 2000 BC:

> Significantly it was a woman who laughed. The Book of Genesis tells us (xviii. 10 ff.) that, when Sarah overheard the Lord inform her husband Abraham she was to have a son, 'Sarah laughed within herself, saying, after I am waxed old shall I have pleasure, my lord being old also?'

Johnson's conclusion is that the first joke was female and was about sex. Sarah tried to keep it to herself; but the men accused her of laughing. She denied it, 'for she was afraid'. It may have seemed a good joke to Sarah in 2000 BC but that does not justify its inclusion today. On the other hand some 3,600 years later, Shakespeare's stage direction 'Exit, pursued by a bear' in *The Winter's Tale*, now a mellow 400 years old, still makes me smile—whether he intended it or not. However, there is no room for all the smiles in Shakespeare. I mourn the passing of 'Nay, faith, let me not play a woman: I have a beard coming,' from the *Dream*, which is warm, funny, and well observed; however, it is preserved in the *Oxford Dictionary of Quotations*.

I have not thought it necessary to reopen the ever-raging debate fought over the boundaries between wit and humour. In introducing his *Anthology of Wit*, Guy Boas derives humour from the supposition that human nature was once held to be determined by the physical 'humours' and fluids which make up the body. Imbalance of these fluids produces (as in Ben Jonson's plays) conduct which was freakish, absurd, or whimsical—provoking laughter at the recognizably humorous situation. The word 'wit', however, stems from the Old English *witan* to know, which lent itself flatteringly to the Anglo-Saxon approximation to Parliament, and implied optimistically the exercise there of the intellect. So wit is associated with the mind's contribution to what is amusing. 'Humour', to Boas, 'is the funny situation or object; wit is the fun which a particular mind subjectively perceives on the situation or object.' There is room in this book for both. So what were the criteria for the quotations which survive?

No such book can afford to ignore perennials like Wilde, Mencken, Coward, Parker, Kaufman, and Shaw; Johnny Speight, the creator of *Till Death Do Us Part* (and therefore, in America, of *All in the Family*) grew up reading collections of quotations and concluded that Bernard Shaw was a gag-writer, which fuelled his own ambitions in the field of comedy. Among phrase-makers in recent years Gore Vidal, Tom Stoppard, Alan Bennett, Russell Baker, P. J. O'Rourke, Stephen Fry, and Craig Brown demand inclusion as new hardy annuals. Some writers are consistently witty, some have a happy inspiration. The former earn more entries than the latter. I did not consider it useful to operate a quota system.

The unintentionally humorous can be as diverting and must also be found a place. With its 'Colemanballs' feature *Private Eye* magazine spotlighted for our superior pleasure the pressure under which sports commentators try and sometimes fail to find the right word—though who can be sure whether 'the batsman's Holding, the bowler's Willey' was Brian Johnston's accidental comment or the result of a confrontation for which he had long been lying in wait. In America there is the famous Phil Rizzuto remark when his commentary was interrupted by the news of the Pope's death: 'that puts a damper, even on a Yankee win.' Dan Quayle and George Bush are modern political stars on the unconscious humour circuit. It is hard to do better than Quayle's alleged hesitation on visiting Latin America, 'not having studied Latin', or his insistence on the 'e' at the end of 'potato'.

Political correctness throws up a shoal of examples of unconscious humour, some of which have found a place. I might have found room for excerpts from the reported BBC *Woman's Hour* directive to new presenters in the early 1990s:

> 3. Do not be surprised that a woman has achieved something . . . 4. Do not be surprised that an older person has achieved something . . . 5. Do not be surprised that a black person has achieved something . . .

but there is a leaden mind behind that directive which does not deserve to be included.

The pronouncements of censors are another rich vein of unconscious humour. In the 1920s Nina Shortt, a daughter of a film censor and ex-Home Secretary, Sir Edward Shortt, refused a certificate to Jean Cocteau's avant-garde movie *The Seashell and the Clergyman*:

> [This film] is so cryptic as to be almost meaningless. If there is a meaning, it is doubtless objectionable.

Lord Tyrell, who succeeded Shortt, went one better in 1937:

> We take pride in observing that there is not a single film showing in London today that deals with any of the burning issues of the hour.

The sublimely named Major de Fonblanque Cox combined censorship with dogbreeding. On his appointment he declared:

> No, my boy, let us show clean films in the old country! I shall judge film stories as I would horseflesh, or a dog. I shall look for clean lines everywhere.

There may be less art in this than in the words which the Grossmiths put into Mr Pooter's mouth, 'I left the room with silent dignity but caught my foot in the mat,' but there is no less humour.

Another *Private Eye* feature, 'Pseud's Corner', is based on yet another sort of unconscious humour. I do not think Professor Karl Miller's verdict on the footballer Paul Gascoigne for *The London Review of Books* found its way there, but it deserved to:

> He was a highly charged spectacle on the field of play: fierce and comic, formidable and vulnerable, urchin-like and waiflike, a strong head and torso with comparatively breakable legs, strange-eyed, pink-faced, fair-haired, tense and upright, a priapic monolith in the Mediterranean sun . . . he is magic, and fairy-tale magic at that.

Of them all, the late Lord Massereene and Ferrard emerges as a new star provider of unintentional amusement, recommending the warning notice, 'Beware of the Agapanthus'.

Quotations are taken from novels, plays, poems, essays, letters, speeches, films, radio and television broadcasts, songs, popular jokes, graffiti, and advertisements, accurately attributed where possible. Some have had to fall by the wayside for reasons for space, or because I could not legitimize them. Under the firm but patient guidance of the Dictionary Department at Oxford University Press, I have endeavoured to help their devoted detectives to verify the quotations chosen in original or authoritative sources.

I have found space for some of the best-known catchphrases which have sprung from radio or television programmes, but sources are so prolific that a general anthology can only hint at the richness—from the inventive conceits of Frank Muir and Denis Norden in *Take It From Here* to the anachronistic whimsies of Ben Elton and Richard Curtis in *Blackadder*. In *Take It From Here* the puns were elaborate, the plotting devious:

> [SILAS THE PURITAN] Thou art spending all the royal coffers on this female person [Nell Gwynne]. But yesterday you sold the Crown Jewels . . . to buy her a sedan chair with a sunshine roof!
> [KING CHARLES II] So I blued a couple of baubles? 'Tis of no account.
> [SILAS] (reproachfully) But you're forever blueing baubles.

In *Blackadder* the humour is starker:

> The Germans are a cruel race. Their operas last for six hours and they have no word for fluffy.

Some catchphrases demand to be included, such as the Chief Whip's notorious response in Michael Dobbs' *House of Cards*:

> You might very well think that. I couldn't possibly comment.

Formula jokes are also generally too plentiful and often too unfunny to earn a place—sick jokes, light-bulb jokes, elephant jokes, and drummer jokes are excluded. I have also resisted the temptation to follow a 1994 trend with the latest fashionable American joke craze, 'Doing the Dozens', allegedly a venerable Afro-American habit of trading insults—preferably about the opponent's mother. For example, 'Your mother is so ugly, when she walks into the bank they turn off the camera,' or 'Your mother is so dumb, she went to the movies and the sign said, "Under 17 not admitted", so she came back with 18 friends.' 'Doing the Dozens' can wait for the slim paperback volume in which these ripostes will doubtless one day be collected by another publisher.

At the moment when I identified a mass-multiplying reproach 'like turkeys voting for Christmas', a scholarly commentator in the *Independent Magazine* traced the birth of this death-wish simile to the late David Penhaligon who used it to highlight his distaste for the British Lib-Lab pact (1977–8). For Penhaligon it emphasized the Prime Minister's (James Callaghan's) certainty that the Liberals would never vote to bring him down. Callaghan himself plundered it the next year to slight the weak position of Scottish Nationalists. It crossed the Irish Sea when a Fianna Fáil member of the Dáil said that, 'a woman voting for divorce is like turkeys . . .' Both the Bruges Group of Conservative MPs and Michael Heseltine rented the phrase for their own ends in 1991. Paddy Ashdown, the leader of Penhaligon's old party, grabbed it to pour scorn on rebel Tories during the Maastricht debate. The Tory Party, he said, would not be defeated by its place-preserving backbenchers. For them to bring the Government down, 'would be like turkeys . . .' he said, 'etc.' The apotheosis of this witfest came when the French awarded a special 'foreign political humour prize' to the British MP Teresa Gorman for trotting out the same rubric, once again in the context of Maastricht. If anyone deserves to accept the prize it is the Widow Penhaligon.

Topicality admitted the inclusion of a borderline case, a version of another cliché-ridden humorous quip which is custom-made for hand-me-down insults. John Major was not being witty or original when he called some of his backbenchers 'a few apples short of a picnic', but the phrase caught the public fancy. I can't remember whether the ex-chairman of Test Selectors, Ted Dexter, said of someone or was described by someone as being, 'a few roos loose in the top paddock'. 'One brick short of a load' and 'One slice short of a sandwich' are in the same vein: but none of them earns inclusion. Victor Lewis-Smith, describing Lord Rees-Mogg as 'two coupons short of a pop-up toaster', gets nearer with a vivid variation but is still disqualified by the curse of formula. Had he been Prime Minister he might have made it.

The files of the OUP Dictionary Department have inevitably provided a mass of material, all providentially sourced. Sadly many of the contributions derived from my own serendipitizing were lodged solely in the mind which failed to remember where I had found them. However, perhaps I should have let stand more of those remarks at whose birth I was present. One example is Anthony Quinton's impromptu comment as solemn music flooded a BBC studio when we were taken off the air for a news bulletin during the Falklands War. 'I know that tune,' he said, 'it's Sibelius' "You Can't Win 'Em All".' I can't think of a better authority.

In culling the new material the decision to organize the book thematically and not to arrange quotations under author headings was often revealing. In the section on **Wealth**, for example, some fun is to be had by the witty at the expense of the wealthy; but I relish the petulant note that invades the voices of the rich from Lord Durham (who in the nineteenth century was known as 'King Jog' because he could 'jog along' on £40,000 a year) through Lord Northcliffe (who said that when he wanted a peerage he would 'buy it like an honest man') and Chips Channon (who found it difficult in 1934 to go out shopping and spend less than £200) to Alan Clark (moaning in his diary in 1987 of the £700,000 in his Abbey National Crazy-High-Interest account, 'but what's the use?'). Sadly I could not confirm the Duke of Marlborough's bleat when urged to sack one of his many Viennese pastry-cooks, 'May not a man have a biscuit?'

Looking at other collections, I was frustrated by innumerable headings which yield very few quotations. Here we have a total of 149 classifications, some of which represent the combination of related headings. For example, **Truth** is linked with **Lies** rather than sitting unhappily in separate beds, while on the other hand the stage is such a productive source that I have separated **Actors and Acting** from **The Theatre**. Appropriate cross-reference entries are supplied, and keyword and author indexes further facilitate the chasing of references. (For a more detailed account, see 'How to Use the Dictionary'.)

I have introduced a large number of quotations from popular songs—so much wit is crammed into the discipline which a lyric writer observes. My selection cannot be comprehensive but it aims to point the road to a Samarkand of riches. Which do you choose from a Sondheim lyric? Look at 'Now', a song from *A Little Night Music*, in which a literary-minded middle-aged husband is trying to decide which gem will turn on his reluctant young wife. I sacrificed:

> The Brontes are grander
> But not very gay.
> Her taste is much blander
> I'm sorry to say,
> But is Hans Christian Ander-
> sen ever risqué?

in favour of:

> And Stendhal would ruin
> The plan of attack,
> As there isn't much blue in
> *The Red and the Black.*

But the whole score is laced with wit.

To backtrack, I was tempted to include the current Professor of Poetry at Oxford's review of Sondheim's *Sweeney Todd* in the *Sunday Times*, 'the worst rhymes in London', along with Dan Quayle's contributions to unconscious humour; but it got away. Coward, Porter, and Hart are dinosaurs in the field but other British and American lyric writers from E. Y. Harburg to Raymond Douglas Davis (The Kinks) deserve a more detailed examination than this book can afford. I hope enough creeps in to point the reader in the right direction.

Songs are easy to source, but an arrangement in themes prompted all sorts of quotations that dance tantalizingly in my magpie memory and have eluded our keenest detectives. Some of recollection's children I cannot legitimize. Some I have had to omit for others more favoured. Here are some of those I mourn:

Lord Thorneycroft's reply to Lord Houghton's letter, 'outlining his massive campaign to put animals into politics':

> Dear Douglas, Thank you for your letter about animals. I do think that the poor creatures have enough to put up with without being put into politics. Yours sincerely . . .

Nietzsche and Michael Frayn on books:

> Books for general reading always smell badly. The odour of the common people hangs about them. (Nietzsche)

> There is something about a blurb-writer paying his respects to a funny book which puts one in mind of a short-sighted Lord Mayor raising his hat to a hippopotamus. (Frayn)

Robert Altman on children:

> If you have a child who is seven feet tall, you don't cut off his head or his legs. You buy him a bigger bed and hope he plays basketball.

Evelyn Waugh on class:

> No writer before the middle of the nineteenth century wrote about the working-class other than as grotesques or as pastoral decorations. Then when they were given the vote, certain writers started to suck up to them.

Ronald Firbank on the country:

> I'd like to spank the white walls of (that shepherd's) cottage.

Antonia Fraser on death:

> Once there was a Drag Hunt Ball, just outside Oxford, to which I had unaccountably failed to be asked. I asked God to do something about it, and God recklessly killed poor King George, as a result of which the Hunt Ball was cancelled.

Mickey Rose on dress-sense:

> Nobody would wear beige to rob a bank.

Lord Rosebery's advice to Queen Victoria:

> There is much exaggeration about the attainments required for a speaker. All Speakers are highly successful, all Speakers are deeply regretted, and are generally announced to be irreplaceable. But a Speaker is soon found, and found, almost invariably, among the mediocrities of the House.

Bernard Levin on Barbara Cartland's grasp of history:

> Miss Cartland insists that Earl Mountbatten helped her with the writing . . . All that expert help, however, has still not managed to correct her apparent belief that Trafalgar came very shortly after Waterloo; perhaps she has confused English history with the London Underground system.

Lily Tomlin on love:

> If love is the answer, could you rephrase the question?

Chekhov on marriage:

> If you're afraid of loneliness, don't marry.

Carl Sandburg on murder:

> Papa loved Mamma
> Mamma loved men
> Mamma's in the graveyard
> Papa's in the pen.

Thomas Beecham on a fellow-musician:

> Sir Adrian Boult came to see me this morning—positively reeking of Horlicks.

J. G. Saxe on the newspaper world:

> Who would not be an Editor? To write
> The magic 'we' of such enormous might.
> To be so great beyond the common span
> It takes the plural to express the Man.

Senator Wyche Fowler on being asked whether, in 'those permissive sixties', he had smoked a marijuana cigarette:

> Only when committing adultery.

Norman Douglas on Suffolk:

> Land of uncomfortable beds, brown sherry, and Perpendicular Gothic.

The Duke of Devonshire on President Nasser and Anthony Eden:

> The camel that broke the straw's back.

P. G. Wodehouse's Sir Roderick Glossop on religion:

> A lay interest in matters to do with liturgical procedure is invariably a prelude to insanity.

Horace Walpole on Queen Charlotte in her later years:

> I do think the *bloom* of her ugliness is going off.

The Prince of Conti, a noted rake, when he at last became aware of his failing sexual prowess:

> It is time for me to retire. Formerly my civilities were taken for declarations of love. Now my declarations of love are taken for civilities.

W. G. Grace, apologizing for his bad fielding in old age:

> It's the ground. It's too far away.

The President of Cornell University on a proposed sporting fixture:

> I shall not permit thirty men to travel four hundred miles (to Michigan) to agitate a ball of wind.

William Faulkner on Henry James:

> One of the nicest old ladies I ever met.

Edith Sitwell and Herman Mankiewicz on modern writers:

> A lot of people writing poetry today would be better employed keeping rabbits. (Sitwell)
>
> 'Tell me, do you know any 75 dollar-a-week writers?'
> 'Yes, I know lots of them. But they're all making 1500 dollars a week.' (Mankiewicz)

I found one aspect of the arrangement of previous dictionaries unsympathetic to humorous quotations. It has been customary to print the quote and follow it with the contextual explanation. This is often like giving the punchline of a joke and then adding the premise. Where appropriate I have put the explanation first, for example this quotation from Thomas Gainsborough:

> *On attempting to paint two actors, David Garrick and Samuel Foote:*
> Rot them for a couple of rogues, they have everybody's faces but their own.

The learned editor of the *Oxford Dictionary of Quotations* has wisely written, 'Ideally, a quotation should be able to float free from its moorings, remaining detached from its original context.' However, one could compare two extracts from a page opened at random in the fourth edition; while the Wolcott Gibbs quote 'Backward ran sentences until reeled the mind' is arresting enough to stand with the subsequent note ('satirizing the style of *Time* magazine'), André Gide's sigh, '*Hugo—hélas!*' would read more entertainingly if the explanation, 'When asked who was the greatest 19th-century poet' preceded it.

I have tried to resist the temptation to admit anecdote where quotation is the brief. Lord Albemarle might have found a place in the unconscious humour section, but the preamble to his striking sentence is too long and involved:

> *The dancer Maude Allen had been accused of lesbianism in an article entitled 'The Cult of the Clitoris', and Miss Allen sued for libel in a much publicized lawsuit which caught the puzzled attention of Lord Albemarle, who complained:*
> I've never heard of this Greek chap Clitoris they're talking about.

However vivid the phrase may be its context is overpoweringly anecdotal. While Lord Macaulay's riposte, aged four, having had hot coffee spilt over his legs, 'Thank you, Madam, the agony is abated,' is a splendid quote preceded to its advantage by a succinct explanation.

I hope that this collection gathers together a vast number of old friends whom it would be disloyal to exclude—conscious that they will still surprise some. I am often astonished at the way an audience can pounce on an over-familiar quip by Coward or Wilde and welcome it as new-minted. It proved particularly enjoyable to hunt for less well-known quotations from established wits. Noël Coward's chestnuts are included, but also his vivid vignette (in spite of Lord Byron's warning, 'Damn description, it is always disgusting'):

> Edith Sitwell, in that great Risorgimento cape of hers, looks as though she were covering a teapot or a telephone.

Less familiar Oscar Wilde contributions include his admonishment to a waiter:

> When I ask for a watercress sandwich, I do not mean a loaf with a field in the middle of it;

his judgement on publishers:

> I suppose all publishers are untrustworthy. They certainly always look it;

and his request to his examiners in his viva at Oxford when he was asked to stop his brilliant translation of the Greek version of the New Testament:

> Oh, do let me go on, I want to see how it ends.

Sydney Smith is sharp on the incongruity of oratorio, 'How absurd to see 500 people fiddling like madmen about Israelites in the Red Sea,' and playful on two Edinburgh women hurling insults at one another across and alleyway, 'Those two women will never agree; they are arguing from different premises.' There is

Whistler on the picture of his mother, 'Yes, one does like to make one's mummy just as nice as possible', and Gore Vidal on ex-President Eisenhower, 'reading a speech with his usual sense of discovery'.

Among the modern phrase-makers I enjoy Jonathan Lynn and Antony Jay in *Yes Minister*:

> I think it will be a clash between the political will and the administrative won't.

Richard Curtis and Ben Elton in *Blackadder*:

> To you, Baldrick, the Renaissance was just something that happened to other people, wasn't it?

Keith Waterhouse in his play *Bookends*:

> Should not the Society of Indexers be known as Indexers, Society of, The?

Joseph O'Connor in his novel *Cowboys and Indians*:

> Buckingham Palace looked like a vast doll's house that some bullying skinhead brother had kicked down the Mall.

Clive James writes of John McEnroe that he 'did his complete Krakatoa number', and John Osborne says of his American producer David Merrick that he 'liked writers in the way a snake likes live rabbits'.

Unlikely candidates include: Lord Tennyson's brother, introducing himself to Dante Gabriel Rossetti:

> I am Septimus, the most morbid of the Tennysons.

Rupert Murdoch, asked to explain Page 3:

> I don't know. The editor did it while I was away.

T. E. Lawrence on reading *Lady Chatterley's Lover*:

> Surely the sex business isn't worth all this damned fuss? I've met only a handful of people who cared a biscuit for it.

Samuel Beckett encouraging an actor who lamented, 'I'm failing':

> Go on failing. Only next time, try to fail better.

C. S. Lewis on desire:

> He that but looketh on a plate of ham and eggs to lust after it, hath already committed breakfast with it in his heart.

There are some new Royal quotes, often falling into the category of unconscious humour. 'Aren't we due a royalty statement?' (Charles, Prince of Wales), 'I know no person so perfectly disagreeable and even dangerous as an author' (William IV), and George V, asked which film he would like to see while convalescing, 'Anything except that damned Mouse,' which makes a change from 'Bugger Bognor.' Furthermore, I have tried to add to the files of the OUP some quotations which are less familiar. This has meant casting a wider net over, for instance, North American sources, and again I have tried to balance the quotations which demand inclusion on account of the fame of their authors—Dorothy Parker, Robert Benchley, Mark Twain, Sam Goldwyn, and S. J. Perelman ('God, whom you doubtless remember as that quaint old subordinate of General Douglas MacArthur'), with the words of modern masters. I have taken pleasure in adding:

Mary McGrory on Watergate:

> Haldeman is the only man in America in this generation who let his hair grow for a courtroom appearance.

P. J. O'Rourke on certainty:

> That happy sense of purpose people have when they are standing up for a principle they haven't really been knocked down for yet.

Bill Bryson on childhood:

> I had always thought that once you grew up you could do anything you wanted—stay up all night or eat ice-cream straight out of the container.

The film critic James Agee on *Tycoon*:

> Several tons of dynamite are set off in this picture: none of it under the right people.

Jackie Mason on the English:

> If an Englishman gets run down by a truck he apologizes to the truck.

Woody Allen, Neil Simon, Fran Lebowitz, and Russell Baker appear *passim*, and for a British angle on America, Anthony Burgess supplies, 'the US Presidency is a Tudor monarchy with telephones.' George Bush ('What's wrong with being a boring kind of guy?') and Dan Quayle supply generous helpings of unconscious humour, such as 'Space is almost infinite. As a matter of fact, we think it is infinite' (Quayle), and are convenient targets, as in 'Poor George [Bush], he can't help it— he was born with a silver foot in his mouth' (Ann Richards). Sports writers like Jimmy Cannon are rewarding on their own craft, 'Let's face it, sports writers, we're not hanging around with brain surgeons'; so, sometimes, can sportsmen be, 'If people don't want to come out to the ball park, nobody's going to stop 'em' (Yogi Berra). Canada supplies both the unconscious humour of Brian Mulroney's 'I am not denying anything I did not say,' and, at the other extreme, Robertson Davies:

> I see Canada as a country torn between a very northern, rather extraordinary, mystical spirit which it fears and its desire to present itself to the world as a Scotch banker.

Australia under Paul Keating has been developing a rich vein of humorous invective like the exchange between the Prime Minister and his opponent John Hewson. Keating's comment:

> [John Hewson] is simply a shiver looking for a spine to run up,

is countered by Hewson with:

> I decided the worst thing you could call Paul Keating, quite frankly, is Paul Keating.

Reflecting on the insularity of his homeland, Clive James has written:

> A broad school of Australian writing has based itself on the assumption that Australia not only has a history worth bothering about, but that all the history worth bothering about happened in Australia.

To verify this range of information would not have been possible without the diligent and imaginative work of the Oxford Dictionary Department researchers. However, the responsibility for the taste and the accuracy must be mine, the only caveat being Simon Strunsky's 'Famous remarks are very seldom quoted correctly.' Above all it is my sense of humour which conditions the final choice and my regret

if your favourite humorous quotation is not recorded here or if you pass too many
entries without amusement.

NED SHERRIN

August 1994

How to Use the Dictionary

The *Oxford Dictionary of Humorous Quotations* is organized by themes, such as **Actors, The Family, Food, Love, Travel and Exploration, The Weather,** and **Writing**. The themes are placed in alphabetical order, and within each theme the quotations are arranged alphabetically according to author.

The themes have been chosen to reflect as wide a range of subjects as possible. Themes such as **Death, Life,** and **Success** emphasize the general rather than the particular, but categories such as **Description, Last Words, People and Personalities,** and **Towns and Cities** have a wider coverage of quotations relevant to specific people, places, and events.

Related topics may be covered by a single theme, such as **Nature and the Environment** and **Sleep and Dreams**, and linked opposites may also be grouped in a single antithetical theme, such as **Heaven and Hell** and **Trust and Treachery**. A cross-reference from the second element of the pair appears in the appropriate place in the alphabetic sequence both in the main text and in the List of Themes.

Where themes are closely related, 'See also' references are given at the head of a scetion, immediately following the theme title and preceding the quotations. The heading **The Family** is thus followed by See also **Children, Parents**.

Each quotation has a marginal note giving the name of the author to whom the quotation is attributed; dates of birth and death (where known) are given. In general, the authors' names are given in the form by which they are best known, so that we have **Saki** rather than 'H. H. Munro'. If the authorship is unknown, 'Anonymous' appears.

A source note, usually including the specific date of the quotation, follows the author information. Quotations which are in general currency but which are not at present traceable to a specific source are indicated by 'attributed' in the source note; quotations which are popularly attributed to an author but whose authenticity is doubted are indicated by a note such as 'perhaps apocryphal'. Contextual information regarded as essential to a full appreciation of the quotation precedes the relevant text in an italicized note; information seen as providing helpful amplification follows in an italicized note.

Allocation of a quotation to an individual theme is inevitably subjective, but the keyword index makes provision for tracing specific items other than by theme titles. Citations by named authors may similarly be traced via the author index. In each case, references show the theme name, sometimes in a shortened form (**Satisfaction** for **Satisfaction and Discontent; Theatre** for **The Theatre**), followed by the number of the quotation within the theme: '**Travel** 7' therefore means the seventh quotation within the theme **Travel and Exploration**.

List of Themes

Quotations

Acting ····➤ Actors, The Theatre

66 There's no business like show business. 99
Irving Berlin

1 This Iago was obviously an intellectual, and refreshingly
unlike the usual furtive dog-stealer who would not impose
upon the most trustful old lady, not to mention an
experienced man of affairs like Othello.
of Neil Porter's Iago in 1927

James Agate 1877–1947: *Brief Chronicles* (1943)

2 *supposed advice to a young actor:*
Try and look as if you had a younger brother in
Shropshire.

J. M. Barrie 1860–1937: Lady Cynthia Asquith diary, 6 January 1918

3 One day they may tell you you will not go far,
That night you open and there you are.
Next day on your dressing room
They hang a star!
Let's go on with the show!

Irving Berlin 1888–1989: 'There's No Business Like Show Business' (1946)

4 *Shakespeare is trying to make a start on Love's Labour Won,
but Burbage interrupts him:*
'I've been thinking,' he said, 'I'd like to play a Dane—
young, intellectual—I see him pale, vacillating, but above
everything sad and prone to soliloquy.' 'I know,' said
Shakespeare. 'Introspective.'

Caryl Brahms 1901–82 and **S. J. Simon** 1904–48: *No Bed for Bacon* (1941)

5 This Thane of Cawdor would be unnerved by Banquo's
valet, never mind Banquo's ghost.
of Michael Hordern in Macbeth in 1959

Alan Brien 1925– : Diana Rigg *No Turn Unstoned* (1982)

6 When I read 'Be real, don't get caught acting,' I thought,
'How the hell do you do that?'

Billy Connolly 1942– : John Miller *Judi Dench: With a Crack in Her Voice* (1998)

7 Don't put your daughter on the stage, Mrs Worthington,
Don't put your daughter on the stage,
One look at her bandy legs should prove
She hasn't got a chance,
In addition to which
The son of a bitch
Can neither sing nor dance.

Noël Coward 1899–1973: 'Mrs Worthington' (1935)

8 CLAUDETTE COLBERT: I knew these lines backwards last
night.
NOËL COWARD: And that's just the way you're saying them
this morning.

Noël Coward 1899–1973: Cole Lesley *The Life of Noel Coward* (1976)

9 Anna Neagle playing Queen Victoria always made me
think that Albert must have married beneath him.

Noël Coward 1899–1973: Sheridan Morley *The Quotable Noël Coward* (1999)

10 There's nothing worse than actors who give the
impression that they've taken on the priesthood. Acting is
really about lying and, in my case, drinking coffee.

Johnny Depp 1963– : in *Radio Times* 18 May 2002

11 She's the only sylph I ever saw, who could stand upon one leg, and play the tambourine on her other knee, like a sylph.

Charles Dickens 1812–70: *Nicholas Nickleby* (1839)

12 I found out that acting was hell. You spend all your time trying to do what they put people in asylums for.

Jane Fonda 1937– : attributed; J. R. Colombo *Wit and Wisdom of the Moviemakers* (1979)

13 *when asked to say something terrifying during rehearsals for Peter Brook's* Oedipus *in 1968:*
We open in two weeks.

John Gielgud 1904–2000: Peter Hay *Theatrical Anecdotes* (1987)

14 I made a great hit in *Macbeth* as the messenger because I took the precaution of running three times round the playground before I made my entrance so that I could deliver the news in a state of exhaustion.
on a school production

Alec Guinness 1914–2000: John Mortimer *Character Parts* (1986)

15 I acted so tragic the house rose like magic,
The audience yelled 'You're sublime.'
They made me a present of Mornington Crescent
They threw it a brick at a time.

W. F. Hargreaves 1846–1919: 'The Night I Appeared as Macbeth' (1922)

16 Acting is the most minor of gifts and not a very high-class way to earn a living. Shirley Temple could do it at the age of four.

Katharine Hepburn 1907–2003: attributed; Nigel Rees *Cassell's Movie Quotations* (2000)

17 If your interpretation of a butterfly at rest brought any money into the coffers of the Communist Party, you contributed directly to the propaganda effort of the Communist Party.
to Zero Mostel, appearing before the House Un-American Activities Committee (HUAC)

Donald L. Jackson: at a hearing of HUAC, 14 October 1955

18 Shakespeare is so tiring. You never get a chance to sit down unless you're a king.

George S. Kaufman 1889–1961 and **Howard Teichmann** 1916–87: *The Solid Gold Cadillac* (1953); spoken by Josephine Hull

19 *watching Spencer Tracy on the set of* Dr Jekyll and Mr Hyde *(1941):*
Which is he playing now?

W. Somerset Maugham 1874–1965: attributed; Leslie Halliwell *The Filmgoer's Book of Quotes* (1978 edn)

20 When you do Shakespeare they think you must be intelligent because they *think* you understand what you're saying.

Helen Mirren 1945– : interviewed on *Ruby Wax Meets . . .* ; in *Mail on Sunday* 16 February 1997 'Night and Day'

21 The only thing wrong with performing was that you couldn't phone it in.

Robert Mitchum 1917–97: attributed; in *Sunday Times* (Magazine section) 11 May 1980

22 I used to work for a living, then I became an actor.

Roger Moore 1927– : in *Independent* 1 July 1989

23 *on the part of Lear:*
When you've the strength for it, you're too young; when you've the age you're too old. It's a bugger, isn't it?

Laurence Olivier 1907–89: in *Sunday Telegraph* 4 May 1986

24 But I have a go, lady, don't I? I 'ave a go. I do.

John Osborne 1929– : *The Entertainer* (1957)

25 Let me know where you are next week! I'll come and see you.

John Osborne 1929– : *The Entertainer* (1957); last lines

26 The difference between being a director and being an actor is the difference between being the carpenter banging the nails into the wood, and being the piece of wood the nails are being banged into.

Sean Penn 1960– : in *Guardian* 28 November 1991

27 Acting is merely the art of keeping a large group of people from coughing.

Ralph Richardson 1902–83: in *New York Herald Tribune* 19 May 1946

28 I don't care for Lady Macbeth in the streetwalking scene.

Edward Linley Sambourne 1844–1910: R. G. C. Price *A History of Punch* (1957)

29 The best actors in the world, either for tragedy, comedy, history, pastoral, pastoral-comical, historical-pastoral, tragical-historical, tragical-comical-historical-pastoral, scene individable, or poem unlimited.

William Shakespeare 1564–1616: *Hamlet* (1601)

30 I could play Ercles rarely, or a part to tear a cat in, to make all split.

William Shakespeare 1564–1616: *A Midsummer Night's Dream* (1595–6)

31 I wish sir, you would practise this without me. I can't stay dying here all night.

Richard Brinsley Sheridan 1751–1816: *The Critic* (1779)

32 I told Mad Frankie Fraser 'I'm doing Hamlet'—he said, 'I'll do him for you.'

Arthur Smith 1954– : *Arthur Smith's Hamlet*

33 *to an over-genteel actress in an Egyptian drama:*
Oh my God! Remember you're in Egypt. The *skay* is only seen in Kensington.

Herbert Beerbohm Tree 1852–1917: M. Peters *Mrs Pat* (1984)

34 *to a motley collection of American females, assembled to play ladies-in-waiting to a queen:*
Ladies, just a little more virginity, if you don't mind.

Herbert Beerbohm Tree 1852–1917: Alexander Woollcott *Shouts and Murmurs* (1923)

35 *definition of acting:*
Shouting in the evenings.

Patrick Troughton 1920–87: recalled as heard in a radio interview; Michael Simkins *What's My Motivation?* (2004)

36 Talk low, talk slow, and don't say much.

John Wayne 1907–79: attributed

37 Acting is like sex. You should do it, not talk about it.

Joanne Woodward 1930– : attributed, 1987; in Nigel Rees *Cassell's Movie Quotations* (2000)

Actors ····▶ Film Stars

❝ Bad as the play was, her acting was worse. ❞
George Bernard Shaw

1 John Hannah has the high cheekbones and low spirits for Inspector Rebus, a man under a cloud. He could also play John Knox, the teenage years.

Nancy Banks-Smith: in *Guardian* 27 April 2000

2 For an actress to be a success, she must have the face of a Venus, the brains of a Minerva, the grace of Terpsichore, the memory of a Macaulay, the figure of Juno, and the hide of a rhinoceros.

Ethel Barrymore 1879–1959: George Jean Nathan *The Theatre in the Fifties* (1953)

3 My only regret in the theatre is that I could never sit out front and watch me.

John Barrymore 1882–1942: Eddie Cantor *The Way I See It* (1959)

4 Every actor has a natural animosity towards every other actor, present or absent, living or dead.

Louise Brooks 1906–85: *Lulu in Hollywood* (1982)

5 Tallulah Bankhead barged down the Nile last night as Cleopatra—and sank.

John Mason Brown 1900–69: in *New York Post* 11 November 1937

6 Like acting with 210 pounds of condemned veal.
   of a dull actor

Coral Browne 1913–91: attributed

7 Like a rat up a rope.
   of an over-busy actor

Coral Browne 1913–91: attributed

8 Tallulah [Bankhead] is always skating on thin ice. Everyone wants to be there when it breaks.

Mrs Patrick Campbell 1865–1940: in *The Times* 13 December 1968

9 I'm out of a job. London wants flappers, and I can't flap.
   of the theatre of 1927

Mrs Patrick Campbell 1865–1940: Margot Peters *Mrs Pat* (1984)

10 She's such a nice woman. If you knew her you'd even admire her acting.
   of another actress

Mrs Patrick Campbell 1865–1940: James Agate diary, 6 May 1937

11 *the daughter of Sybil Thorndike and Lewis Casson explaining to a telephone enquiry why neither of her charitably inclined parents was at home:*
   Daddy is reading Shakespeare Sonnets to the blind and Mummy's playing Shakespeare to the lepers.

Anne Casson: recounted by Emlyn Williams; James Harding *Emlyn Williams* (1987)

12 She [Edith Evans] took her curtain calls as though she had just been un-nailed from the cross.

Noël Coward 1899–1973: diary, 25 October 1964

13 *seeing a poster for 'Michael Redgrave and Dirk Bogarde in* The Sea Shall Not Have Them'*:*
   I fail to see why not; everyone else has.

Noël Coward 1899–1973: Sheridan Morley *The Quotable Noël Coward* (1999)

14 Language was not powerful enough to describe the infant phenomenon.

Charles Dickens 1812–70: *Nicholas Nickleby* (1839)

15 Is it Colman's smile
   That makes life worth while
   Or Crawford's significant form?
   Is it Lombard's lips
   Or Mae West's hips
   That carry you through the storm?

Gavin Ewart 1916–95: 'Verse from an Opera' (1939)

16 *of Creston Clarke as King Lear:*
   He played the King as though under momentary apprehension that someone else was about to play the ace.

Eugene Field 1850–95: review attributed to Field; in *Denver Tribune* c.1880

17 Dear Ingrid—speaks five languages and can't act in any of them.
   of Ingrid Bergman

John Gielgud 1904–2000: Ronald Harwood *The Ages of Gielgud* (1984); attributed

18 People like to hear me say 'shit' in my gorgeous voice.
   of his popularity in America

John Gielgud 1904–2000: in *New Yorker* 10 July 2000; attributed

19 My dear fellow, I never saw anything so funny in my life, and yet it was not in the least bit vulgar.
   of Beerbohm Tree's Hamlet (1892)

W. S. Gilbert 1836–1911: D. Bispham *A Quaker Singer's Recollections* (1920)

20 An actor is a kind of a guy who if you ain't talking about him ain't listening.

George Glass 1910–84: Bob Thomas *Brando* (1973); said to be quoted frequently by Marlon Brando

21 On the stage he was natural, simple, affecting;
'Twas only that when he was off he was acting.
of David Garrick

Oliver Goldsmith 1730–74:
Retaliation (1774)

22 *of Irving as Mephistopheles in Goethe's* Faust:
The actor, of course, at moments presents to the eye a
remarkably sinister figure. He strikes us, however, as
superficial—a terrible fault for an archfiend.

Henry James 1843–1916: *The Scenic
Art* (1948)

23 Massey won't be satisfied until he's assassinated.
on Raymond Massey's success in playing Lincoln

George S. Kaufman 1889–1961:
Howard Teichmann *George S.
Kaufman* (1973)

24 *on being refused membership of an exclusive golf-club:*
I'm *not* an actor, and I enclose my press cuttings to prove
it.

Victor Mature 1915– : Ned Sherrin
Cutting Edge (1984)

25 I have worked with more submarines than leading ladies.

John Mills 1908–2005: in *The Times*
12 February 2000 'Quotes of the
Week'

26 *of Katharine Hepburn at the first night of* The Lake (*1933*)
She ran the whole gamut of the emotions from A to B, and
put some distance between herself and a more experienced
colleague [Alison Skipworth] lest she catch acting from
her.

Dorothy Parker 1893–1967:
attributed

27 It is greatly to Mrs Patrick Campbell's credit that, bad as
the play was, her acting was worse.
review of Sardou Fedora *1 June 1895*

George Bernard Shaw 1856–1950:
Our Theatre in the Nineties (1932)

28 We're *actors*—we're the opposite of people! . . . Think, in
your head, *now*, think of the most . . . *private* . . . *secret* . . .
intimate thing you have ever done secure in the knowledge
of its privacy . . . Are you thinking of it? . . . *Well, I saw
you do it!*

Tom Stoppard 1937– : *Rosencrantz
and Guildenstern Are Dead* (1967)

29 The key to Beatrice Lillie's success is that she ignores her
audience. This is an act of daring that amounts to
revolution.

Kenneth Tynan 1927–80: in *Holiday*
September 1956

30 As Virgilia in *Coriolanus* she yearns so hungrily that I
longed to throw her a fish.
of Claire Bloom in 1955

Kenneth Tynan 1927–80: *Curtains*
(1961)

31 A buxom temptress . . . more impressive in silhouette than
in action.
of Yvonne Furneaux in Giraudoux's Ondine

Kenneth Tynan 1927–80: in *Observer*
23 October 1955

32 ALISON SKIPWORTH: You forget I've been an actress for forty
years.
MAE WEST: Don't worry, dear. I'll keep your secret.

Mae West 1892–1980: G. Eells and S.
Musgrove *Mae West* (1989)

33 *on the Burton-Taylor* Private Lives *in 1964:*
He's miscast and she's Miss Taylor.

Emlyn Williams 1905–87: James
Harding *Emlyn Williams* (1987)

34 They say an actor is only as good as his parts. Well, my
parts have done me pretty well, darling.

Barbara Windsor 1937– : in *The
Times* 13 February 1999

35 She was like a sinking ship firing on the rescuers.
of Mrs Patrick Campbell in her later years

Alexander Woollcott 1887–1943:
While Rome Burns (1944) 'The First
Mrs Tanqueray'

Advertising

❝ the rattling of a stick inside a swill bucket. **❞**
George Orwell

1 While you were out your exterminator called.
heading of leaflet left in a New York letter-box

Anonymous: Sylvia Townsend Warner letter to David Garnett, 12 May 1967

2 The cheap contractions and revised spellings of the advertising world which have made the beauty of the written word almost unrecognizable—surely any society that permits the substitution of 'kwik' for 'quick' and 'e.z.' for 'easy' does not deserve Shakespeare, Eliot or Michener.

Russell Baker 1925– : column in *New York Times*; Ned Sherrin *Cutting Edge* (1984)

3 Blurbs that appear on the back cover and in the advertisements recommending the book in glowing terms . . . are written by friends of the author who haven't read the book but owe the poor guy a favour.

Art Buchwald 1925– : *I Never Danced at the White House* (1974)

4 Advertising is the most fun you can have with your clothes on.

Jerry Della Femina 1936– : *From Those Wonderful Folks Who Gave You Pearl Harbor* (1971)

5 *on a consultant who had given a paper 'Advertising in Medicine':*
It was like listening to a loudspeaker blaring out 'Mum's the word'.

Oliver St John Gogarty 1878–1957: Ulick O'Connor *Oliver St John Gogarty* (1964)

6 It is far easier to write ten passably effective sonnets, good enough to take in the not too enquiring critic, than one effective advertisement that will take in a few thousand of the uncritical buying public.

Aldous Huxley 1894–1963: *On the Margin* (1923) 'Advertisement'

7 Society drives people crazy with lust and calls it advertising.

John Lahr 1941– : in *Guardian* 2 August 1989

8 Advertising may be described as the science of arresting human intelligence long enough to get money from it.

Stephen Leacock 1869–1944: *Garden of Folly* (1924)

9 The explanation of intuition is the same as that of advertisement: tell a man ten thousand times that Pears Soap is good for the complexion and eventually he will have an intuitive certainty of the fact.

W. Somerset Maugham 1874–1965: *A Writer's Notebook* (1949) written in 1901

10 Good wine needs no bush,
And perhaps products that people really want need no hard-sell or soft-sell TV push.
Why not?
Look at pot.

Ogden Nash 1902–71: 'Most Doctors Recommend or Yours For Fast, Fast, Fast Relief' (1972)

11 I think that I shall never see
A billboard lovely as a tree.
Perhaps, unless the billboards fall,
I'll never see a tree at all.

Ogden Nash 1902–71: 'Song of the Open Road' (1933)

12 The consumer isn't a moron; she is your wife.

David Ogilvy 1911– : *Confessions of an Advertising Man* (1963)

13 Advertising is the rattling of a stick inside a swill-bucket.

George Orwell 1903–50: *Keep the Aspidistra Flying* (1936)

14 If the client moans and sighs,
Make his logo twice the size.

John Trench 1920–2003: attributed, perhaps apocryphal; in *The Times* 14 March 2003 (obituary)

15 *asked why he had made a commercial for American Express:*
To pay for my American Express.

Peter Ustinov 1921–2004: in *Ned Sherrin in his Anecdotage* (1993)

America ····> Countries and Peoples, Places

66 High as a flag on the fourth of July. 99
Oscar Hammerstein II

---

1 Every American woman has two souls to call her own, the other being her husband's.

James Agate 1877–1947: diary, 15 May 1937

2 California is a fine place to live—if you happen to be an orange.

Fred Allen 1894–1956: in *American Magazine* December 1945

3 He held, too, in his enlightened way, that Americans have a perfect right to exist. But he did often find himself wishing Mr Rhodes had not enabled them to exercise that right in Oxford.

Max Beerbohm 1872–1956: *Zuleika Dobson* (1911)

4 They're the experts where personality is concerned, the Americans; they've got it down to a fine art.

Alan Bennett 1934– : *Talking Heads* (1988)

5 America is a model of force and freedom and moderation—with all the coarseness and rudeness of its people.

Lord Byron 1788–1824: letter, 12 October 1821

6 I would rather . . . have a nod from an American, than a snuff-box from an Emperor.

Lord Byron 1788–1824: letter, 8 June 1822

7 Your eyes are like the prairie flowers
When they're refreshed by sudden showers,
Next to Texas I love you.

Sammy Cahn 1913– : 'Next to Texas I Love You' (1947)

8 I have always liked Americans, and the sort of man that likes Americans is liable to like Russians.

Claud Cockburn 1904–81: *Crossing the Line* (1958)

9 Father's name was Hezikiah,
Mother's name was Anna Maria,
Yanks, through and through!
Red White and Blue.

George M. Cohan 1878–1942: 'Yankee Doodle Dandy' (1904)

10 I like America . . .
All delegates
From Southern States
Are nervy and distraught.
In New Orleans
The wrought-iron screens
Are dreadfully overwrought . . .
But—I like America,
Every scrap of it,
All the sentimental crap of it.

Noël Coward 1899–1973: 'I like America' (1949)

11 When I was a boy I was told that anybody could become President. I'm beginning to believe it.

Clarence Darrow 1857–1938: Irving Stone *Clarence Darrow for the Defence* (1941)

12 The thing that impresses me most about America is the way parents obey their children.

Edward VIII 1894–1972: in *Look* 5 March 1957

13 Molasses to
Rum to
Slaves!
'Tisn't morals, 'tis money that saves!
Shall we dance to the sound
Of the profitable pound, in
Molasses and
Rum and
Slaves?

Sherman Edwards: 'Molasses to Rum' (1969)

14 When J. P. Morgan bows, I just nod;
Green Pastures wanted me to play God.
But you've got me down hearted
'Cause I can't get started with you.

Ira Gershwin 1896–1983: 'I Can't Get Started' (1936)

15 I'm as corny as Kansas in August
I'm as normal as blueberry pie . . .
. . . High as a flag on the fourth of July.

Oscar Hammerstein II 1895–1960: 'I'm in Love with a Wonderful Guy' (1949)

16 If I had to give a definition of capitalism I would say: the process whereby American girls turn into American women.

Christopher Hampton 1946– : *Savages* (1974)

17 Once we had a Roosevelt
Praise the Lord!
Now we're stuck with Nixon, Agnew, Ford
Brother, can you spare a rope!

E. Y. Harburg 1898–1981: parody of 'Brother Can You Spare a Dime?', written for the *New York Times* at the time of Watergate

18 *Gilbert Harding, applying for a US visa, was irritated by having to fill in a long form with many questions, including 'Is it your intention to overthrow the Government of the United States by force?':*
Sole purpose of visit.

Gilbert Harding 1907–60: W. Reyburn *Gilbert Harding* (1978)

19 I could come back to America . . . to die—but never, never to live.

Henry James 1843–1916: letter to Mrs William James, 1 April 1913

20 To Americans, English manners are far more frightening than none at all.

Randall Jarrell 1914–65: *Pictures from an Institution* (1954)

21 Never criticize Americans. They have the best taste that money can buy.

Miles Kington 1941–2008: *Welcome to Kington* (1989)

22 *the universal philosophy of young America:*
I can do that.

Ed Kleban: song-title (1975)

23 So I really think that American gentlemen are the best after all, because kissing your hand may make you feel very very good but a diamond and safire bracelet lasts forever.

Anita Loos 1893–1981: *Gentlemen Prefer Blondes* (1925)

24 I like to be in America!
O.K. by me in America!
Ev'rything free in America
For a small fee in America!

Stephen Sondheim 1930– : 'America' (1957)

25 In the United States there is more space where nobody is than where anybody is. That is what makes America what it is.

Gertrude Stein 1874–1946: *The Geographical History of America* (1936)

26 In America any boy may become President and I suppose it's just one of the risks he takes!

Adlai Stevenson 1900–65: speech in Detroit, 7 October 1952

27 America is a vast conspiracy to make you happy.

John Updike 1932– : *Problems* (1980) 'How to love America and Leave it at the Same Time'

28 The land of the dull and the home of the literal.

Gore Vidal 1925– : *Reflections upon a Sinking Ship* (1969)

29 The goal of white Americans has always been shining cities on the hill, with converted Indians and imported African slaves to do the heavy lifting.

Gore Vidal 1925– : *Inventing a Nation: Washington* (2003)

30 MRS ALLONBY: They say, Lady Hunstanton, that when good Americans die they go to Paris.
LADY HUNSTANTON: Indeed? And when bad Americans die, where do they go to?
LORD ILLINGWORTH: Oh, they go to America.

Oscar Wilde 1854–1900: *A Woman of No Importance* (1893)

31 The youth of America is their oldest tradition. It has been going on now for three hundred years.

Oscar Wilde 1854–1900: *A Woman of No Importance* (1893)

Anger

66 When very angry, swear. 99
Mark Twain

1 Anger makes dull men witty, but it keeps them poor.

Francis Bacon 1561–1626: *Works* (1859) 'Baconiana'

2 I was angry with my friend;
I told my wrath, my wrath did end.
I was angry with my foe:
I told it not, my wrath did grow.

William Blake 1757–1827: 'A Poison Tree' (1794)

3 I expect to pass through this world but once and therefore if there is anybody that I want to kick in the crutch I had better kick them in the crutch *now*, for I do not expect to pass this way again.
  while lunching at the Reform Club with a bishop at the next table

Maurice Bowra 1898–1971: Arthur Marshall *Life's Rich Pageant* (1984)

4 When you get angry, they tell you, count to five before you reply. Why should I count to five? It's what happens *before* you count to five which makes life interesting.

David Hare 1947– : *The Secret Rapture* (1988)

5 McEnroe . . . did his complete Krakatoa number.
  of John McEnroe disputing a line call at Wimbledon

Clive James 1939– : in *Observer* 5 July 1981

6 It's my rule never to lose me temper till it would be dethrimental to keep it.

Sean O'Casey 1880–1964: *The Plough and the Stars* (1926)

7 I storm and I roar, and I fall in a rage,
And missing my whore, I bugger my page.

Charles Sackville 1638–1706:
'Regime d'vivre' (often attributed to
Lord Rochester, but probably not by
him)

8 Whereat, with blade, with bloody blameful blade,
He bravely broached his boiling bloody breast.

William Shakespeare 1564–1616: *A
Midsummer Night's Dream* (1595–6)

9 He never let the sun go down on his wrath, though there
were some colourful sunsets while it lasted.
of W. G. Grace

A. A. Thomson: Alan Gibson *The
Cricket Captains of England* (1979)

10 When angry, count four; when very angry, swear.

Mark Twain 1835–1910: *Pudd'nhead
Wilson* (1894)

11 The adjective 'cross' as a description of his Jovelike wrath
. . . jarred upon Derek profoundly. It was as though
Prometheus, with the vultures tearing his liver, had been
asked if he were piqued.

P. G. Wodehouse 1881–1975: *Jill the
Reckless* (1922)

Animals ····▸ Birds, Dogs

❝ I am fond of pigs. ❞
Winston Churchill

1 The lion and the calf shall lie down together but the calf
won't get much sleep.

Woody Allen 1935– : in *New
Republic* 31 August 1974

2 *during his time in the Lords the eighth Earl of Arran was
concerned with measures for homosexual reform and the
protection of badgers, interests concisely summed up by a
fellow peer:*
Teaching people not to bugger badgers and not to badger
buggers.

Anonymous: in *Ned Sherrin in his
Anecdotage* (1993)

3 The rabbit has a charming face:
Its private life is a disgrace.
I really dare not name to you
The awful things that rabbits do.

Anonymous: *The Week-End Book*
(1925) 'The Rabbit'

4 *Puella Rigensis ridebat
Quam tigris in tergo vehebat;
Externa profecta,
Interna revecta,
Risusque cum tigre manebat.*

There was a young lady of Riga
Who went for a ride on a tiger;
They returned from the ride
With the lady inside,
And a smile on the face of the tiger.

Anonymous: R. L. Green (ed.) *A
Century of Humorous Verse* (1959)

5 I shoot the Hippopotamus
With bullets made of platinum,
Because if I use leaden ones

Hilaire Belloc 1870–1953: 'The
Hippopotamus' (1896)

His hide is sure to flatten 'em.

6 The Tiger, on the other hand, is kittenish and mild,
He makes a pretty play fellow for any little child;
And mothers of large families (who claim to common
     sense)
Will find a Tiger well repay the trouble and expense.

Hilaire Belloc 1870–1953: 'The Tiger'
(1896)

7 I had an Aunt in Yucatan
Who bought a Python from a man
And kept it for a pet.
She died, because she never knew
These simple little rules and few;—
The Snake is living yet.

Hilaire Belloc 1870–1953: 'The
Python' (1897)

8 It's awf'lly bad luck on Diana,
Her ponies have swallowed their bits;
She fished down their throats with a spanner
And frightened them all into fits.

John Betjeman 1906–84: 'Hunter
Trials' (1954)

9 To my mind, the only possible pet is a cow. Cows love you
. . . They will listen to your problems and never ask a thing
in return. They will be your friends for ever. And when
you get tired of them, you can kill and eat them. Perfect.

Bill Bryson 1951– : *Neither Here Nor
There* (1991)

10 He thought he saw an Elephant,
That practised on a fife:
He looked again, and found it was
A letter from his wife.
'At length I realize,' he said,
'The bitterness of life!'

Lewis Carroll 1832–98: *Sylvie and
Bruno* (1889)

11 I am fond of pigs. Dogs look up to us. Cats look down on
us. Pigs treat us as equal.

Winston Churchill 1874–1965: M.
Gilbert *Never Despair* (1988);
attributed

12 *after an operation to remove a fishbone stuck in her throat:*
After all these years of fishing, the fish are having their
revenge.

Queen Elizabeth, the Queen Mother
1900–2002: in November 1982,
attributed; Christopher Dobson (ed.)
*Queen Elizabeth the Queen Mother:
Chronicle of a Remarkable Life* (2000)

13 The great thing about racehorses is you don't need to take
them for walks.

Albert Finney 1936– : in *The Mail on
Sunday* 9 April 2000

14 Commodus killed a camelopardalis or giraffe . . . the tallest,
the most gentle, and the most useless of the large
quadrupeds. This singular animal, a native only of the
interior parts of Africa, has not been seen in Europe since
the revival of letters, and though M. de Buffon . . . has
endeavoured to describe, he has not ventured to delineate
the giraffe.

Edward Gibbon 1737–94: *The
Decline and Fall of the Roman Empire*
(1776–88)

15 My God . . . The hero is a bee!
*on reading the synopsis of a story by Maurice Maeterlinck in
1920*

Sam Goldwyn 1882–1974: Michael
Freedland *The Goldwyn Touch* (1986)

16 Even the rabbits
Inhibit their habits
On Sunday at Cicero Falls.

E. Y. Harburg 1898–1981: 'Sunday at
Cicero Falls' (1944)

17 Tar-baby ain't sayin' nuthin', en Brer Fox, he lay low.

Joel Chandler Harris 1848–1908: *Uncle Remus and His Legends of the Old Plantation* (1881) 'The Wonderful Tar-Baby Story'

18 Bred en bawn in a brier-patch!

Joel Chandler Harris 1848–1908: *Uncle Remus and His Legends of the Old Plantation* (1881) 'How Mr Rabbit was too Sharp for Mr Fox'

19 What the horse is to the Arab, or the dog is to the Greenlander, the pig is to the Irishman.

J. G. Kohl 1808–78: *Ireland, Scotland and England* (1844)

20 Arabs of means rode none but she-camels, since they . . . were patient and would endure to march long after they were worn out, indeed until they tottered with exhaustion and fell in their tracks and died: whereas the coarser males grew angry, flung themselves down when tired, and from sheer rage would die there unnecessarily.

T. E. Lawrence 1888–1935: *Seven Pillars of Wisdom* (1926)

21 Its tail was a plume of such magnificence that it almost wore the cat.

Hugh Leonard 1926– : *Rover and Other Cats* (1992)

22 Where are you going
With your fetlocks blowing in the . . . wind
I want to shower you with sugar lumps
And ride you over . . . fences
I want to polish your hooves every single day
And bring you to the horse . . . dentist.
　　'My Lovely Horse' as sung by Fathers Ted and Dougal

Graham Linehan and **Arthur Mathews**: 'A Song for Europe' (1996), episode from *Father Ted* (Channel 4 TV, 1994–)

23 A
water bison
is what
yer wash
yer face in.

Roger McGough 1937– : *An Imaginary Menagerie* (1988)

24 Rudolph, the Red-Nosed Reindeer
Had a very shiny nose,
And if you ever saw it,
You would even say it glows.

Johnny Marks 1909–85: 'Rudolph, the Red-Nosed Reindeer' (1949)

25 Outside of a dog, a book is a man's best friend. Inside of a dog, it's too dark to read.

Groucho Marx 1895–1977: Groucho Marx and Stefan Kanfer *The Essential Groucho* (2000)

26 Slow but sure the turtle
Enormously fert'le
Lays her eggs by the dozens,
Maybe some are her cousins,
Even the catamount is nonplussed by that amount
It's Spring, Spring, Spring!

Johnny Mercer 1909–76: 'Spring, Spring, Spring' (1954)

27 Eeyore, the old grey Donkey, stood by the side of the stream, and looked at himself in the water. 'Pathetic,' he said. 'That's what it is. Pathetic.'

A. A. Milne 1882–1956: *Winnie-the-Pooh* (1926)

28 Pooh began to feel a little more comfortable, because when you are a Bear of Very Little Brain, and you Think of Things, you find sometimes that a Thing which seemed very Thingish inside you is quite different when it gets out into the open and has other people looking at it.

A. A. Milne 1882–1956: *The House at Pooh Corner* (1928)

29 One disadvantage of being a hog is that at any moment some blundering fool may try to make a silk purse out of your wife's ear.

J. B. Morton 1893–1975: *By the Way* (1931)

30 God in His wisdom made the fly
And then forgot to tell us why.

Ogden Nash 1902–71: 'The Fly' (1942)

31 The turtle lives 'twixt plated decks
Which practically conceal its sex.
I think it clever of the turtle
In such a fix to be so fertile.

Ogden Nash 1902–71: 'Autres Bêtes, Autres Moeurs' (1931)

32 The cow is of the bovine ilk;
One end is moo, the other, milk.

Ogden Nash 1902–71: 'The Cow' (1931)

33 Four legs good, two legs bad.

George Orwell 1903–50: *Animal Farm* (1945)

34 Your elephant seal . . . is not a natural self-starter. Start him, however, and he goes, not like a rocket, but a sort of turbo-charged mega-caterpillar.

Matthew Parris 1949– : in *Spectator* 17 June 2000

35 Don't go into Mr McGregor's garden: your father had an accident there, he was put into a pie by Mrs McGregor.

Beatrix Potter 1866–1943: *The Tale of Peter Rabbit* (1902)

36 There was one poor tiger that hadn't *got* a Christian.

Punch 1841–1992: vol. 68 (1875)

37 Oh how the family affections combat
Within this heart, and each hour flings a bomb at
My burning soul! Neither from owl or from bat
Can peace be gained until I clasp my wombat.

Dante Gabriel Rossetti 1828–82: on the loss of his pet wombat, and his other pets; 'The Wombat' (1849)

38 I know two things about the horse
And one of them is rather coarse.

Naomi Royde-Smith c.1875–1964: in *Weekend Book* (1928)

39 When a man wants to murder a tiger he calls it sport; when a tiger wants to murder him, he calls it ferocity.

George Bernard Shaw 1856–1950: *Man and Superman* (1903)

40 So, naturalists observe, a flea
Hath smaller fleas that on him prey;
And these have smaller fleas to bite 'em,
And so proceed *ad infinitum*.

Jonathan Swift 1667–1745: 'On Poetry' (1733)

Appearance ····▶ Faces

66 Glamour is on a life-support machine. **99**
Joan Collins

1 It often means vanity and sometimes drink.
explaining his mistrust of 'men with waxed moustaches'

Lord Baden-Powell 1857–1941: *Scouting for Boys* (1908)

2 He had a thin vague beard—or rather, he had a chin on which a large number of hairs weakly curled and clustered to cover its retreat.

Max Beerbohm 1872–1956: 'Enoch Soames' (1912)

3 I know I looked awful because my mother phoned and said I looked lovely.
after getting a makeover on television

Jo Brand 1957– : in *Sunday Telegraph* 28 December 2003

4 I look like an elderly *wasp* in an interesting condition.
of her appearance in her black and yellow costume for False Gods *in 1917*

Mrs Patrick Campbell 1865–1940: Margot Peters *Mrs Pat* (1984)

5 Men who are too good looking are never good in bed because they never had to be.

Cindy Chupack: *Sex and the City* 'Unoriginal Sin' (2002), spoken by Carrie (Sarah Jessica Parker)

6 Glamour is on a life-support machine and not expected to live.

Joan Collins 1933– : in *Independent* 24 April 1999

7 Edith Sitwell, in that great Risorgimento cape of hers, looks as though she were covering a teapot or a telephone.

Noël Coward 1899–1973: William Marchant *The Pleasure of his Company* (1975)

8 I was very plain. My rich mouse hair was straight but my teeth were not. I wore tin-rimmed spectacles.
of himself in youth

Quentin Crisp 1908–99: in *Daily Telegraph* 22 November 1999; obituary

9 I guess a drag queen's like an oil painting: You gotta stand back from it to get the full effect.

Harvey Fierstein 1954– : *Torch Song Trilogy* (1979)

10 I don't trust photographers. I'm now a relaxed, contented 60-year-old, but look at my pictures and you see a crazy, bug-eyed serial killer.
on a photograph accompanying an Independent *article to mark his 60th birthday*

Richard Ingrams 1937– : in *Observer* 24 August 1997

11 RICHARD: You look fabulous!
ALLY: I know, I just got fired for it.

David E. Kelley: *Ally McBeal* (US television series, 1998–2003) episode 1

12 I'm tired of all this nonsense about beauty being only skin-deep. That's deep enough. What do you want—an adorable pancreas?

Jean Kerr 1923–2003: *The Snake has all the Lines* (1958)

13 Her ugliness was destined to bloom late, hidden first by the unformed gawkiness of youth, budding to plainness in young womanhood and now flowering to slow maturity in her early forties.

Brian Moore 1921– : *The Lonely Passion of Judith Hearne* (1955)

14 No power on earth, however, can abolish the merciless class distinction between those who are physically desirable and the lonely, pallid, spotted, silent, unfancied majority.

John Mortimer 1923– : *Clinging to the Wreckage* (1982)

15 Sure, deck your lower limbs in pants;
Yours are the limbs, my sweeting.
You look divine as you advance—
Have you seen yourself retreating?

Ogden Nash 1902–71: 'What's the Use?' (1940)

16 My beauty am faded.

Rudolf Nureyev 1939–93: on being rejected by a young man he had tried to pick up; in *Ned Sherrin in his Anecdotage* (1993)

17 In Los Angeles everyone has perfect teeth. It's crocodile land.

Gwyneth Paltrow 1972– : in *Sunday Times* 3 February 2002

18 I always say beauty is only sin deep.

Saki 1870–1916: *Reginald* (1904)

19 You're welcome to take a bath. You look like the second week of the garbage strike.

Neil Simon 1927– : *The Gingerbread Lady* (1970)

20 Women never look so well as when one comes in wet and dirty from hunting.

R. S. Surtees 1805–64: *Mr. Sponge's Sporting Tour* (1853) ch. 21

21 If beauty is truth, why don't women go to the library to have their hair done?

Lily Tomlin 1939– : Sally Feldman (ed.) *Woman's Hour Book of Humour* (1993)

22 By the time you hit 50, I reckon you've earned your wrinkles, so why not be proud of them?

Twiggy 1949– : in *Observer* 8 September 2002

23 A man who can part the Red Sea but apparently not his own hairpiece.
of Charlton Heston

Dick Vosburgh and **Denis King**: *Beauty and the Beards* (2001)

24 It is better to be beautiful than to be good. But . . . it is better to be good than to be ugly.

Oscar Wilde 1854–1900: *The Picture of Dorian Gray* (1891)

25 I was so ugly when I was born, the doctor slapped my mother.

Henny Youngman 1906–98: in *Times* 26 February 1998; obituary

Architecture

66 We can improve on the igloo. **99**
Abraham Okpik

1 The floozie in the jacuzzi.
popular description of the monument in O'Connell Street, Dublin

Anonymous: comment, c.1988

2 *of the cramped office he shared with Dorothy Parker:*
One square foot less and it would be adulterous.

Robert Benchley 1889–1945: in *New Yorker* 5 January 1946

3 Sir Christopher Wren
Said, 'I am going to dine with some men.
If anybody calls
Say I am designing St Paul's.'

Edmund Clerihew Bentley 1875–1956: 'Sir Christopher Wren' (1905)

4 Ghastly good taste, or a depressing story of the rise and fall of English architecture.

John Betjeman 1906–84: title of book (1933)

5 The existence of St Sophia is atmospheric; that of St Peter's, overpoweringly, imminently substantial. One is a church to God: the other a salon for his agents. One is consecrated to reality, the other, to illusion. St Sophia in fact is large, and St Peter's is vilely, tragically small.

Robert Byron 1905–41: *The Road to Oxiana* (1937)

6 A monstrous carbuncle on the face of a much-loved and elegant friend.

Charles, Prince of Wales 1948– : speech on the proposed extension to the National Gallery, London, 30 May 1984

7 The Pavilion
Cost a million
As a monument to Art,
And the wits here
Say it sits here
Like an Oriental tart!

Noël Coward 1899–1973: on Brighton Pavilion; 'There was Once a Little Village' (1934)

8 O Dome gigantic, Dome immense
Built in defiance of common sense.

P. D. James 1920– : attributed in *Daily Telegraph* 18 May 2000

9 A taste for the grandiose, like a taste for morphia, is, once it has been fully acquired, difficult to keep within limits.

Osbert Lancaster 1908–80: *Homes Sweet Homes* (1939)

10 A lot of nuns in a rugger scrum.
on the Sydney Opera House

George Molnar 1910–98: attributed

11 I am proud to be an Eskimo, but I think we can improve on the igloo as a permanent dwelling.

Abraham Okpik: in *Northern Affairs Bulletin* March 1960

12 A singularly dreary street. What I would term Victorian Varicose.

Peter Shaffer 1926– : *Lettice and Lovage* (rev. ed. 1989)

13 *on Brighton Pavilion:*
As if St Paul's had come down and littered.

Sydney Smith 1771–1845: Peter Virgin *Sydney Smith* (1994)

14 Whatever may be said in favour of the Victorians, it is pretty generally admitted that few of them were to be trusted within reach of a trowel and a pile of bricks.

P. G. Wodehouse 1881–1975: *Summer Moonshine* (1938)

15 The physician can bury his mistakes, but the architect can only advise his client to plant vines.

Frank Lloyd Wright 1867–1959: in *New York Times* 4 October 1953

Argument

66 Reason always means what someone else has got to say. **99**
Elizabeth Gaskell

1 Sir Roger told them, with the air of a man who would not give his judgement rashly, that much might be said on both sides.

Joseph Addison 1672–1719: *The Spectator* 20 July 1711

2 I've never won an argument with her; and the only times I thought I had I found out the argument wasn't over yet.
of his wife Rosalynn

Jimmy Carter 1924– : in *Reader's Digest* March 1979

3 You can't turn a thing upside down if there's no theory about it being the right way up.

G. K. Chesterton 1874–1936: attributed

4 'My idea of an agreeable person,' said Hugo Bohun, 'is a person who agrees with me.'

Benjamin Disraeli 1804–81: *Lothair* (1870)

5 I'll not listen to reason . . . Reason always means what someone else has got to say.

Elizabeth Gaskell 1810–65: *Cranford* (1853)

6 Those who in quarrels interpose,
Must often wipe a bloody nose.

John Gay 1685–1732: *Fables* (1727) 'The Mastiffs'

7 There is no arguing with Johnson; for when his pistol misses fire, he knocks you down with the butt end of it.

Oliver Goldsmith 1730–74: James Boswell *Life of Samuel Johnson* (1934 ed.) 26 October 1769

8 Any stigma, as the old saying is, will serve to beat a dogma.

Philip Guedalla 1889–1944: *Masters and Men* (1923)

9 The concept of two people living together for 25 years without having a cross word suggests a lack of spirit only to be admired in sheep.

A. P. Herbert 1890–1971: in *News Chronicle*, 1940

10 Several excuses are always less convincing than one.

Aldous Huxley 1894–1963: *Point Counter Point* (1928)

11 [Logic] is neither a science nor an art, but a dodge.

Benjamin Jowett 1817–93: Lionel A. Tollemache *Benjamin Jowett* (1895)

12 The only person who listens to both sides of a husband and wife argument is the woman in the next apartment.

Sam Levenson 1911–80: *You Can Say That Again, Sam!* (1975)

13 I think it will be a clash between the political will and the administrative won't.

Jonathan Lynn 1943– and **Antony Jay** 1930– : *Yes Prime Minister* vol. 2 (1987)

14 The first obligation of the demonstrator is to be legible. Miss Manners cannot sympathize with a cause whose signs she cannot make out even with her glasses on.

Judith Martin 1938– : 'Advice from Miss Manners', column in *Washington Post* 1979–82

15 Casuistry has got a bad name in the world, mainly, I suppose, because of the dubious uses to which it was put during the Sixteenth and Seventeenth Centuries by some of its Jesuit practitioners. But it is really a very useful art.

H. L. Mencken 1880–1956: *Minority Report* (1956)

16 I had inherited what my father called the art of the advocate, or the irritating habit of looking for the flaw in any argument.

John Mortimer 1923– : *Clinging to the Wreckage* (1982)

17 Why, i'faith, I believe I am between *both*.
when two royal dukes walking on either side of him told him that they were trying to decide if he was a greater fool or rogue

Richard Brinsley Sheridan 1751–1816: Walter Jerrold *Bon-Mots* (1893)

18 JUDGE: What do you suppose I am on the Bench for, Mr Smith?
SMITH: It is not for me, Your Honour, to attempt to fathom the inscrutable workings of Providence.

F. E. Smith 1872–1930: Lord Birkenhead *F. E.* (1959 ed.)

19 *on seeing two Edinburgh women hurling insults at one another across an alleyway:*
Those two women will never agree; they are arguing from different premises.

Sydney Smith 1771–1845: Peter Virgin *Sydney Smith* (1994)

20 And who are you? said he.—Don't puzzle me, said I.

Laurence Sterne 1713–68: *Tristram Shandy* (1759–67)

21 My uncle Toby would never offer to answer this by any other kind of argument, than that of whistling half a dozen bars of Lillabullero.

Laurence Sterne 1713–68: *Tristram Shandy* (1759–67)

22 I don't take orders from you, you're just a figure-head and I've seen better ones on the sharp end of a dredger.

Tom Stoppard 1937– : *The Dog It Was That Died* (1983)

23 When two strong men stand face to face, each claiming to be Major Brabazon-Plank, it is inevitable that there will be a sense of strain, resulting in a momentary silence.

P. G. Wodehouse 1881–1975: *Uncle Dynamite* (1948)

The Aristocracy ····▸ Class

66 Spurn not the nobly born. 99
W. S. Gilbert

1 The young Sahib shot divinely, but God was very merciful to the birds.

Anonymous: G. W. E. Russell *Collections and Recollections* (1898)

2 *the much-married Duke of Westminster had died the previous*
day:
There was a bad fire next door; lots of smoke, but it turned
out *not* to be the four bereaved Duchesses of Westminster
committing suttee.

Chips Channon 1897–1958: diary, 21
July 1953

3 The Stately Homes of England,
How beautiful they stand,
To prove the upper classes
Have still the upper hand.

Noël Coward 1899–1973: 'The
Stately Homes of England' (1938)

4 Spurn not the nobly born
With love affected,
Nor treat with virtuous scorn
The well-connected.

W. S. Gilbert 1836–1911: *Iolanthe*
(1882)

5 I can trace my ancestry back to a protoplasmal primordial
atomic globule. Consequently, my family pride is
something in-conceivable. I can't help it. I was born
sneering.

W. S. Gilbert 1836–1911: *The
Mikado* (1885)

6 Hearts just as pure and fair
May beat in Belgrave Square
As in the lowly air
Of Seven Dials.

W. S. Gilbert 1836–1911: *Iolanthe*
(1882)

7 They are no members of the common throng;
They are all noblemen who have gone wrong!

W. S. Gilbert 1836–1911: *The Pirates
of Penzance* (1879)

8 There never was a Churchill from John of Marlborough
down that had either morals or principles.

W. E. Gladstone 1809–98: in
conversation in 1882, recorded by
Captain R. V. Briscoe; R. F. Foster *Lord
Randolph Churchill* (1981)

9 I am a well-known élitist. I don't even own a pair of
trainers. If I did, I am sure they would be very fragrant.

Lord Gowrie 1939– : in *Independent*
24 January 1998

10 We don't represent anybody, it's true,
But that's not a thing to regret;
We can say what we think—and I know one or two
Who've never said anything yet.
While the Commons must bray like an ass every day
To appease their electoral hordes,
We don't say a thing till we've something to say—
There's a lot to be said for the Lords.

A. P. Herbert 1890–1971: *Big Ben*
(1946)

11 *replying to Harold Wilson's remark* (*on Home's leading the*
Conservatives to victory in the 1963 election) *that 'the whole*
[democratic] *process has ground to a halt with a fourteenth*
Earl':
As far as the fourteenth earl is concerned, I suppose Mr
Wilson, when you come to think of it, is the fourteenth Mr
Wilson.

Lord Home 1903–95: in *Daily
Telegraph* 22 October 1963

12 I am an ancestor.
reply when taunted on his lack of ancestry, having been
made Duke of Abrantes, 1807

Marshal Junot 1771–1813: attributed

13 We always feel kindly disposed towards noble authors.

Lord Macaulay 1800–59: in
Edinburgh Review January 1833

14 An aristocracy in a republic is like a chicken whose head has been cut off: it may run about in a lively way, but in fact it is dead.

Nancy Mitford 1904–73: *Noblesse Oblige* (1956) 'The English Aristocracy'

15 This world consists of men, women, and Herveys.

Lady Mary Wortley Montagu 1689–1762: attributed by Lord Wharncliffe in *Letters and Works of Lady Mary Wortley Montagu* (1837), 'Herveys' being a reference to John Hervey, Baron Hervey of Ickworth, 1696–1743

16 I'll purge, and leave sack, and live cleanly, as a nobleman should do.

William Shakespeare 1564–1616: *Henry IV, Part 1* (1597)

17 At the palace of the Duke of Ferrara,
Who was prematurely deaf but a dear,
At the palace of the Duke of Ferrara
I acquired some position
Plus a tiny Titian . . .
Liaisons! What's happened to them?

Stephen Sondheim 1930– : 'Liaisons' (1972)

18 LORD ILLINGWORTH: A title is really rather a nuisance in these democratic days. As George Harford I had everything I wanted. Now I have merely everything that other people want.

Oscar Wilde 1854–1900: *A Woman of No Importance* (1893)

The Armed Forces ····> War

‟When the military man approaches, the world locks up its spoons.**”**
George Bernard Shaw

1 On no account is this man to be put in charge of others.
Army selection board on the young Peter Ustinov, c.1942

Anonymous: quoted in *Daily Telegraph* 30 March 2004

2 My home at my uncle's brought me acquainted with a circle of admirals. Of *Rears* and *Vices*, I saw enough. No, do not be suspecting me of a pun, I entreat.
Mary Crawford to a disapproving Edmund

Jane Austen 1775–1817: *Mansfield Park* (1814)

3 We joined the Navy to see the world,
And what did we see? We saw the sea.

Irving Berlin 1888–1989: 'We Saw the Sea' in *Follow the Fleet* (1936)

4 I should like to take the opportunity to correct some widespread misconceptions about the part played in the global struggle by the Irish Navy—a force with whom no one, except the patriots afloat, mucked in at all.

Patrick Campbell 1913–80: *The Campbell Companion* (1994) 'Sean Tar Joins Up'

5 Don't talk to me about naval tradition. It's nothing but rum, sodomy, and the lash.

Winston Churchill 1874–1965: Peter Gretton *Former Naval Person* (1968)

6 I can always guarantee that the Irish Citizen Army will fight, but I cannot guarantee that it will be on time.

James Connolly 1868–1916: Diana Norman *Terrible Beauty* (1987)

7 Have you had any word
Of that bloke in the 'Third',
Was it Southerby, Sedgwick or Sim?

Noël Coward 1899–1973: 'I Wonder What Happened to Him' (1945)

They had him thrown out of the club in Bombay
For, apart from his mess bills exceeding his pay,
He took to pig-sticking in *quite* the wrong way.
I wonder what happened to him!

8 Has anybody seen our ship?
The H.M.S. Peculiar
We've been on shore
For a month or more,
And when we see the Captain we shall get 'what for'.

Noël Coward 1899–1973: 'Has Anybody Seen Our Ship' (1935)

9 Admirals extolled for standing still,
Or doing nothing with a deal of skill.

William Cowper 1731–1800: 'Table Talk' (1782)

10 For a soldier I listed, to grow great in fame,
And be shot at for sixpence a-day.

Charles Dibdin 1745–1814: 'Charity' (1791)

11 *to the Duke of Newcastle, who had complained that General Wolfe was a madman:*
Mad, is he? Then I hope he will *bite* some of my other generals.

George II 1683–1760: Henry Beckles Willson *Life and Letters of James Wolfe* (1909)

12 Stick close to your desks and never go to sea,
And you all may be Rulers of the Queen's Navee!

W. S. Gilbert 1836–1911: *HMS Pinafore* (1878)

13 I'm very good at integral and differential calculus,
I know the scientific names of beings animalculous;
In short, in matters vegetable, animal, and mineral,
I am the very model of a modern Major-General.

W. S. Gilbert 1836–1911: *The Pirates of Penzance* (1879)

14 Fortunately, the army has had much practice at ignoring impossible instructions.

Michael Green 1927– : *The Boy Who Shot Down an Airship* (1988)

15 I had examined myself pretty thoroughly and discovered that I was unfit for military service.

Joseph Heller 1923–99: *Catch-22* (1961)

16 Ben Battle was a soldier bold,
And used to war's alarms:
But a cannon-ball took off his legs,
So he laid down his arms!

Thomas Hood 1799–1845: 'Faithless Nelly Gray' (1826)

17 For here I leave my second leg,
And the Forty-second Foot!

Thomas Hood 1799–1845: 'Faithless Nelly Gray' (1826)

18 My parents were very pleased that I was in the army. The fact that I hated it somehow pleased them even more.

Barry Humphries 1934– : *More Please* (1992)

19 No man will be a sailor who has contrivance enough to get himself into a jail; for being in a ship is being in a jail, with the chance of being drowned . . . A man in a jail has more room, better food, and commonly better company.

Samuel Johnson 1709–84: James Boswell *Life of Samuel Johnson* (1791) 16 March 1759

20 The uniform 'e wore
Was nothin' much before,
An' rather less than 'arf o' that be'ind.

Rudyard Kipling 1865–1936: 'Gunga Din' (1892)

21 Though I've belted you and flayed you,
By the livin' Gawd that made you,
You're a better man than I am, Gunga Din!

Rudyard Kipling 1865–1936: 'Gunga Din' (1892)

22 *as young army musician, having composed a march for his regiment:*
GENERAL: Isn't it a little fast, Korngold? The men can't march to that.

Erich Korngold 1897–1957: Brendan G. Carroll *The Last Prodigy* (1997)

KORNGOLD: Ah yes, well, you see Sir, this was composed for
the retreat!

23 *to a general who sent his dispatches from 'Headquarters in the
Saddle':*
The trouble with Hooker is that he's got his headquarters
where his hindquarters ought to be.

Abraham Lincoln 1809–65: P. M. Zall
Abe Lincoln Laughing (1982)

24 [Haig is] brilliant—to the top of his boots.

David Lloyd George 1863–1945:
Paul Johnson (ed.) *The Oxford Book
of Political Anecdotes* (1986);
attributed

25 If these gentlemen had their way, they would soon be
asking me to defend the moon against a possible attack
from Mars.
*of his senior military advisers, and their tendency to see
threats which did not exist*

Lord Salisbury 1830–1903: Robert
Taylor *Lord Salisbury* (1975)

26 'He's a cheery old card,' grunted Harry to Jack
As they slogged up to Arras with rifle and pack.
But he did for them both by his plan of attack.

Siegfried Sassoon 1886–1967: 'The
General' (1918)

27 I don't consider myself dovish and I certainly don't
consider myself hawkish. Maybe I would describe myself as
owlish—that is, wise enough to understand that you want
to do everything possible to avoid war.

H. Norman Schwarzkopf III 1934– :
in *New York Times* 28 January 1991

28 Napoleon's armies always used to march on their
stomachs shouting: 'Vive l'Intérieur!'

W. C. Sellar 1898–1951 and **R. J.
Yeatman** 1898–1968: *1066 and All
That* (1930)

29 Your friend the British soldier can stand up to anything
except the British War Office.

George Bernard Shaw 1856–1950:
The Devil's Disciple (1901)

30 When the military man approaches, the world locks up its
spoons and packs off its womankind.

George Bernard Shaw 1856–1950:
Man and Superman (1903)

31 Oh, you are a very poor soldier—a chocolate cream
soldier!

George Bernard Shaw 1856–1950:
Arms and the Man (1898)

32 As for being a General, well at the age of four with paper
hats and wooden swords we're all Generals. Only some of
us never grow out of it.

Peter Ustinov 1921–2004: *Romanoff
and Juliet* (1956)

33 The General was essentially a man of peace, except in his
domestic life.

Oscar Wilde 1854–1900. *The
Importance of Being Earnest* (1895)

Art

66 My art belongs to Dada. 99
Cole Porter

1 I'm a guy who can't function well in life, but I can in art.

Woody Allen 1935– : *Deconstructing
Harry* (1997 film)

2 A cow and calf are cut in half
And placed in separate cases
To call it art, however smart
Casts doubt on art's whole basis

Anonymous: unattributed; in
Spectator 5 July 2003

3 *an old lady on Epstein's controversial* Christ in Majesty:
I can never forgive Mr Epstein for his representation of Our
Lord. So very un-English!

Anonymous: in *Ned Sherrin in his Anecdotage* (1993)

4 Oh, I wish I could draw. I've always wanted to draw. I'd
give my right arm to be able to draw. It must be very
relaxing.

Alan Ayckbourn 1939– : *Joking Apart* (1979)

5 All the arts in America are a gigantic racket run by
unscrupulous men for unhealthy women.

Thomas Beecham 1879–1961: in *Observer* 5 May 1946

6 Of course he [William Morris] was a wonderful all-round
man, but the act of walking round him has always tired
me.

Max Beerbohm 1872–1956: letter to S. N. Behrman c.1953; *Conversations with Max* (1960)

7 The artistic temperament is a disease that afflicts
amateurs. It is a disease which arises from men not having
sufficient power of expression to utter and get rid of the
element of art in their being.

G. K. Chesterton 1874–1936: *Heretics* (1905)

8 There are only two styles of portrait painting; the serious
and the smirk.

Charles Dickens 1812–70: *Nicholas Nickleby* (1839)

9 *to a lawyer who had asked him why he laid such stress on 'the painter's eye':*
The painter's eye is to him what the lawyer's tongue is to
you.

Thomas Gainsborough 1727–88: William Hazlitt *Conversations of James Northcote* (1830)

10 *on attempting to paint two actors, David Garrick and Samuel Foote:*
Rot them for a couple of rogues, they have everybody's
faces but their own.

Thomas Gainsborough 1727–88: Allan Cunningham *The Lives of the Most Eminent Painters, Sculptors and Architects* (1829)

11 Then a sentimental passion of a vegetable fashion must
excite your languid spleen,
An attachment à la Plato for a bashful young potato, or a
not too French French bean!
Though the Philistines may jostle, you will rank as an
apostle in the high aesthetic band,
If you walk down Piccadilly with a poppy or a lily in your
medieval hand.

W. S. Gilbert 1836–1911: *Patience* (1881)

12 *a few days after the funeral of Sir William Orpen:*
Our painter! He never got under the surface till he got
under the sod.

Oliver St John Gogarty 1878–1957: Ulick O'Connor *Oliver St John Gogarty* (1964)

13 Yes, Frances [his wife] has the most beautiful hands in the
world—and someday I'm going to have a bust made of
them.

Sam Goldwyn 1882–1974: Michael Freedland *The Goldwyn Touch* (1986)

14 As my poor father used to say
In 1863,
Once people start on all this Art
Goodbye, moralitee!

A. P. Herbert 1890–1971: 'Lines for a Worthy Person' (1930)

15 It's amazing what you can do with an E in A-level art,
twisted imagination and a chainsaw

Damien Hirst 1965– : in *Observer* 3 December 1995 'Sayings of the Week'

16 There is, perhaps, no more dangerous man in the world
than the man with the sensibilities of an artist but without
creative talent. With luck such men make wonderful

Barry Humphries 1934– : *More Please* (1992)

theatrical impresarios and interior decorators, or else they become mass murderers or critics.

17 It is a symbol of Irish art. The cracked lookingglass of a servant.

James Joyce 1882–1941: *Ulysses* (1922)

18 Little bits of porcelain,
Little sticks of Boule
Harmonize with Venuses
Of the Flemish school.

Osbert Lancaster 1908–80: *Homes Sweet Homes* (1939)

19 *of Art Nouveau:*
Certainly no style seems at first glance to provide a richer field for the investigations of Herr Freud.

Osbert Lancaster 1908–80: *Homes Sweet Homes* (1939)

20 Mr Landseer whose only merit as a painter was the tireless accuracy with which he recorded the more revoltingly sentimental aspects of the woollier mammals.

Osbert Lancaster 1908–80: *Homes Sweet Homes* (1939)

21 If a scientist were to cut his ear off, no one would take it as evidence of a heightened sensibility.

Peter Medawar 1915–87: 'J. B. S.' (1968)

22 The perfect aesthete logically feels that the artist is strictly a turkish bath attendant.

Flann O'Brien 1911–66: *The Best of Myles* (1968)

23 *on a South African statue of the Voortrekkers:*
Patriotism is the last refuge of the sculptor.

William Plomer 1903–73: Rupert Hart-Davis letter to George Lyttelton, 13 October 1956

24 My art belongs to Dada.

Cole Porter 1891–1964: attributed

25 If you want art to be like ovaltine, then clearly some art is not for you.

Peter Reading 1946– : in *Critics' Forum*, Radio 3, 22 November 1986; attributed

26 *on the probable reaction to the painting of the subjects of Turner's Girls Surprised while Bathing:*
I should think devilish surprised to see what Turner has made of them.

Dante Gabriel Rossetti 1828–82: O. Doughty *A Victorian Romantic* (1960)

27 I don't know what art is, but I do know what it isn't. And it isn't someone walking around with a salmon over his shoulder, or embroidering the name of everyone they have slept with on the inside of a tent.

Brian Sewell: in *Independent* 26 April 1999

28 I always ask the sitter if they want truth or flattery. They always ask for truth, and I always give them flattery.

Ruskin Spear 1911–90: attributed, in *Sunday Times* (Letters) 4 January 2004

29 I doubt that art needed Ruskin any more than a moving train needs one of its passengers to shove it.

Tom Stoppard 1937– : in *Times Literary Supplement* 3 June 1977

30 *the ingredients for a successful exhibition:*
You've got to have two out of death, sex and jewels.

Roy Strong 1935– : in *Sunday Times* 23 January 1994

31 There is only one position for an artist anywhere: and that is, upright.

Dylan Thomas 1914–53: *Quite Early One Morning* (1954)

32 A genius with the IQ of a moron.
of Andy Warhol

Gore Vidal 1925– : in *Observer* 18 June 1989

33 Painters are so bitchy. Magritte told Miró that Kandinsky had feet of Klee.

Dick Vosburgh: told to the Editor

34 *on a Constable painting of the Thames:*
It is as though Constable had taken a long steady appraising stare at Canaletto and then charged straight through him.

Sylvia Townsend Warner 1893–1978: letter, 6 February 1969

35 Mrs Ballinger is one of the ladies who pursue Culture in bands, as though it were dangerous to meet it alone.

Edith Wharton 1862–1937: *Xingu and Other Stories* (1916)

36 Yes—one does like to make one's mummy just as nice as possible!
on his portrait of his mother

James McNeill Whistler 1834–1903: E. R. and J. Pennell *The Life of James McNeill Whistler* (1908)

37 *in his case against Ruskin, replying to the question: 'For two days' labour, you ask two hundred guineas?':*
No, I ask it for the knowledge of a lifetime.

James McNeill Whistler 1834–1903: D. C. Seitz *Whistler Stories* (1913)

38 *to a lady who had been reminded of his work by an 'exquisite haze in the atmosphere':*
Yes madam, Nature is creeping up.

James McNeill Whistler 1834–1903: D. C. Seitz *Whistler Stories* (1913)

39 All that I desire to point out is the general principle that Life imitates Art far more than Art imitates Life.

Oscar Wilde 1854–1900: *Intentions* (1891) 'The Decay of Lying'

40 *after the death of the outlaw Jesse James relics of his house were sold:*
His sole work of art, a chromo-lithograph of the most dreadful kind, of course was sold at a price which in Europe only a Mantegna or an undoubted Titian can command!

Oscar Wilde 1854–1900: letter 25 April 1882

41 The Sheridan stands in the heart of New York's Bohemian and artistic quarter. If you threw a brick from any of its windows, you would be certain to brain some rising young interior decorator, some Vorticist sculptor or a writer of revolutionary *vers libre*.

P. G. Wodehouse 1881–1975: *The Small Bachelor* (1927)

Autobiography ····> Biography

66 An obituary in serial form with the last instalment missing. **99**
Quentin Crisp

1 Every time somebody's Autobiography comes out I turn to the Index to see if my name occurs, and of course it never does.

James Agate 1877–1947: diary 16 September 1932

2 I used to think I was an interesting person, but I must tell you how sobering a thought it is to realize your life's story fills about thirty-five pages and you have, actually, not much to say.

Roseanne Arnold 1953– : *Roseanne* (1990)

3 *on James Agate's autobiography:*
I did so enjoy your book. Everything that everybody writes in it is so good.

Mrs Patrick Campbell 1865–1940: James Agate diary 6 May 1937

4 The reader need not become uneasy; I do not intend to write of the boy that made good.

Neville Cardus 1889–1975: *Autobiography* (1947)

5 Reformers are always finally neglected, while the memoirs of the frivolous will always eagerly be read.

Chips Channon 1897–1958: diary, 7 July 1936

6 An autobiography should give the reader opportunity to point out the author's follies and misconceptions.

Claud Cockburn 1904–81: *Crossing the Line* (1958)

7 I am really not motivated by revenge of any description
. . . The book is rather gentle.
*on her autobiography, describing the break up of her
marriage to Robin Cook*

Margaret Cook 1944– : in *Guardian* 11 January 1999

8 An autobiography is an obituary in serial form with the
last instalment missing.

Quentin Crisp 1908–99: *The Naked Civil Servant* (1968)

9 *Giles Gordon's father had criticized the length of his son's
entry in* Who's Who:
I've just measured it, with a ruler; it's exactly the same
length as my male organ, which I've also just measured.

Giles Gordon 1940– : *Aren't We Due a Royalty Statement?* (1993)

10 Autobiography is now as common as adultery and hardly
less reprehensible.

John Grigg 1924– : in *Sunday Times* 28 February 1962

11 Next to the writer of real estate advertisements, the
autobiographer is the most suspect of prose artists.

Donal Henahan: in *New York Times* 1977

12 The purpose of the Presidential Office is not power, or
leadership of the Western World, but reminiscence, best-
selling reminiscence.

Roger Jellinek 1938– : in *New York Times Book Review* 1969

13 If a man is to write *A Panegyric* he may keep vices out of
sight; but if he professes to write *A Life*, he must represent
it as it really was.

Samuel Johnson 1709–84: James Boswell *Life of Samuel Johnson* (1791) 1777

14 The reminiscences of Mrs Humphrey Ward . . . convinced
me that autobiography is a sin.

Harold Laski 1893–1950: letter to Oliver Wendell Holmes, 1 December 1918

15 *on Margot Asquith's forthcoming memoirs:*
As scandal is the second breath of life my name is down
for an early copy.

Harold Laski 1893–1950: letter to Oliver Wendell Holmes, 6 March 1920

16 I write no memoirs. I'm a gentleman. I cannot bring
myself to write nastily about persons whose hospitality I
have enjoyed.

John Pentland Mahaffy 1839–1919: W. B. Stanford and R. B. McDowell *Mahaffy* (1971)

17 Like all good memoirs it has not been emasculated by
considerations of good taste.

Peter Medawar 1915–87: review of James D. Watson *The Double Helix* (1968)

18 Every autobiography . . . becomes an absorbing work of
fiction, with something of the charm of a cryptogram.

H. L. Mencken 1880–1956: *Minority Report* (1956)

19 Even when Micheál [MacLíammoir] took in later life to
autobiographies, they were about as reliable as his
hairpieces.

Sheridan Morley 1941– : in *Sunday Times* 6 February 1994

20 To write one's memoirs is to speak ill of everybody except
oneself.

Henri Philippe Pétain 1856–1951: in *Observer* 26 May 1946

21 If you really want to hear about it, the first thing you'll
probably want to know is where I was born, and what my
lousy childhood was like, and how my parents were
occupied and all before they had me, and all that David
Copperfield kind of crap, but I don't feel like going into it.

J. D. Salinger 1919– : *The Catcher in the Rye* (1951)

22 My problem is that I am not frightfully interested in
anything, except myself. And of all forms of fiction
autobiography is the most gratuitous.

Tom Stoppard 1937– : *Lord Malquist and Mr Moon* (1966)

23 Only when one has lost all curiosity about the future has
one reached the age to write an autobiography.

Evelyn Waugh 1903–66: *A Little Learning* (1964)

24 I shall not say why and how I became, at the age of fifteen, the mistress of the Earl of Craven.

Harriette Wilson 1789–1846: opening words of *Memoirs* (1825)

25 *of political memoirists:*
It is an exceptionally inadequate ex-minister who fails to secure a six-figure sum for his work, serialization included.

Hugo Young 1938– : in *Guardian* 20 September 1990

Awards ····➤ Honours

66 Like piles. Sooner or later, every bum gets one. **99**
Maureen Lipman

1 Prizes are like sashes, you can wear them and be Miss World for a bit . . . I've been royally dissed by prizes.

Martin Amis 1949– : in *Observer* 10 March 1996 'Sayings of the Week'

2 My career must be slipping. This is the first time I've been available to pick up an award.

Michael Caine 1933– : at the Golden Globe awards, Beverly Hills, California, 24 January 1999

3 Oscar night at my house is called Passover.

Bob Hope 1903–2003: in *Daily Telegraph* 29 May 2003 (online edition)

4 *suggestion for a winning poem for the competition for Bard of Humberside:*
I put my luncheon in the fridge
and go and look at Humber Bridge.

Philip Larkin 1922–85: in conversation with Andrew Motion; quoted in *Sunday Times* 23 May 1999

5 Awards are like piles. Sooner or later, every bum gets one.

Maureen Lipman 1946– : in *Independent* 31 July 1999

6 It's about time a transvestite potter won the Turner Prize.
accepting the prize, 7 December 2003

Grayson Perry 1960– : in *Daily Telegraph* 8 December 2003 (online edition)

7 The award for travel-writing was for 'people who've been somewhere and written about it.' . . . Veni, vidi, velcro; I came, I saw, I stuck around.

Sandi Toksvig 1959– : in *Daily Telegraph* 20 March 2004

Baseball ····➤ Sports and Games

66 If people don't want to come out to the ball park, nobody's going to stop 'em. **99**
Yogi Berra

1 One of the chief duties of the fan is to engage in arguments with the man behind him. This department of the game has been allowed to run down fearfully.

Robert Benchley 1889–1945: Ralph S. Graben *The Baseball Reader* (1951)

2 Think! How the hell are you gonna think and hit at the same time?

Yogi Berra 1925– : *Nice Guys Finish Seventh* (1976)

3 If people don't want to come out to the ball park, nobody's going to stop 'em.

Yogi Berra 1925– : attributed

4 For those of us who are baseball fans and agnostics, the [Baseball] Hall of Fame is as close to a religious experience as we may ever get.

Bill Bryson 1951– : *The Lost Continent* (1989)

5 If baseball goes for pay television, shouldn't the viewers be given a bonus for watching a ball game between Baltimore and Kansas City?

Jimmy Cannon 1910–73: in *New York Post* 1951–54 'Nobody Asked Me, But . . . '

6 Finally I realized that the gentleman holding the bat is antagonistic to the man throwing the ball.

Lynn Fontanne 1887–1983: Margot Peters *Design for Living* (2003)

7 Baseball is very big with my people. It figures. It's the only way we can get to shake a bat at a white man without starting a riot.

Dick Gregory 1932– : D. H. Nathan (ed.) *Baseball Quotations* (1991)

8 *after leaving his sick-bed in October 1935 to attend the World Baseball Series in Detroit, and betting on the losers:*
I should of stood in bed.

Joe Jacobs 1896–1940: John Lardner *Strong Cigars* (1951)

9 Although he is a bad fielder he is also a poor hitter.
of a baseball player

Ring Lardner 1885–1933: R. E. Drennan *Wit's End* (1973)

10 Take me out to the ball game,
Take me out with the crowd.
Buy me some peanuts and cracker-jack—
I don't care if I never get back.

Jack Norworth 1879–1959: 'Take Me Out to the Ball Game' (1908 song)

11 Don't look back. Something may be gaining on you.
a baseball pitcher's advice

Leroy ('Satchel') Paige 1906–82: in *Collier's* 13 June 1953

12 All you have to do is keep the five players who hate your guts away from the five who are undecided.
a baseball manager's view in 1974

Casey Stengel 1891–1975: John Samuel (ed.) *The Guardian Book of Sports Quotes* (1985)

13 I don't think I can be expected to take seriously any game which takes less than three days to reach its conclusion.
a cricket enthusiast on baseball

Tom Stoppard 1937– : in *Guardian* 24 December 1984 'Sports Quotes of the Year'

14 Baseball, it is said, is only a game. True. And the Grand Canyon is only a hole in Arizona. Not all holes, or games, are created equal.

George F. Will 1941– : *Men At Work: The Craft of Baseball* (1990)

Behaviour

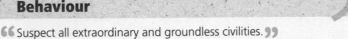

❝ Suspect all extraordinary and groundless civilities. **❞**
Thomas Fuller

1 Thank you for the most *marvellous* interview, darling, you're quite the politest lesbian I've ever met.
calling out in a crowded lobby after a self-righteous reporter

Tallulah Bankhead 1903–68: Bryony Lavery *Tallulah Bankhead* (1999)

2 My grandmother took a bath every year, whether she was dirty or not.

Brendan Behan 1923–64: *Brendan Behan's Island* (1962)

3 It looked bad when the Duke of Fife
Left off using a knife;
But people began to talk
When he left off using a fork.

Edmund Clerihew Bentley 1875–1956: 'The Duke of Fife' (1905)

4 You know what charm is: a way of getting the answer yes without having asked any clear question.

Albert Camus 1913–60: *La Chute* (1956)

5 It isn't etiquette to cut any one you've been introduced to. Remove the joint.

Lewis Carroll 1832–98: *Through the Looking-Glass* (1872)

6 Curtsey while you're thinking what to say. It saves time.

Lewis Carroll 1832–98: *Through the Looking-Glass* (1872)

7 I always take blushing either for a sign of guilt, or of ill breeding.

William Congreve 1670–1729: *The Way of the World* (1700)

8 Don't let us be familiar or fond, nor kiss before folks, like my Lady Fadler and Sir Francis . . . Let us be very strange and well-bred: Let us be as strange as if we had been married a great while, and as well-bred as if we were not married at all.

William Congreve 1670–1729: *The Way of the World* (1700)

9 HECKLER: We expected a better play.
COWARD: I expected better manners.
to a heckler in the audience after Sirocco (*1927*) *was booed*

Noël Coward 1899–1973: Sheridan Morley *A Talent to Amuse* (1969)

10 How would I like to be remembered? By my charm, you silly bugger.

Noël Coward 1899–1973: Sheridan Morley *The Quotable Noël Coward* (1999)

11 I tried to keep in mind the essential rules of British conduct which the Major had carefully instilled in me:
1. The English never speak to anyone unless they have been properly introduced (except in case of shipwreck).
2. You must never talk about God or your stomach.

Pierre Daninos: *Major Thompson and I* (1957)

12 After a brief period of anguish over whether or not to sling out the fish-knives, everyone said, 'Oh, stuff it', and heaved a sigh of relief, and the haut-ton was gone for ever.

Alice Thomas Ellis 1932–2005: in *Independent on Sunday* 2 October 1993

13 He'd say 'Par'n my glove', politely
When he shook my hand.
And he'd pass me the evening paper
When his soup was fanned.
He only used four-letter words
I didn't understand.
He had refinement.

Dorothy Fields 1905–74: 'He Had Refinement' (in *A Tree Grows in Brooklyn*, 1951 musical)

14 You children must be extra polite to strangers because your father's an actor.

Mrs Fields: Dorothy Fields' mother; taped lecture in Caryl Brahms and Ned Sherrin *Song by Song* (1984)

15 Suspect all extraordinary and groundless civilities.

Thomas Fuller 1654–1734: *Gnomologia* (1734)

16 I get too hungry for dinner at eight.
I like the theatre, but never come late.
I never bother with people I hate.
That's why the lady is a tramp.

Lorenz Hart 1895–1943: 'The Lady is a Tramp' (1937)

17 *on Harold Wilson's 'Lavender List'* (*the honours list he drew up on resigning the British premiership in 1976*):
Such a graceful exit. And then he had to go and do this on the doorstep.

John Junor 1919–97: in *Observer* 23 December 1990

18 'What are you doing for dinner tonight?'
'Digesting it.'
to a dinner invitation arriving at 8.30 pm

George S. Kaufman 1889–1961:
Howard Teichmann *George S.
Kaufman* (1973)

19 Eccentricity, to be socially acceptable, had still to have at
least four or five generations of inbreeding behind it.

Osbert Lancaster 1908–80: *All Done
From Memory* (1953)

20 The mayor gave no other answer than that deep guttural
grunt which is technically known in municipal interviews
as refusing to commit oneself.

Stephen Leacock 1869–1944:
*Arcadian Adventures with the Idle
Rich* (1914)

21 I have noticed that the people who are late are often so
much jollier than the people who have to wait for them.

E. V. Lucas 1868–1938: *365 Days and
One More* (1926)

22 *aged four, having had hot coffee spilt over his legs:*
Thank you, madam, the agony is abated.

Lord Macaulay 1800–59: G. O.
Trevelyan *Life and Letters of Lord
Macaulay* (1876)

23 Etiquette, sacred subject of, 1–389.

Judith Martin 1938– : *Miss Manners'
Guide to Rearing Perfect Children*
(1985); index entry

24 Good manners are a combination of intelligence,
education, taste, and style mixed together so that you
don't need any of those things.

P. J. O'Rourke 1947– : *Modern
Manners* (1984)

25 Do you suppose I could buy back my introduction to you?

S. J. Perelman 1904–79 et al.: in
Monkey Business (1931 film)

26 Miss Otis regrets she's unable to lunch today,
Madam.

Cole Porter 1891–1964: 'Miss Otis
Regrets' (1934)

27 In olden days, a glimpse of stocking
Was looked on as something shocking,
But now, God knows,
Anything goes.

Cole Porter 1891–1964: 'Anything
Goes' (1934)

28 One of those telegrams of which M. de Guermantes had
wittily fixed the formula: 'Cannot come, lie follows'.

Marcel Proust 1871–1922: *Le Temps
retrouvé* (Time Regained, 1926)

29 I am a woman of the world, Hector; and I can assure you
that if you will only take the trouble always to do the
perfectly correct thing, and to say the perfectly correct
thing, you can do just what you like.

George Bernard Shaw 1856–1950:
Heartbreak House (1919)

30 These sort of boobies think that people come to balls to do
nothing but dance; whereas everyone knows that the real
business of a ball is either to look out for a wife, to look
after a wife, or to look after somebody else's wife.

R. S. Surtees 1805–64: *Mr Facey
Romford's Hounds* (1865)

31 *Somerset Maugham excused his leaving early when dining
with Lady Tree by saying, 'I must look after my youth':*
Next time do bring him. We adore those sort of people.

Lady Tree 1863–1937: in *Ned Sherrin
in his Anecdotage* (1993); a similar
story is told of Maugham and Lady
Cunard

32 This is a free country, madam. We have a right to share
your privacy in a public place.

Peter Ustinov 1921–2004: *Romanoff
and Juliet* (1956)

33 Orthodoxy is my doxy; heterodoxy is another man's doxy.

William Warburton 1698–1779: to
Lord Sandwich; Joseph Priestley
Memoirs (1807)

34 Manners are especially the need of the plain. The pretty
can get away with anything.

Evelyn Waugh 1903–66: in *Observer*
15 April 1962

35 I am very sorry to hear that Duff [Cooper] was surprised and grieved to hear that I had detested him for 23 years. I must have nicer manners than people normally credit me with.

Evelyn Waugh 1903–66: letter to Lady Diana Cooper, 29 August 1953

36 *hearing someone object that the good manners of the French were all on the surface:*
Well, you know, a very good place to have them.

James McNeill Whistler 1834–1903: E. R. and J. Pennell *The Life of James McNeill Whistler* (1908)

37 It is very vulgar to talk like a dentist when one isn't a dentist. It produces a false impression.

Oscar Wilde 1854–1900: *The Importance of Being Earnest* (1895)

38 Duty is what one expects from others, it is not what one does oneself.

Oscar Wilde 1854–1900: *A Woman of No Importance* (1893)

39 It is a good rule in life never to apologize. The right sort of people do not want apologies, and the wrong sort take a mean advantage of them.

P. G. Wodehouse 1881–1975: *The Man Upstairs* (1914)

40 The confessions of error, as jocular as they are suspect, which the upper class have always associated with good manners.

Hugo Young 1938– : in *Guardian* 20 September 1990

Betting ····> Gambling

66 Horse sense is a good judgement which keeps horses from betting on people. 99
W. C. Fields

1 It's one thing to ask your bank manager for an overdraft to buy 500 begonias for the borders in Haslemere, but quite another to seek financial succour to avail oneself of some of the 5–2 they're offering on Isle de Bourbon for the St Leger.

Jeffrey Bernard 1932–97: in *Guardian* 23 December 1978 'Sports Quotes of the Year'

2 Horse sense is a good judgement which keeps horses from betting on people.

W. C. Fields 1880–1946: attributed; Nigel Rees *Cassell Dictionary of Humorous Quotations* (1999)

3 Don't let's go to the dogs tonight,
For mother will be there.

A. P. Herbert 1890–1971: 'Don't Let's Go to the Dogs Tonight' (1926)

4 I got a horse right here,
The name is Paul Revere,
And here's a guy that says if the weather's clear,
Can do, can do, this guy says the horse can do.

Frank Loesser 1910–69: 'Fugue for Tinhorns' (1950)

5 Not for good old reliable Nathan for it's always just a short walk,
To the oldest established permanent floating crap game in New York.

Frank Loesser 1910–69: 'The Oldest Established' (1950)

6 It may be that the race is not always to the swift, nor the battle to the strong—but that's the way to bet.

Damon Runyon 1884–1946: attributed

7 'You are snatching a hard guy when you snatch Bookie Bob. A very hard guy, indeed. In fact,' I say, 'I hear the softest thing about him is his front teeth.'

Damon Runyon 1884–1946: in *Collier's* 26 September 1931, 'The Snatching of Bookie Bob'

8 My immediate reward for increasing the tax on bookmaking was major vilification. It was confidently asserted in the bookmakers' circles that my mother and father met only once and then for a very brief period.
in 1972, when Chairman of the British Betting Levy Board

George Wigg 1900–83: Jonathon Green and Don Atyeo (eds.) *The Book of Sports Quotes* (1979)

The Bible

66 A lesson in how not to write for the movies. **99**
Raymond Chandler

1 There's a great text in Galatians,
Once you trip on It, entails
Twenty-nine distinct damnations,
One sure, if another fails.

Robert Browning 1812–89: 'Soliloquy of the Spanish Cloister' (1842)

2 *on Moses and the reason why there are only ten commandments:*
He probably said to himself, 'Must stop or I shall be getting silly.'

Mrs Patrick Campbell 1865–1940: James Agate diary, 6 May 1937

3 The Bible . . . is a lesson in how not to write for the movies.

Raymond Chandler 1888–1959: letter to Edgar Carter, 28 March 1947

4 A wonderful book, but there are some very queer things in it.

George V 1865–1936: K. Rose *King George V* (1983)

5 It ain't necessarily so,
It ain't necessarily so—
De t'ings that yo' li'ble
To read in de Bible—
It ain't necessarily so.

Ira Gershwin 1896–1983: 'It Ain't Necessarily So' (1935)

6 The number one book of the ages was written by a committee, and it was called the Bible.

Louis B. Mayer 1885–1957: attributed

7 The Ten Commandments should be treated like an examination. Only six need to be attempted.

Bertrand Russell 1872–1970: attributed, perhaps apocryphal

8 LORD ILLINGWORTH: The Book of Life begins with a man and a woman in a garden.
MRS ALLONBY: It ends with Revelations.

Oscar Wilde 1854–1900: *A Woman of No Importance* (1893)

9 I read the book of Job last night. I don't think God comes well out of it.

Virginia Woolf 1882–1941: letter to Lady Robert Cecil, 12 November 1922

10 It's just called 'The Bible' now. We dropped the word 'Holy' to give it a more mass-market appeal.
a publisher's view

Judith Young: attributed, 1989

Biography ····▸ Autobiography

❝ The mesh through which real life escapes. **❞**
Tom Stoppard

---

1 *to the biographer Richard Holmes, arriving to speak in a tent at the Hay on Wye Literary Festival on a particularly muddy day:*
Perfect biographer's weather. Feet of clay everywhere.

Anonymous: in *Daily Telegraph* 8 March 2003

2 Biography should be written by an acute enemy.

Arthur James Balfour 1848–1930: in *Observer* 30 January 1927

3 Nobody likes being written about in their lifetime, it's as though the FBI and the CIA were suddenly to splash your files in the paper.
on his forthcoming biography

Saul Bellow 1915–2005: in *Guardian* 10 September 1997

4 The Art of Biography
Is different from Geography.
Geography is about Maps,
But Biography is about Chaps.

Edmund Clerihew Bentley 1875–1956: *Biography for Beginners* (1905) introduction

5 *reason for shelving a planned biography of L. P. Hartley:*
I was told I had to track one butler down to a male brothel in Norway.

Penelope Fitzgerald 1916–2000: in *Daily Telegraph* 6 May 2000; obituary

6 Biography, like big game hunting, is one of the recognized forms of sport, and it is as unfair as only sport can be.

Philip Guedalla 1889–1944: *Supers and Supermen* (1920)

7 Do not send me your manuscript. Worse than the practice of writing books about living men is the conduct of living men in supervising such books.
to his would-be biographer Houston Martin

A. E. Housman 1859–1936: letter, 22 March 1936

8 *on hearing that Arthur Benson was to write the life of Rossetti:*
No, no, no, it won't do. *Dear* Arthur, we know just what he can, so beautifully, do, but no, oh no, this is to have the story of a purple man written by a white, or at the most, a pale green man.

Henry James 1843–1916: George Lyttelton letter to Rupert Hart-Davis, 28 February 1957

9 Sir John Malcolm, whose love passes the love of biographers, and who can see nothing but wisdom and justice in the action of his idol.

Lord Macaulay 1800–59: 'Lord Clive' (1840)

10 I never read the life of any important person without discovering that he knew more and could do more than I could ever hope to know or to do in half a dozen lifetimes.

J. B. Priestley 1894–1984: *Apes and Angels* (1928)

11 I have done my best to die before this book is published. It now seems possible that I may not succeed . . . I shall try to keep my sense of humour and the perspective of eternity.
letter to his biographer, Humphrey Carpenter, shortly before publication

Robert Runcie 1921–2000: H. Carpenter *Robert Runcie* (1996)

12 Biography is the mesh through which real life escapes.

Tom Stoppard 1937– : *The Invention of Love* (1997)

13 He's written me a rather plaintive letter, saying will you at least read the typescript to correct any factual errors and I've replied no, I want it to be as inaccurate as possible.
of his response to a would-be and unwanted biographer

Tom Stoppard 1937– : in *Daily Telegraph* 27 February 1999

14 Discretion is not the better part of biography.

Lytton Strachey 1880–1932: Michael Holroyd *Lytton Strachey* (1967)

15 I have a good track record with larger-than-life iron ladies.
on writing the story of the liner QEII

Carol Thatcher 1953– : in *Sunday Times* 19 March 2000 'Talking Heads'

16 Blamelessness runs riot through six hundred pages.
review of Kenneth Harris's biography of Attlee

John Vincent 1937– : in *Sunday Times* 26 September 1982

17 Then there is my noble and biographical friend who has added a new terror to death.

Charles Wetherell 1770–1846: on Lord Campbell's *Lives of the Lord Chancellors* being written without the consent of heirs or executors; also attributed to Lord Lyndhurst (1772–1863)

18 Every great man nowadays has his disciples, and it is always Judas who writes the biography.

Oscar Wilde 1854–1900: *Intentions* (1891) 'The Critic as Artist'

19 *on being lent a hot-from-the-press copy of Lytton Strachey's* Eminent Victorians *in 1918:*
We are in for a bad time.

G. M. Young 1882–1959: attributed

Birds ····▸ Animals

66 A wondrous bird is the pelican! **99**
Dixon Lanier Merritt

1 I am a sundial. Ordinary words
Cannot express my thoughts on Birds.

Hilaire Belloc 1870–1953: 'On Another' (1954)

2 Ornithology used to be an arcane hobby for embittered schoolmasters, dotty spinsters and lonely little boys, but now it is as normal a weekend occupation as rug-making or wife-swapping.

Kyril Bonfiglioli 1928–85: *Don't Point that Thing at Me* (1972)

3 A hen is only an egg's way of making other eggs.

Samuel Butler 1835–1902: *Life and Habit* (1877)

4 *to her husband, a chicken farmer in California, after a flash flood had wiped out his entire flock:*
I told you to stick to ducks.

Marlene Dietrich 1901–92: attributed; Richard Eyre *Diaries* 14 May 1992

5 Get out of town!
And he went, with a quack and a waddle and a quack,
In a flurry of eiderdown.

Frank Loesser 1910–69: 'The Ugly Duckling' (1952)

6 This woodcock, by a happy fluke,
Might have avoided either duke.
Had it the commoner preferred,
It would have been a wiser bird.
Alas, its fate became a cert,
Betwixt Duke Bobo and Duke Bert.

Harold Macmillan 1894–1986: 'Ode to a woodcock which, on emerging from the covert, was fired on simultaneously by the Dukes of Roxburghe and Marlborough'; collected by Peter Fleming from an unidentified gamebook, and quoted by Duff Hart-Davis in *Sunday Telegraph* 6 August 2000

7 Oh, a wondrous bird is the pelican!
His beak holds more than his belican.
He takes in his beak
Food enough for a week.
But I'll be darned if I know how the helican.

Dixon Lanier Merritt 1879–1972: in *Nashville Banner* 22 April 1913

8 Canaries, caged in the house, do it,
When they're out of season, grouse do it.

Cole Porter 1891–1964: 'Let's Do It, Let's Fall in Love' (1928)

9 Phoney-rustic bards,
Spare us your thoughts about birds.

Peter Reading 1946– : 'Nips' in *Collected Poems 1970–1984* (1995)

10 If I were a cassowary
On the plains of Timbuctoo,
I would eat a missionary,
Cassock, band, and hymn-book too.

Samuel Wilberforce 1805–73: impromptu verse, attributed

The Body ····▶ Appearance, Description, Faces

❝I don't really like knees.❞
Yves Saint Laurent

1 My brain? It's my second favourite organ.

Woody Allen 1935– and **Marshall Brickman** 1941– : *Sleeper* (1973 film)

2 The verandah over the toy shop.
Australian term for a beer belly.

Anonymous: Richard Eyre *National Service: Diary of a Decade* (2003)

3 If I had the use of my body I would throw it out of the window.

Samuel Beckett 1906–89: *Malone Dies* (1988)

4 Your private parts have become public property.

Alan Bennett 1934– : *Kafka's Dick* (1987)

5 Hello boys, have a good night's rest? . . . I missed you.
Governor Le Petomane facing his secretary's cleavage

Andrew Bergman 1945– and **Mel Brooks** 1926– : *Blazing Saddles* (1974 film), spoken by Mel Brooks

6 People don't come in my size until they're old . . . I used to think people were born with big bones and large frames, but apparently these grow when you're about sixty-eight.

Maeve Binchy 1940– : *Circle of Friends* (1990)

7 And our carcases, which are to rise again, are they worth raising? I hope, if mine is, that I shall have a better pair of legs than I have moved on these two-and-twenty years, or I shall be sadly behind in the squeeze into Paradise.

Lord Byron 1788–1824: letter, 13 September 1811

8 I've got difficult feet. They're almost round, like an elephant's. Lengthways they're size ten and sideways size twelve.

Patrick Campbell 1913–80: *Gullible Travels* (1969)

9 I'm the female equivalent of a counterfeit $20 bill. Half of what you see is a pretty good reproduction, the rest is a fraud.

Cher 1946– : Doug McClelland *Star Speak: Hollywood on Everything* (1987)

10 Imprisoned in every fat man a thin one is wildly signalling to be let out.

Cyril Connolly 1903–74: *The Unquiet Grave* (1944)

11 I didn't pay three pounds fifty just to see half a dozen acorns and a chipolata.

Noël Coward 1899–1973: on David Storey's *The Changing Room*; attributed

12 He had but one eye, and the popular prejudice runs in favour of two.

Charles Dickens 1812–70: *Nicholas Nickleby* (1839)

13 If you could see my legs when I take my boots off, you'd form some idea of what unrequited affection is.

Charles Dickens 1812–70: *Dombey and Son* (1848)

14 What is man, when you come to think upon him, but a minutely set, ingenious machine for turning, with infinite artfulness, the red wine of Shiraz into urine?

Isak Dinesen 1885–1962: *Seven Gothic Tales* (1934) 'The Dreamers'

15 I wish you could only see Dizzy in his bath, then you would know what a white skin is.
 of her husband

Mary Anne Disraeli d. 1872: attributed; William Gregory *An Autobiography* (1894)

16 *to William Cecil, who suffered from gout:*
 My lord, we make use of you, not for your bad legs, but for your good head.

Elizabeth I 1533–1603: F. Chamberlin *Sayings of Queen Elizabeth* (1923)

17 Being a woman is worse than being a farmer—There is so much harvesting and crop spraying to be done: legs to be waxed, underarms shaved, eyebrows plucked, feet pumiced, skin exfoliated and moisturized, spots cleansed, roots dyed, eyelashes tinted, nails filed, cellulite massaged, stomach muscles exercised . . . Is it any wonder girls have no confidence?

Helen Fielding 1958– : *Bridget Jones's Diary* (1996)

18 I travel light; as light,
 That is, as a man can travel who will
 Still carry his body around because
 Of its sentimental value.

Christopher Fry 1907–2005: *The Lady's not for Burning* (1949)

19 My complexion owes much to my Franco-Slavic mamma and little to my British papa. My waist is my own work.

Mark Gatiss 1966– : *The Vesuvius Club* (2004)

20 I have a left shoulder-blade that is a miracle of loveliness. People come miles to see it. My right elbow has a fascination that few can resist.

W. S. Gilbert 1836–1911: *The Mikado* (1885)

21 There is something between us.

Donald Hall 1928– : 'Breasts' (a one-line poem, 1971)

22 I wouldn't change anything but I could do with sharing my bottom and thighs with at least two other people.

Christine Hamilton: in *Observer* 4 April 2004

23 Lydia, oh Lydia—Say, have you met Lydia?
 Oh, Lydia, the tattooed lady?
 When she stands, her lap grows littler,
 When she sits, she sits on Hitler!

E. Y. Harburg 1898–1981: 'Lydia, the Tattooed Lady' (*A Day at the Circus*, 1939 film)

24 [Alfred Hitchcock] thought of himself as looking like Cary Grant. That's tough, to think of yourself one way and look another.

Tippi Hedren 1935– : interview in California, 1982; P. F. Boller and R. L. Davis *Hollywood Anecdotes* (1988)

25 What they call 'heart' lies much lower than the fourth waistcoat button.

Georg Christoph Lichtenberg 1742–99: notebook (1776–79) in *Aphorisms* (1990)

26 If your mother had married a proper decent Limerickman you wouldn't have this standing up, North of Ireland, Presbyterian hair.

Frank McCourt 1930– : *Angela's Ashes* (1996)

27 *seaside postcard showing a very fat man whose stomach obscures the small boy at his feet:*
Can't see my little Willy.

Donald McGill 1875–1962: caption, c.1910; in 'Quote Unquote Newsletter', July 1994

28 I'd like to borrow his body for just 48 hours. There are three guys I'd like to beat up and four women I'd like to make love to.

Jim Murray: of Muhammad Ali; attributed

29 A bit of talcum
Is always walcum.

Ogden Nash 1902–71: 'The Baby' (1931)

30 In an advanced state of nudity.

Joe Orton 1933–67: *Up Against It*, screenplay written for the Beatles but never filmed

31 If I see something sagging, dragging or bagging, I'm going to have the stuff tucked or plucked.

Dolly Parton 1946– : interview with Larry King, 12 July 2003

32 *a gay friend, patting her bottom, had commented that it was flabby:*
FRIEND: You should feel mine. It's all taut.
JENNIFER PATERSON: Oh really? And who taut it?

Jennifer Paterson 1928–99: in *The Times* 11 August 1999, obituary

33 I'm deeply honoured, but a bit confused. I was only ever a B-cup.
on being voted the sexiest television star 'of all time' by Americans

Diana Rigg 1938– : in *The Times* 3 May 1999

34 I don't really like knees.

Yves Saint Laurent 1936– : in *Observer* 3 August 1958

35 It's hard to be naked and not be upstaged by your nipples.

Susan Sarandon 1946– : in *Independent* 28 December 2002

36 Thou seest I have more flesh than another man, and therefore more frailty.

William Shakespeare 1564–1616: *Henry IV, Part 1* (1597)

37 The body of a young woman is God's greatest achievement . . . Of course, He could have built it to last longer but you can't have everything.

Neil Simon 1927– : *The Gingerbread Lady* (1970)

38 *on seeing her son Toby Stephens appear naked in the television adaptation of* The Camomile Lawn*:*
I hadn't see Toby's willy since he was about two, so you can imagine the terrible shock of it all!

Maggie Smith 1934– : attributed (told to the Editor)

39 Mrs Bennett . . . had but two back teeth in her head, but, thank God, they still met.

Edith Œ. Somerville 1858–1949 and **Martin Ross** 1862–1915: *Some Experiences of an Irish R.M.* (1899)

40 Big breasts à la Pamela Anderson are one thing but ones that look more like old socks with tangerines dropped in the bottom are an entirely different kettle du poisson.

Arabella Weir: *Does My Bum Look Big in This?* (1997)

41 Bah! the thing is not a nose at all, but a bit of primordial chaos clapped on to my face.

H. G. Wells 1866–1946: *Select Conversations with an Uncle* (1895) 'The Man with a Nose'

42 Let's forget the six feet and talk about the seven inches.

Mae West 1892–1980: G. Eells and S. Musgrove *Mae West* (1989)

43 A lot of people are very critical of modern reproductive processes without understanding all the ins and outs.

Lord Winston 1940– : attributed in *Private Eye*, 6 February 2004

44 He was built on large lines, and seemed to fill the room to overflowing. In physique he was not unlike what Primo Carnera would have been if Carnera hadn't stunted his growth by smoking cigarettes when a boy.

P. G. Wodehouse 1881–1975: *Mulliner Nights* (1933)

45 You're a man, and that's a bonus
'Cause when you're swinging your cojones
You'll show 'em what testosterone is.

David Yazbek: 'Man' in *The Full Monty* (musical, 2000)

Books ····▷ Dictionaries, Indexes, Libraries, Literature, Reading, Publishing

❝ One man is as good as another until he has written a book. **❞**
Benjamin Jowett

1 My desire is . . . that mine adversary had written a book.

Bible: *Job*

2 Take care not to understand editions and title-pages too well. It always smells of pedantry, and not always of learning . . . Beware of the *bibliomanie*.

Lord Chesterfield 1694–1773: *Letters to his Son* (1774)

3 *on hearing that a fellow guest was 'writing a book':*
Neither am I.

Peter Cook 1937–95: attributed (disclaimed as original by Cook); Nigel Rees *Cassell Dictionary of Humorous Quotations* (1999)

4 PETER BOGDANOVICH: I'm giving John Wayne a book as a birthday present.
JOHN FORD: He's *got* a book.

John Ford 1895–1973: Peter Bogdanovich *Who the Hell's in It?* (2004)

5 When the [Supreme] Court moved to Washington in 1800, it was provided with no books, which probably accounts for the high quality of early opinions.

Robert H. Jackson 1892–1954: *The Supreme Court in the American System of Government* (1955)

6 One man is as good as another until he has written a book.

Benjamin Jowett 1817–93: Evelyn Abbott and Lewis Campbell (eds.) *Life and Letters of Benjamin Jowett* (1897)

7 This is primarily a picture-book and the letterpress is intended to do no more than provide a small mass of information leavened by a large dose of personal prejudice.

Osbert Lancaster 1908–80: *Pillar to Post* (1938)

8 Synopsis of Previous Chapters: There are no Previous Chapters.

Stephen Leacock 1869–1944: *Nonsense Novels* (1911) 'Gertrude the Governess'

9 Having been unpopular in high school is not just cause for book publication.

Fran Lebowitz 1946– : *Metropolitan Life* (1978)

10 Book—what they make a movie out of for television.

Leonard Louis Levinson: Laurence J. Peter (ed.) *Quotations for our Time* (1977)

11 Things were easier for the old novelists who saw people all of a piece. Speaking generally, their heroes were good through and through, their villains wholly bad.

W. Somerset Maugham 1874–1965: *A Writer's Notebook* (1949) written in 1922

12 I opened it at page 96—the secret page on which I write my name to catch out borrowers and book-sharks.

Flann O'Brien 1911–66: *Myles Away from Dublin* (1990)

13 Some savage faculty for observation told him that most respectable and estimable people usually had a lot of books in their houses.

Flann O'Brien 1911–66: *The Best of Myles* (1968)

14 This is not a novel to be tossed aside lightly. It should be thrown with great force.

Dorothy Parker 1893–1967: R. E. Drennan *Wit's End* (1973)

15 I hate books; they only teach us to talk about things we know nothing about.

Jean-Jacques Rousseau 1712–78: *Émile* (1762)

16 A best-seller is the gilded tomb of a mediocre talent.

Logan Pearsall Smith 1865–1946: *Afterthoughts* (1931) 'Art and Letters'

17 No furniture so charming as books.

Sydney Smith 1771–1845: Lady Holland *Memoir* (1855)

18 A. L. ROWSE: You don't read my books, John. Do you know *Tudor Cornwall?*
JOHN SPARROW: Do you know Stuart Hampshire?

John Sparrow 1906–92: Noel Annan *The Dons* (1999)

19 Digressions, incontestably, are the sunshine;—they are the life, the soul of reading;—take them out of this book for instance,—you might as well take the book along with them.

Laurence Sterne 1713–68: *Tristram Shandy* (1759–67)

20 'Pilgrim's Progress', about a man that left his family it didn't say why . . . The statements was interesting, but tough.

Mark Twain 1835–1910: *The Adventures of Huckleberry Finn* (1884)

21 I haven't been so happy since the day Reader's Digest lost my address.

Dick Vosburgh: *A Saint She Ain't* (1999)

22 In every first novel the hero is the author as Christ or Faust.

Oscar Wilde 1854–1900: attributed

23 There is no such thing as a moral or an immoral book. Books are well written, or badly written.

Oscar Wilde 1854–1900: *The Picture of Dorian Gray* (1891)

24 The good ended happily, and the bad unhappily. That is what fiction means.

Oscar Wilde 1854–1900: *The Importance of Being Earnest* (1895)

25 The scratching of pimples on the body of the bootboy at Claridges.

Virginia Woolf 1882–1941: of James Joyce's *Ulysses*; letter to Lytton Strachey, 24 April 1922

Bores

66 What's wrong with being a boring kind of guy? **99**
George Bush

1 He really is terribly heavy going. Like running up hill in roller skates.

Alan Ayckbourn 1939– : *Living Together* (1975)

2 A person who talks when you wish him to listen.

Ambrose Bierce 1842–c.1914: definition of a bore; *Cynic's Word Book* (1906)

3 What's wrong with being a boring kind of guy?

George Bush 1924– : during the campaign for the Republican nomination; in *Daily Telegraph* 28 April 1988

4 Dullness is so much stronger than genius because there is so much more of it, and it is better organized and more naturally cohesive *inter se*. So the arctic volcano can do nothing against arctic ice.

Samuel Butler 1835–1902: *Notebooks* (1912)

5 VISITOR TO ETON: I hope that I am not boring you.
PROVOST: Not yet.

Lord Hugh Cecil 1869–1956: attributed; in *Dictionary of National Biography* (1917–)

6 He is not only dull in himself, but the cause of dullness in others.
on a dull law lord

Samuel Foote 1720–77: James Boswell *Life of Samuel Johnson* (1934 ed.) 1783

7 Most of my contemporaries at school entered the World of Business, the logical destiny of bores.

Barry Humphries 1934– : *More Please* (1992)

8 He was dull in a new way, and that made many people think him *great*.

Samuel Johnson 1709–84: of Thomas Gray; James Boswell *Life of Samuel Johnson* (1791) 28 March 1775

9 The boredom occasioned by too much restraint is always preferable to that produced by an uncontrolled enthusiasm for a pointless variety.

Osbert Lancaster 1908–80: *Pillar to Post* (1938)

10 A bore is simply a nonentity who resents his humble lot in life, and seeks satisfaction for his wounded ego by forcing himself on his betters.

H. L. Mencken 1880–1956: *Minority Report* (1956)

11 The only rule I have found to have any validity in writing is not to bore yourself.

John Mortimer 1923– : *Clinging to the Wreckage* (1982)

12 He was not only a bore; he bored for England.

Malcolm Muggeridge 1903–90: of Anthony Eden; *Tread Softly* (1966)

13 It is to be noted that when any part of this paper appears dull there is a design in it.

Richard Steele 1672–1729: *The Tatler* 7 July 1709

14 A bore is a man who, when you ask him how he is, tells you.

Bert Leston Taylor 1866–1901: *The So-Called Human Race* (1922)

15 Dylan talked copiously, then stopped. 'Somebody's boring me,' he said, 'I think it's me.'

Dylan Thomas 1914–53: Rayner Heppenstall *Four Absentees* (1960)

16 He is an old bore. Even the grave yawns for him.
of the actor Israel Zangwill

Herbert Beerbohm Tree 1852–1917:
Max Beerbohm *Herbert Beerbohm Tree* (1920)

17 My boredom threshold is low at the best of times but I have spent more time being slowly and excruciatingly bored by children than any other section of the human race.

Jill Tweedie 1936–93: *It's Only Me* (1980)

18 In England people actually try to be brilliant at breakfast. That is so dreadful of them! Only dull people are brilliant at breakfast.

Oscar Wilde 1854–1900: *An Ideal Husband* (1895)

Boxing ····▸ Sports and Games

66 Show business with blood. **99**
David Belasco

1 I figure I'll be champ for about ten years and then I'll let my brother take over—like the Kennedys down in Washington.
before becoming world heavyweight champion in 1964

Muhammad Ali 1942– : attributed, 1979

2 Boxing is show-business with blood.

David Belasco: in 1915; Michael Parkinson *Sporting Lives* (1993); later also used by Frank Bruno

3 And I want to say anything is possible. Comma. You know.

Frank Bruno: in *Guardian* 24 December 1990 'Sports Quotes of the Year'

4 Tall men come down to my height when I hit 'em in the body.

Jack Dempsey 1895–1983: in 1920, attributed

5 The bigger they are, the further they have to fall.

Robert Fitzsimmons 1862–1917: prior to a fight, in *Brooklyn Daily Eagle* 11 August 1900 (similar forms found in proverbs since the 15th century)

6 I want to keep fighting because it is the only thing that keeps me out of the hamburger joints. If I don't fight, I'll eat this planet.

George Foreman 1948– : in *Times* 17 January 1990

7 Putting a fighter in the business world is like putting silk stockings on a pig.
in 1961, a boxing promoter's view

Jack Hurley: attributed, 1979

8 *after Jack Sharkey beat Max Schmeling (of whom Jacobs was manager) in the heavyweight title fight, 21 June 1932:*
We was robbed!

Joe Jacobs 1896–1940: Peter Heller *In This Corner* (1975)

9 *borrowing E. M. Forster's literary maxim during a bad amateur boxing match:*
Only connect.

Philip Larkin 1922–85: attributed; in *Guardian* 3 December 1985 (online edition, obituary by Craig Raine)

10 I miss the things like the cameraderie in the gym. I don't miss being smacked in the mouth every day.
on retirement from the ring

Barry McGuigan 1961– : in *Irish Times* 18 April 1998 'This Week They Said'

11 They're selling video cassettes of the Ali–Spinks fight for $89.95. Hell, for that money Spinks will come to your house.

Ferdie Pacheco: in *Guardian* 23 December 1978 'Sports Quotes of the Year'

12 While Spider McCoy manages a number of fighters, he never gets excited about anything but a heavyweight, and this is the way all fight managers are. A fight manager may have a lightweight champion of the world, but he will get more heated up about some sausage who scarcely knows how to hold his hands up if he is a heavyweight.

Damon Runyon 1884–1946: *Take It Easy* (1938)

Broadcasting ····➤ Television

❝The media. It sounds like a convention of spiritualists.❞
Tom Stoppard

1 Adams' first law of television: the weight of the backside is greater than the force of the intellect.

Phillip Adams 1939– : in 1970; attributed

2 We hope to amuse the customers with music and with rhyme
But ninety minutes is a long, long time.

Noël Coward 1899–1973: '90 Minutes is a Long, Long Time' (1955); opening song for a CBS television live special starring Noël Coward and Mary Martin

3 IAN ST JOHN: Is he speaking to you yet?
JIMMY GREAVES: Not yet, but I hope to be incommunicado with him in a very short space of time.

Jimmy Greaves 1940– : Barry Fantoni (ed.) *Private Eye's Colemanballs 2* (1984)

4 Every time I think that Ned Sherrin is dead I switch on the television and see him in some dreadful, off-colour programme which brings home all too painfully the fact that he is still alive.

Ian Hamilton 1938– : Ned Sherrin *Cutting Edge* (1984); attributed

5 To goad the BBC is a rewarding sport in itself. It makes a tabloid feel like a heavyweight.

Clive James 1939– : *The Dreaming Swimmer* (1992)

6 The media. It sounds like a convention of spiritualists.

Tom Stoppard 1937– : *Night and Day* (1978)

Bureaucracy ····➤ Civil Servants, Management

❝A camel is a horse designed by a committee.❞
Alec Issigonis

1 A memorandum is written not to inform the reader but to protect the writer.

Dean Acheson 1893–1971: in *Wall Street Journal* 8 September 1977

2 MAM: Opportunities calling for devoted self-sacrifice don't turn up every day of the week.
MS CRAIG: Quite. Any really first-rate chance of improving the soul gets snapped up by the social services department.

Alan Bennett 1934– : *Enjoy* (1980)

3 This island is made mainly of coal and surrounded by fish. Only an organizing genius could produce a shortage of coal and fish at the same time.

Aneurin Bevan 1897–1960: speech at Blackpool 24 May 1945

4 Whatever was required to be done, the Circumlocution Office was beforehand with all the public departments in the art of perceiving—HOW NOT TO DO IT.

Charles Dickens 1812–70: *Little Dorrit* (1857)

5 The Pentagon, that immense monument to modern man's subservience to the desk.

Oliver Franks 1905–92: in *Observer* 30 November 1952

6 *his secretary had suggested throwing away out-of-date files:*
A good idea, only be sure to make a copy of everything before getting rid of it.

Sam Goldwyn 1882–1974: Michael Freedland *The Goldwyn Touch* (1986)

7 Official dignity tends to increase in inverse ratio to the importance of the country in which the office is held.

Aldous Huxley 1894–1963: *Beyond the Mexique Bay* (1934)

8 *on his dislike of working in teams:*
A camel is a horse designed by a committee.

Alec Issigonis 1906–88: in *Guardian* 14 January 1991 'Notes and Queries' (attributed)

9 The truth in these matters may be stated as a scientific law: 'The persistence of public officials varies inversely with the importance of the matter on which they are persisting.'

Bernard Levin 1928– : *In These Times* (1986)

10 It is characteristic of committee discussions and decisions that every member has a vivid recollection of them and that every member's recollection differs violently from every other member's recollection.

Jonathan Lynn 1943– and **Antony Jay** 1930– : *Yes Prime Minister* vol. 2 (1987)

11 Perfection of planned layout is achieved only by institutions on the point of collapse.

C. Northcote Parkinson 1909–93: *Parkinson's Law* (1958)

12 Underneath runs the main current of preoccupation, which is keeping one's nose clean at all times. This means that when things go wrong you have to pass the blame along the line, like pass-the-parcel, till the music stops.

Tom Stoppard 1937– : *Neutral Ground* (1983)

Business ····▸ Management

❝ I play it the company way. ❞
Frank Loesser

1 Our clients are coping with the stress of financial loss by soaking in a hot bath scented with my Rose Geranium bath crystals.
on the Wall Street crash

Elizabeth Arden c. 1880–1966: attributed

2 My first rule of consumerism is never to buy anything you can't make your children carry.

Bill Bryson 1951– : *The Lost Continent* (1989)

3 Some accountants are comedians, but comedians are never accountants.
defending Ken Dodd on the charge of tax evasion

George Carman 1930– : in *The Times* 30 August 2000; attributed

4 Accountants are the witch-doctors of the modern world and willing to turn their hands to any kind of magic.

Lord Justice Harman 1894–1970: speech, February 1964

5 The last stage of fitting the product to the market is fitting the market to the product.

Clive James 1939– : in *Observer* 16 October 1989

6 As a simple countryman, he distrusted the use of money and, finding barter cumbersome, preferred to steal.

Miles Kington 1941–2008: *Welcome to Kington* (1989)

7 Doing well by doing good.
now the slogan of Monsanto

Tom Lehrer 1928– : 'The Old Dope Peddler' (1953 song)

8 A: I play it the company way
Where the company puts me, there I'll stay.
B: But what is your point of view?
A: I have no point of view!
Supposing the company thinks . . . I think so too!

Frank Loesser 1910–69: 'The Company Way' (1962)

9 *asked if there were signs of a depression in London:*
If you mean that one could fire a gun across the Savoy Grill without hitting either a diner or an Italian waiter the answer is 'No'

David Montague: attributed, 1963

10 Could Henry Ford produce the Book of Kells? Certainly not. He would quarrel initially with the advisability of such a project and then prove it was impossible.

Flann O'Brien 1911–66: *Myles Away from Dublin* (1990)

11 Jane Austen doesn't sell hi-tech cars. We do the past very well in this country but how can we compete from a high-tech point of view when the rest of the world sees us dressed up in top hats and crinolines all the time?

Roger Puttnam: in *Independent* 7 June 1997

12 We even sell a pair of earrings for under £1, which is cheaper than a prawn sandwich from Marks & Spencers. But I have to say the earrings probably won't last as long.

Gerald Ratner 1949– : speech to the Institute of Directors, Albert Hall, 23 April 1991

13 Running a company on market research is like driving while looking in the rear view mirror.

Anita Roddick 1942–2007: in *Independent* 22 August 1997

14 *the daughter of the Body Shop's founders on her sex emporium:*
We employ Muslim women refugees, use unionised factories, run a 'fair trade' project in Brazil and our wooden dildos are made from naturally felled trees.

Sam Roddick: attributed; in *Times* 3 June 2003

15 Whenever I feel in the least tempted to be methodical or business-like or even decently industrious, I go to Kensal Green and look at the graves of those who died in business.

Saki 1870–1916: *The Square Egg* (1924)

16 Breakages, Limited, the biggest industrial corporation in the country.

George Bernard Shaw 1856–1950: *The Apple Cart* (1930)

17 I long for the day when a new generation of Anita Roddicks can address the AGM in a bright pink dress and strappy sandals.

Alexandra Shulman 1957– : in *Sunday Times* 23 May 1999 'Talking Heads'

18 *definition of insider trading:*
Stealing too fast.

Calvin Trillin 1935– : 'The Inside on Insider Trading' (1987)

19 It's a recession when your neighbour loses his job; it's a depression when you lose yours.

Harry S. Truman 1884–1972: in *Observer* 13 April 1958

20 Put all your eggs in one basket—and WATCH THAT BASKET.

Mark Twain 1835–1910: *Pudd'nhead Wilson* (1894)

21 The public be damned! I'm working for my stockholders.

William H. Vanderbilt 1821–85: comment to a news reporter, 2 October 1882

22 [Commercialism is] doing well that which should not be done at all.

Gore Vidal 1925– : in *Listener* 7 August 1975

23 Go to your business, I say, pleasure, whilst I go to my pleasure, business.

William Wycherley c.1640–1716: *The Country Wife* (1675)

24 Nothing is illegal if one hundred well-placed business men decide to do it.

Andrew Young 1932– : Morris K. Udall *Too Funny to be President* (1988)

Canada

❝ I'm world famous, Dr Parks said, all over Canada. ❞
Mordecai Richler

1 Canada is a country so square that even the female impersonators are women.

Richard Benner: *Outrageous* (1977)

2 *definition of a Canadian:*
Somebody who knows how to make love in a canoe.

Pierre Berton 1920–2004: in *Toronto Star* 22 December 1973

3 I see Canada as a country torn between a very northern, rather extraordinary, mystical spirit which it fears and its desire to present itself to the world as a Scotch banker.

Robertson Davies 1913–95: *The Enthusiasms of Robertson Davies* (1990)

4 Canadians are Americans with no Disneyland.

Margaret Mahy 1937– : *The Changeover* (1984)

5 I'm world famous, Dr Parks said, all over Canada.

Mordecai Richler 1931–2001: *The Incomparable Atuk* (1963)

6 Climb every Mountie.

Dick Vosburgh and **Denis King**: *Beauty and the Beards* (2001)

Catchphrases ····> Comedy Routines and Catchphrases

Censorship

❝ Everybody favours free speech in the slack moments when no axes are being ground. ❞
Heywood Broun

1 She insists on all these torrid romances . . . I have to wrap them round with copies of *Country Life* to carry them home.

Alan Ayckbourn 1939– : *Round and Round the Garden* (1975)

2 There are no alternatives to 'bastard' agreeable to me.
Nevertheless I have offered them 'swine' in its place.
on changes to the text of Endgame *required by the Lord
Chamberlain for the London production, summer 1958*

Samuel Beckett 1906–89: James Knowlson *Damned to Fame* (1996)

3 I'm all in favour of free expression provided it's kept rigidly
under control.

Alan Bennett 1934– : *Forty Years On* (1969)

4 Everybody favours free speech in the slack moments when
no axes are being ground.

Heywood Broun 1888–1939: in *New York World* 23 October 1926

5 It's because it's in English, you can get away with much
more in French. Think what you could get away with in
Japanese!
*on the refusal of the Lord Chamberlain to grant a licence to
Samuel Beckett's* Endgame, *February 1958*

George Devine 1910–66: Irving Wardle *The Theatres of George Devine* (1978)

6 I dislike censorship. Like an appendix it is useless when
inert and dangerous when active.

Maurice Edelman 1911–75: Jonathon Green (ed.) *A Dictionary of Contemporary Quotations* (1982)

7 It's red hot, mate. I hate to think of this sort of book
getting into the wrong hands. As soon as I've finished this,
I shall recommend they ban it.

Ray Galton 1930– and **Alan Simpson** 1929– : *The Missing Page* (1960 BBC television programme) words spoken by Tony Hancock

8 No government ought to be without censors: and where
the press is free, no one ever will.

Thomas Jefferson 1743–1826: letter to George Washington, 9 September 1792

9 No less than twenty-two publishers and printers read the
manuscript of *Dubliners* and when at last it was printed
some very kind person bought out the entire edition and
had it burnt in Dublin.

James Joyce 1882–1941: letter, 2 April 1932

10 Freedom of the press is guaranteed only to those who own
one.

A. J. Liebling 1904–63: 'The Wayward Press: Do you belong in Journalism?' (1960)

11 Careful now!
placard alerting Craggy Island to a banned film

Graham Linehan and **Arthur Mathews**: 'The Passion of St Tibulus' (1994), episode from *Father Ted* (Channel 4 TV, 1994–8)

12 She sits among the cabbages and leeks.
*substitution for 'she sits among the cabbages and peas',
which was supposedly forbidden by a local watch committee*

Marie Lloyd 1870–1922: attributed; Nigel Rees *Cassell Dictionary of Humorous Quotations* (1999)

13 Censorship, like charity, should begin at home, but, unlike
charity, it should end there.

Clare Boothe Luce 1903–87: attributed, 1982

14 We have long passed the Victorian Era when asterisks
were followed after a certain interval by a baby.

W. Somerset Maugham 1874–1965: *The Constant Wife* (1926)

15 *On being appointed Irish film censor:*
I am between the devil and the Holy See . . . [My task is to
prevent] the Californication of Ireland.

James Montgomery: Ulick O'Connor *Oliver St John Gogarty* (1964)

16 I suppose that writers should, in a way, feel flattered by
the censorship laws. They show a primitive fear and dread
at the fearful magic of print.

John Mortimer 1923– : *Clinging to the Wreckage* (1982)

17 Mr de Valera, like Mr Cosgrave, regarded literary censorship as part of our freedom to achieve fuller freedom.

Brendan Ó hEithir 1930– : *The Begrudger's Guide to Irish Politics*

18 A censor is a man who knows more than he thinks you ought to.

Laurence J. Peter 1919– : Jonathon Green (ed.) *A Dictionary of Contemporary Quotations* (1982)

19 Assassination is the extreme form of censorship.

George Bernard Shaw 1856–1950: *The Showing-Up of Blanco Posnet* (1911) 'Limits to Toleration'

20 We are paid to have dirty minds.

John Trevelyan 1903–86: when British Film Censor; in *Observer* 15 November 1959 'Sayings of the Week'

21 'This country [Ireland] . . . has already got a State Censorship of Films which is said to be the strictest in Europe.'
'It's not strict enough.'

Mervyn Wall 1908– : *Leaves for the Burning* (1952)

Certainty ····➤ Religion

❝I deny nothing, but doubt everything.**❞**
Lord Byron

1 He used to be fairly indecisive, but now he's not so certain.

Peter Alliss 1931– : Barry Fantoni (ed.) *Private Eye's Colemanballs 3* (1986)

2 Often undecided whether to desert a sinking ship for one that might not float, he would make up his mind to sit on the wharf for a day.
of Lord Curzon

Lord Beaverbrook 1879–1964: *Men and Power* (1956)

3 ESTRAGON: Charming spot. Inspiring prospects. Let's go.
VLADIMIR: We can't.
ESTRAGON: Why not?
VLADIMIR: We're waiting for Godot.

Samuel Beckett 1906–89: *Waiting for Godot* (1955)

4 Oh! let us never, never doubt
What nobody is sure about!

Hilaire Belloc 1870–1953: 'The Microbe' (1897)

5 You can put up a sign on the door, 'beware of the dog', without having a dog.

Hans Blix 1928– : in *Guardian* (online edition) 18 September 2003

6 *when asked whether he really believed a horseshoe hanging over his door would bring him luck:*
Of course not, but I am told it works even if you don't believe in it.

Niels Bohr 1885–1962: A. Pais *Inward Bound* (1986)

7 There is something pagan in me that I cannot shake off. In short, I deny nothing, but doubt everything.

Lord Byron 1788–1824: letter, 4 December 1811

8 We can dance on pinheads till the cows come home.

Alastair Campbell 1957– : in *The Times* 10 January 2004

9 I don't believe in astrology; I'm a Sagittarius and we're sceptical.

Arthur C. Clarke 1917–2008: attributed; Nigel Rees *Cassell Dictionary of Humorous Quotations* (1999)

10 *of Thomas Arnold, son of Dr Arnold of Rugby, a notable and frequent nineteenth-century convert:*
Poor Tom Arnold has lost his faith *again*.

Eliza Conybeare 1820–1903: Rose Macaulay letter to Father Johnson, 8 April 1951

11 I do not pretend to know where many ignorant men are sure—that is all that agnosticism means.

Clarence Darrow 1857–1938: speech at the trial of John Thomas Scopes, 15 July 1925; *The World's Most Famous Court Trial* (1925)

12 The archbishop [Archbishop Runcie] is usually to be found nailing his colours to the fence.

Frank Field 1942– : attributed in *Crockfords 1987/88* (1987); Geoffrey Madan records in his *Notebooks* that Harry Cust made a similar comment on A. J. Balfour, c.1904.

13 I'll give you a definite maybe.

Sam Goldwyn 1882–1974: attributed

14 PHILIP: I'm sorry. (Pause.) I suppose I'm indecisive. (Pause.) My trouble is, I'm a man of no convictions. (Longish pause.) At least, I think I am.

Christopher Hampton 1946– : *The Philanthropist* (1970)

15 At this moment in time I did not say them things.

Glenn Hoddle 1957– : in *Daily Telegraph* 2 February 1999

16 Certitude is not the test of certainty. We have been cocksure of many things that were not so.

Oliver Wendell Holmes Jr. 1841–1935: 'Natural Law' (1918)

17 A young man who wishes to remain a sound atheist cannot be too careful of his reading.

C. S. Lewis 1898–1963: *Surprised by Joy* (1955)

18 Like all weak men he laid an exaggerated stress on not changing one's mind.

W. Somerset Maugham 1874–1965: *Of Human Bondage* (1915)

19 I wish I was as cocksure of anything as Tom Macaulay is of everything.

Lord Melbourne 1779–1848: Lord Cowper *Preface to Lord Melbourne's Papers* (1889)

20 I am not denying anything I did not say.

Brian Mulroney 1939– : in *The Globe and Mail* 18 September 1986

21 That happy sense of purpose people have when they are standing up for a principle they haven't really been knocked down for yet.

P. J. O'Rourke 1947– : *Give War a Chance* (1992)

22 Well, sir, you never can tell. That's a principle in life with me, sir, if you'll excuse my having such a thing, sir.

George Bernard Shaw 1856–1950: *You Never Can Tell* (1898)

23 All right, have it your own way—you heard a seal bark!

James Thurber 1894–1961: cartoon caption; in *New Yorker* 30 January 1932

24 I would earnestly warn you against trying to find out the reason for and explanation of everything . . . To try and find out the reason for everything is very dangerous and leads to nothing but disappointment and dissatisfaction, unsettling your mind and in the end making you miserable.

Queen Victoria 1819–1901: letter to Princess Victoria of Hesse, 22 August 1883

Character ····> Self-Knowledge and Self-Deception

66 A hellhound is always a hellhound. 99
P. G. Wodehouse

1 He never failed to seek a peaceful solution of a problem when all other possibilities had failed.

Anonymous: Cecil Roth 'Joseph Herman Hertz' (1959) in *The Dictionary of National Biography*

2 Though [Lucia was] essentially autocratic, her subjects were allowed and even encouraged to develop their own minds on their own lines, provided always that those lines met at the junction where she was station-master.

E. F. Benson 1867–1940: *Queen Lucia* (1920)

3 Take care not to be the kind of person for whom the band is always playing in the other room.

Quentin Crisp 1908–99: in *Spectator* 20 November 1999

4 We never knows wot's hidden in each other's hearts; and if we had glass winders there, we'd need keep the shutters up, some on us, I do assure you!

Charles Dickens 1812–70: *Martin Chuzzlewit* (1844)

5 Claudia's the sort of person who goes through life holding on to the sides.

Alice Thomas Ellis 1932–2005: *The Other Side of the Fire* (1983)

6 Clevinger was one of those people with lots of intelligence and no brains, and everyone knew it except those who soon found it out. In short, he was a dope.

Joseph Heller 1923–99: *Catch-22* (1961)

7 Nice guys, when we turn nasty, can make a terrible mess of it, usually because we've had so little practice, and have bottled it up for too long.

Matthew Parris 1949– : in *The Spectator* 27 February 1993

8 He's so wet you could shoot snipe off him.

Anthony Powell 1905–2000: *A Question of Upbringing* (1951)

9 You can tell a lot about a fellow's character by his way of eating jellybeans.

Ronald Reagan 1911– : in *New York Times* 15 January 1981

10 My father named me Autolycus; who being, as I am, littered under Mercury, was likewise a snapper-up of unconsidered trifles.

William Shakespeare 1564–1616: *The Winter's Tale* (1610–11)

11 An unforgiving eye, and a damned disinheriting countenance!

Richard Brinsley Sheridan 1751–1816: *The School for Scandal* (1777)

12 He's too nervous to kill himself. He wears his seat belt in a drive-in movie.

Neil Simon 1927– : *The Odd Couple* (1966)

13 Felix? Playing around? Are you crazy? He wears a vest and galoshes.

Neil Simon 1927– : *The Odd Couple* (1966)

14 I'm told he's [a] decent sort when you get to know him, but no one ever has, so his decency is sort of secret.

Tom Stoppard 1937– : *Neutral Ground* (1983)

15 Then, with that faint fleeting smile playing about his lips, he faced the firing squad; erect and motionless, proud and disdainful, Walter Mitty, the undefeated, inscrutable to the last.

James Thurber 1894–1961: in *New Yorker* 18 March 1939 'The Secret Life of Walter Mitty'

16 Few things are harder to put up with than the annoyance of a good example.

Mark Twain 1835–1910: *Pudd'nhead Wilson* (1894)

17 There, standing at the piano, was the original good time who had been had by all.

Kenneth Tynan 1927–80: at an Oxford Union Debate, while an undergraduate; attributed (also attributed to Bette Davis of a passing starlet)

18 CECIL GRAHAM: What is a cynic?
LORD DARLINGTON: A man who knows the price of everything and the value of nothing.

Oscar Wilde 1854–1900: *Lady Windermere's Fan* (1892)

19 I am afraid that he has one of those terribly weak natures that are not susceptible to influence.

Oscar Wilde 1854–1900: *An Ideal Husband* (1895)

20 I've met a lot of hardboiled eggs in my time, but you're twenty minutes.

Billy Wilder 1906–2002: *Ace in the Hole* (1951 film, co-written with Lesser Samuels and Walter Newman)

21 Slice him where you like, a hellhound is always a hellhound.

P. G. Wodehouse 1881–1975: *The Code of the Woosters* (1938)

Children ····▶ The Family, Parents, Youth

❝ There never was a child so lovely but his mother was glad to get asleep. **❞**
Ralph Waldo Emerson

1 I was very relieved when the child was born at the Chelsea and Westminster hospital. I had thought he would be born in a manger.
on the birth of Leo Blair

Leo Abse 1917– : in *Observer* 28 May 2000 'They said what . . . ?'

2 I sometimes think, Mary, that it is a mistake to have a dog for a nurse.
Mr Darling, of Nana

J. M. Barrie 1860–1937: *Peter Pan* (1928)

3 A Trick that everyone abhors
In Little Girls is slamming Doors.

Hilaire Belloc 1870–1953: 'Rebecca' (1907)

4 And always keep a-hold of Nurse
For fear of finding something worse.

Hilaire Belloc 1870–1953: 'Jim' (1907)

5 I had always thought that once you grew up you could do anything you wanted—stay up all night or eat ice-cream straight out of the container.

Bill Bryson 1951– : *The Lost Continent* (1989)

6 I don't know what Scrope Davies meant by telling you I liked children, I abominate the sight of them so much that I have always had the greatest respect for the character of Herod.

Lord Byron 1788–1824: letter 30 August 1811

7 The place is very well and quiet and the children only scream in a low voice.

Lord Byron 1788–1824: letter 21 September 1813

8 Speak roughly to your little boy,
And beat him when he sneezes;
He only does it to annoy,
Because he knows it teases.

Lewis Carroll 1832–98: *Alice's Adventures in Wonderland* (1865)

9 Timothy Winters comes to school
With eyes as wide as a football-pool,
Ears like bombs and teeth like splinters:
A blitz of a boy is Timothy Winters.

Charles Causley 1917– : 'Timothy Winters' (1957)

10 *on being asked what sort of child he was:*
When paid constant attention, extremely lovable. When not, a pig.

Noël Coward 1899–1973: interview with David Frost in 1969

11 I'll thcream and thcream and thcream till I'm thick. And I can.
Violet Elizabeth Bott's habitual threat

Richmal Crompton 1890–1969: *Still—William* (1925)

12 It's like hanging out with two miniature drunks.
on his two small children

Johnny Depp 1963– : in *Independent* 16 August 2003

13 If men had to have babies, they would only ever have one each.
while in late pregnancy

Diana, Princess of Wales 1961–97: in *Observer* 29 July 1984 'Sayings of the Week'

14 I only know two sorts of boys. Mealy boys, and beef-faced boys.

Charles Dickens 1812–70: *Oliver Twist* (1838)

15 There never was a child so lovely but his mother was glad to get asleep.

Ralph Waldo Emerson 1803–82: *Journal* 1836

16 O'er the rugged mountain's brow
Clara threw the twins she nursed,
And remarked, 'I wonder now
Which will reach the bottom first?'

Harry Graham 1874–1936: 'Calculating Clara' (1899)

17 When Baby's cries grew hard to bear
I popped him in the Frigidaire.
I never would have done so if
I'd known that he'd be frozen stiff.
My wife said, 'George, I'm so unhappé!
Our darling's now completely *frappé*!

Harry Graham 1874–1936: *Ruthless Rhymes for Heartless Homes* (1899) 'L'Enfant glacé'

18 *at the first night of J. M. Barrie's* Peter Pan:
Oh, for an hour of Herod!

Anthony Hope 1863–1933: Denis Mackail *The Story of JMB* (1941)

19 *definition of a baby:*
A loud noise at one end and no sense of responsibility at the other.

Ronald Knox 1888–1957: attributed

20 The realization that it was not people I disliked but children was for me one of those celebrated moments of revelation.
on growing up

Philip Larkin 1922–85: *Required Writing* (1983) 'The Savage Seventh'

21 The parent who could see his boy as he really is, would shake his head and say: 'Willie is no good; I'll sell him.'

Stephen Leacock 1869–1944: *Essays and Literary Studies* (1916)

22 Don't bother discussing sex with small children. They rarely have anything to add.

Fran Lebowitz 1946– : *Social Studies* (1981)

23 *Jack Llewelyn-Davies, stuffing himself with cakes at tea, was warned by his mother Sylvia, 'You'll be sick tomorrow':*
I'll be sick tonight.

Jack Llewelyn-Davies 1894–1959: Andrew Birkin *J. M. Barrie and the Lost Boys* (1979); Barrie used the line in *Little Mary* (1903)

24 Having a baby is like trying to push a grand piano through a transom.

Alice Roosevelt Longworth 1884–1980: Michael Teague *Mrs L* (1981)

25 *a nurse, excusing her illegitimate baby:*
If you please, ma'am, it was a very little one.

Frederick Marryat 1792–1848: *Mr Midshipman Easy* (1836)

26 With the birth of each child you lose two novels.

Candia McWilliam 1955– : in *Guardian* 5 May 1993

27 All bachelors love dogs, and we would love children just as much if they could be taught to retrieve.

P. J. O'Rourke 1947– : *The Bachelor Home Companion* (1987)

28 Every luxury was lavished on you—atheism, breast-feeding, circumcision.

Joe Orton 1933–67: *Loot* (1967)

29 As yet a child, nor yet a fool to fame,
I lisped in numbers, for the numbers came.

Alexander Pope 1688–1744: 'An Epistle to Dr Arbuthnot' (1735)

30 Parents—especially step-parents—are sometimes a bit of a disappointment to their children. They don't fulfil the promise of their early years.

Anthony Powell 1905–2000: *A Buyer's Market* (1952)

31 Go directly—see what she's doing, and tell her she mustn't.

Punch 1841–1992: vol. 63 (1872)

32 The fat greedy owl of the Remove.

Frank Richards 1876–1961: 'Billy Bunter' in *Magnet* (1909)

33 Children with Hyacinth's temperament don't know better as they grow older; they merely know more.

Saki 1870–1916: *Toys of Peace and Other Papers* (1919)

34 Children are given us to discourage our better emotions.

Saki 1870–1916: *Reginald* (1904)

35 Childhood is Last Chance Gulch for happiness. After that, you know too much.

Tom Stoppard 1937– : *Where Are They Now?* (1973)

36 I s'pect I growed. Don't think nobody never made me.

Harriet Beecher Stowe 1811–96: *Uncle Tom's Cabin* (1852)

37 Children can be awe-inspiringly horrible; manipulative, aggressive, rude, and unfeeling to a point where I often think that, if armed, they would make up the most terrifying fighting force the world has ever seen.

Jill Tweedie 1936–93: *It's Only Me* (1980)

38 You will find as the children grow up that as a rule children are a bitter disappointment—their greatest object being to do precisely what their parents do not wish and have anxiously tried to prevent.

Queen Victoria 1819–1901: letter to the Crown Princess of Prussia, 5 January 1876

39 I fear the seventh granddaughter and fourteenth grandchild becomes a very uninteresting thing—for it seems to me to go on like the rabbits in Windsor Park!

Queen Victoria 1819–1901: letter to the Crown Princess of Prussia, 10 July 1868

40 [The baby] romped on my lap like a short stout salmon.

Sylvia Townsend Warner 1893–1978: diary, 13 October 1929

41 Children begin by loving their parents; after a time they judge them; rarely, if ever, do they forgive them.

Oscar Wilde 1854–1900: *A Woman of No Importance* (1893)

Choice

66 Being bitten in half by a shark is a compromise with being swallowed whole. 99
P. J. O'Rourke

1 More than any other time in history, mankind faces a crossroads. One path leads to despair and utter hopelessness. The other, to total extinction. Let us pray we have the wisdom to choose correctly.

Woody Allen 1935– : *Side Effects* (1980)

2 That's a bit like asking a man crawling across the Sahara whether he would prefer Perrier or Malvern Water.
replying to a question by Ian McKellen on his sexual orientation

Alan Bennett 1934– : attributed

3 I would rather have my tongue beaten wafer-thin by a snake tenderiser and then stapled to the floor with a croquet hoop.

Richard Curtis 1956– and **Ben Elton** 1959– : *Blackadder Goes Forth* (1989) 'Major Star'

4 I'll have what she's having.
woman to waiter, seeing Sally acting an orgasm

Nora Ephron 1941– : *When Harry Met Sally* (1989 film)

5 He had polyester sheets and I wanted to get cotton sheets. He discussed it with his shrink many times before he made the switch.

Mia Farrow 1945– : in *Independent* 8 February 1997 'Quote Unquote'

6 *on the contrast between Alec Douglas-Home and Harold Wilson:*
Dull Alec versus Smart Alec.

David Frost 1939– : in *That Was The Week That Was* in 1963

7 *George V was asked which film he would like to see while convalescing:*
Anything except that damned Mouse.

George V 1865–1936: George Lyttelton letter to Rupert Hart-Davis, 12 November 1959

8 'You oughtn't to yield to temptation.' 'Well, somebody must, or the thing becomes absurd,' said I.

Anthony Hope 1863–1933: *The Dolly Dialogues* (1894)

9 Economy is going without something you do want in case you should, some day, want something you probably won't want.

Anthony Hope 1863–1933: *The Dolly Dialogues* (1894)

10 Still raise for good the supplicating voice,
But leave to heaven the measure and the choice.

Samuel Johnson 1709–84: *The Vanity of Human Wishes* (1749)

11 So here I am the victim of my own choices, and I'm just starting.
Ally's view of herself

David E. Kelley: *Ally McBeal* (US television series, 1998–2003) episode 1

12 Too rich and you lose sight of reality; too thin and you end up dead.

Shazia Mirza 1975– : in *Times* 5 February 2004

13 A compromise in the sense that being bitten in half by a shark is a compromise with being swallowed whole.

P. J. O'Rourke 1947– : *Parliament of Whores*

14 *a restaurateur asked for his most unusual request from a customer:*
The table next to Michael Winner, please.

Simon Slater: in *Evening Standard* 27 May 1999

15 *in the post office, pointing at the centre of a sheet of stamps:*
I'll take that one.

Herbert Beerbohm Tree 1852–1917:
Hesketh Pearson *Beerbohm Tree*
(1956)

Christmas

66 A Merry Christmas to all my friends except two. 99
W. C. Fields

1 I have often thought, says Sir Roger, it happens very well
that Christmas should fall out in the Middle of Winter.

Joseph Addison 1672–1719: *The
Spectator* 8 January 1712

2 There are six evacuated children in our house. My wife
and I hate them so much that we have decided to *take
away* something from them for Christmas!

Anonymous: letter from a friend in
the country; James Agate diary 22
December 1939

3 And girls in slacks remember Dad,
And oafish louts remember Mum,
And sleepless children's hearts are glad,
And Christmas-morning bells say 'Come!'
Even to shining ones who dwell
Safe in the Dorchester Hotel.

John Betjeman 1906–84: 'Christmas'
(1954)

And is it true? And is it true,
This most tremendous tale of all,
Seen in a stained-glass window's hue,
A Baby in an ox's stall?
The Maker of the stars and sea
Become a Child on earth for me?

4 Christmas Eve can be hell on earth . . . Everyone running
round doing their last-minute shopping. It's as if Christmas
comes on people by surprise, as it they hadn't known for
weeks it was on its way.

Maeve Binchy 1940– : *The Glass
Lake* (1994)

5 If the Three Wise Men arrived here tonight, the likelihood
is that they would be deported.
advocating an amnesty for asylum-seekers

Proinsias de Rossa: in *Irish Times* 20
December 1997 'This Week They
Said'

6 A Merry Christmas to all my friends except two.

W. C. Fields 1880–1946: attributed

7 I am a poor man, but I would gladly give ten shillings to
find out who sent me the insulting Christmas card I
received this morning.

George Grossmith 1847–1912 and
Weedon Grossmith 1854–1919: *The
Diary of a Nobody* (1894)

8 DRIFTWOOD (Groucho Marx): It's all right. That's—that's in
every contract. That's—that's what they call a sanity
clause.
FIORELLO (Chico Marx): You can't fool me. There ain't no
Sanity Claus.

George S. Kaufman 1889–1961 and
Morrie Ryskind 1895–1985: *Night at
the Opera* (1935 film)

9 A lovely thing about Christmas is that it's compulsory, like
a thunderstorm, and we all go through it together.

Garrison Keillor 1942– : *Leaving
Home* (1987) 'Exiles'

10 I'm walking backwards for Christmas
Across the Irish Sea.

Spike Milligan 1918–2002: 'I'm
Walking Backwards for Christmas'
(1956)

11 Christmas begins about the first of December with an office party and ends when you finally realize what you spent, around April fifteenth of the next year.

P. J. O'Rourke 1947– : *Modern Manners* (1984)

12 Christmas, that time of year when people descend into the bunker of the family.

Byron Rogers: in *Daily Telegraph* 27 December 1993

The Cinema ····➤ Acting, Actors, Film, Film Producers, Film Stars, Hollywood

❝ The trouble with this business is the dearth of bad pictures. ❞
Samuel Goldwyn

---

1 *an assistant director trying to encourage some uninspired extras during the filming of* Julius Caesar (*1953*):
All right, kids. It's Rome, it's hot and here comes Julius!

Anonymous: recounted by John Gielgud; in *Ned Sherrin in his Anecdotage* (1993)

2 There are no rules in filmmaking. Only sins. And the cardinal sin is dullness.

Frank Capra 1897–1991: in *People* 16 September 1991

3 Bring on the empty horses!

Michael Curtiz 1888–1962: said while directing the 1936 film *The Charge of the Light Brigade*; David Niven *Bring on the Empty Horses* (1975)

4 It might be a fight like you see on the screen
A swain getting slain for the love of a Queen,
Some great Shakespearean scene
Where a ghost and a prince meet
And everyone ends as mince-meat . . .

Howard Dietz 1896–1983: 'That's Entertainment' (1953)

5 'She reads at such a pace,' she complained, 'and when I asked her *where* she had learnt to read so quickly, she replied "On the screens at cinemas."'

Ronald Firbank 1886–1926: *The Flower Beneath the Foot* (1923)

6 The movies are the only court where the judge goes to the lawyer for advice.

F. Scott Fitzgerald 1896–1940: *The Crack-up* (1945)

7 Will Hays is my shepherd, I shall not want, He maketh me to lie down in clean postures.
on the establishment of the 'Hays Office' in 1922 to monitor the Hollywood film industry

Gene Fowler: Clive Marsh and Gaye Ortiz (eds.) *Explorations in Theology and Film* (1997)

8 GEORGES FRANJU: Movies should have a beginning, a middle and an end.
JEAN-LUC GODARD: Certainly. But not necessarily in that order.

Jean-Luc Godard 1930– : in *Time* 14 September 1981

9 *told that he could not film Radclyffe Hall's* The Well of Loneliness *as it dealt with lesbians:*
So, make them Latvians.

Sam Goldwyn 1882–1974: attributed; Topol *A Treasury of Jewish Wit, Wisdom and Humour* (1999)

10 The trouble with this business is the dearth of bad pictures.

Sam Goldwyn 1882–1974: after making *The Goldwyn Follies* in 1937; Michael Freedland *The Goldwyn Touch* (1986)

11 Our comedies are not to be laughed at.

Sam Goldwyn 1882–1974: N. Zierold *Hollywood Tycoons* (1969)

12 Pictures are for entertainment, messages should be delivered by Western Union.

Sam Goldwyn 1882–1974: Arthur Marx *Goldwyn* (1976)

13 This business is dog eat dog and nobody is gonna eat me.

Sam Goldwyn 1882–1974: Michael Freedland *The Goldwyn Touch* (1986)

14 Let's have some new clichés.

Sam Goldwyn 1882–1974: attributed, perhaps apocryphal

15 A verbal contract isn't worth the paper it is written on.

Sam Goldwyn 1882–1974: Alva Johnston *The Great Goldwyn* (1937)

16 What we need is a story that starts with an earthquake and works its way up to a climax.

Sam Goldwyn 1882–1974: attributed, perhaps apocryphal

17 The trouble with this business is that the stars keep 90% of the money.

Lew Grade 1906–98: attributed; Nigel Rees *Cassell Dictionary of Humorous Quotations* (1999)

18 'Do you have a leading lady for your film?'
'We're trying for the Queen, she sells.'

George Harrison 1943–2001: at a press conference in the 1960s; Ned Sherrin *Cutting Edge* (1984)

19 Porn? That's films where the plot doesn't thicken.

Sean Lock: *No Flatley! I am Lord of the Dance* (Edinburgh Festival, August 2000)

20 Life in the movies is like the beginning of a love affair. It's full of surprises and you're constantly getting —ed.

David Mamet 1947– : *Speed-the-Plow* (1988)

21 This might have been good for a picture—except it has too many characters in it.
to Jack Warner, on the LA telephone directory

Wilson Mizner 1876–1933: Max Wilk *The Wit and Wisdom of Hollywood* (1972)

22 The writer, in the eyes of many film producers, still seems to occupy a position of importance somewhere between the wardrobe lady and the tea boy, with this difference: it's often quite difficult to replace the wardrobe lady.

John Mortimer 1923– : *Clinging to the Wreckage* (1982)

23 Oh come, my love, and join with me
The oldest infant industry.
Come seek the bourne of palm and pearl
The lovely land of Boy-Meets-Girl.
Come grace this lotus-laden shore,
This Isle of Do-What's-Done-Before.
Come, curb the new, and watch the old win,
Out where the streets are paved with Goldwyn.

Dorothy Parker 1893–1967: 'The Passionate Screen Writer to His Love' (1937)

24 STUDIO EXECUTIVE: Where would you say the centre of your script was?
JACK ROSENTHAL: Somewhere in the middle.

Jack Rosenthal 1931–2004: in *Independent Review* 9 September 2004

25 *on the take-over of United Artists by Charles Chaplin, Mary Pickford, Douglas Fairbanks and D. W. Griffith:*
The lunatics have taken charge of the asylum.

Richard Rowland c.1881–1947: Terry Ramsaye *A Million and One Nights* (1926)

26 The trouble, Mr Goldwyn, is that you are only interested in art and I am only interested in money.
telegraphed version of the outcome of a conversation between Shaw and Sam Goldwyn

George Bernard Shaw 1856–1950: Alva Johnson *The Great Goldwyn* (1937)

27 I wouldn't say when you've seen one Western you've seen the lot; but when you've seen the lot you get the feeling you've seen one.

Katharine Whitehorn 1926– : *Sunday Best* (1976) 'Decoding the West'

Cities ····> Towns and Cities

Civil Servants

66 Grouped with mothers-in-law and Wigan Pier as one of the recognized objects of ridicule. 99
Edward Bridges

1 A mechanism that prides itself on being a Rolls-Royce appeared more like an old banger.
of the Foreign Office's handling of the arms-to-Africa affair

Donald Anderson 1939– : in *Guardian* 10 February 1999

2 Going about persecuting civil servants.
assessment by one unidentified senator of how politicians spend their time

Anonymous: R. F. Foster *Modern Ireland* (1988)

3 I confidently expect that we [civil servants] shall continue to be grouped with mothers-in-law and Wigan Pier as one of the recognized objects of ridicule.

Edward Bridges 1892–1969: *Portrait of a Profession* (1950)

4 Give a civil servant a good case and he'll wreck it with clichés, bad punctuation, double negatives and convoluted apology.

Alan Clark 1928–99: diary 22 July 1983

5 A civil servant doesn't make jokes.

Eugène Ionesco 1912–94: *Tueur sans gages* (The Killer, 1958)

6 May I hasten to support Mrs McGurgle's contention that civil servants are human beings, and must be treated as such?

J. B. Morton 1893–1975: M. Frayn (ed.) *The Best of Beachcomber* (1963)

7 By the time the civil service has finished drafting a document to give effect to a principle, there may be little of the principle left.

Lord Reith 1889–1971: *Into the Wind* (1949)

8 Here lies a civil servant. He was civil
To everyone, and servant to the devil.

C. H. Sisson 1914– : *The London Zoo* (1961)

Class ····> The Aristocracy, Snobbery

66 Mankind is divisible into two great classes: hosts and guests. 99
Max Beerbohm

1 A gentleman never eats. He breakfasts, he lunches, he dines, but he *never* eats!

Anonymous: Cole Porter's headmaster, *c.*1910; Caryl Brahms and Ned Sherrin *Song by Song* (1984)

2 His lordship may compel us to be equal upstairs, but there will never be equality in the servants' hall.

J. M. Barrie 1860–1937: *The Admirable Crichton* (performed 1902)

3 Mankind is divisible into two great classes: hosts and guests.

Max Beerbohm 1872–1956: *And Even Now* (1920)

4 Like many of the Upper Class
He liked the Sound of Broken Glass.

Hilaire Belloc 1870–1953: 'About John' (1930)

5 If you bed people of below-stairs class, they will go to the papers.

Jane Clark: in *Daily Telegraph* 31 May 1994

6 A branch of one of your antediluvian families, fellows that the flood could not wash away.

William Congreve 1670–1729: *Love for Love* (1695)

7 I came upstairs into the world; for I was born in a cellar.

William Congreve 1670–1729: *Love for Love* (1695)

8 Today it may be three white feathers,
But yesterday it was three brass balls.

Noël Coward 1899–1973: 'Three White Feathers' (1932)

9 Dear me, I never knew that the lower classes had such white skins.

Lord Curzon 1859–1925: K. Rose *Superior Person* (1969)

10 Gentlemen do not take soup at luncheon.

Lord Curzon 1859–1925: E. L. Woodward *Short Journey* (1942)

11 All men fall into two main divisions: those who value human relationships, and those who value social or financial advancement. The first division are gentlemen; the second division are cads.

Norman Douglas 1868–1952: *An Almanac* (1941)

12 He [Lord Home] is used to dealing with estate workers. I cannot see how anyone can say he is out of touch.
comment on her father's becoming Prime Minister

Caroline Douglas-Home 1937– : in *Daily Herald* 21 October 1963

13 If they could see me now,
My little dusty group,
Traipsing 'round this
Million-dollar chicken coop!
I'd hear those thrift shop cats say:
'Brother! Get her!'
Draped on a bedspread made from
Three kinds of fur.

Dorothy Fields 1905–74: 'If my Friends could See Me Now' (1966)

14 We are all Adam's children but silk makes the difference.

Thomas Fuller 1654–1734: *Gnomologia* (1732)

15 Boston social zones
Are changing social habits,
And I hear the Cohns
Are taking up the Cabots.

Ira Gershwin 1896–1983: 'Love is Sweeping the Country' (1931)

16 The Earl, the Marquis, and the Dook,
The Groom, the Butler, and the Cook— ...
The Aristocrat who banks with Coutts ...
The Aristocrat who cleans our boots—
They all shall equal be.

W. S. Gilbert 1836–1911: *The Gondoliers* (1889)

17 Bow, bow, ye lower middle classes!
Bow, bow, ye tradesmen, bow, ye masses.

W. S. Gilbert 1836–1911: *Iolanthe* (1882)

18 When every one is somebodee,
Then no one's anybody.

W. S. Gilbert 1836–1911: *The Gondoliers* (1889)

19 When the idle poor become the idle rich
You'll never know just who is who or who is which.

E. Y. Harburg 1898–1981: 'When the Idle Poor become the Idle Rich' (1947)

20 Finer things are for the finer folk
Thus society began
Caviar for peasants is a joke
It's too good for the average man.

Lorenz Hart 1895–1943: 'Too Good for the Average Man' (1936)

21 There are those who think that Britain is a class-ridden society, and those who think it doesn't matter either way as long as you know your place in the set-up.

Miles Kington 1941–2008: Welcome to Kington (1989)

22 Of all the hokum with which this country [America] is riddled the most odd is the common notion that it is free of class distinctions.

W. Somerset Maugham 1874–1965: A Writer's Notebook (1949) written in 1941

23 I no longer keep the coal in the bath. I keep it in the bidet.

John Prescott 1938– : in Independent 3 July 1999

24 'She's leaving her present house and going to Lower Seymour Street.' 'I dare say she will, if she stays there long enough.'

Saki 1870–1916: The Toys of Peace (1919)

25 I don't want to talk grammar, I want to talk like a lady.

George Bernard Shaw 1856–1950: Pygmalion (1916)

26 He's a gentleman: look at his boots.

George Bernard Shaw 1856–1950: preface to Pygmalion (1916)

27 Mr Knox . . . was a fair, spare young man, who looked like a stableboy among gentlemen, and a gentleman among stableboys.

Edith Œ. Somerville 1858–1949 and Martin Ross 1862–1915: Some Experiences of an Irish R.M. (1899)

28 She sits
At The Ritz
With her splits
Of Mum's
And starts to pine
For a Stein
With her Village chums.
But with a Schlitz
In her mitts
Down in Fitz—
Roy's Bar,
She thinks of the Ritz—oh,
It's so
Schizo.

Stephen Sondheim 1930– : 'Uptown Downtown', song rejected from Follies (1971); composer's archive

29 The only infallible rule we know is, that the man who is always talking about being a gentleman never is one.

R. S. Surtees 1805–64: Ask Mamma (1858)

30 The so called immorality of the lower classes is not to be named on the same day with that of the higher and highest. This is a thing which makes my blood boil, and they will pay for it.

Queen Victoria 1819–1901: letter to the Crown Princess of Prussia, 26 June 1872

31 I expect you'll be becoming a schoolmaster, sir. That's what most of the gentlemen does, sir, that gets sent down for indecent behaviour.

Evelyn Waugh 1903–66: Decline and Fall (1928)

32 Really, if the lower orders don't set us a good example, what on earth is the use of them?

Oscar Wilde 1854–1900: The Importance of Being Earnest (1895)

The Clergy ····> Religion

66 The parson knows enough who knows a duke. 99
William Cowper

---

1 A priest is a man who is called Father by everyone except his own children who are obliged to call him Uncle.

Anonymous: said to be an Italian saying found in a French novel; Rupert Hart-Davis letter to George Lyttelton, 15 July 1956

2 As for the British churchman, he goes to church as he goes to the bathroom, with the minimum of fuss and with no explanation if he can help it.

Ronald Blythe 1922– : *The Age of Illusion* (1963)

3 Don't like bishops. Fishy lot. Blessed are the meek my foot! They're all on the climb. Ever heard of meekness stopping a bishop from becoming a bishop? Nor have I.

Maurice Bowra 1898–1971: in conversation while lunching at the Reform Club with a bishop at the next table; Arthur Marshall *Life's Rich Pageant* (1984)

4 Poor Uncle Harry
Having become a missionary
Found the natives' morals rather crude.
He and Aunt Mary
Quickly imposed an arbitrary
Ban upon them shopping in the nude.
They all considered this silly and they didn't take it well,
They burnt his boots and several suits and wrecked the
    Mission Hotel,
They also burnt his mackintosh, which made a disgusting
    smell . . .
Uncle Harry's not a missionary now.

Noël Coward 1899–1973: 'Uncle Harry' (1946)

5 The parson knows enough who knows a duke.

William Cowper 1731–1800: 'Tirocinium' (1785)

6   As a priest,
A piece of mere church furniture at best.

William Cowper 1731–1800: 'Tirocinium' (1785)

7 Mr Doctor, that loose gown becomes you so well I wonder your notions should be so narrow.
to the Puritan Dr Humphreys, as he was about to kiss her hand on her visit to Oxford in 1566

Elizabeth I 1533–1603: F. Chamberlin *Sayings of Queen Elizabeth* (1923)

8 I remember the average curate at home as something between a eunuch and a snigger.

Ronald Firbank 1886–1926: *The Flower Beneath the Foot* (1923)

9 I was a pale young curate then.

W. S. Gilbert 1836–1911: *The Sorcerer* (1877)

10 As I take my shoes from the shoemaker, and my coat from the tailor, so I take my religion from the priest.

Oliver Goldsmith 1730–74: James Boswell *Life of Samuel Johnson* (1934 ed.) 9 April 1773

11 The crisis of the Church of England is that too many of its bishops, and some would say of its archbishops, don't quite realise that they are atheists, but have begun to suspect it.

Clive James 1939– : *The Dreaming Swimmer* (1992)

12 This merriment of parsons is mighty offensive.

Samuel Johnson 1709–84: James Boswell *Life of Samuel Johnson* (1791) March 1781

13 Evangelical vicar, in want of a portable, second-hand font, would dispose, for the same, of a portrait, in frame, of the Bishop, elect, of Vermont.
advertisement placed in a newspaper

Ronald Knox 1888–1957: W. S. Baring-Gould *The Lure of the Limerick* (1968)

14 It's great being a priest, isn't it, Ted?

Graham Linehan and **Arthur Mathews**: 'Good Luck, Father Ted' (1994), episode from *Father Ted* (Channel 4 TV, 1994–8)

15 *on the appointment of Michael Ramsey to succeed Geoffrey Fisher as Archbishop of Canterbury:*
We have had enough of Martha and it is time for some Mary.

Harold Macmillan 1894–1986: attributed

16 *to a clergyman who thanked him for the enjoyment he'd given the world:*
And I want to thank you for all the enjoyment you've taken out of it.

Groucho Marx 1895–1977: Joe Adamson *Groucho, Harpo, Chico and sometimes Zeppo* (1973)

17 As the French say, there are three sexes—men, women, and clergymen.

Sydney Smith 1771–1845: Lady Holland *Memoir* (1855)

18 I have seen nobody since I saw you, but persons in orders. My only varieties are vicars, rectors, curates, and every now and then (by way of turbot) an archdeacon.

Sydney Smith 1771–1845: letter to Miss Berry, 28 January 1843

19 A Curate—there is something which excites compassion in the very name of a Curate!!!

Sydney Smith 1771–1845: *Edinburgh Review* (1822) 'Persecuting Bishops'

20 There is a species of person called a 'Modern Churchman' who draws the full salary of a beneficed clergyman and need not commit himself to any religious belief.

Evelyn Waugh 1903–66: *Decline and Fall* (1928)

21 *Merit*, indeed! . . . We are come to a pretty pass if they talk of *merit* for a bishopric.

Lord Westmorland 1759–1841: Lady Salisbury, diary, 9 December 1835

22 The Bishop . . . was talking to the local Master of Hounds about the difficulty he had in keeping his vicars off the incense.

P. G. Wodehouse 1881–1975: *Mr. Mulliner Speaking* (1929)

Colours

❝ Any colour—so long as it's black. ❞
Henry Ford

1 I was shown round Tutankhamun's tomb in the 1920s. I saw all this wonderful pink on the walls and the artefacts. I was so impressed that I vowed to wear it for the rest of my life.

Barbara Cartland 1901–2000: in *Irish Times* 28 March 1998 'This Week They Said'

2 I cannot pretend to feel impartial about the colours. I rejoice with the brilliant ones, and am genuinely sorry for the poor browns.

Winston Churchill 1874–1965: *Thoughts and Adventures* (1932)

3 Gentlemen never wear brown in London.

Lord Curzon 1859–1925: attributed; Nigel Rees *Cassell Dictionary of Humorous Quotations* (1999)

4 *on the choice of colour for the Model T Ford:*
Any colour—so long as it's black.

Henry Ford 1863–1947: Allan Nevins *Ford* (1957)

5 It's just my colour: it's *beige!*
   a fashionable interior decorator's first view of the Parthenon

Elsie Mendl 1865–1950: Osbert Sitwell *Rat Week: An Essay on the Abdication* (1986)

6 A brilliant blue garment that was an offence alike to her convictions and her complexion.

Edith Œ. Somerville 1858–1949 and **Martin Ross** 1862–1915: *Further Experiences of an Irish R.M.* (1908)

7 If I could find anything blacker than black, I'd use it.

J. M. W. Turner 1775–1851: remark, 1844

8 Pink is the navy blue of India.

Diana Vreeland 1903–89: attributed, 1977

9 I think it pisses God off if you walk by the colour purple in a field somewhere and don't notice it.

Alice Walker 1944– : *The Colour Purple* (1982)

Comedy Routines and Catchphrases

66 Just like that! 99
Tommy Cooper

1 CECIL: After you, Claude.
   CLAUDE: No, after you, Cecil.

Ted Kavanagh 1892–1958: catchphrase in *ITMA* (BBC radio programme, 1939–49)

2 Can I do you now, sir?

Ted Kavanagh 1892–1958: catchphrase spoken by 'Mrs Mopp' in *ITMA* (BBC radio programme, 1939–49)

3 Collapse of Stout Party.
   supposed standard dénouement in Victorian humour

Anonymous: R. Pearsall *Collapse of Stout Party* (1975) introduction

4 D'oh!
   Homer J. Simpson's habitual expression of annoyance

Matt Groening 1954– : *The Simpsons* (American TV series, 1990–)

5 Don't forget the diver.

Ted Kavanagh 1892–1958: catchphrase spoken by 'The Diver' in *ITMA* (BBC radio programme, 1939–49)

6 Don't have a cow, man.

Matt Groening 1954– : catchphrase associated with Bart Simpson; *The Simpsons* (American TV series, 1990–)

7 Drink! Drink!
   habitual cry of Father Jack

Graham Linehan and **Arthur Mathews**: 'New Jack City' (1996), episode from *Father Ted* (Channel 4 TV, 1994–8)

8 Eat my shorts!

Matt Groening 1954– : catchphrase associated with Bart Simpson; *The Simpsons* (American TV series, 1990–)

9 Ee, it was agony, Ivy.

Ted Ray 1906–77: catchphrase in *Ray's a Laugh* (BBC radio programme, 1949–61)

10 'Er indoors.

Leon Griffiths 1928–92: used in ITV television series *Minder* (1979 onwards) by Arthur Daley (played by George Cole) to refer to his wife

11 Fact.
   David Brent's favourite assurance

Ricky Gervais 1961– and **Stephen Merchant**: *The Office* (2001–3)

12 George—don't do that.

Joyce Grenfell 1910–79: used as a recurring line in monologues about a nursery school, from the 1950s

13 A good idea—son.

Eric Sykes and **Max Bygraves** 1922– : *Educating Archie*, 1950–3 BBC radio comedy series

14 Good morning, sir—was there something?

Richard Murdoch 1907–90 and **Kenneth Horne** 1900–69: catchphrase used by Sam Costa in radio comedy series *Much-Binding-in-the-Marsh* (started 2 January 1947)

15 BURNS: Say goodnight, Gracie.
   ALLEN: Goodnight, Gracie.

George Burns 1896–1996: said to be customary conclusion to *The George Burns and Gracie Allen Show* (1950–58), although Burns in *Gracie: a Love Story* (1990) described this as a showbusiness myth

16 Grazie, grazie, you have-a brought great joy to this old Italian stereotype.

Matt Groening 1954– : Springfield's local Mafia leader, Don Vittorio; *The Simpsons* (American TV series, 1990–)

17 Have you read any good books lately?

Richard Murdoch 1907–90 and **Kenneth Horne** 1900–69: catchphrase used by Richard Murdoch in radio comedy series *Much-Binding-in-the-Marsh* (started 2 January 1947)

18 Heeere's . . . Johnny!

Ed McMahon: introducing Johnny Carson on the NBC TV *Tonight Show* (1962–92); catchphrase later used by Jack Nicholson in the *The Shining* (1980 horror film)

19 Hello, I'm Julian and this is my friend, Sandy.

Barry Took 1928–2002 and **Marty Feldman** 1933–83: catchphrase in *Round the Horne* (BBC radio series, 1965–8)

20 Hello possums!

Barry Humphries 1934– : Dame Edna's habitual greeting to her fans; *The Barry Humphries Show: Dame Edna Everage*

21 He's loo-vely, Mrs Hoskin . . . he's loo-ooo-vely!

Ted Ray 1906–77: catchphrase in *Ray's a Laugh* (BBC radio programme, 1949–61)

22 I 'ate you, Butler.

Ronald Wolfe and **Ronald Chesney**: Inspector Blake (Stephen Lewis) to Stan Butler (Reg Varney) in *On the Buses* (1969–73).

23 I didn't get where I am today without —.

David Nobbs 1935– : habitual boast of Reggie Perrin's boss CJ in BBC television series *The Fall and Rise of Reginald Perrin*, 1976–80

24 I don't mind if I do.

Ted Kavanagh 1892–1958: catchphrase spoken by 'Colonel Chinstrap' in *ITMA* (BBC radio programme, 1939–49)

25 If you've got it, flaunt it!

Mel Brooks 1926– : *The Producers* (1967 film)

26 I go—I come back.

Ted Kavanagh 1892–1958: catchphrase spoken by 'Ali Oop' in *ITMA* (BBC radio programme, 1939–49)

27 I have a cunning plan.

Richard Curtis 1956– and **Ben Elton** 1959– : *Blackadder II* (1987) television series; Baldrick's habitual overoptimistic promise

28 I'm free!

David Croft 1922– and **Jeremy Lloyd**: cry of 'Mr Humphries' (played by John Inman) of Grace Brothers, in *Are You Being Served?* (1973–83).

29 It's being so cheerful as keeps me going.

Ted Kavanagh 1892–1958: catchphrase spoken by 'Mona Lott' in *ITMA* (BBC radio programme, 1939–49)

30 It's *sooo* unfair!

Harry Enfield 1961– : habitual complaint of Kevin the Teenager; *Harry Enfield and Chums* (BBC TV, 1994)

31 I've arrived and to prove it I'm here!

Eric Sykes and **Max Bygraves** 1922– : *Educating Archie*, 1950–3 BBC radio comedy series

32 Just like that!

Tommy Cooper 1921–84: catchphrase associated with Tommy Cooper

33 Meredith, we're in!

Fred Kitchen 1872–1950: catchphrase originating in *The Bailiff* (1907 stage sketch)

34 Mind my bike!

Jack Warner 1895–1981: catchphrase used in the BBC radio series *Garrison Theatre*, 1939 onwards

35 My arse!
Jim Royle's usual sceptical comment on people or circumstances

Caroline Aherne 1963– , **Craig Cash**, and **Henry Normal**: *The Royle Family* (BBC television series, 1998–2000); spoken by Ricky Tomlinson

36 Nobody expects the Spanish Inquisition! Our chief weapon is surprise—surprise and fear . . . fear and surprise . . . our two weapons are fear and surprise—and ruthless efficiency . . . our *three* weapons are fear and surprise and ruthless efficiency and an almost fanatical devotion to the Pope . . . our *four* . . . no . . . *Amongst* our weapons—amongst our weaponry—are such elements as fear, surprise . . . I'll come in again.

Graham Chapman 1941–89, **John Cleese** 1939– , et al.: *Monty Python's Flying Circus* (BBC TV programme, 1970)

37 No sex, please—we're British.

Anthony Marriott 1931– and **Alistair Foot**: title of play (1971)

38 Oh, calamity!

Robertson Hare 1891–1979: catchphrase in *Yours Indubitably* (1956)

39 Oh, groovy baby, yeah!

Mike Myers 1963– : Austin Powers (Mike Myers) in *Austin Powers—International Man of Mystery* (1996 film)

40 Ohhh, I don't *believe* it!

David Renwick 1951– : Victor Meldrew in *One Foot in the Grave* (BBC television series, 1989–)

41 Pass the sick bag, Alice.

John Junor 1919–97: referring to a canteen lady at the old *Express* building in Fleet Street, who conveyed plates of egg and chips to journalists at their desks; in *Sunday Express* 28 December 1980

42 Respect!
Ali G acknowledges quality

Ali G (Sacha Baron Cohen) 1970– : *Da Ali G Show* (2000–1)

43 Shoulders back, lovely boy!

Jimmy Perry 1923– and **David Croft** 1922– : Sergeant-Major Williams (Windsor Davies) to his concert party in *It Ain't Half Hot, Mum* (1974–81)

44 So Harry says, 'You don't like me any more. Why not?' And he says, 'Because you've got so terribly pretentious.' And Harry says, 'Pretentious? *Moi?*'

John Cleese 1939– and **Connie Booth**: *Fawlty Towers* (BBC TV programme, 1979)

45 Seriously, though, he's doing a grand job!

David Frost 1939– : catchphrase written by Waterhouse and Hall for Roy Kinnear's sketch 'The Safe Comedian', and adopted by David Frost for 'That Was The Week That Was', on BBC Television, 1962–3

46 Shome mishtake, shurely?

Anonymous: catchphrase in *Private Eye* magazine, 1980s

47 Stop messing about!

Ray Galton 1930– and **Alan Simpson** 1929– : protest of Snide (Kenneth Williams) in *Hancock's Half Hour* (1954–9).

48 STRIKER: Surely you can't be serious.
DR RUMACK: I am serious. And don't call me Shirley.

Jim Abrahams, **David Zucker**, and **Jerry Zucker**: *Airplane!* (1980 film)

49 Take my wife—please!

Henny Youngman 1906–98: in *Times* 26 February 1998; obituary

50 Very interesting . . . but stupid.

Dan Rowan 1922–87 and **Dick Martin** 1923– : catchphrase in *Rowan and Martin's Laugh-In* (American television series, 1967–73)

51 ABBOTT: Now, on the St Louis team we have Who's on first, What's on second, I Don't Know is on third.
COSTELLO: That's what I want to find out.

Bud Abbott 1895–1974 and **Lou Costello** 1906–59: *Naughty Nineties* (1945)

52 SEAGOON: Ying tong iddle I po.

Spike Milligan 1918–2002: *The Dreaded Batter Pudding Hurler* in *The Goon Show* (BBC radio series) 12 October 1954; catchphrase also used in *The Ying Tong Song* (1956)

53 You can't get the wood, you know.

Spike Milligan 1918–2002: *The Goon Show* (BBC radio, 1951–61)

54 You dirty old man!

Ray Galton 1930– and **Alan Simpson** 1929– : Harold Steptoe (Harry H. Corbett) to his father Albert in *Steptoe and Son* (1962–5 and 1970–4).

55 You might very well think that. I couldn't possibly comment.

Michael Dobbs 1948– : *House of Cards* (televised 1990); the Chief Whip's habitual response to questioning

56 You plonker!

John Sullivan: Del Boy Trotter (David Jason) to his brother Rodney (Nicholas Lyndhurst) in *Only Fools and Horses* (1987–)

46 You stupid boy!

Jimmy Perry 1923– and **David Croft** 1922– : Captain Mainwaring (Arthur Lowe) to Private Pike (Ian Lavender), *Dad's Army* (1968–77).

Computers ····▸ Science, Technology

❝ Hovers between the obsolescent and the nonexistent. ❞
Sydney Brenner

1 To err is human but to really foul things up requires a computer.

Anonymous: in *Farmers' Almanac for 1978*

2 A modern computer hovers between the obsolescent and the nonexistent.

Sydney Brenner 1927– : in *Science* 5 January 1990; attributed

3 I am afraid it is a non-starter. I cannot even use a bicycle pump.
when asked whether she uses e-mail

Judi Dench 1934– : in *The Times* 13 February 1999

4 This Ken Starr report is now posted on the Internet. I'll bet Clinton's glad he put a computer in every classroom.

Jay Leno 1950– : in *Sunday Times* 20 September 1998

5 We've all heard that a million monkeys banging on a million typewriters will eventually reproduce the entire works of Shakespeare. Now, thanks to the Internet, we know this is not true.

Robert Wilensky 1951– : in *Mail on Sunday* 16 February 1997 'Quotes of the Week'

6 I should prefer to have a politician who regularly went to a massage parlour than one who promised a laptop computer for every teacher.

A. N. Wilson 1950– : in *Observer* 21 March 1999

Conversation ····▶ Speeches

❝ How time flies when you's doin' all the talking. ❞
Harvey Fierstein

1 Don't speak!

Woody Allen 1935– and **Douglas McGrath**: leading lady Helen Sinclair (Dianne Wiest) in *Bullets over Broadway* (1994 film)

2 It was such a voice as icebergs might be supposed to use to speak to each other as they passed by night in the Arctic Sea.

E. F. Benson 1867–1940: *Miss Mapp* (1922)

3 Although there exist many thousand subjects for elegant conversation, there are persons who cannot meet a cripple without talking about feet.

Ernest Bramah 1868–1942: *The Wallet of Kai Lung* (1900)

4 When you were quite a little boy somebody ought to have said 'hush' just once!

Mrs Patrick Campbell 1865–1940: letter to George Bernard Shaw, 1 November 1912

5 'Then you should say what you mean,' the March Hare went on. 'I do,' Alice hastily replied; 'at least—at least I mean what I say—that's the same thing, you know.' 'Not the same thing a bit!' said the Hatter. 'Why, you might just as well say that "I see what I eat" is the same thing as "I eat what I see!" '

Lewis Carroll 1832–98: *Alice's Adventures in Wonderland* (1865)

6 *on visiting Lord Alfred Douglas:*
We had resolved not to mention Oscar Wilde, prison, Winston, Robbie Ross or Frank Harris, but we were soon well embarked on all five subjects, though not at once.

Chips Channon 1897–1958: diary, 10 October 1942

7 It makes a change from talking to plants.
being photographed with penguins in the Falklands

Charles, Prince of Wales 1948– : in *Sunday Times* 21 March 1999 'Talking Heads'

8 Too much agreement kills a chat.

Eldridge Cleaver 1935– : *Soul on Ice* (1968)

9 Is it possible to cultivate the art of conversation when living in the country all the year round?

E. M. Delafield 1890–1943: *The Diary of a Provincial Lady* (1930)

10 The fun of talk is to find what a man really thinks, and then contrast it with the enormous lies he has been telling all dinner, and, perhaps, all his life.

Benjamin Disraeli 1804–81: *Lothair* (1870)

11 How time flies when you's doin' all the talking.

Harvey Fierstein 1954– : *Torch Song Trilogy* (1979)

12 If you are ever at a loss to support a flagging conversation, introduce the subject of eating.

Leigh Hunt 1784–1859: J. A. Gere and John Sparrow (eds.) *Geoffrey Madan's Notebooks* (1981); attributed

13 I've just spent an hour talking to Tallulah for a few minutes.

Fred Keating: Denis Brian *Tallulah, Darling* (1980)

14 My ear is open like a greedy shark
To catch the tunings of a voice divine.

John Keats 1795–1821: *Poems* (1817) 'Woman! when I behold thee'

15 There are two things in ordinary conversation which ordinary people dislike—information and wit.

Stephen Leacock 1869–1944: *The Boy I Left Behind Me* (1947)

16 The opposite of talking isn't listening. The opposite of talking is waiting.

Fran Lebowitz 1946– : *Social Studies* (1981)

17 Considering how foolishly people act and how pleasantly they prattle, perhaps it would be better for the world if they talked more and did less.

W. Somerset Maugham 1874–1965: *A Writer's Notebook* (1949) written in 1892

18 She plunged into a sea of platitudes, and with the powerful breast stroke of a channel swimmer made her confident way towards the white cliffs of the obvious.

W. Somerset Maugham 1874–1965: *A Writer's Notebook* (1949) written in 1919

19 It is clear enough that you are making some distinction in what you said, that there is some nicety of terminology in your words. I can't quite follow you.

Flann O'Brien 1911–66: *The Dalkey Archive* (1964)

20 With first-rate sherry flowing into second-rate whores,
And third-rate conversation without one single pause:
Just like a young couple
Between the wars.

William Plomer 1903–73: 'Father and Son: 1939' (1945)

21 If you have nothing to say, or, rather, something extremely stupid and obvious, say it, but in a 'plonking' tone of voice—i.e. roundly, but hollowly and dogmatically.

Stephen Potter 1900–69: *Lifemanship* (1950)

22 He never knew what to say. If life was a party, he wasn't even in the kitchen.

Terry Pratchett 1948– : *Thief of Time* (2001)

23 *commenting that George Bernard Shaw's wife was a good listener:*
God knows she had plenty of practice.

J. B. Priestley 1894–1984: *Margin Released* (1962)

24 You talkin' to me?

Paul Schrader 1946– : *Taxi Driver* (1976 film); spoken by Robert de Niro as Travis Bickle

25 [Macaulay] has occasional flashes of silence, that make his conversation perfectly delightful.

Sydney Smith 1771–1845: Lady Holland *Memoir* (1855)

26 —d! said my mother, 'what is all this story about?'— 'A Cock and a Bull,' said Yorick.

Laurence Sterne 1713–68: *Tristram Shandy* (1759–67)

27 *You* talked animatedly for some time about language being the aniseed trail that draws the hounds of heaven when the metaphysical fox has gone to earth; he must have thought you were barmy.

Tom Stoppard 1937– : *Jumpers* (rev. ed. 1986)

28 Faith, that's as well said, as if I had said it myself.

Jonathan Swift 1667–1745: *Polite Conversation* (1738)

29 I re-iterate. You remember, I iterated before.

Dick Vosburgh: *A Saint She Ain't* (1999)

30 If one plays good music, people don't listen and if one plays bad music people don't talk.

Oscar Wilde 1854–1900: *The Importance of Being Earnest* (1895)

31 If one could only teach the English how to talk, and the Irish how to listen, society here would be quite civilized.

Oscar Wilde 1854–1900: *An Ideal Husband* (1895)

32 'What ho!' I said.
'What ho!' said Motty.
'What ho! What ho!'
'What ho! What ho! What ho!'
After that it seemed rather difficult to go on with the conversation.

P. G. Wodehouse 1881–1975: *My Man Jeeves* (1919)

Cookery ····▶ Diets, Food

❝ Those who can make omelettes properly can do nothing else. **❞**
Hilaire Belloc

1 Anyone who tells a lie has not a pure heart, and cannot make a good soup.

Ludwig van Beethoven 1770–1827: Ludwig Nohl *Beethoven Depicted by his Contemporaries* (1880)

2 Be content to remember that those who can make omelettes properly can do nothing else.

Hilaire Belloc 1870–1953: *A Conversation with a Cat* (1931)

3 My mother tells me she's worn out pouring tinned sauce over the frozen chicken.

Maeve Binchy 1940– : *Evening Class* (1996)

4 The discovery of a new dish does more for the happiness of mankind than the discovery of a new star.

Anthelme Brillat-Savarin 1755–1826: *Physiologie du Goût* (1826)

5 He said, 'I look for butterflies
That sleep among the wheat:
I make them into mutton-pies,
And sell them in the street.'

Lewis Carroll 1832–98: *Through the Looking-Glass* (1872)

6 Great cookery is making doughnuts like Fanny's.
comment on one of his wife Fanny Cradock's televised cookery programmes; David Coleman is said to have introduced the following 'Match of the Day' with the words, 'For those of you who watched the last programme, I hope all your doughnuts turn out like Fanny's.'

Johnny Cradock c.1904–87: attributed, perhaps apocryphal

7 Heaven sends us good meat, but the Devil sends cooks.

David Garrick 1717–79: 'On Doctor Goldsmith's Characteristical Cookery' (1777)

8 The difference between a chef and a cook is the difference between a wife and a prostitute. Cooks do meals for people they know and love. Chefs do it anonymously for anyone who's got the price.

A. A. Gill 1954– : in *Independent* 4 November 1998

9 We could not have had a better dinner had there been a *Synod of Cooks*.

Samuel Johnson 1709–84: James Boswell *Life of Samuel Johnson* (1791) 5 August 1763

10 A cucumber should be well sliced, and dressed with pepper and vinegar, and then thrown out, as good for nothing.

Samuel Johnson 1709–84: James Boswell *Journal of a Tour to the Hebrides* (1785) 5 October 1773

11 *watching the TV chef Michael Barry prepare a venison dish:* Bambi—see the movie! Eat the cast!

Henry Kelly: in *Daily Telegraph* 26 February 1994

12 The tragedy of English cooking is that 'plain' cooking cannot be entrusted to 'plain' cooks.

Countess Morphy fl. 1930–50: *English Recipes* (1935)

13 Sorry, I don't do offal.
invited to help improve the food in the Westminster kitchens

Jamie Oliver 1975– : in *Mail on Sunday* 15 June 2003

14 The vulgar boil, the learned roast, an egg.

Alexander Pope 1688–1744: *Imitations of Horace* (1738)

15 Her cooking is the missionary position of cooking. That is how everybody starts.
defending Delia Smith

Egon Ronay: in *Independent on Sunday* 1 November 1998

16 The cook was a good cook, as cooks go; and as cooks go, she went.

Saki 1870–1916: *Reginald* (1904)

17 'But why should you want to shield him?' cried Egbert; 'the man is a common murderer.' 'A common murderer, possibly, but a very uncommon cook.'

Saki 1870–1916: *Beasts and Super-Beasts* (1914)

18 You won't be surprised that diseases are innumerable— count the cooks.

Seneca c.4 BC–AD 65: *Epistles*

19 I want to focus on my salad.
when asked about a congressional investigation into her sale of shares

Martha Stewart 1941– : interviewed on *The Early Show* (CBS) 25 June 2002

20 The most remarkable thing about my mother is that for 30 years she served nothing but leftovers. The original meal was never found.

Tracey Ullman 1959– : in *Observer* 23 May 1999 'Sayings of the Week'

21 And now with some pleasure I find that it's seven; and must cook dinner. Haddock and sausage meat. I think it is true that one gains a certain hold on sausage and haddock by writing them down.

Virginia Woolf 1882–1941: diary, 8 March 1941

Countries and Peoples ····▶ America, Canada, France, Places, Russia

❝ I like my 'abroad' to be Catholic and sensual. **❞**
Chips Channon

1 That Britain was no part of Europe was his conviction.
of Lord Milner

Lord Beaverbrook 1879–1964: *Men and Power* (1956)

2 It's like Bob Benchley's remark on India—'India, what does the name *not* suggest?' To which Benchley himself gives the answer—'a hell of a lot of things.'

Robert Benchley 1889–1945: Stephen Leacock *The Boy I Left Behind Me* (1947); attributed

3 It's where they commit suicide and the king rides a bicycle, Sweden.

Alan Bennett 1934– : *Enjoy* (1980)

4 Germans are flummoxed by humour, the Swiss have no concept of fun, the Spanish think there is nothing at all ridiculous about eating dinner at midnight, and the Italians should never, ever have been let in on the invention of the motor car.

Bill Bryson 1951– : *Neither Here Nor There* (1991)

5 The perpetual lamentations after beef and beer, the stupid bigoted contempt for every thing foreign, and insurmountable incapacity of acquiring even a few words of any language, rendered him like all other English servants, an encumbrance.

Lord Byron 1788–1824: letter, 14 January 1811

6 I like my 'abroad' to be Catholic and sensual.

Chips Channon 1897–1958: diary 18 January 1924

7 Belgium has only one real claim to fame. Thanks to all the wars that have been fought on its soil, there are more dead people there than anywhere else in the world. So, while there's no quality of life in Belgium, there is a simply wonderful quality of death.

Jeremy Clarkson 1960– : in *Sunday Times* 18 July 1999

8 They're Germans. Don't mention the war.

John Cleese 1939– and **Connie Booth**: *Fawlty Towers* (BBC TV programme, 1975)

9 *the French jazz critic Hugues Panassie had given Condon a generally favourable notice:*
I don't see why we need a Frenchman to come over here and tell us how to play American music. I wouldn't think of going to France and telling him how to jump on a grape.

Eddie Condon 1905–73: Bill Crow *Jazz Anecdotes* (1990)

10 To speak with your mouth full
And swallow with greed
Are national traits
Of the travelling Swede.

Duff Cooper 1890–1954: Philip Ziegler *Diana Cooper* (1981)

11 In a bar on the Piccola Marina
Life called to Mrs Wentworth-Brewster,
Fate beckoned her and introduced her
Into a rather queer
Unfamiliar atmosphere . . .
Just for fun three young sailors from Messina
Bowed low to Mrs Wentworth-Brewster,
Said 'Scusi' and politely goosed her.
Then there was quite a scena.
Her family, in floods of tears, cried,
'Leave these men, Mama.'
She said, 'They're just high-spirited, like all Italians are
And most of them have a great deal more to offer than
Papa,
In a bar on the Piccola Marina.'

Noël Coward 1899–1973: 'A Bar on the Piccola Marina' (1954)

12 Don't let's be beastly to the Germans
When our Victory is ultimately won.
It was just those nasty Nazis who persuaded them to fight
And their Beethoven and Bach are really far worse than
their bite,
Let's be meek to them—
And turn the other cheek to them
And try to bring out their latent sense of fun.

Noël Coward 1899–1973: 'Don't Let's
Be Beastly to the Germans' (1943)

13 Some people . . . may be Rooshans, and others may be
Prooshans; they are born so, and will please themselves.
Them which is of other naturs thinks different.

Charles Dickens 1812–70: *Martin
Chuzzlewit* (1844)

14 When you enter a house you take your shoes off
It's better with your shoes off! . . .
Get yourself a Geisha. The flower of Asia,
She's one with whom to take up.
At night your bed she'll make up,
And she'll be there when you wake up.

Howard Dietz 1896–1983: 'Get
Yourself a Geisha' (1935)

15 The Arabs are only Jews upon horseback.

Benjamin Disraeli 1804–81: *Tancred*
(1847)

16 *to a Boer who had told her that he could never quite forgive the
British for having conquered his country:*
I understand that perfectly. We feel very much the same in
Scotland.

Queen Elizabeth, the Queen Mother
1900–2002: Elizabeth Longford (ed.)
The Oxford Book of Royal Anecdotes
(1989)

17 I'm not Jewish. I only look intelligent.
German cabaret artist to Nazis in his audience, 1931

Werner Finck 1902– : Humphrey
Carpenter *That Was Satire That Was*
(2000)

18 We sing you the Song of the Rhineland—
Europe's beauty spot . . .
That wonderful pretzel-and-stein land
Can never be forgot!

Ira Gershwin 1896–1983: 'Song of
the Rhineland' (1945)

19 What cleanliness everywhere! You dare not throw your
cigarette into the lake. No graffiti in the urinals.
Switzerland is proud of this; but I believe this is just what
she lacks: manure.

André Gide 1869–1951: diary,
Lucerne, 10 August 1917

20 For he might have been a Roosian,
A French, or Turk, or Proosian,
Or perhaps Ital-ian!
But in spite of all temptations
To belong to other nations,
He remains an Englishman!

W. S. Gilbert 1836–1911: *HMS
Pinafore* (1878)

21 Australia is a huge rest home, where no unwelcome news
is ever wafted on to the pages of the worst newspapers in
the world.

Germaine Greer 1939– : in *Observer*
1 August 1982

22 Holland . . . lies so low they're only saved by being
dammed.

Thomas Hood 1799–1845: *Up the
Rhine* (1840) 'Letter from Martha
Penny to Rebecca Page'

23 Then brim the bowl with atrabilious liquor!
We'll pledge our Empire vast across the flood:
For Blood, as all men know, than Water's thicker,
But Water's wider, thank the Lord, than Blood.

Aldous Huxley 1894–1963: 'Ninth
Philosopher's Song' (1920)

24 The best thing I know between France and England is—the sea.

Douglas Jerrold 1803–57: *The Wit and Opinions of Douglas Jerrold* (1859) 'The Anglo-French Alliance'

25 Earth is here so kind, that just tickle her with a hoe and she laughs with a harvest.

Douglas Jerrold 1803–57: *The Wit and Opinions of Douglas Jerrold* (1859) 'A Land of Plenty' (Australia)

26 And we will all go together when we go— Every Hottentot and every Eskimo.

Tom Lehrer 1928– : 'We Will All Go Together When We Go' (1953)

27 ELIZA: The Rain in Spain stays mainly in the plain. HIGGINS: By George, she's got it!

Alan Jay Lerner 1918–86: 'The Rain in Spain' (1956)

28 I'd love to get you On a slow boat to China, All to myself, alone.

Frank Loesser 1910–69: 'On a Slow Boat to China' (1948)

29 'We went in [to the European Community],' he said, 'to screw the French by splitting them off from the Germans. The French went in to protect their inefficient farmers from commercial competition. The Germans went in to cleanse themselves of genocide and apply for readmission to the human race.'

Jonathan Lynn 1943– and **Antony Jay** 1930– : *Yes, Minister* vol. 2 (1982)

30 In fact, I'm not really a *Jew*. Just Jew-*ish*. Not the whole hog, you know.

Jonathan Miller 1934– : *Beyond the Fringe* (1960 review) 'Real Class'

31 Frogs . . . are slightly better than Huns or Wops, but abroad is unutterably bloody and foreigners are fiends.

Nancy Mitford 1904–73: *The Pursuit of Love* (1945)

32 I have to spend so much time explaining to Americans that I am not English and to Englishmen that I am not American that I have little time left to be Canadian . . . (On second thought, I am a true cosmopolitan—unhappy anywhere.)

Laurence J. Peter 1919– : *Quotations for our Time* (1977)

33 The Dutch in old Amsterdam do it, Not to mention the Finns, Folks in Siam do it, Think of Siamese twins. Some Argentines, without means, do it, People say, in Boston, even beans do it Let's do it, let's fall in love.

Cole Porter 1891–1964: 'Let's Do It, Let's Fall in Love' (1928)

34 If you come on a camel, you can park it, So come to the supermarket And see Pe- king.

Cole Porter 1891–1964: 'Come to the Supermarket in Old Peking' (1958)

35 In Australia, *Inter alia*, Mediocrities Think they're Socrates.

Peter Porter 1929– : unpublished clerihew; Stephen Murray-Smith (ed.) *The Dictionary of Australian Quotations* (1984)

36 The people of Crete unfortunately make more history than they can consume locally.

Saki 1870–1916: *Chronicles of Clovis* (1911)

37 All my wife has ever taken from the Mediterranean—from that whole vast intuitive culture—are four bottles of Chianti to make into lamps.

Peter Shaffer 1926– : *Equus* (1973)

38 That's the main trouble with the two nations: bad Brits are snobs, bad Americans are slobs.

Peter Shaffer 1926– : *Whom Do I Have the Honour of Addressing?* (1990)

39 I think he bought his doublet in Italy, his round hose in France, his bonnet in Germany, and his behaviour everywhere.

William Shakespeare 1564–1616: *The Merchant of Venice* (1596–8)

40 England and America are two countries divided by a common language.

George Bernard Shaw 1856–1950: attributed in this and other forms, but not found in Shaw's published writings

41 I look upon Switzerland as an inferior sort of Scotland.

Sydney Smith 1771–1845: letter to Lord Holland, 1815

42 Yesterday, the President met with a group he calls the coalition of the willing. Or, as the rest of the world calls them, Britain and Spain.

Jon Stewart 1962– : *The Daily Show* March 2003

43 *a travelling companion on the Alps:*
They say if the Swiss had designed these mountains, um, they'd be rather flatter.

Paul Theroux 1941– : 'Misery on the Orient Express' in *Atlantic Monthly* July 1975

44 Lump the whole thing! say that the Creator made Italy from designs by Michael Angelo!

Mark Twain 1835–1910: *The Innocents Abroad* (1869)

45 I don't like Norwegians at all. The sun never sets, the bar never opens, and the whole country smells of kippers.

Evelyn Waugh 1903–66: letter to Lady Diana Cooper, 13 July 1934

46 In Italy for thirty years under the Borgias they had warfare, terror, murder, bloodshed—they produced Michelangelo, Leonardo da Vinci and the Renaissance. In Switzerland they had brotherly love, five hundred years of democracy and peace and what did that produce . . . ? The cuckoo clock.

Orson Welles 1915–85: *The Third Man* (1949 film); words added by Welles to Graham Greene's script

47 *of art and the Swiss:*
The sons of patriots are left with the clock that turns the mill, and the sudden cuckoo, with difficulty restrained in its box!
For this was Tell a hero! For this did Gessler die!

James McNeill Whistler 1834–1903: lecture in London, 20 February 1885; in *Mr Whistler's 'Ten O'Clock'* (1888)

48 I don't like Switzerland: it has produced nothing but theologians and waiters.

Oscar Wilde 1854–1900: letter from Switzerland, 20 March 1899

The Country

❝ So *that's* what hay looks like. ❞
Queen Mary

1 He likes the country, but in truth must own,
Most likes it, when he studies it in town.

William Cowper 1731–1800: 'Retirement' (1782)

2 God made the country, and man made the town.

William Cowper 1731–1800: *The Task* (1785)

3 Having always been told that living at Crowborough was 'living in the country' I wrongly identified English country life with interminable calls on elderly ladies whose favourite topic was the servant problem.

Tom Driberg 1905–76: *The Best of Both Worlds* (1953)

4 'You are a pretty urban sort of person though, wouldn't you say?'
'Only nor'nor'east,' I said. 'I know a fox from a fax-machine.'

Stephen Fry 1957– : *The Hippopotamus* (1994)

5 A weekend in the country—
Trees in the orchard call.
When you've examined one tree,
Then you've examined them all.

Ira Gershwin 1896–1983: 'A Weekend in the Country' (*The Barkleys of Broadway*, 1949 film)

6 June is bustin' out all over
The sheep aren't sleepin' any more!
All the rams that chase the ewe sheep
Are determined there'll be new sheep
And the ewe sheep aren't even keepin' score!

Oscar Hammerstein II 1895–1960: 'June is Bustin' Out All Over' (1945)

7 In a mountain greenery
Where God paints the scenery—.

Lorenz Hart 1895–1943: 'Mountain Greenery' (1926)

8 There is nothing good to be had in the country, or if there is, they will not let you have it.

William Hazlitt 1778–1830: *The Round Table* (1817)

9 The Farmer will never be happy again;
He carries his heart in his boots;
For either the rain is destroying his grain
Or the drought is destroying his roots.

A. P. Herbert 1890–1971: 'The Farmer' (1922)

10 Hey, buds below, up is where to grow,
Up with which below can't compare with.
Hurry! It's lovely up here! *Hurry!*

Alan Jay Lerner 1918–86: 'It's Lovely Up Here' (1965)

11 So *that's* what hay looks like.
said at Badminton House, where she was evacuated during the Second World War

Queen Mary 1867–1953: James Pope-Hennessy *Life of Queen Mary* (1959)

12 It is no good putting up notices saying 'Beware of the bull' because very rude things are sometimes written on them. I have found that one of the most effective notices is 'Beware of the Agapanthus'.

Lord Massereene and Ferrard 1914–93: speech on the Wildlife and Countryside Bill, House of Lords 16 December 1980

13 Very few people have settled entirely in the country but have grown at length weary of one another. The lady's conversation generally falls into a thousand impertinent effects of idleness, and the gentleman falls in love with his dogs and horses, and out of love with every thing else.

Lady Mary Wortley Montagu 1689–1762: letter to Edward Wortley Montagu, 12 August 1712

14 Whose woods are whose everybody knows exactly, and everybody knows who got them rezoned for a shopping mall and who couldn't get the financing to begin construction and why it was he couldn't get it.
on a traditional New England community, with reference to Robert Frost's 'Whose woods these are I think I know'

P. J. O'Rourke 1947– : *Parliament of Whores* (1991)

15 A farm is an irregular patch of nettles bounded by short-term notes, containing a fool and his wife who didn't know enough to stay in the city.

S. J. Perelman 1904–79: *The Most of S. J. Perelman* (1959) 'Acres and Pains'

16 Farming, that's the fashion,
Farming, that's the passion
Of our great celebrities of today.
Kit Cornell is shellin' peas,
Lady Mendl's climbin' trees,
Dear Mae West is at her best in the hay . . .
The natives think it's utterly utter
When Margie Hart starts churning her butter . . .
Miss Elsa Maxwell, so the folks tattle,
Got well-goosed while dehorning her cattle . . .
Liz Whitney has, on her bin of manure, a
Clip designed by the Duke of Verdura,
Farming is so charming, they all say.

Cole Porter 1891–1964: 'Farming' (1941)

17 Sylvia . . . was accustomed to nothing much more sylvan than 'leafy Kensington'. She looked on the country as something excellent and wholesome in its way, which was apt to become troublesome if you encouraged it overmuch.

Saki 1870–1916: *The Chronicles of Clovis* (1911)

18 I have no relish for the country; it is a kind of healthy grave.

Sydney Smith 1771–1845: letter to Miss G. Harcourt, 1838

19 Anybody can be good in the country.

Oscar Wilde 1854–1900: *The Picture of Dorian Gray* (1891)

20 What do we see at once but a little robin! There is no need to burst into tears fotherington-tomas swete tho he be. Nor to buzz a brick at it, molesworth 2.

Geoffrey Willans 1911–58 and **Ronald Searle** 1920– : a nature walk at St Custards; *Down with Skool!* (1953)

Cricket ····> Sports and Games

❝ Organized loafing. ❞
William Temple

1 *when playing in a Lancashire league game, Dennis Lillee's ball hit the batsman on the leg. Although given out, the batsman remained at the crease, and Lillee insisted forcefully that he must go:*
I'd love to go Dennis but I daren't move. I think you've broken my bloody leg.

Anonymous: Michael Parkinson *Sporting Lives* (1993)

2 *in Australian cricket, traditional line of wicket-keeper to new batsman:*
How's the wife and my kids?

Anonymous: Simon Hughes *Yakking Around the World* (2000)

3 Life as we know it is over.
an unnamed member of the Marylebone Cricket Club, after the MCC voted to admit women members

Anonymous: in *Irish Times* 3 October 1998 'This Week They Said'

4 *the umpire to the bowler, after 'not out' was called when W. G. Grace was unexpectedly bowled first ball:*
They have paid to see Dr Grace bat, not to see you bowl.

Anonymous: Harry Furniss *A Century of Grace* (1985); perhaps apocryphal

5 *on being approached for a contribution to W. G. Grace's*
testimonial:
It's not in support of cricket but as an earnest protest
against golf.

Max Beerbohm 1872–1956:
attributed

6 Broken marriages, conflicts of loyalty, the problems of
everyday life fall away as one faces up to Thomson.
on Jeff Thomson's bowling

Mike Brearley 1942– : Ned Sherrin
Cutting Edge (1984)

7 *reflecting on the cricketer Billy Barnes who had made a*
century at Lord's while tipsy:
The modern professional cricketer does not get drunk at
Lord's or often get a century there, or anywhere else,
before lunch.

Neville Cardus 1889–1975:
Autobiography (1947)

8 The last positive thing England did for cricket was to
invent it.

Ian Chappell 1943– : in *Mail on
Sunday* 6 January 2002

9 I couldn't bat for the length of time required to score 500.
I'd get bored and fall over.

Denis Compton 1918– : to Brian
Lara; in *Daily Telegraph* 27 June 1994

10 That's the trouble with these West Country teams. They
bowl and field beautifully for an hour, and then—They
begin to think of apples.

C. B. Fry 1872–1956: Iain Wilton *C. B.
Fry* (1999)

11 Never read print, it spoils one's eye for the ball.
habitual advice to his players

W. G. Grace 1848–1915: Harry
Furniss *A Century of Grace* (1985)

12 Cricket—a game which the English, not being a spiritual
people, have invented in order to give themselves some
conception of eternity.

Lord Mancroft 1914– : *Bees in Some
Bonnets* (1979)

13 He is also too daring for the majority of the black-beards,
the brown-beards and the no-beards, and the all-beards,
who sit in judgement on batsmen; in short, too daring for
those who have never known what it is to dare in cricket.
Only for those who have not yet grown to the tyranny of
the razor is Gimblett possibly not daring enough.
on Harold Gimblett, sometimes accused of being 'too daring
for the greybeards'

R. C. Robertson-Glasgow 1901–65:
Cricket Prints (1943)

14 He loved to walk sideways towards them, like a grimly
playful crab.
of George Gunn's approach to faster bowlers

R. C. Robertson-Glasgow 1901–65:
Cricket Prints (1943)

15 He mistrusts anyone who reads past the sports pages of the
tabloids.
of Michael Stewart, the former English Test team manager

Peter Roebuck 1956– : in *Ned
Sherrin in his Anecdotage* (1993)

16 Personally, I have always looked upon cricket as organized
loafing.
view of a future archbishop of Canterbury in 1925

William Temple 1881–1944: Michael
Parkinson *Sporting Lives* (1993)

17 I need nine wickets from this match, and you buggers had
better start drawing straws to see who I don't get.
to an opposing team

Freddie Trueman 1931– : in *Ned
Sherrin in his Anecdotage* (1993)

18 It's a well-known fact that, when I'm on 99, I'm the best
judge of a run in all the bloody world.
to Cyril Washbrook

Alan Wharton 1923–93: Freddie
Trueman *You Nearly Had Me That
Time* (1978)

19 Cricket is basically baseball on valium.

Robin Williams 1952– : attributed

Crime ····> The Law, Judges, Punishment

66 What is robbing a bank compared with founding a bank? 99
Bertolt Brecht

1 *Mafia hitman, on trial in Sicily for a double murder:*
It was not me who killed those two men because that
night I was shooting two other men.

Anonymous: in *Mail on Sunday* 4
January 2004 'Quotes of the Year'

2 Sammy, you've already lost one eye. D'you wanna go for
two?
   gangster threatening Sammy Davis Jr

Anonymous: Donald Zec *Put the
Knife in Gently* (2003)

3 When their lordships asked Bacon
How many bribes he had taken
He had at least the grace
To get very red in the face.

Edmund Clerihew Bentley
1875–1956: 'Bacon' (1939)

4 Since it is probable that any book flying a bullet in its title
is going to produce a corpse sooner or later—here it is.

Caryl Brahms 1901–82 and **S. J.
Simon** 1904–48: *A Bullet in the Ballet*
(1937)

5 What is robbing a bank compared with founding a bank?

Bertolt Brecht 1898–1956: *Die
Dreigroschenoper* (1928)

6 Thieves respect property. They merely wish the property to
become their property that they may more perfectly
respect it.

G. K. Chesterton 1874–1936: *The
Man who was Thursday* (1908)

7 Thou shalt not steal; an empty feat,
When it's so lucrative to cheat.

Arthur Hugh Clough 1819–61: 'The
Latest Decalogue' (1862)

8 Here in our city
We're all of us pretty
Well sure that vice
Will in a trice
Be bundled out of sight,
Old men in lobbies
With dubious hobbies
Can still get the deuce of a fright
In London at night.

Noël Coward 1899–1973: 'London at
Night' (1953)

9 Three juvenile delinquents,
Juvenile delinquents,
Happy as can be—we
Waste no time
On the wherefores and whys of it;
We like crime
And that's about the size of it.

Noël Coward 1899–1973: 'Three
Juvenile Delinquents' (1949)

10 *of a burglar:*
He found it inconvenient to be poor.

William Cowper 1731–1800:
'Charity' (1782)

11 *a prisoner before Mr Justice Darling objected to being called 'a
professional crook':*
PRISONER: I've only done two jobs, and each time I've been
nabbed.
LORD DARLING: It has never been suggested that you are
successful in your profession.

Lord Darling 1849–1936: Edward
Maltby *Secrets of a Solicitor* (1929)

12 It is quite a three-pipe problem, and I beg that you won't speak to me for fifty minutes.

Arthur Conan Doyle 1859–1930: *The Adventures of Sherlock Holmes* (1892) 'The Red-Headed League'

13 'Excellent,' I cried. 'Elementary,' said he.

Arthur Conan Doyle 1859–1930: *The Memoirs of Sherlock Holmes* (1894) 'The Crooked Man'. 'Elementary, my dear Watson' is not found in any book by Conan Doyle

14 Major Strasser has been shot. Round up the usual suspects.

Julius J. Epstein 1909– et al.: *Casablanca* (1942 film)

15 It was beautiful and simple as all truly great swindles are.

O. Henry 1862–1910: *Gentle Grafter* (1908) 'Octopus Marooned'

16 The Warden threw a party at the county jail,
The prison band was there an' they began to wail.
The brass band was jumpin' an' the joint began to swing
You should have heard those knocked out jail birds sing.

Jerry Leiber 1933– and **Mike Stoller** 1933– : 'Jailhouse Rock' (1957)

17 If you import cannabis you get 25 years—is importation of cannabis four times as bad as rape?

Lord McCluskey 1914– : speech, Edinburgh, 12 July 1999

18 Let it appear in a criminal trial that the accused is a Sunday-school superintendent, and the jury says guilty almost automatically.

H. L. Mencken 1880–1956: *Minority Report* (1956)

19 When I heard the words criminal investigation my mindset changed considerably.

Oliver North 1943– : in *New York Times* 10 July 1987 'Quotation of the Day'

20 If I ever hear you accuse the police of using violence on a prisoner in custody again, I'll take you down to the station and beat the eyes out of your head.

Joe Orton 1933–67: *Loot* (1966)

21 The most peaceable way for you, if you do take a thief, is, to let him show himself what he is and steal out of your company.

William Shakespeare 1564–1616: *Much Ado About Nothing* (1598–9)

22 She starts to tell me how she's . . . married to an Italian with four restaurants on Long Island and right away I dig he's in with the mob. I mean one restaurant, you're in business, four restaurants it's the Mafia.

Neil Simon 1927– : *The Gingerbread Lady* (1970)

Critics

66 Send me no more reviews of any kind. **99**
Lord Byron

1 A bad review may spoil your breakfast but you shouldn't allow it to spoil your lunch.

Kingsley Amis 1922–95: Giles Gordon *Aren't We Due a Royalty Statement?* (1993); attributed

2 Full many a gallant man lies slain
On Waterloo's ensanguined plain,
But none by bullet or by shot
Fell half so flat as Walter Scott.
*comment on Scott's poem 'The Field of Waterloo' (1815),
sometimes attributed to Thomas Erskine*

Anonymous: Una Pope-Hennessy *The Laird of Abbotsford* (1932)

3 I have always thought it was a sound impulse by which he
[Kipling] was driven to put his 'Recessional' into the
waste-paper basket, and a great pity that Mrs Kipling
fished it out and made him send it to *The Times*.

Max Beerbohm 1872–1956: letter 30 October 1913

4 *apparent reassurance to a leading lady after a particularly bad
first night:*
My dear, good is not the word.

Max Beerbohm 1872–1956: attributed; Nigel Rees *Cassell Dictionary of Humorous Quotations* (1999)

5 Critics are like eunuchs in a harem; they know how it's
done, they've seen it done every day, but they're unable to
do it themselves.

Brendan Behan 1923–64: Jonathon Green (ed.) *A Dictionary of Contemporary Quotations* (1982)

6 Hebrews 13.8. [Jesus Christ, the same yesterday, and
today, and forever.]
summing up the long-running 1920s Broadway hit Abie's
Irish Rose

Robert Benchley 1889–1945: Peter Hay *Theatrical Anecdotes* (1987)

7 Listen, dear, you couldn't write 'fuck' in the dust on a
Venetian blind.
*to a Hollywood writer who had criticized Alan Bennett's 'An
Englishman Abroad'*

Coral Browne 1913–91: attributed

8 Send me no more reviews of any kind.—I will read no
more of evil or good in that line.—Walter Scott has not
read a review of *himself* for *thirteen years*.

Lord Byron 1788–1824: letter to his publisher John Murray, 3 November 1821

9 You know who the critics are? The men who have failed
in literature and art.

Benjamin Disraeli 1804–81: *Lothair* (1870)

10 One of the most characteristic sounds of the English
Sunday is the sound of Harold Hobson barking up the
wrong tree.

Penelope Gilliatt 1933–93: in *Encore* November–December 1959

11 Asking a working writer what he thinks about critics is
like asking a lamp-post how it feels about dogs.

Christopher Hampton 1946– : in *Sunday Times Magazine* 16 October 1977

12 When I read something saying I've not done anything as
good as *Catch-22* I'm tempted to reply, Who has?'

Joseph Heller 1923–99: in *The Times* 9 June 1993

13 There is a sort of savage nobility about his firm reliance on
his own bad taste.
of Richard Bentley's edition of Paradise Lost

A. E. Housman 1859–1936: 'Introductory Lecture' (1892)

14 Criticism is a study by which men grow important and
formidable at very small expense.

Samuel Johnson 1709–84: *The Idler* 9 June 1759

15 The quickest way to start a punch-up between two British
literary critics is to ask them what they think of the poems
of Sir John Betjeman

Philip Larkin 1922–85: introduction to *Collected Poems* (1971)

16 He took the praise as a greedy boy takes apple pie, and the
criticism as a good dutiful boy takes senna-tea.
of Bulwer Lytton, whose novels he had criticized

Lord Macaulay 1800–59: letter, 5 August 1831

17 He takes the long review of things;
He asks and gives no quarter.
And you can sail with him on wings
Or read the book. It's shorter.

David McCord 1897– : 'To A Certain Most Certainly Certain Critic' (1945)

18 Reviewing here [in Baltimore] is a hazardous occupation. Once I spoke harshly of an eminent American novelist, and he retaliated by telling a very charming woman that I was non compos penis. In time she came to laugh at him as a liar.

H. L. Mencken 1880–1956: letter to Hugh Walpole, 1922

19 The lot of critics is to be remembered by what they failed to understand.

George Moore 1852–1933: *Impressions and Opinions* (1891) 'Balzac'

20 And it is that word 'hummy', my darlings, that marks the first place in 'The House at Pooh Corner' at which Tonstant Weader fwowed up.

Dorothy Parker 1893–1967: review in *New Yorker* 20 October 1928

21 At ev'ry word a reputation dies.

Alexander Pope 1688–1744: *The Rape of the Lock* (1714)

22 For 18 years he *started the day* by reading a French novel (in preparation for his history of them) an act so unnatural to man as to amount almost to genius.

Stephen Potter 1900–69: of the critic G. E. B. Saintsbury; *The Muse in Chains* (1937)

23 GLAND: I would say it's somehow redolent, and full of vitality.
HILDA: Well, I would say it's got about as much life in it as a potted shrimp.
GLAND: Well, I think we're probably both trying to say the same thing in different words.

Henry Reed 1914–86: *The Primal Scene, as it were* (1958 radio play)

24 Let my people go!
at a viewing of Exodus

Mort Sahl 1926– : attributed, 1961; Nigel Rees *Cassell Dictionary of Humorous Quotations* (1999)

25 Last year I gave several lectures on 'Intelligence and the Appreciation of Music Among Animals'. Today I am going to speak to you about 'Intelligence and the Appreciation of Music Among Critics'. The subject is very similar.

Erik Satie 1866–1925: Nat Shapiro (ed.) *An Encyclopedia of Quotations about Music* (1978)

26 Criticism is not only medicinally salutary: it has positive popular attractions in its cruelty, its gladiatorship, and the gratification given to envy by its attacks on the great, and to enthusiasm by its praises.

George Bernard Shaw 1856–1950: preface to *Plays Unpleasant* (1898)

27 Never pay any attention to what critics say . . . A statue has never been set up in honour of a critic!

Jean Sibelius 1865–1957: Bengt de Törne *Sibelius: A Close-Up* (1937)

28 I never read a book before reviewing it; it prejudices a man so.

Sydney Smith 1771–1845: H. Pearson *The Smith of Smiths* (1934)

29 As learned commentators view
In Homer more than Homer knew.

Jonathan Swift 1667–1745: 'On Poetry' (1733)

30 *John Churton Collins, a rival of Edmund Gosse, launched a bitter critical attack on him. When Gosse took tea with Tennyson he found an ally who defined Collins as:*
A louse in the locks of literature.

Alfred, Lord Tennyson 1809–92: Evan Charteris *Life and Letters of Sir Edmund Gosse* (1931)

31 My dear Sir: I have read your play. Oh, my dear Sir! Yours faithfully.
rejecting a play

Herbert Beerbohm Tree 1852–1917: Peter Hay *Theatrical Anecdotes* (1987)

32 A critic is a man who knows the way but can't drive the car.

Kenneth Tynan 1927–80: in *New York Times Magazine* 9 January 1966

33 The original Greek is of great use in elucidating Browning's translation of the *Agamemnon*.

Robert Yelverton Tyrrell 1844–1914: habitual remark to students; Ulick O'Connor *Oliver St John Gogarty* (1964)

34 Critics search for ages for the wrong word which, to give them credit, they eventually find.

Peter Ustinov 1921–2004: Ned Sherrin *Cutting Edge* (1984)

35 *Norman Mailer, annoyed at Vidal's literary style of criticism, hit him over the head with a glass tumbler:*
Ah, Mailer is, as usual, lost for words.

Gore Vidal 1925– : attributed; in *Guardian* 27 February 1999

36 WILDE: I shall always regard you as the best critic of my plays.
TREE: But I have never criticized your plays.
WILDE: That's why.

Oscar Wilde 1854–1900: conversation with Beerbohm Tree after the first-night success of *A Woman of No Importance*; Hesketh Pearson *Beerbohm Tree* (1956)

37 One must have a heart of stone to read the death of Little Nell without laughing.

Oscar Wilde 1854–1900: Ada Leverson *Letters to the Sphinx* (1930)

Dance

" A perpendicular expression of a horizontal desire. "
George Bernard Shaw

1 I made the little buggers hop.

Thomas Beecham 1879–1961: on conducting the Diaghilev Ballet; attributed

2 We are told that her supporting company are all relations, and I dare say they do better than yours or mine would under the circumstances.
of Carmen Armaya's Spanish Gypsy Dancers at the Prince's Theatre

Caryl Brahms 1901–82: in *Evening Standard* 1948

3 *The ballet designer Benois:*
Benois . . . If 'e come.

Caryl Brahms 1901–82 and **S. J. Simon** 1904–48: *A Bullet in the Ballet* (1937)

4 Will you, won't you, will you, won't you, will you join the dance?

Lewis Carroll 1832–98: *Alice's Adventures in Wonderland* (1865)

5 Though no one ever could be keener
Than little Nina
On quite a number
Of very eligible men who did the Rhumba
When they proposed to her she simply left them flat.
She said that love should be impulsive
But not compulsive
And syncopation
Has a discouraging effect on procreation
And that she'd rather read a book—and that was that!

Noël Coward 1899–1973: 'Nina' (1945)

6 Do you want the whole countryside to be laughing at us?—women of our years?—mature women, *dancing*?

Brian Friel 1929– : *Dancing at Lughnasa* (1990)

7 Stately as a galleon, I sail across the floor,
Doing the Military Two-step, as in the days of yore . . .
So gay the band,
So giddy the sight,
Full evening dress is a must,
But the zest goes out of a beautiful waltz
When you dance it bust to bust.

Joyce Grenfell 1910–79: 'Stately as a Galleon' (1978)

8 No. You see there are portions of the human anatomy which would keep swinging after the music had finished.
reply to question on whether the fashion for nudity would extend to dance

Robert Helpmann 1909–86: Elizabeth Salter *Helpmann* (1978)

9 Cheek to Cheek
Toes to Toes
Here's a dance you can do on a dime
Knees to Knees
Nose to Nose
Slowly move, and you're doin' 'The Slime'.

Jerry Leiber 1933– : 'The Slime' (1942)

10 He waltzes like a Protestant curate.

Kate O'Brien 1897–1974: *The Last of Summer* (1943)

11 Everyone else at the table had got up to dance, except him and me. There I was, trapped. Trapped like a trap in a trap.

Dorothy Parker 1893–1967: *After Such Pleasures* (1933)

12 I wish I could shimmy like my sister Kate,
She shivers like the jelly on a plate.

Armand J. Piron: 'Shimmy like Kate' (1919)

13 If the Louvre custodian can,
If the Guard Republican can,
If Van Gogh and Matisse and Cézanne can,
Baby, you can can-can too . . .
Lovely Duse in Milan can,
Lucien Guitry and Réjane can,
Sarah Bernhardt upon a divan can,
Baby, you can can-can too.

Cole Porter 1891–1964: 'Can-Can' (1953)

14 [Dancing is] a perpendicular expression of a horizontal desire.

George Bernard Shaw 1856–1950: in *New Statesman* 23 March 1962

15 On the church gate a hand-painted notice with two spelling mistakes announced that owing to the welcome presence of the Redemptorist Fathers in the town there would be no dance on Sunday.

Honor Tracy 1915– : *Mind You, I've Said Nothing* (1953)

Death ····▶ Epitaphs, Funerals, Last Words, Murder

❝ Nothing can be said to be certain, except death and taxes. ❞
Benjamin Franklin

1 It's not that I'm afraid to die. I just don't want to be there when it happens.

Woody Allen 1935– : *Death* (1975)

2 *of suicide:*
There have been times when I've thought about it—but with my luck it would probably turn out to be only a temporary solution.

Woody Allen 1935– : attributed; Milton Shulman *It Takes All Sorts* (2003)

3 I don't want to achieve immortality through my work . . . I want to achieve it through not dying.

Woody Allen 1935– : Eric Lax *Woody Allen and his Comedy* (1975)

4 Death has got something to be said for it:
There's no need to get out of bed for it;
Wherever you may be,
They bring it to you, free.

Kingsley Amis 1922–95: 'Delivery Guaranteed' (1979)

5 Regret to inform you Hand that rocked the cradle kicked the bucket.

Anonymous: reported telegram; in *Ned Sherrin in his Anecdotage* (1993)

6 [Death is] nature's way of telling you to slow down.

Anonymous: American life insurance proverb, in *Newsweek* 25 April 1960

7 *on spiritualism:*
I always knew the living talked rot, but it's nothing to the rot the dead talk.

Margot Asquith 1864–1945: Chips Channon diary, 20 December 1937

8 We met . . . Dr Hall in such very deep mourning that either his mother, his wife, or himself must be dead.

Jane Austen 1775–1817: letter to Cassandra Austen, 17 May 1799

9 Even death is unreliable: instead of zero it may be some ghastly hallucination, such as the square root of minus one.

Samuel Beckett 1906–89: attributed

10 When I came back to Dublin, I was courtmartialled in my absence and sentenced to death in my absence, so I said they could shoot me in my absence.

Brendan Behan 1923–64: *Hostage* (1958)

11 Lord Finchley tried to mend the Electric Light
Himself. It struck him dead: And serve him right!
It is the business of the wealthy man
To give employment to the artisan.

Hilaire Belloc 1870–1953: 'Lord Finchley' (1911)

12 When I am dead, I hope it may be said:
'His sins were scarlet, but his books were read.'

Hilaire Belloc 1870–1953: 'On His Books' (1923)

13 What I like about Clive
Is that he is no longer alive.
There is a great deal to be said
For being dead.

Edmund Clerihew Bentley 1875–1956: 'Clive' (1905)

14 I believe in reincarnation, so I've left all my money to myself.

Tony Blackburn 1943– : in *The Oldie* May 2003

15 Thou shalt not kill; but need'st not strive
Officiously to keep alive.

Arthur Hugh Clough 1819–61: 'The Latest Decalogue' (1862)

16 Swans sing before they die: 'twere no bad thing
Should certain persons die before they sing.

Samuel Taylor Coleridge 1772–1834: 'On a Volunteer Singer' (1834)

17 I'm amazed he was such a good shot.
on being told that his accountant had blown his brains out

Noël Coward 1899–1973: in *Ned Sherrin's Theatrical Anecdotes* (1991)

18 I read the *Times* and if my name is not in the obits I proceed to enjoy the day.

Noël Coward 1899–1973: attributed

19 *before his death, Lord Curzon had informed his second wife of his arrangements for her burial in the family vault at Kedleston, when he 'placing his hand on one of the niches, said*

Lord Curzon 1859–1925: Harold Nicolson diary, 13 January 1934

*"This, Gracie dearest, is reserved for you."' In fact he had
already placed in the niche 'a large Foreign Office envelope on
which he had scrawled in blue pencil':*
Reserved for the second Lady Curzon.

20 He'd make a lovely corpse.

Charles Dickens 1812–70: *Martin Chuzzlewit* (1844)

21 Take away that emblem of mortality.
   on being offered an air cushion to sit on, 1881

Benjamin Disraeli 1804–81: Robert Blake *Disraeli* (1966)

22 When I die I want to decompose in a barrel of porter and
have it served in all the pubs in Dublin. I wonder would
they know it was me?

J. P. Donleavy 1926– : *Ginger Man* (1955)

23 In this world nothing can be said to be certain, except
death and taxes.

Benjamin Franklin 1706–90: letter to Jean Baptiste Le Roy, 13 November 1789

24 Bombazine would have shown a deeper sense of her loss.

Elizabeth Gaskell 1810–65: *Cranford* (1853)

25 He makes a very handsome corpse and becomes his coffin
prodigiously.

Oliver Goldsmith 1730–74: *The Good-Natured Man* (1768)

26 The babe with a cry brief and dismal,
   Fell into the water baptismal;
   Ere they gathered its plight,
   It had sunk out of sight,
   For the depth of the font was abysmal.

Edward Gorey 1925– : *The Listing Attic* (1954)

27 'There's been an accident,' they said,
   'Your servant's cut in half; he's dead!'
   'Indeed!' said Mr Jones, 'and please,
   Send me the half that's got my keys.'

Harry Graham 1874–1936: 'Mr Jones' (1899)

28 Billy, in one of his nice new sashes,
   Fell in the fire and was burnt to ashes;
   Now, although the room grows chilly,
   I haven't the heart to poke poor Billy.

Harry Graham 1874–1936: 'Tender-Heartedness' (1899)

29 *Richard Harris, who died of cancer, to diners, while being
carried on a stretcher out of the Savoy:*
It was the food. It was the food.

Richard Harris 1930–2002: in *Limerick Leader* (online edition) 7 December 2002

30 The best of us being unfit to die, what an inexpressible
absurdity to put the worst to death!

Nathaniel Hawthorne 1804–64: diary, 13 October 1851

31 Once you're dead, you're made for life.

Jimi Hendrix 1942–70: c.1968, attributed; Nigel Rees *Cassell Dictionary of Humorous Quotations* (1999)

32 *during his last illness:*
   If Mr Selwyn calls again, show him up: if I am alive I shall
   be delighted to see him; and if I am dead he would like to
   see me.

Lord Holland 1705–74: J. H. Jesse *George Selwyn and his Contemporaries* (1844)

33 His death, which happened in his berth,
   At forty-odd befell:
   They went and told the sexton, and
   The sexton tolled the bell.

Thomas Hood 1799–1845: 'Faithless Sally Brown' (1826)

34 I still go up my 44 stairs two at a time, but that is in hopes
of dropping dead at the top.

A. E. Housman 1859–1936: letter to Laurence Housman, 9 June 1935

35 At his funeral in Omaha he filled the church to capacity. He was a draw right to the finish.
after the death of the boxer Vince Foster in 1949

Jack Hurley: Jonathon Green and Don Atyeo (eds.) *The Book of Sports Quotes* (1979)

36 But there, everything has its drawbacks, as the man said when his mother-in-law died, and they came down upon him for the funeral expenses.

Jerome K. Jerome 1859–1927: *Three Men in a Boat* (1889)

37 Depend upon it, Sir, when a man knows he is to be hanged in a fortnight, it concentrates his mind wonderfully.

Samuel Johnson 1709–84: James Boswell *Life of Samuel Johnson* (1791) 19 September 1777

38 *ex-President Eisenhower's death prevented her photograph appearing on the cover of* Newsweek:
Fourteen heart attacks and he had to die in my week. In MY week.

Janis Joplin 1943–70: in *New Musical Express* 12 April 1969

39 *on how he would kill himself:*
With kindness.

George S. Kaufman 1889–1961: Howard Teichmann *George S. Kaufman* (1973)

40 I detest life-insurance agents; they always argue that I shall some day die, which is not so.

Stephen Leacock 1869–1944: *Literary Lapses* (1910)

41 Death is the most convenient time to tax rich people.

David Lloyd George 1863–1945: in *Lord Riddell's Intimate Diary of the Peace Conference and After, 1918–23* (1933)

42 Alas! Lord and Lady Dalhousie are dead, and buried at last,
Which causes many people to feel a little downcast.

William McGonagall c.1825–1902: 'The Death of Lord and Lady Dalhousie'

43 Beautiful Railway Bridge of the Silv'ry Tay!
Alas, I am very sorry to say
That ninety lives have been taken away
On the last Sabbath day of 1879,
Which will be remembered for a very long time.

William McGonagall c.1825–1902: 'The Tay Bridge Disaster'

44 There is nothing like a morning funeral for sharpening the appetite for lunch.

Arthur Marshall 1910–89: *Life's Rich Pageant* (1984)

45 Either he's dead, or my watch has stopped.

Groucho Marx 1895–1977: in *A Day at the Races* (1937 film; script by Robert Pirosh, George Seaton, and George Oppenheimer)

46 BLUEBOTTLE: You rotten swines. I told you I'd be deaded.

Spike Milligan 1918–2002: *The Hastings Flyer* in *The Goon Show* (BBC radio series) 3 January 1956

47 Death and taxes and childbirth! There's never any convenient time for any of them.

Margaret Mitchell 1900–49: *Gone with the Wind* (1936)

48 Jimmy Hoffa's most valuable contribution to the American labour movement came at the moment he stopped breathing—on July 30th, 1975.

Don E. Moldea: *The Hoffa Wars* (1978)

49 One dies only once, and it's for such a long time!

Molière 1622–73: *Le Dépit amoureux* (performed 1656, published 1662)

50 *on his deathbed, asked by an acquaintance how he was:*
Hovering between wife and death.

James Montgomery: Ulick O'Connor *Oliver St John Gogarty* (1964)

51 *during the Boxer rising it was erroneously reported that those besieged in the Legation quarter of Peking, including the* Times *correspondent Dr Morrison, had been massacred. Morrison cabled the paper:*
Have just read obituary in the Times. Kindly adjust pay to suit.

George Ernest Morrison 1862–1920: Claud Cockburn *In Time of Trouble* (1956); attributed

52 Drink and dance and laugh and lie
Love, the reeling midnight through
For tomorrow we shall die!
(But, alas, we never do.)

Dorothy Parker 1893–1967: 'The Flaw in Paganism' (1937)

53 *on being told by Robert Benchley that Calvin Coolidge had died:*
DOROTHY PARKER: How can they tell?
ROBERT BENCHLEY: He had an erection.

Dorothy Parker 1893–1967: Ned Sherrin in *The Listener* 8 January 1987; Benchley's final remark vouched for by his grandson Peter on the authority of Benchley's widow.

54 Guns aren't lawful;
Nooses give;
Gas smells awful;
You might as well live.

Dorothy Parker 1893–1967: 'Résumé' (1937)

55 Here am I, dying of a hundred good symptoms.

Alexander Pope 1688–1744: to George, Lord Lyttelton, 15 May 1744

56 Not louder shrieks to pitying heav'n are cast,
When husbands or when lapdogs breathe their last.

Alexander Pope 1688–1744: *The Rape of the Lock* (1714)

57 But thousands die, without or this or that,
Die, and endow a college, or a cat.

Alexander Pope 1688–1744: *Epistles to Several Persons* 'To Lord Bathurst' (1733)

58 [Memorial services are the] cocktail parties of the geriatric set.

Ralph Richardson 1902–83: Ruth Dudley Edwards *Harold Macmillan* (1983)

59 The cemetery is a sort of Mayfair of the dead, the most expensive real estate in Buenos Aires.
of the Recoleta Cemetery in Buenos Aires

Robert Robinson 1927– : in *The Times* 22 July 1978

60 *the aged President of Magdalen was told of a Fellow's suicide by two colleagues anxious that the news would distress him:*
Don't tell me. Let me guess.

Martin Routh 1755–1854: Dacre Balsdon *Oxford Life* (1957)

61 Waldo is one of those people who would be enormously improved by death.

Saki 1870–1916: *Beasts and Super-Beasts* (1914)

62 Ain't it grand to be blooming well dead?

Leslie Sarony 1897–1985: title of song (1932)

63 The thought of death has now become a part of my life. I read the obituaries every day just for the satisfaction of not seeing my name there.

Neil Simon 1927– : *Last of the Red Hot Lovers* (1970)

64 Well, it only proves what they always say—give the public something they want to see, and they'll come out for it.
on the crowds attending the funeral of the movie tycoon Harry Cohn, 2 March 1958

Red Skelton 1913– : attributed

65 Death is always a great pity of course but it's not as though the alternative were immortality.

Tom Stoppard 1937– : *Jumpers* (rev. ed. 1986)

66 Early to rise and early to bed makes a male healthy and wealthy and dead.

James Thurber 1894–1961: 'The Shrike and the Chipmunks'; in *New Yorker* 18 February 1939

67 He was just teaching me my death duties.
on her deathbed, having been visited by her solicitor to put her affairs in order

Lady Tree 1863–1937: in *Ned Sherrin in his Anecdotage* (1993)

68 The report of my death was an exaggeration.
usually quoted as, 'Reports of my death have been greatly exaggerated'

Mark Twain 1835–1910: in *New York Journal* 2 June 1897

69 I refused to attend his funeral, but I wrote a very nice letter explaining that I approved of it.
on hearing of the death of a corrupt politician

Mark Twain 1835–1910: James Munson (ed.) *The Sayings of Mark Twain* (1992)

70 *of Truman Capote's death:*
Good career move.

Gore Vidal 1925– : attributed

71 You're here to stay until the rustle in your dying throat relieves you!

H. M. Walker: addressed to Laurel and Hardy in *Beau Hunks* (1931 film; re-named *Beau Chumps* for British audiences)

72 Just think who we'd have been seen dead with!
on discovery that her name, with Noël Coward's, had been on the Nazi blacklist for arrest and probable execution

Rebecca West 1892–1983: postcard to Noël Coward, 1945

73 *at the mention of a huge fee for a surgical operation:*
Ah, well, then, I suppose that I shall have to die beyond my means.

Oscar Wilde 1854–1900: R. H. Sherard *Life of Oscar Wilde* (1906)

74 *of the wallpaper in the room where he was dying:*
One of us must go.

Oscar Wilde 1854–1900: attributed, probably apocryphal

Debt ····> Money, Poverty

66 If I hadn't my debts I shouldn't have anything to think about. **99**
Oscar Wilde

1 Cohen owes me ninety-seven dollars.

Irving Berlin 1888–1989: song-title (1913)

2 *on Allied war debts:*
They hired the money, didn't they?

Calvin Coolidge 1872–1933: John H. McKee *Coolidge: Wit and Wisdom* (1933)

3 Any further letters and I shall remove my overdraft.
telegram, c.1959, to his bankers, who had become alarmed at his expensive undergraduate lifestyle

Bobby Corbett 1940–99: in his obituary, *Daily Telegraph* 13 March 1999

4 My feet want to dance in the sun.
My head wants to rest in the shade.
The Lord says, 'Go out and have fun'.
But the Landlord says,
'Your rent ain't paid.'

E. Y. Harburg 1898–1981: 'Necessity' (1947)

5 [My father] taught me two things about bills; always query them and never pay till you have no alternative.

Miles Kington 1941–2008: *Welcome to Kington* (1989)

6 If the spoken word is repeated often enough, it is eventually written and thus made permanent . . . Many a decent man who has written a bad cheque knows the truth of that.

Flann O'Brien 1911–66: *Myles Away from Dublin* (1990)

7 I feel these days like a very large flamingo. No matter what way I turn, there is always a very large bill.

Joseph O'Connor 1963– : *The Secret World of the Irish Male* (1994)

8 The National Debt is a very Good Thing and it would be dangerous to pay it off, for fear of Political Economy.

W. C. Sellar 1898–1951 and **R. J. Yeatman** 1898–1968: *1066 and All That* (1930)

9 One must have some sort of occupation nowadays. If I hadn't my debts I shouldn't have anything to think about.

Oscar Wilde 1854–1900: *A Woman of No Importance* (1893)

Democracy ····> Government, Politics

“ It is only effective if you can stop people talking. **”**
Clement Attlee

---

1 Elections are won by men and women chiefly because most people vote against somebody rather than for somebody.

Franklin P. Adams 1881–1960: *Nods and Becks* (1944)

2 If the Archangel Gabriel had stood with the name of Winston Churchill, Ken would still have won.
of Ken Livingstone's candidacy as Mayor of London

Jeffrey Archer 1940– : in *Independent on Sunday* 7 May 2000

3 Democracy means government by discussion, but it is only effective if you can stop people talking.

Clement Attlee 1883–1967: speech at Oxford, 14 June 1957

4 The worst thing I can say about democracy is that it has tolerated the Right Honourable Gentleman [Neville Chamberlain] for four and a half years.

Aneurin Bevan 1897–1960: speech in the House of Commons 23 July 1929

5 A majority is always the best repartee.

Benjamin Disraeli 1804–81: *Tancred* (1847)

6 Hell, I never vote *for* anybody. I always vote *against*.

W. C. Fields 1880–1946: Robert Lewis Taylor *W. C. Fields* (1950)

7 Democracy is the name we give the people whenever we need them.

Robert, Marquis de Flers 1872–1927 and **Armand de Caillavet** 1869–1915: *L'habit vert* (1913)

8 I always voted at my party's call,
And I never thought of thinking for myself at all.

W. S. Gilbert 1836–1911: *HMS Pinafore* (1878)

9 *on John F. Kennedy's electoral victory in Wisconsin:*
A triumph for democracy. It proves that a millionaire has just as good a chance as anybody else.

Bob Hope 1903–2003: TV programme (1960); William Robert Faith *Bob Hope* (1983)

10 Democracy is the theory that the common people know what they want, and deserve to get it good and hard.

H. L. Mencken 1880–1956: *A Little Book in C major* (1916)

11 Under democracy one party always devotes its energies to trying to prove that the other party is unfit to rule—and both commonly succeed and are right.

H. L. Mencken 1880–1956: *Minority Report* (1956)

12 Every government is a parliament of whores. The trouble is, in a democracy the whores are us.

P. J. O'Rourke 1947– : *Parliament of Whores* (1991)

13 All animals are equal but some animals are more equal than others.

George Orwell 1903–50: *Animal Farm* (1945)

14 *on the death of a supporter of Proportional Representation:*
He has joined what even he would admit to be the majority.

John Sparrow 1906–92: J. A. Gere and John Sparrow (eds.) *Geoffrey Madan's Notebooks* (1981)

15 It's not the voting that's democracy, it's the counting.

Tom Stoppard 1937– : *Jumpers* (1972)

16 Democracy is the recurrent suspicion that more than half of the people are right more than half of the time.

E. B. White 1899–1985: in *New Yorker* 3 July 1944

17 Democracy means simply the bludgeoning of the people by the people for the people.

Oscar Wilde 1854–1900: *Sebastian Melmoth* (1891)

18 *a voter canvassed by Wilkes had declared that he would sooner vote for the devil:*
And if your friend is not standing?

John Wilkes 1727–97: Raymond Postgate *'That Devil Wilkes'* (1956 rev. ed.)

Description

❝ Damn description, it is always disgusting. **❞**
Lord Byron

1 Though I yield to no one in my admiration for Mr Coolidge, I do wish he did not look as if he had been weaned on a pickle.

Anonymous: remark recorded in Alice Roosevelt Longworth *Crowded Hours* (1933)

2 Diana Manners has no heart but her brains are in the right place.

Cyril Asquith 1890–1954: J. A. Gere and John Sparrow (eds.) *Geoffrey Madan's Notebooks* (1981)

3 *after a party given by Dorothy Parker:*
The less I behave like Whistler's Mother the night before, the more I look like her the morning after.

Tallulah Bankhead 1903–68: R. E. Drennan *Wit's End* (1973)

4 About as cuddly as a cornered ferret.
of Anne Robinson

Lynn Barber 1944– : in *The Times* 27 October 2001

5 Housman's cap, like a damp bun or pad of waste which engine-drivers clean their hands on.

A. C. Benson 1862–1925: J. A. Gere and John Sparrow (eds.) *Geoffrey Madan's Notebooks* (1981)

6 His smile bathed us like warm custard.

Basil Boothroyd 1910–88: *Let's Move House* (1977)

7 A high altar on the move.
of Edith Sitwell

Elizabeth Bowen 1899–1973: V. Glendinning *Edith Sitwell* (1981)

8 Damn description, it is always disgusting.

Lord Byron 1788–1824: letter 6 August 1809

9 What can you do with a man who looks like a female llama surprised when bathing?
of Charles de Gaulle

Winston Churchill 1874–1965: in conversation, c.1944; David Fraser *Alanbrooke* (1982)

10 The effect is of a Womble taking Cerberus for a walk.
of Roy Hattersley and his dog Buster

Will Cohn: interview in *Daily Telegraph* 19 September 1998

11 Two bursts in a sofa.
of a lady spectator at Wimbledon with pronouncedly hirsute armpits

Bobby Corbett 1940–99: in his obituary, *Daily Telegraph* 13 March 1999

12 The Henry Fondas lay on the evening like a damp mackintosh.

Noël Coward 1899–1973: diary, 8 May 1960

13 Like the silver plate on a coffin.
describing Robert Peel's smile

John Philpot Curran 1750–1817: quoted by Daniel O'Connell, House of Commons 26 February 1835

14 A day away from Tallulah is like a month in the country.

Howard Dietz 1896–1983: *Dancing in the Dark* (1974)

15 The ministers [on the Treasury Bench] reminded me of one of those marine landscapes not very uncommon on the coast of South America. You behold a range of exhausted volcanoes. Not a flame flickers on a single pallid crest.

Benjamin Disraeli 1804–81: speech at Manchester, 3 April 1872

16 Monsignor was forty-four then, and bustling—a trifle too stout for symmetry, with hair the colour of spun gold, and a brilliant, enveloping personality. When he came into a room clad in his full purple regalia from thatch to toe, he resembled a Turner sunset.

F. Scott Fitzgerald 1896–1940: *This Side of Paradise* (1921)

17 You are so graceful, have you wings?
You have a faceful of nice things
You have no speaking voice, dear . . .
With every word it sings.

Lorenz Hart 1895–1943: 'Thou Swell' (1927)

18 *of Arnold Schwarzenegger:*
I once described him as looking like a brown condom full of walnuts

Clive James 1939– : in *Daily Mail* 20 August 2003

19 A man who so much resembled a Baked Alaska—sweet, warm and gungy on the outside, hard and cold within.
of C. P. Snow

Francis King 1923– : *Yesterday Came Suddenly* (1993)

20 His appearance with his large features and rich mane of hair suggested the attempt of some archaic sculptor only acquainted with sheep to achieve a lion by hearsay.

Osbert Lancaster 1908–80: *All Done From Memory* (1953)

21 Springing from the grassroots of the country clubs of America.
of Wendell Willkie

Alice Roosevelt Longworth 1884–1980: Michael Teague *Mrs L* (1981)

22 [He looks like] an explosion in a pubic hair factory.
of Paul Johnson

Jonathan Miller 1934– : Alan Watkins *Brief Lives* (1982)

23 Her face showed the kind of ferocious disbelief with which Goneril must have taken the news that her difficult old father King Lear had decided to retire and move in with her.

Frank Muir 1920–98: *The Walpole Orange* (1993)

24 Rudyard Kipling's eyebrows are very odd indeed! They curl up black and furious like the moustache of a Neapolitan tenor.

Harold Nicolson 1886–1968: diary 8 January 1930

25 The beach was almost deserted. The tide was out. Turnstones were turning stones. Oystercatchers were catching oysters. In the marshalling yards, shunting engines were shunting and marshalling.

David Nobbs 1935– : *Going Gently* (2000)

26 The place smelt of apple-scented air freshener, not like apples, but like a committee's idea of what apples smell like.

Joseph O'Connor 1963– : *Cowboys and Indians* (1992)

27 Buckingham Palace looked a vast doll's house that some bullying skinhead big brother had kicked down the Mall.

Joseph O'Connor 1963– : *Cowboys and Indians* (1992)

28 The butler who answered the door—and he took his time about it—looked like a Road Company Robert Morley at the Paper Mill Playhouse.

S. J. Perelman 1904–79: 'Call Me Monty and Grovel Freely'

29 A rose-red sissy half as old as time.

William Plomer 1903–73: 'Playboy of the Demi-World: 1938' (1945)

30 The Cavaliers (Wrong but Wromantic) and the Roundheads (Right but Repulsive).

W. C. Sellar 1898–1951 and **R. J. Yeatman** 1898–1968: *1066 and All That* (1930)

31 Hotter than Uncle Bud's pants on lesbian mud-wrestling night.

Mark Steyn: in *Spectator* 2 October 1999

32 I don't think I have ever seen a Silver Band so nonplussed. It was as though a bevy of expectant wolves had overtaken a sleigh and found no Russian peasant on board.

P. G. Wodehouse 1881–1975: *Uncle Dynamite* (1948)

33 I turned to Aunt Agatha, whose demeanour was now rather like that of one who, picking daisies on the railway, has just caught the down express in the small of the back.

P. G. Wodehouse 1881–1975: *The Inimitable Jeeves* (1923)

34 She fitted into my biggest armchair as if it had been built round her by someone who knew they were wearing armchairs tight about the hips that season.

P. G. Wodehouse 1881–1975: *My Man Jeeves* (1919)

35 Roderick Spode? Big chap with a small moustache and the sort of eye that can open an oyster at sixty paces?

P. G. Wodehouse 1881–1975: *The Code of the Woosters* (1938)

Despair ····> Hope and Despair

Diaries

66 Keep a diary and some day it'll keep you. 99
Mae West

1 Now that I am finishing the damned thing I realise that diary-writing isn't wholly good for one, that too much of it leads to living for one's diary instead of living for the fun of living as ordinary people do.

James Agate 1877–1947: letter, 7 December 1946

2 A page of my Journal is like a cake of portable soup. A little may be diffused into a considerable portion.

James Boswell 1740–95: *Journal of a Tour to the Hebrides* (1785)

3 What is more dull than a discreet diary? One might just as well have a discreet soul.

Chips Channon 1897–1958: diary, 26 July 1935

4 It is a fair proposition, I think, that the diaries of men who enjoy their own nudity ought not to be published unless they are as interesting as Pepys. Otherwise it is really too distressing for the observer.

Harold Laski 1893–1950: letter to Oliver Wendell Holmes, 23 October 1927

5 To write a diary every day is like returning to one's own vomit.

Enoch Powell 1912–98: interview in *Sunday Times* 6 November 1977

6 I have decided to keep a full journal, in the hope that my life will perhaps seem more interesting when it is written down.

Sue Townsend 1946– : *Adrian Mole: The Wilderness Years* (1993)

7 I always say, keep a diary and some day it'll keep you.

Mae West 1892–1980: *Every Day's a Holiday* (1937 film)

8 I never travel without my diary. One should always have something sensational to read in the train.

Oscar Wilde 1854–1900: *The Importance of Being Earnest* (1895)

Dictionaries

❝ A writer of dictionaries, a harmless drudge. ❞
Samuel Johnson

1 You can file Madonna's quote in the dictionary of clichés under 'pot and kettle'.
response to her reported comment that he and Jennifer Lopez had courted media attention

Ben Affleck 1972– : in *Sunday Times* 20 June 2004 'Talking Heads'

2 Big dictionaries are nothing but storerooms with infrequently visited and dusty corners.

Richard W. Bailey 1939– : *Images of English* (1991)

3 They are strange beings, these lexicographers.

John Brown 1810–82: *Horae Subsecivae* (rev. ed. 1884)

4 Like Webster's Dictionary, we're Morocco bound.

Johnny Burke 1908–64: *The Road to Morocco* (1942 film), title song

5 The greatest masterpiece in literature is only a dictionary out of order.

Jean Cocteau 1889–1963: attributed

6 The Dictionary has not attempted to rival some of its predecessors in deliberate humour . . . Such rare occasions for a smile as may be found in it are unintentional.

W. A. Craigie 1867–1967: of the *New English Dictionary*; in *The Periodical* 15 February 1928

7 Short dictionaries should be improved because they are intended for people who actually need help.

William Empson 1906–84: attributed

8 *Lexicographer.* A writer of dictionaries, a harmless drudge.

Samuel Johnson 1709–84: *A Dictionary of the English Language* (1755)

9 *of his coinage of the phrase 'life's rich pageant':*
As far as I know, I didn't borrow the words from anywhere else and no less a body than the compilers of *The Oxford Dictionary of Quotations* have since taken an interest in the matter. They have finally decided that the phrase, such as it is, was my own invention and it is to be credited

Arthur Marshall 1910–89: *Life's Rich Pageant* (1984)

to me. Let me assure you that this small feather in my cap has not gone, so to speak, to my head.

10 A bad business, opening dictionaries; a thing I very rarely do. I try to make it a rule never to open my mouth, dictionaries, or hucksters' shops.

Flann O'Brien 1911–66: *The Best of Myles* (1968)

11 I suppose that so long as there are people in the world, they will publish dictionaries defining what is unknown in terms of something equally unknown.

Flann O'Brien 1911–66: *Myles Away from Dublin* (1990)

12 *Henry Liddell (1811–98) and Robert Scott (1811–87) were co-authors of the Greek Lexicon (1843), Liddell being in the habit of ascribing to his co-author usages which he criticized in his pupils, and which they said that they had culled from the* Lexicon:
Two men wrote a lexicon, Liddell and Scott;
Some parts were clever, but some parts were not.
Hear, all ye learned, and read me this riddle,
How the wrong part wrote Scott, and the right part wrote Liddell.

Edward Waterfield: L. E. Tanner *Westminster School: A History* (1934)

13 I've been in *Who's Who*, and I know what's what, but it'll be the first time I ever made the dictionary.

Mae West 1892–1980: letter to the RAF, early 1940s, on having an inflatable life jacket named after her

Diets

66 They are wonderful things for other people to go on. 99
Jean Kerr

1 In Lent she ate onion soup and gave up drink; but otherwise she must have drunk the maximum compatible with survival and sanity.
of the television cook, Jennifer Paterson

Anonymous: obituary of Jennifer Paterson, in *Daily Telegraph* 11 August 1999

2 I'm afraid I'm addicted to fat and love British beef. BSE holds no terror for me because . . . I am as likely to get it as win the National Lottery.
on her main difficulty in following a healthy diet

Joan Bakewell 1933– : in *Independent* 30 August 1997 'Quote Unquote'

3 You die of a heart attack but so what? You die thin.
on the Atkins diet

Bob Geldof 1954– : in *Independent* 23 August 2003

4 I feel about airplanes the way I feel about diets. It seems to me that they are wonderful things for other people to go on.

Jean Kerr 1923–2003: *The Snake Has All the Lines* (1958)

5 Life, if you're fat, is a minefield—you have to pick your way, otherwise you blow up.

Miriam Margolyes 1941– : in *Observer* 9 June 1991

6 Free your mind, and your bottom will follow.

Sarah, Duchess of York 1959– : slimming advice, 2001

Diplomacy ····> Politics

66 An ambassador is an honest man sent to lie abroad for the good of his country. 99
Henry Wotton

---

1 The Prime Minister rather enjoyed being led up the garden path by the Taoiseach, but she didn't much like the garden when she got there.

Anonymous: unnamed civil servant on negotiations between Margaret Thatcher and Charles Haughey; in *Daily Telegraph* 14 August 1993

2 *on the Council of Europe:*
If you open that Pandora's Box, you never know what Trojan 'orses will jump out.

Ernest Bevin 1881–1951: Roderick Barclay *Ernest Bevin and the Foreign Office* (1975)

3 We exchanged many frank words in our respective languages.

Peter Cook 1937–95: *Beyond the Fringe* (1961 revue)

4 American *diplomacy*. It's like watching somebody trying to do joinery with a chainsaw.

James Hamilton-Paterson 1941– : *Griefwork* (1993)

5 Diplomacy—lying in state.

Oliver Herford 1863–1935: Laurence J. Peter (ed.) *Quotations for Our Time* (1977)

6 There cannot be a crisis next week. My schedule is already full.

Henry Kissinger 1923– : in *New York Times Magazine* 1 June 1969

7 *on the life of a Foreign Secretary:*
Forever poised between a cliché and an indiscretion.

Harold Macmillan 1894–1986: in *Newsweek* 30 April 1956

8 *On the Hoare-Laval pact:*
Sam Hoare was certified by his doctors as unfit for public business, and on his way to the sanatorium he stops off in Paris and allows Laval to do him down.

Harold Nicolson 1886–1968: diary 12 December 1935

9 The French are masters of 'the dog ate my homework' school of diplomatic relations.

P. J. O'Rourke 1947– : *Holidays in Hell* (1988)

10 Wherever there is suffering, injustice and oppression, the Americans will show up, six months late, and bomb the country next to where it's happening.

P. J. O'Rourke 1947– : *Peace Kills* (2004)

11 Lord Palmerston, with characteristic levity had once said that only three men in Europe had ever understood [the Schleswig-Holstein question], and of these the Prince Consort was dead, a Danish statesman (unnamed) was in an asylum, and he himself had forgotten it.

Lord Palmerston 1784–1865: R. W. Seton-Watson *Britain in Europe 1789–1914* (1937)

12 I was wisely seen as unsuitable.
admitting he was once rejected by the Diplomatic Corps

Jeremy Paxman 1950– : in *Observer* 2 May 1999 'Sayings of the Week'

13 The chief distinction of a diplomat is that he can say no in such a way that it sounds like yes.

Lester Bowles Pearson 1897–1972: a Canadian Prime Minister's view; Geoffrey Pearson *Seize the Day* (1993)

14 In return for a handsomely bound facsimile of Palestrina's music, the Vicar of God was rewarded with a signed photograph of the Grocer and a gramophone record of himself conducting an orchestra.
of a meeting between the Pope and Edward Heath

Nicholas Shakespeare 1957– : in *The Spectator* 19/26 December 1992

15 There is a story that when Mrs Thatcher first met Gorbachev he gave her a ball-point and she offered him Labour-voting Scotland.

Nicholas Shakespeare 1957– : in *The Spectator* 19/26 December 1992

16 A diplomat these days is nothing but a head-waiter who's allowed to sit down occasionally.

Peter Ustinov 1921–2004: *Romanoff and Juliet* (1956)

17 An ambassador is an honest man sent to lie abroad for the good of his country.

Henry Wotton 1568–1639: written in the album of Christopher Fleckmore in 1604

Discontent ····▶ Satisfaction and Discontent

Dogs

❝ A door is what a dog is perpetually on the wrong side of. ❞
Ogden Nash

1 I look like a young wolf — cuddly in a frightening sort of way.
Buster's view of himself

Roy Hattersley 1932– : *Buster's Diaries* (1998)

2 Dogs who earn their living by appearing in television commercials in which they constantly and aggressively demand meat should remember that in at least one Far Eastern country they *are* meat.

Fran Lebowitz 1946– : *Social Studies* (1981)

3 A door is what a dog is perpetually on the wrong side of.

Ogden Nash 1902–71: 'A Dog's Best Friend is his Illiteracy' (1953)

4 I think Crab my dog be the sourest-natured dog that lives.

William Shakespeare 1564–1616: *The Two Gentlemen of Verona* (1592–3)

5 That indefatigable and unsavoury engine of pollution, the dog.

John Sparrow 1906–92: letter to *The Times* 30 September 1975

6 The more one gets to know of men, the more one values dogs.

A. Toussenel 1803–85: *L'Esprit des bêtes* (1847); attributed to Mme Roland in the form 'The more I see of men, the more I like dogs'

7 They say a reasonable amount o' fleas is good fer a dog— keeps him from broodin' over bein' a dog, mebbe.

Edward Noyes Westcott 1846–98: *David Harum* (1898)

Doubt ····▶ Certainty and Doubt

Dreams ····▶ Sleep and Dreams

Dress

" Never have your best trousers on when you go out to fight for freedom and truth. **"**
Henrik Ibsen

1 I had spent the whole of my savings . . . on a suit for the wedding—a remarkable piece of apparel with lapels that had been modelled on the tail fins of a 1957 Coupe de Ville and trousers so copiously flared that when I walked you didn't see my legs move.

Bill Bryson 1951– : *Neither Here Nor There* (1991)

2 *on being told that several of his fly-buttons were undone:*
No matter. The dead bird does not leave the nest.

Winston Churchill 1874–1965: Rupert Hart-Davis letter to George Lyttelton, 5 January 1957

3 You've got so much ice on your hands I could skate on them.
to Liberace

John Curry 1949–94: Ned Sherrin *Cutting Edge* (1984)

4 *to Sir Frederick Ponsonby, who had proposed accompanying him in a tail-coat:*
I thought everyone must know that a *short* jacket is always worn with a silk hat at a private view in the morning.

Edward VII 1841–1910: Philip Magnus *Edward VII* (1964)

5 *when Lord Harris appeared at Ascot in a brown bowler:*
Goin' rattin', 'Arris?

Edward VII 1841–1910: Michael Hill *Right Royal Remarks* (2003)

6 When he buys his ties he has to ask if gin will make them run.

F. Scott Fitzgerald 1896–1940: *Notebooks* (1978)

7 People always look askance at someone on the left who doesn't go around in sackcloth and ashes. I've always taken the view: why should the Devil have all the best suits?

George Galloway 1954– : interviewed by John Humphrys, *On the Ropes* (BBC Radio 4) 17 June 2003

8 *Lord Charles Russell had appeared incorrectly dressed at a Court Ball:*
Good evening, sir, I suppose you are the regimental doctor.

George IV 1762–1830: Michael Hill (ed.) *Right Royal Remarks* (2003)

9 *Dame Edna to Judy Steel:*
Tell me the history of that frock, Judy. It's obviously an old favourite. You were wise to remove the curtain rings.

Barry Humphries 1934– : *Another Audience with Dame Edna* (TV, 1984); Nigel Rees (ed.) *Cassell Dictionary of Humorous Quotations* (1999)

10 You should never have your best trousers on when you go out to fight for freedom and truth.

Henrik Ibsen 1828–1906: *An Enemy of the People* (1882)

11 Satan himself can't save a woman who wears thirty-shilling corsets under a thirty-guinea costume.

Rudyard Kipling 1865–1936: *Debits and Credits* (1926)

12 A silk dress in four sections, and shoes with high heels that would have broken the heart of John Calvin.

Stephen Leacock 1869–1944: *Arcadian Adventures with the Idle Rich* (1914)

13 I am not . . . totally unreceptive to colour providing it makes its appearance quietly, deferentially, and without undue fanfare.

Fran Lebowitz 1946– : *Metropolitan Life* (1978)

14 *of 'Fred Fernackerpan, a Mystery Goblin', who walked about the town with his trousers deployed à la Grand Old Duke of York:*
And when they were up they were up
And when they were down they were down
And when they were only half way up
He was arrested.

Spike Milligan 1918–2002: Alexander Games *The Essential Spike Milligan* (2002)

15 *on being asked what she wore in bed:*
Chanel No. 5.

Marilyn Monroe 1926–62: Pete Martin *Marilyn Monroe* (1956)

16 The officers of this branch of the Force [the Obscene Publications Squad at Scotland Yard] have a discouraging club tie, on which a book is depicted being cut in half by a larger pair of scissors.

John Mortimer 1923– : *Clinging to the Wreckage* (1982)

17 The only really firm rule of taste about cross dressing is that neither sex should ever wear anything they haven't yet figured out how to go to the bathroom in.

P. J. O'Rourke 1947– : *Modern Manners* (1984)

18 Fur is a subject that makes sensitive toes curl in their leather shoes.
introducing a discussion on fur coats

Jeremy Paxman 1950– : in *The Mail on Sunday* 13 February 2000 'Quotes of the Week'

19 I like curious clothes. Back in Dublin I stayed in my riding breeches, bought at a cheap shop in Dublin, and wore them for weeks after, as an enjoyable symbol of the Irish habit of life, until someone tactfully suggested I looked like a stable boy.

V. S. Pritchett 1900–97: *Midnight Oil* (1971)

20 She wears her clothes, as if they were thrown on her with a pitchfork.

Jonathan Swift 1667–1745: *Polite Conversation* (1738)

21 She wore far too much rouge last night, and not quite enough clothes. That is always a sign of despair in a woman.

Oscar Wilde 1854–1900: *An Ideal Husband* (1895)

Drink

66 I have taken more out of alcohol than alcohol has taken out of me. **99**
Winston Churchill

1 R-E-M-O-R-S-E!
Those dry Martinis did the work for me;
Last night at twelve I felt immense,
Today I feel like thirty cents.
My eyes are bleared, my coppers hot,
I'll try to eat, but I cannot.
It is no time for mirth and laughter,
The cold, grey dawn of the morning after.

George Ade 1866–1944: *The Sultan of Sulu* (1903)

2 Let's get out of these wet clothes and into a dry Martini.

Anonymous: line coined in the 1920s by Robert Benchley's press agent and adopted by Mae West in *Every Day's a Holiday* (1937 film)

3 Somewhere in the limbo which divides perfect sobriety from mild intoxication.

Cyril Asquith 1890–1954: J. A. Gere and John Sparrow (eds.) *Geoffrey Madan's Notebooks* (1981)

4 At Dirty Dick's and Sloppy Joe's
We drank our liquor straight,
Some went upstairs with Margery,
And some, alas, with Kate.

W. H. Auden 1907–73: 'The Sea and the Mirror' (1944)

5 I saw a notice which said 'Drink Canada Dry' and I've just started.

Brendan Behan 1923–64: attributed (probably not original); Nigel Rees *Cassell Dictionary of Humorous Quotations* (1999)

6 *asked to devise an advertising slogan for Guinness:*
Guinness makes you drunk.

Brendan Behan 1923–64: attributed, perhaps apocryphal

7 *on being told that the particular drink he was consuming was slow poison:*
So who's in a hurry?

Robert Benchley 1889–1945: Nathaniel Benchley *Robert Benchley* (1955)

8 Often Daddy sat up very late working on a case of Scotch.

Robert Benchley 1889–1945: *Pluck and Luck* (1925)

9 An admirable man, who puts down half a bottle of whisky a day and has two convictions for drunken driving, but otherwise a pillar of society.

Alan Bennett 1934– : *Getting On* (1972)

10 One evening in October, when I was one-third sober,
An' taking home a 'load' with manly pride;
My poor feet began to stutter, so I lay down in the gutter,
And a pig came up an' lay down by my side;
Then we sang 'It's all fair weather when good fellows get together,'
Till a lady passing by was heard to say:
'You can tell a man who "boozes" by the company he chooses'
And the pig got up and slowly walked away.

Benjamin Hapgood Burt 1880–1950: 'The Pig Got Up and Slowly Walked Away' (1933)

11 'Take some more tea,' the March Hare said to Alice, very earnestly. 'I've had nothing yet,' Alice replied in an offended tone, 'so I can't take more.' 'You mean you can't take *less*,' said the Hatter: 'it's very easy to take *more* than nothing.'

Lewis Carroll 1832–98: *Alice's Adventures in Wonderland* (1865)

12 Tea, although an Oriental,
Is a gentleman at least.
Cocoa is a cad and coward
Cocoa is a vulgar beast.

G. K. Chesterton 1874–1936: 'A Song of Right and Wrong' (1914)

13 I have taken more out of alcohol than alcohol has taken out of me.

Winston Churchill 1874–1965: Quentin Reynolds *By Quentin Reynolds* (1964)

14 *on being invited by a friend to dine at a Middle Eastern restaurant:*
The aftertaste of foreign food spoils the clean, pure flavour of gin for hours.

Eddie Condon 1905–73: Bill Crow *Jazz Anecdotes* (1990)

15 *when seriously ill and given a blood transfusion:*
This must be Fats Waller's blood. I'm getting high.

Eddie Condon 1905–73: Bill Crow *Jazz Anecdotes* (1990)

16 Take the juice of two quarts of whisky.
recommended hangover cure

Eddie Condon 1905–73: in *New York Sunday News* 10 June 1951

17 Sure I eat what I advertise. Sure I eat Wheaties for breakfast. A good bowl of Wheaties with Bourbon can't be beat.
a baseball star's comment

Dizzy Dean: in *Guardian* 23 December 1978 'Sports Quotes of the Year'

18 Therefore I *do* require it, which I makes confession, to be brought reg'lar and draw'd mild.

Charles Dickens 1812–70: *Martin Chuzzlewit* (1844)

19 'Mrs Harris,' I says, 'leave the bottle on the chimley-piece, and don't ask me to take none, but let me put my lips to it when I am so dispoged.'

Charles Dickens 1812–70: *Martin Chuzzlewit* (1844)

20 There is wan thing, an' on'y wan thing, to be said in favour iv dhrink, an' that is that it has caused manny a lady to be loved that otherwise might've died single.

Finley Peter Dunne 1867–1936: *Mr. Dooley Says* (1910)

21 A man shouldn't fool with booze until he's fifty; then he's a damn fool if he doesn't.

William Faulkner 1897–1962: James M. Webb and A. Wigfall Green *William Faulkner of Oxford* (1965)

22 Some weasel took the cork out of my lunch.

W. C. Fields 1880–1946: *You Can't Cheat an Honest Man* (1939 film)

23 I always keep a supply of stimulant handy in case I see a snake—which I also keep handy.

W. C. Fields 1880–1946: Corey Ford *Time of Laughter* (1970); attributed

24 A woman drove me to drink and I never even had the courtesy to thank her.

W. C. Fields 1880–1946: attributed

25 Best while you have it use your breath,
There is no drinking after death.

John Fletcher 1579–1625: *The Bloody Brother*, or *Rollo Duke of Normandy* (with Ben Jonson and others, performed *c*.1616)

26 And he that will go to bed sober,
Falls with the leaf still in October.

John Fletcher 1579–1625: *The Bloody Brother*, or *Rollo Duke of Normandy* (with Ben Jonson and others, performed *c*.1616)

27 There is no such thing as a small whisky.

Oliver St John Gogarty 1878–1957: attributed

28 From the bathing machine came a din
As of jollification within;
It was heard far and wide,
And the incoming tide
Had a definite flavour of gin.

Edward Gorey 1925– : *The Listing Attic* (1954)

29 The House of Lords is sitting in its judicial capacity this afternoon, and while I may be drunk as a lord I must be sober as a judge.
refusing another drink from the political journalist Robin Oakley

Lord Hailsham 1907–2001: anecdote; in *Spectator* 5 April 2003

30 Licker talks mighty loud w'en it git loose fum de jug.

Joel Chandler Harris 1848–1908: *Uncle Remus: His Songs and His Sayings* (1880) 'Plantation Proverbs'

31 I felt that the assortment of tablets that I had been given may have been mis-prescribed, since they seemed to interfere with the pleasant effects of alcohol. In the interests of my health, therefore, I stopped taking them.

Barry Humphries 1934– : *More Please* (1992)

32 We drink one another's healths, and spoil our own.

Jerome K. Jerome 1859–1927: *Idle Thoughts of an Idle Fellow* (1886)

33 Claret is the liquor for boys; port, for men; but he who aspires to be a hero (smiling) must drink brandy.

Samuel Johnson 1709–84: James Boswell *Life of Samuel Johnson* (1791) 7 April 1779

34 When I makes tea I makes tea, as old mother Grogan said. And when I makes water I makes water . . . *Begob, ma'am,* says Mrs Cahill, *God send you don't make them in the one pot.*

James Joyce 1882–1941: *Ulysses* (1922)

35 The Lord above made liquor for temptation
To see if man could turn away from sin.
The Lord above made liquor for temptation—but
With a little bit of luck,
With a little bit of luck,
When temptation comes you'll give right in!

Alan Jay Lerner 1918–86: 'With a Little Bit of Luck' (1956)

36 I don't drink liquor. I don't like it. It makes me feel good.

Oscar Levant 1906–72: in *Time* 5 May 1958

37 Heineken refreshes the parts other beers cannot reach.

Terry Lovelock: slogan for Heineken lager, 1975 onwards

38 Love makes the world go round? Not at all. Whisky makes it go round twice as fast.

Compton Mackenzie 1883–1972: *Whisky Galore* (1947)

39 Prohibition makes you want to cry into your beer and denies you the beer to cry into.

Don Marquis 1878–1937: *Sun Dial Time* (1936)

40 You're not drunk if you can lie on the floor without holding on.

Dean Martin 1917– : Paul Dickson *Official Rules* (1978)

41 Just a wee deoch-an-doris,
Just a wee yin, that's a'.
Just a wee deoch-an-doris,
Before we gang awa'.
There's a wee wifie waitin',
In a wee but-an-ben;
If you can say
'It's a braw bricht moonlicht nicht',
Ye're a' richt, ye ken.

R. F. Morrison: 'Just a Wee Deoch-an-Doris' (1911); popularized by Harry Lauder

42 If one glass of stout on a Sunday night is not enough, his spiritual home is the bodega.

J. B. Morton 1893–1975: M. Frayn *The Best of Beachcomber* (1963)

43 Candy
Is dandy
But liquor
Is quicker.

Ogden Nash 1902–71: 'Reflections on Ice-breaking' (1931)

44 *on the water content of a glass of whiskey:*
True, it is nearly impossible to avoid absorbing water in one form or another. But are you quite sane to be paying four shillings for a modest glasheen of it?

Flann O'Brien 1911–66: *Myles Away from Dublin* (1990)

45 Sometimes I have a sherry before dinner.
 a notable understatement

Charlie Parker 1920–55: Bill Crow *Jazz Anecdotes* (1990)

46 You can always tell that the crash is coming when I start getting tender about Our Dumb Friends. Three highballs and I think I'm St Francis of Assisi.

Dorothy Parker 1893–1967: *Here Lies* (1939)

47 One more drink and I'd have been under the host.

Dorothy Parker 1893–1967: Howard Teichmann *George S. Kaufman* (1973)

48 So make it another old-fashioned, please.
Leave out the cherry,
Leave out the orange,
Leave out the bitters,
Just make it a straight rye!

Cole Porter 1891–1964: 'Make it Another Old-Fashioned, Please' (1940)

49 Look here, Steward, if this is coffee, I want tea; but if this is tea, then I wish for coffee.

Punch 1841–1992: vol. 123 (1902)

50 And the sooner the tea's out of the way, the sooner we can get out the gin, eh?

Henry Reed 1914–86: *Private Life of Hilda Tablet* (1954 radio play)

51 Doth it not show vilely in me to desire small beer?

William Shakespeare 1564–1616: *Henry IV, Part 2* (1597)

52 PORTER: Drink, sir, is a great provoker of three things.
MACDUFF: What three things does drink especially provoke?
PORTER: Marry, sir, nose-painting, sleep, and urine. Lechery, sir, it provokes, and unprovokes; it provokes the desire, but it takes away the performance.

William Shakespeare 1564–1616: *Macbeth* (1606)

53 Alcohol . . . enables Parliament to do things at eleven at night that no sane person would do at eleven in the morning.

George Bernard Shaw 1856–1950: *Major Barbara* (1907)

54 Gin was mother's milk to her.

George Bernard Shaw 1856–1950: *Pygmalion* (1916)

55 A bumper of good liquor
Will end a contest quicker
Than justice, judge, or vicar.

Richard Brinsley Sheridan 1751–1816: *The Duenna* (1775)

56 But I'm not so think as you drunk I am.

J. C. Squire 1884–1958: 'Ballade of Soporific Absorption' (1931)

57 There are two things that will be believed of any man whatsoever, and one of them is that he has taken to drink.

Booth Tarkington 1869–1946: *Penrod* (1914)

58 [An alcoholic:] A man you don't like who drinks as much as you do.

Dylan Thomas 1914–53: Constantine Fitzgibbon *Life of Dylan Thomas* (1965)

59 *of Edvard Grieg:*
Checking into the Betty Fjord Clinic.

Dick Vosburgh and **Denis King**: *Beauty and the Beards* (2001)

60 What have you been doing in my absinthe?

Dick Vosburgh: *A Saint She Ain't* (1999)

61 I have a rare intolerance to herbs which means I can only drink fermented liquids, such as gin.

Julie Walters 1950– : in *Observer* 14 March 1999 'Sayings of the Week'

62 It was my Uncle George who discovered that alcohol was a food well in advance of medical thought.

P. G. Wodehouse 1881–1975: *The Inimitable Jeeves* (1923)

63 At the present moment, the whole Fleet's lit up. When I say 'lit up', I mean lit up by fairy lamps.
engaged to make a live outside broadcast of the Spithead Review, Woodrooffe was so overcome by his reunion with many old Naval colleagues that the celebrations sabotaged his ability to commentate

Thomas Woodrooffe 1899–1978: reporting on the Spithead Review, 20 May 1937

Drugs

66 I didn't inhale. **99**
Bill Clinton

1 LSD? Nothing much happened, but I did get the distinct
   impression that some birds were trying to communicate
   with me.

   W. H. Auden 1907–73: George
   Plimpton (ed.) *The Writer's Chapbook*
   (1989)

2 Cocaine habit-forming? Of course not. I ought to know.
   I've been using it for years.

   Tallulah Bankhead 1903–68: *Tallulah*
   (1952)

3 I'll die young, but it's like kissing God.
   on his drug addiction

   Lenny Bruce 1925–66: attributed

4 I experimented with marijuana a time or two. And I didn't
   like it, and I didn't inhale.

   Bill Clinton 1946– : in *Washington
   Post* 30 March 1992

5 In 1979 the way to tell an English gentleman is by the
   quality of his drugs.

   Lord Hesketh 1950– : Alexander
   Chancellor *Some Times in America*
   (1999); attributed, perhaps
   apocryphal

6 Drugs have taught an entire generation of English kids the
   metric system.

   P. J. O'Rourke 1947– : *Modern
   Manners* (1984, UK ed.)

7 Sure thing, man. I used to be a laboratory myself once.
   on being asked to autograph a fan's school chemistry book

   Keith Richards 1943– : in
   Independent on Sunday 7 August
   1994

8 Reality is a crutch for people who can't cope with drugs.

   Lily Tomlin 1939– : attributed; Phil
   Hammond and Michael Mosley *Trust
   Me (I'm a Doctor)* 1999

9 A drug is neither moral or immoral—it's a chemical
   compound. The compound itself is not a menace to society
   until a human being treats it as if consumption bestowed a
   temporary licence to act like an asshole.

   Frank Zappa 1940–93: *The Real
   Frank Zappa Book* (1989)

Economics ····➤ Money

66 Expenditure rises to meet income. **99**
C. Northcote Parkinson

1 No real English gentleman, in his secret soul, was ever
   sorry for the death of a political economist.

   Walter Bagehot 1826–77: *Estimates
   of some Englishmen and Scotchmen*
   (1858) 'The First Edinburgh
   Reviewers'

2 A man explained inflation to his wife thus: 'When we
   married you measured 36-24-36. Now you're 42-42-42.
   There's more of you, but you're not worth as much.'

   Joel Barnett 1923– : attributed; in
   Mail on Sunday 5 October 2003

3 John Stuart Mill,
By a mighty effort of will,
Overcame his natural *bonhomie*
And wrote 'Principles of Political Economy'.

Edmund Clerihew Bentley
1875–1956: 'John Stuart Mill' (1905)

4 It's the economy, stupid.
slogan on a sign put up at the Clinton presidential campaign headquarters

James Carville 1944– : campaign slogan, 1992

5 I never could make out what those damned dots meant.
as Chancellor, on decimal points

Lord Randolph Churchill 1849–94: W. S. Churchill *Lord Randolph Churchill* (1906)

6 Trickle-down theory—the less than elegant metaphor that if one feeds the horse enough oats, some will pass through to the road for the sparrows.

J. K. Galbraith 1908–2006: *The Culture of Contentment* (1992)

7 I could seek to ease his pain, but only by giving him an aspirin.
the Governor of the Bank of England on economic problems of the small businessman

Eddie George 1938– : interview on *The Money Programme* BBC2 TV, 28 February 1999

8 Balancing the budget is like going to heaven. Everybody wants to do it, but nobody wants to do what you have to do to get there.

Phil Gramm 1942– : in a television interview, 16 September 1990

9 In '29 when the banks went bust,
Our coins still read 'In God We Trust'.

E. Y. Harburg 1898–1981: 'Federal Reserve' (1965)

10 If economists could manage to get themselves thought of as humble, competent people, on a level with dentists, that would be splendid!

John Maynard Keynes 1883–1946: 'Economic Possibilities for our Grandchildren'; David Howell *Blind Victory* (1986)

11 People don't realize that the Victorian age was simply an interruption in British history . . . It's exciting living on the edge of bankruptcy.

Harold Macmillan 1894–1986: in conversation in 1961; Anthony Sampson *Macmillan* (1967)

12 Expenditure rises to meet income.

C. Northcote Parkinson 1909–93: *The Law and the Profits* (1960)

13 Nothink for nothink 'ere, and precious little for sixpence.

Punch 1841–1992: vol. 57 (1869)

14 Greed—for lack of a better word—is good. Greed is right. Greed works.

Stanley Weiser and **Oliver Stone** 1946– : *Wall Street* (1987 film)

Education ····> Examinations

❝ He who can, does. He who cannot, teaches. ❞
George Bernard Shaw

1 He shows great originality which must be curbed at all costs.
an early school report on Peter Ustinov

Anonymous: Catherine Hurley *Could Do Better* (2003)

2 I read Shakespeare and the Bible and I can shoot dice. That's what I call a liberal education.

Tallulah Bankhead 1903–68: attributed

3 Exeter is the second oldest college in Oxford—unless you count lodging houses, in which case it is the fourth.

Eric Arthur Barber 1888–1965: the Rector of Exeter's welcoming speech to undergraduates in 1951

4 I was not unpopular [at school] . . . It is Oxford that has made me insufferable.

Max Beerbohm 1872–1956: *More* (1899) 'Going Back to School'

5 Someone once said, Rumbold, that education is what is left when you have forgotten all you have ever learned. You appear to be trying to circumvent the process by learning as little as possible.

Alan Bennett 1934– : *Forty Years On* (1969)

6 Education with socialists, it's like sex, all right so long as you don't have to pay for it.

Alan Bennett 1934– : *Getting On* (1972)

7 I went to public school, of course. But looking back on it, I think it may have been Borstal.

Alan Bennett 1934– : *Getting On* (1972)

8 Gentlemen: I have not had your advantages. What poor education I have received has been gained in the University of Life.

Horatio Bottomley 1860–1933: speech at the Oxford Union, 2 December 1920

9 I won't say ours was a tough school, but we had our own coroner. We used to write essays like: What I'm going to be if I grow up.

Lenny Bruce 1925–66: attributed

10 In my day, the principal concerns of university students were sex, smoking dope, rioting and learning. Learning was something you did only when the first three weren't available.

Bill Bryson 1951– : *The Lost Continent* (1989)

11 *of Cambridge University:*
This place is the Devil, or at least his principal residence, they call it the University, but any other appellation would have suited it much better, for study is the last pursuit of the society; the Master eats, drinks, and sleeps, the Fellows drink, dispute and pun, the employments of the undergraduates you will probably conjecture without my description.

Lord Byron 1788–1824: letter, 23 November 1805

12 No academic person is ever voted into the chair until he has reached an age at which he has forgotten the meaning of the word 'irrelevant'.

Francis M. Cornford 1874–1943: *Microcosmographia Academica* (1908)

13 C-l-e-a-n, clean, verb active, to make bright, to scour. W-i-n, win, d-e-r, der, winder, a casement. When the boy knows this out of the book, he goes and does it.

Charles Dickens 1812–70: *Nicholas Nickleby* (1839)

14 EDUCATION.—At Mr Wackford Squeers's Academy, Dotheboys Hall, at the delightful village of Dotheboys, near Greta Bridge in Yorkshire, Youth are boarded, clothed, booked, furnished with pocket-money, provided with all necessaries, instructed in all languages living and dead, mathematics, orthography, geometry, astronomy, trigonometry, the use of the globes, algebra, single stick (if required), writing, arithmetic, fortification, and every other branch of classical literature. Terms, twenty guineas per annum. No extras, no vacations, and diet unparalleled.

Charles Dickens 1812–70: *Nicholas Nickleby* (1839)

15 Ev'ry pedagogue
Goes to bed agog at night—
Doing Collegiana . . . .

Dorothy Fields 1905–74: 'Collegiana' (1924)

16 The clever men at Oxford
Know all that there is to be knowed.
But they none of them know one half as much
As intelligent Mr Toad!

Kenneth Grahame 1859–1932: *The Wind in the Willows* (1908)

17 Common to all staff was a conviction that they could have done better outside education. The teachers believed in a mysterious world outside the school called 'business' where money was handed out freely.

Michael Green 1927– : *The Boy Who Shot Down an Airship* (1988)

18 Education in those elementary subjects which are ordinarily taught to our defenceless children, as reading, writing, and arithmetic.

A. P. Herbert 1890–1971: *Misleading Cases* (1935)

19 Beauty school report
No graduation day for you
Beauty school dropout
Mixed your mid-terms and flunked shampoo.

Jim Jacobs and **Warren Casey**: 'Beauty School Dropout' (1972)

20 [JOHNSON:] I had no notion that I was wrong or irreverent to my tutor.
[BOSWELL:] That, Sir, was great fortitude of mind.
[JOHNSON:] No, Sir; stark insensibility.

Samuel Johnson 1709–84: James Boswell *Life of Samuel Johnson* (1791) 31 October 1728

21 That state of resentful coma that . . . dons dignify by the name of research.

Harold Laski 1893–1950: letter to Oliver Wendell Holmes, 10 October 1922

22 Most people tire of a lecture in ten minutes; clever people can do it in five. Sensible people never go to lectures at all.

Stephen Leacock 1869–1944: *My Discovery of England* (1922)

23 If you are truly serious about preparing your child for the future, don't teach him to subtract—teach him to deduct.

Fran Lebowitz 1946– : *Social Studies* (1981)

24 Stand firm in your refusal to remain conscious during algebra. In real life, I assure you, there is no such thing as algebra.

Fran Lebowitz 1946– : *Social Studies* (1981)

25 Who walks in the classroom cool and slow?
Who calls his English teacher Daddy-O?

Jerry Leiber 1933– and **Mike Stoller** 1933– : 'Charlie Brown' (1959)

26 University seems to have turned them into Conan the Grammarians, who fret over perfect sentence construction.
of writer friends with degrees in English

Kathy Lette 1958– : in *Daily Telegraph* 30 November 2002

27 At school I never minded the lessons. I just resented having to work terribly hard at playing.

John Mortimer 1923– : *A Voyage Round My Father* (1971)

28 The Socratic method is a game at which only one (the professor) can play.

Ralph Nader 1934– : Joel Seligman *The High Citadel* (1978)

29 Liberals have invented whole college majors—psychology, sociology, women's studies— to prove that nothing is anybody's fault.

P. J. O'Rourke 1947– : *Give War a Chance* (1992)

30 The schoolteacher is certainly underpaid as a childminder, but ludicrously overpaid as an educator.

John Osborne 1929– : in *Observer* 21 July 1985 'Sayings of the Week'

31 I don't think one 'comes down' from Jimmy's university. According to him, it's not even red brick, but white tile.

John Osborne 1929– : *Look Back in Anger* (1956)

32 Oxford's instinctive hatred of any branch of education which is directly useful, superficially easy, or attractive, which above all has connections with universities younger than itself.

Stephen Potter 1900–69: *The Muse in Chains* (1937)

33 Good gracious, you've got to educate him first. You can't expect a boy to be vicious till he's been to a good school.

Saki 1870–1916: *Reginald in Russia* (1910)

34 For every person who wants to teach there are approximately thirty who don't want to learn—much.

W. C. Sellar 1898–1951 and **R. J. Yeatman** 1898–1968: *And Now All This* (1932) introduction

35 Very nice sort of place, Oxford, I should think, for people that like that sort of place. They teach you to be a gentleman there. In the Polytechnic they teach you to be an engineer or such like.

George Bernard Shaw 1856–1950: *Man and Superman* (1903)

36 He who can, does. He who cannot, teaches.

George Bernard Shaw 1856–1950: *Man and Superman* (1903) 'Maxims: Education'

37 *Educ*: during the holidays from Eton.

Osbert Sitwell 1892–1969: entry in *Who's Who* (1929)

38 *replying to Woodrow Wilson's 'And what in your opinion is the trend of the modern English undergraduate?':* Steadily towards drink and women, Mr President.

F. E. Smith 1872–1930: attributed

39 To me education is a leading out of what is already there in the pupil's soul. To Miss Mackay it is a putting in of something that is not there, and that is not what I call education, I call it intrusion.

Muriel Spark 1918–2006: *The Prime of Miss Jean Brodie* (1961)

40 I am putting old heads on your young shoulders . . . all my pupils are the crème de la crème.

Muriel Spark 1918–2006: *The Prime of Miss Jean Brodie* (1961)

41 Soap and education are not as sudden as a massacre, but they are more deadly in the long run.

Mark Twain 1835–1910: *A Curious Dream* (1872) 'Facts concerning the Recent Resignation'

42 'We class schools, you see, into four grades: Leading School, First-rate School, Good School, and School. Frankly,' said Mr Levy, 'School is pretty bad.'

Evelyn Waugh 1903–66: *Decline and Fall* (1928)

43 Any one who has been to an English public school will always feel comparatively at home in prison. It is the people brought up in the gay intimacy of the slums, Paul learned, who find prison so soul-destroying.

Evelyn Waugh 1903–66: *Decline and Fall* (1928)

44 Assistant masters came and went . . . Some liked little boys too little and some too much.

Evelyn Waugh 1903–66: *A Little Learning* (1964)

45 In England, at any rate, education produces no effect whatsoever. If it did, it would prove a serious danger to the upper classes, and probably lead to acts of violence in Grosvenor Square.

Oscar Wilde 1854–1900: *The Importance of Being Earnest* (1895)

46 'Didn't Frankenstein get married?'
'Did he?' said Eggy. 'I don't know. I never met him. Harrow man, I expect.'

P. G. Wodehouse 1881–1975: *Laughing Gas* (1936)

47 A pretty example he sets to this Infants' Bible Class of which he speaks! A few years of sitting at the feet of Harold Pinker and imbibing his extraordinary views on

P. G. Wodehouse 1881–1975: *The Code of the Woosters* (1938)

morality and ethics, and every bally child on the list will be serving a long stretch at Wormwood Scrubs for blackmail.

Enemies

A man cannot be too careful in the choice of his enemies.
Oscar Wilde

1 I wouldn't piss in his ear if his brain was on fire.
indicating your level of dislike for someone

Anonymous: quoted as a traditional expression of the Southern US; Bill Clinton *My Life* (2004)

2 I do not love thee, Dr Fell.
The reason why I cannot tell;
But this I know, and know full well,
I do not love thee, Dr Fell.

Thomas Brown 1663–1704: written while an undergraduate at Christ Church, Oxford, of which Dr Fell was Dean

3 Rejoice, rejoice, rejoice.
telephone call to his office on hearing of Margaret Thatcher's fall from power in 1990

Edward Heath 1916–2005: attributed; in *Daily Telegraph* 24 September 1998 (online edition)

4 I detest him more than cold boiled veal.

Lord Macaulay 1800–59: of the Tory essayist and politician John Wilson Croker; letter 5 August 1831

5 People wish their enemies dead—but I do not; I say give them the gout, give them the stone!

Lady Mary Wortley Montagu 1689–1762: W. S. Lewis et al. (eds.) *Horace Walpole's Correspondence* (1973)

6 Any kiddie in school can love like a fool,
But hating, my boy, is an art.

Ogden Nash 1902–71: 'Plea for Less Malice Toward None' (1933)

7 I find that forgiving one's enemies is a most curious morbid pleasure; perhaps I should check it.

Oscar Wilde 1854–1900: letter ?20 April 1894

8 A man cannot be too careful in the choice of his enemies.

Oscar Wilde 1854–1900: *The Picture of Dorian Gray* (1891)

England ····➤ Countries and Peoples, Places

Mad dogs and Englishmen Go out in the midday sun.
Noël Coward

1 Boasting about modesty is typical of the English.

Anonymous: unattributed; in *Mail on Sunday* 21 February 1999 'Quotes of the Week'

2 An Englishman considers himself a self-made man, and thereby relieves the Almighty of a dreadful responsibility.

Anonymous: unattributed; in *The Times* 23 February 1999

3 The English may not like music, but they absolutely love the noise it makes.

Thomas Beecham 1879–1961: in *New York Herald Tribune* 9 March 1961

4 He was born an Englishman and remained one for years.

Brendan Behan 1923–64: *Hostage* (1958)

5 We English are of course the chosen race; but we should be none the worse for a little intellectual apprehension.

A. C. Benson 1862–1925: *From a College Window* (1906)

6 Think of what our Nation stands for,
Books from Boots' and country lanes,
Free speech, free passes, class distinction,
Democracy and proper drains.
Lord, put beneath Thy special care
One-eighty-nine Cadogan Square.

John Betjeman 1906–84: 'In Westminster Abbey' (1940)

7 For 'tis a low, newspaper, humdrum, lawsuit Country.

Lord Byron 1788–1824: *Don Juan* (1819–24)

8 Mad dogs and Englishmen
Go out in the midday sun.
The Japanese don't care to,
The Chinese wouldn't dare to,
The Hindus and Argentines sleep firmly from twelve to one,
But Englishmen detest a siesta.
In the Philippines, there are lovely screens
To protect you from the glare;
In the Malay states, they have hats like plates
Which the Britishers won't wear.
At twelve noon, the natives swoon,
And no further work is done;
But mad dogs and Englishmen go out in the midday sun.

Noël Coward 1899–1973: 'Mad Dogs and Englishmen' (1931)

9 The English can be explained by their Anglo-Saxon heritage and the influence of the Methodists. But I prefer to explain them in terms of tea, roast beef and rain. A people is first what it eats, drinks and gets pelted with.

Pierre Daninos: *Major Thompson and I* (1957)

10 There is in the Englishman a combination of qualities, a modesty, an independence, a responsibility, a repose, combined with an absence of everything calculated to call a blush into the cheek of a young person, which one would seek in vain among the Nations of the Earth.

Charles Dickens 1812–70: *Our Mutual Friend* (1865)

11 But 'tis the talent of our English nation,
Still to be plotting some new reformation.

John Dryden 1631–1700: 'The Prologue at Oxford, 1680'

12 Stiff upper lip! Stout fella!
Carry on, old fluff!
Chin up! Keep muddling through!
Stiff upper lip! Stout fella!
When the going's rough—
Pip-pip to Old Man Trouble—and a toodle-oo, too!

Ira Gershwin 1896–1983: 'Stiff Upper Lip' (1937)

13 He is an Englishman!
For he himself has said it,
And it's greatly to his credit,
That he is an Englishman!

W. S. Gilbert 1836–1911: *HMS Pinafore* (1878)

14 Contrary to popular belief, English women do not wear tweed nightgowns.

Hermione Gingold 1897–1987: in *Saturday Review* 16 April 1955

15 The truth is that every Englishman's house is his hospital, particularly the bathroom. Patent medicine is the English patent.

Oliver St John Gogarty 1878–1957: *As I Was Going Down Sackville Street* (1937)

16 Even crushed against his brother in the Tube, the average Englishman pretends desperately that he is alone.

Germaine Greer 1939– : *The Female Eunuch* (1970)

17 My parents were English. We were too poor to be British. *on his British origins*

Bob Hope 1903–2003: in *The Times* 29 July 2003

18 Not to be English was for my family so terrible a handicap as almost to place the sufferer in the permanent invalid class.

Osbert Lancaster 1908–80: *All Done From Memory* (1953)

19 The old English belief that if a thing is unpleasant it is automatically good for you.

Osbert Lancaster 1908–80: *Homes Sweet Homes* (1939)

20 In England it is very dangerous to have a sense of humour.

E. V. Lucas 1868–1938: *365 Days and One More* (1926)

21 If an Englishman gets run down by a truck he apologizes to the truck.

Jackie Mason 1931– : in *Independent* 20 September 1990

22 An Englishman, even if he is alone, forms an orderly queue of one.

George Mikes 1912–87: *How to be an Alien* (1946)

23 The English are busy; they don't have time to be polite.

Montesquieu 1689–1755: *Pensées et fragments inédits . . .* (1901)

24 Let us pause to consider the English,
Who when they pause to consider themselves they get all reticently thrilled and tinglish,
Because every Englishman is convinced of one thing, viz.:
That to be an Englishman is to belong to the most exclusive club there is.

Ogden Nash 1902–71: 'England Expects' (1938)

25 But we, brave Britons, foreign laws despised,
And kept unconquered, and uncivilized.

Alexander Pope 1688–1744: *An Essay on Criticism* (1711)

26 Good evening, England. This is Gillie Potter speaking to you in English.

Gillie Potter 1887–1975: *Heard at Hogsnorton* (opening words of broadcasts, 6 June 1946 and 11 November 1947)

27 It is hard to tell where the MCC ends and the Church of England begins.

J. B. Priestley 1894–1984: in *New Statesman* 20 July 1962

28 She comes from the North, where they live in the fear of Heaven and the Earl of Durham.

Saki 1870–1916: *Reginald* (1904) 'Reginald on Christmas Presents'

29 The Roman Conquest was, however, a *Good Thing*, since the Britons were only natives at the time.

W. C. Sellar 1898–1951 and **R. J. Yeatman** 1898–1968: *1066 and All That* (1930)

30 We really *like* dowdiness in England. It's absolutely incurable in us, I believe.

Peter Shaffer 1926– : *Whom Do I Have the Honour of Addressing?* (1990)

31 An Englishman thinks he is moral when he is only uncomfortable.

George Bernard Shaw 1856–1950: *Man and Superman* (1903)

32 Englishmen never will be slaves: they are free to do whatever the Government and public opinion allow them to do.

George Bernard Shaw 1856–1950: *Man and Superman* (1903)

33 This Englishwoman is so refined
She has no bosom and no behind.

Stevie Smith 1902–71: 'This Englishwoman' (1937)

34 What two ideas are more inseparable than Beer and Britannia?

Sydney Smith 1771–1845: Hesketh Pearson *The Smith of Smiths* (1934)

35 What a pity it is that we have no amusements in England but vice and religion!

Sydney Smith 1771–1845: Hesketh Pearson *The Smith of Smiths* (1934)

36 I think for my part one half of the nation is mad—and the other not very sound.

Tobias Smollett 1721–71: *The Adventures of Sir Launcelot Greaves* (1762)

37 As an Englishman does not travel to see Englishmen, I retired to my room.

Laurence Sterne 1713–68: *A Sentimental Journey* (1768)

38 Now hang it! quoth I, as I looked towards the French coast—a man should know something of his own country too, before he goes abroad.

Laurence Sterne 1713–68: *Tristram Shandy* (1759–67)

39 No little lily-handed baronet he,
A great broad-shouldered genial Englishman,
A lord of fat prize-oxen and of sheep,
A raiser of huge melons and of pine,
A patron of some thirty charities,
A pamphleteer on guano and on grain.

Alfred, Lord Tennyson 1809–92: *The Princess* (1847)

40 *on the suggestion that, in his books, washing has some symbolic significance:*
I've noticed that the British are not given to it.

Gore Vidal 1925– : attributed; in *Guardian* 27 February 1999

41 Any who have heard that sound will shrink at the recollection of it; it is the sound of English county families baying for broken glass.

Evelyn Waugh 1903–66: *Decline and Fall* (1928)

42 Other nations use 'force'; we Britons alone use 'Might'.

Evelyn Waugh 1903–66: *Scoop* (1938)

43 He is a typical Englishman, always dull and usually violent.

Oscar Wilde 1854–1900: *An Ideal Husband* (1895)

44 You should study the Peerage, Gerald . . . It is the best thing in fiction the English have ever done.

Oscar Wilde 1854–1900: *A Woman of No Importance* (1893)

45 I like a man to be a clean, strong, upstanding Englishman who can look his gnu in the face and put an ounce of lead in it.

P. G. Wodehouse 1881–1975: *Mr. Mulliner Speaking* (1929)

Environment ····> Nature and the Environment

Epitaphs ····> Death

66 Excuse My Dust. 99
Dorothy Parker

1 Whoever treadeth on this stone
I pray you tread most neatly
For underneath this stone do lie

Anonymous: gravestone at Stepney, London, 10 November 1683; Fritz Spiegl (ed.) *A Small Book of Grave Humour* (1971)

Your honest friend
WILL WHEATLEY.

2 In bloom of life
  She's snatched from hence
  She had not room
  To make defence;
  For Tiger fierce
  Took life away,
  And here she lies
  In a bed of clay
  Until the Resurrection Day.

Anonymous: gravestone in Malmesbury churchyard to Hannah Twynnoy, who had been attacked by an escaped tiger from a travelling circus in 1703

3 Here lies a poor woman who always was tired,
  For she lived in a place where help wasn't hired.
  Her last words on earth were, Dear friends I am going
  Where washing ain't done nor sweeping nor sewing,
  And everything there is exact to my wishes,
  For there they don't eat and there's no washing of dishes
    . . .
  Don't mourn for me now, don't mourn for me never,
  For I'm going to do nothing for ever and ever.

Anonymous: epitaph in Bushey churchyard, before 1860; destroyed by 1916

4 Here lies Fred,
  Who was alive and is dead:
  Had it been his father,
  I had much rather;
  Had it been his brother,
  Still better than another;
  Had it been his sister,
  No one would have missed her;
  Had it been the whole generation,
  Still better for the nation:
  But since 'tis only Fred,
  Who was alive and is dead,—
  There's no more to be said.

Anonymous: epitaph for Frederick, Prince of Wales, killed by a cricket ball in 1751; Horace Walpole *Memoirs of George II* (1847)

5 I should like my epitaph to say, 'He helped people see God in the ordinary things of life, and he made children laugh.'

Revd W. Awdry 1911–97: in *Independent* 22 March 1997

6 *suggested epitaph for an unnamed movie queen whose love-life had been notorious:*
  She sleeps alone at last.

Robert Benchley 1889–1945: attributed

7 John Adams lies here, of the parish of Southwell,
  A carrier who carried his can to his mouth well;
  He carried so much, and he carried so fast,
  He could carry no more—so was carried at last;
  For the liquor he drank, being too much for one,
  He could not carry off—so he's now carri-on.

Lord Byron 1788–1824: 'Epitaph on John Adams of Southwell, a Carrier who Died of Drunkenness' (1807)

8 Alan died suddenly at Saltwood on Sunday 5th September. He said he would like it to be stated that he regarded himself as having gone to join Tom and the other dogs.

Alan Clark 1928–99: announcement in *The Times* 8 September 1999

9 *on the death of US President Warren G. Harding:*
  The only man, woman or child who wrote a simple declarative sentence with seven grammatical errors is dead.

e. e. cummings 1894–1962: attributed

10 Believing that his hate for queers
Proclaimed his love for God,
He now (of all queer things, my dears)
Lies under his first sod.
  on John Gordon (1890-1974), editor of the Sunday
  Express

Paul Dehn 1912–76: Nigel Rees
*Cassell Dictionary of Humorous
Quotations* (1999)

11 Under this stone, Reader, survey
Dead Sir John Vanbrugh's house of clay.
Lie heavy on him, Earth! for he
Laid many heavy loads on thee!

Abel Evans 1679–1737: 'Epitaph on
Sir John Vanbrugh, Architect of
Blenheim Palace'

12 Here lies W. C. Fields. I would rather be living in
Philadelphia.

W. C. Fields 1880–1946: suggested
epitaph for himself; in *Vanity Fair* June
1925

13 Here Skugg
Lies snug
As a bug
In a rug.

Benjamin Franklin 1706–90: letter to
Georgiana Shipley on the death of her
squirrel, 26 September 1772

14 Here lies Nolly Goldsmith, for shortness called Noll,
Who wrote like an angel, but talked like poor Poll.

David Garrick 1717–79: 'Impromptu
Epitaph' (written 1773/4)

15 John Le Mesurier wishes it to be known that he conked out
on November 15th. He sadly misses family and friends.

John Le Mesurier 1912–83: obituary
notice in *The Times* 16 November
1983

16 Poor G.K.C., his day is past—
Now God will know the truth at last.

E. V. Lucas 1868–1938: mock epitaph
for G. K. Chesterton; Dudley Barker
G. K. Chesterton (1973)

17 *epitaph for a waiter:*
By and by
God caught his eye.

David McCord 1897– : 'Remainders'
(1935)

18 Here lie I, Martin Elginbrodde:
Hae mercy o' my soul, Lord God;
As I wad do, were I Lord God,
And ye were Martin Elginbrodde.

George MacDonald 1824–1905:
David Elginbrod (1863)

19 *his chosen epitaph*
Here lies Spike Milligan. I told you I was ill.

Spike Milligan 1918–2002: in *Daily
Telegraph* 28 February 2002

20 Beneath this slab
John Brown is stowed.
He watched the ads,
And not the road.

Ogden Nash 1902–71: 'Lather as You
Go' (1942)

21 Excuse My Dust.

Dorothy Parker 1893–1967:
suggested epitaph for herself;
Alexander Woollcott *While Rome
Burns* (1934) 'Our Mrs Parker'

22 *epitaph for Maurice Bowra:*
Without you, Heaven would be too dull to bear,
And Hell would not be Hell if you are there.

John Sparrow 1906–92: in *Times
Literary Supplement* 30 May 1975

23 He gave the little wealth he had
To build a house for fools and mad;
And showed, by one satiric touch,
No nation wanted it so much.

Jonathan Swift 1667–1745: 'Verses
on the Death of Dr Swift' (1731)

24 Poor Pope will grieve a month, and Gay
A week, and Arbuthnot a day.
St John himself will scarce forbear
To bite his pen, and drop a tear.
The rest will give a shrug, and cry,
'I'm sorry—but we all must die!'

Jonathan Swift 1667–1745: 'Verses
on the Death of Dr Swift' (1731)

25 There was a poor poet named Clough,
Whom his friends all united to puff,
But the public, though dull,
Had not such a skull
As belonged to believers in Clough.

Algernon Charles Swinburne
1837–1909: *Essays and Studies*
(1875)

26 *when asked what he would like to see on his tombstone:*
Keep off the grass.

Peter Ustinov 1921–2004:
attributed; in *Mail on Sunday* 4 April
2004

27 I always thought I'd like my tombstone to be blank. No
epitaph, and no name. Well, actually I'd like it to say
'figment'.

Andy Warhol 1927–87: *America*
(1985)

28 His friends he loved. His direst earthly foes—
Cats—I believe he did but feign to hate.
My hand will miss the insinuated nose,
Mine eyes the tail that wagged contempt at Fate.

William Watson 1858–1936: 'An
Epitaph'

29 Here lies Mr Chesterton,
who to heaven might have gone,
but didn't, when he heard the news
that the place was run by Jews.

Humbert Wolfe 1886–1940: 'G. K.
Chesterton' (1925)

Examinations

❝ Those who do not wish to know ask questions of those who cannot tell. ❞
Walter Raleigh

1 I wrote my name at the top of the page. I wrote down the
number of the question '1'. After much reflection I put a
bracket round it thus '(1)'. But thereafter I could not think
of anything connected with it that was either relevant or
true. . . . It was from these slender indications of
scholarship that Mr Welldon drew the conclusion that I
was worthy to pass into Harrow. It is very much to his
credit.

Winston Churchill 1874–1965: *My
Early Life* (1930)

2 He had ambitions, at one time, to become a sex maniac,
but he failed his practical.

Les Dawson 1934–93: attributed;
Fred Metcalf (ed.) *Penguin Dictionary
of Modern Humorous Quotations*
(1987)

3 *explaining why he performed badly in the Civil Service
examinations:*
I evidently knew more about economics than my
examiners.

John Maynard Keynes 1883–1946:
Roy Harrod *Life of John Maynard
Keynes* (1951)

4 In examinations those who do not wish to know ask
questions of those who cannot tell.

Walter Raleigh 1861–1922: *Laughter
from a Cloud* (1923) 'Some Thoughts
on Examinations'

5 Do not on any account attempt to write on both sides of the paper at once.

W. C. Sellar 1898–1951 and **R. J. Yeatman** 1898–1968: *1066 and All That* (1930) 'Test Paper 5'

6 *Whistler had been found 'deficient in chemistry' in a West Point examination:*
Had silicon been a gas, I would have been a major-general by now.

James McNeill Whistler 1834–1903: E. R. and J. Pennell *The Life of James McNeill Whistler* (1908)

7 *in his viva at Oxford Wilde was required to translate a passage from the Greek version of the New Testament. Having acquitted himself well, he was stopped:*
Oh, do let me go on, I want to see how it ends.

Oscar Wilde 1854–1900: James Sutherland (ed.) *The Oxford Book of Literary Anecdotes* (1975)

Exploration ····> Travel and Exploration

Faces

❝ The sort of face that makes you realise God does have a sense of humour. **❞**
Bill Bryson

1 My face looks like a wedding cake left out in the rain.

W. H. Auden 1907–73: Humphrey Carpenter *W. H. Auden* (1981)

2 In appearance Dior is like a bland country curate made out of pink marzipan.
of Christian Dior

Cecil Beaton 1904–80: *The Glass of Fashion* (1954)

3 He had the sort of face that makes you realise God does have a sense of humour.

Bill Bryson 1951– : *Neither Here Nor There* (1991)

4 *of W. H. Auden's heavily wrinkled face:*
Were a fly to attempt to cross it, it would break its leg.

Lord David Cecil 1902–86: A. L. Rowse diary, 30 May 1960

5 I kept thinking, if his face was that wrinkled, what did his balls look like?
after drawing W. H. Auden

David Hockney 1937– : attributed

6 My general appearance, and especially my face, have always been a source of depression to me.

William Orpen 1878–1931: *Stories of Old Ireland and Myself* (1924)

Failure

❝ If at first you don't succeed, failure may be your style. **❞**
Quentin Crisp

1 *during a rehearsal at the Royal Court, Beckett encouraged an actor who had lamented, 'I'm failing':*
Go on failing. Go on. Only next time, try to fail better.

Samuel Beckett 1906–89: Tony Richardson *Long Distance Runner* (1993)

2 In the end we are all sacked and it's always awful.

Alan Clark 1928–99: diary 21 June 1983

3 If at first you don't succeed, failure may be your style.

Quentin Crisp 1908–99: in *Sunday Telegraph* 28 September 1999

4 I don't think we have failed, we have just found another way that doesn't work.
on the ending of an attempted round-the-world balloon flight

Andy Ellson: comment, Hamamatsu, Japan, 7 March 1999

5 If at first you don't succeed, try, try again. Then quit. No use being a damn fool about it.

W. C. Fields 1880–1946: attributed

6 Come forth, Lazarus! And he came fifth and lost the job.

James Joyce 1882–1941: *Ulysses* (1922)

7 Anybody seen in a bus over the age of 30 has been a failure in life.

Loelia, Duchess of Westminster 1902–93: in *The Times* 4 November 1993; habitual remark

Fame

66 One day you are a signature, next day you're an autograph. **99**
Billy Wilder

1 A celebrity is a person who works hard all his life to become well known, and then wears dark glasses to avoid being recognized.

Fred Allen 1894–1956: Laurence J. Peter (ed.) *Quotations for our Time* (1977)

2 To live in *Who's Who*
And to die in *The Times*,
To be one of the few
To live in *Who's Who*,
What would I not do?—
I'd commit frightful crimes
To live in *Who's Who*
And to die in *The Times*

Anonymous: unattributed; in *The Times* 3 January 2004

3 I go in and out of fashion like a double-breasted suit.

Alan Ayckbourn 1939– : in *Observer* 13 August 2000 'They said what . . . ?'

4 Stardom isn't a profession; it's an accident.

Lauren Bacall 1924– : in *Observer* 19 March 1995 'Sayings of the Week'

5 *asked at a press conference what it was like to act with a 'screen legend' like Nicole Kidman:*
She's not a legend, she's a beginner. You can't be a legend at whatever age she is.

Lauren Bacall 1924– : in *Sunday Telegraph* 12 September 2004

6 Being a legend is a hazardous thing if you're *only* a legend. If you can keep updating yourself, then being a legend is just an added bonus.

Joan Baez 1941– : in *Independent* 19 January 2004

7 Oh, the self-importance of fading stars. Never mind, they will be black holes one day.

Jeffrey Bernard 1932–97: in *The Spectator* 18 July 1992

8 Oblivion . . . fame's eternal dumping ground.

Ambrose Bierce 1842–c.1914: *The Enlarged Devil's Dictionary* (1967)

9 A legend in his own lunchtime.
of Dennis Main Wilson

David Climie: Ned Sherrin *Theatrical Anecdotes* (1991); also attributed to Christopher Wordsworth of Clifford Makins

10 *refusing to allow his biographer Sheridan Morley to out him as a homosexual, despite the example of the theatre critic T. C. Worsley:*
You forget that the great British public would not care if Cuthbert Worsley had slept with mice.

Noël Coward 1899–1973: in *Independent on Sunday Magazine* 12 November 1995

11 Fancy being remembered around the world for the invention of a mouse!

Walt Disney 1901–66: during his last illness; Leonard Mosley *Disney's World* (1985)

12 It's the first time I've opened a pier. Nothing can really prepare you, though last night I opened a tin of tomatoes and declared my bathroom open.
at the official reopening of Cromer's Pier Pavilion, 27 June 2004

Stephen Fry 1957– : in *Sunday Times* 4 July 2004 'Talking Heads'

13 ARTHUR: I think I'll take a bath.
HOBSON: I'll alert the media.

Steve Gordon: *Arthur* (1981 film); Dudley Moore as Arthur Bach, and John Gielgud as his valet Hobson

14 The best fame is a writer's fame: it's enough to get a table at a good restaurant, but not enough that you get interrupted when you eat.

Fran Lebowitz 1946– : in *Observer* 30 May 1993 'Sayings of the Week'

15 *on being asked what it was like to be famous:*
It's like having a string of pearls given you. It's nice, but after a while, if you think of it at all, it's only to wonder if they're real or cultured.

W. Somerset Maugham 1874–1965: *A Writer's Notebook* (1949) written in 1941

16 You can't shame or humiliate modern celebrities. What used to be called shame and humiliation is now called publicity.

P. J. O'Rourke 1947– : *Give War a Chance* (1992)

17 *autographing a book for a dissatisfied customer:*
CUSTOMER: But usen't you to be J. B. Priestley?
PRIESTLAND: That was a long time ago.

Gerald Priestland 1927–91: *Something Understood* (1986)

18 The people, they need to adore me,
So Christian Dior me.

Tim Rice 1944– : *Evita* (1979)

19 Well, not exactly a big star . . . But I once had a sandwich named after me at the Stage Delicatessen.

Neil Simon 1927– : *The Gingerbread Lady* (1970)

20 *to Labour MP Chris Bryant, whose photograph in his Y-fronts had appeared on a gay website:*
Ah, Bryant, there you are. Nearly didn't recognise you with your clothes on.

Nicholas Soames 1948– : attributed; in *Mail on Sunday* 4 January 2004

21 Fame is like V.D. Everybody wants to fuck you until they see what they get.

Sylvester Stallone 1946– : quoted by Sharon Stone, *Graham Norton Show* (Channel 4 TV) 18 December 2003

22 Celebrity is good for kick-starting ideas, but often celebrity is a lead weight around your neck. It's like you pointing at the moon, but people are looking at your finger.
on campaigning

Sting 1951– : in *Mojo* February 1995

23 One day you are a signature, next day you're an autograph.

Billy Wilder 1906–2002: Charlotte Chandler *Nobody's Perfect* (2002)

The Family ····> Children, Parents

66 Accidents will occur in the best-regulated families. **99**
Charles Dickens

---

1 What is wrong with a little incest? It is both handy and cheap.

James Agate 1877–1947: on *The Barretts of Wimpole Street*; attributed, perhaps apocryphal

2 And my parents finally realize that I'm kidnapped and they snap into action immediately: They rent out my room.

Woody Allen 1935– : Eric Lax *Woody Allen and his Comedy* (1975)

3 Could you possibly whistle your father and put him back on his lead, please.

Alan Ayckbourn 1939– : *Sisterly Feelings* (1981)

4 Daughters are best. They don't migrate.

Alan Bennett 1934– : *Talking Heads* (1988)

5 My mother-in-law broke up my marriage. My wife came home from work one day and found us in bed together.

Lenny Bruce 1925–66: attributed; Fred Metcalf (ed.) *The Penguin Dictionary of Modern Humorous Quotations*

6 I should, many a good day, have blown my brains out, but for the recollection that it would have given pleasure to my mother-in-law; and, even *then*, if I could have been certain to haunt her . . .

Lord Byron 1788–1824: letter, 28 January 1817

7 We must all be very kind to Auntie Jessie,
For she's never been a Mother or a Wife,
You mustn't throw your toys at her
Or make a vulgar noise at her,
She hasn't led a very happy life.

Noël Coward 1899–1973: 'We Must All be Very Kind to Auntie Jessie' (c.1924)

8 My sister and my sister's child,
Myself and children three,
Will fill the chaise; so you must ride
On horseback after we.

William Cowper 1731–1800: 'John Gilpin' (1785)

9 If you must go flopping yourself down, flop in favour of your husband and child, and not in opposition to 'em.

Charles Dickens 1812–70: *A Tale of Two Cities* (1859)

10 Your sister is given to government.

Charles Dickens 1812–70: *Great Expectations* (1861)

11 Accidents will occur in the best-regulated families.

Charles Dickens 1812–70: *David Copperfield* (1850)

12 We do everything alike
We look alike, we dress alike,
We walk alike, we talk alike,
and what is more we hate each other very much.

Howard Dietz 1896–1983: 'Triplets' (1937)

13 John Donne, Anne Donne, Un-done.
in a letter to his wife, on being dismissed from the service of his father-in-law, Sir George More

John Donne 1572–1631: Izaak Walton *The Life of Dr Donne* (first printed in *LXXX Sermons*, 1640)

14 You know what they say, if at first you don't succeed, you're not the eldest son.

Stephen Fry 1957– : *Paperweight* (1992)

15 A man . . . is *so* in the way in the house!

Elizabeth Gaskell 1810–65: *Cranford* (1853)

16 He will be six foot two,
My son-in-law;
His haircut will be crew,
My son-in-law.

Ira Gershwin 1896–1983: 'My Son-in-Law' (1946)

17 And so do his sisters, and his cousins and his aunts!
His sisters and his cousins,
Whom he reckons up by dozens,
And his aunts!

W. S. Gilbert 1836–1911: *HMS Pinafore* (1878)

18 T'Morra, t'morra,
Lookin' for t'morra,
My aunt became a spinster that way.

E. Y. Harburg 1898–1981: 'T'Morra' (1944)

19 I'm also told that the latest popular game in America is called Incest—all the family can join in!

Rupert Hart-Davis 1907–99: letter to George Lyttelton, 14 November 1959

20 If Gloria hadn't divorced me she might never have become her own daughter-in-law.
of his ex-wife, Gloria Grahame, who had married her former stepson

Cy Howard: in *Ned Sherrin in his Anecdotage* (1993)

21 'It wouldn't hurt us to be nice, would it?'
'That depends on your threshold of pain.'
on being told his aunt was coming to visit

George S. Kaufman 1889–1961: Howard Teichmann *George S. Kaufman* (1973)

22 *of his appointment of his brother Robert:*
I see nothing wrong with giving Robert some legal experience as Attorney General before he goes out to practice law.

John F. Kennedy 1917–63: Bill Adler *The Complete Kennedy Wit* (1967)

23 BARBARA WALTERS: What would be your first act on becoming President?
JOHN F. KENNEDY JNR: Call Uncle Teddy and gloat.

John F. Kennedy Jnr. 1960–99: in *Sunday Telegraph* 25 July 1999; recalled by Ted Kennedy at his nephew's memorial service on 23 July 1999

24 My grandfather had displayed that Jovelike side to his character of which his family were always nervously aware.

Osbert Lancaster 1908–80: *All Done From Memory* (1953)

25 Few misfortunes can befall a boy which bring worse consequences than to have a really affectionate mother.

W. Somerset Maugham 1874–1965: *A Writer's Notebook* (1949), written in 1896

26 One would be in less danger
From the wiles of the stranger
If one's own kin and kith
Were more fun to be with.

Ogden Nash 1902–71: 'Family Court' (1931)

27 Uncle Carl Laemmle,
Has a very large faemmle.
of a Hollywood mogul much given to nepotism

Ogden Nash 1902–71: Philip French *The Movie Moguls* (1969)

28 A home keeps you from living with your parents.

P. J. O'Rourke 1947– : *The Bachelor Home Companion* (1987)

29 Bury her naked? My own mum? It's a Freudian nightmare.

Joe Orton 1933–67: *Loot* (1967)

30 We kept Mommy on a pedestal—it was the only way we could keep Daddy off her.
  of family life as one of twelve children

Dolly Parton 1946– : review of her show at the Hammersmith Apollo, London; in *Observer* 24 November 2002

31 I want to spend more time with my family, but I'm not sure they want to spend more time with me.

Esther Rantzen 1940– : in *Independent* 29 April 2000

32 To your tents, O Israel!
  to his wife's Rothschild relations one evening at Mentmore

Lord Rosebery 1847–1929: Robert Rhodes James *Rosebery* (1963); perhaps apocryphal

33 I find it difficult to take much interest in a man whose father was a dragon.
  apologizing for his inability to appreciate William Morris's epic poem Sigurd the Volsung (*1876*)

Dante Gabriel Rossetti 1828–82: Osbert Sitwell *Noble Essences* (1950)

34 *Chutzpa* is that quality enshrined in a man who, having killed his mother and father, throws himself on the mercy of the court as an orphan.

Leo Rosten 1908– : *The Joys of Yiddish* (1968)

35 *questionnaire for would-be Kings in the Wars of the Roses:* What have you done with your mother? (If *Nun*, write *None.*)

W. C. Sellar 1898–1951 and R. J. Yeatman 1898–1968: *1066 and All That* (1930)

36 It is a wise father that knows his own child.

William Shakespeare 1564–1616: *The Merchant of Venice* (1596–8)

37 Parentage is a very important profession, but no test of fitness for it is ever imposed in the interest of the children.

George Bernard Shaw 1856–1950: *Everybody's Political What's What?* (1944)

38 My father is a bastard
  My Ma's an S.O.B.
  My Grandpa's always plastered
  My Grandma pushes tea
  My sister wears a moustache
  My brother wears a dress
  Goodness gracious, that's why I'm a mess.

Stephen Sondheim 1930– : 'Gee, Officer Krupke' (1957)

39 'Never was born!' persisted Topsy . . . 'never had no father, nor mother, nor nothin'. I was raised by a speculator, with lots of others.'

Harriet Beecher Stowe 1811–96: *Uncle Tom's Cabin* (1852)

40 The young ladies entered the drawing-room in the full fervour of sisterly animosity.

R. S. Surtees 1805–64: *Mr Sponge's Sporting Tour* (1853)

41 I am Septimus, the most morbid of the Tennysons.
  introducing himself to Dante Gabriel Rossetti

Septimus Tennyson 1815–66: Peter Levi *Tennyson* (1993)

42 If a man's character is to be abused, say what you will, there's nobody like a relation to do the business.

William Makepeace Thackeray 1811–63: *Vanity Fair* (1847–8)

43 We have become a grandmother.

Margaret Thatcher 1925– : in *The Times* 4 March 1989

44 I'm off to see if X Mansions is really razed to the ground, as I have an uncle who lives there and I know I'm in his will!

Ernest Thesiger 1879–1961: during the war; in *Ned Sherrin in his Anecdotage* (1993)

45 I'm Charley's aunt from Brazil—where the nuts come from.

Brandon Thomas 1856–1914: *Charley's Aunt* (1892)

46 I suppose that the high-water mark of my youth in Columbus, Ohio, was the night the bed fell on my father.

James Thurber 1894–1961: *My Life and Hard Times* (1933)

47 All happy families resemble one another, but each unhappy family is unhappy in its own way.

Leo Tolstoy 1828–1910: *Anna Karenina* (1875–7)

48 Familiarity breeds contempt—and children.

Mark Twain 1835–1910: *Notebooks* (1935)

49 To lose one parent, Mr Worthing, may be regarded as a misfortune; to lose both looks like carelessness.

Oscar Wilde 1854–1900: *The Importance of Being Earnest* (1895)

50 To be born, or at any rate bred, in a hand-bag, whether it had handles or not, seems to me to display a contempt for the ordinary decencies of family life that reminds one of the worst excesses of the French Revolution.

Oscar Wilde 1854–1900: *The Importance of Being Earnest* (1895)

51 It is no use telling me that there are bad aunts and good aunts. At the core, they are all alike. Sooner or later, out pops the cloven hoof.

P. G. Wodehouse 1881–1975: *The Code of the Woosters* (1938)

52 To my daughter Leonora without whose never-failing sympathy and encouragement this book would have been finished in half the time.

P. G. Wodehouse 1881–1975: dedication to *The Heart of a Goof* (1926)

53 As a rule, you see, I'm not lugged into Family Rows. On the occasions when Aunt is calling to Aunt like mastodons bellowing across primeval swamps and Uncle James's letter about Cousin Mabel's peculiar behaviour is being shot round the family circle . . . the clan has a tendency to ignore me.

P. G. Wodehouse 1881–1975: *The Inimitable Jeeves* (1923)

54 It was that strange, almost unearthly light which comes into the eyes of wronged uncles when they see a chance of getting a bit of their own back from erring nephews.

P. G. Wodehouse 1881–1975: *Uncle Dynamite* (1948)

Fashion ····▷ Dress

❝ He feels a dedicated follower of fashion. **❞**
Raymond Douglas Davies

1 It is totally impossible to be well dressed in cheap shoes.

Hardy Amies 1909–2003: *The Englishman's Suit* (1994)

2 *of Asquith's first wife:*
She lived in Hampstead and had no clothes.

Margot Asquith 1864–1945: Chips Channon diary, 31 October 1937

3 I never cared for fashion much. Amusing little seams and witty little pleats. It was the girls I liked.

David Bailey 1938– : in *Independent* 5 November 1990

4 *of Dior's New Look:*
   Clothes by a man who doesn't know women, never had
   one, and dreams of being one!

Coco Chanel 1883–1971: in *Vanity Fair* June 1994

5 He thinks he is a flower to be looked at
   And when he pulls his frilly nylon pants right up tight
   He feels a dedicated follower of fashion.

Raymond Douglas Davies: 'A Dedicated Follower of Fashion' (1966)

6 I guess I'll have to change my plan
   I should have realized there'd be another man
   Why did I buy those blue pyjamas
   Before the big affair began?
   I guess I'll have to change my plan.

Howard Dietz 1896–1983: 'I Guess I'll Have to Change My Plan' (1929)

7 Uncool people never hurt anybody—all they do is collect
   stamps, read science-fiction books and stand on the end of
   railway platforms staring at trains.

Ben Elton 1959– : in *Radio Times* 18/24 April 1998

8 There are easier things in this life than being a drag queen.
   But, I ain't got no choice. Try as I may, I just can't walk in
   flats.

Harvey Fierstein 1954– : *Torch Song Trilogy* (1979)

9 *when a waiter at Buckingham Palace spilled soup on her dress:*
   Never darken my Dior again!

Beatrice Lillie 1894–1989: *Every Other Inch a Lady* (1973)

10 A woman's dress should be like a barbed wire fence:
   serving its purpose without obstructing the view.

Sophia Loren 1934– : in *Mail on Sunday* 30 March 2003

11 *on reports that 'style guru' Carole Caplin had dressed President
   Putin's wife for the Russian state visit:*
   She made her look like a lampshade in a curry house.

Andrew Marr 1959– : in *Daily Telegraph* 2 July 2003 (online edition)

12 Elizabeth Taylor is wearing Orson Welles designer jeans.

Joan Rivers 1933– : attributed; Ned Sherrin *Cutting Edge* (1984)

13 PIRATE: I'm gonna teach you the meaning of pain.
   ELIZABETH: You like pain? Try wearing a corset.

Terry Rossio and **Ted Elliott**: *Pirates of the Caribbean* (2003)

14 I wish I had invented blue jeans.
   on his only regret

Yves Saint Laurent 1936– : interview in *Harper's & Queen*; in *Independent on Sunday* 29 November 1998

15 His socks compelled one's attention without losing one's
   respect.

Saki 1870–1916: *Chronicles of Clovis* (1911)

16 Her frocks are built in Paris, but she wears them with a
   strong English accent.

Saki 1870–1916: *Reginald* (1904)

17 If Botticelli were alive today he'd be working for *Vogue*.

Peter Ustinov 1921–2004: in *Observer* 21 October 1962 'Sayings of the Week'

18 I like to dress egos. If you haven't got an ego today, you
   can forget it.

Gianni Versace 1949–97: in *Guardian* 16 July 1997; obituary

19 It is charming to totter into vogue.

Horace Walpole 1717–97: letter to George Selwyn, 2 December 1765

20 *to Ada Leverson, who with her husband visited Wilde on the
   morning he left Pentonville:*
   How marvellous of you to know exactly the right hat to
   wear at seven o'clock in the morning to meet a friend who
   has been away.

Oscar Wilde 1854–1900: Rupert Hart-Davis (ed.) *Selected Letters of Oscar Wilde* (1979)

Film ····❯ The Cinema, Film Producers, Film Stars

❝ Let's bring it up to date with some snappy 19th-century dialogue. **❞**
Sam Goldwyn

---

1 Several tons of dynamite are set off in this picture [*Tycoon*]; none of it under the right people.

James Agee 1909–55: in *The Nation* 14 February 1948

2 *Adolph Zukor had protested at the escalating costs of* The Ten Commandments:
What do you want me to do? Stop shooting now and release it as *The Five Commandments*?

Cecil B. De Mille 1881–1959: M. LeRoy *Take One* (1974)

3 A movie so good they named a country after it.
on his film Brazil

Terry Gilliam 1940– : in *Mail on Sunday* 22 August 1999, attributed

4 Let's bring it up to date with some snappy 19th-century dialogue.

Sam Goldwyn 1882–1974: King Vidor *A Tree is a Tree* (1953)

5 *of one of his own films:*
It's more than magnificent, it's mediocre.

Sam Goldwyn 1882–1974: attributed, perhaps apocryphal

6 GOLDWYN: I hope you didn't think it was too blood and thirsty.
THURBER: Not only did I think so but I was horror and struck.
of The Secret Life of Walter Mitty, *Goldwyn's 1947 film of Thurber's story*

Sam Goldwyn 1882–1974: Michael Freedland *The Goldwyn Touch* (1986)

7 It would have been cheaper to lower the Atlantic!
of the disaster movie Raise the Titanic

Lew Grade 1906–98: *Still Dancing: My Story* (1987)

8 *of the film* Lock, Stock and Two Smoking Barrels *starring Vinnie Jones:*
Think of it as a carefully constructed entertainment for the benefit of people who really, really like beer commercials.

Anthony Lane: in *New Yorker* 8 March 1999

9 Do you have any idea how bad the picture is? I'll tell you. Stay away from the neighbourhood where it's playing— don't even go near that street! It might rain—you could get caught in the downpour, and to keep dry you'd have to go inside the theatre.

Herman J. Mankiewicz 1897–1953: attributed

10 I'm not [biting my fingernails]. I'm biting my knuckles. I finished the fingernails months ago.

Joseph L. Mankiewicz 1909– : while directing *Cleopatra* (1963); Dick Sheppard *Elizabeth* (1975)

11 The slaves . . . are so cordial and upbeat about having their lives and property gentrified in 1776 that you fear for the entire future of the blues.
of The Patriot

Wesley Morris: in *San Francisco Examiner* 28 June 2000

12 It was a cute picture. They used the basic story of *Wuthering Heights* and worked in surfriders.

Neil Simon 1927– : *Last of the Red Hot Lovers* (1970)

13 Anything but Beethoven. Nobody wants to see a movie about a blind composer.

Jack Warner 1892–1978: J. Lawrence *Actor* (1975)

14 I didn't have to act in 'Tarzan, the Ape Man'—just said, 'Me Tarzan, you Jane.'

Johnny Weissmuller 1904–84: in *Photoplay Magazine* June 1932 (the words 'Me Tarzan, you Jane' do not occur in the 1932 film)

15 *asking Graham Greene to give a final polish to a rewrite of the last part of the screenplay for* Ben Hur*:* You see, we find a kind of anticlimax after the Crucifixion.

Sam Zimbalist: Graham Greene *Ways of Escape* (1980)

Film Producers and Directors ····> The Cinema, Film

❝ I like the old masters, by which I mean John Ford, John Ford, and John Ford. **❞**
Orson Welles

1 Cecil B. de Mille
Rather against his will,
Was persuaded to leave Moses
Out of 'The Wars of the Roses'.

Anonymous: J. W. Carter (ed.) *Clerihews* (1938); attributed to Nicolas Bentley

2 Ah don't believe Ah know which pictures are yours. Do you make the Mickey Mouse brand?
   to Irving Thalberg

William Faulkner 1897–1962: Max Wilk *The Wit and Wisdom of Hollywood* (1972)

3 *resigning from the Motion Picture Producers and Distributors of America in 1933:*
Gentlemen, include me out.

Sam Goldwyn 1882–1974: Michael Freedland *The Goldwyn Touch* (1986)

4 PRODUCTION ASSISTANT: But Mr Goldwyn, you said you wanted a spectacle.
   GOLDWYN: Yes, but goddam it, I wanted an intimate spectacle!

Sam Goldwyn 1882–1974: attributed, perhaps apocryphal

5 That's the way with these directors, they're always biting the hand that lays the golden egg.

Sam Goldwyn 1882–1974: Alva Johnston *The Great Goldwyn* (1937)

6 A pig in a silk suit who sends flowers.
   of Sam Spiegel

Katharine Hepburn 1907–2003: Natasha Fraser-Cavassoni *Sam Spiegel* (2003)

7 If I made Cinderella, the audience would immediately be looking for a body in the coach.

Alfred Hitchcock 1899–1980: in *Newsweek* 11 June 1956

8 I can't tell you [the perfect ending to a script] . . . I thought of the answer after 5.30.
   to Jack Warner, who imposed a strict nine-to-five-thirty schedule on his scriptwriters

Norman Krasna 1909–84: M. Freedland *Warner Brothers* (1983)

9 Jack Warner has oilcloth pockets so he can steal soup.

Wilson Mizner 1876–1933: Max Wilk *The Wit and Wisdom of Hollywood* (1972)

10 Tsar of all the rushes.
   of Louis B. Mayer

B. P. Schulberg d. 1957: Norman Zierold *The Hollywood Tycoons* (1969)

11 Once a month the sky falls on my head, I come to, and I see another movie I want to make.

Steven Spielberg 1947– : in *Time* 8 June 1998

12 To Raoul Walsh a tender love scene is burning down a whorehouse.

Jack Warner 1892–1978: P. F. Boller and R. L. Davis *Hollywood Anecdotes* (1988)

13 I like the old masters, by which I mean John Ford, John Ford, and John Ford.

Orson Welles 1915–85: P. F. Boller and R. L. Davis *Hollywood Anecdotes* (1988)

14 Johnny, it's the usual slashed-wrist shot . . . Keep it out of focus. I want to win the foreign picture award.

Billy Wilder 1906–2002: to his lighting cameraman, John Seitz, when filming *Sunset Boulevard* (1950); P. F. Boller and R. L. Davis *Hollywood Anecdotes* (1988)

15 A modern-day Robin Hood, who steals from the rich and steals from the poor.
of Sam Spiegel

Billy Wilder 1906–2002: Natasha Fraser-Cavassoni *Sam Spiegel* (2003)

16 Anonymous: What is an associate producer?
Billy Wilder: Anybody who's prepared to associate with a producer.

Billy Wilder 1906–2002: attributed

17 He could do more with a closed door than other directors could do with an open fly.
of Ernst Lubitsch

Billy Wilder 1906–2002: attributed

18 The first nine commandments for a director are 'Thou shalt not bore.' The tenth is 'Thou shalt have the right of final cut.'

Billy Wilder 1906–2002: attributed, perhaps apocryphal

Film Stars ····> The Cinema, Film

66 All Americans born between 1890 and 1945 wanted to be movie stars. 99
Gore Vidal

1 Can't act. Slightly bald. Also dances.
studio official's comment on Fred Astaire

Anonymous: Bob Thomas *Astaire* (1985)

2 They used to shoot her through gauze. You should shoot me through linoleum.
on Shirley Temple

Tallulah Bankhead 1903–68: attributed

3 Joe Gillis: You used to be in pictures. You used to be big.
Norma Desmond: I am big. It's the pictures that got small.

Charles Brackett 1892–1969 and **Billy Wilder** 1906–2002: *Sunset Boulevard* (1950 film)

4 When he meets Garbo in a suit of corduroy,
He gives a little frown
And knocks her down.
Oh dear, oh dear, I'm mad about the boy.

Noël Coward 1899–1973: 'Mad About the Boy' (1932)

5 *asked what it was like to kiss Marilyn Monroe:*
It's like kissing Hitler.

Tony Curtis 1925– : A. Hunter *Tony Curtis* (1985)

6 Nowadays Mitchum doesn't so much act as point his suit at people.

Russell Davies 1946– : in *Sunday Times* 18 September 1983

7 *during the making of* Lifeboat *in 1944, Mary Anderson asked Hitchcock what he thought her 'best side' for photography was:* My dear, you're sitting on it.

Alfred Hitchcock 1899–1980: D. Spoto *Life of Alfred Hitchcock* (1983)

8 That man's ears make him look like a taxi-cab with both doors open.
of Clark Gable

Howard Hughes Jr. 1905–76: Charles Higham and Joel Greenberg *Celluloid Muse* (1969)

9 She is a phenomenon of nature, like Niagara Falls or the Grand Canyon. You can't talk to it. It can't talk to you. All you can do is stand back and be awed by it.
of Marilyn Monroe

Nunnally Johnson 1897–1977: Peter Harry Brown and Patte B. Barham *Marilyn, the Last Take* (1990)

10 To work as hard as I've worked to accomplish anything and then have some yo-yo come up and say 'Take off those dark glasses and let's have a look at those blue eyes' is really discouraging.

Paul Newman 1925– : in *Observer* 5 October 1986 'Sayings of the Week'

11 Elizabeth [Taylor] is a wonderful movie actress: she has a deal with the film lab—she gets better in the bath overnight.

Mike Nichols 1931– : in *Vanity Fair* June 1994

12 Wet, she was a star—dry she ain't.
of the swimmer Esther Williams and her 1940s film career

Joe Pasternak 1901–91: attributed

13 There are times when Richard Gere has the warm effect of a wind tunnel at dawn, waiting for work, all sheen, inner curve, and posed emptiness.

David Thomson 1941– : *A Biographical Dictionary of Film* (1994)

14 All Americans born between 1890 and 1945 wanted to be movie stars.

Gore Vidal 1925– : *Pink Triangle and Yellow Star* (1982)

15 *on hearing that Ronald Reagan was seeking nomination as Governor of California:*
No, no. Jimmy Stewart for governor—Reagan for his best friend.

Jack Warner 1892–1978: Max Wilk *The Wit and Wisdom of Hollywood* (1972)

16 It's not what I do, but the way I do it. It's not what I say, but the way I say it.

Mae West 1892–1980: G. Eells and S. Musgrove *Mae West* (1989)

17 *on Marilyn Monroe's unpunctuality:*
My Aunt Minnie would always be punctual and never hold up production, but who would pay to see my Aunt Minnie?

Billy Wilder 1906–2002: P. F. Boller and R. L. Davis *Hollywood Anecdotes* (1988)

18 The question is whether Marilyn [Monroe] is a person at all or one of the greatest Dupont products ever invented. She has breasts like granite and a brain like Swiss cheese, full of holes.

Billy Wilder 1906–2002: E. Goodman *The Fifty-Year Decline and Fall of Hollywood* (1961)

Fishing

66 Transcendental meditation with a punch-line. **99**
Billy Connolly

1 If fishing is a religion, fly fishing is high church.

Tom Brokaw 1940– : in *International Herald Tribune* 10 September 1991

2 I love fishing. It's like transcendental meditation with a punch-line.

Billy Connolly 1942– : *Gullible's Travels* (1982)

3 Fishing is unquestionably a form of madness but, happily, for the once-bitten there is no cure.

Lord Home 1903–95: *The Way the Wind Blows* (1976)

4 Fly fishing may be a very pleasant amusement; but angling or float fishing I can only compare to a stick and a string, with a worm at one end and a fool at the other.

Samuel Johnson 1709–84: attributed; Hawker *Instructions to Young Sportsmen* (1859); also attributed to Jonathan Swift

5 It is to be observed that 'angling' is the name given to fishing by people who can't fish.

Stephen Leacock 1869–1944: attributed

Flattery ····▷ Praise and Flattery

Food ····▷ Cookery, Diets

❝ Of soup and love, the first is best. **❞**
Thomas Fuller

1 I've eaten shepherd's pie at The Ivy and the Savoy, but I've never seen anything like Belmarsh's version.

Jeffrey Archer 1940– : prison diaries, in *Independent* 28 December 2002

2 Shake and shake
The catsup bottle,
None will come,
And then a lot'll.

Richard Armour: Laurence J. Peter (ed.) *Quotations for our Time* (1977)

3 A gourmet can tell from the flavour whether a woodcock's leg is the one on which the bird is accustomed to roost.

Lucius Beebe 1902– : Laurence J. Peter (ed.) *Quotations for our Time* (1977)

4 WAITER WITH FISH ORDER: Are you smelt, sir?
JOHN BETJEMAN: Only by the discerning.

John Betjeman 1906–84: Bevis Hillier *Betjeman: the Bonus of Laughter* (2004)

5 Good to eat, and wholesome to digest, as a worm to a toad, a toad to a snake, a snake to a pig, a pig to a man, and a man to a worm.
on the cycle of digestion

Ambrose Bierce 1842–c.1914: *The Enlarged Devil's Dictionary* (1967)

6 One of the sauces which serve the French in place of a state religion.
on mayonnaise

Ambrose Bierce 1842–c.1914: *The Enlarged Devil's Dictionary* (1967)

7 Sir Walter Raleigh gripped his seat under the table. He had sailed halfway round the world to find this root, he had faced great perils to bring it back, he had withstood the blandishments of the most expert cajolers at Court, and had not even hinted at the secret of its flavour, he had changed his chef six times, and now Elizabeth of England was tasting it.
He looked at her.
Elizabeth of England spat.
'Not enough salt,' she said.

Caryl Brahms 1901–82 and **S. J. Simon** 1904–48: *No Bed for Bacon* (1941)

8 Where else can you see, at a table for six, six grey suits?

Seymour Britchky: of the men at '21'; *The Restaurants of New York* (1974 ed.)

9 Some of the waiters discuss the menu with you as if they were sharing wisdom picked up in the Himalayas.

Seymour Britchky: *The Restaurants of New York* (1981 ed.)

10 *Leo Bloom on life in Rio with Swedish Ulla:*
Breakfast on our terrace—many different kinds of herring.

Mel Brooks 1926– and **Thomas Meehan**: *The Producers* (musical, 2001)

11 I'm President of the United States, and I'm not going to eat any more broccoli!

George Bush 1924– : in *New York Times* 23 March 1990

12 The healthy stomach is nothing if not conservative. Few radicals have good digestions.

Samuel Butler 1835–1902: *Notebooks* (1912)

13 Day will break and you'll awake and start to bake a sugar cake for all the boys to see.

Irving Caesar 1895– : 'Tea for Two' (1925)

14 'There's nothing like eating hay when you're faint' . . . 'I didn't say there was nothing *better*,' the King replied, 'I said there was nothing *like* it.'

Lewis Carroll 1832–98: *Through the Looking-Glass* (1872)

15 Take away that pudding—it has no theme.

Winston Churchill 1874–1965: Lord Home *The Way the Wind Blows* (1976)

16 Open up the caviare
And say Thank God.

Noël Coward 1899–1973: 'Alice is At It Again' (1954)

17 I never see an egg brought on my table but I feel penetrated with the wonderful change it would have undergone but for my gluttony; it might have been a gentle useful hen, leading her chickens with a care and vigilance which speaks shame to many women.

St John de Crévècoeur 1735–1813: *Letters from an American Farmer* (1782)

18 'It's very easy to talk,' said Mrs Mantalini. 'Not so easy when one is eating a demnition egg,' replied Mr Mantalini; 'for the yolk runs down the waistcoat, and yolk of egg does not match any waistcoat but a yellow waistcoat, demmit.'

Charles Dickens 1812–70: *Nicholas Nickleby* (1839)

19 It's a wery remarkable circumstance . . . that poverty and oysters always seem to go together.

Charles Dickens 1812–70: *Pickwick Papers* (1837)

20 Please, sir, I want some more.

Charles Dickens 1812–70: *Oliver Twist* (1838)

21 [Cheese is] milk's leap toward immortality.

Clifton Fadiman 1904–99: *Any Number Can Play* (1957)

22 Roast Beef, Medium, is not only a food. It is a philosophy.

Edna Ferber 1887–1968: foreword to *Roast Beef, Medium* (1911)

23 Ask for heron's eggs whipped with wine into an amber foam.
when asked by a friend what to order in a Lyons teashop

Ronald Firbank 1886–1926: Mervyn Horder *Ronald Firbank: Memoirs and Critiques* (1977)

24 Last night we went to a Chinese dinner at six and a French dinner at nine, and I can feel the sharks' fins navigating unhappily in the Burgundy.

Peter Fleming 1907–71: letter from Yunnanfu, 20 March 1938

25 Of soup and love, the first is the best.

Thomas Fuller 1654–1734: *Gnomologia* (1732)

26 You like potato and I like po-tah-to,
You like tomato and I like to-mah-to;
Potato, po-tah-to, tomato, to-mah-to—
Let's call the whole thing off!

Ira Gershwin 1896–1983: 'Let's Call the Whole Thing Off' (1937)

27 The best number for a dinner party is two—myself and a dam' good head waiter.

Nubar Gulbenkian 1896–1972: in *Daily Telegraph* 14 January 1965

28 'For what we are about to receive,
Oh Lord, 'tis Thee we thank,'
Said the cannibal as he cut a slice
Of the missionary's shank.

E. Y. Harburg 1898–1981: 'The Realist' (1965)

29 I ate his liver with some fava beans and a nice chianti.

Thomas Harris 1940– and **Ted Tally** 1952– : *The Silence of the Lambs* (1991 film)

30 Oh, I was down by Manly Pier
Drinking tubes of ice-cold beer
With a bucket full of prawns upon me knee.
But when I'd swallowed the last prawn
I had a technicolour yawn
And I chundered in the old Pacific sea.

Barry Humphries 1934– : 'Chunder Down Under' (1964)

31 What proper man would plump for bints
Ahead of After-Eight thin mints?
True pleasure for a man of parts
Is tarts in him, not him in tarts.

Clive James 1939– : Ned Sherrin *Cutting Edge* (1984)

32 Mr Leopold Bloom ate with relish the inner organs of beasts and fowls. He liked thick giblet soup, nutty gizzards, a stuffed roast heart, liverslices fried with crustcrumbs, fried hencod's roes. Most of all he liked grilled mutton kidneys which gave to his palate a fine tang of faintly scented urine.

James Joyce 1882–1941: *Ulysses* (1922)

33 Lunch Hollywood-style—a hot dog and vintage wine.

Harry Kurnitz 1907–68: Max Wilk *The Wit and Wisdom of Hollywood* (1971)

34 It has nothing to do with frogs' legs. No amphibian is harmed in the making of this dish.
explaining toad-in-the-hole to an American audience

Nigella Lawson 1960– : in *Sunday Times* 6 October 2002

35 Cannibalism went right out as soon as the American canned food came in.

Stephen Leacock 1869–1944: *The Boy I Left Behind Me* (1947)

36 Large, naked, raw carrots are acceptable as food only to those who live in hutches eagerly awaiting Easter.

Fran Lebowitz 1946– : *Metropolitan Life* (1978)

37 The piece of cod passeth all understanding.

Edwin Lutyens 1869–1944: Robert Lutyens *Sir Edwin Lutyens* (1942)

38 You are offered a piece of bread and butter that feels like a damp handkerchief and sometimes, when cucumber is added to it, like a wet one.

Compton Mackenzie 1883–1972: *Vestal Fire* (1927)

39 Sushi, crab claws, caviar, little heaps of pink glop . . . A taste of dank rock pools fills my mouth.

Liz McManus 1947– : 'Dwelling Below the Skies' (1997)

40 It's all right, the white wine came up with the fish.
at a formal dinner at the home of the producer Arthur Hornblow Jr., having left the dinner table to be sick

Herman J. Mankiewicz 1897–1953: Max Wilk *The Wit and Wisdom of Hollywood* (1972); also claimed by Howard Dietz

41 'Can I have a table near the floor?'
'Certainly, I'll have the waiter saw the legs off.'

Groucho Marx 1895–1977:
attributed

42 [England] is the only country in the world where the food
is more dangerous than sex. I mean, a hard cheese will kill
you, but a soft cheese will kill you in *seconds*.

Jackie Mason 1931– : in
Independent 17 February 1989

43 People often feed the hungry so that nothing may disturb
their own enjoyment of a good meal.

W. Somerset Maugham 1874–1965:
A Writer's Notebook (1949) written in
1896

44 *to a friend who had said that he hated English food:*
All you have to do is eat breakfast three times a day.

W. Somerset Maugham 1874–1965:
Ted Morgan *Somerset Maugham*
(1980)

45 *explaining her dislike of soup:*
I do not believe in building a meal on a lake.

Elsie Mendl 1865–1950: Elsie de
Wolfe *After All* (1935)

46 Sue wants a barbecue, Sam wants to boil a ham,
Grace votes for bouillabaisse stew,
Jake wants a weeny-bake, steak and a layer cake,
He'll get a tummy ache too.

Johnny Mercer 1909–76: 'In the
Cool, Cool, Cool of the Evening'
(1951)

47 Long as there is chicken and gravy on your rice
Ev'rything is nice.

Johnny Mercer 1909–76: 'Lazybones'
(1932)

48 Parsley
Is gharsley.

Ogden Nash 1902–71: 'Further
Reflections on Parsley' (1942)

49 *of the wartime food at his prep school:*
There was greasy toad in an equally greasy hole, and a
bacon and egg pie so dry and powdery that it was like
eating a crumbling 17th-century wattle and daub cottage.

David Nobbs 1935– : *I Didn't Get
Where I Am Today* (2003)

50 Never serve oysters in a month that has no paycheck in it.

P. J. O'Rourke 1947– : *The Bachelor
Home Companion* (1987)

51 I'll take a lemonade! . . . In a dirty glass!

Norman Panama 1914– and **Melvin
Frank** 1913–88: in *Road to Utopia*
(1946 film; words spoken by Bob
Hope)

52 I had never had a piece of toast
Particularly long and wide,
But fell upon the sanded floor,
And always on the buttered side.

James Payn 1830–98: in *Chambers's
Journal* 2 February 1884

53 The mountain sheep are sweeter,
But the valley sheep are fatter;
We therefore deemed it meeter
To carry off the latter.

Thomas Love Peacock 1785–1866:
'The War-Song of Dinas Vawr' (1823)

54 The divine took his seat at the breakfast-table, and began
to compose his spirits by the gentle sedative of a large cup
of tea, the demulcent of a well-buttered muffin, and the
tonic of a small lobster.

Thomas Love Peacock 1785–1866:
Crotchet Castle (1831)

55 There is no danger of my getting scurvy [while in
England], as I have to consume at least two gin-and-limes
every evening to keep the cold out.

S. J. Perelman 1904–79: letter, 13
December 1953

56 I've had a taste of society
And society has had a taste of me.
the oyster ending up back in the sea after a day of social climbing

Cole Porter 1891–1964: 'The Tale of the Oyster' (1929)

57 It just proves that fifty million Frenchmen can't be wrong. They eat horses instead of ride them.
having been crippled in a riding accident in 1937

Cole Porter 1891–1964: G. Eells *The Life that Late He Led* (1967)

58 It is said that the effect of eating too much lettuce is 'soporific'.

Beatrix Potter 1866–1943: *The Tale of the Flopsy Bunnies* (1909)

59 Dinner at the Huntercombes' possessed 'only two dramatic features—the wine was a farce and the food a tragedy'.

Anthony Powell 1905–2000: *The Acceptance World* (1955)

60 Botticelli isn't a wine, you Juggins! Botticelli's a *cheese*!

Punch 1841–1992: vol. 106 (1894)

61 BISHOP: I'm afraid you've got a bad egg, Mr Jones.
CURATE: Oh no, my Lord, I assure you! Parts of it are excellent!

Punch 1841–1992: vol. 109 (1895)

62 Cheese it is a peevish elf
It digests all things but itself.

John Ray 1627–1705: *English Proverbs* (1670)

63 Does the spearmint lose its flavour on the bedpost overnight?

Billy Rose 1899–1966 and **Marty Bloom**: title of song (1924); revived in 1959 by Lonnie Donegan with the title 'Does your chewing-gum lose its flavour on the bedpost overnight?'

64 Like a purée of white kid gloves.
of a dish of lobster Newburg

Philip Sassoon 1888–1939: Chips Channon, diary, 3 June 1939

65 Methinks I have a great desire to a bottle of hay: good hay, sweet hay, hath no fellow.

William Shakespeare 1564–1616: *A Midsummer Night's Dream* (1595–6)

66 A plague o' these pickle herring!

William Shakespeare 1564–1616: *Twelfth Night* (1601)

67 Then my stomach must digest its waistcoat.
when told that drinking would ruin the coat of his stomach

Richard Brinsley Sheridan 1751–1816: in *Sheridaniana* (1826)

68 OSCAR: I got brown sandwiches and green sandwiches . . . Well, what do you say?
MURRAY: What's the green?
OSCAR: It's either very new cheese or very old meat.

Neil Simon 1927– : *The Odd Couple* (1966)

69 Serenely full, the epicure would say,
Fate cannot harm me, I have dined to-day.

Sydney Smith 1771–1845: Lady Holland *Memoir* (1855) 'Receipt for a Salad'

70 If there is a pure and elevated pleasure in this world it is a roast pheasant with bread sauce. Barn door fowls for dissenters but for the real Churchman, the thirty-nine times articled clerk—the pheasant, the pheasant.

Sydney Smith 1771–1845: letter to R. H. Barham, 15 November 1841

71 Shepherd's pie peppered with actual shepherd on top.
one of Mrs Lovett's variations on Sweeney Todd's human meat pies

Stephen Sondheim 1930– : 'A Little Priest' (1979)

72 Have an egg roll, Mr Goldstone,
Have a napkin, have a chopstick, have a chair!
Have a sparerib, Mr Goldstone—
Any sparerib that I can spare, I'd be glad to share!

Stephen Sondheim 1930– : 'Mr Goldstone, I Love You' (1959)

73 For the edible and the readable we give thanks to God, the Author of Life.

Mervyn Stockwood 1913–95: grace for a literary lunch, in Ned Sherrin *Cutting Edge* (1984)

74 I'll fill hup the chinks wi' cheese.

R. S. Surtees 1805–64: *Handley Cross* (1843)

75 MARGARET THATCHER: This food is absolutely delicious.
DENIS THATCHER: So it should be. They're charging like the Light Brigade.
eating in Harry's Bar

Denis Thatcher 1915–2003: attributed; in *Spectator* 20 March 2004

76 *dining with her Cabinet:*
MRS THATCHER: Steak.
WAITER: And the vegetables?
MRS THATCHER: Oh, they'll have steak too.

Margaret Thatcher 1925– : attributed, probably apocryphal

77 *offered jugged hare by his hostess Margaret Taylor, he finally agreed:*
[To] eat the hare of the bitch that dogs me.

Dylan Thomas 1914–53: attributed; Andrew Lycett 'Thomas Untutored' in *Oxford Today* Hilary 2004 (online edition)

78 Cauliflower is nothing but cabbage with a college education.

Mark Twain 1835–1910: *Pudd'nhead Wilson* (1894)

79 'Turbot, Sir,' said the waiter, placing before me two fishbones, two eyeballs, and a bit of black mackintosh.

Thomas Earle Welby 1881–1933: *The Dinner Knell* (1932) 'Birmingham or Crewe?'

80 Beulah, peel me a grape.

Mae West 1892–1980: in *I'm No Angel* (1933 film)

81 MOTHER: It's broccoli, dear.
CHILD: I say it's spinach, and I say the hell with it.

E. B. White 1899–1985: cartoon caption in *New Yorker* 8 December 1928

82 When I ask for a watercress sandwich, I do not mean a loaf with a field in the middle of it.

Oscar Wilde 1854–1900: Max Beerbohm letter to Reggie Turner, 15 April 1893

83 I was so darned sorry for poor old Corky that I hadn't the heart to touch my breakfast. I told Jeeves to drink it himself.

P. G. Wodehouse 1881–1975: *My Man Jeeves* (1919)

84 The lunches of fifty-seven years had caused his chest to slip down into the mezzanine floor.

P. G. Wodehouse 1881–1975: *The Heart of a Goof* (1926)

85 What with excellent browsing and sluicing and cheery conversation and what-not, the afternoon passed quite happily.

P. G. Wodehouse 1881–1975: *My Man Jeeves* (1919)

86 JACKIE: Pity there's no such thing as Sugar Replacement Therapy.
VICTORIA: There is. It's called chocolate.

Victoria Wood 1953– : *Mens Sana in Thingummy Doodah* (1990)

87 If you dine out of tins, you should have the labels served up with the grub.

Jack B. Yeats 1871–1957: *The Charmed Life* (1938)

88 One doughnut doesn't do a thing. You've got to eat 20 a day for five weeks before you get results.
preparing to play Bridget Jones

Renee Zellweger 1969– : in *Mail on Sunday* 15 June 2003

Foolishness ····▸ Ignorance, Stupidity

66 As any fule kno. **99**

Geoffrey Willans and Ronald Searle

---

1 *New Year Resolutions*
   1. To refrain from saying witty, unkind things, unless they are really witty and irreparably damaging.
   2. To tolerate fools more gladly, provided this does not encourage them to take up more of my time.

James Agate 1877–1947: diary 2 January 1942

2 Fools have this happiness—to be easy with themselves, and let other people blush for 'em.

Anonymous: in *The Female Tatler* July–August 1709

3 I sometimes wonder if the manufacturers of foolproof items keep a fool or two on their payroll to test things.

Alan Coren 1938–2007: *Seems Like Old Times* (1989)

4 How much a dunce that has been sent to roam
Excels a dunce that has been kept at home?

William Cowper 1731–1800: 'The Progress of Error' (1782)

5 I believe they talked of me, for they laughed consumedly.

George Farquhar 1678–1707: *The Beaux' Stratagem* (1707)

6 The idiot who praises, with enthusiastic tone,
All centuries but this, and every country but his own.

W. S. Gilbert 1836–1911: *The Mikado* (1885)

7 Oh, innocent victims of Cupid,
Remember this terse little verse;
To let a fool kiss you is stupid,
To let a kiss fool you is worse.

E. Y. Harburg 1898–1981: 'Inscriptions on a Lipstick' (1965)

8 The Lord made Adam,
The Lord made Eve,
He made 'em both a little naïve.

E. Y. Harburg 1898–1981: 'The Begat' (1947)

9 You've heard of people living in a fool's paradise? Well, Leonora has a duplex there.
   of Leonora Corbett

George S. Kaufman 1889–1961: Howard Teichmann *George S. Kaufman* (1973)

10 I could name eight people—half of those eight are barmy. How many apples short of a picnic?
   on Tory critics

John Major 1943– : comment, 19 September 1993

11 A man may be a fool and not know it, but not if he is married.

H. L. Mencken 1880–1956: Laurence J. Peter (ed.) *Quotations for our Time* (1977)

12 What a waste it is to lose one's mind, or not to have a mind. How true that is.

Dan Quayle 1947– : speech to the United Negro College Fund, whose slogan is 'a mind is a terrible thing to waste'; in *The Times* 26 May 1989

13 He does it with a better grace, but I do it more natural.

William Shakespeare 1564–1616: *Twelfth Night* (1601)

14 *Sheridan's son Tom announced that when he became an MP he would proclaim his independence of party by writing 'To Let' on his forehead:*
And, under that, Tom, write 'unfurnished'.

Richard Brinsley Sheridan 1751–1816: Walter Jerrold *Bon-Mots* (1893)

15 'A soldier,' cried my Uncle Toby, interrupting the corporal, 'is no more exempt from saying a foolish thing, Trim, than a man of letters.'—'But not so often, an' please your honour,' replied the corporal.

Laurence Sterne 1713–68: *Tristram Shandy* (1759–67)

16 Major Yammerton was rather a peculiar man, inasmuch as he was an ass, without being a fool.

R. S. Surtees 1805–64: *Ask Mamma* (1858)

17 How haughtily he lifts his nose,
To tell what every schoolboy knows.

Jonathan Swift 1667–1745: 'The Journal' (1727)

18 Hain't we got all the fools in town on our side? and ain't that a big enough majority in any town?

Mark Twain 1835–1910: *The Adventures of Huckleberry Finn* (1884)

19 Man is without any doubt the most interesting fool there is. Also the most eccentric. He hasn't a single written law, in his Bible or out of it, which has any but one purpose and intention—to *limit or defeat a law of God*.

Mark Twain 1835–1910: *Letters from the Earth* (1905–09)

20 As any fule kno.

Geoffrey Willans 1911–58 and **Ronald Searle** 1920– : *Down with Skool!* (1953)

Football ····> Sports and Games

66 The natural state of the football fan is bitter disappointment. **99**
Nick Hornby

1 You've got DiCanio, we've
nicked your stereo!
   football chant sung by Liverpool fans to West Ham fans to the tune of La donna e mobile

Anonymous: in *Sunday Times* 30 November 2003

2 Why is there only one ball for 22 players? If you gave a ball to each of them, they'd stop fighting for it.
   comment of a football widow, posted on an anti-World Cup website

Anonymous: in *Daily Telegraph* 28 December 1998 'Sporting Quotes of the Year'

3 If I had the wings of a sparrow
If I had the arse of a crow
I'd fly over Tottenham tomorrow
And shit on the bastards below.

Anonymous: frequently sung on the Chelsea terraces; Ned Sherrin *Cutting Edge* (1984)

4 In our Coventry homes.
   football chant sung by Coventry City fans to the tune of In our Liverpool Homes

Anonymous: in *Sunday Times* 30 November 2003

5 He's blond, he's quick,
his name's a porno flick
Emmanuel, Emmanuel.
He's quick, he's he's blond, he's
won the Coupe du Monde
   football chant sung by Arsenal fans when Emmanuel Petit played at Highbury

Anonymous: in *Sunday Times* 30 November 2003

6 I hate manly men. Four men in a car talking about football is my idea of hell.

David Bailey 1938– : in *Observer* 2 May 1999 'Sayings of the Week'

7 *George Best was often told by Matt Busby not to bother to turn up for Busby's team talks to Manchester United:*
It wasn't worth his coming. It was a very simple team talk. All I used to say was: 'Whenever possible, give the ball to George.'

Matt Busby 1909–94: Michael Parkinson *Sporting Lives* (1993)

8 *on meetings with players:*
We talk about it for 20 minutes and then we decide I was right.

Brian Clough 1935–2004: attributed; in *Channel 4 News* 20 September 2004 (online edition)

9 Football's football; if that weren't the case, it wouldn't be the game it is.

Garth Crooks 1958– : Barry Fantoni (ed.) *Private Eye's Colemanballs 2* (1984)

10 United will no longer be a football club, it will be a giant Old Trafford fruit machine.

Tommy Docherty 1928– : in *Mail on Sunday* 13 September 1998 'Quotes of the Week'

11 *of Stan Bowles:*
If only he could pass a betting shop like he does a football.

Reg Drury 1928–2003: in *Times* 28 June 2003 (obituary)

12 One is not amused at that.
reported comment when the disallowing of a goal put England out of the World Cup

Elizabeth II 1926– : in *Daily Telegraph* 28 December 1998 'Sporting Quotes of the Year'

13 Football, wherein is nothing but beastly fury, and extreme violence, whereof proceedeth hurt, and consequently rancour and malice do remain with them that be wounded.

Thomas Elyot 1499–1546: *Book of the Governor* (1531)

14 The only thing that Norwich didn't get was the goal that they finally got.

Jimmy Greaves 1940– : Barry Fantoni (ed.) *Private Eye's Colemanballs 2* (1984)

15 What makes a sane and rational person subject himself to such humiliation? Why on earth does anyone want to become a football referee?

Roy Hattersley 1932– : in *Sunday Times* 7 April 2002 'Talking Heads'

16 The natural state of the football fan is bitter disappointment, no matter what the score.

Nick Hornby 1957– : *Fever Pitch* (1992)

17 I got into moisturiser when I played football. If you're out in all weathers you have to take care of your face.

Vinnie Jones 1965– : in *Independent* 28 December 2002

18 The nice aspect about football is that, if things go wrong, it's the manager who gets the blame.
before his first match as captain of England

Gary Lineker 1960– : in *Independent* 12 September 1990

19 Oh, he's football crazy, he's football mad
And the football it has robbed him o' the wee bit sense he had.
And it would take a dozen skivvies, his clothes to wash and scrub,
Since our Jock became a member of that terrible football club.

Jimmy McGregor: 'Football Crazy' (1960)

20 What's a geriatric? A German footballer scoring three goals.

Bob Monkhouse 1928–2003: attributed; in *BBC News* (UK edition, online) 29 December 2003

21 Nobody cares if Le Saux is gay or not. It is the fact that he openly admits to reading *The Guardian* that makes him the most reviled man in football.

Piers Morgan 1965– : letter to *Guardian*, 5 March 1999

22 To say that these men paid their shillings to watch twenty-two hirelings kick a ball is merely to say that a violin is wood and catgut, that *Hamlet* is so much paper and ink. For a shilling the Bruddersford United AFC offered you Conflict and Art.

J. B. Priestley 1894–1984: *Good Companions* (1929)

23 We didn't underestimate them. They were a lot better than we thought.
on Cameroon's football team

Bobby Robson 1933– : in *Guardian* 24 December 1990 'Sports Quotes of the Year'

24 I don't drop players. I make changes.
a football manager's view

Bill Shankly 1914–81: in *Guardian* 24 December 1973 'Sports Quotes of the Year'

25 Some people think football is a matter of life and death . . . I can assure them it is much more serious than that.

Bill Shankly 1914–81: in *Guardian* 24 December 1973 'Sports Quotes of the Year'

26 [Gary Lineker is] the Queen Mother of football.

Arthur Smith 1954– and **Chris England**: *An Evening with Gary Lineker* (1990)

27 The English football team—brilliant on paper, shit on grass.

Arthur Smith 1954– and **Chris England**: *An Evening with Gary Lineker* (1990)

28 Football and cookery are the two most important subjects in the country.
having been appointed a director of Norwich City football club

Delia Smith 1941– : in *Observer* 23 February 1997 'Said and Done'

29 We're having a philosophical discussion about the yob ethics of professional footballers.

Tom Stoppard 1937– : *Professional Foul* (1978)

30 Me and the wife are breeding our own team. When I get home tonight it'll be 'c'mon hen, we need a centre-back.'
comment by the manager of Coventry, whose son is a Sky Blues youth-team player

Gordon Strachan (1957–): in *Daily Telegraph* 28 December 1998 'Sporting Quotes of the Year'

France

66 How can you govern a country which has 246 varieties of cheese? **99**
Charles de Gaulle

1 France is the only place where you can make love in the afternoon without people hammering on your door.

Barbara Cartland 1901–2000: in *Guardian* 24 December 1984

2 Every wise and thoroughly worldly wench
Knows there's always something fishy about the French!

Noël Coward 1899–1973: 'There's Always Something Fishy about the French' (1933)

3 How can you govern a country which has 246 varieties of cheese?

Charles de Gaulle 1890–1970: Ernest Mignon *Les Mots du Général* (1962)

4 I hate the French, I hate them all,
From Toulouse Lafucking Trec to Charles de Gaulle.

Paul Scott Goodman: 'I Hate the French' (*Bright Lights, Big City*, 1988 musical, from the book by Jay McInerney)

5 Bonjourr, you cheese-eating surrender monkeys.
Groundskeeper Willie as French teacher

Matt Groening 1954– : *The Simpsons* (1995) 'Round Springfield'

6 No matter how politely or distinctly you ask a Parisian a question he will persist in answering you in French.

Fran Lebowitz 1946– : *Metropolitan Life* (1978)

7 Yet, who can help loving the land that has taught us Six hundred and eighty-five ways to dress eggs?

Thomas Moore 1779–1852: *The Fudge Family in Paris* (1818)

8 They order, said I, this matter better in France.

Laurence Sterne 1713–68: opening words of *A Sentimental Journey* (1768)

9 Paris last year. Wonderful town but the French are awful, the waiters and so on, they're tip mad.

Tom Stoppard 1937– : *Neutral Ground* (1983)

10 France is a country where the money falls apart in your hands and you can't tear the toilet paper.

Billy Wilder 1906–2002: Leslie Halliwell *The Filmgoer's Book of Quotes* (1973)

Friends ····➤ Enemies

❝God's apology for relations.❞
Hugh Kingsmill

1 I may be wrong, but I have never found deserting friends conciliates enemies.

Margot Asquith 1864–1945: *Lay Sermons* (1927)

2 Champagne for my real friends, and real pain for my sham friends.
his favourite toast

Francis Bacon 1909–92: Michael Peppiatt *Francis Bacon* (1996)

3 It may be more difficult to make new friends as you get older but it is some consolation to know how easy it is to lose them when you are young.

Jeffrey Bernard 1932–97: in *The Spectator* 17 August 1985

4 A person whom we know well enough to borrow from, but not well enough to lend to. A degree of friendship called slight when its object is poor or obscure, and intimate when he is rich or famous.

Ambrose Bierce 1842–c.1914: definition of an acquaintance; *The Cynic's Word Book* (1906)

5 *of a rival:*
Such a clever actress. Pity she does her hair with Bovril.

Mrs Patrick Campbell 1865–1940: in *Ned Sherrin in his Anecdotage* (1993); attributed

6 *during an audience with the Pope:*
I expect you know my friend Evelyn Waugh, who, like your holiness, is a Roman Catholic.

Randolph Churchill 1911–68: attributed; in *Penguin Dictionary of Modern Quotations* (1971)

7 To find a friend one must close one eye. To keep him— two.

Norman Douglas 1868–1952: *Almanac* (1941)

8 [Friends are] God's apology for relations.

Hugh Kingsmill 1889–1949: Michael Holroyd *The Best of Hugh Kingsmill* (1970)

9 Money couldn't buy friends but you got a better class of enemy.

Spike Milligan 1918–2002: *Puckoon* (1963)

10 Scratch a lover, and find a foe.

Dorothy Parker 1893–1967: 'Ballade of a Great Weariness' (1937)

11 If it is abuse,—why one is always sure to hear of it from one damned goodnatured friend or another!

Richard Brinsley Sheridan 1751–1816: *The Critic* (1779)

12 We were in some little time fixed in our seats, and sat with that dislike which people not too good-natured usually conceive of each other at first sight.

Richard Steele 1672–1729: *The Spectator* 1 August 1711

13 You had only two friends in the world, and having killed one you can't afford to irritate the other.

Tom Stoppard 1937– : *Artist Descending a Staircase* (1973)

14 *on Harold Macmillan's sacking seven of his Cabinet on 13 July 1962:*
Greater love hath no man than this, that he lay down his friends for his life.

Jeremy Thorpe 1929– : D. E. Butler and Anthony King *The General Election of 1964* (1965)

15 It takes your enemy and your friend, working together, to hurt you to the heart: the one to slander you and the other to get the news to you.

Mark Twain 1835–1910: *Following the Equator* (1897)

16 Unfortunately we have little in common except a mutual knowledge of a story by Charlotte Yonge in which the hero is an albino curate with eyes like rubies. This is cordial, but not enough.

Sylvia Townsend Warner 1893–1978: letter, 31 October 1967

17 He [Bernard Shaw] hasn't an enemy in the world, and none of his friends like him.

Oscar Wilde 1854–1900: George Bernard Shaw *Sixteen Self Sketches* (1949)

18 *I* go to the OP club [a theatrical society where he would have faced a hostile audience]? I should be like a poor lion in a den of Daniels.

Oscar Wilde 1854–1900: Ford Madox Ford *Return to Yesterday* (1931)

Funerals

❝ I have nothing against undertakers personally. **❞**
Jessica Mitford

1 You can't get buried quickly at Bexhill on Sea—it's like getting a table at the Caprice.

David Hare 1947– : Richard Eyre *National Service: Diary of a Decade* (2003)

2 *fax sent to Harry Secombe:*
I hope you go before me because I don't want you singing at my funeral.

Spike Milligan 1918–2002: attributed; in *Daily Telegraph* 28 February 2002

3 I have nothing against undertakers personally. It's just that I wouldn't want one to bury my sister.

Jessica Mitford 1917–96: in *Saturday Review* 1 February 1964

4 *on Teddy Kennedy arriving for Aristotle Onassis's funeral:*
Looking like a priestly hustler peddling indulgences.

Christina Onassis 1950–88: Peter Evans *Nemesis: the True Story of Aristotle* (2004)

The Future ····> Past and Present

66 You can only predict things after they have happened. 99
Eugène Ionesco

1 Fascism is not in itself a new order of society. It is the future refusing to be born.

Aneurin Bevan 1897–1960: Leon Harris *The Fine Art of Political Wit* (1965)

2 That period of time in which our affairs prosper, our friends are true, and our happiness is assured.

Ambrose Bierce 1842–c.1914: *The Cynic's Word Book* (1906)

3 Predictions can be very difficult—especially about the future.

Niels Bohr 1885–1962: attributed

4 Posterity is as likely to be wrong as anybody else.

Heywood Broun 1888–1939: *Sitting on the World* (1924)

5 I never think of the future. It comes soon enough.

Albert Einstein 1879–1955: interview given on the *Belgenland*, December 1930

6 Why should I write for posterity?
What, if I may be free
To ask a ridiculous question,
Has posterity done for me?

E. Y. Harburg 1898–1981: 'Posterity is Right Around the Corner' (1976)

7 This very remarkable man
Commends a most practical plan:
You can do what you want
If you don't think you can't,
So don't think you can't think you can.

Charles Inge 1868–1957: 'On Monsieur Coué' (1928)

8 You can only predict things after they have happened.

Eugène Ionesco 1912–94: *Le Rhinocéros* (1959)

9 Cheer up! the worst is yet to come!

Philander Chase Johnson 1866–1939: in *Everybody's Magazine* May 1920

10 The bridge to the future is the phallus.

D. H. Lawrence 1885–1930: *Sex, Literature and Censorship* (1955)

11 Soon we'll be sliding down the razor-blade of life.

Tom Lehrer 1928– : 'Bright College Days' (c.1960)

12 *supposed opening words of a letter of dismissal to the* Sun's *astrologer:*
As you will no doubt have foreseen . . .

Kelvin Mackenzie 1946– : attributed, probably apocryphal

Gambling

66 All life is 6 to 5 against. 99
Damon Runyon

1 I have a notion that gamblers are as happy as most people—being always excited.

Lord Byron 1788–1824: 'Detached Thoughts' 15 October 1821

2 Rowe's Rule: the odds are five to six that the light at the end of the tunnel is the headlight of an oncoming train.

Paul Dickson 1939– : in *Washingtonian* November 1978

3 Never give a sucker an even break.

W. C. Fields 1880–1946: title of a W. C. Fields film (1941); the catch-phrase (Fields's own) is said to have originated in the musical comedy *Poppy* (1923)

4 GAMBLER: Say, is this a game of chance?
CUTHBERT J. TWILLIE: Not the way I play it.

W. C. Fields 1880–1946: *My Little Chickadee* (1940 film), spoken by W. C. Fields

5 Two-up is Australia's very own way of parting a fool and his money.

Germaine Greer 1939– : in *Observer* 1 August 1982

6 *asked how his bridge-partner should have played a hand:*
Under an assumed name.

George S. Kaufman 1889–1961: Scott Meredith *George S. Kaufman and the Algonquin Round Table* (1974)

7 I long ago come to the conclusion that all life is 6 to 5 against.

Damon Runyon 1884–1946: in *Collier's* 8 September 1934, 'A Nice Price'

Games ····> Sports and Games

Gardens

❝ I'm not a dirt gardener. ❞
Hardy Amies

1 I'm not a dirt gardener. I sit with my walking stick and point things out that need to be done. After many years, the garden is now totally obedient.

Hardy Amies 1909–2003: in *Sunday Times* 11 July 1999

2 Everyone with a garden, however small, should have a few acres of woodland.

Anonymous: saying, sometimes attributed to Lord Rothschild or to an unidentified Director of the Royal Horticultural Society

3 One thimbleful of water every blue moon does not constitute expertise. Otherwise we should all be fellows of the Royal Horticultural Society.

Alan Bennett 1934– : *Getting On* (1972)

4 Laid to lawn? This is laid to adventure playground.

Basil Boothroyd 1910–88: *Let's Move House* (1977)

5 A delectable sward, shaved as close as a bridegroom and looking just as green.

Basil Boothroyd 1910–88: *Let's Move House* (1977)

6 Gr-r-r—there go, my heart's abhorrence!
Water your damned flower-pots, do!
If hate killed men, Brother Lawrence,
God's blood, would not mine kill you!

Robert Browning 1812–89: 'Soliloquy of the Spanish Cloister' (1842)

7 I will keep returning to the virtues of sharp and swift
drainage, whether a plant prefers to be wet or dry . . . I
would have called this book Better Drains, but you would
never have bought it or borrowed it for bedtime.

Robin Lane Fox 1946– : *Better Gardening* (1982)

8 I was dosing the greenfly . . . with that frightfully good
aerosol defoliant that Picarda got the recipe for from some
boffin on the run from Porton Down.

Richard Ingrams 1937– and **John Wells** 1936– : *The Other Half* (1981); 'Dear Bill' letters

9 Mad fools of gardeners go out in the pouring rain
To prove they're Anglo-Saxon
They rarely put their macks on;
Each puts on rubber boots and squelches through moist
terrain,
Then leaves the mud and silt on
The Wilton.

Alan Melville 1910–83: *Gnomes and Gardens* (1983)

10 'I distinguish the picturesque and the beautiful, and I add
to them, in the laying out of the grounds, a third and
distinct character, which I call *unexpectedness*.'
'Pray, Sir,' said Mr Milestone, 'by what name do you
distinguish this character, when a person walks round
the grounds for a second time?'

Thomas Love Peacock 1785–1866: *Headlong Hall* (1816)

11 'All really grim gardeners possess a keen sense of humus.'
Capt. W. D. Pontoon.

W. C. Sellar 1898–1951 and **R. J. Yeatman** 1898–1968: *Garden Rubbish* (1930); chapter heading

12 'A garden is a loathsome thing—so what?' Capt. W. D.
Pontoon.

W. C. Sellar 1898–1951 and **R. J. Yeatman** 1898–1968: *Garden Rubbish* (1930); chapter heading

13 'I want to be a lawn.' Greta Garbo.

W. C. Sellar 1898–1951 and **R. J. Yeatman** 1898–1968: *Garden Rubbish* (1930); chapter heading

14 Perennials are the ones that grow like weeds, biennials are
the ones that die this year instead of next and hardy
annuals are the ones that never come up at all.

Katharine Whitehorn 1926– : *Observations* (1970)

The Generation Gap ····▸ Children, Parents

66 The one war in which everyone changes sides. 99
Cyril Connolly

1 Time is the one thing you have got. If there's one thing I
envy you for, it's not your cool and your easy birds . . . it's
time.

Alan Bennett 1934– : *Getting On* (1972)

2 They're both on drugs, they both detest you, and neither
of them has a job.
on the similarities between teenagers and their grandparents

Jasper Carrott 1945– : in *Observer* 11 January 2004

3 It is the one war in which everyone changes sides.

Cyril Connolly 1903–74: Tom Driberg, speech in House of Commons, 30 October 1959

4 Grown-ups never understand anything for themselves, and it is tiresome for children to be always and forever explaining things to them.

Antoine de Saint-Exupéry 1900–44: *Le Petit Prince* (1943)

5 When I was young, the old regarded me as an outrageous young fellow, and now that I'm old the young regard me as an outrageous old fellow.

Fred Hoyle 1915–2001: in *Scientific American* March 1995

6 What is a teenager in San Francisco to rebel against, for pity's sake? Their parents are all so busy trying to be non-judgemental, it's no wonder they take to dyeing their hair green.

Molly Ivins 1944–2007: in *Dallas Times Herald* 3 February 1987

7 I . . . remember how I regarded adults when I was small. They seemed a grey crew to me, too fond of sitting down, too keen on small talk, too accustomed to having nothing to look forward to.

Ian McEwan 1948– : *Enduring Love* (1998)

8 Remember the battle between the generations twenty-some years ago . . . Well, our parents won. They're out there living the American dream on some damned golf course, and we're stuck with the jobs and haircuts.

P. J. O'Rourke 1947– : *Parliament of Whores* (1991)

9 The young have aspirations that never come to pass, the old have reminiscences of what never happened.

Saki 1870–1916: *Reginald* (1904)

10 The denunciation of the young is a necessary part of the hygiene of older people, and greatly assists the circulation of their blood.

Logan Pearsall Smith 1865–1946: *Afterthoughts* (1931) 'Age and Death'

11 There is more felicity on the far side of baldness than young men can possibly imagine.

Logan Pearsall Smith 1865–1946: *Afterthoughts* (1931) 'Age and Death'

12 When I was a boy of 14, my father was so ignorant I could hardly stand to have the old man around. But when I got to be 21, I was astonished at how much the old man had learned in seven years.

Mark Twain 1835–1910: attributed in *Reader's Digest* September 1939, but not traced in his works

13 Two things my parents did for me as a child stand head and shoulders above what parents usually do for their children. They had me in Egypt and they set me a vivid example of everything I didn't want to be when I grew up.

Jill Tweedie 1936–93: *Eating Children* (1993)

14 When I was your age . . . I had been an inconsolable widower for three months, and was already paying my addresses to your admirable mother.

Oscar Wilde 1854–1900: *An Ideal Husband* (1895)

God ····▸ Religion

66 God will pardon me, it is His trade. 99
Heinrich Heine

1 If it turns out that there is a God, I don't think that he's evil. But the worst that you can say about him is that basically he's an underachiever.

Woody Allen 1935– : *Love and Death* (1975 film)

2 If only God would give me some clear sign! Like making a large deposit in my name at a Swiss bank.

Woody Allen 1935– : 'Selections from the Allen Notebooks' in *New Yorker* 5 November 1973

3 God is silent, now if only we can get Man to shut up.

Woody Allen 1935– : 'Remembering Needleman' (1976)

4 I expect to see God in a five-button suit.

Hardy Amies 1909–2003: quoted in service of thanksgiving Order of Service, 17 July 2003

5 God is not dead but alive and working on a much less ambitious project.

Anonymous: graffito quoted in *Guardian* 26 November 1975

6 Dear Sir,
Your astonishment's odd:
I am always about in the Quad.
And that's why the tree
Will continue to be,
Since observed by
Yours faithfully,
God.

Anonymous: reply to verse by Ronald Knox (see **God** 32); Langford Reed *Complete Limerick Book* (1924)

7 Not odd
Of God:
Goyim
Annoy 'im.

Anonymous: in *Leo Rosten's Book of Laughter* (1986); see **God** 14, 24

8 If I were Her what would really piss me off the worst is that they cannot even get My gender right for Christsakes.

Roseanne Arnold 1953– : *Roseanne* (1990)

9 CLAIRE: How do you know you're . . . God?
EARL OF GURNEY: Simple. When I pray to Him I find I'm talking to myself.

Peter Barnes 1931– : *The Ruling Class* (1969)

10 Let us pray to God . . . the bastard! He doesn't exist!

Samuel Beckett 1906–89: *Endgame* (1958)

11 *replying to the Master of Trinity College Cambridge, H. M. Butler, who in proposing the health of the College had said that 'it was well to remember that, at this moment, both the Sovereign and the Prime Minister are Trinity men':*
The Master should have added that he can go further, for it is obvious that the affairs of the world are built upon the momentous fact that God also is a Trinity man.

Augustine Birrell 1850–1933: Harold Laski, letter to Oliver Wendell Holmes, 4 December 1926

12 *Birrell once saw a man treat George Eliot rudely:*
I sat down in a corner and prayed to God to blast him. God did nothing, and ever since I have been an agnostic.

Augustine Birrell 1850–1933: Harold Laski, letter to Oliver Wendell Holmes, 21 January 1928

13 *Boswell's daughter had concluded that God did not exist:*
I looked into Cambrai's *Education of a Daughter*, hoping to have found some simple argument for the being of God. But it is taken for granted.

James Boswell 1740–95: diary, 20 December 1779

14 But not so odd
As those who choose
A Jewish God,
But spurn the Jews.

Cecil Browne 1932– : reply to verse by William Norman Ewer; see **God** 7, 24

15 An apology for the Devil: It must be remembered that we have only heard one side of the case. God has written all the books.

Samuel Butler 1835–1902: *Notebooks* (1912)

16 God will not always be a Tory.

Lord Byron 1788–1824: letter, 2 February 1821

17 I'm sorry, we don't do God.
when Tony Blair was asked about his Christian faith in an interview for Vanity Fair *magazine*

Alastair Campbell 1957– : in *Daily Telegraph* 5 May 2003

18 He's not the Messiah! He's a very naughty boy!
Brian's mother to his would-be followers

Graham Chapman 1941–89, **John Cleese** 1939– , et al.: *Monty Python's Life of Brian* (1979 film)

19 Isn't God a shit?
while reading the Bible straight through for a bet

Randolph Churchill 1911–68: Evelyn Waugh, diary 11 November 1944

20 Thou shalt have one God only; who
Would be at the expense of two?

Arthur Hugh Clough 1819–61: 'The Latest Decalogue' (1862)

21 Do I believe in God? Let's say we have a working relationship.

Noël Coward 1899–1973: Sheridan Morley *The Quotable Noël Coward* (1999)

22 I don't believe in God because I don't believe in Mother Goose.

Clarence Darrow 1857–1938: speech in Toronto in 1930

23 Our only hope rests on the off-chance that God does exist.

Alice Thomas Ellis 1932–2005: *Unexplained Laughter* (1985)

24 How odd
Of God
To choose
The Jews.

William Norman Ewer 1885–1976: *Week-End Book* (1924); see **God** 7, 14

25 Forgive, O Lord, my little jokes on Thee
And I'll forgive Thy great big one on me.

Robert Frost 1874–1963: 'Cluster of Faith' (1962)

26 Did God who gave us flowers and trees,
Also provide the allergies?

E. Y. Harburg 1898–1981: 'A Nose is a Nose is a Nose' (1965)

27 God will pardon me, it is His trade.

Heinrich Heine 1797–1856: on his deathbed, in Alfred Meissner *Heinrich Heine. Erinnerungen* (1856)

28 The great act of faith is when a man decides he is not God.

Oliver Wendell Holmes Jr. 1841–1935: letter to William James, 24 March 1907

29 *to an undergraduate trying to excuse himself from attendance at early morning chapel on the plea of loss of faith:*
You will find God by tomorrow morning, or leave this college.

Benjamin Jowett 1817–93: Kenneth Rose *Superior Person* (1969)

30 Zeus, 'the God of wine and whoopee'.

Garrison Keillor 1942– : *The Book of Guys* (1994)

31 The peculiar, even unsatisfactory system whereby God never communicated direct with his chosen people but preferred to give the Israelite leaders an off-the-record briefing.

Miles Kington 1941–2008: *Welcome to Kington* (1989)

32 There once was a man who said, 'God
Must think it exceedingly odd
If he finds that this tree
Continues to be
When there's no one about in the Quad.'

Ronald Knox 1888–1957: Langford Reed *Complete Limerick Book* (1924); see **God** 6

33 I don't know why it is that the religious never ascribe common sense to God.

W. Somerset Maugham 1874–1965: *A Writer's Notebook* (1949) written in 1941

34 The chief contribution of Protestantism to human thought is its massive proof that God is a bore.

H. L. Mencken 1880–1956: *Minority Report* (1956)

35 It is impossible to imagine the universe run by a wise, just and omnipotent God, but it is quite easy to imagine it run by a board of gods. If such a board actually exists it operates precisely like the board of a corporation that is losing money.

H. L. Mencken 1880–1956: *Minority Report* (1956)

36 God, to whom, if he existed, I felt I should have nothing very polite to say.

John Mortimer 1923– : *Clinging to the Wreckage* (1982)

37 Satan probably wouldn't have talked so big if God had been his wife.

P. J. O'Rourke 1947– : *Modern Manners* (1984)

38 God is an elderly or, at any rate, middle-aged male, a stern fellow, patriarchal rather than paternal and a great believer in rules and regulations.

P. J. O'Rourke 1947– : *Parliament of Whores* (1991)

39 God, whom you doubtless remember as that quaint old subordinate of General Douglas MacArthur.

S. J. Perelman 1904–79: letter to Mel Elliott, 24 April 1951

40 I've made a lot of mistakes, but, boy, you've made a lot more.
on what he plans to say to God when they meet

Burt Reynolds 1936– : in *Sunday Times* 17 February 2002

41 Those who set out to serve both God and Mammon soon discover that there is no God.

Logan Pearsall Smith 1865–1946: *Afterthoughts* (1931) 'Other People'

42 For ten years of my life, three times a day, I thanked the Lord for what I was about to receive and thanked him again for what I had just received, and then we lost touch—and I suddenly thought, *where is He now?*

Tom Stoppard 1937– : *Where Are They Now?* (1973)

43 Only one thing, is impossible for God: to find any sense in any copyright law on the planet.

Mark Twain 1835–1910: Notebook 23 May 1903

44 God was left out of the Constitution but was furnished a front seat on the coins of the country.

Mark Twain 1835–1910: *Mark Twain in Eruption* (1940)

45 Even God has become female. God is no longer the bearded patriarch in the sky. He has had a sex change and turned into Mother Nature.

Fay Weldon 1931– : in *The Times* 29 August 1998

Golf ····➤ Sports and Games

❝A good walk spoiled.❞
Mark Twain

1 His drive has gone to pieces, largely through having more hinges in it than a sardine tin. But he could always play his iron shots, and his never-ending chatter must be worth at least two holes to his side.

James Agate 1877–1947: diary, 7 August 1938

2 *on the golf course, on being asked by Nancy Cunard, 'What is your handicap?'*
Drink and debauchery.

Lord Castlerosse 1891–1943: Philip Ziegler *Diana Cooper* (1981)

3 QUESTION: What is your handicap?
ANSWER: I'm a colored, one-eyed Jew—do I need anything else?

Sammy Davis Jnr. 1925–90: *Yes I Can* (1965)

4 Of course I want to win it . . . I'm not here to have a good time, nor to keep warm and dry.
while leading the field, in wet weather, during the 1996 PGA Championship

Nick Faldo 1957– : in *Guardian* 25 May 1996

5 One who has to shout 'Fore' when he putts.
definition of a Coarse Golfer

Michael Green 1927– : *The Art of Coarse Golf* (1967)

6 Men who would face torture without a word become blasphemous at the short fourteenth. It is clear that the game of golf may well be included in that category of intolerable provocations which may legally excuse or mitigate behaviour not otherwise excusable.

A. P. Herbert 1890–1971: *Misleading Cases* (1935)

7 If you watch a game, it's fun. If you play it, it's recreation. If you work at it, it's golf.

Bob Hope 1903–2003: in *Reader's Digest* October 1958

8 While tearing off
A game of golf
I may make a play for the caddy.
But when I do
I don't follow through
'Cause my heart belongs to Daddy.

Cole Porter 1891–1964: 'My Heart belongs to Daddy' (1938)

9 I'm playing like Tarzan and scoring like Jane.

Chi Chi Rodrigues 1935– : attributed, 1982

10 Golf is a good walk spoiled.

Mark Twain 1835–1910: Alex Ayres *Greatly Exaggerated: the Wit and Wisdom of Mark Twain* (1988); attributed

11 The uglier a man's legs are, the better he plays golf—it's almost a law.

H. G. Wells 1866–1946: *Bealby* (1915)

12 The least thing upset him on the links. He missed short putts because of the uproar of the butterflies in the adjoining meadows.

P. G. Wodehouse 1881–1975: *The Clicking of Cuthbert* (1922)

13 Golf . . . is the infallible test. The man who can go into a patch of rough alone, with the knowledge that only God is watching him, and play his ball where it lies, is the man who will serve you faithfully and well.

P. G. Wodehouse 1881–1975: *The Clicking of Cuthbert* (1922)

Gossip

❝ What you say about the objects of flattery when they aren't present. **❞**
P. J. O'Rourke

1 I know that's a secret, for it's whispered every where.

William Congreve 1670–1729: *Love for Love* (1695)

2 They come together like the Coroner's Inquest, to sit upon the murdered reputations of the week.

William Congreve 1670–1729: *The Way of the World* (1700)

3 A secret in the Oxford sense: you may tell it to only one person at a time.

Oliver Franks 1905–92: in *Sunday Telegraph* 30 January 1977

4 It's the gossip columnist's business to write about what is none of his business.

Louis Kronenberger 1904– : *The Cart and the Horse* (1964)

5 I hate to spread rumours, but what else can one do with them?

Amanda Lear: in an interview in 1978; Jonathon Green (ed.) *A Dictionary of Contemporary Quotations* (1978)

6 If you haven't got anything good to say about anyone come and sit by me.

Alice Roosevelt Longworth 1884–1980: maxim embroidered on a cushion; Michael Teague *Mrs L: Conversations with Alice Roosevelt Longworth* (1981)

7 She proceeds to dip her little fountain-pen filler into pots of oily venom and to squirt this mixture at all her friends.
   of the society hostess Mrs Ronnie Greville

Harold Nicolson 1886–1968: diary, 20 July 1937

8 Gossip is what you say about the objects of flattery when they aren't present.

P. J. O'Rourke 1947– : *Modern Manners* (1984)

9 You have dished me up, like a savoury omelette, to gratify the appetite of the reading rabble for gossip.

Thomas Love Peacock 1785–1866: *Crotchet Castle* (1831)

10 I hope there's a tinge of disgrace about me. Hopefully, there's one good scandal left in me yet.

Diana Rigg 1938– : in *The Times* 3 May 1999

11 I'm called away by particular business—but I leave my character behind me.

Richard Brinsley Sheridan 1751–1816: *The School for Scandal* (1777)

12 Here is the whole set! a character dead at every word.

Richard Brinsley Sheridan 1751–1816: *The School for Scandal* (1777)

13 It is perfectly monstrous the way people go about, nowadays, saying things against one behind one's back that are absolutely and entirely true.

Oscar Wilde 1854–1900: *A Woman of No Importance* (1893)

14 There is only one thing in the world worse than being talked about, and that is not being talked about.

Oscar Wilde 1854–1900: *The Picture of Dorian Gray* (1891)

Government ····> Democracy, Politics

66 I don't mind how much my Ministers talk, so long as they do what I say. 99
Margaret Thatcher

1 The first requirement of a statesman is that he be dull.

Dean Acheson 1893–1971: in *Observer* 21 June 1970

2 There's only one minister in this department with any brains, and he's mad.
unidentified senior civil servant at the Ministry of Defence to Max Hastings at the time of the first Gulf War, when Tom King was the Secretary of State and Alan Clark a junior Minister

Anonymous: quoted in *Guardian* 24 May 2004

3 There is, in fact, no law or government at all [in Italy]; and it is wonderful how well things go on without them.

Lord Byron 1788–1824: letter, 2 January 1821

4 Democracy means government by the uneducated, while aristocracy means government by the badly educated.

G. K. Chesterton 1874–1936: in *New York Times* 1 February 1931

5 And they that rule in England,
In stately conclaves met,
Alas, alas for England
They have no graves as yet.

G. K. Chesterton 1874–1936: 'Elegy in a Country Churchyard' (1922)

6 Like most Chief Whips he [Michael Jopling] knew who the shits were.

Alan Clark 1928–99: diary, 17 June 1987

7 A wartime Minister of Information is compelled, in the national interest, to such continuous acts of duplicity that even his natural hair must grow to resemble a wig.
of Brendan Bracken

Claud Cockburn 1904–81: *Crossing the Line* (1958)

8 MRS THATCHER: I do not create peers to have them vote against me in the House of Lords.
LORD DENHAM: Prime Minister, even you should know better than to expect me to find you a majority during Gold Cup week.
exchange between the Prime Minister and the Leader of the House of Lords

Lord Denham 1927– : Peter Hennessy *The Prime Minister* (2000)

9 Distrust of authority should be the first civic duty.

Norman Douglas 1868–1952: *An Almanac* October (1941)

10 A woolsack without a Lord Chancellor resplendent in his wig will be like Ascot without the hats and morning coats.

Lord Falkland 1935– : in *Independent* 5 July 2003 'Quotes of the Week'

11 Ambassadors cropped up like hay,
Prime Ministers and such as they
Grew like asparagus in May,
And dukes were three a penny.

W. S. Gilbert 1836–1911: *The Gondoliers* (1889)

12 But the privilege and pleasure
That we treasure beyond measure
Is to run on little errands for the Ministers of State.

W. S. Gilbert 1836–1911: *The Gondoliers* (1889)

13 The House of Peers, throughout the war,
Did nothing in particular,
And did it very well.

W. S. Gilbert 1836–1911: *Iolanthe* (1882)

14 'Do you pray for the senators, Dr Hale?' 'No, I look at the senators and I pray for the country.'

Edward Everett Hale 1822–1909: Van Wyck Brooks *New England Indian Summer* (1940)

15 This we learn from Watergate
That almost any creep'll
Be glad to help the Government
Overthrow the people.

E. Y. Harburg 1898–1981: 'History Lesson' (1976)

16 This high official, all allow,
Is grossly overpaid;
There wasn't any Board, and now
There isn't any Trade.

A. P. Herbert 1890–1971: 'The President of the Board of Trade' (1922)

17 People must not do things for fun. We are not here for fun. There is no reference to fun in any Act of Parliament.

A. P. Herbert 1890–1971: *Uncommon Law* (1935) 'Is it a Free Country?'

18 *Alan Clark, then a Parliamentary Under-Secretary at the Department of Employment, asked Douglas Hogg, then a junior Whip, how he was 'keeping all the new boys in order':*
By offering them your job.

Douglas Hogg 1945– : Alan Clark, diary, 28 July 1983

19 Office hours are from 12 to 1 with an hour off for lunch.
of the US Senate

George S. Kaufman 1889–1961: Howard Teichmann *George S. Kaufman* (1973)

20 We are a government of laws. Any laws some government hack can find to louse up a man who's down.

Murray Kempton 1917– : in *New York Post* 21 December 1955

21 I work for a Government I despise for ends I think criminal.

John Maynard Keynes 1883–1946: letter to Duncan Grant, 15 December 1917

22 How is the world ruled and how do wars start? Diplomats tell lies to journalists and then believe what they read.

Karl Kraus 1874–1936: *Aphorisms and More Aphorisms* (1909)

23 Office tends to confer a dreadful plausibility on even the most negligible of those who hold it.

Mark Lawson: Joe Queenan *Imperial Caddy* (1992); introduction

24 *on suggestions that the US should draft a Constitution for Iraq:*
We might as well give them ours. We aren't using it.

Jay Leno 1950– : attributed; in *Mail on Sunday* 7 September 2003

25 One of these days the people of Louisiana are going to get good government—and they aren't going to like it.

Huey Long 1893–1935: attributed

26 He [Calvin Coolidge] slept more than any other President, whether by day or by night. Nero fiddled, but Coolidge only snored.

H. L. Mencken 1880–1956: in *American Mercury* April 1933

27 The worst government is often the most moral. One composed of cynics is often very tolerant and humane. But when fanatics are on top there is no limit to oppression.

H. L. Mencken 1880–1956: *Minority Report* (1956)

28 There are two reasons for making an appointment. Either there was nobody else; or there *was* somebody else.

Lord Normanbrook 1902–67: Anthony Sampson *The Changing Anatomy of Britain* (1982)

29 *criticism of an opposition motion to declare general warrants illegal, 17 February 1764:*
If I was a Judge, I should pay no more regard to this resolution than to that of a drunken porter.

Fletcher Norton 1716–1789: Horace Walpole *Memoirs of the Reign of George III* (1845)

30 Whatever it is that the government does, sensible Americans would prefer that the government does it to somebody else. This is the idea behind foreign policy.

P. J. O'Rourke 1947– : *Parliament of Whores* (1991)

31 Feeling good about government is like looking on the bright side of any catastrophe. When you quit looking on the bright side, the catastrophe is still there.

P. J. O'Rourke 1947– : *Parliament of Whores* (1991)

32 Are you labouring under the impression that I read these memoranda of yours? I can't even lift them.
to Leon Henderson

Franklin D. Roosevelt 1882–1945: J. K. Galbraith *Ambassador's Journal* (1969)

33 We all know that Prime Ministers are wedded to the truth, but like other married couples they sometimes live apart.

Saki 1870–1916: *The Unbearable Bassington* (1912)

34 Members [of civil service orders] rise from CMG (known sometimes in Whitehall as 'Call Me God') to the KCMG ('Kindly Call Me God') to—for a select few governors and super-ambassadors—the GCMG ('God Calls Me God').

Anthony Sampson 1926–2004: *Anatomy of Britain* (1962)

35 The art of government is the organization of idolatry.

George Bernard Shaw 1856–1950: *Man and Superman* (1903) 'Maxims: Idolatry'

36 A government which robs Peter to pay Paul can always depend on the support of Paul.

George Bernard Shaw 1856–1950: *Everybody's Political What's What?* (1944)

37 Back in the East you can't do much without the right papers, but *with* the right papers you can do *anything*. They *believe* in papers. Papers are power.

Tom Stoppard 1937– : *Neutral Ground* (1983)

38 The House of Lords, an illusion to which I have never been able to subscribe—responsibility without power, the prerogative of the eunuch throughout the ages.

Tom Stoppard 1937– : *Lord Malquist and Mr Moon* (1966)

39 I don't mind how much my Ministers talk, so long as they do what I say.

Margaret Thatcher 1925– : in *Observer* 27 January 1980

40 That loyal retainer of the Chase Manhattan Bank, the American president.

Gore Vidal 1925– : in *Esquire* August 1980

41 *of his first Cabinet meeting as Prime Minister:*
An extraordinary affair. I gave them their orders and they wanted to stay and discuss them.

Duke of Wellington 1769–1852: Peter Hennessy *Whitehall* (1990)

42 I accept that anomalies exist but I would not wish to remove them by taking something from people who already have it.
on the television license fee

William Whitelaw 1918–99: in House of Commons, 1 December 1981

43 Now that the House of Commons is trying to become useful, it does a great deal of harm.

Oscar Wilde 1854–1900: *An Ideal Husband* (1895)

44 *the White House in the time of President Eisenhower:*
The Tomb of the Well-Known Soldier.

Emlyn Williams 1905–87: James Harding *Emlyn Williams* (1987)

Grammar

❝ I was born to be a punctuation vigilante. **❞**
Lynne Truss

1 Sentence structure is innate but whining is acquired.

Woody Allen 1935– : 'Remembering Needleman' (1976)

2 I did spend a lot of time making sure his sentences always had verbs . . . I'm sorry to see he's slipped in recent years.
on teaching English to the young Tony Blair

Eric Anderson 1936– : in *Daily Telegraph* 25 October 1997

3 Would you convey my compliments to the purist who reads your proofs and tell him or her that I write in a sort of broken-down patois which is something like the way a

Raymond Chandler 1888–1959: letter to Edward Weeks, 18 January 1947

Swiss waiter talks, and that when I split an infinitive, God damn it, I split it so it will stay split.

4 The subjunctive mood is in its death throes, and the best thing to do is to put it out of its misery as soon as possible.

W. Somerset Maugham 1874–1965: *A Writer's Notebook* (1949) written in 1941

5 Save the gerund and screw the whale.

Tom Stoppard 1937– : *The Real Thing* (1988 rev. ed.)

6 I was born to be a punctuation vigilante.

Lynne Truss: *Eats, Shoots and Leaves* (2003)

7 *on the first-person plural pronoun:*
Only presidents, editors, and people with tapeworms have the right to use the editorial 'we'.

Mark Twain 1835–1910: attributed

8 Good intentions are invariably ungrammatical.

Oscar Wilde 1854–1900: attributed

Handwriting

66 Like a fly which has been trained at the Russian ballet. 99
James Agate

1 That exquisite handwriting like a fly which has been trained at the Russian ballet.
of George Bernard Shaw's handwriting

James Agate 1877–1947: diary, 22 September 1944

2 I never saw Monty James's writing but doubt whether he can have been more illegible than Lady Colefax: the only hope of deciphering *her* invitations, someone said, was to pin them up on the wall and *run* past them!

Rupert Hart-Davis 1907–99: letter to George Lyttelton, 13 November 1955

3 The dawn of legibility in his handwriting has revealed his utter inability to spell.

Ian Hay 1876–1952: attributed; perhaps used in a dramatization of *The Housemaster* (1938)

4 Did you ever get a letter from Monty James? I once had a note from him inviting us to dinner—we guessed that the time was 8 and not 3, as it appeared to be, but all we could tell about the day was that it was not Wednesday.

George Lyttelton 1883–1962: letter to Rupert Hart-Davis, 9 November 1955

5 *of Foreign Office handwriting:*
Iron railings leaning out of the perpendicular.

Lord Palmerston 1784–1865: J. A. Gere and John Sparrow (eds.) *Geoffrey Madan's Notebooks* (1981)

6 No individual word was decipherable, but, with a bold reader, groups could be made to conform to a scheme based on probabilities.

Edith Œ. Somerville 1858–1949 and **Martin Ross** 1862–1915: *In Mr Knox's Country* (1915)

7 I know that handwriting . . . I remember it perfectly. The ten commandments in every stroke of the pen, and the moral law all over the page.

Oscar Wilde 1854–1900: *An Ideal Husband* (1895)

8 As regards the mode of copying: of course it is too long for any amanuensis to attempt: and your own handwriting, dear Robbie, in your last letter seems specially designed to remind me that the task is not to be yours.

Oscar Wilde 1854–1900: letter to Robert Ross from Reading Prison, 1 April 1897

Happiness ····▸ Hope and Despair, Satisfaction and Discontent

❝ A lifetime of happiness! No man alive could bear it. ❞
George Bernard Shaw

---

1 No pleasure is worth giving up for the sake of two more years in a geriatric home in Weston-super-Mare.

Kingsley Amis 1922–95: in *The Times* 21 June 1994; attributed

2 Happy as a bastard on Father's Day.
Australian expression

Anonymous: Richard Eyre *National Service: Diary of a Decade* (2003)

3 You have flair . . . It's handed out at birth . . . And as always happens in these cases, it's always given to the very people who in my opinion do least to earn it. It's taken me forty-two years to think of that and I'm very depressed.

Alan Ayckbourn 1939– : *Joking Apart* (1979)

4 When people say, 'You're breaking my heart,' they do in fact usually mean that you're breaking their genitals.

Jeffrey Bernard 1932–97: in *Spectator* 31 May 1986

5 Let us have wine and women, mirth and laughter, Sermons and soda-water the day after.

Lord Byron 1788–1824: *Don Juan* (1819–24)

6 MEDVEDENKO: Why do you wear black all the time?
MASHA: I'm in mourning for my life, I'm unhappy.

Anton Chekhov 1860–1904: *The Seagull* (1896)

7 When constabulary duty's to be done, A policeman's lot is not a happy one.

W. S. Gilbert 1836–1911: *The Pirates of Penzance* (1879)

8 I can imagine no more comfortable frame of mind for the conduct of life than a humorous resignation.

W. Somerset Maugham 1874–1965: *A Writer's Notebook* (1949) written in 1903

9 The fact that I have no remedy for the sorrows of the world is no reason for my accepting yours. It simply supports the strong probability that yours is a fake.

H. L. Mencken 1880–1956: *Minority Report* (1956)

10 I told him that if somebody liked to dress up in chamois leather and be stung by wasps, I really couldn't see why one should stop him.
recalling a conversation with Lord Longford on pornography

Robert Morley 1908–92: Kenneth Tynan diary, 31 March 1975

11 He's simply got the instinct for being unhappy highly developed.

Saki 1870–1916: *Chronicles of Clovis* (1911)

12 But a lifetime of happiness! No man alive could bear it: it would be hell on earth.

George Bernard Shaw 1856–1950: *Man and Superman* (1903)

13 There are two tragedies in life. One is not to get your heart's desire. The other is to get it.

George Bernard Shaw 1856–1950: *Man and Superman* (1903)

14 MRS BAKER is a woman who has managed to find a little misery in the best of things. Sorrow and trouble are the only things that can make her happy.

Neil Simon 1927– : *Come Blow Your Horn* (1961)

15 Life would be very pleasant if it were not for its enjoyments.

R. S. Surtees 1805–64: *Mr Facey Romford's Hounds* (1865)

16 Have some fun. Buy a big gun.

Richard Thomas and **Stewart Lee**:
Jerry Springer—the Opera (2003)

17 Let us all be happy, and live within our means, even if we have to borrer the money to do it with.

Artemus Ward 1834–67: *Artemus Ward in London* (1867)

18 A cigarette is the perfect type of a perfect pleasure. It is exquisite, and it leaves one unsatisfied. What more can one want?

Oscar Wilde 1854–1900: *The Picture of Dorian Gray* (1891)

19 All the things I really like to do are either illegal, immoral, or fattening.

Alexander Woollcott 1887–1943: R. E. Drennan *Wit's End* (1973)

Health ····➤ Medicine, Sickness

" The two best exercises in the world are making love and dancing. **"**
Barbara Cartland

---

1 I feel as young as I ever did, apart from the occasional heart attack.

Robert Benchley 1889–1945: attributed

2 The two best exercises in the world are making love and dancing but a simple one is to stand on tiptoe.

Barbara Cartland 1901–2000: in 1972, attributed; in *Guardian* 22 May 2000

3 In the face of such overwhelming statistical possibilities, hypochondria has always seemed to me to be the only rational position to take on life.

John Diamond: *C: Because Cowards Get Cancer Too* (1998)

4 Exercise is the yuppie version of bulimia.

Barbara Ehrenreich 1941– : *The Worst Years of Our Lives* (1991) 'Food Worship'

5 *on Warren Clarke's portrayal of Hill's Superintendent Dalziel:*
REGINALD HILL: For the sake of my art you should be seven stones heavier.
WARREN CLARKE: For the sake of my heart, I shouldn't.

Reginald Hill 1936– : in *Mail on Sunday* 30 July 2000

6 Aromatherapy is like going into the countryside and smelling flowers. It should be available in Parliament. They already have it in some mental hospitals.

Simon Hughes 1951– : in *Independent* 24 January 1998

7 It's no longer a question of staying healthy. It's a question of finding a sickness you like.

Jackie Mason 1934– : attributed

8 My uterine contractions have been bogus for sometime.

Joe Orton 1933–67: *What the Butler Saw* (1969)

9 The only exercise I take is walking behind the coffins of friends who took exercise.

Peter O'Toole 1932– : in *Mail on Sunday* 27 December 1998 'Quotes of the Year'

10 Avoid running at all times.

Leroy ('Satchel') Paige 1906–82: *How To Stay Young* (1953)

11 At 70, I'm in fine fettle for my age, sleep like a babe and feel around 12. The secret? Lots of meat, drink and cigarettes and not giving in to things.

Jennifer Paterson 1928–99: in *Daily Mail* 18 August 1998

12 If God had wanted us to bend over, He would have put diamonds on the floor.

Joan Rivers 1933– : attributed

13 I try to keep fit. I've got these parallel bars at home. I run at them and try to buy a drink from both of them.

Arthur Smith 1954– : attributed

14 When people discussed tonics, pick-me-ups after a severe illness, she kept to herself the prescription of a quick dip in bed with someone you liked but were not in love with. A shock of sexual astonishment which could make you feel astonishingly well and high spirited.

Mary Wesley 1912– : *Not That Sort of Girl* (1987)

Heaven and Hell

❝ I have friends in both places. ❞
Mark Twain

1 *of Lord Curzon, who at the age of thirty-nine had been created Viceroy of India:*
For all the rest of his life Curzon was influenced by his sudden journey to heaven at the age of thirty-nine, and then by his return seven years later to earth, for the remainder of his mortal existence.

Lord Beaverbrook 1879–1964: *Men and Power* (1956)

2 All are inclined to believe what they covet, from a lottery-ticket up to a passport to Paradise,—in which, from description, I see nothing very tempting.

Lord Byron 1788–1824: diary 27 November 1813

3 I always say, as you know, that if my fellow citizens want to go to Hell I will help them. It's my job.

Oliver Wendell Holmes Jr. 1841–1935: letter to Harold Laski, 4 March 1920

4 The Devil himself had probably re-designed Hell in the light of information he had gained from observing airport layouts.

Anthony Price 1928– : *The Memory Trap* (1989)

5 My idea of heaven is, eating *pâté de foie gras* to the sound of trumpets.

Sydney Smith 1771–1845: view ascribed by Smith to his friend Henry Luttrell; Peter Virgin *Sydney Smith* (1994)

6 I have friends in both places.

Mark Twain 1835–1910: Archibald Henderson *Mark Twain* (1911)

7 If Max [Beaverbrook] gets to Heaven he won't last long. He will be chucked out for trying to pull off a merger between Heaven and Hell . . . after having secured a controlling interest in key subsidiary companies in both places, of course.

H. G. Wells 1866–1946: A. J. P. Taylor *Beaverbrook* (1972)

History

66 History is more or less bunk. 99
Henry Ford

1 I want to see the hand of history on his collar.
   woman queueing to see the Prime Minister at the Hutton Inquiry
   Anonymous: in *Mail on Sunday* 31 August 2003

2 History is a commentary on the various and continuing incapabilities of men. What is history? History is women following behind with the buckets.
   Alan Bennett 1934– : *The History Boys* (2004)

3 An account, mostly false, of events, mostly unimportant, which are brought about by rulers, mostly knaves, and soldiers, mostly fools.
   definition of history
   Ambrose Bierce 1842–c.1914: *The Cynic's Word Book* (1906)

4 History repeats itself; historians repeat one other.
   Rupert Brooke 1887–1915: letter to Geoffrey Keynes, 4 June 1906

5 People who make history know nothing about history. You can see that in the sort of history they make.
   G. K. Chesterton 1874–1936: J. A. Gere and John Sparrow (eds.) *Geoffrey Madan's Notebooks* (1981)

6 History teaches us that men and nations behave wisely once they have exhausted all other alternatives.
   Abba Eban 1915– : speech in London 16 December 1970

7 History is more or less bunk.
   Henry Ford 1863–1947: in *Chicago Tribune* 25 May 1916

8 History is not what you thought. *It is what you can remember.*
   W. C. Sellar 1898–1951 and **R. J. Yeatman** 1898–1968: *1066 and All That* (1930) 'Compulsory Preface'

9 AMERICA was thus clearly top nation, and History came to a .
   W. C. Sellar 1898–1951 and **R. J. Yeatman** 1898–1968: *1066 and All That* (1930)

10 SWINDON: What will history say?
   BURGOYNE: History, sir, will tell lies as usual.
   George Bernard Shaw 1856–1950: *The Devil's Disciple* (1901)

11 Like most of those who study history, he [Napoleon III] learned from the mistakes of the past how to make new ones.
   A. J. P. Taylor 1906–90: in *Listener* 6 June 1963

12 History gets thicker as it approaches recent times.
   A. J. P. Taylor 1906–90: *English History 1914–45* (1965), bibliography

13 *on being asked what would have happened in 1963, had Khrushchev and not Kennedy been assassinated:*
   With history one can never be certain, but I think I can safely say that Aristotle Onassis would not have married Mrs Khrushchev.
   Gore Vidal 1925– : in *Sunday Times* 4 June 1989

14 Thanks to modern technology . . . history now comes equipped with a fast-forward button.
   Gore Vidal 1925– : *Screening History* (1992)

15 Human history becomes more and more a race between education and catastrophe.
   H. G. Wells 1866–1946: *Outline of History* (1920)

16 The one duty we owe to history is to rewrite it.

Oscar Wilde 1854–1900: *Intentions* (1891) 'The Critic as Artist' pt. 1

17 History started badly and hav been geting steadily worse.

Geoffrey Willans 1911–58 and **Ronald Searle** 1920– : *Down with Skool!* (1953)

Holidays

66 Sand in the porridge and sand in the bed. **99**
Noël Coward

1 The sort of place to send your mother-in-law for a month, all expenses paid.
of Pakistan, in a BBC Radio interview, 17 March 1984; in April 1984 he was fined £1000 for making the remark by the Test and County Cricket Board

Ian Botham 1955– : in *The Times* 20 March 1984

2 I would love . . . a one-year break doing absolutely nothing. Now whether, as I say to my friends, I will take to the gin bottle at 11 o'clock in the morning, and drink myself or smoke myself to death, I don't know—but I'd love to find out.

Gay Byrne 1934– : in *Irish Post* 16 May 1998

3 What kind of holiday can you take when you live in almost continual sunshine in an olive grove in the mountains, which is only twenty minutes away from the beaches and the sea?

Patrick Campbell 1913–80: *Gullible Travels* (1969)

4 There's sand in the porridge and sand in the bed, And if this is pleasure we'd rather be dead.

Noël Coward 1899–1973: 'The English Lido' (1928)

5 Cannot avoid contrasting deliriously rapid flight of time when on a holiday with very much slower passage of days, and even hours, in other and more familiar surroundings.

E. M. Delafield 1890–1943: *The Diary of a Provincial Lady* (1930)

6 It will give the public a rest as much it will reward his family.
on the question of Tony Blair's taking paternity leave

Frank Field 1942– : in *Observer* 14 May 2000 'They said what . . . ?'

7 I don't think we can do better than 'Good old Broadstairs'.

George Grossmith 1847–1912 and **Weedon Grossmith** 1854–1919: *The Diary of a Nobody* (1894)

8 I suppose we all have our recollections of our earlier holidays, all bristling with horror.

Flann O'Brien 1911–66: *Myles Away from Dublin* (1990)

9 I like to have exciting evenings on holiday, because after you've spent 8 hours reading on the beach you don't feel like turning in early with a good book.

Arthur Smith 1954– : *The Live Bed Show* (1995)

10 A weekend in the country
With the panting
And the yawns
With the crickets and the pheasants
And the orchards and the hay,

Stephen Sondheim 1930– : 'A Weekend in the Country' (1972)

With the servants and the peasants,
We'll be laying our plans
While we're playing croquet
For a weekend in the country
So inactive one has to lie down.
A weekend in the country
Where we're twice as upset
As in town.

11 The Victorians had not been anxious to go away for the weekend. The Edwardians, on the contrary, were nomadic.

T. H. White 1906–64: *Farewell Victoria* (1933)

12 I wish I'd given Spain a miss this year—I nearly plumped for a crochet week in Rhyl. I was going to have a stab at a batwing blouson.

Victoria Wood 1953– : *Mens Sana in Thingummy Doodah* (1990)

Hollywood ····> The Cinema, Film

❝ A trip through a sewer in a glass-bottomed boat. ❞
Wilson Mizner

1 Hollywood is a place where people from Iowa mistake each other for stars.

Fred Allen 1894–1956: Maurice Zolotow *No People like Show People* (1951)

2 I'm not very keen on Hollywood. I'd rather have a nice cup of cocoa really.

Noël Coward 1899–1973: letter to his mother, 1937; Cole Lesley *The Life of Noel Coward* (1976)

3 Remember all the time . . . that Hollywood is an Oriental city. As long as you do that you might survive.

Olivia De Havilland 1916– : Dirk Bogarde *Snakes and Ladders* (1978)

4 Hollywood is bounded on the north, south, east, and west by agents.

William Fadiman: *Hollywood Now* (1972)

5 Working in Hollywood does give one a certain expertise in the field of prostitution.

Jane Fonda 1937– : J. R. Colombo *Wit and Wisdom of the Moviemakers* (1979)

6 The only place you can wake up in the morning and hear the birds coughing in the trees.

Joe Frisco: attributed

7 Hollywood is strange when you're in trouble. Everyone is afraid it's contagious.

Judy Garland 1922–69: Simon Rose *Classic Film Guide* (1995)

8 The most beautiful slave-quarters in the world.

Moss Hart 1904–61: attributed

9 There's lots of nice guys walking around Hollywood, but they ain't eating.

Henry Hathaway 1898–1985: in *The Times* 22 March 1969

10 Every country gets the circus it deserves. Spain gets bullfights. Italy gets the Catholic Church. America Hollywood.

Erica Jong 1942– : *How to Save Your Own Life* (1977)

11 Behind the phoney tinsel of Hollywood lies the real tinsel.

Oscar Levant 1906–72: Laurence J. Peter (ed.) *Quotations for our Time* (1977)

12 Being a writer in Hollywood is like going into Hitler's Eagle's Nest with a great idea for a bar-mitzvah.

David Mamet 1947– : in *Sunday Times* 1 August 2004

13 Hooray for Hollywood,
Where you're terrific if you're even good!

Johnny Mercer 1909–76: 'Hooray for Hollywood' (*Hollywood Hotel*, 1938 musical)

14 A trip through a sewer in a glass-bottomed boat.

Wilson Mizner 1876–1933: Alva Johnston *The Legendary Mizners* (1953), reworked by Mayor Jimmy Walker into 'A reformer is a guy who rides through a sewer in a glass-bottomed boat'

15 Hollywood is a place where they'll pay you a thousand dollars for a kiss and fifty cents for your soul.

Marilyn Monroe 1926–62: J. R. Colombo *Wit and Wisdom of the Moviemakers* (1979)

16 Hollywood, the Versailles of Los Angeles.

Jan Morris 1926– : Destinations (1980)

17 The only 'ism' in Hollywood is plagiarism.

Dorothy Parker 1893–1967: attributed

18 Oh, it's all right. You make a little money and get caught up on your debts. We're up to 1912 now . . .

Dorothy Parker 1893–1967: Max Wilk *The Wit and Wisdom of Hollywood* (1972)

19 Hollywood money isn't money. It's congealed snow, melts in your hand, and there you are.

Dorothy Parker 1893–1967: Malcolm Cowley (ed.) *Writers at Work* 1st Series (1958)

20 Hollywood: They know only one word of more than one syllable here, and that is fillum.

Louis Sherwin: Laurence J. Peter (ed.) *Quotations for our Time* (1977)

21 This is the biggest electric train any boy ever had!

Orson Welles 1915–85: Leo Rosten *Hollywood* (1941)

The Home ····> Housework

66 All I need is room enough to lay a hat and a few friends. 99
Dorothy Parker

1 Here was situated the famous smoking-parlour, with rushes on the floor, and a dresser ranged with pewter tankards, and leaded lattice-windows of glass so antique that it was practically impossible to see out of them.

E. F. Benson 1867–1940: *Queen Lucia* (1920)

2 The premises are so delightfully extensive, that two people might live together without ever seeing, hearing, or meeting.
of Newstead Abbey

Lord Byron 1788–1824: letter 30 (31?) August 1811

3 They tell me there is no more toilet paper in the house. How can I be expected to act a romantic part and remember to order TOILET PAPER!

Mrs Patrick Campbell 1865–1940: Margot Peters *Mrs Pat* (1984)

4 My old man said, 'Follow the van,
  Don't dilly-dally on the way!'
  Off went the cart with the home packed in it,
  I walked behind with my old cock linnet.
  But I dillied and dallied, dallied and dillied,
  Lost the van and don't know where to roam.

Charles Collins: 'Don't Dilly-Dally on the Way' (1919, with Fred Leigh); popularized by Marie Lloyd

5 Love and a cottage! Eh, Fanny! Ah, give me indifference
  and a coach and six!

George Colman, the Elder 1732–94 and **David Garrick** 1717–79: *The Clandestine Marriage* (1766)

6 Tho' the pipes that supply the bathroom burst
  And the lavatory makes you fear the worst,
  It was used by Charles the First
  Quite informally,
  And later by George the Fourth
  On a journey North.

Noël Coward 1899–1973: 'The Stately Homes of England' (1938)

7 Though the fact that they have to be rebuilt
  And frequently mortgaged to the hilt
  Is inclined to take the gilt
  Off the gingerbread,
  And certainly damps the fun
  Of the eldest son.

Noël Coward 1899–1973: 'The Stately Homes of England' (1938)

8 Thus first necessity invented stools,
  Convenience next suggested elbow-chairs,
  And luxury the accomplished sofa last.

William Cowper 1731–1800: *The Task* (1785)

9 Mrs Crupp had indignantly assured him that there wasn't
  room to swing a cat there; but, as Mr Dick justly observed
  to me, sitting down on the foot of the bed, nursing his leg,
  'You know, Trotwood, I don't want to swing a cat. I never
  do swing a cat. Therefore, what does that signify to *me*!'

Charles Dickens 1812–70: *David Copperfield* (1850)

10 *congratulating Margaret Thatcher on 10 Downing Street:*
   I never seem to meet a good estate agent.

John Gielgud 1904–2000: Sheridan Morley *Asking for Trouble* (2002)

11 There's no greater bliss in life than when the plumber
   eventually comes to unblock your drains. No writer can
   give that sort of pleasure.

Victoria Glendinning 1937– : in *Observer* 3 January 1993

12 What's the good of a home if you are never in it?

George Grossmith 1847–1912 and **Weedon Grossmith** 1854–1919: *The Diary of a Nobody* (1894)

13 I want a house that has got over all its troubles; I don't
   want to spend the rest of my life bringing up a young and
   inexperienced house.

Jerome K. Jerome 1859–1927: *They and I* (1909)

14 Although very few people are actually called upon to live
   in palaces a very large number are unwilling to admit the
   fact.

Osbert Lancaster 1908–80: *Homes Sweet Homes* (1939)

15 All I need is room enough to lay a hat and a few friends.

Dorothy Parker 1893–1967: R. E. Drennan *Wit's End* (1973)

16 *on a guest who had outstayed his welcome:*
   There is a mad artist named Inchbold,
   With whom you must be at a pinch bold:
   Or you may as well score
   The brass plate on your door
   With the name of J. W. Inchbold.

Dante Gabriel Rossetti 1828–82: limerick written c.1870

17 Home life as we understand it is no more natural to us than a cage is natural to a cockatoo.

George Bernard Shaw 1856–1950: *Getting Married* (1911) preface 'Hearth and Home'

18 *on being encountered drinking a glass of wine in the street, while watching his theatre, the Drury Lane, burn down, on 24 February 1809:*
A man may surely be allowed to take a glass of wine by his own fireside.

Richard Brinsley Sheridan 1751–1816: T. Moore *Life of Sheridan* (1825)

19 Is that bottle just going to sit up there or are you going to turn it into a lamp?

Neil Simon 1927– : *Last of the Red Hot Lovers* (1970)

20 It looks different when you're sober. I thought I had twice as much furniture.

Neil Simon 1927– : *The Gingerbread Lady* (1970)

21 I have heard of a man who had a mind to sell his house, and therefore carried a piece of brick in his pocket, which he shewed as a pattern to encourage purchasers.

Jonathan Swift 1667–1745: *The Drapier's Letters* (1724)

22 *asked who wore the trousers at home:*
I do. I wear the trousers. And I wash and iron them, too.

Denis Thatcher 1915–2003: attributed; in *The Times* 27 June 2003

23 The national sport of England is obstacle racing. People fill their rooms with useless and cumbersome furniture, and spend the rest of their lives in trying to dodge it.

Herbert Beerbohm Tree 1852–1917: Hesketh Pearson *Beerbohm Tree* (1956)

24 I am returned to my own Lares and Penates—to my dogs and cats.

Horace Walpole 1717–97: letter, 25 October 1775

Honours ····▷ Awards

❝ You should always accept because of the pain it brings to your enemies. ❞
Maurice Bowra

1 Gongs and medals and ribbons really belong on a Christmas tree.

J. G. Ballard 1930– : in *Independent* 14 July 2004

2 You should always accept because of the pain it brings to your enemies.

Maurice Bowra 1898–1971: quoted by Peter Hennessy in evidence to the House of Commons Select Committee on Public Administration, 11 March 2004

3 Had they sent me ¼ lb of good tobacco, the addition to my happiness had probably been suitabler and greater!
on being awarded the Prussian Order of Merit

Thomas Carlyle 1795–1881: letter to his brother John Carlyle, 14 February 1874

4 Now Mr Schlesinger, we must try and get this *straight*.
adjusting the ribbon of a CBE round the sizeable neck of John Schlesinger; he took it as a tactful recognition of his sexual orientation

Elizabeth II 1926– : Alan Bennett diary 2003, in *London Review of Books* 8 January 2004

5 I feel very humble. But I think I have the strength of character to fight it.
on receiving a Congressional Gold Medal from President Kennedy

Bob Hope 1903–2003: attributed; in *The Times* 29 July 2003

6 *on his acceptance of an OBE:*
Someone had to accept one, otherwise there would be shelves full of them left.

Roy Hudd 1936– : in *Sunday Times* 4 January 2004

7 I can't see the sense in it really. It makes me a Commander of the British Empire. They might as well make me a Commander of Milton Keynes—at least that exists.
on receiving an honorary CBE in 1992

Spike Milligan 1918–2002: attributed; in *Daily Telegraph* 28 February 2002

8 In the end I accepted the honour, because during dinner Venables told me, that, if I became Poet Laureate, I should always when I dined out be offered the liver-wing of a fowl.
on being made Poet Laureate in 1850

Alfred, Lord Tennyson 1809–92: in *Alfred Lord Tennyson: A Memoir by his Son* (1897) vol. 1

9 *congratulated on being awarded a baronetcy:*
Thanks—but more importantly than that, I have just been elected a member of Sunningdale Golf Club.

Denis Thatcher 1915–2003: attributed; in *The Times* 27 June 2003

10 The cross of the Legion of Honour has been conferred upon me. However, few escape that distinction.

Mark Twain 1835–1910: *A Tramp Abroad* (1880)

11 People fail you, children disappoint you, thieves break in, moths corrupt, but an OBE goes on for ever.

Fay Weldon 1931– : *Praxis* (1978)

Hope and Despair ····▷ Happiness, Satisfaction and Discontent

❝There are bad times just around the corner.❞
Noël Coward

1 *seeing a commemorative stone engraved 'Laid by the Poet Laureate' (John Masefield):*
Every nice girl's ambition.

John Betjeman 1906–84: Bevis Hillier *Betjeman: the Bonus of Laughter* (2004)

2 A minor form of despair, disguised as a virtue.
definition of patience

Ambrose Bierce 1842–c.1914: *The Devil's Dictionary* (1911)

3 We seek to find peace of mind in the word, the formula, the ritual. The hope is an illusion.

Benjamin N. Cardozo 1870–1938: *The Growth of the Law* (1924)

4 There are bad times just around the corner,
There are dark clouds travelling through the sky
And it's no good whining
About a silver lining
For we know from experience that they won't roll by,
With a scowl and a frown
We'll keep our peckers down
And prepare for depression and doom and dread,
We're going to unpack our troubles from our old kitbag
And wait until we drop down dead.

Noël Coward 1899–1973: 'There are Bad Times Just Around the Corner' (1953)

5 I have known him come home to supper with a flood of tears, and a declaration that nothing was now left but a jail; and go to bed making a calculation of the expense of putting bow-windows to the house, 'in case anything turned up,' which was his favourite expression.

Charles Dickens 1812–70: *David Copperfield* (1850)

6 but wotthehell
archy wotthehell
it s cheerio
my deario that
pulls a lady through.

Don Marquis 1878–1937: *archy and mehitabel* (1927) 'cheerio my deario'

7 but wotthehell archy wotthehell
jamais triste archy jamais triste
that is my motto.

Don Marquis 1878–1937: *archy and mehitabel* (1927) 'mehitabel sees paris'

8 When I am sad and weary
When I think all hope has gone
When I walk along High Holborn
I think of you with nothing on.

Adrian Mitchell 1932– : 'Celia, Celia'

9 'Blessed is the man who expects nothing, for he shall never be disappointed' was the ninth beatitude.

Alexander Pope 1688–1744: letter to Fortescue, 23 September 1725

10 Why, even the janitor's wife
Has a perfectly good love life
And here am I
Facing tomorrow
Alone with my sorrow
Down in the depths on the ninetieth floor.

Cole Porter 1891–1964: 'Down in the Depths' (1936)

11 'Do you know what a pessimist is?' 'A man who thinks everybody is as nasty as himself, and hates them for it.'

George Bernard Shaw 1856–1950: *An Unsocial Socialist* (1887)

Hospitality

❝ A host is like a general: misfortunes often reveal his genius. ❞
Horace

1 *opening a lecture at Strathclyde University, immediately after her husband's trial for perjury; the audience included many journalists:*
Good morning, and a special welcome to those of you who are new to the field of quantum solar energy conversion.

Mary Archer 1944– : in *Sunday Times* 29 July 2001

2 *an assiduous hostess:*
She arranged that motor-cars, golf-caddies and fishing gillies were lurking like wild beasts round the corner, ready to pounce.

E. F. Benson 1867–1940: *The Climber* (1908)

3 *instructions to strangers trying to find their way around Drumlanrig Castle:*
Turn right at the Rembrandt then left at the Leonardo.

Jane, Duchess of Buccleuch and Queensberry: attributed; in *Mail on Sunday* 31 August 2003

4 Hospitality consists in a little fire, a little food, and an immense quiet.

Ralph Waldo Emerson 1803–82: journal, 1865

5 Here you are again, older faces and younger clothes.
a famous hostess's habitual greeting to guests

Mamie Stuyvesant Fish 1853–1915: attributed

6 A host is like a general: misfortunes often reveal his genius.

Horace 65–8 BC: *Satires* bk 2

7 *when visiting Chequers:*
Come on, young Blair, where's the whisky?

Derry Irvine 1940– : attributed;
Anthony Howard in *The Times* 10
June 2003

Hotels

❛❛ There is a French widow in every bedroom. ❜❜
Gerard Hoffnung

1 All through the night there's a friendly receptionist
Welcome to Holiday Inn.

Dorothy Fields 1905–74: 'Welcome
to Holiday Inn' (1973)

2 The cushions had cushions, the curtains looked like
duvets.
of a typical English country house hotel

A. A. Gill 1954– : *Starcrossed* (1999)

3 The chambermaid is very kind,
She always thinks we're so refined.
Of course, she's deaf and dumb and blind—
No fools we—
In our little den of iniquity.

Lorenz Hart 1895–1943: 'In Our Little
Den of Iniquity' (*Pal Joey*, 1940
musical)

4 *supposedly quoting a letter from a Tyrolean landlord:*
Standing among savage scenery, the hotel offers
stupendous revelations. There is a French widow in every
bedroom, affording delightful prospects.

Gerard Hoffnung 1925–59: speech at
the Oxford Union, 4 December 1958

5 We were served the sort of dinner you might get in a
remarkably well-run open prison.

Alexei Sayle 1952– : *Overtaken*
(2003)

6 The great advantage of a hotel is that it's a refuge from
home life.

George Bernard Shaw 1856–1950:
You Never Can Tell (1898)

Housework

❛❛ It expands to fill the time available plus half an hour. ❜❜
Shirley Conran

1 All the house-parlourmaids have evaporated into thin air!
without a word. Ethics and manners have vanished in this
particular pursuit.

Violet Bonham Carter 1887–1969:
Diaries and Letters, 1946–1969
(2000)

2 Conran's Law of Housework—it expands to fill the time
available plus half an hour.

Shirley Conran 1932– : *Superwoman
2* (1977)

3 *of Greta Garbo:*
A rather boring old Swede, but luckily she loves doing the
washing-up.

Gladys Cooper 1888–1971: Sheridan
Morley *Asking for Trouble* (2002)

4 There was no need to do any housework at all. After the
first four years the dirt doesn't get any worse.

Quentin Crisp 1908–99: *The Naked
Civil Servant* (1968)

5 I hate housework! You make the beds, you do the dishes—
and six months later you have to start all over again.

Joan Rivers 1933– : attributed, 1984

6 Hatred of domestic work is a natural and admirable result of civilization.

Rebecca West 1892–1983: in *The Freewoman* 6 June 1912

7 Everything's getting on top of me. I can't switch off. I've got a self-cleaning oven—I have to get up in the night to see if it's doing it.

Victoria Wood 1953– : *Mens Sana in Thingummy Doodah* (1990)

The Human Race

66 Man is the Only Animal that Blushes. Or needs to. 99
Mark Twain

1 Well, of course, people are only human . . . But it really does not seem much for them to be.

Ivy Compton-Burnett 1884–1969: *A Family and a Fortune* (1939)

2 They are usually a mistake.
of other people

Quentin Crisp 1908–99: in *Spectator* 20 November 1999

3 I got disappointed in human nature as well and gave it up because I found it too much like my own.

J. P. Donleavy 1926– : *A Fairy Tale of New York* (1973)

4 Certainty generally is illusion, and repose is not the destiny of man.

Oliver Wendell Holmes Jr. 1841–1935: 'The Path of the Law' (1897)

5 That habit of treading in ruts and trooping in companies which men share with sheep.

A. E. Housman 1859–1936: 'The Editing of Juvenal' (1905)

6 Men have an extraordinarily erroneous opinion of their position in nature; and the error is ineradicable.

W. Somerset Maugham 1874–1965: *A Writer's Notebook* (1949) written in 1896

7 Man is one of the toughest of animated creatures. Only the anthrax bacillus can stand so unfavourable an environment for so long a time.

H. L. Mencken 1880–1956: *Minority Report* (1956)

8 I wish I loved the Human Race;
I wish I loved its silly face;
I wish I liked the way it walks;
I wish I liked the way it talks;
And when I'm introduced to one
I wish I thought *What Jolly Fun!*

Walter Raleigh 1861–1922: 'Wishes of an Elderly Man' (1923)

9 I'm dealing in rock'n'roll. I'm, like, I'm not a bona fide human being.

Phil Spector 1940– : attributed

10 He's an animal lover . . . People he don't like so much.

Tom Stoppard 1937– : *Neutral Ground* (1983)

11 The only man who wasn't spoilt by being lionized was Daniel.

Herbert Beerbohm Tree 1852–1917: Hesketh Pearson *Beerbohm Tree* (1956)

12 Man is the Only Animal that Blushes. Or needs to.

Mark Twain 1835–1910: *Following the Equator* (1897)

13 Reality is something the human race doesn't handle very well.

Gore Vidal 1925– : in *Radio Times* 3 January 1990

14 This world is a comedy to those that think, a tragedy to those that feel.

Horace Walpole 1717–97: letter to Anne, Countess of Upper Ossory, 16 August 1776

15 'Have you ever seen Spode eat asparagus?'
'No.'
'Revolting. It alters one's whole conception of Man as Nature's last word.'

P. G. Wodehouse 1881–1975: *The Code of the Woosters* (1938)

Humility

❝ If you've got an opinion, why be humble about it? **❞**
Joan Baez

1 I've never had a humble opinion. If you've got an opinion, why be humble about it?

Joan Baez 1941– : in *Observer* 29 February 2004

2 In 1969 I published a small book on Humility. It was a pioneering work which has not, to my knowledge, been superseded.

Lord Longford 1905–2001: in *The Tablet* 22 January 1994

3 *Wayne and Garth meet Alice Cooper:*
We're not worthy! We're not worthy!

Mike Myers 1963– : *Wayne's World* (1992 film)

4 Do you imagine I am going to pronounce the name of my beautiful theatre in a hired cab?
refusing to give directions to His Majesty's theatre to a cab-driver

Herbert Beerbohm Tree 1852–1917: Neville Cardus *Sir Thomas Beecham* (1961)

5 Charity, dear Miss Prism, charity! None of us are perfect. I myself am peculiarly susceptible to draughts.

Oscar Wilde 1854–1900: *The Importance of Being Earnest* (1895)

Humour ····▶ Wit and Wordplay

❝ Without humour you cannot run a sweetie-shop, let alone a nation. **❞**
John Buchan

1 Among all kinds of writing, there is none in which authors are more apt to miscarry than in works of humour, as there is none in which they are more ambitious to excel.

Joseph Addison 1672–1719: *The Spectator* 10 April 1711

2 The marvellous thing about a joke with a double meaning is that it can only mean one thing.

Ronnie Barker 1929–2005: *Sauce* (1977)

3 In Milwaukee last month a man died laughing over one of his own jokes. That's what makes it so tough for us outsiders. We have to fight home competition.

Robert Benchley 1889–1945: R. E. Drennan *Wit's End* (1973)

4 Mark my words, when a society has to resort to the lavatory for its humour, the writing is on the wall.

Alan Bennett 1934– : *Forty Years On* (1969)

5 The world dwindles daily for the humorist . . . Jokes are fast running out, for a joke must transform real life in some perverse way, and real life has begun to perform the same operation perfectly professionally upon itself.

Craig Brown 1957– : *Craig Brown's Greatest Hits* (1993)

6 When you tell an Iowan a joke, you can see a kind of race going on between his brain and his expression.

Bill Bryson 1951– : *The Lost Continent* (1989)

7 Without humour you cannot run a sweetie-shop, let alone a nation.

John Buchan 1875–1940: *Castle Gay* (1930)

8 Good jests ought to bite like lambs, not dogs: they should cut, not wound.

Charles II 1630–85: attributed; Stephen Leacock 'A Rehabilitation of Charles II' in *Essays and Literary Studies* (1916)

9 A joke's a very serious thing.

Charles Churchill 1731–64: *The Ghost* (1763)

10 Reality goes bounding past the satirist like a cheetah laughing as it lopes ahead of the greyhound.

Claud Cockburn 1904–81: *Crossing the Line* (1958)

11 Freud's theory was that when a joke opens a window and all those bats and bogeymen fly out, you get a marvellous feeling of relief and elation. The trouble with Freud is that he never had to play the old Glasgow Empire on a Saturday night after Rangers and Celtic had both lost.

Ken Dodd 1931– : in *Guardian* 30 April 1991 (quoted in many, usually much contracted, forms since the mid-1960s)

12 A difference of taste in jokes is a great strain on the affections.

George Eliot 1819–80: *Daniel Deronda* (1876)

13 Comedy, like sodomy, is an unnatural act.

Marty Feldman 1933–83: in *The Times* 9 June 1969

14 The funniest thing about comedy is that you never know why people laugh. I know *what* makes them laugh but trying to get your hands on the *why* of it is like trying to pick an eel out of a tub of water.

W. C. Fields 1880–1946: Richard J. Anobile *A Flask of Fields* (1972)

15 It is easy to forget that the most important aspect of comedy, after all, its great saving grace, is its ambiguity. You can simultaneously laugh at a situation, *and* take it seriously.

Stephen Fry 1957– : *Paperweight* (1992)

16 There's a weight of intellect behind my comedy.
David Brent's self-analysis

Ricky Gervais 1961– and **Stephen Merchant**: *The Office* (Series 1, Episode 2; 2001)

17 'Tis ever thus with simple folk—an accepted wit has but to say 'Pass the mustard', and they roar their ribs out!

W. S. Gilbert 1836–1911: *The Yeoman of the Guard* (1888)

18 The Irish have wit but little humour. They cannot laugh at the battle while they are involved in the broil of life.

Oliver St John Gogarty 1878–1957: *Tumbling in the Hay* (1939)

19 What do you mean, funny? Funny-peculiar or funny ha-ha?

Ian Hay 1876–1952: *The Housemaster* (1938)

20 A sober God-fearing man whose idea of a good joke was to lie about his age.

Joseph Heller 1923–99: *Catch-22* (1961)

21 You need real surprise. It's like poetry. A good joke turns life inside out.

Terry Jones 1942– : interview, in *Guardian* 4 October 2002

22 My idea of an ideal programme would be a show where I would have all the questions and some other bastard would have to figure out the funny answers.

Groucho Marx 1895–1977: letter, 10 October 1940

23 It's an odd job, making decent people laugh.

Molière 1622–73: *La Critique de l'école des femmes* (1663)

24 They laughed when I said I was going to be a comedian . . . They're not laughing now.

Bob Monkhouse 1928–2003: attributed; *BBC News* 29 December 2003 (online edition)

25 I knew nothing about farce until I read [Feydeau's] *Puce à l'Oreille*, and had no idea what a deadly serious business it is.

John Mortimer 1923– : *Clinging to the Wreckage* (1982)

26 Good taste and humour . . . are a contradiction in terms, like a chaste whore.

Malcolm Muggeridge 1903–90: in *Time* 14 September 1953

27 Another day gone and no jokes.

Flann O'Brien 1911–66: *The Best of Myles* (1968)

28 That's the Irish people all over—they treat a joke as a serious thing and a serious thing as a joke.

Sean O'Casey 1880–1964: *The Shadow of a Gunman* (1923)

29 Humour is, by its nature, more truthful than factual.

P. J. O'Rourke 1947– : *Parliament of Whores* (1991)

30 Laughter is pleasant, but the exertion is too much for me.

Thomas Love Peacock 1785–1866: *Nightmare Abbey* (1818)

31 Everything is funny as long as it is happening to Somebody Else.

Will Rogers 1879–1935: *The Illiterate Digest* (1924) 'Warning to Jokers: lay off the prince'

32 All humour is based on hostility—that's why World War Two was funny.

Neil Simon 1927– : *Laughter on the 23rd Floor* (1993)

33 There are three basic rules for great comedy. Unfortunately no-one can remember what they are.

Arthur Smith 1954– : attributed

34 For every ten jokes, thou hast got an hundred enemies.

Laurence Sterne 1713–68: *Tristram Shandy* (1769)

35 It would be a sad reflection on any satirical programme if no one ended up taking offence at some point.

Meera Syal 1963– : in *Independent* 30 November 2002

36 Humour is emotional chaos remembered in tranquillity.

James Thurber 1894–1961: in *New York Post* 29 February 1960

37 That joke was lost on the foreigner—guides cannot master the subtleties of the American joke.

Mark Twain 1835–1910: *The Innocents Abroad* (1869)

38 Laughter would be bereaved if snobbery died.

Peter Ustinov 1921–2004: in *Observer* 13 March 1955

39 Mucky jokes. Obscenity—it's all the go nowadays. By law, you see. You're allowed to do it. You can say bum, you can say po, you can say anything . . . Well, he said it! The thin one! He said bum one night. I heard him! Satire!

Keith Waterhouse 1929– and **Willis Hall**: 'Close Down' in David Frost and Ned Sherrin *That Was The Week That Was* (1963)

40 It's hard to be funny when you have to be clean.

Mae West 1892–1980: Joseph Weintraub *The Wit and Wisdom of Mae West* (1967)

41 Madeleine Bassett laughed the tinkling, silvery laugh that had got her so disliked by the better element.

P. G. Wodehouse 1881–1975: *The Code of the Woosters* (1938)

42 She had a penetrating sort of laugh. Rather like a train going into a tunnel.

P. G. Wodehouse 1881–1975: *The Inimitable Jeeves* (1923)

Hypocrisy

66 Most people sell their souls, and live with a good conscience on the proceeds. 99
Logan Pearsall Smith

1 There are moments when we in the British press can show extraordinary sensitivity; these moments usually coincide with the death of a proprietor, or a proprietor's wife.

Craig Brown 1957– : *Craig Brown's Greatest Hits* (1993)

2 In England the only homage which they pay to Virtue—is hypocrisy.

Lord Byron 1788–1824: letter, 11 May 1821

3 *speaking against the Welsh Disestablishment Bill, F. E. Smith had called it 'a Bill which has shocked the conscience of every Christian community in Europe':*
Talk about the pews and steeples
and the Cash that goes therewith!
But the souls of Christian people . . .
Chuck it, Smith!

G. K. Chesterton 1874–1936: 'Antichrist, or the Reunion of Christendom: An Ode' (1912)

4 We are so very 'umble.
Uriah Heep

Charles Dickens 1812–70. *David Copperfield* (1850)

5 He combines the manners of a Marquis with the morals of a Methodist.

W. S. Gilbert 1836–1911: *Ruddigore* (1887)

6 Hypocrisy is not generally a social sin, but a virtue.

Judith Martin 1938– : *Miss Manners' Guide to Rearing Perfect Children* (1985)

7 *the hypocritical Quaker, Ephraim Smooth, hears violin music:*
I must shut my ears. The man of sin rubbeth the hair of the horse to the bowels of the cat.

John O'Keeffe 1747–1833: *Wild Oats* (1791)

8 Most people sell their souls, and live with a good conscience on the proceeds.

Logan Pearsall Smith 1865–1946: *Afterthoughts* (1931) 'Other People'

9 Of all the cants which are canted in this canting world,— though the cant of hypocrites may be the worst,—the cant of criticism is the most tormenting!

Laurence Sterne 1713–68: *Tristram Shandy* (1759–67)

10 I hope you have not been leading a double life, pretending to be wicked and being really good all the time. That would be hypocrisy.

Oscar Wilde 1854–1900: *The Importance of Being Earnest* (1895)

Ideas

66 There are some ideas so wrong that only a very intelligent person could believe in them. 99
George Orwell

1 I ran into Isosceles. He has a great idea for a new triangle!

Woody Allen 1935– : *If the Impressionists had been Dentists*

2 An original idea. That can't be too hard. The library must be full of them.

Stephen Fry 1957– : *The Liar* (1991)

3 I had a monumental idea this morning, but I didn't like it.

Sam Goldwyn 1882–1974: N. Zierold *Hollywood Tycoons* (1969)

4 The chief end of man is to frame general ideas—and . . . no general idea is worth a damn.

Oliver Wendell Holmes Jr. 1841–1935: letter to Morris R. Cohen, 12 April 1915

5 It is better to entertain an idea than to take it home to live with you for the rest of your life.

Randall Jarrell 1914–65: *Pictures from an Institution* (1954)

6 A household where a total unawareness of the world of ideas not only existed but was regarded as a matter for congratulation.

Osbert Lancaster 1908–80: *All Done From Memory* (1953)

7 There are some ideas so wrong that only a very intelligent person could believe in them.

George Orwell 1903–50: attributed

8 The English approach to ideas is not to kill them, but to let them die of neglect.

Jeremy Paxman 1950– : *The English: a portrait of a people* (1998)

Ignorance

66 Ignorance, madam, pure ignorance. 99
Samuel Johnson

1 Mr Kremlin himself was distinguished for ignorance, for he had only one idea,—and that was wrong.

Benjamin Disraeli 1804–81: *Sybil* (1845)

2 *on being asked why he had defined* pastern *as the 'knee' of a horse:*
Ignorance, madam, pure ignorance.

Samuel Johnson 1709–84: James Boswell *Life of Samuel Johnson* (1791) 1755

3 *in response to the comment on another lawyer, 'It may be doubted whether any man of our generation has plunged more deeply into the sacred fount of learning':*
Or come up drier.

Abraham Lincoln 1809–65: Leon Harris *The Fine Art of Political Wit* (1965)

4 A bishop wrote gravely to the *Times* inviting all nations to destroy 'the formula' of the atomic bomb. There is no simple remedy for ignorance so abysmal.

Peter Medawar 1915–87: *The Hope of Progress* (1972)

5 What's it all about . . . ?

Bill Naughton 1910–92: *Alfie* (1966 film); spoken by Michael Caine as Alfie

6 You know everybody is ignorant, only on different subjects.

Will Rogers 1879–1935: in *New York Times* 31 August 1924

7 Reports that say that something hasn't happened are always interesting to me, because as we know, there are known knowns; there are things we know we know. We also know there are known unknowns; that is to say we know there are some things we do not know. But there are also unknown unknowns—the ones we don't know we don't know.

Donald Rumsfeld 1932– : news briefing, February 2002; the statement won the Plain English Campaign's Foot in Mouth award

8 Ignorance is like a delicate exotic fruit; touch it and the bloom is gone.

Oscar Wilde 1854–1900: *The Importance of Being Earnest* (1895)

Indexes ····> Books

❝ I wasn't even in the index. **❞**
Edwina Currie

1 If you don't find it in the Index, look very carefully through the entire catalogue.

Anonymous: in *Consumer's Guide, Sears, Roebuck and Co.* (1897); Donald E. Knuth *Sorting and Searching* (1973)

2 Whenever I am sent a new book on the lively arts, the first thing I do is look for myself in the index.

Julie Burchill 1960– : *The Spectator* 16 January 1992

3 I wasn't even in the index.
on John Major's autobiography

Edwina Currie 1946– : in *The Times* 28 September 2002

4 *the Editors' acknowledgements:*
Their thanks are also due to their wife for not preparing the index wrong. There is no index.

W. C. Sellar 1898–1951 and **R. J. Yeatman** 1898–1968: *1066 and All That* (1930)

5 An index is a great leveller.

George Bernard Shaw 1856–1950: G. N. Knight *Indexing* (1979); attributed, perhaps apocryphal

6 Should not the Society of Indexers be known as Indexers, Society of, The?

Keith Waterhouse 1929– : *Bookends* (1990)

Insults and Invective

❝ I married beneath me, all women do. **❞**
Nancy Astor

1 Lord Birkenhead is very clever but sometimes his brains go to his head.

Margot Asquith 1864–1945: in *Listener* 11 June 1953 'Margot Oxford' by Lady Violet Bonham Carter

2 The *t* is silent, as in *Harlow*.
to Jean Harlow, who had been mispronouncing her first name

Margot Asquith 1864–1945: T. S. Matthews *Great Tom* (1973)

3 I married beneath me, all women do.

Nancy Astor 1879–1964: in *Dictionary of National Biography 1961–1970* (1981)

4 NANCY ASTOR: If I were your wife I would put poison in your coffee!
WINSTON CHURCHILL: And if I were your husband I would drink it.

Nancy Astor 1879–1964: Consuelo Vanderbilt Balsan *Glitter and Gold* (1952)

5 I didn't know he'd been knighted. I knew he'd been doctored.

Thomas Beecham 1879–1961: on Malcolm Sargent's knighthood; attributed

6 The 'g' is silent—the only thing about her that is.
of Camille Paglia

Julie Burchill 1960– : in *The Spectator* 16 January 1992

7 Lillian Gish may be a charming person, but she is not Ophelia. She comes on stage as if she had been sent for to sew rings on the new curtains.

Mrs Patrick Campbell 1865–1940: Margot Peters *Mrs Pat* (1984)

8 [Clement Attlee is] a modest man who has a good deal to be modest about.

Winston Churchill 1874–1965: in *Chicago Sunday Tribune Magazine of Books* 27 June 1954

9 A sheep in sheep's clothing.
of Clement Attlee

Winston Churchill 1874–1965: Lord Home *The Way the Wind Blows* (1976)

10 BESSIE BRADDOCK: Winston, you're drunk.
CHURCHILL: Bessie, you're ugly. But tomorrow I shall be sober.

Winston Churchill 1874–1965: an exchange with the Labour MP Bessie Braddock; J. L. Lane (ed.) *Sayings of Churchill* (1992)

11 *Henry Clay of Virginia unexpectedly moved out of the way of his political rival, John Randolph of Roanoke:*
JOHN RANDOLPH: I never sidestep skunks.
HENRY CLAY: I always do.

Henry Clay 1777–1852: Robert V. Remini *Henry Clay* (1991)

12 A sophistical rhetorician, inebriated with the exuberance of his own verbosity.
of Gladstone

Benjamin Disraeli 1804–81: in *The Times* 29 July 1878

13 [*The Sun Also Rises* is about] bullfighting, bullslinging, and bull—.

Zelda Fitzgerald 1900–47: Marion Meade *What Fresh Hell Is This?* (1988)

14 A very weak-minded fellow I am afraid, and, like the feather pillow, bears the marks of the last person who has sat on him!
of Lord Derby

Earl Haig 1861–1928: letter to Lady Haig, 14 January 1918

15 His thoughts are seldom consecutive.
He just can write.
I know a movie executive
Who's twice as bright.

Lorenz Hart 1895–1943: 'Take Him' (*Pal Joey*, 1940 musical)

16 *on being criticized by Geoffrey Howe:*
Like being savaged by a dead sheep.

Denis Healey 1917– : speech, House of Commons 14 June 1978

17 Some men are born mediocre, some men achieve mediocrity, and some men have mediocrity thrust upon them. With Major Major it had been all three.

Joseph Heller 1923–99: *Catch-22* (1961)

18 Such cruel glasses.
  of Robin Day

Frankie Howerd 1922–92: in *That Was The Week That Was* (BBC television series, from 1963)

19 So dumb he can't fart and chew gum at the same time.
  of Gerald Ford

Lyndon Baines Johnson 1908–73: Richard Reeves *A Ford, not a Lincoln* (1975)

20 Is not a Patron, my Lord, one who looks with unconcern on a man struggling for life in the water, and, when he has reached ground, encumbers him with help? The notice which you have been pleased to take of my labours, had it been early, had been kind; but it has been delayed till I am indifferent, and cannot enjoy it; till I am solitary, and cannot impart it; till I am known, and do not want it.

Samuel Johnson 1709–84: letter to Lord Chesterfield, 7 February 1755; James Boswell *Life of Samuel Johnson* (1791)

21 This man [Lord Chesterfield] I thought had been a Lord among wits; but, I find, he is only a wit among Lords.

Samuel Johnson 1709–84: James Boswell *Life of Samuel Johnson* (1791) (1754)

22 This little flower, this delicate little beauty, this cream puff, is supposed to be beyond personal criticism . . . He is simply a shiver looking for a spine to run up.
  of John Hewson, the Australian Liberal leader

Paul Keating 1944– : in *Ned Sherrin in his Anecdotage* (1993)

23 The truckman, the trashman and the policeman on the block may call me Alice but you may not.
  to Senator Joseph McCarthy

Alice Roosevelt Longworth 1884–1980: Michael Teague *Mrs. L* (1981)

24 *on hearing that a Hollywood agent had swum safely in shark-infested waters:*
  I think that's what they call professional courtesy.

Herman J. Mankievicz 1897–1953: attributed; Nigel Rees *Cassell Dictionary of Humorous Quotations* (1999)

25 I never forget a face, but in your case I'll be glad to make an exception.

Groucho Marx 1895–1977: Leo Rosten *People I have Loved, Known or Admired* (1970) 'Groucho'

26 The majority of the members of the Irish parliament are professional politicians, in the sense that otherwise they would not be given jobs minding mice at crossroads.

Flann O'Brien 1911–66: *The Hair of the Dogma* (1977)

27 If you say a modern celebrity is an adulterer, a pervert and a drug addict, all it means is that you've read his autobiography.

P. J. O'Rourke 1947– : *Give War a Chance* (1992)

28 *to Clare Boothe Luce, who had stood aside for her saying, 'Age before Beauty':*
  Pearls before swine.

Dorothy Parker 1893–1967: R. E. Drennan *Wit's End* (1973)

29 The affair between Margot Asquith and Margot Asquith will live as one of the prettiest love stories in all literature.

Dorothy Parker 1893–1967: review of Margot Asquith's *Lay Sermons*; in *New Yorker* 22 October 1927

30 I'm not offended at all, because I know I'm not a dumb blonde. I also know I'm not blonde.

Dolly Parton 1946– : M. Palmer *Small Talk, Big Names: 40 Years of Rock Quotes* (1993)

31 Let Sporus tremble—'What? that thing of silk, Sporus, that mere white curd of ass's milk? Satire or sense, alas! can Sporus feel? Who breaks a butterfly upon a wheel?'

Alexander Pope 1688–1744: of Lord Hervey; 'An Epistle to Dr Arbuthnot' (1735)

32 A cherub's face, a reptile all the rest.

Alexander Pope 1688–1744: of Lord Hervey; 'An Epistle to Dr Arbuthnot' (1735)

33 A wit with dunces, and a dunce with wits.

Alexander Pope 1688–1744: *The Dunciad* (1742)

34 Don't look at me, Sir, with—ah—in that tone of voice.

Punch 1841–1992: vol. 87 (1884)

35 BEATRICE: I wonder that you will still be talking, Signior Benedick: nobody marks you.
BENEDICK: What! my dear Lady Disdain, are you yet living?

William Shakespeare 1564–1616: *Much Ado About Nothing* (1598–9)

36 Diana Rigg is built like a brick mausoleum with insufficient flying buttresses.
review of Abelard and Heloise *in 1970*

John Simon 1925– : Diana Rigg *No Turn Unstoned* (1982)

37 *on being approached by the secretary of the Athenaeum, which he had been in the habit of using as a convenience on the way to his office:*
Good God, do you mean to say this place is a club?

F. E. Smith 1872–1930: attributed

38 JUDGE: You are extremely offensive, young man.
SMITH: As a matter of fact, we both are, and the only difference between us is that I am trying to be, and you can't help it.

F. E. Smith 1872–1930: Lord Birkenhead *Earl of Birkenhead* (1933)

39 *on a proposal to surround St Paul's with a wooden pavement:*
Let the Dean and Canons lay their heads together and the thing will be done.

Sydney Smith 1771–1845: H. Pearson *The Smith of Smiths* (1934)

40 Science is his forte, and omniscience his foible.

Sydney Smith 1771–1845: of William Whewell, master of Trinity College, Cambridge; Isaac Todhunter *William Whewell* (1876)

41 I regard you with an indifference closely bordering on aversion.

Robert Louis Stevenson 1850–94: *New Arabian Nights* (1882)

42 *when pressed by a gramophone company for a written testimonial:*
Sirs, I have tested your machine. It adds a new terror to life and makes death a long-felt want.

Herbert Beerbohm Tree 1852–1917: Hesketh Pearson *Beerbohm Tree* (1956)

43 *to Richard Adams, who had described Vidal's novel on Lincoln as 'meretricious'*
Really? Well, meretricious and a happy New Year to you too!
earlier uses of the response are attributed to Franklin P. Adams in the 1930s, and the NBC radio show starring the Marx Brothers, Flywheel, Shyster and Flywheel, *in 1933*

Gore Vidal 1925– : on *Start the Week*, BBC radio, 1970s

44 Every other inch a gentleman.

Rebecca West 1892–1983: of Michael Arlen; Victoria Glendinning *Rebecca West* (1987)

45 CECILY: When I see a spade I call it a spade.
GWENDOLEN: I am glad to say that I have never seen a spade.

Oscar Wilde 1854–1900: *The Importance of Being Earnest* (1895)

46 [EARL OF SANDWICH:] 'Pon my soul, Wilkes, I don't know whether you'll die upon the gallows or of the pox.
[WILKES:] That depends, my Lord, whether I first embrace your Lordship's principles, or your Lordship's mistresses.

John Wilkes 1727–97: Charles Petrie *The Four Georges* (1935); probably apocryphal

Intelligence and Intellectuals ····> The Mind

66 I have nothing to declare except my genius. 99
Oscar Wilde

1 To the man-in-the-street, who, I'm sorry to say,
Is a keen observer of life,
The word 'Intellectual' suggests straight away
A man who's untrue to his wife.

W. H. Auden 1907–73: *New Year Letter* (1941)

2 Men of genius are so few that they ought to atone for their fewness by being at any rate ubiquitous.

Max Beerbohm 1872–1956: letter to W. B. Yeats, 11 July 1911

3 But—Oh! ye lords of ladies intellectual,
Inform us truly, have they not hen-pecked you all?

Lord Byron 1788–1824: *Don Juan* (1819–24)

4 Genius is one per cent inspiration, ninety-nine per cent perspiration.

Thomas Alva Edison 1847–1931: said c.1903; in *Harper's Monthly Magazine* September 1932

5 With the thoughts I'd be thinkin'
I could be another Lincoln,
If I only had a brain.

E. Y. Harburg 1898–1981: 'If I Only Had a Brain' (1939)

6 Zip! Walter Lippman wasn't brilliant today,
Zip! Will Saroyan ever write a great play?
Zip! I was reading Schopenhauer last night.
Zip! And I think that Schopenhauer was right!
satirizing the intellectual pretensions of Gypsy Rose Lee

Lorenz Hart 1895–1943: 'Zip' (1940)

7 Probably the greatest concentration of talent and genius in this house except for perhaps those times when Thomas Jefferson ate alone.
of a dinner for Nobel Prizewinners at the White House

John F. Kennedy 1917–63: in *New York Times* 30 April 1962

8 *I think, therefore I am* is the statement of an intellectual who underrates toothaches.

Milan Kundera 1929– : *Immortality* (1991)

9 No one in this world, so far as I know—and I have searched the records for years, and employed agents to help me—has ever lost money by underestimating the intelligence of the great masses of the plain people.

H. L. Mencken 1880–1956: in *Chicago Tribune* 19 September 1926

10 You can persuade a man to believe almost anything provided he is clever enough, but it is much more difficult to persuade someone less clever.

Tom Stoppard 1937– : *Professional Foul* (1978)

11 What is a highbrow? He is a man who has found something more interesting than women.

Edgar Wallace 1875–1932: in *New York Times* 24 January 1932

12 I have nothing to declare except my genius.

Oscar Wilde 1854–1900: at the New York Custom House; Frank Harris *Oscar Wilde* (1918)

13 'Jeeves is a wonder.'
'A marvel.'
'What a brain.'
'Size nine-and-a-quarter, I should say.'
'He eats a lot of fish.'

P. G. Wodehouse 1881–1975: *Thank You, Jeeves* (1934)

14 'Well, I think you're a pig.'
'A pig, maybe, but a shrewd, levelheaded pig. I wouldn't touch the project with a bargepole.'

P. G. Wodehouse 1881–1975: *The Code of the Woosters* (1938)

15 I know I've got a degree. Why does that mean I have to spend my life with intellectuals? I've got a life-saving certificate but I don't spend my evenings diving for a rubber brick with my pyjamas on.

Victoria Wood 1953– : *Mens Sana in Thingummy Doodah* (1990)

Invective ····▶ Insults and Invective

Ireland and the Irish ····▶ Countries and Peoples, Places

❝ I'm Irish. We think sideways. **❞**
Spike Milligan

1 PAT: He was an Anglo-Irishman.
MEG: In the blessed name of God what's that?
PAT: A Protestant with a horse.

Brendan Behan 1923–64: *Hostage* (1958)

2 We've never been cool, we're hot. Irish people are Italians who can't dress, Jamaicans who can't dance.

Bono 1960– : interview, 25 February 2001; in *Independent* 26 February 2001

3 Where would the Irish be without someone to be Irish at?

Elizabeth Bowen 1899–1973: *The House in Paris* (1935)

4 We rose to bring about Eutopia,
But all we got was Dev's myopia.

Oliver St John Gogarty 1878–1957: letter to James Montgomery; Ulick O'Connor *Oliver St John Gogarty* (1964)

5 Ireland is a small but insuppressible island half an hour nearer the sunset than Great Britain.

Thomas Kettle 1880–1916: 'On Crossing the Irish Sea'

6 The Irish, he says, don't care for clean government; they want Irish government.

Stephen Leacock 1869–1944: *Arcadian Adventures with the Idle Rich* (1914)

7 I'm Irish. We think sideways.

Spike Milligan 1918–2002: in *Independent on Sunday* 20 June 1999

8 Our ancestors believed in magic, prayers, trickery, browbeating and bullying: I think it would be fair to sum that list up as 'Irish politics'.

Flann O'Brien 1911–66: *The Hair of the Dogma* (1977)

9 He'd . . . settled into a life of Guinness, sarcasm and late late nights, the kind of life that American academics think real Dubliners lead.

Joseph O'Connor 1963– : *Cowboys and Indians* (1991)

10 Gladstone . . . spent his declining years trying to guess the answer to the Irish Question; unfortunately whenever he was getting warm, the Irish secretly changed the Question.

W. C. Sellar 1898–1951 and **R. J. Yeatman** 1898–1968: *1066 and All That* (1930)

11 An Irishman's heart is nothing but his imagination.

George Bernard Shaw 1856–1950: *John Bull's Other Island* (1907)

12 *denying that he was Irish:*
Because a man is born in a stable, that does not make him a horse.

Duke of Wellington 1769–1852: Paul Johnson (ed.) *The Oxford Book of Political Anecdotes* (1986)

Journalism ····> Newspapers

66 Comment is free but facts are on expenses. 99
Tom Stoppard

---

1 At certain times each year, we journalists do almost nothing except apply for the Pulitzers and several dozen other major prizes. During these times you could walk right into most newsrooms and commit a multiple axe murder naked, and it wouldn't get reported in the paper because the reporters and editors would all be too busy filling out prize applications.

Dave Barry 1948– : in *Miami Herald* 29 March 1987

2 *to Nicholas Phipps, who had announced that he was an efficient hack rather than a creative writer:*
Creative writers are two a penny. Efficient hacks are very rare.

Lord Beaverbrook 1879–1964: in *Daily Telegraph* 17 July 2004 (obituary of Nicholas Phipps)

3 When a dog bites a man, that is not news, because it happens so often. But if a man bites a dog, that is news.

John B. Bogart 1848–1921: F. M. O'Brien *The Story of the* [New York] *Sun* (1918); often attributed to Charles A. Dana

4 *on being asked whether George Mair had been a fastidious journalist:*
He once telephoned a semicolon from Moscow.

James Bone: James Agate diary, 31 October 1935

5 A would-be satirist, a hired buffoon,
A monthly scribbler of some low lampoon,
Condemned to drudge, the meanest of the mean,
And furbish falsehoods for a magazine.
of journalists

Lord Byron 1788–1824: 'English Bards and Scotch Reviewers' (1809)

6 Let's face it, sports writers, we're not hanging around with brain surgeons.

Jimmy Cannon 1910–73: attributed

7 *explaining the craft of sports writers:*
We work in the toy department.

Jimmy Cannon 1910–73: Michael Parkinson *Sporting Lives* (1993)

8 When seagulls follow a trawler, it is because they think sardines will be thrown into the sea.

Eric Cantona 1966– : at the end of a press conference, 31 March 1995

9 Journalism largely consists in saying 'Lord Jones Dead' to people who never knew that Lord Jones was alive.

G. K. Chesterton 1874–1936: *Wisdom of Father Brown* (1914)

10 You are misunderstood, maligned, viewed by the press as a Pulitzer Prize ready to be won.
on the problems of investigative journalism for politicians

Lawton Chiles 1930– : in *St Petersburg (Florida) Times* 6 March 1991

11 The first law of journalism—to confirm existing prejudice rather than contradict it.

Alexander Cockburn 1941– : in 1974; Jonathon Green *Says Who?* (1988)

12 Thou god of our idolatry, the press . . .
Thou fountain, at which drink the good and wise;
Thou ever-bubbling spring of endless lies;
Like Eden's dread probationary tree,
Knowledge of good and evil is from thee.

William Cowper 1731–1800: 'The Progress of Error' (1782)

13 If you lose your temper at a newspaper columnist, he'll be rich, or famous, or both.

James Hagerty 1936– : the view of President Eisenhower's press secretary; Jonathon Green *Says Who?* (1988)

14 Power without responsibility: the prerogative of the harlot throughout the ages.
summing up the view of Lord Beaverbrook, who had said to Kipling: 'What I want is power. Kiss 'em one day and kick 'em the next'; Stanley Baldwin, Kipling's cousin, subsequently obtained permission to use the phrase in a speech in London on 18 March 1931

Rudyard Kipling 1865–1936: in *Kipling Journal* December 1971

15 I think it well to remember that, when writing for the newspapers, we are writing for an elderly lady in Hastings who has two cats of which she is passionately fond. Unless our stuff can successfully compete for her interest with those cats, it is no good.

Willmott Lewis 1877–1950: Claud Cockburn *In Time of Trouble* (1957)

16 I like to do my principal research in bars, where people are more likely to tell the truth or, at least, lie less convincingly than they do in briefings and books.

P. J. O'Rourke 1947– : *Holidays in Hell* (1988)

17 No government in history has been as obsessed with public relations as this one . . . Speaking for myself, if there is a message I want to be off it.

Jeremy Paxman 1950– : in *Daily Telegraph* 3 July 1998

18 More like a gentleman than a journalist.

J. B. Priestley 1894–1984: of Bruce Richmond, editor of *The Times Literary Supplement*; letter to Edward Davison, 23 June 1924

19 Comment is free but facts are on expenses.

Tom Stoppard 1937– : *Night and Day* (1978)

20 For a slashing article, sir, there's nobody like the Capting.

William Makepeace Thackeray 1811–63: *Pendennis* (1848–50)

21 Up to a point, Lord Copper.

Evelyn Waugh 1903–66: *Scoop* (1938)

22 A journalist is somebody who possesses himself of a fantasy and lures the truth towards it.

Arnold Wesker 1932– : *Journey into Journalism* (1977)

23 There is a journalistic curse of Eve. The woman who writes is always given anti-feminist books to review.

Rebecca West 1892–1983: in *The Clarion* 21 November 1913

24 *the difference between journalism and literature:*
Journalism is unreadable, and literature is not read.

Oscar Wilde 1854–1900: 'The Critic as Artist' (1891)

25 You cannot hope
to bribe or twist,
thank God! the
British journalist.
But, seeing what
the man will do
unbribed, there's
no occasion to.

Humbert Wolfe 1886–1940: 'Over the Fire' (1930)

26 Rock journalism is people who can't write interviewing people who can't talk for people who can't read.

Frank Zappa 1940–93: Linda Botts *Loose Talk* (1980)

Judges ····▶ Crime and Punishment, The Law

❝I could have been a judge but I never had the Latin.**❞**
Peter Cook

---

1 Reform! Reform! Aren't things bad enough already?

Mr Justice Astbury 1860–1939: attributed

2 *affecting not to recognize Lord Campbell, the newly appointed Lord Chancellor, whom he encountered enveloped in a huge fur coat:*
I beg your pardon, My Lord. I mistook you for the Great Seal.

Richard Bethell 1800–73: J. B. Atlay *Victorian Chancellors* (1908)

3 CONVICTED CRIMINAL: As God is my judge—I am innocent.
LORD BIRKETT: He isn't; I am, and you're not!

Lord Birkett 1883–1962: attributed; Matthew Parris *Scorn* (1994)

4 I always approach Judge [Lemuel] Shaw as a savage approaches his fetish, knowing that he is ugly but feeling that he is great.

Rufus Choate 1799–1859: Van Wyck Brooks *The Flowering of New England* (1936)

5 I don't want to know what the law is, I want to know who the judge is.

Roy M. Cohn 1927–86: in *New York Times Book Review* 3 April 1988

6 Did you mail that cheque to the Judge?

Roy M. Cohn 1927–86: spoken to an aide, at breakfast with Ned Sherrin, 1978

7 Yes, I could have been a judge but I never had the Latin, never had the Latin for the judging, I just never had sufficient of it to get through the rigorous judging exams. They're noted for their rigour. People come staggering out saying, 'My God, what a rigorous exam'—and so I became a miner instead.

Peter Cook 1937–95: *Beyond the Fringe* (1961 revue)

8 *the judge Sir James Mansfield had suggested that the Court might sit on Good Friday:*
If your Lordship pleases. But your Lordship will be the first judge who has done so since Pontius Pilate.

William Davy d. 1780: Edward Parry *The Seven Lamps of Advocacy* (1923); the Court did *not* sit

9 Judges commonly are elderly men, and are more likely to hate at sight any analysis to which they are not accustomed, and which disturbs repose of mind, than to fall in love with novelties.

Oliver Wendell Holmes Jr. 1841–1935: in *Harvard Law Review* 1899

10 *of Judges Learned and Augustus Hand:*
Quote Learned, and follow 'Gus'.

Robert H. Jackson 1892–1954: Hershel Shanks *The Art and Craft of Judging* (1968)

11 I always feel that there should be some comfort derived from any question from the bench. It is clear proof that the inquiring Justice is not asleep.

Robert H. Jackson 1892–1954: 'Advocacy before the Supreme Court: Suggestions for Effective Presentation' (1951)

12 Mr Justice Cocklecarrot began the hearing of a very curious case yesterday. A Mrs Tasker is accused of continually ringing the doorbell of a Mrs Renton, and then, when the door is opened, pushing a dozen red-bearded dwarfs into the hall and leaving them there.

J. B. Morton 1893–1975: *Diet of Thistles* (1938)

13 Poor fellow, I suppose he fancied he was on the bench.
on hearing that a judge had slept through his play Pizarro

Richard Brinsley Sheridan 1751–1816: Walter Jerrold *Bon-Mots* (1893)

14 JUDGE: I have read your case, Mr Smith, and I am no wiser now than I was when I started.
SMITH: Possibly not, My Lord, but far better informed.

F. E. Smith 1872–1930: Lord Birkenhead *F. E.* (1959)

15 JUDGE WILLIS: Mr Smith, have you ever heard of a saying by Bacon—the great Bacon—that youth and discretion are ill-wed companions?
SMITH: Indeed I have, your Honour; and has your Honour ever heard of a saying by Bacon—the great Bacon—that a much talking Judge is like an ill-tuned cymbal?

F. E. Smith 1872–1930: Lord Birkenhead *F. E.* (1959)

Language ····▸ Grammar, Languages, Words

❝ The sort of English up with which I will not put. ❞
Winston Churchill

1 Don't swear, boy. It shows a lack of vocabulary.

Alan Bennett 1934– : *Forty Years On* (1969)

2 This is the sort of English up with which I will not put.

Winston Churchill 1874–1965: Ernest Gowers *Plain Words* (1948) 'Troubles with Prepositions'

3 Stars, Charlie had noticed before, always spoke slowly. Listening to Warren Beatty being interviewed was like waiting for speech to finish being invented.

Ray Connally: *Shadows on a Wall* (1994)

4 Where in this small-talking world can I find
A longitude with no platitude?

Christopher Fry 1907–2005: *The Lady's not for Burning* (1949)

5 Backward ran sentences until reeled the mind.
satirizing the style of Time *magazine*

Wolcott Gibbs 1902–58: in *New Yorker* 28 November 1936 'Time . . . Fortune . . . Life . . . Luce'

6 When you're lying awake with a dismal headache, and repose is taboo'd by anxiety,
I conceive you may use any language you choose to indulge in, without impropriety.

W. S. Gilbert 1836–1911: *Iolanthe* (1882)

7 Though 'Bother it' I may
Occasionally say,
I never use a big, big D—

W. S. Gilbert 1836–1911: *HMS Pinafore* (1878)

8 The minute a phrase becomes current it becomes an apology for not thinking accurately to the end of the sentence.

Oliver Wendell Holmes Jr. 1841–1935: letter to Harold Laski, 2 July 1917

9 My spelling is Wobbly. It's good spelling but it Wobbles, and the letters get in the wrong places.

A. A. Milne 1882–1956: *Winnie-the-Pooh* (1926)

10 'Feather-footed through the plashy fen passes the questing vole' . . . 'Yes,' said the Managing Editor. 'That must be good style.'

Evelyn Waugh 1903–66: *Scoop* (1938)

Languages ····▸ Language, Words

❝ Speak in French when you can't think of the English. ❞
Lewis Carroll

1 The Norwegian language has been described as German spoken underwater.

Anonymous: Nigel Rees *Cassell Dictionary of Humorous Quotations* (1999)

2 If you understand English, press 1. If you do not understand English, press 2.
recorded message on Australian tax helpline

Anonymous: in *Mail on Sunday* 30 July 2000 'Quotes of the Week'

3 The letter is written in the tongue of the Think Tanks, a language more difficult to master than Basque or Navaho and spoken only where strategic thinkers clump together in Institutes.

Russell Baker 1925– : in *New York Times* 8 April 1981

4 Albanian . . . a language that sounded comic with all its pffts, pees, wees, pings and fitts.

Cecil Beaton 1904–80: diary, August 1940

5 Is there no Latin word for Tea? Upon my soul, if I had known that I would have let the vulgar stuff alone.

Hilaire Belloc 1870–1953: 'On Tea' (1908)

6 You know the trouble with the French, they don't even have a word for entrepeneur.

George W. Bush 1946– : attributed, probably apocryphal

7 JOSEPHINE BAKER: Donnez moi une tasse de café, s'il vous plait.
MARY CAMPBELL: Honey, talk out of the mouth you was born with.
exchange between Josephine Baker, who had moved to France from America, and who was staying with Lorenz Hart's parents, and Mary Campbell, who was the Harts' cook

Mary Campbell: Samuel Marx and Jan Clayton *Rodgers and Hart* (1975)

8 Speak in French when you can't think of the English for a thing.

Lewis Carroll 1832–98: *Through the Looking-Glass* (1872)

9 *on speaking French fluently rather than correctly:*
It's nerve and brass, *audace* and disrespect, and leaping-before-you-look and what-the-hellism, that must be developed.

Diana Cooper 1892–1986: Philip Ziegler *Diana Cooper* (1981)

10 Anglish is what we don' know
Spanglish is langlish we know.

Dorothy Fields 1905–74: 'Spanglish' (1973)

11 I hear it's the Hebrew in Heaven, sir. Spanish is seldom spoken.

Ronald Firbank 1886–1926: *Concerning the Eccentricities of Cardinal Pirelli* (1926)

12 'Basta!' his master replied, with all the brilliant glibness of the Berlitz-school.

Ronald Firbank 1886–1926: *The Flower Beneath the Foot* (1923)

13 Weep not for little Léonie
Abducted by a French Marquis!
Though loss of honour was a wrench
Just think how it's improved her French.

Harry Graham 1874–1936: 'Compensation' (1930)

14 All pro athletes are bilingual. They speak English and profanity.

Gordie Howe 1928– : in *Toronto Star* 27 May 1975

15 There even are places where English completely disappears.
In America, they haven't used it for years!
Why can't the English teach their children how to speak?

Alan Jay Lerner 1918–86: 'Why Can't the English?' (1956)

16 *when Khrushchev began banging his shoe on the desk:*
Perhaps we could have a translation, I could not quite follow.

Harold Macmillan 1894–1986: during his speech to the United Nations, 29 September 1960

17 Listen, someone's screaming in agony—fortunately I speak it fluently.

Spike Milligan 1918–2002: *The Goon Show* 'The Scarlet Capsule' (BBC Radio, 1959)

18 I can speak Esperanto like a native.

Spike Milligan 1918–2002: attributed; in *Daily Telegraph* 28 February 2002

19 Waiting for the German verb is surely the ultimate thrill.

Flann O'Brien 1911–66: *The Hair of the Dogma* (1977)

20 *on being told there was no English word equivalent to* sensibilité:
Yes we have. Humbug.

Lord Palmerston 1784–1865: attributed

21 KENNETH: If you're so hot, you'd better tell me how to say she has ideas above her station.
BRIAN: Oh, yes, I forgot. It's fairly easy, old boy. *Elle a des idées au-dessus de sa gare.*
KENNETH: You can't do it like that. You can't say *au-dessus de sa gare*. It isn't that sort of station.

Terence Rattigan 1911–77: *French without Tears* (1937)

22 Remember that you are a human being with a soul and the divine gift of articulate speech: that your native language is the language of Shakespeare and Milton and The Bible; and don't sit there crooning like a bilious pigeon.

George Bernard Shaw 1856–1950: *Pygmalion* (1916)

23 Egad I think the interpreter is the hardest to be understood of the two!

Richard Brinsley Sheridan 1751–1816: *The Critic* (1779)

24 They spell it Vinci and pronounce it Vinchy; foreigners always spell better than they pronounce.

Mark Twain 1835–1910: *The Innocents Abroad* (1869)

25 I once heard a Californian student in Heidelberg say, in one of his calmest moods, that he would rather decline two drinks than one German adjective.

Mark Twain 1835–1910: *A Tramp Abroad* (1880)

26 An unalterable and unquestioned law of the musical world required that the German text of French operas sung by Swedish artists should be translated into Italian for the clearer understanding of English-speaking audiences.

Edith Wharton 1862–1937: *The Age of Innocence* (1920)

Last Words ····> Death

66 Die, my dear Doctor, that's the last thing I shall do! **99**
Lord Palmerston

1 I will not go down to posterity talking bad grammar.

Benjamin Disraeli 1804–81: while correcting proofs of his last Parliamentary speech, 31 March 1881; Robert Blake *Disraeli* (1966)

2 No it is better not. She would only ask me to take a message to Albert.
near death, declining a proposed visit from Queen Victoria

Benjamin Disraeli 1804–81: Robert Blake *Disraeli* (1966)

3 *on his deathbed in 1936, when someone remarked 'Cheer up, your Majesty, you will soon be at Bognor again':*
Bugger Bognor.

George V 1865–1936: Kenneth Rose *King George V* (1983); attributed

4 'Hallelujah!', Was the only observation
That escaped Lieutenant-Colonel Mary Jane
When she tumbled off the platform in the station,
And was cut in little pieces by the train.
Mary Jane, the train is through yer:
Hallelujah, Hallelujah!
We will gather up the fragments that remain.

A. E. Housman 1859–1936: 'Hallelujah!'

5 *Lady Eldon had suggested that she should read to him from his own New Testament:*
No . . . Awfully jolly of you to suggest it, though.

Ronald Knox 1888–1957: Evelyn Waugh *Life of Ronald Knox*

6 Die, my dear Doctor, that's the last thing I shall do!

Lord Palmerston 1784–1865: E. Latham *Famous Sayings and their Authors* (1904)

7 Put that bloody cigarette out!
before being shot by a sniper in World War One

Saki 1870–1916: attributed, perhaps apocryphal

8 They couldn't hit an elephant at this distance.
immediately prior to being killed by enemy fire at the battle of Spotsylvania in the American Civil War, May 1864

John Sedgwick d. 1864: Robert E. Denney *The Civil War Years* (1992)

9 If this is dying, then I don't think much of it.

Lytton Strachey 1880–1932: Michael Holroyd *Lytton Strachey* (1967)

10 I find, then, I am but a bad anatomist.
cutting his throat in prison, he severed his windpipe instead of his jugular, and lingered for several days

Wolfe Tone 1763–98: Oliver Knox *Rebels and Informers* (1998)

11 This is no time for making new enemies.
on being asked to renounce the Devil, on his deathbed

Voltaire 1694–1778: attributed

The Law ····> Crime and Punishment, Judges

66 The law is a ass—a idiot. 99

Charles Dickens

---

1 I have knowingly defended a number of guilty men. But the guilty never escape unscathed. My fees are sufficient punishment for anyone.

F. Lee Bailey 1933– : in *Los Angeles Times* 9 January 1972

2 Equity does not demand that its suitors shall have led blameless lives.

Louis Brandeis 1856–1941: in *Loughran v. Loughran* 1934

3 Lawyers charge a fortune to handle a bond offering. You know what it takes to handle a bond offering? The mental capacities of a filing cabinet.

Jimmy Breslin 1929– : in *Legal Times* 17 January 1983

4 As a moth is drawn to the light, so is a litigant drawn to the United States. If he can only get his case into their courts, he stands to win a fortune.

Lord Denning 1899–1999: *Smith Kline & French Laboratories Ltd. v. Bloch* 1983

5 'Little to do, and plenty to get, I suppose?' said Sergeant Buzfuz, with jocularity. 'Oh, quite enough to get, sir, as the soldier said ven they ordered him three hundred and fifty lashes,' replied Sam. 'You must not tell us what the soldier, or any other man, said, sir,' interposed the judge; 'it's not evidence.'

Charles Dickens 1812–70: *Pickwick Papers* (1837)

6 'If the law supposes that,' said Mr Bumble . . . 'the law is a ass—a idiot.'

Charles Dickens 1812–70: *Oliver Twist* (1838)

7 The one great principle of the English law is, to make business for itself.

Charles Dickens 1812–70: *Bleak House* (1853)

8 This contract is so one-sided that I am surprised to find it written on both sides of the paper.

Lord Evershed 1899–1966: Lord Denning *Closing Chapter* (1983)

9 I was sued by a woman who claimed that she became pregnant because she watched me on the television and I bent her contraceptive coil.

Uri Geller 1946– : in *Sunday Times* 17 December 2000

10 When I was a lad I served a term
As office boy to an Attorney's firm.
I cleaned the windows and I swept the floor,
And I polished up the handle of the big front door.
I polished up that handle so carefullee
That now I am the Ruler of the Queen's Navee!

W. S. Gilbert 1836–1911: *HMS Pinafore* (1878)

11 The Law is the true embodiment
Of everything that's excellent.
It has no kind of fault or flaw,
And I, my Lords, embody the Law.

W. S. Gilbert 1836–1911: *Iolanthe* (1882)

12 Let's find out what everyone is doing,
And then stop everyone from doing it.

A. P. Herbert 1890–1971: 'Let's Stop Somebody from Doing Something' (1930)

13 *an attempt is made to write a cheque on a cow:*
'Was the cow crossed?'
'No, your worship, it was an open cow.'

A. P. Herbert 1890–1971: *Uncommon Law* (1935) 'The Negotiable Cow'

14 *on the award of £600,000 libel damages to Sonia Sutcliffe against* Private Eye*:*
If this is justice, I am a banana.

Ian Hislop 1960– : in *Guardian* 25 May 1989

15 Legal writing is one of those rare creatures, like the rat and the cockroach, that would attract little sympathy even as an endangered species.

Richard Hyland 1949– : 'A Defense of Legal Writing' (1986)

16 Johnson observed, that 'he did not care to speak ill of any man behind his back, but he believed the gentleman was an *attorney*.'

Samuel Johnson 1709–84: James Boswell *Life of Samuel Johnson* (1791) 1770

17 *when Knox was Attorney General Theodore Roosevelt requested a legal justification for his acquisition of the Panama Canal:*
Oh, Mr President, do not let so great an achievement suffer from any taint of legality.

Philander C. Knox 1853–1921: Tyler Dennett *John Hay: From Poetry to Politics*

18 If you want to get ahead in this world get a lawyer—not a book.

Fran Lebowitz 1946– : on self-help books; *Social Studies* (1981)

19 Whatever fees we [Judge Logan and I] earn at a distance, if not paid *before*, we notice we never hear of after the work is done. We therefore, are growing a little sensitive on the point.

Abraham Lincoln 1809–65: letter 2 November 1842

20 Sue me, sue me
Shoot bullets through me
I love you.

Frank Loesser 1910–69. 'Sue Me' (1950)

21 However harmless a thing is, if the law forbids it most people will think it wrong.

W. Somerset Maugham 1874–1965: *A Writer's Notebook* (1949) written in 1896

22 Injustice is relatively easy to bear; what stings is justice.

H. L. Mencken 1880–1956: *Prejudices, Third Series* (1922)

23 Here [in Paris] they hang a man first, and try him afterwards.

Molière 1622–73: *Monsieur de Pourceaugnac* (1670)

24 I don't know as I want a lawyer to tell me what I cannot do. I hire him to tell me how to do what I want to do.

J. P. Morgan 1837–1913: Ida M. Tarbell *The Life of Elbert H. Gary* (1925)

25 No brilliance is needed in the law. Nothing but common sense, and relatively clean finger nails.

John Mortimer 1923– : *A Voyage Round My Father* (1971)

26 As it was once put to me, always remember that [as a barrister] you are in the position of a cabman on the rank, bound to answer the first hail.

Ralph Neville: in *The Times* 16 June 1913

27 The Polis as Polis, in this city, is Null an' Void!

Sean O'Casey 1880–1964: *Juno and the Paycock* (1925)

28 Policemen, like red squirrels, must be protected.

Joe Orton 1933–67: *Loot* (1967)

29 I have always noticed that any time a man can't come and settle with you without bringing his lawyer, why, look out for him.

Will Rogers 1879–1935: 'Slipping the Lariat Over' 14 January 1923

30 Went down and spoke at some lawyers' meeting last night. They didn't think much of my little squib yesterday about driving the shysters out of their profession. They seemed to kinder doubt just who would have to leave.

Will Rogers 1879–1935: 'Mr. Rogers is Hob Nobbing With Leaders of the Bar'

31 The first thing we do, let's kill all the lawyers.

William Shakespeare 1564–1616: *Henry VI, Part 2* (1592)

32 The sound of tireless voices is the price we pay for the right to hear the music of our own opinions.

Adlai Stevenson 1900–65: *The Guide to American Law* (1984)

33 Some circumstantial evidence is very strong, as when you find a trout in the milk.

Henry David Thoreau 1817–62: diary, 11 November 1850

34 What chance has the ignorant, uncultivated liar against the educated expert? What chance have I . . . against a lawyer?

Mark Twain 1835–1910: 'On the Decay of the Art of Lying' (1882)

35 Whenever a copyright law is to be made or altered, then the idiots assemble.

Mark Twain 1835–1910: *Notebook* 23 May 1903

36 There's a lot of law at the end of a nightstick.

Grover A. Whalen 1886–1962: Quentin Reynolds *Courtroom* (1950)

37 Asking the ignorant to use the incomprehensible to decide the unknowable.

Hiller B. Zobel 1932– : 'The Jury on Trial' in *American Heritage* July–August 1995; see **Sports and Games** 38

Leisure ····> Work and Leisure

Letters

66 All the pith is in the postscript. **99**
William Hazlitt

1 *formula with which to return unsolicited manuscripts:*
Mr James Agate regrets that he has no time to bother about the enclosed in which he has been greatly interested.

James Agate 1877–1947: diary, 3 January 1936

2 It would have been less heterodox
If he had put the letter in the letter-o-box.

Brian Brindley: the Babes-in-the-Wood discovering a letter pinned to a tree by Robin Hood, in an Oxford pantomime in 1953; Ned Sherrin *Cutting Edge* (1984)

3 I am not a cautious letter-writer and generally say what comes uppermost at the moment.

Lord Byron 1788–1824: letter to Mary Shelley, 9 October 1822

4 WITWOUD: Madam, do you pin up your hair with all your letters?
MILLAMANT: Only with those in verse, Mr Witwoud. I never pin up my hair with prose.

William Congreve 1670–1729: *The Way of the World* (1700)

5 Regarding yours, dear Mrs Worthington, of Wednesday the 23rd.

Noël Coward 1899–1973: 'Mrs Worthington' (1935)

6 Dear 338171 (May I call you 338?).

Noël Coward 1899–1973: letter to T. E. Lawrence, 25 August 1930

7 Sir, My pa requests me to write to you, the doctors considering it doubtful whether he will ever recuvver the use of his legs which prevents his holding a pen.

Charles Dickens 1812–70: *Nicholas Nickleby* (1839)

8 It is wonderful how much news there is when people write every other day; if they wait for a month, there is nothing that seems worth telling.

O. Douglas 1877–1948: *Penny Plain* (1920)

9 [Charles Lamb's] sayings are generally like women's letters; all the pith is in the postscript.

William Hazlitt 1778–1830: *Conversations of James Northcote* (1826–7)

10 A man seldom puts his authentic self into a letter. He writes it to amuse a friend or to get rid of a social or business obligation, which is to say, a nuisance.

H. L. Mencken 1880–1956: *Minority Report* (1956)

11 I have made this [letter] longer than usual, only because I have not had the time to make it shorter.

Blaise Pascal 1623–62: *Lettres Provinciales* (1657)

12 Laura's repeated assurances to me that she had both replied to your letter and that she was about to do so are, I think, characteristic of a mind at bay.

S. J. Perelman 1904–79: letter 17 October 1948

13 *responding to a savage review by Rudolph Louis in* München Neueste Nachrich *7 February 1906:*
I am sitting in the smallest room of my house. I have your review before me. In a moment it will be behind me.

Max Reger 1873–1916: Nicolas Slonimsky *Lexicon of Musical Invective* (1953)

14 *circular sent out to forestall unwanted visitors:*
Mr J. Ruskin is about to begin a work of great importance and therefore begs that in reference to calls and correspondence you will consider him dead for the next two months.

John Ruskin 1819–1900: attributed

15 *Wilde had sent a letter on 'Fashion in Dress' to the* Daily Telegraph, *but explained in a covering letter to the proprietor:*
I don't wish to sign my name, though I am afraid everybody will know who the writer is: one's style is one's signature always.

Oscar Wilde 1854–1900: letter, 2 February 1891

16 I have no need of your God-damned sympathy. I only wish to be entertained by some of your grosser reminiscences.

Alexander Woollcott 1887–1943: letter to Rex O'Malley, 1942

Libraries ····▸ Books

66 File your waste-paper basket for 50 years. **99**
Tony Benn

1 RUTH: They'll sack you.
NORMAN: They daren't. I reorganized the Main Index. When I die, the secret dies with me.

Alan Ayckbourn 1939– : *Round and Round the Garden* (1975)

2 If you file your waste-paper basket for 50 years, you have a public library.

Tony Benn 1925– : in *Daily Telegraph* 5 March 1994

3 What a sad want I am in of libraries, of books to gather facts from! Why is there not a Majesty's library in every county town? There is a Majesty's jail and gallows in every one.

Thomas Carlyle 1795–1881: diary, 18 May 1832

4 There is nowhere in the world where sleep is so deep as in the libraries of the House of Commons.

Chips Channon 1897–1958: diary, 16 December 1937

5 Th' first thing to have in a libry is a shelf. Fr'm time to time this can be decorated with lithrachure. But th' shelf is th' main thing.

Finley Peter Dunne 1867–1936: *Mr Dooley Says* (1910)

6 I've been drunk for about a week now, and I thought it might sober me up to sit in a library.

F. Scott Fitzgerald 1896–1940: *The Great Gatsby* (1925)

7 Mr Cobb took me into his library and showed me his books, of which he had a complete set.

Ring Lardner 1885–1933: R. E. Drennan *Wit's End* (1973)

8 'Our library,' said the president, 'two hundred thousand volumes!' 'Aye,' said the minister, 'a powerful heap of rubbish, I'll be bound!'

Stephen Leacock 1869–1944: *Arcadian Adventures with the Idle Rich* (1914)

9 E. W. B. Nicholson [Bodley's Librarian] spending three days at the London Docks, watching outgoing ships, after losing a book from Bodley, which was afterwards discovered slightly out of place on the shelf.

Falconer Madan 1851–1935: J. A. Gere and John Sparrow (eds.) *Geoffrey Madan's Notebooks* (1981)

10 Those dreadful detective stories. Another corpse in the library this evening. Really, you know, too much of a good thing. Fourth this week. No doubt trouble is shortage of libraries.

Flann O'Brien 1911–66: *The Best of Myles* (1968)

11 The Librarian was, of course, very much in favour of reading in general, but readers in particular got on his nerves . . . He liked people who loved and respected books, and the best way to do that, in the Librarian's opinion, was to leave them on the shelves where Nature intended them to be.

Terry Pratchett 1948– : *Men at Arms* (1993)

Lies ····▶ Truth

❝ Enough white lies to ice a wedding cake. **❞**
Margot Asquith

1 It reminds me of the small boy who jumbled his biblical quotations and said: 'A lie is an abomination unto the Lord, and a very present help in trouble.'

Anonymous: recalled by Adlai Stevenson; Billl Adler *The Stevenson Wit* (1966)

2 She [Lady Desborough] tells enough white lies to ice a wedding cake.

Margot Asquith 1864–1945: Lady Violet Bonham Carter 'Margot Oxford' in *Listener* 11 June 1953

3 Matilda told such Dreadful Lies,
It made one Gasp and Stretch one's Eyes;
Her Aunt, who, from her Earliest Youth,

Hilaire Belloc 1870–1953: 'Matilda' (1907)

Had kept a Strict Regard for Truth,
Attempted to Believe Matilda:
The effort very nearly killed her.

4 For every time She shouted 'Fire!'
They only answered 'Little Liar!'
And therefore when her Aunt returned,
Matilda, and the House, were Burned.

Hilaire Belloc 1870–1953: 'Matilda'
(1907)

5 That branch of the art of lying which consists in very
nearly deceiving your friends without quite deceiving your
enemies.
   of propaganda

Francis M. Cornford 1874–1943:
Microcosmographia Academica (1922
ed.)

6 There are three kinds of lies: lies, damned lies and
statistics.

Benjamin Disraeli 1804–81:
attributed to Disraeli in Mark Twain
Autobiography (1924)

7 What you take for lying in an Irishman is only his attempt
to put an herbaceous border on stark reality.

Oliver St John Gogarty 1878–1957:
Going Native (1940)

8 By the time you say you're his,
Shivering and sighing
And he vows his passion is
Infinite, undying—
Lady, make a note of this:
One of you is lying.

Dorothy Parker 1893–1967:
'Unfortunate Coincidence' (1937)

9 *on being told that Lord Astor claimed that her allegations,*
concerning himself and his house parties at Clivedon, were
untrue:
He would, wouldn't he?

Mandy Rice-Davies 1944– : in
Guardian 1 July 1963

10 A little inaccuracy sometimes saves tons of explanation.

Saki 1870–1916: *The Square Egg*
(1924)

11 I don't think the son of a bitch knows the difference
between telling the truth and lying.
   of Richard Nixon

Harry S. Truman 1884–1972: Merle
Miller *Plain Speaking* (1974)

12 In exceptional circumstances it is necessary to say
something that is untrue in the House of Commons.

William Waldegrave 1946– : in
Guardian 9 March 1994

13 Untruthful! My nephew Algernon? Impossible! He is an
Oxonian.

Oscar Wilde 1854–1900: *The*
Importance of Being Earnest (1895)

Life ····▶ Lifestyle

❝ Just one damned thing after another. ❞
Elbert Hubbard

1 Alun's life was coming to consist more and more
exclusively of being told at dictation speed what he knew.

Kingsley Amis 1922–95: *The Old*
Devils (1986)

2 Life is a sexually transmitted disease.

Anonymous: graffito found on the London Underground

3 The only thing I regret about my life is the length of it. If I had to live my life again I'd make all the same mistakes—only sooner.

Tallulah Bankhead 1903–68: Laurence J. Peter (ed.) *Quotations for our Time* (1977)

4 Brought up in the provinces in the forties and fifties one learned early the valuable lesson that life is generally something that happens elsewhere.

Alan Bennett 1934– : introduction to *Talking Heads* (1988)

5 It's as large as life, and twice as natural!

Lewis Carroll 1832–98: *Through the Looking-Glass* (1872)

6 Life is the funny thing that happens to you on the way to the grave.

Quentin Crisp 1908–99: in *Spectator* 20 November 1999

7 It's a funny old world—a man's lucky if he gets out of it alive.

Walter de Leon and **Paul M. Jones**: *You're Telling Me* (1934 film); spoken by W. C. Fields

8 'Sairey,' says Mrs Harris, 'sech is life. Vich likeways is the hend of all things!'

Charles Dickens 1812–70: *Martin Chuzzlewit* (1844)

9 Life is a Cabaret, old chum
Come to the Cabaret.

Fred Ebb: 'Cabaret' (1965)

10 Life is just one damned thing after another.

Elbert Hubbard 1859–1915: in *Philistine* December 1909, (often attributed to Frank Ward O'Malley)

11 Life is something to do when you can't get to sleep.

Fran Lebowitz 1946– : *Metropolitan Life* (1978)

12 Laugh it off, laugh it off; it's all part of life's rich pageant.

Arthur Marshall 1910–89: *The Games Mistress* (recorded monologue, 1937)

13 Moderation in all things. Not too much of life. It often lasts too long.

H. L. Mencken 1880–1956: *Minority Report* (1956)

14 Life is a shit sandwich and every day you take another bite.
a pro football player's view

Joe Schmidt: Jonathon Green and Don Atyeo (eds.) *The Book of Sports Quotes* (1979)

15 I *love* living. I have some problems with my *life*, but living is the best thing they've come up with so far.

Neil Simon 1927– : *Last of the Red Hot Lovers* (1970)

16 Life is a gamble at terrible odds—if it was a bet, you wouldn't take it.

Tom Stoppard 1937– : *Rosencrantz and Guildenstern are Dead* (1967)

17 Above all, gentlemen, not the slightest zeal.

Charles-Maurice de Talleyrand 1754–1838: P. Chasles *Voyages d'un critique à travers la vie et les livres* (1868)

18 Oh, isn't life a terrible thing, thank God?

Dylan Thomas 1914–53: *Under Milk Wood* (1954)

19 What a queer thing Life is! So unlike anything else, don't you know, if you see what I mean.

P. G. Wodehouse 1881–1975: *My Man Jeeves* (1919)

Lifestyle

66 Never try to keep up with the Joneses. Drag them down to your level. 99
Quentin Crisp

1 Have fun. And go home when you're tired.

George Abbott 1887–1995: in obituary, *New York Times* 2 February 1995

2 Never try to keep up with the Joneses. Drag them down to your level. It's cheaper that way.

Quentin Crisp 1908–99: in *The Times* 22 November 1999

3 If *A* is a success in life, then *A* equals *x* plus *y* plus *z*. Work is *x*; *y* is play; and *z* is keeping your mouth shut.

Albert Einstein 1879–1955: in *Observer* 15 January 1950

4 There's nothing in the middle of the road but yellow stripes and dead armadillos.

Jim Hightower 1943– : attributed, 1984

5 Puberty is a phase . . . Fifteen years of rejection is a lifestyle.

Susan Kolinsky: *Sex and the City* 'The Turtle and the Hare'(1998), spoken by Stanford (Willie Garson)

6 Why is he living among those men
Who talk like Barbie and look like Ken?
on the last straight man in gay Chelsea

Glenn Slater: *The New Yorkers* (2000)

7 As life goes on, don't you find that all you need is about two real friends, a regular supply of books, and a Peke?

P. G. Wodehouse 1881–1975: letter 28 October 1930

8 The others had their drugs and booze. I had my women. I thought that was safer: you can't overdose on women.

Bill Wyman 1936– : in *Independent* 26 October 2002

Literature ····> Books, Poetry and Poets, Writers and Writing

66 A good card to play for honours. 99
Arnold Bennett

1 *on literature as taught in school:*
Schoolteachers seemed determined to persuade me that 'classic' is a synonym for 'narcotic'.

Russell Baker 1925– : in *New York Times* 14 April 1982

2 A swear-word in a rustic slum
A simple swear-word is to some,
To Masefield something more.

Max Beerbohm 1872–1956: *Fifty Caricatures* (1912)

3 The literary gift is a mere accident—is as often bestowed on idiots who have nothing to say worth hearing as it is denied to strenuous sages.

Max Beerbohm 1872–1956: letter to George Bernard Shaw, 21 September 1903

4 Remote and ineffectual Don
That dared attack my Chesterton.

Hilaire Belloc 1870–1953: 'Lines to a Don' (1910)

5 We were put to Dickens as children but it never quite took. That unremitting humanity soon had me cheesed off.

Alan Bennett 1934– : *The Old Country* (1978)

6 Literature's always a good card to play for Honours. It makes people think that Cabinet ministers are educated.

Arnold Bennett 1867–1931: *The Title* (1918)

7 Dr Weiss, at forty, knew that her life had been ruined by literature.

Anita Brookner 1928– : *A Start in Life* (1981)

8 'The whole of this unfortunate business,' said Dr Lyster, 'has been the result of PRIDE AND PREJUDICE.'

Fanny Burney 1752–1840: *Cecilia* (1782)

9 I hate things all fiction . . . there should always be some foundation of fact for the most airy fabric—and pure invention is but the talent of a liar.

Lord Byron 1788–1824: letter to his publisher John Murray, 2 April 1817

10 We learn from Horace, Homer sometimes sleeps; We feel without him: Wordsworth sometimes wakes.

Lord Byron 1788–1824: *Don Juan* (1819–24)

11 You praise the firm restraint with which they write— I'm with you there, of course: They use the snaffle and the curb all right, But where's the bloody horse?

Roy Campbell 1901–57: 'On Some South African Novelists' (1930)

12 'What is the use of a book', thought Alice, 'without pictures or conversations?'

Lewis Carroll 1832–98: *Alice's Adventures in Wonderland* (1865)

13 If my books had been any worse, I should not have been invited to Hollywood, and if they had been any better, I should not have come.

Raymond Chandler 1888–1959: letter to Charles W. Morton, 12 December 1945

14 A literary man—*with* a wooden leg.

Charles Dickens 1812–70: *Our Mutual Friend* (1865)

15 When I want to read a novel, I write one.

Benjamin Disraeli 1804–81: W. Monypenny and G. Buckle *Life of Benjamin Disraeli* (1920)

16 *listening to readings from Tolkien's* Lord of the Rings: Oh fuck, not another elf!

Hugo Dyson 1896–1975: A. N. Wilson *C. S. Lewis* (1990)

17 The mama of dada. *of Gertrude Stein*

Clifton Fadiman 1904–99: *Party of One* (1955)

18 How rare, how precious is frivolity! How few writers can prostitute all their powers! They are always implying, 'I am capable of higher things.'

E. M. Forster 1879–1970: *Abinger Harvest* (1936)

19 The work of Henry James has always seemed divisible by a simple dynastic arrangement into three reigns: James I, James II, and the Old Pretender.

Philip Guedalla 1889–1944: *Supers and Supermen* (1920) 'Some Critics'

20 The cheerful clatter of Sir James Barrie's cans as he went round with the milk of human kindness.

Philip Guedalla 1889–1944: *Supers and Supermen* (1920) 'Some Critics'

21 He knew everything about literature except how to enjoy it.

Joseph Heller 1923–99: *Catch-22* (1961)

22 It takes a great deal of history to produce a little literature.

Henry James 1843–1916: *Hawthorne* (1879)

23 A beginning, a muddle, and an end. *on the 'classic formula' for a novel*

Philip Larkin 1922–85: in *New Fiction* January 1978

24 From the moment I picked up your book until I laid it down, I was convulsed with laughter. Some day I intend reading it.

Groucho Marx 1895–1977: a blurb written for S. J. Perelman's 1928 book *Dawn Ginsberg's Revenge*

25 A novelist must preserve a childlike belief in the importance of things which common sense considers of no great consequence.

W. Somerset Maugham 1874–1965: *A Writer's Notebook* (1949) written in 1933

26 *explaining to Queen Victoria why he did not wish to read* Oliver Twist:
It's all among workhouses and Coffin Makers and Pickpockets . . . I wish to avoid them.

Lord Melbourne 1779–1848: A. N. Wilson *The Victorians* (2002)

27 I have only ever read one book in my life, and that is *White Fang*. It's so frightfully good I've never bothered to read another.
     Uncle Matthew's view of literature

Nancy Mitford 1904–73: *Love in a Cold Climate* (1949)

28 And I'll stay off Verlaine too; he was always chasing Rimbauds.

Dorothy Parker 1893–1967: 'The Little Hours' (1939)

29 If, with the literate, I am
Impelled to try an epigram,
I never seek to take the credit;
We all assume that Oscar said it.

Dorothy Parker 1893–1967: 'A Pig's-Eye View of Literature' (1937)

30 Nearly all our best men are dead! Carlyle, Tennyson, Browning, George Eliot!—I'm not feeling very well myself.

Punch 1841–1992: vol. 104 (1893)

31 I have known her pass the whole evening without mentioning a single book, or *in fact anything unpleasant*, at all.

Henry Reed 1914–86: *A Very Great Man Indeed* (1953)

32 In view of her penchant
For something romantic,
De Sade is too trenchant
And Dickens too frantic,
And Stendhal would ruin
The plan of attack
As there isn't much blue in
The Red and the Black.

Stephen Sondheim 1930– : 'Now' (1972)

33 I should have no objection to this method, but that I think it must smell too strong of the lamp.

Laurence Sterne 1713–68: *Tristram Shandy* (1759–67)

34 You're familiar with the tragedies of antiquity, are you? The great homicidal classics?

Tom Stoppard 1937– : *Rosencrantz and Guildenstern are Dead* (1967)

35 I don't give a toss about writing really. It's a bit ironic that the things I'm really into are music and football, and I have never really been good at either.

Irvine Welsh 1957– : in *The Times* 1999, attributed

36 Any writer worth his salt knows that only a small proportion of literature does more than partly compensate people for the damage they have suffered in learning to read.

Rebecca West 1892–1983: Peter Vansittart *Path from a White Horse* (1985), author's note

37 Meredith's a prose Browning, and so is Browning.

Oscar Wilde 1854–1900: *Intentions* (1891) 'The Critic as Artist'

Living ····≻ Life and Living

Love ·····> Marriage, Sex

❝ The magic of first love is our ignorance that it can ever end. **❞**
Benjamin Disraeli

1 We men have got love well weighed up; our stuff
Can get by without it.
Women don't seem to think that's good enough;
They write about it.

Kingsley Amis 1922–95: 'A Bookshop Idyll' (1956)

2 Even logical positivists are capable of love.

A. J. Ayer 1910–89: Kenneth Tynan *Profiles* (1989)

3 Women who love the same man have a kind of bitter freemasonry.

Max Beerbohm 1872–1956: *Zuleika Dobson* (1911)

4 Make love to every woman you meet. If you get five percent on your outlays it's a good investment.

Arnold Bennett 1867–1931: Laurence J. Peter (ed.) *Quotations for our Time* (1977)

5 Miss Joan Hunter Dunn, Miss Joan Hunter Dunn,
How mad I am, sad I am, glad that you won.
The warm-handled racket is back in its press,
But my shock-headed victor, she loves me no less.

John Betjeman 1906–84: 'A Subaltern's Love-Song' (1945)

6 The ability to make love frivolously is the chief characteristic which distinguishes human beings from beasts.

Heywood Broun 1888–1939: Howard Teichmann *George S. Kaufman* (1973)

7 Would I were free from this restraint,
Or else had hopes to win her;
Would she could make of me a saint,
Or I of her a sinner.

William Congreve 1670–1729: 'Pious Selinda Goes to Prayers' (song)

8 If this be not love, it is madness, and then it is pardonable.

William Congreve 1670–1729: *The Old Bachelor* (1693)

9 An affair between a mad rocking horse and a rawhide suitcase.
on Jeanette MacDonald and Nelson Eddy

Noël Coward 1899–1973: diary, 1 July 1946

10 They made love as though they were an endangered species.

Peter de Vries 1910–93: Laurence J. Peter (ed.) *Quotations for our Time* (1977)

11 Did you ever hear of Captain Wattle?
He was all for love, and a little for the bottle.

Charles Dibdin 1745–1814: 'Captain Wattle and Miss Roe' (1797)

12 Barkis is willin'.

Charles Dickens 1812–70: *David Copperfield* (1850)

13 Oh, Mrs Corney, what a prospect this opens! What a opportunity for a jining of hearts and house-keepings!

Charles Dickens 1812–70: *Oliver Twist* (1838)

14 The magic of first love is our ignorance that it can ever end.

Benjamin Disraeli 1804–81: *Henrietta Temple* (1837)

15 What is commonly called love, namely the desire of satisfying a voracious appetite with a certain quantity of delicate white human flesh.

Henry Fielding 1707–54: *Tom Jones* (1749)

16 I'm afraid I was very much the traditionalist. I went down on one knee and dictated a proposal which my secretary faxed over straight away.

Stephen Fry 1957– and **Hugh Laurie**: *A Bit More Fry and Laurie* (1991)

17 How happy could I be with either,
Were t'other dear charmer away!

John Gay 1685–1732: *The Beggar's Opera* (1728)

18 Holding hands at midnight
'Neath a starry sky . . .
Nice work if you can get it,
And you can get it if you try.

Ira Gershwin 1896–1983: 'Nice Work If You Can Get It' (1937)

19 With love to lead the way,
I've found more clouds of grey
Than any Russian play
Could guarantee . . .
. . . When ev'ry happy plot
Ends with the marriage knot—
And there's no knot for me.

Ira Gershwin 1896–1983: 'But Not For Me' (1930)

20 Love is sweeping the country;
Waves are hugging the shore;
All the sexes
From Maine to Texas
Have never known such love before.

Ira Gershwin 1896–1983: 'Love is Sweeping the Country' (1931)

21 So I fell in love with a rich attorney's
Elderly ugly daughter.

W. S. Gilbert 1836–1911: *Trial by Jury* (1875)

22 I never meant to marry my second wife. I only meant to rob her.

Rich Hall 1954– : *Otis Lee Crenshaw: I Blame Society*

23 In the spring a young man's fancy lightly turns to thoughts of love;
And in summer,
and in autumn,
and in winter—
See above.

E. Y. Harburg 1898–1981: 'Tennyson Anyone?' (1965)

24 When I'm not near the girl I love,
I love the girl I'm near.
. . . When I can't fondle the hand I'm fond of
I fondle the hand at hand.

E. Y. Harburg 1898–1981: 'When I'm Not Near the Girl I Love' (1947)

25 The broken dates,
The endless waits,
The lovely loving and the hateful hates,
The conversation and the flying plates—
I wish I were in love again.

Lorenz Hart 1895–1943: 'I Wish I Were in Love Again' (1937)

26 When love congeals
It soon reveals
The faint aroma of performing seals,
The double crossing of a pair of heels.
I wish I were in love again!

Lorenz Hart 1895–1943: 'I Wish I Were in Love Again' (1937)

27 Love's like the measles—all the worse when it comes late in life.

Douglas Jerrold 1803–57: *The Wit and Opinions of Douglas Jerrold* (1859) 'Love'

28 Another bride, another June,
Another sunny honeymoon,
Another season, another reason,
For makin' whoopee!

Gus Kahn 1886–1941: 'Makin' Whoopee' (1928)

29 Snug as two baboons—in a bamboo tree
I'll bamboozle you
And you'll bamboozle me
By a goona goona goona,
by a goona goona goona lagoon.

John Latouche 1917–56: 'The Goona Goona Goona Lagoon' (*The Golden Apple*, 1954 musical)

30 You ain't nothin' but a hound dog,
Quit snoopin' round my door
You can wag your tail but I ain't gonna feed you no more.

Jerry Leiber 1933– and **Mike Stoller** 1933– : 'Hound Dog' (1956)

31 Tell me, George, if you had to do it all over would you fall in love with yourself again.
to George Gershwin

Oscar Levant 1906–72: David Ewen *The Story of George Gershwin* (1943)

32 Love's a disease. But curable.

Rose Macaulay 1881–1958: *Crewe Train* (1926)

33 Bed. No woman is worth more than a fiver unless you're in love with her. Then she's worth all she costs you.

W. Somerset Maugham 1874–1965: *A Writer's Notebook* (1949) written in 1903

34 Love is the delusion that one woman differs from another.

H. L. Mencken 1880–1956: *Chrestomathy* (1949)

35 You want to get three feet up a bull's ass, just listen to the whisperings of sweethearts.

Anthony Minghella 1954–2008: *Cold Mountain* (2003 film); spoken by Ruby Thewes (Renee Zellweger)

36 Oh, life is a glorious cycle of song,
A medley of extemporanea;
And love is a thing that can never go wrong;
And I am Marie of Roumania.

Dorothy Parker 1893–1967: 'Comment' (1937)

37 Four be the things I'd been better without:
Love, curiosity, freckles, and doubt.

Dorothy Parker 1893–1967: 'Inventory' (1937)

38 Most gentlemen don't like love,
They just like to kick it around.

Cole Porter 1891–1964: 'Most Gentlemen don't like Love' (1938)

39 I get no kick from champagne,
Mere alcohol doesn't thrill me at all,
So tell me why should it be true
That I get a kick out of you?

Cole Porter 1891–1964: 'I Get a Kick Out of You' (1934)

40 There are various ways of mending a broken heart, but perhaps going to a learned conference is one of the more unusual.

Barbara Pym 1913–80: *No Fond Return of Love* (1961)

41 I was adored once too.

William Shakespeare 1564–1616: *Twelfth Night* (1601)

42 ELAINE: *Romantic?* In your mother's clean apartment with two glasses from Bloomingdale's and your rubbers dripping on the newspaper?
BARNEY: It was my belief that romance is inspired by the participants and not the accoutrements.

Neil Simon 1927– : *Last of the Red Hot Lovers* (1970)

43 Loving you
Is not a choice
And not much reason
To rejoice.

Stephen Sondheim 1930– : *Passion* (1994) 'Loving You'

44 Out upon it, I have loved
Three whole days together;
And am like to love three more,
If it prove fair weather.

Time shall moult away his wings,
Ere he shall discover
In the whole wide world again
Such a constant lover.

John Suckling 1609–42: 'A Poem with the Answer' (1659)

45 Love is the fart
Of every heart:
It pains a man when 'tis kept close,
And others doth offend, when 'tis let loose.

John Suckling 1609–42: 'Love's Offence' (1646)

46 If love is the answer, could you rephrase the question?

Lily Tomlin 1939– : attributed; David Housham and John Frank-Keyes *Funny Business* (1992)

47 Love conquers all things—except poverty and toothache.

Mae West 1892–1980: attributed

48 To love oneself is the beginning of a lifelong romance.

Oscar Wilde 1854–1900: *An Ideal Husband* (1895)

49 For the first time since sudden love had thrown them into each other's arms, she had found herself beginning to wonder if her Blair was quite the godlike superman she had supposed. There even flashed through her mind a sinister speculation as to whether, when you came right down to it, he wasn't something of a pill.

P. G. Wodehouse 1881–1975: *Hot Water* (1932)

50 LILL: He loves me. He's just waiting till the children are settled.
VICTORIA: What in—sheltered housing?

Victoria Wood 1953– : *Mens Sana in Thingummy Doodah* (1990)

Management ····> Bureaucracy

66 Don't say yes until I finish talking! 99
Darryl F. Zanuck

1 Assistant heads must roll!
traditional solution to management problems in broadcasting

Anonymous: in *Guardian* 30 June 2004

2 We trained hard . . . but it seemed that every time we were beginning to form up into teams we would be reorganized. I was to learn later in life that we tend to meet any new situation by reorganizing; and a wonderful method it can be for creating the illusion of progress while producing confusion, inefficiency, and demoralization.

Anonymous: modern saying, frequently (and wrongly) attributed to Petronius Arbiter

3 When people say. 'Oh, would you rather be thought of as a funny man or a great boss?' My answer's always the same: to me they're not mutually exclusive.
David Brent as manager

Ricky Gervais 1961– and **Stephen Merchant**: *The Office* (Series 1, Episode 2; 2001)

4 Only the paranoid survive.
dictum on which he has long run his company, the Intel Corporation

Andrew Grove 1936– : in *New York Times* 18 December 1994

5 The man who is denied the opportunity of taking decisions of importance begins to regard as important the decisions he is allowed to take.

C. Northcote Parkinson 1909–93: *Parkinson's Law* (1958)

6 Lunch is for wimps.

Stanley Weiser and **Oliver Stone** 1946– : *Wall Street* (1987 film)

7 Don't say yes until I finish talking!
characteristic instruction

Darryl F. Zanuck 1902–79: Mel Gussow *Don't Say Yes Until I Finish Talking* (1971)

Marriage ····▷ Love, Sex

66 A feast where the grace is sometimes better than the dinner. **99**
Charles Caleb Colton

1 If it were not for the presents, an elopement would be preferable.

George Ade 1866–1944: *Forty Modern Fables* (1901)

2 It was partially my fault that we got divorced . . . I tended to place my wife under a pedestal.

Woody Allen 1935– : 'I Had a Rough Marriage' (monologue, 1964)

3 My wife was an immature woman . . . I would be home in the bathroom, taking a bath, and my wife would walk in whenever she felt like it and sink my boats.

Woody Allen 1935– : 'I Had a Rough Marriage' (monologue, 1964)

4 Your experience will be a lesson to all us men to be careful not to marry ladies in very high positions.
to Lord Snowdon on the break-up of his marriage to Princess Margaret

Idi Amin 1925– : attributed; Nigel Rees *Cassell Dictionary of Humorous Quotations* (1999)

5 Egghead weds hourglass.
on the marriage of Arthur Miller and Marilyn Monroe

Anonymous: headline in *Variety* 1956; attributed

6 [Marriage is] the only war where one sleeps with the enemy.

Anonymous: Mexican saying; Ned Sherrin *Cutting Edge* (1984)

7 Bigamy is having one husband too many. Monogamy is the same.

Anonymous: Erica Jong *Fear of Flying* (1973)

8 I think we explored the further reaches of 'for better or for worse'.
on her marriage during the 1980s

Mary Archer 1944– : at Jeffrey Archer's trial for perjury, London, 29 June 2001

9 It is a truth universally acknowledged, that a single man in possession of a good fortune, must be in want of a wife.

Jane Austen 1775–1817: *Pride and Prejudice* (1813)

10 A fate worse than marriage. A sort of eternal engagement.

Alan Ayckbourn 1939– : *Living Together* (1975)

11 Marriage is very difficult if you're a woman and a writer. No wonder Virginia Woolf committed suicide.

Beryl Bainbridge 1933– : attributed

12 A man cannot marry before he has studied anatomy and has dissected at the least one woman.

Honoré de Balzac 1799–1850: *Physiology of Marriage* (1904)

13 Opposites, opposites,
Where Momma won't sit Poppa sits.

Lionel Bart 1930– : *Blitz!* (1962)

14 I've known for years our marriage has been a mockery.
My body lying there night after night in the wasted
moonlight. I know now how the Taj Mahal must feel.

Alan Bennett 1934– : *Habeas Corpus*
(1973)

15 Being a husband is a whole-time job. That is why so many
husbands fail. They cannot give their entire attention to it.

Arnold Bennett 1867–1931: *The Title*
(1918)

16 Never marry a man who hates his mother, because he'll
end up hating you.

Jill Bennett 1931–90: in *Observer* 12
September 1982 'Sayings of the
Week'

17 My wife's gone to the country
Hooray! Hooray!
She thought it best, I need a rest,
That's why she's gone away.

Irving Berlin 1888–1989 and **George
Whiting**: 'My Wife's Gone To The
Country' (1910)

18 They stood before the altar and supplied
The fire themselves in which their fat was fried.

Ambrose Bierce 1842–c.1914: *The
Enlarged Devil's Dictionary* (1967)

19 Love matches are formed by people who pay for a month
of honey with a life of vinegar.

Countess of Blessington 1789–1849:
Desultory Thoughts and Reflections
(1839)

20 Even quarrels with one's husband are preferable to the
ennui of a solitary existence.
*view of the estranged American wife of Napoleon
Bonaparte's brother Jerome*

Elizabeth Patterson Bonaparte
1785–1879: Eugene L. Didier *The Life
and Letters of Madame Bonaparte*
(1879)

21 'Vladimir,' said Natasha, 'do you love me?' 'Toujours,'
said Stroganoff, with wariness. An unusual emotion for a
honeymooning husband when this particular question
crops up. But Stroganoff was lying in the upper berth of a
railway compartment and Natasha was in the lower berth
so the question could not be an overture to a delightful
interlude but merely the prelude to some less delightful
demand.

Caryl Brahms 1901–82 and **S. J.
Simon** 1904–48: *Six Curtains for
Stroganova* (1945)

22 *to his butler, who had resigned because of Lady Braxfield's
constant scolding:*
Lord! ye've little to complain o': ye may be thankfu' ye're
no married to her.

Lord Braxfield 1722–99: Henry
Cockburn *Memorials of his Time*
(1856)

23 It was very good of God to let Carlyle and Mrs Carlyle
marry one another and so make only two people miserable
instead of four.

Samuel Butler 1835–1902: letter, 21
November 1884

24 Think you, if Laura had been Petrarch's wife,
He would have written sonnets all his life?

Lord Byron 1788–1824: *Don Juan*
(1819–24)

25 I am about to be married—and am of course in all the
misery of a man in pursuit of happiness.

Lord Byron 1788–1824: letter, 15
October 1814

26 I have great hopes that we shall love each other all our
lives as much as if we had never married at all.

Lord Byron 1788–1824: letter to
Annabella Milbanke, 5 December
1814

27 Love and marriage, love and marriage,
Go together like a horse and carriage.

Sammy Cahn 1913– : 'Love and
Marriage' (1955)

28 The deep, deep peace of the double-bed after the hurly-
burly of the chaise-longue.

Mrs Patrick Campbell 1865–1940:
Alexander Woollcott *While Rome
Burns* (1934) 'The First Mrs
Tanqueray'

29 Translations (like wives) are seldom strictly faithful if they are in the least attractive.

Roy Campbell 1901–57: in *Poetry Review* June–July 1949

30 I am not at all the sort of person you and I took me for.

Jane Carlyle 1801–66: letter to Thomas Carlyle, 7 May 1822

31 Yblessed be god that I have wedded fyve!
Welcome the sixte, whan that evere he shal.

Geoffrey Chaucer c.1343–1400: *The Canterbury Tales* 'The Wife of Bath's Prologue'

32 *of her future son-in-law John Betjeman:*
We invite people like that to our houses, but we don't marry them.

Lady Chetwode d. 1946: Maurice Bowra *Memories 1898–1939* (1966)

33 Every woman should marry an archaeologist because she grows increasingly attractive to him as she grows increasingly to resemble a ruin.

Agatha Christie 1890–1976: Russell H. Fitzgibbon *The Agatha Christie Companion* (1980); attributed, perhaps apocryphal

34 The most happy marriage I can picture or imagine to myself would be the union of a deaf man to a blind woman.

Samuel Taylor Coleridge 1772–1834: Thomas Allsop *Letters, Conversations, and Recollections of S. T. Coleridge* (1836)

35 Marriage is a feast where the grace is sometimes better than the dinner.

Charles Caleb Colton 1780–1832: *Lacon* (1822)

36 Courtship to marriage, as a very witty prologue to a very dull play.

William Congreve 1670–1729: *The Old Bachelor* (1693)

37 Nay, for my part I always despised Mr Tattle of all things; nothing but his being my husband could have made me like him less.

William Congreve 1670–1729: *Love for Love* (1695)

38 Tho' marriage makes man and wife one flesh, it leaves 'em still two fools.

William Congreve 1670–1729: *The Double Dealer* (1694)

39 SHARPER: Thus grief still treads upon the heels of pleasure: Married in haste, we may repent at leisure.
SETTER: Some by experience find those words mis-placed: At leisure married, they repent in haste.

William Congreve 1670–1729: *The Old Bachelor* (1693)

40 The figure is unbelievable—just because she cooked a few meals now and again and wrote a few books.
   on the £10 million divorce settlement awarded to Caroline Conran

Terence Conran 1931– : in *Mail on Sunday* 6 July 1997 'Quotes of the Week'

41 Marriage is a wonderful invention; but, then again, so is a bicycle repair kit.

Billy Connolly 1942– : Duncan Campbell *Billy Connolly* (1976)

42 There is no more sombre enemy of good art than the pram in the hall.

Cyril Connolly 1903–74: *Enemies of Promise* (1938)

43 One of those looks which only a quarter-century of wedlock can adequately marinate.

Alan Coren 1938–2007: *Seems Like Old Times* (1989)

44 'What are your views on marriage?'
'Rather garbled.'

Noël Coward 1899–1973: in *Ned Sherrin's Theatrical Anecdotes* (1991); attributed

45 She very soon married this short young man
Who talked about soldiers all day
But who wasn't above
Making passionate love
In a coarse, rather Corsican way.

Noël Coward 1899–1973: 'Josephine' (1946)

46 How was the wedding?
Brief, to the point and not unduly musical.

Noël Coward 1899–1973: *Shadow Play*

47 So basically you're saying marriage is just a way of getting out of an embarrassing pause in conversation.

Richard Curtis 1956– : *Four Weddings and a Funeral* (1994 film)

48 All these years we've been single and proud of it—never noticed that two of us were to all intents and purposes married all this time.

Richard Curtis 1956– : *Four Weddings and a Funeral* (1994 film)

49 It's my old girl that advises. She has the head. But I never own to it before her. Discipline must be maintained.

Charles Dickens 1812–70: *Bleak House* (1853)

50 I revere the memory of Mr F. as an estimable man and most indulgent husband, only necessary to mention Asparagus and it appeared to hint at any little delicate thing to drink and it came like magic in a pint bottle it was not ecstasy but it was comfort.

Charles Dickens 1812–70: *Little Dorrit* (1857)

51 I have always thought that every woman should marry, and no man.

Benjamin Disraeli 1804–81: *Lothair* (1870)

52 No man is regular in his attendance at the House of Commons until he is married.

Benjamin Disraeli 1804–81: Hesketh Pearson *Dizzy* (1951)

53 Here lies my wife; here let her lie!
Now she's at peace and so am I.

John Dryden 1631–1700: epitaph; attributed but not traced in his works

54 I don't think matrimony consistent with the liberty of the subject.

George Farquhar 1678–1707: *The Twin Rivals* (1703)

55 His designs were strictly honourable, as the phrase is; that is, to rob a lady of her fortune by way of marriage.

Henry Fielding 1707–54: *Tom Jones* (1749)

56 I love to cry at weddings, anybody's weddings anytime!
. . . anybody's weddings just so long as it's not mine!

Dorothy Fields 1905–74: 'I Love to Cry at Weddings' (1966)

57 The awe and dread with which the untutored savage contemplates his mother-in-law are amongst the most familiar facts of anthropology.

James George Frazer 1854–1941: *The Golden Bough* (2nd ed., 1900)

58 He taught me housekeeping; when I divorce I keep the house.

Zsa Zsa Gabor 1919– : of her fifth husband; Ned Sherrin *Cutting Edge* (1984)

59 A man in love is incomplete until he has married. Then he's finished.

Zsa Zsa Gabor 1919– : in *Newsweek* 28 March 1960

60 *when asked how many husbands she had had:*
You mean apart from my own?

Zsa Zsa Gabor 1919– : K. Edwards *I Wish I'd Said That* (1976)

61 The comfortable estate of widowhood, is the only hope that keeps up a wife's spirits.

John Gay 1685–1732: *The Beggar's Opera* (1728)

62 Do you think your mother and I should have lived comfortably so long together, if ever we had been married?

John Gay 1685–1732: *The Beggar's Opera* (1728)

63 POLLY: Then all my sorrows are at an end.
MRS PEACHUM: A mighty likely speech, in troth, for a wench who is just married!

John Gay 1685–1732: *The Beggar's Opera* (1728)

64 Imagine signing a lease together;
And hanging a Matisse together;
Being alone and baking bread together.

Ira Gershwin 1896–1983: 'There's Nothing Like Marriage for People' (1946)

Reading the *New Yorker* in bed together!
Starting a family tree together!
Voting for the GOP together!

65 By god, D. H. Lawrence was right when he had said there must be a dumb, dark, dull, bitter belly-tension between a man and a woman, and how else could this be achieved save in the long monotony of marriage?

Stella Gibbons 1902–89: *Cold Comfort Farm* (1932)

66 I . . . chose my wife, as she did her wedding gown, not for a fine glossy surface, but such qualities as would wear well.

Oliver Goldsmith 1730–74: *The Vicar of Wakefield* (1766)

67 It seemed to me pretty plain, that they had more of love than matrimony in them.

Oliver Goldsmith 1730–74: *The Vicar of Wakefield* (1766)

68 My mother said it was simple to keep a man, you must be a maid in the living room, a cook in the kitchen and a whore in the bedroom. I said I'd hire the other two and take care of the bedroom bit.

Jerry Hall 1956– : in *Observer* 6 October 1985 'Sayings of the Week'

69 I married many men,
A ton of them,
And yet I was untrue to none of them
Because I bumped off ev'ry one of them
To keep my love alive.
Sir Paul was frail,
He looked a wreck to me.
At night he was a horse's neck to me.
So I performed an appendectomy
To keep my love alive.

Lorenz Hart 1895–1943: 'To Keep My Love Alive' (1943)

70 It was not totally inconceivable that she could have joined me as my wife at No. 10.
on the TV starlet Jayne Mansfield

Edward Heath 1916–2005: in *Sunday Times* 6 February 2000

71 The critical period in matrimony is breakfast-time.

A. P. Herbert 1890–1971: *Uncommon Law* (1935) 'Is Marriage Lawful?'

72 Holy deadlock.

A. P. Herbert 1890–1971: title of novel (1934)

73 A TV host asked my wife, 'Have you ever considered divorce?' She replied: 'Divorce never, murder often.'

Charlton Heston 1924– : in *Independent* 21 July 1999

74 Who weddeth or he be wise shall die ere he thrive.

John Heywood c.1497–c.1580: *A Dialogue of Proverbs* (1546)

75 Hogamus, higamous
Man is polygamous
Higamus, hogamous
Woman monogamous.

William James 1842–1910: in *Oxford Book of Marriage* (1990)

76 *of a man who remarried immediately after the death of a wife with whom he had been unhappy:*
The triumph of hope over experience.

Samuel Johnson 1709–84: James Boswell *Life of Samuel Johnson* (1791) 1770

77 I want you to assist me in forcing her on board the lugger; once there, I'll frighten her into marriage.

John Benn Johnstone 1803–91: *The Gipsy Farmer* (performed 1845); since quoted as 'Once aboard the lugger and the maid is mine'

78 I'm getting married in the morning!
Ding dong! The bells are gonna chime.
Pull out the stopper!
Let's have a whopper!
But get me to the church on time!

Alan Jay Lerner 1918–86: 'Get Me to the Church on Time' (1956)

79 I've been married six months. She looks like a million dollars, but she only knows a hundred and twenty words and she's only got two ideas in her head.

Eric Linklater 1899–1974: *Juan in America* (1931)

80 Did you ever look through a microscope at a drop of pond water? You see plenty of love there. All the amoebae getting married. I presume they think it very exciting and important. We don't.

Rose Macaulay 1881–1958: *Crewe Train* (1926)

81 Don't worry if you never marry. It will save you a lot of vexation.
last words of advice to Petronella Wyatt

Princess Margaret 1930–2002: in *Sunday Times* 17 February 2002

82 *to her husband, who had asked the age of a flirtatious starlet with noticeably thick legs:*
For God's sake, Walter, why don't you chop off her legs and read the rings?

Carol Matthau: Truman Capote *Answered Prayers* (1986)

83 No matter how happily a woman may be married, it always pleases her to discover that there is a nice man who wishes she were not.

H. L. Mencken 1880–1956: *Chrestomathy* (1949)

84 Kissing don't last: cookery do!

George Meredith 1828–1909: *The Ordeal of Richard Feverel* (1859)

85 There once was an old man of Lyme
Who married three wives at a time,
When asked 'Why a third?'
He replied, 'One's absurd!
And bigamy, Sir, is a crime!'

William Cosmo Monkhouse 1840–1901: *Nonsense Rhymes* (1902)

86 One doesn't have to get anywhere in a marriage. It's not a public conveyance.

Iris Murdoch 1919–99: *A Severed Head* (1961)

87 I'm Henery the Eighth, I am!
Henery the Eighth, I am, I am!
I got married to the widow next door,
She's been married seven times before.
Every one was a Henery,
She wouldn't have a Willie or a Sam.
I'm her eighth old man named Henery
I'm Henery the Eighth, I am!

Fred Murray: 'I'm Henery the Eighth, I Am!' (1911)

88 To keep your marriage brimming
With love in the loving cup,
Whenever you're wrong, admit it,
Whenever you're right, shut up.

Ogden Nash 1902–71: 'A Word to Husbands' (1957)

89 To Wanda, the only item of essential equipment—apart from a Rolex watch (boiled in a stew by Afghans to test its waterproof qualities)—not lost, stolen or simply worn out in the course of some thirty years of travel together.

Eric Newby 1919– : *On the Shores of the Mediterranean* (1984); dedication to his wife

90 *to his wife Vita Sackville-West:*
A crushed life is what I lead, similar to that of the hen you ran over the other day.

Harold Nicolson 1886–1968: diary, 8 October 1958

91 'It was she as set her bonnet at him!' cried Mrs Williams, who had never yet let her husband finish a sentence since his 'I will' at Trinity Church, Plymouth Dock, in 1782 [eighteen years before].

Patrick O'Brian 1914–2000: *Master and Commander* (1970)

92 *agreeing with the comment, at her remarriage to Alan Campbell in 1950, that some of those present had not spoken to each other for years:*
Including the bride and groom.

Dorothy Parker 1893–1967: Marion Meade *What Fresh Hell Is This?* (1988)

93 Marriage may often be a stormy lake, but celibacy is almost always a muddy horsepond.

Thomas Love Peacock 1785–1866: *Melincourt* (1817)

94 Strange to say what delight we married people have to see these poor fools decoyed into our condition.

Samuel Pepys 1633–1703: diary, 25 December 1665

95 My wife, who, poor wretch, is troubled with her lonely life.

Samuel Pepys 1633–1703: diary, 19 December 1662

96 Tolerance is the one essential ingredient . . . You can take it from me that the Queen has the quality of tolerance in abundance.
his recipe for a successful marriage, 19 November 1997, marking their golden wedding anniversary

Prince Philip, Duke of Edinburgh 1921– : in *The Times* 20 November 1997

97 They dream in courtship, but in wedlock wake.

Alexander Pope 1688–1744: *Translations from Chaucer* (1714)

98 HE: Have you heard Professor Munch
Ate his wife and divorced his lunch?
SHE: Well, did you evah!
What a swell party this is.

Cole Porter 1891–1964: 'Well, Did You Evah!' (1939)

99 It feels so fine to be a bride,
And how's the groom? Why, he's slightly fried,
It's delightful, it's delicious, it's de-lovely.

Cole Porter 1891–1964: 'It's De-lovely' (1936)

100 I'm a maid who would marry
And will take with no qualm
Any Tom, Dick or Harry,
Any Harry, Dick or Tom.

Cole Porter 1891–1964: 'Tom, Dick or Harry' (1948)

101 WIFE OF TWO YEARS' STANDING: Oh yes! I'm sure he's not so fond of me as at first. He's away so much, neglects me dreadfully, and he's so cross when he comes home. What *shall* I do?
WIDOW: Feed the brute!

Punch 1841–1992: vol. 89 (1885)

102 Advice to persons about to marry.—'Don't.'

Punch 1841–1992: vol. 8 (1845)

103 BISHOP: Who is it that sees and hears all we do, and before whom even I am but as a crushed worm?
PAGE: The Missus, my Lord.

Punch 1841–1992: vol. 79 (1880)

104 A husband is what is left of a lover, after the nerve has been extracted.

Helen Rowland 1875–1950: *A Guide to Men* (1922)

105 *the Lord Chief Justice was once asked by a lady what was the maximum punishment for bigamy:*
Two mothers-in-law.

Lord Russell of Killowen 1832–1900: Edward Abinger *Forty Years at the Bar* (1930)

106 I think that gay marriage is something that should be between a man and a woman.

Arnold Schwarzenegger 1947– : in *CCN.com* (online edition) 28 August 2003

107 But for marriage 'tis good for nothing, but to make friends fall out.

Thomas Shadwell c.1642–92: *The Sullen Lovers* (1668)

108 A young man married is a man that's marred.

William Shakespeare 1564–1616: *All's Well that Ends Well* (1603–4)

109 Many a good hanging prevents a bad marriage.

William Shakespeare 1564–1616: *Twelfth Night* (1601)

110 It is a woman's business to get married as soon as possible, and a man's to keep unmarried as long as he can.

George Bernard Shaw 1856–1950: *Man and Superman* (1903)

111 Marriage is popular because it combines the maximum of temptation with the maximum of opportunity.

George Bernard Shaw 1856–1950: *Man and Superman* (1903) 'Maxims: Marriage'

112 'Tis safest in matrimony to begin with a little aversion.

Richard Brinsley Sheridan 1751–1816: *The Rivals* (1775)

113 Take care of him. And make him feel important. And if you can do that, you'll have a happy and wonderful marriage. Like two out of every ten couples.

Neil Simon 1927– : *Barefoot in the Park* (1964)

114 PAUL: You want me to be rich and famous, don't you?
CORRIE: During the day. At night I want you to be here and sexy.

Neil Simon 1927– : *Barefoot in the Park* (1964)

115 My definition of marriage . . . it resembles a pair of shears, so joined that they cannot be separated; often moving in opposite directions, yet always punishing anyone who comes between them.

Sydney Smith 1771–1845: Lady Holland *Memoir* (1855)

116 The concerts you enjoy together
Neighbours you annoy together
Children you destroy together,
That keep marriage intact.

Stephen Sondheim 1930– : 'The Little Things You Do Together' (1970)

117 My brother Toby, quoth she, is going to be married to Mrs Wadman. Then he will never, quoth my father, lie *diagonally* in his bed again as long as he lives.

Laurence Sterne 1713–68: *Tristram Shandy* (1759–67)

118 Even if we take matrimony at its lowest, even if we regard it as no more than a sort of friendship recognised by the police.

Robert Louis Stevenson 1850–94: *Virginibus Puerisque* (1881)

119 A woman with fair opportunities and without a positive hump, may marry whom she likes.

William Makepeace Thackeray 1811–63: *Vanity Fair* (1847–8)

120 A husband should not insult his wife publicly, at parties. He should insult her in the privacy of the home.

James Thurber 1894–1961: *Thurber Country* (1953)

121 That's my first wife up there and this is the *present* Mrs Harris.

James Thurber 1894–1961: cartoon caption in *New Yorker* 16 March 1933

122 Don't get mad, get everything.
advice to wronged wives

Ivana Trump 1949– : spoken in *The First Wives Club* (film, 1996)

123 LADY BRUTE: 'Tis a hard fate I should not be believed.
SIR JOHN: 'Tis a damned atheistical age, wife.

John Vanbrugh 1664–1726: *The Provoked Wife* (1697)

124 Marriage isn't a word . . . it's a *sentence*!

King Vidor 1895–1982: in *The Crowd* (1928 film)

125 He is dreadfully married. He's the most married man I ever saw in my life.

Artemus Ward 1834–67: *Artemus Ward's Lecture* (1869) 'Brigham Young's Palace'

126 *telegram supposedly sent to Tom Driberg on the occasion of Driberg's wedding:*
I pray that the church is not struck by lightning.

Evelyn Waugh 1903–66: attributed; Nigel Rees (ed.) *Cassell Dictionary of Humorous Quotations* (1999)

127 Marriage is a great institution, but I'm not ready for an institution yet.

Mae West 1892–1980: Laurence J. Peter (ed.) *Quotations for our Time* (1977); attributed

128 An engagement should come on a young girl as a surprise, pleasant or unpleasant, as the case may be.

Oscar Wilde 1854–1900: *The Importance of Being Earnest* (1895)

129 Twenty years of romance make a woman look like a ruin; but twenty years of marriage make her something like a public building.

Oscar Wilde 1854–1900: *A Woman of No Importance* (1893)

130 GERRY: We can't get married at all . . . I'm a man.
OSGOOD: Well, nobody's perfect.

Billy Wilder 1906–2002 and **I. A. L. Diamond** 1915–88: *Some Like It Hot* (1959 film; closing words)

131 *when courting his future wife (whom he married in 1949):*
I would worship the ground you walk on, Audrey, if you only lived in a better neighbourhood.

Billy Wilder 1906–2002: M. Zolotow *Billy Wilder in Hollywood* (1977)

132 Marriage is a bribe to make a housekeeper think she's a householder.

Thornton Wilder 1897–1975: *The Merchant of Yonkers* (1939)

133 Chumps always make the best husbands. When you marry, Sally, grab a chump. Tap his forehead first, and if it rings solid, don't hesitate. All the unhappy marriages come from the husbands having brains.

P. G. Wodehouse 1881–1975: *The Adventures of Sally* (1920)

134 There are men who fear repartee in a wife more keenly than a sword.

P. G. Wodehouse 1881–1975: *Jill the Reckless* (1922)

135 'Tis my maxim, he's a fool that marries, but he's a greater that does not marry a fool.

William Wycherley c.1640–1716: *The Country Wife* (1675)

Medicine ·····▶ Sickness and Health

❝ I don't believe in vitamin pills. I swear by men. ❞
Joan Collins

1 *doctor's advice to Bond star Roger Moore after he had been fitted with a heart pacemaker:*
Keep paying the electricity bill.

Anonymous: in *Mail on Sunday* 4 January 2004 'Quotes of the Year'

2 She has her high days and low days, a bit like the church. It depends what miracle drug the doctor's currently got her on.

Alan Ayckbourn 1939– : *Joking Apart* (1979)

3 Medicinal discovery,
It moves in mighty leaps,
It leapt straight past the common cold
And gave it us for keeps.

Pam Ayres 1947– : 'Oh no, I got a cold' (1976)

4 Hark! the herald angels sing!
Beecham's Pills are just the thing,
Two for a woman, one for a child . . .
Peace on earth and mercy mild!

Thomas Beecham 1879–1961: advertising jingle devised for his father, but not used; Neville Cardus *Sir Thomas Beecham* (1961)

5 Physicians of the Utmost Fame
Were called at once; but when they came
They answered, as they took their Fees,
'There is no Cure for this Disease.'

Hilaire Belloc 1870–1953: 'Henry King' (1907)

6 Dr Sillitoes's got him on tablets for depression. It's not mental, in fact it's quite widespread. A lot of better-class people get it apparently.

Alan Bennett 1934– : *Enjoy* (1980)

7 I was in for ten hours and had 40 pints, beating my previous record by 20 minutes.
comparing transfusions with drinking, during the BBC's Sports Personality of the Year Awards

George Best 1946–2005: in *Mail on Sunday* 15 December 2002

8 I don't believe in vitamin pills. I swear by men, darling—and as many as possible.

Joan Collins 1933– : in *Independent* 10 June 2000 'Quotes of the Week'

9 And, on the label of the stuff,
He wrote this verse;
Which one would think was clear enough,
And terse:—
When taken,
To be well shaken.

George Colman the Younger 1762–1836: 'The Newcastle Apothecary' (1797)

10 Meaty jelly, too, especially when a little salt, which is the case when there's ham, is mellering to the organ.

Charles Dickens 1812–70: *Our Mutual Friend* (1865)

11 *epigram on Dr John Lettsom, who would sign his prescriptions 'I. Lettsom':*
Whenever patients come to I,
I physics, bleeds, and sweats 'em;
If after that they choose to die,
What's that to me!—I *letts 'em.*

Thomas Erskine 1750–1823: *Poetical Works* (1823)

12 A cousin of mine who was a casualty surgeon in Manhattan tells me that he and his colleagues had a one-word nickname for bikers: Donors. Rather chilling.

Stephen Fry 1957– : *Paperweight* (1992)

13 I came in here in all good faith to help my country. I don't mind giving a reasonable amount [of blood], but a pint . . . why that's very nearly an armful. I'm sorry. I'm not walking around with an empty arm for anybody.

Ray Galton 1930– and **Alan Simpson** 1929– : *The Blood Donor* (1961 television programme, words spoken by Tony Hancock)

14 Any man who goes to a psychiatrist should have his head examined.

Sam Goldwyn 1882–1974: Norman Zierold *Moguls* (1969)

15 If you have a stomach ache, in France you get a suppository, in Germany a health spa, in the United States they cut your stomach open and in Britain they put you on a waiting list.

Phil Hammond 1955– and **Michael Mosley** : *Trust Me (I'm a Doctor)* (1999)

16 Hungry Joe collected lists of fatal diseases and arranged them in alphabetical order so that he could put his finger without delay on any one he wanted to worry about.

Joseph Heller 1923–99: *Catch-22* (1961)

17 The kind of doctor I want is one who, when he's not examining me, is home studying medicine.

George S. Kaufman 1889–1961: Howard Teichmann *George S. Kaufman* (1973)

18 In disease Medical Men guess: if they cannot ascertain a disease, they call it nervous.

John Keats 1795–1821: J. A. Gere and John Sparrow (eds.) *Geoffrey Madan's Notebooks* (1981); attributed

19 Dr Milton's really lost it . . . his brow lifts are getting scary. He cuts way too much and makes everybody look either frightened or surprised.

Jay McInerney 1955– : *How It Ended* (2000)

20 The medics can now stretch your life out an additional dozen years but they don't tell you that most of these years are going to be spent flat on your back while some ghoul with thick glasses and a matted skull peers at you through a machine that's hot out of 'Space Patrol'.

Groucho Marx 1895–1977: letter 23 December 1954

21 All the errors that lead to burst appendixes are made by family doctors. The patient usually is sick enough to call for help, but by the time he gets to the specialist he is too far gone for it.

H. L. Mencken 1880–1956: *Minority Report* (1956)

22 GÉRONTE: It seems to me you are locating them wrongly: the heart is on the left and the liver is on the right.
SGANARELLE: Yes, in the old days that was so, but we have changed all that, and we now practise medicine by a completely new method.

Molière 1622–73: *Le Médecin malgré lui* (1667)

23 I only take Viagra when I'm with more than one woman.

Jack Nicholson 1937– : in *Mail on Sunday* 8 February 2004

24 I fear that being a patient in any hospital in Ireland calls for two things—holy resignation and an iron constitution.

Flann O'Brien 1911–66: *Myles Away from Dublin* (1990)

25 The desire to take medicine is perhaps the greatest feature which distinguishes man from animals.

William Osler 1849–1919: H. Cushing *Life of Sir William Osler* (1925)

26 As for consulting a dentist regularly, my punctuality practically amounted to a fetish. Every twelve years I would drop whatever I was doing and allow wild Caucasian ponies to drag me to a reputable orthodontist.

S. J. Perelman 1904–79: *The Most of S. J. Perelman* (1959) 'Dental or Mental, I Say It's Spinach'

27 He said my bronchial tubes were entrancing,
My epiglottis filled him with glee,
He simply loved my larynx
And went wild about my pharynx,
But he never said he loved me.

Cole Porter 1891–1964: 'The Physician' (1933)

28 Cured yesterday of my disease,
I died last night of my physician.

Matthew Prior 1664–1721: 'The Remedy Worse than the Disease' (1727)

29 Being hugged by Diana Rigg is worth three sessions of chemotherapy.
after his appearance on Loose Ends *with Diana Rigg, 15 April 2000*

Robert Runcie 1921–2000: letter to the Editor, April 2000

30 There would never be any public agreement among doctors if they did not agree to agree on the main point of the doctor being always in the right.

George Bernard Shaw 1856–1950: preface to *The Doctor's Dilemma* (1911)

31 There is at bottom only one genuinely scientific treatment for all diseases, and that is to stimulate the phagocytes.

George Bernard Shaw 1856–1950: *The Doctor's Dilemma* (1911)

32 I can't stand whispering. Every time a doctor whispers in the hospital, next day there's a funeral.

Neil Simon 1927– : *The Gingerbread Lady* (1970)

33 A psychiatrist is a man who goes to the Folies-Bergère and looks at the audience.

Mervyn Stockwood 1913–95: in *Observer* 15 October 1961

34 Take anything that is either nasty, expensive or difficult to obtain, wrap it up in mystery and you have a cure.

Richard Totman: Phil Hammond and Michael Mosley *Trust Me (I'm a Doctor)* (1999)

35 Randolph Churchill went into hospital . . . to have a lung removed. It was announced that the trouble was not 'malignant' . . . it was a typical triumph of modern science to find the only part of Randolph that was not malignant and remove it.

Evelyn Waugh 1903–66: 'Irregular Notes 1960–65'; diary March 1964

36 Sir Roderick Glossop . . . is always called a nerve specialist, because it sounds better, but everybody knows that he's really a sort of janitor to the looney-bin.

P. G. Wodehouse 1881–1975: *The Inimitable Jeeves* (1923)

37 *on being given aspirin from a small tin box by Jeeves:*
Thank you, Jeeves. Don't slam the lid.

P. G. Wodehouse 1881–1975: *Ring for Jeeves* (1953) ch. 18

Men ····▸ Men and Women

❝A hard man is good to find.❞
Mae West

1 Nobody ever, unless he is very wicked, deliberately tries to hurt anybody. It's just that men cannot help not loving you or behaving badly.

Beryl Bainbridge 1933– : interview in *Daily Telegraph* 10 September 1996

2 Women were brought up to believe that men were the answer. They weren't. They weren't even one of the questions.

Julian Barnes 1946– : *Staring at the Sun* (1986)

3 You cannot make a man by standing a sheep on its hind-legs. But by standing a flock of sheep in that position you can make a crowd of men.

Max Beerbohm 1872–1956: *Zuleika Dobson* (1911)

4 My mother wanted me to be a nice boy. I didn't let her down. I don't smoke, drink or mess around with women.

Julian Clary 1959– : in *Independent* 2 March 1996 'Quote Unquote'

5 Faded boys, jaded boys, come what may,
Art is our inspiration,
And as we are the reason for the 'Nineties' being gay,
We all wear a green carnation.

Noël Coward 1899–1973: 'Green Carnation' (1929)

6 We are lads. We have burgled houses and nicked car stereos, and we like girls and swear and go to the football and take the piss.

Noel Gallagher 1967– : interview in *Melody Maker* 30 March 1996

7 Francesca di Rimini, miminy, piminy,
Je-ne-sais-quoi young man!

W. S. Gilbert 1836–1911: *Patience* (1881)

8 A greenery-yallery, Grosvenor Gallery,
Foot-in-the-grave young man!

W. S. Gilbert 1836–1911: *Patience* (1881)

9 Men are animals and as such are entitled to humane treatment and should not be trapped or shot or bred for food or fur.

Germaine Greer 1939– : in *Mail on Sunday* 7 March 1999 'Quotes of the Week'

10 *asked about his hard-man image:*
Neanderthal. A glowering thug, the Terminator in shorts. And that's just my wife's opinion.

Martin Johnson 1970– : Martin Johnson *Autobiography* (2003)

11 Years ago, manhood was an opportunity for achievement, and now it is a problem to be overcome.

Garrison Keillor 1942– : *The Book of Guys* (1994)

12 There is nothing about which men lie so much as about their sexual powers. In this at least every man is, what in his heart he would like to be, a Casanova.

W. Somerset Maugham 1874–1965: *A Writer's Notebook* (1949) written in 1941

13 He's an oul' butty o' mine—oh, he's a darlin' man, a daarlin' man.

Sean O'Casey 1880–1964: *Juno and the Paycock* (1925)

14 The follies which a man regrets most, in his life, are those which he didn't commit when he had the opportunity.

Helen Rowland 1875–1950: *A Guide to Men* (1922)

15 God made him, and therefore let him pass for a man.

William Shakespeare 1564–1616: *The Merchant of Venice* (1596–8)

16 To be a well-favoured man is the gift of fortune; but to write and read comes by nature.

William Shakespeare 1564–1616: *Much Ado About Nothing* (1598–9)

17 You men are unaccountable things; mad till you have your mistresses, and then stark mad till you are rid of 'em again.

John Vanbrugh 1664–1726: *The Provoked Wife* (1697)

18 A hard man is good to find.

Mae West 1892–1980: attributed

Men and Women ····▸ Men, Women and Woman's Role

❝ The female sex has no greater fan than I, and I have the bills to prove it. ❞
Alan Jay Lerner

---

1 *'Mrs Merton' to Debbie McGee:*
But what first, Debbie, attracted you to millionaire Paul Daniels?

Caroline Aherne 1963– : *The Mrs Merton Show* (BBC TV)

2 *announcing the break-up of Ken and Barbie's 43-year romance:*
Like other Hollywood couples, their celebrity romance has come to an end.

Russell Arons: in *CNN.com* (online edition) 12 February 2004

3 Women love scallywags, but some marry them and then try to make them wear a blazer.

David Bailey 1938– : in *Mail on Sunday* 16 February 1997 'Quotes of the Week'

4 All women dress like their mothers, that is their tragedy. No man ever does. That is his.

Alan Bennett 1934– : *Forty Years On* (1969)

5 We sat in the car park till twenty to one
And now I'm engaged to Miss Joan Hunter Dunn.

John Betjeman 1906–84: 'A Subaltern's Love-Song' (1945)

6 Too many rings around Rosie
Never got Rosie a ring.

Irving Caesar 1895– : 'Too Many Rings around Rosie' (1925)

7 AMANDA: I've been brought up to believe that it's beyond the pale, for a man to strike a woman.
ELYOT: A very poor tradition. Certain women should be struck regularly, like gongs.

Noël Coward 1899–1973: *Private Lives* (1930)

8 ''Cos a coachman's a privileged indiwidual,' replied Mr Weller, looking fixedly at his son. ''Cos a coachman may do vithout suspicion wot other men may not; 'cos a coachman may be on the wery amicablest terms with eighty mile o' females, and yet nobody think that he ever means to marry any vun among them.'

Charles Dickens 1812–70: *Pickwick Papers* (1837)

9 The feminist movement seems to have beaten the manners out of men, but I didn't see them put up a lot of resistance.

Clarissa Dickson Wright: in *Mail on Sunday* 24 September 2000 'Quotes of the Week'

10 *a fellow Congressman attacked a piece of women's rights legislation with the words, 'I've always thought of women as kissable, cuddly, and smelling good*':
That's what I feel about men. I only hope you haven't been disappointed as often as I have.

Millicent Fenwick 1910– : in *Ned Sherrin in his Anecdotage* (1993)

11 I will not . . . sulk about having no boyfriend, but develop inner poise and authority and sense of self as woman of substance, complete *without* boyfriend, as best way to obtain boyfriend.

Helen Fielding 1958– : *Bridget Jones's Diary* (1996)

12 The minute you walked in the joint,
I could see you were a man of distinction,
A real big spender.
Good looking, so refined,
Say, wouldn't you like to know what's going on in my mind?
So let me get right to the point.
I don't pop my cork for every guy I see.
Hey! big spender, spend a little time with me.

Dorothy Fields 1905–74: 'Big Spender' (1966)

13 A fine romance with no kisses.
A fine romance, my friend, this is.
We should be like a couple of hot tomatoes,
But you're as cold as yesterday's mashed potatoes.

Dorothy Fields 1905–74: 'A Fine Romance' (1936)

14 *estranged husband of Liza Minnelli:*
I'd give up all my Shirley Temple dolls to get Liza back.

David Gest: attributed; in *Sunday Times* 14 December 2003 'Talking Heads'

15 If they ever invent a vibrator that can open pickle jars, we've had it.
on the bleak future facing men

Jeff Green: in *Mail on Sunday* 21 March 1999 'Quotes of the Week'

16 Our days will be so ecstatic
Our nights will be so exotic
For I'm a neurotic erratic
And you're an erratic erotic.

E. Y. Harburg 1898–1981: 'Courtship in Greenwich Village' (1965)

17 I'm wild again,
Beguiled again,
A simpering, whimpering child again—
Bewitched, bothered and bewildered am I.
Couldn't sleep
And wouldn't sleep

Lorenz Hart 1895–1943: 'Bewitched, Bothered and Bewildered' (1940)

Until I could sleep where I shouldn't sleep—
Bewitched, bothered and bewildered am I.

18 Take him, I won't put a price on him
Take him, he's yours
Take him, pyjamas look nice on him
But how he snores!

Lorenz Hart 1895–1943: 'Take Him'
(1940)

19 KATHARINE HEPBURN: I fear I may be too tall for you, Mr.
Tracy.
SPENCER TRACY: Don't worry, I'll cut you down to my size.
*apocryphal account of their first meeting in 1942; it was
the film director Joe Mankiewicz who said to Hepburn, 'He'll
cut you down to size'*

Katharine Hepburn 1909–2003: Bill
Davidson *Spencer Tracy* (1987)

20 A woman's mind is cleaner than a man's; she changes it
more often.

Oliver Herford 1863–1935:
attributed; Evan Esar and Nicolas
Bentley (eds.) *Treasury of Humorous
Quotations* (1951)

21 Brought up in an epoch when ladies apparently rolled
along on wheels, Mr Quarles was peculiarly susceptible to
calves.

Aldous Huxley 1894–1963: *Point
Counter Point* (1928)

22 If men could get pregnant, abortion would be a sacrament.

Florynce Kennedy 1916–2001: 'The
Verbal Karate of Florynce R. Kennedy'
(1973)

23 Being kissed by a man who *didn't* wax his moustache
was—like eating an egg without salt.

Rudyard Kipling 1865–1936: *The
Story of the Gadsbys* (1889) 'Poor
Dear Mamma'

24 The female sex has no greater fan than I, and I have the
bills to prove it.

Alan Jay Lerner 1918–86: *The Street
Where I Live* (1978)

25 Yes, why can't a woman be more like a man?
Men are so honest, so thoroughly square;
Eternally noble, historically fair;
Who when you win will always give your back a pat—
Why can't a woman be like that?

Alan Jay Lerner 1918–86: 'A Hymn
to Him' (1956)

26 But let a woman in your life
And your serenity is through!
She'll redecorate your home
From the cellar to the dome;
Then get on to the enthralling
Fun of overhauling
You.

Alan Jay Lerner 1918–86: 'I'm an
Ordinary Man' (1956)

27 *comment made by the estranged wife of Selwyn Lloyd:*
How could any woman love a man who wears a cardigan
over his pyjamas?

Elizabeth Lloyd 1928– : attributed;
Alan Watkins in *Spectator* 14 June
2003

28 Brother, do you know a nicer occupation,
Matter of fact, neither do I,
Than standing on the corner
Watching all the girls go by?

Frank Loesser 1910–69: 'Standing on
the Corner' (1956)

29 Oh! to be loved by a man I respect,
To bask in the glow of his perfectly understandable
neglect.

Frank Loesser 1910–69: 'Happy to
Keep his Dinner Warm' (1961)

30 When you meet a gent paying all sorts of rent
For a flat that would flatten the Taj Mahal,
Call it sad, call it funny
But it's better than even money
That the guy's only doing it for some doll.

Frank Loesser 1910–69: 'Guys and Dolls' (1950)

31 So then he said that he used to be a member of the choir himself, so who was he to cast the first rock at a girl like I.

Anita Loos 1893–1981: *Gentlemen Prefer Blondes* (1925)

32 *approaching an unwelcoming Greta Garbo and peering up under the brim of her floppy hat:*
Pardon me, Ma'am . . . I thought you were a guy I knew in Pittsburgh.

Groucho Marx 1895–1977: David Niven *Bring on the Empty Horses* (1975)

33 I suppose true sexual equality will come when a general called Anthea is found having an unwise lunch with a young, unreliable male model from Spain.

John Mortimer 1923– : in *The Spectator* 26 March 1994

34 He tells you when you've got on too much lipstick,
And helps you with your girdle when your hips stick.

Ogden Nash 1902–71: 'The Perfect Husband' (1949)

35 A little incompatibility is the spice of life, particularly if he has income and she is pattable.

Ogden Nash 1902–71: *Versus* (1949)

36 Twenty years ago when we had no respect for women they just used to say, 'You're chucked.' And now we do respect them we have to lie to them sensitively.

Simon Nye 1958– : *Men Behaving Badly* (ITV, series 1, 1992) 'Intruders'

37 I killin' meself workin', an' he shruttin' about from mornin' till night like a paycock!

Sean O'Casey 1880–1964: *Juno and the Paycock* (1925)

38 Men seldom make passes
At girls who wear glasses.

Dorothy Parker 1893–1967: 'News Item' (1937)

39 Woman lives but in her lord;
Count to ten, and man is bored.
With this the gist and sum of it,
What earthly good can come of it?

Dorothy Parker 1893–1967: 'General Review of the Sex Situation' (1937)

40 Some get a kick from cocaine.
I'm sure that if I took even one sniff
That would bore me terrific'ly too,
Yet I get a kick out of you.

Cole Porter 1891–1964: 'I Get a Kick out of You' (1934)

41 Of course, I'm awf'ly glad that Mother had to marry Father,
But I hate men.

Cole Porter 1891–1964: 'I Hate Men' (1948)

42 The breeze is chasing the zephyr,
The moon is chasing the sea,
The bull is chasing the heifer,
But nobody's chasing me.

Cole Porter 1891–1964: 'Nobody's Chasing Me' (1950)

43 You're the Nile,
You're the Tow'r of Pisa,
You're the smile
On the Mona Lisa.
I'm a worthless check, a total wreck, a flop,
But if, baby, I'm the bottom
You're the top!

Cole Porter 1891–1964: 'You're the Top' (1934)

44 Only the male intellect, clouded by sexual impulse, could call the undersized, narrow-shouldered, broad-hipped, and short-legged sex the fair sex.

Arthur Schopenhauer 1788–1860: 'On Women' (1851), tr. E. Belfort Bax

45 A bunch of the boys were whooping it up in the Malamute saloon;
The kid that handles the music-box was hitting a jag-time tune;
Back of the bar, in a solo game, sat Dangerous Dan McGrew,
And watching his luck was his light-o'-love, the lady that's known as Lou.

Robert W. Service 1874–1958: 'The Shooting of Dan McGrew' (1907)

46 Say that she rail; why then I'll tell her plain
She sings as sweetly as a nightingale:
Say that she frown; I'll say she looks as clear
As morning roses newly washed with dew:
Say she be mute and will not speak a word;
Then I'll commend her volubility,
And say she uttereth piercing eloquence.

William Shakespeare 1564–1616: *The Taming of the Shrew* (1592)

47 *an unknown woman wrote to Shaw suggesting that as he had the greatest brain in the world, and she the most beautiful body, they ought to produce the most perfect child:*
What if the child inherits my body and your brains?

George Bernard Shaw 1856–1950: Hesketh Pearson *Bernard Shaw* (1942)

48 You think that you are Ann's suitor; that you are the pursuer and she the pursued . . . Fool: it is you who are the pursued, the marked down quarry, the destined prey.

George Bernard Shaw 1856–1950: *Man and Superman* (1903)

49 Won't you come into the garden? I would like my roses to see you.

Richard Brinsley Sheridan 1751–1816: to a young lady; attributed

50 You've got to understand, in a way a thirty-three-year-old guy is a lot younger than a twenty-four-year-old girl. That is, he may not be ready for marriage yet.

Neil Simon 1927– : *Come Blow Your Horn* (1961)

51 From my experience of life I believe my personal motto should be 'Beware of men bearing flowers.'

Muriel Spark 1918–2006: *Curriculum Vitae* (1992)

52 A lady, if surprised by melancholy, might go to bed with a chap, once; or a thousand times if consumed by passion. But twice . . . *twice* . . . A lady might think she'd been taken for a tart.

Tom Stoppard 1937– : *Night and Day* (1978)

53 Yes, I am a fatal man, Madame Fribsbi. To inspire hopeless passion is my destiny.

William Makepeace Thackeray 1811–63: *Pendennis* (1848–50)

54 Werther had a love for Charlotte
Such as words could never utter;
Would you know how first he met her?
She was cutting bread and butter.

William Makepeace Thackeray 1811–63: 'Sorrows of Werther' (1855)

55 In Europe, when a rich woman has an affair with a conductor, they have a baby. In America, she endows an orchestra for him.

Edgar Varèse 1885–1965: Herman G. Weinberg *Saint Cinema* (1970)

56 I don't want anyone to notice that I've been chucked, well, not even chucked, to be chucked you have to have been going out with someone, I've been . . . sort of sampled.

Arabella Weir: *Does My Bum Look Big in This?* (1997)

57 A man has one hundred dollars and you leave him with two dollars, that's subtraction.

Mae West 1892–1980: Joseph Weintraub *Peel Me a Grape* (1975)

58 Is that a gun in your pocket, or are you just glad to see me?

Mae West 1892–1980: Joseph Weintraub *Peel Me a Grape* (1975), usually quoted as 'Is that a pistol in your pocket . . . '

59 When women go wrong, men go right after them.

Mae West 1892–1980: in *She Done Him Wrong* (1933 film)

60 *asked by the gossip columnist Hedda Hopper how she knew so much about men:*
Baby, I went to night school.

Mae West 1892–1980: Max Wilk *The Wit and Wisdom of Hollywood* (1972)

61 Whatever women do they must do twice as well as men to be thought half as good. Luckily, this is not difficult.

Charlotte Whitton 1896–1975: in *Canada Month* June 1963

62 A man can be happy with any woman as long as he does not love her.

Oscar Wilde 1854–1900: *The Picture of Dorian Gray* (1891)

63 All women become like their mothers. That is their tragedy. No man does. That's his.

Oscar Wilde 1854–1900: *The Importance of Being Earnest* (1895); the same words occur in dialogue form in *A Woman of No Importance* (1893)

64 Girls are just friends who give you erections.
reporting his teenage son's words

Nigel Williams 1948– : *Fortysomething* (1999)

65 A mistress should be like a little country retreat near the town, not to dwell in constantly, but only for a night and away.

William Wycherley c.1640–1716: *The Country Wife* (1675)

Middle Age ····> Old Age, Youth

66 I recently turned 60. Practically a third of my life is over. 99
Woody Allen

1 Years ago we discovered the exact point, the dead centre of middle age. It occurs when you are too young to take up golf and too old to rush up to the net.

Franklin P. Adams 1881–1960: *Nods and Becks* (1944)

2 I recently turned 60. Practically a third of my life is over.

Woody Allen 1935– : in *Observer* 'Sayings of the Week' 10 March 1996

3 You are thirty-two. You are rapidly approaching the age when your body, whether it embarrasses you or not, begins to embarrass other people.

Alan Bennett 1934– : *Getting On* (1972)

4 Whenever the talk turns to age, I say I am 49 plus VAT.

Lionel Blair 1936– : in *Mail on Sunday* 6 June 1999

5 After forty a woman has to choose between losing her figure or her face. My advice is to keep your face, and stay sitting down.

Barbara Cartland 1901–2000: Libby Purves 'Luncheon à la Cartland'; in *The Times* 6 October 1993

6 Middle age is when your broad mind and narrow waist begin to change places.

E. Joseph Crossman: attributed

7 Nobody loves a fairy when she's forty.

Arthur W. D. Henley: title of song (1934)

8 When grown-ups pretend they are in playschool they are either trying to cheat you or are terrified to death.

P. J. Kavanagh 1931– : in *The Spectator* 5 December 1992

9 20 to 40 is the fillet steak of life. After that it's all short cuts.

Philip Larkin 1922–85: comment, in *Philip Larkin Documentary* (Channel 4 TV) 6 July 2003

10 *of Zsa Zsa Gabor:*
She's discovered the secret of perpetual middle age.

Oscar Levant 1906–72: attributed

11 I have a bone to pick with Fate.
Come here and tell me, girlie,
Do you think my mind is maturing late,
Or simply rotted early?

Ogden Nash 1902–71: 'Lines on Facing Forty' (1942)

12 As invariably happens after one passes 40, the paper sagged open to the obituary page.

S. J. Perelman 1904–79: 'Swindle Sheet with Blueblood Engrailed Arrant Fibs Rampant'

13 When I was cuter,
Each night meant another suitor,
I sleep easier now.

Cole Porter 1891–1964: 'I Sleep Easier Now' (1950)

14 As we get older we do not get any younger.
Seasons return, and today I am fifty-five,
And this time last year I was fifty-four,
And this time next year I shall be sixty-two.

Henry Reed 1914–86: 'Chard Whitlow (Mr Eliot's Sunday Evening Postscript)' (1946)

15 It is one of the consolations of middle-aged reformers that the good they inculcate must live after them if it is to live at all.

Saki 1870–1916: *Beasts and Super-Beasts* (1914)

16 Maturity is a high price to pay for growing up.

Tom Stoppard 1937– : *Where Are They Now?* (1973)

17 From birth to 18 a girl needs good parents. From 18 to 35, she needs good looks. From 35 to 55, good personality. From 55 on, she needs good cash.

Sophie Tucker 1884–1966: Michael Freedland *Sophie* (1978)

18 Thirty-five is a very attractive age. London society is full of women of the very highest birth who have, of their own free choice, remained thirty-five for years.

Oscar Wilde 1854–1900: *The Importance of Being Earnest* (1895)

The Mind ····▶ Intelligence and Intellectuals

❝A neurosis is a secret you don't know you're keeping.❞
Kenneth Tynan

1 If I am out of my mind, it's all right with me, thought Moses Herzog.

Saul Bellow 1915–2005: *Herzog* (1961) opening sentence

2 The asylums of this country are full of the sound of mind disinherited by the out of pocket.

Alan Bennett 1934– : *The Madness of George III* (performed 1991)

3 An apparatus with which we think that we think.
definition of the brain

Ambrose Bierce 1842–c.1914: *Cynic's Word Book* (1906)

4 *Charles Condomine declining psychoanalysis:*
I refuse to endure months of expensive humiliation only to be told at the end of it that at the age of four I was in love with my rocking-horse.

Noël Coward 1899–1973: *Blithe Spirit* (1941)

5 'I am inclined to think—' said I [Dr Watson]. 'I should do so,' Sherlock Holmes remarked, impatiently.

Arthur Conan Doyle 1859–1930: *The Valley of Fear* (1915)

6 There was only one catch and that was Catch-22, which specified that a concern for one's own safety in the face of dangers that were real and immediate was the process of a rational mind . . . Orr would be crazy to fly more missions and sane if he didn't, but if he was sane he had to fly them. If he flew them he was crazy and didn't have to; but if he didn't want to he was sane and had to.

Joseph Heller 1923–99: *Catch-22* (1961)

7 Psychiatry is a waste of good couches. Why should I make a psychiatrist laugh, and then pay him?

Kathy Lette 1958– : in *The Times* 27 October 2001

8 Insanity is hereditary. You can get it from your children.

Sam Levenson 1911–80: *You Can Say That Again, Sam!* (1975)

9 If the nineteenth century was the age of the editorial chair, ours is the century of the psychiatrist's couch.

Marshall McLuhan 1911–80: *Understanding Media* (1964)

10 'Do you know if there was any insanity in her family?' 'Insanity? No, I never heard of any. Her father lives in West Kensington, but I believe he's sane on all other subjects.'

Saki 1870–1916: *Beasts and Super-Beasts* (1914)

11 O Lord, Sir—when a heroine goes mad she always goes into white satin.

Richard Brinsley Sheridan 1751–1816: *The Critic* (1779)

12 Not body enough to cover his mind decently with; his intellect is improperly exposed.

Sydney Smith 1771–1845: Lady Holland *Memoir* (1855)

13 I must have a prodigious quantity of mind; it takes me as much as a week, sometimes, to make it up.

Mark Twain 1835–1910: *The Innocents Abroad* (1869)

14 A neurosis is a secret you don't know you're keeping.

Kenneth Tynan 1927–80: Kathleen Tynan *Life of Kenneth Tynan* (1987)

15 Dr Tayler's thoughts are very white and pure, recalling in their disorder a draper's shop on the last day of a great white sale.

Rebecca West 1892–1983: in *The Clarion* 7 March 1913

Mistakes and Misfortunes

66 My misdeeds are accidental happenings. **99**
Jeffrey Bernard

1 Instead of being arrested, as we stated, for kicking his wife down a flight of stairs and hurling a lighted kerosene lamp after her, the Revd James P. Wellman died unmarried four years ago.

Anonymous: from an American newspaper, quoted by Burne-Jones in a letter to Lady Horner; J. A. Gere and John Sparrow (eds.) *Geoffrey Madan's Notebooks* (1981)

2 I'm not going to make the same mistake once.
  on marriage

Warren Beatty 1937– : attributed; Bob Chieger *Was It Good For You Too?* (1983)

3 My only solution for the problem of habitual accidents . . .
  is to stay in bed all day. Even then, there is always the
  chance that you will fall out.

Robert Benchley 1889–1945: *Chips off the old Benchley* (1949) 'Safety Second'

4 George the Third
  Ought never to have occurred.
  One can only wonder
  At so grotesque a blunder.

Edmund Clerihew Bentley 1875–1956: 'George the Third' (1929)

5 The younger Van Eyck
  Was christened Jan, and not Mike,
  The thought of this curious mistake
  Often kept him awake.

Edmund Clerihew Bentley 1875–1956: 'Van Eyck' (1905)

6 My misdeeds are accidental happenings and merely the
  result of having been in the wrong bar or bed at the wrong
  time, say most days between midday and midnight.

Jeffrey Bernard 1932–97: in *The Spectator* 18 July 1992

7 Calamities are of two kinds: misfortune to ourselves, and
  good fortune to others.

Ambrose Bierce 1842–c.1914: *The Cynic's Word Book* (1906)

8 *on premature calls of a win in Florida in the presidential
  election of 2000:*
  We don't just have egg on our face. We have omelette all
  over our suits.

Tom Brokaw 1940– : in *Atlanta Constitution-Journal* 9 November 2000 (online edition)

9 Of all the horrid, hideous notes of woe,
  Sadder than owl-songs or the midnight blast,
  Is that portentous phrase, 'I told you so.'

Lord Byron 1788–1824: *Don Juan* (1819–24)

10 *Edith Evans repeatedly inserted the word 'very' into a line of*
  Hay Fever:
  No, no, Edith. The line is, 'You can see as far as Marlow
  on a clear day.' On a *very* clear day you can see Marlow
  and Beaumont and Fletcher.

Noël Coward 1899–1973: Cole Lesley *The Life of Noël Coward* (1976)

11 It was a moment of madness for which I have
  subsequently paid a very, very heavy price.
  *of the episode on Clapham Common leading to his
  resignation as Welsh Secretary*

Ron Davies 1946– : interview with BBC Wales and HTV, 30 October 1998

12 He has gone to the demnition bow-wows.

Charles Dickens 1812–70: *Nicholas Nickleby* (1839)

13 If Gladstone fell into the Thames, that would be
  misfortune; and if anybody pulled him out, that, I
  suppose, would be a calamity.

Benjamin Disraeli 1804–81: Leon Harris *The Fine Art of Political Wit* (1965)

14 Something nasty in the woodshed.

Stella Gibbons 1902–89: *Cold Comfort Farm* (1932)

15 I left the room with silent dignity, but caught my foot in
  the mat.

George Grossmith 1847–1912 and **Weedon Grossmith** 1854–1919: *The Diary of a Nobody* (1894)

16 I was mistaken for a prostitute once in the last war. When a GI asked me what I charged, I said, 'Well, dear, what do your mother and sisters normally ask for?'

Thora Hird 1911–2003: in *Independent* 27 February 1999

17 Higgledy—Piggledy
Andrea Doria
Lines in the name of this
Glorious boat.
As I sit writing these
Non-navigational
Verses a—CRASH! BANG! BLURP!
GLUB . . . (end of quote).

John Hollander 1929– : 'Last Words' (1966)

18 Well, I'm still here.
after erroneous reports of his death, marked by tributes paid to him in Congress

Bob Hope 1903–2003: in *Mail on Sunday* 7 June 1998 'Quotes of the Week'

19 When I make a mistake, it's a beaut.

Fiorello H. La Guardia 1882–1947: on his appointment of Herbert O'Brien as a judge; William Manners *Patience and Fortitude* (1976)

20 I've no sympathy with people to whom things happen. It may be that their luck was bad, but is that to count in their favour?

Cormac McCarthy 1933– : *All the Pretty Horses* (1993)

21 now and then
there is a person born
who is so unlucky
that he runs into accidents
which started to happen
to somebody else.

Don Marquis 1878–1937: *archys life of mehitabel* (1933) 'archy says'

22 *a postcard of the Venus de Milo sent to his niece:*
See what'll happen to you if you don't stop biting your finger-nails.

Will Rogers 1879–1935: Bennett Cerf *Shake Well Before Using* (1948)

23 *For* Pheasant *read* Peasant, throughout.

W. C. Sellar 1898–1951 and **R. J. Yeatman** 1898–1968: *1066 and All That* (1930); errata

24 Misery acquaints a man with strange bedfellows.

William Shakespeare 1564–1616: *The Tempest* (1611)

25 *when the news that Sheridan's Drury Lane theatre was on fire reached the House of Commons, a motion was made to adjourn the debate on the campaign in Spain:*
Whatever might be the extent of the individual calamity, I do not consider it of a nature worthy to interrupt the proceedings on so great a national question.

Richard Brinsley Sheridan 1751–1816: speech, House of Commons, 24 February 1809

26 Well, if I called the wrong number, why did you answer the phone?

James Thurber 1894–1961: cartoon caption in *New Yorker* 5 June 1937

27 Wardrobe malfunction.
explanation for the exposure of Janet Jackson's right breast on prime time American television during the Super Bowl

Justin Timberlake 1981– : in *Daily Telegraph* 3 February 2004 (online edition)

28 *to his troop sergeant after sustaining serious wounds trying to unblock a jammed machine gun:*
Kiss me, Chudleigh

Auberon Waugh 1939–2001: anecdote; in *Daily Telegraph* 18 January 2001

Money ····▶ Debt, Poverty, Wealth

66 What you'd get on beautifully without if only other people weren't so crazy about it. **99**
Margaret Case Harriman

---

1 Money is better than poverty, if only for financial reasons.

Woody Allen 1935– : *Without Feathers* (1976) 'Early Essays'

2 Money, it turned out, was exactly like sex, you thought of nothing else if you didn't have it and thought of other things if you did.

James Baldwin 1924–87: in *Esquire* May 1961 'Black Boy looks at the White Boy'

3 I'm tired of Love: I'm still more tired of Rhyme.
But Money gives me pleasure all the time.

Hilaire Belloc 1870–1953: 'Fatigued' (1923)

4 HOLDUP MAN: Quit stalling—I said your money or your life.
JACK BENNY: I'm thinking it over!

Jack Benny 1894–1974: one of Jack Benny's most successful gags; Irving Fein *Jack Benny* (1976)

5 'First you schange me schmall scheque?' 'No.'

Caryl Brahms 1901–82 and **S. J. Simon** 1904–48: *A Bullet in the Ballet* (1937)

6 I never loved a dear gazelle—
Nor anything that cost me much:
High prices profit those who sell,
But why should I be fond of such?

Lewis Carroll 1832–98: 'Tema con Variazioni'

7 Annual income twenty pounds, annual expenditure nineteen nineteen six, result happiness. Annual income twenty pounds, annual expenditure twenty pounds ought and six, result misery.

Charles Dickens 1812–70: *David Copperfield* (1850)

8 When you don't have any money, the problem is food. When you have money, it's sex. When you have both it's health.

J. P. Donleavy 1926– : *The Ginger Man* (1955)

9 I like Chopin and Bizet, and the voice of Doris Day,
Gershwin songs and old forgotten carols.
But the music that excels is the sound of oil wells
As they slurp, slurp, slurp into the barrels.

My little home will be quaint as an old parasol,
Instead of fitted carpets I'll have money wall to wall.
I want an old-fashioned house
With an old-fashioned fence
And an old-fashioned millionaire.

Marve Fisher: 'An Old-Fashioned Girl' (1954)

10 Economy was always 'elegant', and money-spending always 'vulgar' and ostentatious— a sort of sour-grapeism, which made us very peaceful and satisfied.

Elizabeth Gaskell 1810–65: *Cranford* (1853)

11 Money, wife, is the true fuller's earth for reputations, there is not a spot or a stain but what it can take out.

John Gay 1685–1732: *The Beggar's Opera* (1728)

12 The shares are a penny, and ever so many are taken by Rothschild and Baring,
And just as a few are allotted to you, you awake with a shudder despairing.

W. S. Gilbert 1836–1911: *Iolanthe* (1882)

13 Good news rarely comes in a brown envelope.

Henry D'Avigdor Goldsmid 1909–76: John Betjeman, letter to Tom Driberg, 21 July 1976

14 *on being told that money doesn't buy happiness:*
But it upgrades despair so beautifully.

Richard Greenberg: *Hurrah at Last* (1999)

15 Money is what you'd get on beautifully without if only other people weren't so crazy about it.

Margaret Case Harriman: Laurence J. Peter (ed.) *Quotations for our Time* (1977)

16 A bank is a place that will lend you money if you can prove that you don't need it.

Bob Hope 1903–2003: Alan Harrington *Life in the Crystal Palace* (1959)

17 Men are more often bribed by their loyalties and ambitions than money.

Robert H. Jackson 1892–1954: dissenting opinion in *United States v. Wunderlich* 1951

18 *to Joynson-Hicks, who had acquired his double-barrelled surname through marriage with an heiress:*
On the spur of the moment I can think of no better example of unearned increment than the hyphen in the right honourable gentleman's name.

David Lloyd George 1863–1945: Leon Harris *The Fine Art of Political Wit* (1965)

19 I am in an age group where it is rude to discuss money, and now it is all anyone cares about.

Jack Nicholson 1937– ; in *Observer* 3 January 1999 'Sayings of the Week'

20 There's only one thing to do with loose change of course. Tighten it.

Flann O'Brien 1911–66: *The Best of Myles* (1968)

21 'My boy,' he says, 'always try to rub up against money, for if you rub up against money long enough, some of it may rub off on you.'

Damon Runyon 1884–1946: in *Cosmopolitan* August 1929, 'A Very Honourable Guy'

22 *on being asked what* Rosencrantz and Guildenstern are Dead *was about:*
It's about to make me very rich.

Tom Stoppard 1937– : attributed; in *Daily Telegraph* 27 February 1999

23 The elegant simplicity of the three per cents.

Lord Stowell 1745–1836: Lord Campbell *Lives of the Lord Chancellors* (1857)

24 Money won't buy happiness, but it will pay the salaries of a large research staff to study the problem.

Bill Vaughan: Laurence J. Peter (ed.) *Quotations for Our Time* (1977)

Morality ····▶ Virtue and Vice

❝ I probably have a different sense of morality to most people. ❞
Alan Clark

1 *asking Robbie Ross to keep away from the scandal-touched Reggie Turner:*
He is very weak and you, if I remember rightly, are wicked.

Max Beerbohm 1872–1956: letter, spring 1895

2 Morality's *not* practical. Morality's a gesture. A complicated gesture learned from books.

Robert Bolt 1924–95: *A Man for All Seasons* (1960)

3 I am all for morality now—and shall confine myself henceforward to the strictest adultery—which you will please recollect is all that that virtuous wife of mine has left me.

Lord Byron 1788–1824: letter 29 October 1819

4 I probably have a different sense of morality to most people.

Alan Clark 1928–99: in *The Times* 2 June 1994

5 To be absolutely honest, what I feel really bad about is that I don't feel worse. That's the ineffectual liberal's problem in a nutshell.

Michael Frayn 1933– : in *Observer* 8 August 1965

6 If people want a sense of purpose, they should get it from their archbishops. They should not hope to receive it from their politicians.

Harold Macmillan 1894–1986: in conversation 1963; Henry Fairlie *The Life of Politics* (1968)

7 Providing you have enough courage—or money—you can do without a reputation.
said by Rhett Butler

Margaret Mitchell 1900–49: *Gone with the Wind* (1936)

8 I think fidelity is a very good idea—now that I can't walk.

John Mortimer 1923– : in *Mail on Sunday* 4 January 2004 'Quotes of the Year'

9 I'm very mild, I'm very meek,
My will is strong, but my won't is weak;
So don't look at me that way!

Cole Porter 1891–1964: 'Don't Look at Me That Way' (*Paris*, 1928 musical)

10 People will do things from a sense of duty which they would never attempt as a pleasure.

Saki 1870–1916: *The Chronicles of Clovis* (1911)

11 There is such a thing as letting one's aesthetic sense override one's moral sense . . . I believe you would have condoned the South Sea Bubble and the persecution of the Albigenses if they had been carried out in effective colour schemes.

Saki 1870–1916: *The Toys of Peace* (1919)

12 Dost thou think, because thou art virtuous, there shall be no more cakes and ale?

William Shakespeare 1564–1616: *Twelfth Night* (1601)

13 When a stupid man is doing something he is ashamed of, he always declares that it is his duty.

George Bernard Shaw 1856–1950: *Caesar and Cleopatra* (1901)

14 PICKERING: Have you no morals, man?
DOOLITTLE: Can't afford them, Governor.

George Bernard Shaw 1856–1950: *Pygmalion* (1916)

15 If your morals make you dreary, depend upon it they are wrong.

Robert Louis Stevenson 1850–94: *Across the Plains* (1892)

16 BELINDA: Ay, but you know we must return good for evil.
LADY BRUTE: That may be a mistake in the translation.

John Vanbrugh 1664–1726: *The Provoked Wife* (1697)

17 Moral indignation is jealousy with a halo.

H. G. Wells 1866–1946: *The Wife of Sir Isaac Harman* (1914)

18 On an occasion of this kind it becomes more than a moral duty to speak one's mind. It becomes a pleasure.

Oscar Wilde 1854–1900: *The Importance of Being Earnest* (1895)

Murder

❝ You can always count on a murderer for a fancy prose style. **❞**
Vladimir Nabokov

1 Lizzie Borden took an axe
And gave her mother forty whacks;
When she saw what she had done
She gave her father forty-one!

Anonymous: popular rhyme in circulation after the acquittal of Lizzie Borden, in June 1893, from the charge of murdering her father and stepmother at Fall River, Massachusetts on 4 August 1892

2 I feel we are so busy compromising at every turn that we can't say 'murder is wrong' in case it upsets some murderers.

Alan Ayckbourn 1939– : in *Guardian* 4 September 2002

3 You can't chop your poppa up in Massachusetts,
Not even if it's planned as a surprise
No you can't chop your poppa up in Massachusetts
You know how neighbours love to criticize.

Michael Brown: 'Lizzie Borden' (1952)

4 The Stately Homes of England,
Tho' rather in the lurch,
Provide a lot of chances
For Psychical Research —
There's the ghost of a crazy younger son
Who murdered, in thirteen fifty-one,
An extremely rowdy Nun
Who resented it,
And people who come to call
Meet her in the hall.

Noël Coward 1899–1973: *The Stately Homes of England* (1938)

5 *on being asked whether he thought that Dr John Bodkin Adams, acquitted of murdering an elderly female patient, had actually been guilty:*
He must have had quite a lot of explaining to do to the recording angel.

Lord Hailsham 1907–2001: in an interview; John Mortimer *Character Parts* (1986)

6 Television has brought back murder into the home— where it belongs.

Alfred Hitchcock 1899–1980: in *Observer* 19 December 1965

7 It was not until several weeks after he had decided to murder his wife that Dr Bickleigh took any active steps in the matter. Murder is a serious business.

Francis Iles 1893–1970: *Malice Aforethought* (1931)

8 The National Rifle Association says guns don't kill people, people do. But I think the gun helps. Just standing there, going 'Bang!'—that's not going to kill too many people.

Eddie Izzard 1962– : *Dress to Kill* (stageshow, San Francisco, 1998)

9 We'll murder them all amid laughter and merriment,
Except for a few we'll take home to experiment.
My pulse will be quickenin' with each drop of strychnine
    we feed to a pigeon.
(It just takes a smidgin!)
To poison a pigeon in the park.

Tom Lehrer 1928– : 'Poisoning Pigeons in the Park' (1953)

10 You can always count on a murderer for a fancy prose style.

Vladimir Nabokov 1899–1977: *Lolita* (1955)

11 *Julius Caesar of his assassins:*
Infamy, infamy, they've all got it in for me!

Talbot Rothwell 1916–74: *Carry on, Cleo* (1964); according to Frank Muir's letter to the *Guardian*, 22 July 1995, the line had actually been written by him and Denis Norden for a radio sketch for 'Take It From Here', and was later used by Rothwell with their permission

12 I met Murder on the way—
He had a mask like Castlereagh.

Percy Bysshe Shelley 1792–1822: 'The Mask of Anarchy' (1819)

13 By the argument of counsel it was shown that at half-past ten in the morning on the day of the murder . . . [the defendant] became insane, and remained so for eleven and a half hours exactly.

Mark Twain 1835–1910: 'A New Crime' (1875)

14 *justification for poisoning his sister-in-law*
She had very thick ankles.

Thomas Griffiths Wainewright 1794–1852: in *Dictionary of National Biography* (1917–)

Music ····▶ Musicians, Songs and Singing

66 Two golden rules for an orchestra: start together and finish together. **99**
Thomas Beecham

1 I can't listen to too much Wagner, ya know? I start to get the urge to conquer Poland.

Woody Allen 1935– : *Manhattan Murder Mystery* (1998 film)

2 All music is folk music, I ain't never heard no horse sing a song.

Louis Armstrong 1901–71: in *New York Times* 7 July 1971

3 *when asked what jazz is:*
If you still have to ask . . . shame on you.

Louis Armstrong 1901–71: Max Jones et al. *Salute to Satchmo* (1970) (sometimes quoted 'Man, if you gotta ask you'll never know')

4 I love Wagner, but the music I prefer is that of a cat hung up by its tail outside a window and trying to stick to the panes of glass with its claws.

Charles Baudelaire 1821–67: Nat Shapiro (ed.) *An Encyclopedia of Quotations about Music* (1978)

5 What can you do with it? It's like a lot of yaks jumping about.
on the third movement of Beethoven's Seventh Symphony

Thomas Beecham 1879–1961: Harold Atkins and Archie Newman *Beecham Stories* (1978)

6 Why do we have to have all these third-rate foreign conductors around—when we have so many second-rate ones of our own?

Thomas Beecham 1879–1961: L. Ayre *Wit of Music* (1966)

7 The musical equivalent of the Towers of St Pancras Station.

Thomas Beecham 1879–1961: describing Elgar's 1st Symphony; Neville Cardus *Sir Thomas Beecham* (1961)

8 There are two golden rules for an orchestra: start together and finish together. The public doesn't give a damn what goes on in between.

Thomas Beecham 1879–1961: Harold Atkins and Archie Newman *Beecham Stories* (1978)

9 [The piano is] a parlour utensil for subduing the impenitent visitor. It is operated by depressing the keys of the machine and the spirits of the audience.

Ambrose Bierce 1842–c.1914: *The Enlarged Devil's Dictionary* (1967)

10 Extraordinary how potent cheap music is.

Noël Coward 1899–1973: *Private Lives* (1930); see **Music** 57

11 The tuba is certainly the most intestinal of instruments— the very lower bowel of music.

Peter de Vries 1910–93: *The Glory of the Hummingbird* (1974)

12 Dumb as a drum vith a hole in it, sir.

Charles Dickens 1812–70: *Pickwick Papers* (1837)

13 I don't like composers who think. It gets in the way of their plagiarism.

Howard Dietz 1896–1983: *Dancing in the Dark* (1974)

14 *a trumpet player had been suggested with the endorsement 'he's a nice guy':*
Nice guys are a dime a dozen! Get me a prick that can play!

Tommy Dorsey 1905–56: Bill Crow *Jazz Anecdotes* (1990)

15 I hate music, especially when it's played.

Jimmy Durante 1893–1980: Nat Shapiro (ed.) *An Encyclopedia of Quotations about Music* (1978)

16 Playing 'Bop' is like scrabble with all the vowels missing.

Duke Ellington 1899–1974: in *Look* 10 August 1954

17 'Tis wonderful how soon a piano gets into a log hut on the frontier.

Ralph Waldo Emerson 1803–82: 'Civilization' (1870)

18 Slap that bass—
Use it like a tonic.
Slap that bass
Keep your Philharmonic.
Zoom, zoom, zoom—
And the milk and honey'll flow!

Ira Gershwin 1896–1983: 'Slap that Bass' (1937)

19 The music-hall singer attends a series
Of masses and fugues and 'ops'
By Bach, interwoven
With Spohr and Beethoven,
At classical Monday Pops.

W. S. Gilbert 1836–1911: *The Mikado* (1885)

20 Then they began to sing
That extremely lovely thing,
'Scherzando! ma non troppo ppp.'

W. S. Gilbert 1836–1911: 'Story of Prince Agib' (1869)

21 What I love best about music is the women who listen to it.

Jules Goncourt 1830–70: Nat Shapiro (ed.) *An Encyclopedia of Quotations about Music* (1978)

22 I only know two tunes. One of them is 'Yankee Doodle' and the other isn't.

Ulysses S. Grant 1822–85: Nat Shapiro (ed.) *An Encyclopedia of Quotations about Music* (1978)

23 Music helps not the toothache.

George Herbert 1593–1633: *Outlandish Proverbs* (1640)

24 Classic music is th'kind that we keep thinkin'll turn into a tune.

Frank McKinney Hubbard 1868–1930: *Comments of Abe Martin and His Neighbors* (1923)

25 A pianoforte is a harp in a box.

Leigh Hunt 1784–1859: *The Seer* (1840)

26 *On the performance of a celebrated violinist:*
Difficult do you call it, Sir? I wish it were impossible.

Samuel Johnson 1709–84: William Seward *Supplement to the Anecdotes of Distinguished Persons* (1797)

27 If you play that score one more time before we open, people are going to think we're doing a revival.
to George Gershwin

George S. Kaufman 1889–1961: Howard Teichmann *George S. Kaufman* (1973)

28 HAMMERSTEIN: Here is a story laid in China about an Italian told by an Irishman. What kind of music are you going to write?
KERN: It'll be good Jewish music.
in the 1930s, discussing with Oscar Hammerstein II a musical to be based on Donn Byrne's novel Messer Marco Polo

Jerome Kern 1885–1945: Gerald Bordman *Jerome Kern* (1980)

29 A carpenter's hammer, in a warm summer noon, will fret me into more than midsummer madness. But those unconnected, unset sounds are nothing to the measured malice of music.

Charles Lamb 1775–1834: *Elia* (1823)

30 A squeak's heard in the orchestra
The leader draws across
The intestines of the agile cat
The tail of the noble hoss.

G. T. Lanigan 1845–86: *The Amateur Orlando* (1875)

31 Mine was the kind of piece in which nobody knew what was going on, including the composer, the conductor, and the critics. Consequently I got pretty good notices.

Oscar Levant 1906–72: *A Smattering of Ignorance* (1940)

32 If I play Tchaikovsky I play his melodies and skip his spiritual struggles . . . If there's any time left over I fill in with a lot of runs up and down the keyboard.

Liberace 1919–87: Stuart Hall and Paddy Whannel (eds.) *The Popular Arts* (1964)

33 I don't like my music, but what is my opinion against that of millions of others.

Frederick Loewe 1904–88: Nat Shapiro (ed.) *An Encyclopedia of Quotations about Music* (1978)

34 On seeing Niagara Falls, Mahler exclaimed: 'Fortissimo at last!'

Gustav Mahler 1860–1911: K. Blaukopf *Gustav Mahler* (1973)

35 If you're in jazz and more than ten people like you, you're labelled commercial.

Herbie Mann 1930– : Henry Pleasants *Serious Music and all that Jazz!* (1969)

36 If I had the power, I would insist on all oratorios being sung in the costume of the period—with a possible exception in the case of *The Creation*.

Ernest Newman 1868–1959: in *New York Post* 1924; Nat Shapiro (ed.) *An Encyclopedia of Quotations about Music* (1978)

37 I have been told that Wagner's music is better than it sounds.

Bill Nye 1850–96: Mark Twain *Autobiography* (1924)

38 What a terrible revenge by the culture of the Negroes on that of the whites!

Ignacy Jan Paderewski 1860–1941: of jazz; Nat Shapiro (ed.) *An Encyclopedia of Quotations about Music* (1978)

39 *Parsifal* is the kind of opera that starts at six o'clock. After it has been going three hours, you look at your watch and it says 6.20.

David Randolph 1914– : Nat Shapiro (ed.) *An Encyclopedia of Quotations about Music* (1978)

40 Of course we've all *dreamed* of reviving the *castrati*; but it's needed Hilda to take the first practical steps towards making them a reality . . . She's drawn up a list of well-known singers who she thinks would benefit . . . It's only a question of getting them to agree.

Henry Reed 1914–86: *Private Life of Hilda Tablet* (1954)

41 To the social-minded, a definition for Concert is: that which surrounds an intermission.

Ned Rorem 1923– : *The Final Diary* (1974)

42 It is a music one must hear several times. I am not going again.
  of Tannhäuser

Gioacchino Rossini 1792–1868: L. de Hegermann-Lindencrone *In the Courts of Memory* (1912)

43 Wagner has lovely moments but awful quarters of an hour.

Gioacchino Rossini 1792–1868: to Emile Naumann, April 1867

44 Applause is a receipt, not a note of demand.

Artur Schnabel 1882–1951: in *Saturday Review of Literature* 29 September 1951

45 I know two kinds of audiences only—one coughing, and one not coughing.

Artur Schnabel 1882–1951: *My Life and Music* (1961)

46 You are there and I am here; but where is Beethoven?
  to his conductor during a Beethoven rehearsal

Artur Schnabel 1882–1951: Nat Shapiro (ed.) *An Encyclopedia of Quotations about Music* (1978)

47 I have a reasonable good ear in music: let us have the tongs and the bones.

William Shakespeare 1564–1616: *A Midsummer Night's Dream* (1595–6)

48 Hell is full of musical amateurs: music is the brandy of the damned.

George Bernard Shaw 1856–1950: *Man and Superman* (1903)

49 I absolutely forbid such outrage. If *Pygmalion* is not good enough for your friends with its own verbal music . . . let them try Mozart's *Cosi Fan Tutti*, or at least Offenbach's *Grand Duchess*.

George Bernard Shaw 1856–1950: refusing to allow a musical based on *Pygmalion*; Caryl Brahms and Ned Sherrin *Song by Song* (1984)

50 If one will only take the precaution to go in long enough after it commences and to come out long before it is over you will not find it wearisome.

George Bernard Shaw 1856–1950: of Gounod's *La Rédemption*; in *The World* 22 February 1893

51 Nothing can be more disgusting than an oratorio. How absurd to see 500 people fiddling like madmen about Israelites in the Red Sea!

Sydney Smith 1771–1845: Hesketh Pearson *The Smith of Smiths* (1934)

52 Jazz will endure, just as long as people hear it through their feet instead of their brains.

John Philip Sousa 1854–1932: Nat Shapiro (ed.) *An Encyclopedia of Quotations about Music* (1978)

53 Satisfied great success.
  reply to telegram from Billy Rose, suggesting that reorchestration by Robert Russell Bennett might make a ballet which was 'a great success' even more successful

Igor Stravinsky 1882–1971: in *Ned Sherrin in his Anecdotage* (1993)

54 I would like to thank Beethoven, Brahms, Wagner, Strauss, Rimsky-Korsakov.

Dmitri Tiomkin 1899–1979: Oscar acceptance speech for the score of *The High and the Mighty* in 1955; Nat Shapiro (ed.) *An Encyclopedia of Quotations about Music* (1978)

55 I assure you that the typewriting machine, when played with expression, is not more annoying than the piano when played by a sister or near relation.

Oscar Wilde 1854–1900: letter to Robert Ross from Reading Prison, 1 April 1897

56 Musical people are so absurdly unreasonable. They always want one to be perfectly dumb at the very moment when one is longing to be absolutely deaf.

Oscar Wilde 1854–1900: *An Ideal Husband* (1895)

57 He reminds us how cheap potent music can be.
of the popular pianist Richard Clayderman

Richard Williams: Ned Sherrin *Cutting Edge* (1984); see **Music** 10

Musictans ····➤ Music

❝ The first requirement for a composer is to be dead. **❞**
Arthur Honegger

---

1 The music teacher came twice each week to bridge the awful gap between Dorothy and Chopin.

George Ade 1866–1944: Nat Shapiro (ed.) *An Encyclopedia of Quotations about Music* (1978)

2 There's no need for Peter Pears
To give himself airs.
He has them written
By Benjamin Britten.

Anonymous: a verse from *Punch*; in *Ned Sherrin in his Anecdotage* (1993)

3 I prefer to face the wrath of the police than the wrath of Sir John Barbirolli.
a member of the Hallé orchestra on a speeding charge

Anonymous: Ned Sherrin *Cutting Edge* (1984)

4 *printed notice in an American dancing saloon:*
Please do not shoot the pianist. He is doing his best.

Anonymous: Oscar Wilde *Impressions of America* 'Leadville' (c.1882–3)

5 A musicologist is a man who can read music but can't hear it.

Thomas Beecham 1879–1961: H. Proctor-Gregg *Beecham Remembered* (1976)

6 Tchaikovsky thought of committing suicide for fear of being discovered as a homosexual, but today, if you are a composer and *not* homosexual, you might as well put a bullet through your head.

Sergei Diaghilev 1872–1929: Vernon Duke *Listen Here!* (1963)

7 QUESTION: Mr. Sullivan's music . . . reminds me so much of dear Baytch [Bach]. Do tell me: what is Baytch doing just now? Is he still composing?
ANSWER: Just now, as a matter of fact, dear Baytch is by way of decomposing.

W. S. Gilbert 1836–1911: Hesketh Pearson *Gilbert and Sullivan* (1947)

8 There is no doubt that the first requirement for a composer is to be dead.

Arthur Honegger 1892–1955: *Je suis compositeur* (1951)

9 A review in the *Financial Times* said I was an extremely funky pub pianist. That was a good summing-up of what I am.

Elton John 1947– : in *Independent* 13 September 1997 'Quote Unquote'

10 Some cry up Haydn, some Mozart,
Just as the whim bites; for my part
I care not a farthing candle
For either of them, or for Handel.

Charles Lamb 1775–1834: 'Free Thoughts on Several Eminent Composers' (1830)

11 Leonard Bernstein has been disclosing musical secrets that have been known for over four hundred years.

Oscar Levant 1906–72: *Memoirs of an Amnesiac* (1965)

12 I'm told that Saint-Saëns has informed a delighted public that since the war began he has composed music for the stage, melodies, an elegy and a piece for the trombone. If he'd been making shell-cases instead it might have been all the better for music.

Maurice Ravel 1875–1937: letter to Jean Marnold, 7 October 1916

13 Ravel refuses the Legion of Honour, but all his music accepts it.

Erik Satie 1866–1925: Jean Cocteau *Le Discours d'Oxford* (1956)

14 *asked how he could play so well when he was loaded:*
I practise when I'm loaded.

Zoot Sims 1925–85: Bill Crow *Jazz Anecdotes* (1990)

15 'What do you think of Beethoven?'
'I love him, especially his poems.'

Ringo Starr 1940– : at a press conference during the Beatles' first American tour in 1964; Hunter Davies *The Beatles* (1985)

16 On matters of intonation and technicalities I am more than a martinet—I am a martinetissimo!

Leopold Stokowski 1882–1977: Nat Shapiro (ed.) *An Encyclopedia of Quotations about Music* (1978)

17 After I die, I shall return to earth as the doorkeeper of a bordello and I won't let one of you in.

Arturo Toscanini 1867–1957: to his orchestra during a difficult rehearsal; Nat Shapiro (ed.) *An Encyclopedia of Quotations about Music* (1978)

Names

66 Every Tom, Dick and Harry is called Arthur. **99**
Sam Goldwyn

1 Can I speak to Mr S. P. Eagle—this is Mr C. O. Hen.
friend's joke on Sam Spiegel's change of name

Anonymous: Natasha Fraser-Cavassoni *Sam Spiegel* (2003)

2 The reason Michael Jackson entitled his album *Bad* was because he couldn't spell *Indescribable*.

Anonymous: in 1987; Nigel Rees (ed.) *Cassell Dictionary of Humorous Quotations* (1999)

3 *of Arianna Stassinopoulos:*
So boring you fall asleep halfway through her name.

Alan Bennett 1934– : attributed; in *Observer* 18 September 1983

4 'You mustn't mention the Shah out loud.' . . . 'We had better call him Marjoribanks, if we want to remember who we mean.'

Robert Byron 1905–41: *The Road to Oxiana* (1937)

5 *fashionable children's names of which Camden disapproved:*
The new names, Free-gift, Reformation, Earth, Dust, Ashes . . . which have lately been given by some to their children.

William Camden 1551–1623: *Remains* (1605)

6 They *will* call me Mrs Pat. I can't stand it. The 'Pat' is the last straw that breaks the Campbell's back.

Mrs Patrick Campbell 1865–1940: attributed

7 *of Alfred Bossom:*
Who is this man whose name is neither one thing nor the other?

Winston Churchill 1874–1965: attributed

8 *nickname for Cecil Beaton:*
Malice in Wonderland.

Jean Cocteau 1889–1963: attributed;
Hugo Young in *Guardian* 24 January
2004

9 Rip-Van-With-It
nickname for Cecil Beaton

Cyril Connolly 1903–74: Hugo
Vickers (ed.) *The Unexpurgated
Beaton* (2002)

10 One theory is that I was named after the opera and the
other that my mum was sitting in her boudoir wondering
what to call me and glanced at her Carmen rollers. I prefer
the Bizet theory.

Carmen Ejogo: in *Observer* 26 March
2000 'They said what . . . ?'

11 *on J. P. Horrocks-Taylor's slipping Mick English's rugby tackle
to score:*
Horrocks went one way, Taylor went the other, and I was
left holding his bloody hyphen.

Mick English: in *Sunday Times* 2
September 1990

12 Every Tom, Dick and Harry is called Arthur.

Sam Goldwyn 1882–1974: to Arthur
Hornblow, who was planning to
name his son Arthur; Michael
Freedland *The Goldwyn Touch* (1986)

13 *Yossarian*—the very sight of the name made him shudder.
There were so many esses in it. It just had to be
subversive.

Joseph Heller 1923–99: *Catch-22*
(1961)

14 It was an odious, alien, distasteful name, that just did not
inspire confidence. It was not at all like such clean, crisp,
honest, American names as Cathcart, Peckem and
Dreedle.

Joseph Heller 1923–99: *Catch-22*
(1961)

15 The batsman's Holding, the bowler's Willey.

Brian Johnson: attributed; comment
at a Test Match as Michael Holding
faced Peter Willey

16 In the last Parliament, the House of Commons had more
MPs called John than all the women MPs put together.

Tessa Jowell 1947– : in *Independent
on Sunday* 14 March 1999 'Quotes'

17 If you should have a boy do not christen him John . . . 'Tis
a bad name and goes against a man. If my name had been
Edmund I should have been more fortunate.

John Keats 1795–1821: letter to his
sister-in-law, 13 January 1820

18 One day I'll be famous! I'll be proper and prim;
Go to St James so often I will call it St Jim!

Alan Jay Lerner 1918–86: 'Just You
Wait' (*My Fair Lady*, 1956 musical)

19 *pointing out that if she had kept her first husband's name she
would still be 'Mrs Wisdom':*
That would have been asking for trouble.

Doris Lessing 1919– : in *The Times*
15 July 2000

20 Obadiah Bind-their-kings-in-chains-and-their-nobles-with-
links-of-iron.

Lord Macaulay 1800–59: 'The Battle
of Naseby' (1824), fictitious author's
name

21 EUNICE GRAYSON: Mr—?
SEAN CONNERY: Bond. James Bond.

**Richard Maibaum, Johanna
Harwood**, and **Berkley Mather**
1909–96: *Dr No* (1962 film, based on
the novel by Ian Fleming; origin of
Bond's trademark introduction, 'The
name is Bond. James Bond.'

22 No, I'm breaking it in for a friend.
when asked if Groucho were his real name

Groucho Marx 1895–1977:
attributed

23 *on why she had named her canary 'Onan':*
Because he spills his seed on the ground.

Dorothy Parker 1893–1967: John Keats *You Might as Well Live*

24 Why should people I have never met, who read me in bed and in the bathtub, think of me as 'Sam'.
insisting that his first name be represented by the initial 'S.' on the title-pages of his books

Samuel ('Sam') Schoenbaum 1927–96: in *The Times* 25 April 1996; obituary

25 *of Jeffrey Archer's title:*
Lord Archer of Weston-Super-Mare—the only seaside pier on which Danny La Rue has not performed.

Neil Shand: *Loose Ends* monologue, 1999

26 *wondering why, since he was Irish, he was not O'Sheridan:*
For in truth we owe everybody.

Richard Brinsley Sheridan 1751–1816: Walter Jerrold *Bon-Mots* (1893)

27 I remember your name perfectly; but I just can't think of your face.

William Archibald Spooner 1844–1930: attributed; in *Penguin Dictionary of Quotations* (1960)

28 Bingo Bolger-Baggins a bad name. Let Bingo = Frodo.
on the first draft of The Lord of the Rings

J. R. R. Tolkien 1892–1973: note, c.1938; Humphrey Carpenter *J. R. R. Tolkien* (1977)

29 We do have these extraordinary names . . . When you see the sign 'African Primates Meeting' you expect someone to produce bananas.
address at his retirement service, Cape Town, 23 June 1996

Desmond Tutu 1931– : in *Daily Telegraph* 24 June 1996

30 *on being asked by William Carlos Williams how he had chosen the name 'West':*
Horace Greeley said, 'Go West, young man. So I did.'

Nathanael West 1903–40: Jay Martin *Nathanael West* (1970)

Nature and the Environment

❝ When the sukebind hangs heavy from the wains. ❞
Stella Gibbons

1 Every year, in the fulness o' summer, when the sukebind hangs heavy from the wains . . . 'tes the same. And when the spring comes her hour is upon her again. 'Tes the hand of Nature and we women cannot escape it.

Stella Gibbons 1902–89: *Cold Comfort Farm* (1932)

2 What do we chop, when we chop a tree?
A thousand things that you daily see.
A baby's crib, the poet's chair,
The soap box down in Union Square.
A pipe for Dad, a bat for brother,
An extra broom for dear old mother.

E. Y. Harburg 1898–1981: 'Song of the Woodman' (1936)

3 Man he eat the barracuda,
Barracuda eat the bass
Bass he eat the little flounder,
'Cause the flounder lower class.
Little flounder eat the sardine
That's nature's plan.
Sardine eat the little worm,
Little worm eat man.

E. Y. Harburg 1898–1981: 'For Every Fish' (1957)

4 I find it hard to accept, difficult to swallow, the new term 'ecology' which has come to us . . . It sounds a little too much like being sick.

Stephen Leacock 1869–1944: *The Boy I Left Behind Me* (1947)

5 Worship of nature may be ancient, but seeing nature as cuddlesome, hug-a-bear and too cute for words is strictly a modern fashion.

P. J. O'Rourke 1947– : *Parliament of Whores* (1991)

6 [Richard Nixon is] the kind of politician who would cut down a redwood tree, and then mount the stump and make a speech on conservation.

Adlai Stevenson 1900–65: Fawn M. Brodie *Richard Nixon* (1983)

7 *on the Falklands campaign, 1982:*
It is exciting to have a real crisis on your hands, when you have spent half your political life dealing with humdrum issues like the environment.

Margaret Thatcher 1925– : speech to Scottish Conservative Party conference, 14 May 1982

8 BRICK: Well, they say nature hates a vacuum, Big Daddy.
BIG DADDY: That's what they say, but sometimes I think that a vacuum is a hell of a lot better than some of the stuff that nature replaces it with.

Tennessee Williams 1911–83: *Cat on a Hot Tin Roof* (1955)

Newspapers ····▸ Journalism

❝My one form of continuous fiction.❞
Aneurin Bevan

1 HONG KONG POOH-POOHS NICHI NICHI'S DUM-DUMS.
reported headline in Australian newspaper, referring to reports that Hong Kong police denied a claim by the Japanese paper Nichi Nichi Shimbun *that they had used soft-nosed bullets against rioters*

Anonymous: attributed; in *Spectator* 19 December 1998

2 Sticks nix hick pix.

Anonymous: front-page headline on the lack of enthusiasm for farm dramas among rural populations; in *Variety* 17 July 1935

3 It's The Sun Wot Won It.
following the 1992 general election

Anonymous: headline in *Sun* 11 April 1992

4 NUT SCREWS WASHERS AND BOLTS.
reported headline in a Chinese newspaper above the story of an escapee from an asylum who broke into a laundry and raped several laundresses before escaping

Anonymous: Claud Cockburn *I, Claud* (1967)

5 If Kinnock wins today will the last person to leave Britain please turn out the lights.
on election day, showing Neil Kinnock's head inside a light bulb

Anonymous: headline in *Sun* 9 April 1992

6 If I rescued a child from drowning, the Press would no doubt headline the story 'Benn grabs child.'

Tony Benn 1925– : in *Observer* 2 March 1975

7 I read the newspapers avidly. It is my one form of continuous fiction.

Aneurin Bevan 1897–1960: in *The Times* 29 March 1960

8 More than one newspaper has been ruined by the brilliant writer in the editor's chair.

Lord Camrose 1879–1954: Leonard Russell et al. *The Pearl of Days: An Intimate Memoir of the Sunday Times* (1972)

9 *with which Cockburn claimed to have won a competition at* The Times *for the dullest headline:*
Small earthquake in Chile. Not many dead.

Claud Cockburn 1904–81: *In Time of Trouble* (1956)

10 'I believe that nothing in the newspapers is ever true,' said Madame Phoebus. 'And that is why they are so popular,' added Euphrosyne, 'the taste of the age being decidedly for fiction.'

Benjamin Disraeli 1804–81: *Lothair* (1870)

11 Where it will all end, knows God!
satirizing the style of Time *magazine*

Wolcott Gibbs 1902–58: in *New Yorker* 28 November 1936

12 The witness replied that his leading articles [in *The Observer*] were half-way between a cold bath and a religious exercise, and that this was the place which they occupied, very fitly, in the life of the nation.

A. P. Herbert 1890–1971: *Misleading Cases* (1935)

13 Editor: a person employed by a newspaper, whose business it is to separate the wheat from the chaff, and to see that the chaff is printed.

Elbert Hubbard 1859–1915: *The Roycroft Dictionary* (1914)

14 A newspaper which weighs as much as the *Oxford Dictionary of Quotations* and a very large haddock.
of the Sunday edition of the New York Times

Bernard Levin 1928– : *In These Times* (1986)

15 The British Press is always looking for stuff to fill the space between their cartoons.

Bernadette Devlin McAliskey 1947– : comment, 1970

16 You should always believe all you read in the newspapers, as this makes them more interesting.

Rose Macaulay 1881–1958: *A Casual Commentary* (1926)

17 People don't actually read newspapers. They get into them every morning, like a hot bath.

Marshall McLuhan 1911–80: in 1965; Jonathon Green (ed.) *A Dictionary of Contemporary Quotations* (1982)

18 The art of newspaper paragraphing is to stroke a platitude until it purrs like an epigram.

Don Marquis 1878–1937: E. Anthony *O Rare Don Marquis* (1962)

19 When newspapers became solvent they lost a good deal of their old venality, but at the same time they became increasingly cautious, for capital is always timid.

H. L. Mencken 1880–1956: *Minority Report* (1956)

20 Whenever I see a newspaper I think of the poor trees. As trees they provide beauty, shade and shelter. But as paper all they provide is rubbish.

Yehudi Menuhin 1916– : Jonathon Green (ed.) *Contemporary Quotations* (1982)

21 Exclusives aren't what they used to be. We tend to put 'exclusive' on everything just to annoy other papers. I once put 'exclusive' on the weather by mistake.

Piers Morgan 1965– : in *Independent on Sunday* 14 March 1999 'Quotes'

22 SIXTY HORSES WEDGED IN CHIMNEY
The story to fit this sensational headline has not turned up yet.

J. B. Morton 1893–1975: Michael Frayn (ed.) *The Best of Beachcomber* (1963)

23 *asked why he had allowed Page 3 to develop:*
I don't know. The editor did it when I was away.

Rupert Murdoch 1931– : in *Guardian* 25 February 1994

24 *on being telephoned by the* Sunday Express *to ask what was his main wish for 1956:*
Not to be telephoned by the *Sunday Express* when I am busy.

Harold Nicolson 1886–1968: diary, 29 December 1955

25 If a newspaper prints a sex crime, it is smut: but when the *New York Times* prints it it is a sociological study.

Adolph S. Ochs 1858–1935: Laurence J. Peter (ed.) *Quotations for our Time* (1977)

26 No self-respecting fish would be wrapped in a Murdoch newspaper.

Mike Royko 1932– : before resigning from the Chicago *Sun-Times* when the paper was sold to Rupert Murdoch in 1984; Karl E. Meyer (ed.) *Pundits, Poets, and Wits* (1990)

27 *of the Daily Mail:*
By office boys for office boys.

Lord Salisbury 1830–1903: H. Hamilton Fyfe *Northcliffe, an Intimate Biography* (1930)

28 The newspapers! Sir, they are the most villainous—licentious—abominable—infernal—Not that I ever read them—No—I make it a rule never to look into a newspaper.

Richard Brinsley Sheridan 1751–1816: *The Critic* (1779)

29 Accuracy to a newspaper is what virtue is to a lady; but a newspaper can always print a retraction.

Adlai Stevenson 1900–65: *The Wit and Wisdom of Adlai Stevenson* (1965)

30 I'm with you on the free press. It's the newspapers I can't stand.

Tom Stoppard 1937– : *Night and Day* (1978)

31 Freedom of the press in Britain means freedom to print such of the proprietor's prejudices as the advertisers don't object to.

Hannen Swaffer 1879–1962: Tom Driberg *Swaff* (1974)

32 It is part of the social mission of every great newspaper to provide a refuge and a home for the largest possible number of salaried eccentrics.

Lord Thomson of Fleet 1894–1976: in *Observer* 22 November 1959 'Sayings of the Week'

33 There are laws to protect the freedom of the press's speech, but none that are worth anything to protect the people from the press.

Mark Twain 1835–1910: 'License of the Press' (1873)

34 *The Beast* stands for strong mutually antagonistic governments everywhere . . . Self-sufficiency at home, self-assertion abroad.

Evelyn Waugh 1903–66: *Scoop* (1938)

35 Newspapers, even, have degenerated. They may now be absolutely relied upon.

Oscar Wilde 1854–1900: *The Decay of Lying* (1891)

New York

❝ A helluva town. **❞**
Betty Comden and Adolph Green

1 New York makes one think of the collapse of civilization, about Sodom and Gomorrah, the end of the world. The end wouldn't come as a surprise here. Many people already bank on it.

Saul Bellow 1915–2005: *Mr Sammler's Planet* (1970)

2 New York, New York,—a helluva town,
The Bronx is up but the Battery's down,
And people ride in a hole in the ground:
New York, New York,—It's a helluva town.

Betty Comden 1917–2006 and **Adolph Green** 1915–2002: 'New York, New York' (1945)

3 Nearly all th' most foolish people in th' counthry an' manny iv th' wisest goes to Noo York. Th' wise people ar-re there because th' foolish wint first. That's th' way th' wise men make a livin'.

Finley Peter Dunne 1867–1936: *Mr. Dooley's Opinions* (1902)

4 Broadway's turning into Coney,
Champagne Charlie's drinking gin.
Old New York is new and phoney—
Give it back to the Indians.

Lorenz Hart 1895–1943: 'Give it back to the Indians' (1940)

5 There are no available men in their thirties in New York. Giuliani had them removed along with the homeless.

Michael Patrick King: *Sex and the City* 'Valley of the Twenty-Something Guys' (1998); spoken by Miranda

6 When people start writing about New York, they tend to go get a thesaurus and find all the synonyms for dysfunctional.

James J. Lack: in *The Times* 22 October 2002

7 *sitting in a New York bar in the 1940s:*
Oh, to be back in Hollywood, wishing I was back in New York.

Herman J. Mankiewicz 1897–1953: James Sanders *Celluloid Skyline: New York and the Movies* (2001)

Old Age ····> Middle Age, Youth

66 Always fifteen years older than I am. **99**
Bernard Baruch

---

1 If you want to be adored by your peers and have standing ovations wherever you go—live to be over ninety.

George Abbott 1887–1995: in *The Times* 2 February 1995; obituary

2 Mr Salteena was an elderly man of 42.

Daisy Ashford 1881–1972: *The Young Visiters* (1919)

3 To me old age is always fifteen years older than I am.

Bernard Baruch 1870–1965: in *Newsweek* 29 August 1955

4 In England, you see, age wipes the slate clean . . . If you live to be ninety in England and can still eat a boiled egg they think you deserve the Nobel Prize.

Alan Bennett 1934– : *An Englishman Abroad* (1989)

5 Here I sit, alone and sixty,
Bald, and fat, and full of sin,
Cold the seat and loud the cistern,
As I read the Harpic tin.

Alan Bennett 1934– : 'Place Names of China' (parody of John Betjeman)

6 *on reaching the age of 100:*
If I'd known I was gonna live this long, I'd have taken better care of myself.

Eubie Blake 1883–1983: in *Observer* 13 February 1983 'Sayings of the Week'; also claimed by Adolph Zukor on reaching 100

7 'You are old, Father William,' the young man said,
'And your hair has become very white;
And yet you incessantly stand on your head—
Do you think, at your age, it is right?'

Lewis Carroll 1832–98: *Alice's Adventures in Wonderland* (1865)

8 I'll tell thee everything I can:
There's little to relate.
I saw an aged, aged man,
A-sitting on a gate.

Lewis Carroll 1832–98: *Through the Looking-Glass* (1872)

9 Old age is the outpatients' department of Purgatory.

Lord Hugh Cecil 1869–1956: John Betjeman, letter to Tom Driberg, 21 July 1976

10 *in his old age Churchill overheard one of two new MPs whisper to the other, 'They say the old man's getting a bit past it':*
And they say the old man's getting deaf as well.

Winston Churchill 1874–1965: K. Halle *The Irrepressible Churchill* (1985)

11 *it was pointed out to the aged Winston Churchill that his fly-button was undone:*
No matter. The dead bird does not leave the nest.

Winston Churchill 1874–1965: Rupert Hart-Davis letter to George Lyttelton, 5 January 1957

12 How foolish to think that one can ever slam the door in the face of age. Much wiser to be polite and gracious and ask him to lunch in advance.

Noël Coward 1899–1973: diary, 3 June 1956

13 To what do I attribute my longevity? Bad luck.

Quentin Crisp 1908–99: in *Spectator* 20 November 1999

14 *approaching his 80th birthday:*
While there's snow on the roof, it doesn't mean the fire has gone out in the furnace.

John G. Diefenbaker 1895–1979: attributed, 1991

15 Before I go to meet my Maker,
I want to use the salt left in my shaker.
I want to find out if it's true
The Blue Danube is really blue,
Before I kiss the world goodbye.

Howard Dietz 1896–1983: 'Before I Kiss the World Goodbye' (1963)

16 He who anticipates his century is generally persecuted when living, and is always pilfered when dead.

Benjamin Disraeli 1804–81: *Vivian Grey* (1826)

17 Being an old maid is like death by drowning, a really delightful sensation after you cease to struggle.

Edna Ferber 1887–1968: R. E. Drennan *Wit's End* (1973)

18 After the age of 80, you seem to be having breakfast every five minutes.

Christopher Fry 1907–2005: attributed; in *Spectator* 7 December 2002

19 Methus'lah live nine hundred years,
Methus'lah live nine hundred years
But who calls dat livin'
When no gal'll give in
To no man what's nine hundred years?

Ira Gershwin 1896–1983: 'It Ain't Necessarily So' (1935)

20 I've got to take under my wing,
Tra la,
A most unattractive old thing,
Tra la,
With a caricature of a face.

W. S. Gilbert 1836–1911: *The Mikado* (1885)

21 At forty I lost my illusions,
At fifty I lost my hair,
At sixty my hope and teeth were gone,
And my feet were beyond repair.
At eighty life has clipped my claws,
I'm bent and bowed and cracked;
But I can't give up the ghost because
My follies are intact.

E. Y. Harburg 1898–1981: 'Gerontology or Springtime for Senility' (1965)

22 When our organs have been transplanted
And the new ones made happy to lodge in us,
Let us pray one wish be granted—
We retain our zones erogenous.

E. Y. Harburg 1898–1981: 'Seated One Day at the Organ' (1965)

23 W'en folks git ole en strucken wid de palsy, dey mus speck ter be laff'd at.

Joel Chandler Harris 1848–1908: *Nights with Uncle Remus* (1883)

24 Nobody in Beverly Hills grows old. It's a violation of a city ordinance.

Bob Hope 1903–2003: attributed; in *The Times* 24 September 2003

25 Amidst the mortifying circumstances attendant upon growing old, it is something to have seen the *School for Scandal* in its glory.

Charles Lamb 1775–1834: *Elia* (1823)

26 H: We met at nine
G: We met at eight
H: I was on time
G: No, you were late
H: Ah yes! I remember it well.

Alan Jay Lerner 1918–86: 'I Remember It Well' (1957)

27 The fountain of youth is dull as paint.
Methuselah is my favourite saint.
I've never been so comfortable before.
Oh I'm so glad I'm not young any more.

Alan Jay Lerner 1918–86: 'I'm Glad I'm Not Young Any More' (1957)

28 The thing about getting old is the number of things you think that you can't say aloud because it would be too shocking.

Doris Lessing 1919– : in *The Times* 15 July 2000

29 *of an elderly guest:*
Talk about over 70. She can do 8 times more than I can and reduces me to a pudding of exhaustion.

Nancy Mitford 1904–73: letter 15 October 1953

30 There's one more terrifying fact about old people: I'm going to be one soon.

P. J. O'Rourke 1947– : *Parliament of Whores* (1991)

31 When men grow virtuous in their old age, they only make a sacrifice to God of the devil's leavings.

Alexander Pope 1688–1744: *Miscellanies* (1727) 'Thoughts on Various Subjects'

32 Growing old is like being increasingly penalized for a crime you haven't committed.

Anthony Powell 1905–2000: *Temporary Kings* (1973)

33 As I grow older and older,
And totter towards the tomb,
I find that I care less and less
Who goes to bed with whom.

Dorothy L. Sayers 1893–1957: 'That's Why I Never Read Modern Novels'; Janet Hitchman *Such a Strange Lady* (1975)

34 A good old man, sir; he will be talking: as they say, 'when the age is in, the wit is out.'

William Shakespeare 1564–1616: *Much Ado About Nothing* (1598–9)

35 *a final letter to a young correspondent, a year before his death:*
Dear Elise,
Seek younger friends; I am extinct.

George Bernard Shaw 1856–1950: letter, 1949

36 The House of Lords is a perfect eventide home.

Baroness Stocks 1891–1975: *My Commonplace Book* (1970)

37 *to a young diplomat who boasted of his ignorance of whist:*
What a sad old age you are preparing for yourself.

Charles-Maurice de Talleyrand 1754–1838: J. Amédée Pichot *Souvenirs Intimes sur M. de Talleyrand* (1870)

38 *on growing old:*
I feel I can talk with more authority, especially when I say, 'I don't know'.
   at the age of 78

Peter Ustinov 1921–2004: interview in *Independent* 28 July 1999

39 One should never make one's début with a scandal. One should reserve that to give an interest to one's old age.

Oscar Wilde 1854–1900: *The Picture of Dorian Gray* (1891)

40 Though well stricken in years the old blister becomes on these occasions as young as he feels, which seems to be about twenty-two.

P. G. Wodehouse 1881–1975: *Uncle Dynamite* (1948)

Opera

❝ Opera is when a guy gets stabbed in the back and, instead of bleeding, he sings. ❞
Ed Gardner

---

1 I do not mind what language an opera is sung in so long as it is a language I don't understand.

Edward Appleton 1892–1965: in *Observer* 28 August 1955

2 The opera ain't over 'til the fat lady sings.

Dan Cook: in *Washington Post* 3 June 1978

3 People are wrong when they say that the opera isn't what it used to be. It is what it used to be—that's what's wrong with it.

Noël Coward 1899–1973: *Design for Living* (1933)

4 Opera is when a guy gets stabbed in the back and, instead of bleeding, he sings.

Ed Gardner 1901–63: *Duffy's Tavern* (US radio programme, 1940s)

5 Opera in English is, in the main, just about as sensible as baseball in Italian.

H. L. Mencken 1880–1956: Laurence J. Peter (ed.) *Quotations for our Time* (1977)

6 *view of opera before he met Maria Callas:*
Italian chefs screaming risotto recipes at each other.

Aristotle Onassis 1906–75: Peter Evans *Nemesis: the True Story of Aristotle* (2004)

7 The first act of the three occupied two hours. I enjoyed that in spite of the singing.

Mark Twain 1835–1910: *What is Man?* (1906)

Parents ····▸ Children, The Family

❝ Mothers go on getting blamed until they're eighty, but shouldn't take it personally. ❞
Katharine Whitehorn

---

1 Money—the one thing that keeps us in touch with our children.

Gyles Brandreth 1948– : in *The Times* 2 February 2002

2 The authoritarian, didactic, primitive Irish parent is world famous—as is his frequently neurotic, deceitful and anxious child.

Noel Browne 1915–97: in 1973, attributed

3 My parents and his mother ganged up and had pan-parent meetings.

Katy Hayes: *Forecourt* (1995)

4 *to his daughter's date:*
Anything happens to my daughter, I got a .45 and a shovel. I doubt anybody would miss you.

Amy Heckering: *Clueless* (1995 film); spoken by Mel Horowitz (Dan Hedeya)

5 Mom and Pop were just a couple of kids when they got married. He was eighteen, she was sixteen, and I was three.

Billie Holiday 1915–59: *Lady Sings the Blues* (1958) opening words

6 *on hearing a report that his son Charles James Fox was to be married:*
He will be obliged to go to bed at least one night of his life.

Lord Holland 1705–74: Christopher Hobhouse *Fox* (1934)

7 If I'm more of an influence to your son as a rapper than you are as a father . . . you got to look at yourself as a parent.

Ice Cube 1970– : to Mike Sager in *Rolling Stone* 4 October 1990

8 In case it is one of mine.
patting children in Chelsea on the head as he passed by

Augustus John 1878–1961: Michael Holroyd *Augustus John* (1975)

9 *to Nina Hamnett:*
We have become, Nina, the sort of people our parents warned us about.

Augustus John 1878–1961: attributed; Nigel Rees *Cassell Dictionary of Humorous Quotations* (1999)

10 Fathers don't curse, they disinherit. Mothers curse.

Irma Kurtz: *Malespeak* (1986)

11 *explaining her mother's insistence on taking her own bidet with her when she travelled:*
My poor, dear mother suffers from a bidet-fixe.

Karen Lancaster d. 1964: Osbert Lancaster *With an Eye to the Future* (1967)

12 They fuck you up, your mum and dad.
They may not mean to, but they do.
They fill you with the faults they had
And add some extra, just for you.

Philip Larkin 1922–85: 'This Be The Verse' (1974)

13 Parents should conduct their arguments in quiet, respectful tones, but in a foreign language. You'd be surprised what an inducement that is to the education of children.

Judith Martin 1938– : 'Advice from Miss Manners', column in *Washington Post* 1979–82

14 Because of their size, parents may be difficult to discipline properly.

P. J. O'Rourke 1947– : *Modern Manners* (1984)

15 A Jewish man with parents alive is a fifteen-year-old boy, and will remain a fifteen-year-old boy until *they die*!

Philip Roth 1933– : *Portnoy's Complaint* (1967)

16 I did not throw myself into the struggle for life: I threw my mother into it. I was not a staff to my father's old age: I hung on to his coat tails.

George Bernard Shaw 1856–1950: preface to *The Irrational Knot* (1905)

17 I wish either my father or my mother, or indeed both of them, as they were in duty both equally bound to it, had minded what they were about when they begot me.

Laurence Sterne 1713–68: *Tristram Shandy* (1759–67)

18 And her mother came too!

Dion Titheradge: title of song (1921)

19 I have four sons and three stepsons. I have learnt what it is like to step on Lego with bare feet.

Fay Weldon 1931– : in *Independent* 6 July 2002

20 In our society . . . mothers go on getting blamed until they're eighty, but shouldn't take it personally.

Katharine Whitehorn 1926– : *Observations* (1970)

Parties ····> Society and Social Life

66 Unless your life is going well you don't dream of giving a party. 99
Carol Shields

1 I've been to a marvellous party,
We didn't start dinner till ten
And young Bobbie Carr
Did a stunt at the bar
With a lot of extraordinary men.

Noël Coward 1899–1973: 'I've been to a Marvellous Party' (1938)

2 You know I hate parties. My idea of hell is a very large party in a cold room, where everybody has to play hockey properly.

Stella Gibbons 1902–89: *Cold Comfort Farm* (1932)

3 Home is heaven and orgies are vile,
But you *need* an orgy, once in a while.

Ogden Nash 1902–71: 'Home, 99⁴⁴⁄₁₀₀% Sweet Home' (1935)

4 Unless your life is going well you don't dream of giving a party. Unless you can look in the mirror and see a benign and generous and healthy human being, you shrink from acts of hospitality.

Carol Shields 1935–2003: *Larry's Party* (1997)

5 Gee, what a terrific party. Later on we'll get some fluid and embalm each other.

Neil Simon 1927– : *The Gingerbread Lady* (1970)

6 I made a terrible social gaffe. I went to a Ken and Barbie party dressed as Klaus Barbie.

Arthur Smith 1954– and **Chris England**: *An Evening with Gary Lineker* (1990)

7 An office party is not, as is sometimes supposed, the Managing Director's chance to kiss the tea-girl. It is the tea-girl's chance to kiss the Managing Director.

Katharine Whitehorn 1926– : *Roundabout* (1962) 'The Office Party'

8 Of course I don't want to go to a cocktail party . . . If I wanted to stand around with a load of people I don't know eating bits of cold toast I can get caught shoplifting and go to Holloway.

Victoria Wood 1953– : *Mens Sana in Thingummy Doodah* (1990)

Past and Present ····> The Future

66 On balance Right Now is preferable to the Good Old Days. 99
Maeve Binchy

1 'The first ten million years were the worst,' said Marvin, 'and the second ten million years, they were the worst too. The third ten million I didn't enjoy at all. After that I went into a bit of a decline.'

Douglas Adams 1952–2001: *Restaurant at the End of the Universe* (1980)

2 Nostalgia isn't what it used to be.

Anonymous: graffito (taken as title of book by Simone Signoret, 1978)

3 The world has turned upside down. The best golfer in the world is black; the best rapper in the world is white; and now there is a war and, guess what, Germany doesn't want to be in it.

Alan Bennett 1934– : diary 2003, in *London Review of Books* 8 January 2004

4 It's not perfect, but to me on balance Right Now is a lot better than the Good Old Days.

Maeve Binchy 1940– : in *Irish Times* 15 November 1997

5 The rule is, jam to-morrow and jam yesterday—but never jam today.

Lewis Carroll 1832–98: *Through the Looking-Glass* (1872)

6 What a Royal Academy,
Too Alma-Tademy,
Practical, mystical,
Over-artistical,
Highly pictorial,
Albert Memorial
Century this has been.

Noël Coward 1899–1973: 'What a Century' (1953)

7 I do not know which makes a man more conservative—to know nothing but the present, or nothing but the past.

John Maynard Keynes 1883–1946: *The End of Laissez-Faire* (1926)

8 Industrial archaeology . . . believes that a thing that doesn't work any more is far more interesting than a thing that still works.

Miles Kington 1941–2008: *Nature Made Ridiculously Simple* (1983)

9 Weren't the eighties grand? Cash grew on trees or, anyway, coca bushes. The rich roamed the land in vast herds hunted by proud, free tribes of investment brokers who lived a simple life in tune with money.

P. J. O'Rourke 1947– : introduction to the second edition of *The Bachelor Home Companion* (1993)

10 They spend their time mostly looking forward to the past.

John Osborne 1929– : *Look Back in Anger* (1956)

11 There's a million more important things going on in the world today. New countries are being born. They're getting ready to send men to the moon. I just can't get excited about making wax fruit.

Neil Simon 1927– : *Come Blow Your Horn* (1961)

12 It used to be a good hotel, but that proves nothing—I used to be a good boy.

Mark Twain 1835–1910: *The Innocents Abroad* (1869)

13 It is the spirit of the age to believe that any fact, no matter how suspect, is superior to any imaginative exercise, no matter how true.

Gore Vidal 1925– : in *Encounter* December 1967

14 We mustn't prejudge the past.

William Whitelaw 1918–99: in *The Times* 2 July 1999; attributed

15 Hindsight is always twenty-twenty.

Billy Wilder 1906–2002: J. R. Columbo *Wit and Wisdom of the Moviemakers* (1979)

People and Personalities

❝ Peter Mandelson is someone who can skulk in broad daylight. ❞
Simon Hoggart

1 This was an actress who, for twenty years, had the world at her feet. She kicked it away, and the ball rolled out of her reach.
of Mrs Patrick Campbell

James Agate 1877–1947: diary, 12 April 1940

2 *of Gordon Brown:*
A man who can lighten a room by leaving it.

Anonymous: Tom Bower *Gordon Brown* (2004)

3 My name is George Nathaniel Curzon,
I am a most superior person.
My face is pink, my hair is sleek,
I dine at Blenheim once a week.
of Lord Curzon

Anonymous: *The Masque of Balliol* (c.1870), in W. G. Hiscock *The Balliol Rhymes* (1939, the last two lines are a later addition); see **People** 29

4 My God, there are two of them!
cry from the gallery of the Glasgow Empire as Mike Winters followed Bernie Winters on to the stage

Anonymous: unattributed

5 *on Vita Sackville-West's appearance in a* tableau vivant:
Dear old Vita, all aqua, no vita, was as heavy as frost.

Margot Asquith 1864–1945: Philip Ziegler *Diana Cooper* (1981)

6 He came to see me this morning—positively reeking of Horlicks.
of Adrian Boult

Thomas Beecham 1879–1961: Ned Sherrin *Cutting Edge* (1984)

7 Byron!—he would be all forgotten today if he had lived to be a florid old gentleman with iron-grey whiskers, writing very long, very able letters to *The Times* about the Repeal of the Corn Laws.

Max Beerbohm 1872–1956: *Zuleika Dobson* (1911)

8 He's always backing into the limelight.
of T. E. Lawrence

Lord Berners 1883–1950: oral tradition

9 The meringue-utan.
of Rosamond Lehmann

Maurice Bowra 1898–1971: in *Spectator* 17 July 1999; attributed

10 *jumping from a second storey window:*
I'm Superjew!

Lenny Bruce 1925–66: in *Observer* 21 August 1966

11 I kind of like ducking questions.

George W. Bush 1946– : in April 2004; Graydon Carter *What We've Lost* (2004)

12 That's the trouble with Anthony—half mad baronet, half beautiful woman.
of Anthony Eden

R. A. Butler 1902–82: attributed

13 He is a person of very *epic* appearance—and has a fine head as far as the outside goes—and wants nothing but taste to make the inside equally attractive.
of Robert Southey

Lord Byron 1788–1824: letter, 30 September 1813

14 *of the vegetarian George Bernard Shaw:*
If you give him meat no woman in London will be safe.

Mrs Patrick Campbell 1865–1940: Frank Harris *Contemporary Portraits* (1919)

15 I do not wear a bleeper. I can't speak in soundbites. I refuse to repeat slogans. . . . I hate focus groups. I absolutely hate image consultants.

Kenneth Clarke 1940– : in *New Statesman* 12 February 1999

16 I had to pull him out, otherwise nobody would have believed I didn't push him in.
on rescuing David Frost from drowning

Peter Cook 1937–95: Nigel Rees (ed.) *A Year of Stings and Squelches* (1985)

17 I view this able and energetic man with some detachment. He is loyal to his own career but only incidentally to anything or anyone else.
of Richard Crossman

Hugh Dalton 1887–1962: diary 17 September 1941

18 The laugh in mourning.
of Eamonn de Valera

Oliver St John Gogarty 1878–1957: Ulick O'Connor *Oliver St John Gogarty* (1964)

19 Peter Mandelson is someone who can skulk in broad daylight.

Simon Hoggart 1946– : in *Guardian* 10 July 1998

20 A First Minister whose self-righteous stubbornness has not been equalled, save briefly by Neville Chamberlain, since Lord North.
of Margaret Thatcher

Roy Jenkins 1920–2003: in *Observer* 11 March 1990

21 I'd rather be Frank Capra than God. If there is a Frank Capra.

Garson Kanin 1912–99: in *The Times* 16 March 1999; attributed

22 It was like watching someone organize her own immortality. Every phrase and gesture was studied. Now and again, when she said something a little out of the ordinary, she wrote it down herself in a notebook.
of Virginia Woolf

Harold Laski 1893–1950: letter to Oliver Wendell Holmes, 30 November 1930

23 Many people see Eva Peron as either a saint or the incarnation of Satan. That means I can definitely identify with her.

Madonna 1958– : in *Newsweek* 5 February 1996

24 There were three things that Chico was always on—a phone, a horse or a broad.

Groucho Marx 1895–1977: Ned Sherrin *Cutting Edge* (1984)

25 Nothing ever made me more doubtful of T. E. Lawrence's genuineness than that he so heartily trusted two persons whom I knew to be bogus.

W. Somerset Maugham 1874–1965: *A Writer's Notebook* (1949) written in 1941

26 *Asked if she really had nothing on in the* [calendar] *photograph:*
I had the radio on.

Marilyn Monroe 1926–62: in *Time* 11 August 1952

27 The triumph of sugar over diabetes.
of J. M. Barrie

George Jean Nathan 1882–1958: Robin May *The Wit of the Theatre* (1969)

28 A big cat detained briefly in a poodle parlour, sharpening her claws on the velvet.
of Lady Thatcher in the House of Lords

Matthew Parris 1949– : *Look Behind You!* (1993)

29 My name is Mandy: Peter B.
I'm back in charge—don't mess with me.
My cheeks are drawn, my face is bony,
The line I take comes straight from Tony.

Matthew Parris 1949– : in *The Times* 21 October 1999; see **People** 3

30 An elderly fallen angel travelling incognito.
of André Gide

Peter Quennell 1905– : *The Sign of the Fish* (1960)

31 Any man who hates dogs and babies can't be all bad.
of W. C. Fields, and often attributed to him

Leo Rosten 1908– : speech at Masquers' Club dinner, 16 February 1939

32 Through it all, I have remained consistently and nauseatingly adorable. In fact, I have been known to cause diabetes.

Meg Ryan 1961– : at Women in Hollywood luncheon, 1999

33 He [Macaulay] is like a book in breeches.

Sydney Smith 1771–1845: Lady Holland *Memoir* (1855)

34 Daniel Webster struck me much like a steam-engine in trousers.

Sydney Smith 1771–1845: Lady Holland *Memoir* (1855)

35 That great Cham of literature, Samuel Johnson.

Tobias Smollett 1721–71: letter to John Wilkes, 16 March 1759

36 Her conception of God was certainly not orthodox. She felt towards Him as she might have felt towards a glorified sanitary engineer; and in some of her speculations she seems hardly to distinguish between the Deity and the Drains.
of Florence Nightingale

Lytton Strachey 1880–1932: *Eminent Victorians* (1918)

37 [Charles Laughton] walks top-heavily, like a salmon standing on its tail.

Kenneth Tynan 1927–80: *Profiles* (ed. Kathleen Tynan, 1989)

38 Forty years ago he was Slightly in *Peter Pan*, and you might say that he has been wholly in *Peter Pan* ever since.
of Noël Coward

Kenneth Tynan 1927–80: *Curtains* (1961)

39 A triumph of the embalmer's art.
of Ronald Reagan

Gore Vidal 1925– : in *Observer* 26 April 1981

40 Of course, I believe in the Devil. How otherwise would I account for the existence of Lord Beaverbrook?

Evelyn Waugh 1903–66: L. Gourlay *The Beaverbrook I Knew* (1984)

41 *to a gentleman who had accosted him in the street saying, 'Mr Jones, I believe?':*
If you believe that, you'll believe anything.

Duke of Wellington 1769–1852: Elizabeth Longford *Pillar of State* (1972); George Jones RA (1786–1869), painter of military subjects, bore a striking resemblance to Wellington

42 The only Greek Tragedy I know.
of Spyros Skouras, Head of Fox Studios

Billy Wilder 1906–2002: attributed, perhaps apocryphal

43 She is so odd a blend of Little Nell and Lady Macbeth. It is not so much the familiar phenomenon of a hand of steel in a velvet glove as a lacy sleeve with a bottle of vitriol concealed in its folds.
of Dorothy Parker

Alexander Woollcott 1887–1943: *While Rome Burns* (1934)

Peoples ····▸ Countries and Peoples

Personalities ····▸ People and Personalities

Philosophy

66 Cheerfulness was always breaking in. **99**
Oliver Edwards

1 *intervening at a New York party between Mike Tyson and Naomi Campbell:*
TYSON: Do you know who the f— I am? I'm the heavyweight champion of the world.
AYER: And I am the former Wykeham Professor of Logic. We are both pre-eminent in our field. I suggest we talk about this like rational men.

A. J. Ayer 1910–89: Ben Rogers *A. J. Ayer: a Life* (1999)

2 I have tried too in my time to be a philosopher; but, I don't know how, cheerfulness was always breaking in.

Oliver Edwards 1711–91: James Boswell *Life of Samuel Johnson* (1934 ed.) 17 April 1778

3 The philosopher is like a mountaineer who has with difficulty climbed a mountain for the sake of the sunrise, and arriving at the top finds only fog . . . He must be an honest man if he doesn't tell you that the spectacle was stupendous.

W. Somerset Maugham 1874–1965: *A Writer's Notebook* (1949) written in 1896

4 Philosophy consists very largely of one philosopher arguing that all others are jackasses. He usually proves it, and I should add that he usually proves that he is one himself.

H. L. Mencken 1880–1956: *Minority Report* (1956)

5 Apart from the known and the unknown, what else is there?

Harold Pinter 1930– : *The Homecoming* (1965)

6 Sometimes I sits and thinks, and then again I just sits.

Punch 1841–1992: vol. 131 (1906)

7 *on the speaker's choice of subject at university:*
Almost everyone who didn't know what to do, did philosophy. Well, that's logical.

Tom Stoppard 1937– : *Albert's Bridge* (1969)

8 The safest general characterization of the European philosophical tradition is that it consists of a series of footnotes to Plato.

Alfred North Whitehead 1861–1947: *Process and Reality* (1929)

9 What is your aim in philosophy?—To show the fly the way out of the fly-bottle.

Ludwig Wittgenstein 1889–1951: *Philosophische Untersuchungen* (1953)

10 You would not like Nietzsche, sir. He is fundamentally unsound.

P. G. Wodehouse 1881–1975: *My Man Jeeves* (1919)

Places ····▶ America, Countries, England, Ireland, Scotland, Wales

❝ Very flat, Norfolk. **❞**
Noël Coward

1 He was glued to Soho, a fairly common but chronic attachment some of us formed. There is no known cure for it except the road to Golders Green.

Jeffrey Bernard 1932–97: in *The Spectator* 8 March 1986

2 For Cambridge people rarely smile,
Being urban, squat, and packed with guile.

Rupert Brooke 1887–1915: 'The Old Vicarage, Grantchester' (1915)

3 I had forgotten just how flat and empty it [middle America] is. Stand on two phone books almost anywhere in Iowa and you get a view.

Bill Bryson 1951– : *The Lost Continent* (1989)

4 *of Herat:*
Here at last is Asia without an inferiority complex.

Robert Byron 1905–41: *The Road to Oxiana* (1937)

5 BASIL: May I ask what you were hoping to see out of a Torquay bedroom window? Sydney Opera House, perhaps? The Hanging Gardens of Babylon? Herds of wildebeeste sweeping majestically . . .

John Cleese 1939– and **Connie Booth**: *Fawlty Towers* (1979) 'Communication Problems'

6 Very flat, Norfolk.

Noël Coward 1899–1973: *Private Lives* (1930)

7 In Manhattan, every flat surface is a potential stage and every inattentive waiter an unemployed, possibly unemployable, actor.

Quentin Crisp 1908–99: 'Love Lies Bleeding' (Channel 4 TV), 6 August 1991; Nigel Rees (ed.) *Cassell Dictionary of Humorous Quotations* (1999)

8 Kent, sir—everybody knows Kent—apples, cherries, hops, and women.

Charles Dickens 1812–70: *Pickwick Papers* (1837)

9 There's a famous seaside place called Blackpool,
That's noted for fresh air and fun,
And Mr and Mrs Ramsbottom
Went there with young Albert, their son.

Marriott Edgar 1880–1951: 'The Lion and Albert' (1932)

10 They used to say that Cambridge was the first stopping place for the wind that swept down from the Urals: in the thirties that was as true of the politics as the weather.

Stephen Fry 1957– : *The Liar* (1991)

11 The Pacific Ocean was a body of water surrounded on all sides by elephantiasis and other dread diseases.

Joseph Heller 1923–99: *Catch-22* (1961)

12 Broadbosomed, bold, becalm'd, benign
Lies Balham foursquare on the Northern Line.
Matched by no marvel save in Eastern scene,
A rose-red city half as gold as green.

Frank Muir 1920–98 and **Denis Norden** 1922– : 'Balham—Gateway to the South' *Third Division* (BBC Third Programme, 1948); Nigel Rees (ed.) *Cassell Dictionary of Humorous Quotations* (1999)

13 The lush pastrami beds of the West Forties knew him not.

S. J. Perelman 1904–79: 'The Swirling Cape and the Low Bow'

14 Addresses are given to us to conceal our whereabouts.

Saki 1870–1916: *Reginald in Russia* (1910)

15 Wensleydale lies between Tuesleydale and Thursleydale.

Arthur Smith 1954– : attributed

Poetry ····➤ Literature, Poets, Writers and Writing

66 The only art people haven't yet learnt to consume like soup. **99**
W. H. Auden

1 There was a young man called MacNabbiter
Who had an organ of prodigious diameter.
But it was not the size
That gave girls the surprise,
'Twas his rhythm—Iambic Pentameter.

Anonymous: in *Ned Sherrin in his Anecdotage* (1993)

2 There was a young man from Peru
Whose limericks stopped at line two.

Anonymous: Harry Mathews and Alastair Brotchie (eds) *Oulipo Compendium* (1998)

3 Poetry is the only art people haven't yet learnt to consume like soup.

W. H. Auden 1907–73: in *New York Times* 1960

4 I have but with some difficulty *not* added any more to this snake of a poem [*The Giaour*]—which has been lengthening its rattles every month.

Lord Byron 1788–1824: letter 26 August 1813

5 '*I* can repeat poetry as well as other folk if it comes to that—' 'Oh, it needn't come to that!' Alice hastily said.

Lewis Carroll 1832–98: *Through the Looking-Glass* (1872)

6 'By God,' quod he, 'for pleynly, at a word,
Thy drasty rymyng is nat worth a toord!'

Geoffrey Chaucer c.1343–1400: *The Canterbury Tales* 'Sir Thopas'

7 Sometimes poetry is emotion recollected in a highly emotional state.

Wendy Cope 1945– : 'An Argument with Wordsworth' (1992)

8 *Laman Blanchard, a young poet, had submitted some verses entitled 'Orient Pearls at Random Strung' to* Household Words:
Dear Blanchard, too much string—Yours. C.D.

Charles Dickens 1812–70: Frederick Locker-Lampson *My Confidences* (1896)

9 So poetry, which is in Oxford made
An art, in London only is a trade.

John Dryden 1631–1700: 'Prologue to the University of Oxon . . . at the Acting of *The Silent Woman*' (1673)

10 Immature poets imitate; mature poets steal.

T. S. Eliot 1888–1965: *The Sacred Wood* (1920) 'Philip Massinger'

11 I'd as soon write free verse as play tennis with the net down.

Robert Frost 1874–1963: Edward Lathem *Interviews with Robert Frost* (1966)

12 There are the women whose husbands I meet on aeroplanes
Who close their briefcases and ask, 'What are *you* in?'
I look in their eyes, I tell them I am in poetry . . . .

Donald Hall 1928– : 'To a Waterfowl' (1971)

13 I did not begin to write poetry in earnest until the really emotional part of my life was over; and my poetry, so far as I could make out, sprang chiefly from physical conditions, such as a relaxed sore throat during my most prolific period.

A. E. Housman 1859–1936: letter, 5 February 1933

14 Mr Stone's hexameters are verses of no sort, but prose in ribands.

A. E. Housman 1859–1936: in *Classical Review* 1899

15 The notion of expressing sentiments in short lines having similar sounds at their ends seems as remote as mangoes on the moon.

Philip Larkin 1922–85: letter to Barbara Pym, 22 January 1975

16 Writing a book of poetry is like dropping a rose petal down the Grand Canyon and waiting for the echo.

Don Marquis 1878–1937: E. Anthony *O Rare Don Marquis* (1962)

17 My favourite poem is the one that starts 'Thirty days hath September' because it actually tells you something.

Groucho Marx 1895–1977: Ned Sherrin *Cutting Edge* (1984); attributed

18 All that is not prose is verse; and all that is not verse is prose.

Molière 1622–73: *Le Bourgeois Gentilhomme* (1671)

19 M. JOURDAIN: What? when I say: 'Nicole, bring me my slippers, and give me my night-cap,' is that prose?
PHILOSOPHY TEACHER: Yes, Sir.
M. JOURDAIN: Good heavens! For more than forty years I have been speaking prose without knowing it.

Molière 1622–73: *Le Bourgeois Gentilhomme* (1671)

20 And he, whose fustian's so sublimely bad,
It is not poetry, but prose run mad.

Alexander Pope 1688–1744: 'An Epistle to Dr Arbuthnot' (1735)

21 Of all the literary scenes
Saddest this sight to me:
The graves of little magazines
Who died to make verse free.

Keith Preston 1884–1927: 'The Liberators'

22 I picture him as short and tan.
We'd meet, perhaps, in Hindustan.
I'd say, with admirable *élan*,
'Ah, Anantanarayanan—'.

John Updike 1932– : 'I Missed His Book, But I Read His Name' (1964)

23 All bad poetry springs from genuine feeling.

Oscar Wilde 1854–1900: 'The Critic as Artist' (1891)

24 Peotry is sissy stuff that rhymes. Weedy people sa la and fie and swoon when they see a bunch of daffodils.

Geoffrey Willans 1911–58 and **Ronald Searle** 1920– : *Down with Skool!* (1953)

Poets ····> Poetry

❝ Be poignant, man, be poignant! ❞
P. G. Wodehouse

1 The Edinburgh praises Jack Keats or Ketch or whatever his names are;—why his is the Onanism of poetry.

Lord Byron 1788–1824: letter to his publisher John Murray, 4 November 1820

2 I used to think all poets were Byronic —
Mad, bad and dangerous to know.
And then I met a few. Yes it's ironic —
I used to think all poets were Byronic.
They're mostly wicked as a ginless tonic
And wild as pension plans.

Wendy Cope 1945– : 'Triolet' (1986)

3 *the young Stephen Spender had told Eliot of his wish to become a poet:*
I can understand your wanting to write poems, but I don't quite know what you mean by 'being a poet' . . .

T. S. Eliot 1888–1965: Stephen Spender *World within World* (1951)

4 Osbert was wonderful, as you would expect, and Edith, of course, but then we had this rather lugubrious man in a suit, and he read a poem . . . I think it was called The Desert. And first the girls got the giggles and then I did and then even the King.
of an evening at Windsor during the war, arranged by Osbert Sitwell, at which T. S. Eliot read from 'The Waste Land' to the King and Queen and the Princesses

Queen Elizabeth, the Queen Mother 1900–2002: private conversation, reported in *Spectator* 30 June 1990

5 What is a modern poet's fate?
To write his thoughts upon a slate;
The critic spits on what is done,
Gives it a wipe—and all is gone.

Thomas Hood 1799–1845: 'A Joke', in Hallam Tennyson *Alfred Lord Tennyson* (1897); not found in Hood's *Complete Works*

6 *a nineteenth-century headmaster of Eton:*
I wish Shelley had been at Harrow.

James John Hornby 1826–1909: Henry S. Salt *Percy Bysshe Shelley* (1896)

7 In barrenness, at any rate, I hold a high place among English poets, excelling even Gray.

A. E. Housman 1859–1936: letter 28 February 1910

8 Dr Donne's verses are like the peace of God; they pass all understanding.

James I 1566–1625: remark recorded by Archdeacon Plume (1630–1704)

9 *on the relative merits of two minor poets:*
Sir, there is no settling the point of precedency between a louse and a flea.

Samuel Johnson 1709–84: James Boswell *Life of Samuel Johnson* (1791) 1783

10 We had the old crow over at Hull recently, looking like a Christmas present from Easter Island.
  of Ted Hughes

Philip Larkin 1922–85: letter, 1975

11 *on being asked by Stephen Spender in the 1930s how best a poet could serve the Communist cause:*
Go to Spain and get killed. The movement needs a Byron.

Harry Pollitt 1890–1960: Frank Johnson *Out of Order* (1982); attributed, perhaps apocryphal

12 While pensive poets painful vigils keep,
Sleepless themselves, to give their readers sleep.

Alexander Pope 1688–1744: *The Dunciad* (1742)

13 Sir, I admit your gen'ral rule
That every poet is a fool:
But you yourself may serve to show it,
That every fool is not a poet.

Alexander Pope 1688–1744: 'Epigram from the French' (1732)

14 For years a secret shame destroyed my peace—
I'd not read Eliot, Auden or MacNeice.
But then I had a thought that brought me hope—
Neither had Chaucer, Shakespeare, Milton, Pope.

Justin Richardson: 'Take Heart, Illiterates' (1966)

15 I made my then famous declaration (among 100 people) 'I am a Socialist, an Atheist and a Vegetarian' (ergo, a true Shelleyan), whereupon two ladies who had been palpitating with enthusiasm for Shelley under the impression that he was a devout Anglican, resigned on the spot.

George Bernard Shaw 1856–1950: letter 1 March 1908

16 Life's a curse, love's a blight, God's a blaggard, cherry blossom is quite nice.
  on A. E. Housman

Tom Stoppard 1937– : *The Invention of Love* (1997)

17 I may as well tell you, here and now, that if you are going about the place thinking things pretty, you will never make a modern poet. Be poignant, man, be poignant!

P. G. Wodehouse 1881–1975: *The Small Bachelor* (1927)

Political Parties

66 A liberal is a man who leaves the room before the fight begins. **99**
Heywood Broun

1 I realize I am about as welcome in the Tory party as Banquo's ghost.

Jonathan Aitken 1942– : in *Sunday Times* 15 February 2004

2 CHILD: Mamma, are Tories born wicked, or do they grow wicked afterwards?
MOTHER: They are born wicked, and grow worse.

Anonymous: G. W. E. Russell *Collections and Recollections* (1898)

3 Don't be stupid, be a smarty,
Come and join the Nazi Party.

Mel Brooks 1926– : 'Springtime for Hitler', lyric from *The Producers* (2001 musical)

4 A liberal is a man who leaves the room before the fight begins.

Heywood Broun 1888–1939: R. E. Drennan *Wit's End* (1973)

5 'A sound Conservative government,' said Taper, musingly. 'I understand: Tory men and Whig measures.'

Benjamin Disraeli 1804–81: *Coningsby* (1844)

6 The right hon. Gentleman caught the Whigs bathing, and walked away with their clothes.
  on Sir Robert Peel's abandoning protection in favour of free trade, traditionally the policy of the [Whig] *Opposition*

Benjamin Disraeli 1804–81: speech, House of Commons 28 February 1845

7 I did not vote Labour because they've heard of Oasis and nobody is going to vote Tory because William Hague has got a baseball cap.

Ben Elton 1959– : in *Radio Times* 18 April 1998

8 I never dared be radical when young
For fear it would make me conservative when old.

Robert Frost 1874–1963: 'Precaution' (1936)

9 I often think it's comical
How Nature always does contrive
That every boy and every gal,
That's born into the world alive,
Is either a little Liberal,
Or else a little Conservative!

W. S. Gilbert 1836–1911: *Iolanthe* (1882)

10 Conservatives do not believe that the political struggle is the most important thing in life . . . The simplest of them prefer fox-hunting—the wisest religion.

Lord Hailsham 1907–2001: *The Case for Conservatism* (1947)

11 *at a photocall when Lady Thatcher said to him* 'You should be on my right':
That would be difficult.

Edward Heath 1916–2005: in *The Times* 24 April 1999 'Quotes of the Week'

12 Testators would do well to provide some indication of the particular Liberal Party which they have in mind, such as a telephone number or a Christian name.

A. P. Herbert 1890–1971: *Misleading Cases* (1935)

13 The Tory Party only panics in a crisis.

Iain Macleod 1913–70: attributed

14 Labour is led by an upper-class public school man, the Tories by a self-made grammar school lass who worships her creator, though she is democratic enough to talk down to anyone.

Austin Mitchell 1934– : *Westminster Man* (1982)

15 I have only one firm belief about the American political system, and that is this: God is a Republican and Santa Claus is a Democrat.

P. J. O'Rourke 1947– : *Parliament of Whores* (1991)

16 Having committed political suicide, the Conservative Party is now living to regret it.

Chris Patten 1944– : attributed, 2003; the remark was subsequently considered for a Plain English Foot in Mouth Award

17 Tory and Whig in turns shall be my host,
I taste no politics in boiled and roast.

Sydney Smith 1771–1845: letter to John Murray, November 1834

18 I like a lot of Republicans . . . Indeed, there are some I would trust with anything—anything, that is, except public office.

Adlai Stevenson 1900–65: in *New York Times* 15 August 1952

19 The Labour Party is going around stirring up apathy.

William Whitelaw 1918–99: recalled by Alan Watkins as a characteristic 'Willieism', in *Observer* 1 May 1983

20 The average footslogger in the New South Wales Right . . . generally speaking carries a dagger in one hand and a Bible in the other and doesn't put either to really elegant use.

Neville Wran 1926– : in 1973; Michael Gordon *A Question of Leadership* (1993)

Politicians ····> People and Personalities, Politics, Presidents, Prime Ministers

66 A statesman is a politician who's been dead 10 or 15 years. 99
Harry S. Truman

---

1 In good King Charles's golden days,
  When loyalty no harm meant;
  A furious High-Churchman I was,
  And so I gained preferment.
  Unto my flock I daily preached,
  Kings are by God appointed,
  And damned are those who dare resist,
  Or touch the Lord's Anointed.
  And this is law, I will maintain,
  Unto my dying day, Sir,
  That whatsoever King shall reign,
  I will be the Vicar of Bray, sir!

  Anonymous: *British Musical Miscellany* (1734) 'The Vicar of Bray'

2 They [parliament] are a lot of hard-faced men who look as if they had done very well out of the war.

  Stanley Baldwin 1867–1947: J. M. Keynes *Economic Consequences of the Peace* (1919)

3 Beaverbrook is so pleased to be in the Government that he is like the town tart who has finally married the Mayor!

  Beverley Baxter 1891–1964: Chips Channon diary 12 June 1940

4 I am the very master of the multipurpose metaphor,
  I put them into speeches which I always feel the better for.
  The speed of my delivery is totally vehicular,
  I'm burning with a passion about nothing in particular.
  I'm well acquainted too with matters technological,
  I'm able to explain myself in phrases tautological.
  My language is poetical and full of hidden promises . . .
  It's like the raging torrent of a thousand Dylan Thomases.

  Alistair Beaton: 'I am the very Model . . . ', sung by Pooh-Bach (*Minister for everything else*. Formerly Neil Kinnock) in Ned Sherrin and Alistair Beaton *The Metropolitan Mikado* (1985)

5 Always threatening resignation, he never signed off.
  of Lord Derby

  Lord Beaverbrook 1879–1964: *Men and Power* (1956)

6 Sir! you have disappointed us!
  We had intended you to be
  The next Prime Minister but three:
  The stocks were sold; the Press was squared;
  The Middle Class was quite prepared.
  But as it is! . . . My language fails!
  Go out and govern New South Wales!

  Hilaire Belloc 1870–1953: 'Lord Lundy' (1907)

7 I am not going to spend any time whatsoever in attacking the Foreign Secretary . . . If we complain about the tune, there is no reason to attack the monkey when the organ grinder is present.

  Aneurin Bevan 1897–1960: during a debate on the Suez crisis, House of Commons 16 May 1957

8 The right kind of leader for the Labour Party . . . a desiccated calculating machine.
  generally taken as referring to Hugh Gaitskell, although Bevan specifically denied it in an interview with Robin Day on 28 April 1959

  Aneurin Bevan 1897–1960: Michael Foot *Aneurin Bevan* (1973) vol. 2

9 *Attlee is said to have remarked that Herbert Morrison was his own worst enemy:*
Not while I'm alive he ain't.

Ernest Bevin 1881–1951: Paul Johnson (ed.) *The Oxford Book of Political Anecdotes* (1986), introduction; also attributed to Bevin of Aneurin Bevan

10 *of the popularity of Margaret Thatcher:*
The further you got from Britain, the more admired you found she was.

James Callaghan 1912–2005: in *Spectator* 1 December 1990

11 Labour spin doctors aren't supposed to like Tory MPs. But Alan Clark was an exceptional man.

Alastair Campbell 1957– : in *Daily Mirror* 8 September 1999

12 QUESTION: What are the desirable qualifications for any young man who wishes to become a politician?
MR CHURCHILL: It is the ability to foretell what is going to happen tomorrow, next week, next month, and next year. And to have the ability afterwards to explain why it didn't happen.

Winston Churchill 1874–1965: B. Adler *Churchill Wit* (1965)

13 There but for the grace of God, goes God.
of Stafford Cripps

Winston Churchill 1874–1965: P. Brendon *Churchill* (1984)

14 a politician is an arse upon
which everyone has sat except a man.

e. e. cummings 1894–1962: *1 x 1* (1944)

15 It is not necessary that every time he rises he should give his famous imitation of a semi-house-trained polecat.
of Norman Tebbit

Michael Foot 1913– : speech in the House of Commons 2 March 1978

16 *on being asked immediately after the Munich crisis if he were not worn out by the late nights:*
No, not exactly. But it spoils one's eye for the high birds.

Lord Halifax 1881–1959: Paul Johnson (ed.) *The Oxford Book of Political Anecdotes* (1986)

17 *having been dissuaded from writing a story which would have been soundly based:*
I decided that for Peter Mandelson the truth was like a second home: he didn't live there all the time.

Trevor Kavanagh 1943– : in *The Times* 7 May 2003

18 did you ever
notice that when
a politician
does get an idea
he usually
gets it all wrong.

Don Marquis 1878–1937: *archys life of mehitabel* (1933) 'archygrams'

19 He had the geniality of the politician who for years has gone out of his way to be cordial with everyone he meets.

W. Somerset Maugham 1874–1965: *A Writer's Notebook* (1949) written in 1938

20 If I saw Mr Haughey buried at midnight at a crossroads, with a stake driven through his heart—politically speaking—I should continue to wear a clove of garlic round my neck, just in case.

Conor Cruise O'Brien 1917– : in *Observer* 10 October 1982

21 DEMOSTHENES: The Athenians will kill thee, Phocion, should they go crazy.
PHOCION: But they will kill thee, should they come to their senses.

Phocion c.402–317 BC: Plutarch *Life of Phocion and Cato the Younger* (Loeb ed., 1919)

22 He may be a son of a bitch, but he's our son of a bitch.
on President Somoza of Nicaragua, 1938

Franklin D. Roosevelt 1882–1945: Jonathon Green *The Book of Political Quotes* (1982)

23 He didn't inhale, he didn't insert. He won't invade.
on Bill Clinton and Kosovo

Neil Shand: *Loose Ends* monologue, 1999

24 *explaining to his fellow columnist Simon Hoggart why he avoided meeting MPs:*
If I knew them, it might spoil the purity of my hatred.

Norman Shrapnel 1912–2004: in *Guardian* 3 February 2004

25 Austen [Chamberlain] always played the game, and he always lost it.

F. E. Smith 1872–1930: Lord Beaverbrook *Men and Power* (1956)

26 A politician is a man who understands government, and it takes a politician to run a government. A statesman is a politician who's been dead 10 or 15 years.

Harry S. Truman 1884–1972: in *New York World Telegram and Sun* 12 April 1958

27 I never saw so many shocking bad hats in my life.
on seeing the first Reformed Parliament

Duke of Wellington 1769–1852: W. Fraser *Words on Wellington* (1889)

28 If the country doesn't go to the dogs or the Radicals, we shall have you Prime Minister, some day.

Oscar Wilde 1854–1900: *An Ideal Husband* (1895)

Politics ····> Democracy, Diplomacy, Government, Presidents, Prime Ministers

❝The only safe pleasure for a parliamentarian is a bag of boiled sweets.❞
Julian Critchley

---

1 Being an MP is the sort of job all working-class parents want for their children—clean, indoors and no heavy lifting.

Diane Abbott 1953– : in *Observer* 30 January 1994 'Sayings of the Week'

2 When the political columnists say 'Every thinking man' they mean themselves, and when candidates appeal to 'Every intelligent voter' they mean everybody who is going to vote for them.

Franklin P. Adams 1881–1960: *Nods and Becks* (1944)

3 Practical politics consists in ignoring facts.

Henry Brooks Adams 1838–1918: *The Education of Henry Adams* (1907)

4 *annotation to a ministerial brief, said to have been read out inadvertently in the House of Lords:*
This is a rotten argument, but it should be good enough for their lordships on a hot summer afternoon.

Anonymous: Lord Home *The Way the Wind Blows* (1976)

5 Revolutions are not made with rosewater.

Anonymous: used by Disraeli in a speech at High Wycombe in 1847; Hesketh Pearson *Dizzy* (1951)

6 *Je suis Marxiste—tendance Groucho.*
I am a Marxist—of the Groucho tendency.

Anonymous: slogan found at Nanterre in Paris, 1968

7 [The War Office kept three sets of figures:] one to mislead the public, another to mislead the Cabinet, and the third to mislead itself.

Herbert Asquith 1852–1928: Alistair Horne *Price of Glory* (1962)

8 From politics, it was an easy step to silence.

Jane Austen 1775–1817: *Northanger Abbey* (1818)

9 There are three classes which need sanctuary more than others—birds, wild flowers, and Prime Ministers.

Stanley Baldwin 1867–1947: in *Observer* 24 May 1925

10 Vote for the man who promises least; he'll be the least disappointing.

> **Bernard Baruch** 1870–1965: Meyer Berger *New York* (1960)

11 Damn it all, you can't have the crown of thorns *and* the thirty pieces of silver.
> *on his position in the Labour Party, c.1956*

> **Aneurin Bevan** 1897–1960: Michael Foot *Aneurin Bevan* (1973) vol. 2

12 There are two ways of getting into the Cabinet—you can crawl in or kick your way in.

> **Aneurin Bevan** 1897–1960: attributed

13 A strife of interests masquerading as a contest of principles. The conduct of public affairs for private advantage.

> **Ambrose Bierce** 1842–c.1914: *The Enlarged Devil's Dictionary* (1967)

14 My God! They've shot our fox!
> *on hearing of the resignation of Hugh Dalton, Chancellor of the Exchequer in the Labour Government, after a leakage of Budget secrets*

> **Nigel Birch** 1906–81: on 13 November 1947

15 Have you ever seen a candidate talking to a rich person on television?

> **Art Buchwald** 1925– : Laurence J. Peter (ed.) *Quotations for our Time* (1977)

16 The US presidency is a Tudor monarchy plus telephones.

> **Anthony Burgess** 1917–93: George Plimpton (ed.) *Writers at Work* 4th Series (1977)

17 In politics you must always keep running with the pack. The moment that you falter and they sense that you are injured, the rest will turn on you like wolves.

> **R. A. Butler** 1902–82: Dennis Walters *Not Always with the Pack* (1989)

18 *to Franklin Roosevelt on the likely duration of the Yalta conference with Stalin:*
I do not see any other way of realizing our hopes about World Organization in five or six days. Even the Almighty took seven.

> **Winston Churchill** 1874–1965: *The Second World War* (1954) vol. 6

19 Politics are almost as exciting as war and quite as dangerous. In war you can only be killed once, but in politics—many times.

> **Winston Churchill** 1874–1965: attributed

20 There are no true friends in politics. We are all sharks circling, and waiting, for traces of blood to appear in the water.

> **Alan Clark** 1928–99: diary, 30 November 1990

21 There's nothing so improves the mood of the Party as the imminent execution of a senior colleague.

> **Alan Clark** 1928–99: diary, 13 July 1990

22 Safe is spelled D-U-L-L. Politics has got to be a fun activity.
> *on being selected as parliamentary candidate for Kensington and Chelsea, 24 January 1997*

> **Alan Clark** 1928–99: in *Daily Telegraph* 25 January 1997

23 M is for Marx
And Movement of Masses
And Massing of Arses.
And Clashing of Classes.

> **Cyril Connolly** 1903–74: 'Where Engels Fears to Tread'

24 The only safe pleasure for a parliamentarian is a bag of boiled sweets.

> **Julian Critchley** 1930–2000: in *Listener* 10 June 1982

25 The duty of an Opposition [is] very simple . . . to oppose everything, and propose nothing.

> **Lord Derby** 1799–1869: quoting 'Mr Tierney, a great Whig authority'; House of Lords 4 June 1841

26 'It's always best on these occasions to do what the mob do.' 'But suppose there are two mobs?' suggested Mr Snodgrass. 'Shout with the largest,' replied Mr Pickwick.

Charles Dickens 1812–70: *Pickwick Papers* (1837)

27 'I am all for a religious cry,' said Taper. 'It means nothing, and, if successful, does not interfere with business when we are in.'

Benjamin Disraeli 1804–81: *Coningsby* (1844)

28 Men destined to the highest places should beware of badinage . . . An insular country subject to fogs, and with a powerful middle class, requires grave statesmen.

Benjamin Disraeli 1804–81: *Endymion* (1880)

29 Think of it! A second Chamber selected by the Whips. A seraglio of eunuchs.

Michael Foot 1913– : speech in the House of Commons 3 February 1969

30 The prospect of a lot
Of dull MPs in close proximity,
All thinking for themselves is what
No man can face with equanimity.

W. S. Gilbert 1836–1911: *Iolanthe* (1882)

31 When in that House MPs divide,
If they've a brain and cerebellum too,
They have to leave that brain outside,
And vote just as their leaders tell 'em to.

W. S. Gilbert 1836–1911: *Iolanthe* (1882)

32 Once the toothpaste is out of the tube, it is awfully hard to get it back in.

H. R. Haldeman 1929–93: to John Dean; *Hearings Before the Select Committee on Presidential Campaign Activities of US Senate: Watergate and Related Activities* (1973)

33 Fat filibusterers begat
Income tax adjusterers begat
'Twas Natchaler and Natchaler to
Begat
And sometimes a bachelor, he begat . . .

E. Y. Harburg 1898–1981: 'The Begat' (1947)

34 DEALER: How about Dave Zimmerman?
BEN: Davie's too bright.
2: What about Walt Gustafson?
BEN: Walt died last night.
3: How about Frank Monohan?
4: What about George Gale?
BEN: Frank ain't a citizen
And George is in jail.
5: We could run Al Wallenstein.
BEN: He's only twenty three.
DEALER: How about Ed Peterson?
2: You idiot, that's me!
ALL: Politics and Poker . . .

Sheldon Harnick 1924– : 'Politics and Poker' (1959)

35 I cannot and will not cut my conscience to fit this year's fashions.

Lillian Hellman 1905–84: letter to John S. Wood, 19 May 1952, in *US Congress Committee Hearing on Un-American Activities* (1952)

36 *of Labour's 'prawn cocktail offensive' prior to the 1992 election campaign:*
Never before have so many crustaceans died in vain.

Michael Heseltine 1933– : speech, 1992

37 A little rebellion now and then is a good thing.

Thomas Jefferson 1743–1826: letter to James Madison, 30 January 1787

38 BOSWELL: So, Sir, you laugh at schemes of political improvement.
JOHNSON: Why, Sir, most schemes of political improvement are very laughable things.

Samuel Johnson 1709–84: James Boswell *Life of Samuel Johnson* (1791) 26 October 1769

39 Gratitude is not a normal feature of political life.

Lord Kilmuir 1900–67: *Political Adventure* (1964)

40 Since when was fastidiousness a quality useful for political advancement?

Bernard Levin 1928– : *If You Want My Opinion* (1992)

41 If voting changed anything they'd abolish it.

Ken Livingstone 1945– : in *Independent* 12 April 1996

42 If you want to succeed in politics, you must keep your conscience well under control.

David Lloyd George 1863–1945: Lord Riddell diary 23 April 1919

43 As usual the Liberals offer a mixture of sound and original ideas. Unfortunately none of the sound ideas is original and none of the original ideas is sound.

Harold Macmillan 1894–1986: speech to London Conservatives, 7 March 1961

44 *on privatization:*
First of all the Georgian silver goes, and then all that nice furniture that used to be in the saloon. Then the Canalettos go.

Harold Macmillan 1894–1986: speech to the Tory Reform Group, 8 November 1985

45 *statement at London airport on leaving for a Commonwealth tour, 7 January 1958, following the resignation of the Chancellor of the Exchequer and others:*
I thought the best thing to do was to settle up these little local difficulties, and then turn to the wider vision of the Commonwealth.

Harold Macmillan 1894–1986: in *The Times* 8 January 1958

46 It has always seemed to me more artistic, when the curtain falls on the last performance, to accept the inevitable *E finita la commedia*. It is tempting, perhaps, but unrewarding to hang about the greenroom after final retirement from the stage.

Harold Macmillan 1894–1986: *At the End of the Day* (1973)

47 There are three bodies no sensible man directly challenges: the Roman Catholic Church, the Brigade of Guards and the National Union of Mineworkers.

Harold Macmillan 1894–1986: in *Observer* 22 February 1981

48 I have never found in a long experience of politics that criticism is ever inhibited by ignorance.

Harold Macmillan 1894–1986: Leon Harris *The Fine Art of Politcal Wit* (1965)

49 A political culture that has no time for lunch is no culture at all.

Andrew Marr 1959– : in *Independent* 11 January 2003

50 I thought you were the original professor of rotational medicine.
to Bernard Ingham, who was appearing before the Commons public administration select committee

Rhodri Morgan 1939– : in *Mail on Sunday* 7 June 1998 'Quotes of the Week'

51 I'm not going to rearrange the furniture on the deck of the Titanic.
having lost five of the last six primaries as President Ford's campaign manager

Rogers Morton 1914–79: in *Washington Post* 16 May 1976

52 Politics is the diversion of trivial men who, when they succeed at it, become important in the eyes of more trivial men.

George Jean Nathan 1882–1958: attributed

53 *Nigel Nicolson, who in 1956 abstained from voting with the Government on the Suez Crisis and subsequently lost his seat, reflecting on the Maastricht vote:*
One final tip to rebels: always have a second profession in reserve.

Nigel Nicolson 1917– : in *The Spectator* 7 November 1992

54 I will be sad if I either look up or down after my death and don't see my son fast asleep on the same benches on which I have slept.

Lord Onslow 1938– : in *Times* 31 October 1998 'Quotes of the Week'

55 Politics are, like God's infinite mercy, a last resort.

P. J. O'Rourke 1947– : *Parliament of Whores* (1991)

56 Men enter local politics solely as a result of being unhappily married.

C. Northcote Parkinson 1909–93: *Parkinson's Law* (1958)

57 Being an MP feeds your vanity and starves your self-respect.

Matthew Parris 1949– : in *The Times* 9 February 1994

58 Politics is supposed to be the second oldest profession. I have come to realize that it bears a very close resemblance to the first.

Ronald Reagan 1911– : at a conference in Los Angeles, 2 March 1977

59 The more you read and observe about this Politics thing, you got to admit that each party is worse than the other.

Will Rogers 1879–1935: *The Illiterate Digest* (1924)

60 It's not cricket to picket.

Harold Rome 1908– : song-title (1937)

61 Sing us a song
Of social significance.
All other tunes are taboo
It must be packed with social fact
Or we won't love you!

Harold Rome 1908– : 'Sing a Song of Social Significance' (1937)

62 He knows nothing; and he thinks he knows everything. That points clearly to a political career.

George Bernard Shaw 1856–1950: *Major Barbara* (1907)

63 Anarchism is a game at which the police can beat you.

George Bernard Shaw 1856–1950: *Misalliance* (1914)

64 Nature has no cure for this sort of madness [Bolshevism], though I have known a legacy from a rich relative work wonders.

F. E. Smith 1872–1930: *Law, Life and Letters* (1927)

65 Minorities . . . are almost always in the right.

Sydney Smith 1771–1845: H. Pearson *The Smith of Smiths* (1934)

66 *on the quality of debate in the House of Lords:*
It is, I think, good evidence of life after death.

Donald Soper 1903–98: in *Listener* 17 August 1978

67 An independent is a guy who wants to take the politics out of politics.

Adlai Stevenson 1900–65: Bill Adler *The Stevenson Wit* (1966)

68 I will make a bargain with the Republicans. If they will stop telling lies about Democrats, we will stop telling the truth about them.

Adlai Stevenson 1900–65: speech during 1952 Presidential campaign; Leon Harris *The Fine Art of Political Wit* (1965)

69 *on why he did not become a politician:*
I could not stand the strain of having to be right all the time.

Peter Ustinov 1921–2004: in *Saga Magazine* August 1999

70 If you want to rise in politics in the United States there is one subject you must stay away from, and that is politics.

Gore Vidal 1925– : in *Observer* 28 June 1987 'Sayings of the Week'

71 The public say they are getting cynical about politicians; they should hear how politicians talk about them.

George Walden 1939– : *Lucky George* (1999)

Poverty ····▸ Debt, Money

66 Poverty is no disgrace to a man, but it is confoundedly inconvenient. 99
Sydney Smith

1 She was poor but she was honest
Victim of a rich man's game.
First he loved her, then he left her,
And she lost her maiden name . . .
It's the same the whole world over,
It's the poor wot gets the blame,
It's the rich wot gets the gravy.
Ain't it all a bleedin' shame?

Anonymous: 'She was Poor but she was Honest'; sung by British soldiers in the First World War

2 Anyone who has ever struggled with poverty knows how extremely expensive it is to be poor.

James Baldwin 1924–87: *Nobody Knows My Name* (1961) 'Fifth Avenue, Uptown: a letter from Harlem'

3 Come away; poverty's catching.

Aphra Behn 1640–89: *The Rover* (1681)

4 The murmuring poor, who will not fast in peace.

George Crabbe 1754–1832: 'The Newspaper' (1785)

5 There is a wealth of poverty in Northern Ireland which must be overcome.

Lord Enniskillen 1918–89: speech in the House of Lords, 3 December 1968

6 Gee, I'd like to see you looking swell, Baby,
Diamond bracelets Woolworth doesn't sell, Baby,
Till that lucky day, you know darned well, Baby
I can't give you anything but love.

Dorothy Fields 1905–74: 'I Can't Give You Anything But Love' (1928)

7 What throws a monkey wrench in
A fella's good intention?
That nasty old invention—
Necessity!

E. Y. Harburg 1898–1981: 'Necessity' (1947)

8 It's no disgrace t'be poor, but it might as well be.

Frank McKinney Hubbard 1868–1930: *Short Furrows* (1911)

9 There seems to be much more in the New Testament in praise of poverty than we like to acknowledge.

Benjamin Jowett 1817–93: Kenneth Rose *Superior Person* (1969)

10 Everyone was poor and proud. My parents didn't know anything to be proud of, so they just carried on.

Patrick Kavanagh 1904–67: *The Green Fool* (1938)

11 Up and down the City Road,
In and out the Eagle,
That's the way the money goes—
Pop goes the weasel!

W. R. Mandale: 'Pop Goes the Weasel' (1853); also attributed to Charles Twiggs

12 If only Bapu [Gandhi] knew the cost of setting him up in poverty!

Sarojini Naidu 1879–1949: A. Campbell-Johnson *Mission with Mountbatten* (1951)

13 Look at me. Worked myself up from nothing to a state of extreme poverty.

S. J. Perelman 1904–79, **Will B. Johnstone**, and **Arthur Sheekman**: *Monkey Business* (1931 film)

14 LABRAX: One letter more than a medical man, that's what I am.
GRIPUS: Then you're a mendicant?
LABRAX: You've hit the point.

Plautus c.250–184 BC: *Rudens*

15 How can I ever start
To tell what's in my heart
At the sight of a dime
Of a shiny new dime.

Harold Rome 1908– : 'The Face on the Dime' (1946)

16 The greatest of evils and the worst of crimes is poverty . . . our first duty—a duty to which every other consideration should be sacrificed—is not to be poor.

George Bernard Shaw 1856–1950: *Major Barbara* (1907) preface

17 You may tempt the upper classes
With your villainous demi-tasses,
But: Heaven will protect a working-girl!

Edgar Smith 1857–1938: 'Heaven Will Protect the Working-Girl' (1909)

18 Poverty is no disgrace to a man, but it is confoundedly inconvenient.

Sydney Smith 1771–1845: J. Potter Briscoe *Sydney Smith: His Wit and Wisdom* (1900)

19 I am pent up in frowzy lodgings, where there is not room enough to swing a cat.

Tobias Smollett 1721–71: *Humphry Clinker* (1771)

20 He was a gentleman who was generally spoken of as having nothing a-year, paid quarterly.

R. S. Surtees 1805–64: *Mr Sponge's Sporting Tour* (1853)

21 How to live well on nothing a year.

William Makepeace Thackeray 1811–63: *Vanity Fair* (1847–8)

22 As for the virtuous poor, one can pity them, of course, but one cannot possibly admire them.

Oscar Wilde 1854–1900: *Sebastian Melmoth* (1891)

23 Like dear St Francis of Assisi I am wedded to Poverty: but in my case the marriage is not a success.

Oscar Wilde 1854–1900: letter June 1899

Power

❝ I'll make him an offer he can't refuse. **❞**
Mario Puzo

1 Whatever happens we have got
The Maxim Gun, and they have not.

Hilaire Belloc 1870–1953: *The Modern Traveller* (1898)

2 Anybody that wants the presidency so much that he'll spend two years organizing and campaigning for it is not to be trusted with the office.

David Broder 1929– : in *Washington Post* 18 July 1973

3 She cannot see an institution without hitting it with her handbag.
of Margaret Thatcher

Julian Critchley 1930–2000: in *The Times* 21 June 1982

4 So long as men worship the Caesars and Napoleons, Caesars and Napoleons will duly arise and make them miserable.

Aldous Huxley 1894–1963: *Ends and Means* (1937)

5 I don't want loyalty. I want *loyalty*. I want him to kiss my ass in Macy's window at high noon and tell me it smells like roses. I want his pecker in my pocket.

Lyndon Baines Johnson 1908–73: David Halberstam *The Best and the Brightest* (1972)

6 Better to have him inside the tent pissing out, than outside pissing in.
of J. Edgar Hoover

Lyndon Baines Johnson 1908–73: David Halberstam *The Best and the Brightest* (1972)

7 I'll make him an offer he can't refuse.

Mario Puzo 1920–99: *The Godfather* (1969)

8 Seven months ago I could give a single command and 541,000 people would immediately obey it. Today I can't get a plumber to come to my house.

H. Norman Schwarzkopf III 1934– : in *Newsweek* 11 November 1991; see **Presidents** 21

9 The Pope! How many divisions has *he* got?
on being asked to encourage Catholicism in Russia by way of conciliating the Pope

Joseph Stalin 1879–1953: on 13 May 1935

10 He seemed much greater than a private citizen while he still was a private citizen, and by everyone's consent capable of reigning if only he had not reigned.
of the Emperor Galba

Tacitus AD 56–after 117: *Histories*

11 Children and zip fasteners do not respond to force . . . Except occasionally.

Katharine Whitehorn 1926– : *Observations* (1970)

Praise and Flattery

66 Flattery hurts no one, that is, if he doesn't inhale. 99
Adlai Stevenson

1 We authors, Ma'am.
to Queen Victoria after the publication of Leaves from the Journal of our Life in the Highlands *in 1868*

Benjamin Disraeli 1804–81: Elizabeth Longford *Victoria R.I.* (1964); attributed

2 Your Majesty is the head of the literary profession.
to Queen Victoria after the publication of Leaves from the Journal of our Life in the Highlands *in 1868*

Benjamin Disraeli 1804–81: Hesketh Pearson *Dizzy* (1951); attributed

3 Please don't be too effusive.
adjuration to the Prime Minister, at their weekly meeting on the speech he was to make to celebrate her golden wedding; see **Prime Ministers** 6

Elizabeth II 1926– : in *Daily Telegraph* 21 November 1997

4 I live for your agglomerated lucubrations.
to H. G. Wells

Henry James 1843–1916: letter, 18 November 1902

5 Consider with yourself what your flattery is worth before you bestow it so freely.
to Hannah More

Samuel Johnson 1709–84: James Boswell *Life of Johnson* (1791)

6 You're the top! You're the Coliseum,
You're the top! You're the Louvre Museum,
You're a melody
From a symphony by Strauss,
You're a Bendel bonnet,
A Shakespeare sonnet,
You're Mickey Mouse!

Cole Porter 1891–1964: 'You're the Top' (1934)

7 I used your soap two years ago; since then I have used no other.

Punch 1841–1992: vol. 86 (1884)

8 What really flatters a man is that you think him worth flattering.

George Bernard Shaw 1856–1950: *John Bull's Other Island* (1907)

9 Among the smaller duties of life, I hardly know one more important than that of not praising where praise is not due.

Sydney Smith 1771–1845: Saba Holland *Memoir* (1855)

10 I suppose flattery hurts no one, that is, if he doesn't inhale.

Adlai Stevenson 1900–65: television broadcast, 30 March 1952

Prejudice and Tolerance

66 Tolerance is only another name for indifference. 99
W. Somerset Maugham

1 Being a star has made it possible for me to get insulted in places where the average Negro could never *hope* to go and get insulted.

Sammy Davis Jnr. 1925–90: *Yes I Can* (1965)

2 I always suspected she had Scotch blood in her veins, anything else I could have looked over in her from a regard to the family.

Maria Edgeworth 1767–1849: *Castle Rackrent* (1800)

3 CONGRESSMAN STARNES: You are quoting from this Marlowe. Is he a Communist?
HALLIE FLANAGAN: I am very sorry. I was quoting from Christopher Marlowe.

Hallie Flanagan 1890–1969: in hearing on the Federal Theatre Project by the House Un-American Activities Committee, 6 December 1938

4 CONGRESSMAN STARNES: I believe Mr Euripides was guilty of teaching class consciousness also, wasn't he?
HALLIE FLANAGAN: I believe that was alleged against all the Greek dramatists.

Hallie Flanagan 1890–1969: in hearing on the Federal Theatre Project by the House Un-American Activities Committee, 6 December 1938

5 Wouldn't it be a hell of a thing if all this was burnt cork and you people were being tolerant for nothing?

Dick Gregory 1932– : *Nigger* (1965)

6 You gotta say this for the white race—its self-confidence knows no bounds. Who else could go to a small island in the South Pacific where there's no poverty, no crime, no unemployment, no war and no worry—and call it a 'primitive society'?

Dick Gregory 1932– : *From the Back of the Bus* (1962)

7 Without the aid of prejudice and custom, I should not be able to find my way across the room.

William Hazlitt 1778–1830: 'On Prejudice' (1830)

8 'It's powerful,' he said.
'What?'
'That one drop of Negro blood—because just *one* drop of black blood makes a man coloured. *One* drop—you are a Negro!'

Langston Hughes 1902–67: *Simple Takes a Wife* (1953)

9 If there were any of Australia's original inhabitants living in Melbourne they were kept well out of the way of nice people; unless, of course, they could sing.

Barry Humphries 1934– : *More Please* (1992)

10 When they call you articulate, that's another way of saying 'He talks good for a black guy'.

Ice-T 1958– : in *Independent* 30 December 1995 'Interviews of the Year'

11 *refused admittance to a smart Californian beach club:*
Since my daughter is only half-Jewish, could she go in the water up to her knees?

Groucho Marx 1895–1977: in *Observer* 21 August 1977

12 Tolerance is only another name for indifference.

W. Somerset Maugham 1874–1965: *A Writer's Notebook* (1949) written in 1896

13 The South African police would leave no stone unturned to see that nothing disturbed the even terror of their lives.

Tom Sharpe 1928– : *Indecent Exposure* (1973)

14 You must always look for the *Ulsterior motive*.
of C. S. Lewis as an Ulsterman

J. R. R. Tolkien 1892–1973: A. N. Wilson *Life of C. S. Lewis* (1986)

15 I have a distinct impression that the anthropologists' version of that famous quote from Alexander Pope's essay runs: 'The proper study of mankind is *black* man, or if not actually black, at least poor and a long way off.'

Jill Tweedie 1936–93: *It's Only Me* (1980)

Present ····▶ Past and Present

Presidents ····▶ Politicians, Politics

66 The pay is good and I can walk to work. 99
John F. Kennedy

1 Richard Nixon impeached himself. He gave us Gerald Ford as his revenge.

Bella Abzug 1920– : in *Rolling Stone*; Linda Botts *Loose Talk* (1980)

2 *of Woodrow Wilson:*
When the President proposed to the second Mrs Wilson, she was so surprised that she fell out of bed.

Anonymous: anecdote, probably apocryphal; recalled by Anthony Howard in *The Times* 1 April 2003

3 God Almighty was satisfied with Ten Commandments. Mr Wilson requires Fourteen Points.

Georges Clemenceau 1841–1929: during the Peace Conference negotiations in 1919; Leon Harris *The Fine Art of Political Wit* (1965)

4 A hard dog to keep on the porch.
on her husband, Bill Clinton

Hillary Rodham Clinton 1947– : in *Guardian* 2 August 1999

5 Mr Speaker, the Honourable Gentleman has conceived three times and brought forth nothing.
when Lincoln, making his first speech in the Illinois legislature, had three times begun 'Mr Speaker, I conceive'

Stephen A. Douglas 1813–61: Leon Harris *The Fine Art of Political Wit* (1965)

6 *on his office:*
The vice-presidency isn't worth a pitcher of warm piss.

John Nance Garner 1868–1967: O. C. Fisher *Cactus Jack* (1978) ch. 11

7 Higgledy-Piggledy
Benjamin Harrison
Twenty-third President,
Was, and, as such,
Served between Clevelands, and
Save for this trivial
Idiosyncrasy
Didn't do much.

John Hollander 1929– : 'Historical Reflections' (1966)

8 I performed for twelve presidents and entertained six.

Bob Hope 1903–2003: in *The Times* 29 July 2003

9 Ronald Reagan, the President who never told bad news to the American people.

Garrison Keillor 1942– : *We Are Still Married* (1989), introduction

10 The pay is good and I can walk to work.

John F. Kennedy 1917–63: attributed; James B. Simpson (ed.) *Simpson's Contemporary Quotations* (1988)

11 Many a time have I stood on one side of the counter and sold whiskey to Mr Douglas, but the difference between us now is this. I have left my side of the counter, but Mr Douglas still sticks to his as tenaciously as ever.
during a debate with Stephen A. Douglas in 1858

Abraham Lincoln 1809–65: Leon Harris *The Fine Art of Political Wit* (1965)

12 If there had been any formidable body of cannibals in the country he would have promised to provide them with free missionaries fattened at the taxpayer's expense.
of Harry Truman's success in the 1948 presidential campaign

H. L. Mencken 1880–1956: in *Baltimore Sun* 7 November 1948

13 The battle for the mind of Ronald Reagan was like the trench warfare of World War I. Never have so many fought so hard for such barren terrain.

Peggy Noonan 1950– : *What I Saw at the Revolution* (1990)

14 I trust Bush with my daughter, but I trust Clinton with my job.

Craig Paterson: in *Independent* 1 February 2003

15 Poor George, he can't help it—he was born with a silver foot in his mouth.
of George Bush Snr

Ann Richards 1933–2006: keynote speech at the Democratic convention, in *Independent* 20 July 1988

16 McKinley has no more backbone than a chocolate éclair!

Theodore Roosevelt 1858–1919: Harry Thurston Peck *Twenty Years of the Republic* (1906)

17 *on being a father as well as President*
I can do one of two things. I can be president of the United States or I can control Alice. I cannot possibly do both.

Theodore Roosevelt 1858–1919: John Lewis-Stempel *Fatherhood: An Anthology* (2001)

18 If I talk over people's heads, Ike must talk under their feet.

Adlai Stevenson 1900–65: during the Presidential campaign of 1952; Bill Adler *The Stevenson Wit* (1966)

19 *of Eisenhower's presidential campaign in 1956:*
The General has dedicated himself so many times he must feel like the cornerstone of a public building.

Adlai Stevenson 1900–65: Leon Harris *The Fine Art of Political Wit* (1965)

20 We elected a President, not a Pope.
to journalists at the White House, 5 February 1998

Barbra Streisand 1942– : reported by James Naughtie, BBC Radio 4, Today programme, 6 February 1998

21 He'll sit right here and he'll say do this, do that! And nothing will happen. Poor Ike—it won't be a bit like the Army.

Harry S. Truman 1884–1972: *Harry S. Truman* (1973); see **Power** 8

Pride ····> Humility

❝ I have often wished I had time to cultivate modesty. **❞**
Edith Sitwell

1 His opinion of himself, having once risen, remained at 'set fair'.

Arnold Bennett 1867–1931: *The Card* (1911)

2 *on stepping from his bath in the presence of a startled President Roosevelt:*
The Prime Minister has nothing to hide from the President of the United States.

Winston Churchill 1874–1965: as recalled by Roosevelt's son in *Churchill* (BBC television series presented by Martin Gilbert, 1992)

3 Every day when he looked into the glass, and gave the last touch to his consummate toilette, he offered his grateful thanks to Providence that his family was not unworthy of him.

Benjamin Disraeli 1804–81: *Lothair* (1870)

4 Modest? My word, no . . . He was an all-the-lights-on man.

Henry Reed 1914–86: *A Very Great Man Indeed* (1953 radio play) in *Hilda Tablet and Others*

5 But be not afraid of greatness: some men are born great, some achieve greatness, and some have greatness thrust upon them.

William Shakespeare 1564–1616: *Twelfth Night* (1601)

6 I have often wished I had time to cultivate modesty . . . But I am too busy thinking about myself.

Edith Sitwell 1887–1964: in *Observer* 30 April 1950

7 I am the Dean of Christ Church, Sir:
There's my wife; look well at her.
She's the Broad and I'm the High;
We are the University.

Cecil Spring-Rice 1859–1918: *The Masque of Balliol* (composed by and current among members of Balliol College, Oxford, in the 1870s); the first couplet was unofficially altered to: 'I am the Dean, and this is Mrs Liddell; / She the first, and I the second fiddle.'

8 Of all my verse, like not a single line;
But like my title, for it is not mine.
That title from a better man I stole;
Ah, how much better, had I stol'n the whole!

Robert Louis Stevenson 1850–94: *Underwoods* (1887) foreword

9 When I pass my name in such large letters I blush, but at the same time instinctively raise my hat.

Herbert Beerbohm Tree 1852–1917: Hesketh Pearson *Beerbohm Tree* (1956)

10 *on being asked to name the best living author writing in English:*
No one working in the English language now comes close to my exuberance, my passion, my fidelity to words.

Jeanette Winterson 1959– : in *Sunday Times* 13 March 1994

Prime Ministers ····> Politicians, Politics

66 Mr Blair is not the Archangel Gabriel. 99
Tam Dalyell

1 It is fitting that we should have buried the Unknown Prime Minister [Bonar Law] by the side of the Unknown Soldier.

Herbert Asquith 1852–1928: Robert Blake *The Unknown Prime Minister* (1955)

2 He [Lloyd George] can't see a belt without hitting below it.

Margot Asquith 1864–1945: in *Listener* 11 June 1953 'Margot Oxford' by Lady Violet Bonham Carter

3 Few thought he was even a starter
There were many who thought themselves smarter
But he ended PM
CH and OM
An earl and a knight of the garter.

Clement Attlee 1883–1967: describing himself; letter to Tom Attlee, 8 April 1956

4 [Lloyd George] did not seem to care which way he travelled providing he was in the driver's seat.

Lord Beaverbrook 1879–1964: *The Decline and Fall of Lloyd George* (1963)

5 Listening to a speech by Chamberlain is like paying a visit to Woolworth's: everything in its place and nothing above sixpence.

Aneurin Bevan 1897–1960: Michael Foot *Aneurin Bevan* (1962) vol.1

6 I am from the Disraeli school of Prime Ministers in their relations with the Monarch.
at the Queen's golden wedding celebration; see **Praise** 3

Tony Blair 1953– · speech, 20 November 1997

7 If he ever went to school without any boots it was because he was too big for them.
referring to Harold Wilson in a speech at the Conservative Party Conference

Ivor Bulmer-Thomas 1905–93: in *Manchester Guardian* 13 October 1949

8 *on the younger Pitt's maiden speech:*
Not merely a chip of the old 'block', but the old block itself.

Edmund Burke 1729–97: N. W. Wraxall *Historical Memoirs of My Own Time* (1904 ed.)

9 Pitt is to Addington
As London is to Paddington.

George Canning 1770–1827: 'The Oracle' (c.1803)

10 For the purposes of recreation he [Gladstone] has selected the felling of trees, and we may usefully remark that his amusements, like his politics, are essentially destructive . . . The forest laments in order that Mr Gladstone may perspire.

Lord Randolph Churchill 1849–94: speech on Financial Reform, delivered in Blackpool, 24 January 1884

11 I remember, when I was a child, being taken to the celebrated Barnum's circus, which contained an exhibition of freaks and monstrosities, but the exhibit on the programme which I most desired to see was the one described as 'The Boneless Wonder'. My parents judged that that spectacle would be too revolting and demoralizing for my youthful eyes, and I have waited 50 years to see the boneless wonder sitting on the Treasury Bench.
of Ramsay Macdonald

Winston Churchill 1874–1965: speech in the House of Commons 28 January 1931

12 In the depths of that dusty soul is nothing but abject
surrender.
   of Neville Chamberlain

Winston Churchill 1874–1965: Leon
Harris *The Fine Art of Political Wit*
(1965)

13 Tony Blair has now had 10 years as a leader of the party
and been Prime Minister since 1997. That's enough for
the Archangel Gabriel. And Mr Blair is not the Archangel
Gabriel.

Tam Dalyell 1932– : in *Guardian* 5
March 2004 (online edition)

14 Palmerston is now seventy. If he could prove evidence of
his potency in his electoral address he'd sweep the
country.
   *to the suggestion that capital could be made from one of
   Palmerston's affairs*

Benjamin Disraeli 1804–81: Hesketh
Pearson *Dizzy* (1951); attributed,
probably apocryphal

15 *Disraeli was asked on what, offering himself for Marylebone,
he intended to stand:*
On my head.

Benjamin Disraeli 1804–81: *Lord
Beaconsfield's Correspondence with
his Sister 1832–1852* (1886)

16 INTERVIEWER: What three skills should every great Prime
Minister have? Did you have them?
HEATH: Patience, stamina and good luck. Two out of three
isn't bad!

Edward Heath 1916–2005: in
Independent 25 November 1998

17 JOHN MAJOR: Tell me, do you mind dreadfully not having
been Prime Minister?
ROY JENKINS: No not at all—but tell me, do *you* mind
dreadfully actually having been Prime Minister?

Roy Jenkins 1920–2003: anecdote
recalled by Anthony Howard, in *The
Times* 1 April 2003

18 *of Tony Blair:*
He believes in magic. That if you say a thing, it is true.
He's not very bright.

Doris Lessing 1919– : in *Sunday
Times* 28 March 2004

19 *on being asked what place Arthur Balfour would have in
history:*
He will be just like the scent on a pocket handkerchief.

David Lloyd George 1863–1945:
Thomas Jones diary, 9 June 1922

20 [Churchill] would make a drum out of the skin of his
mother in order to sound his own praises.

David Lloyd George 1863–1945:
Paul Johnson (ed.) *The Oxford Book
of Political Anecdotes* (1986)

21 He might make an adequate Lord Mayor of Birmingham in
a lean year.
   of Neville Chamberlain

David Lloyd George 1863–1945:
Leon Harris *The Fine Art of Political
Wit* (1965)

22 Well, it was the best I could do, seated as I was between
Jesus Christ and Napoleon Bonaparte.
   *on the outcome of the Peace Conference negotiations in
   1919 between himself, Woodrow Wilson, and Georges
   Clemenceau*

David Lloyd George 1863–1945:
Leon Harris *The Fine Art of Political
Wit* (1965)

23 *after forming the National Government, 25 August 1931:*
Tomorrow every Duchess in London will be wanting to
kiss me!

Ramsay MacDonald 1866–1937:
Viscount Snowden *An Autobiography*
(1934)

24 Every Prime Minister needs a Willie.
   at the farewell dinner for William Whitelaw

Margaret Thatcher 1925– : in
Guardian 7 August 1991

25 I think sometimes the Prime Minister should be
intimidating. There's not much point being a weak, floppy
thing in the chair, is there?

Margaret Thatcher 1925– : on 'The
Thatcher Years' (BBC 1), 21 October
1993

Prizes ····> Awards and Prizes

Progress ····> Science, Technology

66 Mechanics, not microbes, are the menace to civilization. 99
Norman Douglas

1 Everywhere one looks, decadence. I saw a bishop with a moustache the other day.

Alan Bennett 1934– : *Forty Years On* (1969)

2 All progress is based upon a universal innate desire on the part of every organism to live beyond its income.

Samuel Butler 1835–1902: *Notebooks* (1912)

3 Now, *here*, you see, it takes all the running *you* can do, to keep in the same place. If you want to get somewhere else, you must run at least twice as fast as that!

Lewis Carroll 1832–98: *Through the Looking-Glass* (1872)

4 To you, Baldrick, the Renaissance was just something that happened to other people, wasn't it?

Richard Curtis 1956– and **Ben Elton** 1959– : *Blackadder II* (1987) television series

5 Mechanics, not microbes, are the menace to civilization.

Norman Douglas 1868–1952: introduction to *The Norman Douglas Limerick Book* (1967)

6 Think what we would have missed if we had never . . . used a mobile phone or surfed the Net—or, to be honest, listened to other people talking about surfing the Net.
reflecting on developments in the past 50 years

Elizabeth II 1926– : in *Daily Telegraph* 21 November 1997

7 The civilized man has built a coach, but has lost the use of his feet.

Ralph Waldo Emerson 1803–82: 'Self-Reliance' (1841)

8 *on being asked what he thought of modern civilization:*
That would be a good idea.
while visiting England in 1930

Mahatma Gandhi 1869–1948: E. F. Schumacher *Good Work* (1979)

9 They all laughed at Christopher Columbus
When he said the world was round
They all laughed when Edison recorded sound
They all laughed at Wilbur and his brother
When they said that man could fly;
They told Marconi
Wireless was a phony—
It's the same old cry!

Ira Gershwin 1896–1983: 'They All Laughed' (1937)

10 Don't get smart alecksy,
With the galaxy
Leave the atom alone.

E. Y. Harburg 1898–1981: 'Leave the Atom Alone' (1957)

11 Push de button!
Up de elevator!
Push de button!
Out de orange juice!
Push de button!
From refrigerator
Come banana short-cake and frozen goose!

E. Y. Harburg 1898–1981: 'Push de Button' (1957)

12 You can't say civilization don't advance, however, for in every war they kill you in a new way.

Will Rogers 1879–1935: in *New York Times* 23 December 1929

13 The cry was for vacant freedom and indeterminate progress: *Vorwärts! Avanti! Onwards! Full speed ahead!*, without asking whether directly before you was not a bottomless pit.

George Santayana 1863–1952: *My Host the World* (1953)

14 You started something which you can't stop. You want a self-limiting revolution but it's like trying to limit influenza.

Tom Stoppard 1937– : *Squaring the Circle* (1984)

15 A swell house with . . . all the modern inconveniences.

Mark Twain 1835–1910: *Life on the Mississippi* (1883)

Publishing

66 Now Barabbas was a publisher. 99
Thomas Campbell

---

1 If I had been someone not very clever, I would have done an easier job like publishing. That's the easiest job I can think of.

A. J. Ayer 1910–89: attributed

2 Times have changed since a certain author was executed for murdering his publisher. They say that when the author was on the scaffold he said goodbye to the minister and to the reporters, and then he saw some publishers sitting in the front row below, and to them he did not say goodbye. He said instead, 'I'll see you later.'

J. M. Barrie 1860–1937: speech at Aldine Club, New York, 5 November 1896

3 In a profession where simple accountancy is preferable to a degree in English, illiteracy is not considered to be a great drawback.

Dominic Behan 1928– : *The Public World of Parable Jones* (1989)

4 The ever-increasing dullness and oddity of Oxford books is an old favourite among humorists, who are always trying to think up new and hilariously tedious 'The Oxford Book of . . . ' titles.

Craig Brown 1957– : *Craig Brown's Greatest Hits* (1993)

5 I have seen enough of my publishers to know that they have no ideas of their own about literature save what they can clutch at as believing it to be a straight tip from a business point of view.

Samuel Butler 1835–1902: *Notebooks* (1912)

6 The poem will please if it is lively—if it is stupid it will fail—but I will have none of your damned cutting and slashing.

Lord Byron 1788–1824: letter to his publisher John Murray, 6 April 1819

7 *at a literary dinner during the Napoleonic Wars, Thomas Campbell proposed a toast to Napoleon:*
Gentlemen, you must not mistake me. I admit that the French Emperor is a tyrant. I admit he is a monster. I admit that he is the sworn foe of our nation, and, if you will, of the whole human race. But, gentlemen, we must be just to our great enemy. We must not forget that he once shot a bookseller.

Thomas Campbell 1777–1844: G. O. Trevelyan *The Life of Lord Macaulay* (1876)

8 Now Barabbas was a publisher.

Thomas Campbell 1777–1844: attributed, in Samuel Smiles *A Publisher and his Friends: Memoir and Correspondence of the late John Murray* (also attributed, wrongly, to Byron); see **Publishing** 11

9 Aren't we due a royalty statement?
to his literary agent

Charles, Prince of Wales 1948– : Giles Gordon *Aren't We Due a Royalty Statement?* (1993)

10 *on being sent the manuscript of* Travels with my Aunt, *Greene's American publishers had cabled, 'Terrific book, but we'll need to change the title':*
No need to change title. Easier to change publishers.

Graham Greene 1904–91: telegram to his American publishers in 1968; Giles Gordon *Aren't We Due a Royalty Statement?* (1993)

11 I always thought Barabbas was a much misunderstood man . . .
a publisher's view

Peter Grose: letter, 25 May 1983; see **Publishing** 8

12 You cannot or at least you should not try to argue with authors. Too many are like children whose tears can suddenly be changed to smiles if they are handled in the right way.
a publisher's view

Michael Joseph 1897–1958: *The Adventure of Publishing* (1949)

13 The relationship of an agent to a publisher is that of a knife to a throat.
an American agent's view

Marvin Josephson: Ned Sherrin *Cutting Edge* (1984)

14 A publisher who writes is like a cow in a milk bar.

Arthur Koestler 1905–83: Jonathon Green (ed.) *A Dictionary of Contemporary Quotations* (1982)

15 There is some kind of notion abroad that because a book is humorous the publisher has to be funnier and madder than hell in marketing it.

S. J. Perelman 1904–79: letter to Bennett Cerf, 23 July 1937

16 I suppose publishers are untrustworthy. They certainly always look it.

Oscar Wilde 1854–1900: letter February 1898

17 All a publisher has to do is write cheques at intervals, while a lot of deserving and industrious chappies rally round and do the real work.

P. G. Wodehouse 1881–1975: *My Man Jeeves* (1919)

18 Being published by the Oxford University Press is rather like being married to a duchess: the honour is almost greater than the pleasure.

G. M. Young 1882–1959: Rupert Hart-Davis letter to George Lyttelton, 29 April 1956

Punishment ····> Crime, The Law

❝Something lingering, with boiling oil.❞
W. S. Gilbert

1 *to a prison visitor who asked if he were sewing:*
No, reaping.

Horatio Bottomley 1860–1933: S. T. Felstead *Horatio Bottomley* (1936)

2 It's over, and can't be helped, and that's one consolation, as they always says in Turkey, ven they cuts the wrong man's head off.

Charles Dickens 1812–70: *Pickwick Papers* (1837)

3 Thwackum was for doing justice, and leaving mercy to heaven.

Henry Fielding 1707–54: *Tom Jones* (1749)

4 Hanging is too good for him. He must be posted to the infantry.
on being asked to endorse the execution of a cavalryman who sodomized his horse

Frederick the Great 1712–86: Giles MacDonogh *Frederick the Great: a Life in Deed and Letters* (1999)

5 Awaiting the sensation of a short, sharp shock,
From a cheap and chippy chopper on a big black block.

W. S. Gilbert 1836–1911: *The Mikado* (1885)

6 As some day it may happen that a victim must be found,
I've got a little list—I've got a little list
Of society offenders who might well be under ground
And who never would be missed—who never would be missed!

W. S. Gilbert 1836–1911: *The Mikado* (1885)

7 Something lingering, with boiling oil in it, I fancy.

W. S. Gilbert 1836–1911: *The Mikado* (1885)

8 *on the campaign trail for Mayor of London:*
Death to anyone who drops chewing gum.

Steven Norris 1945– : in *Sunday Times* 13 June 2004

9 In sentencing a man for one crime, we may well be putting him beyond the reach of the law in respect of those crimes which he has not yet had an opportunity to commit. The law, however, is not to be cheated in this way. I shall therefore discharge you.

N. F. Simpson 1919– : *One Way Pendulum* (1960)

10 *Alf Garnett's view:*
Better to hang somebody than not to hang anybody at all.

Johnny Speight 1920–1998: *In Sickness and in Health* (1985–92); spoken by Warren Mitchell

Quotations

“ Next to the originator of a good sentence is the first quoter of it. ”
Ralph Waldo Emerson

1 To-day I am a lamppost against which no anthologist lifts his leg.

James Agate 1877–1947: diary, 21 August 1941

2 Ah, yes! I wrote the 'Purple Cow'—
I'm sorry, now, I wrote it!
But I can tell you anyhow,
I'll kill you if you quote it!

Gelett Burgess 1866–1951: *The Burgess Nonsense Book* (1914) 'Confessional'

3 For quotable good things, for pregnant aphorisms, for touchstones of ready application, the opinions of the English judges are a mine of instruction and a treasury of joy.

Benjamin N. Cardozo 1870–1938: *Law and Literature* (1931)

4 It would be nice if sometimes the kind things I say were considered worthy of quotation. It isn't difficult, you know, to be witty or amusing when one has something to

Noël Coward 1899–1973: William Marchant *The Pleasure of His Company* (1981)

say that is destructive, but damned hard to be clever and quotable when you are singing someone's praises.

5 I know heaps of quotations, so I can always make quite a fair show of knowledge.

O. Douglas 1877–1948: *The Setons* (1917)

6 Next to the originator of a good sentence is the first quoter of it.

Ralph Waldo Emerson 1803–82: *Letters and Social Aims* (1876)

7 *advice for House of Commons quotations:*
No Greek; as much Latin as you like: never French in any circumstance: no English poet unless he has completed his century.

Charles James Fox 1749–1806: J. A. Gere and John Sparrow (eds.) *Geoffrey Madan's Notebooks* (1981)

8 A cannibal, but one with better table manners.
of the editor of the Oxford Dictionary of Twentieth Century Quotations

Bevis Hillier 1940– : in *Spectator* 19 December 1998

9 But I have long thought that if you knew a column of advertisements by heart, you could achieve unexpected felicities with them. You can get a happy quotation anywhere if you have the eye.

Oliver Wendell Holmes Jr. 1841–1935: letter to Harold Laski, 31 May 1923

10 You must not treat my immortal works as quarries to be used at will by the various hacks whom you may employ to compile anthologies.

A. E. Housman 1859–1936: letter to his publisher Grant Richards, 29 June 1907

11 He wrapped himself in quotations—as a beggar would enfold himself in the purple of emperors.

Rudyard Kipling 1865–1936. *Many Inventions* (1893)

12 There is no reason why a book of quotations should be dull; it has its uses in idleness as well as in study.

H. L. Mencken 1880–1956: introduction to *H. L. Mencken's Dictionary of Quotations* (1942)

13 My favourite quotation is eight pounds ten for a second-hand suit.

Spike Milligan 1918–2002: on *Quote . . . Unquote* (BBC Radio) 1 January 1979; Nigel Rees (ed.) *Cassell Dictionary of Humorous Quotations* (1999)

14 He liked those literary cooks
Who skim the cream of others' books;
And ruin half an author's graces
By plucking bon-mots from their places.

Hannah More 1745–1833: *Florio* (1786)

15 His works contain nothing worth quoting; and a book that furnishes no quotations is, *me judice*, no book—it's a plaything.

Thomas Love Peacock 1785–1866: *Crotchet Castle* (1831)

16 Misquotation is, in fact, the pride and privilege of the learned. A widely-read man never quotes accurately, for the rather obvious reason that he has read too widely.

Hesketh Pearson 1887–1964: *Common Misquotations* (1934) introduction

17 An anthology is like all the plums and orange peel picked out of a cake.

Walter Raleigh 1861–1922: letter to Mrs Robert Bridges, 15 January 1915

18 I always have a quotation for everything—it saves original thinking.

Dorothy L. Sayers 1893–1957: *Have His Carcase* (1932)

19 It seems pointless to be quoted if one isn't going to be quotable . . . It's better to be quotable than honest.

Tom Stoppard 1937– : in *Guardian* 21 March 1973

20 What a good thing Adam had. When he said a good thing he knew nobody had said it before.

Mark Twain 1835–1910: *Notebooks* (1935)

Reading

❝ People say that life is the thing, but I prefer reading. **❞**
Logan Pearsall Smith

1 The world may be full of fourth-rate writers but it's also full of fourth-rate readers.

Stan Barstow 1928– : in *Daily Mail* 15 August 1989

2 *on hearing that* Watership Down *was a novel about rabbits written by a civil servant:*
I would rather read a novel about civil servants written by a rabbit.

Craig Brown 1957– : attributed; probably apocryphal

3 The ideal reader of my novels is a lapsed Catholic and a failed musician, short-sighted, colour-blind, auditorily biased, who has read the books that I have read. He should also be about my age.

Anthony Burgess 1917–93: George Plimpton (ed.) *Writers at Work* 4th Series (1977)

4 You couldn't even read the Gettysburg Address. So who cares anyway where Gettysburg lived?

Betty Comden 1917–2006 and **Adolph Green** 1915–2002: *Singin' in the Rain* (1952)

5 Arrival of Book of the Month choice, and am disappointed. History of a place I am not interested in, by an author I do not like.

E. M. Delafield 1890–1943: *The Diary of a Provincial Lady* (1930)

6 *to an author who had presented him with an unwelcome book:*
Many thanks. I shall lose no time in reading it.

Benjamin Disraeli 1804–81: Wilfrid Meynell *The Man Disraeli* (1903)

7 *on the difficulties of reading the novels of Sir Walter Scott:*
He shouldn't have written in such small print.

O. Douglas 1877–1948: *The Setons* (1917)

8 I read part of it all the way through.

Sam Goldwyn 1882–1974: N. Zierold *Hollywood Tycoons* (1969)

9 Henry Kissinger may be a great writer, but anyone who finishes his book is definitely a great reader.

Walter Isaacson: in *The Week* 20 March 1999 'Wit and Wisdom'

10 [ELPHINSTON:] What, have you not read it through?
[JOHNSON:] No, Sir, do *you* read books *through*?

Samuel Johnson 1709–84: James Boswell *Life of Samuel Johnson* (1791) 19 April 1773

11 [*The Compleat Angler*] is acknowledged to be one of the world's books. Only the trouble is that the world doesn't read its books, it borrows a detective story instead.

Stephen Leacock 1869–1944: *The Boy I Left Behind Me* (1947)

12 We shouldn't trust writers, but we should read them.

Ian McEwan 1948– : in BBC2 'Late Show' 7 February 1990

13 Don't read much but love books about homos.
to Gore Vidal, on her taste in reading

Ethel Merman 1909–84: Fred Kaplan *Gore Vidal* (1999)

14 Reading isn't an occupation we encourage among police officers. We try to keep the paper work down to a minimum.

Joe Orton 1933–67: *Loot* (1967)

15 What really knocks me out is a book that, when you're all done reading it, you wish the author that wrote it was a terrific friend of yours and you could call him up on the phone whenever you felt like it.

J. D. Salinger 1919– : *Catcher in the Rye* (1951)

16 People say that life is the thing, but I prefer reading.

Logan Pearsall Smith 1865–1946: *Afterthoughts* (1931) 'Myself'

17 '*Classic.*' A book which people praise and don't read.

Mark Twain 1835–1910: *Following the Equator* (1897)

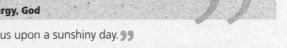

Religion ····▷ The Clergy, God

❝ I am always most religious upon a sunshiny day. ❞
Lord Byron

1 We have in England a particular bashfulness in every thing that regards religion.

Joseph Addison 1672–1719: *The Spectator* 15 August 1712

2 As Sir Roger is landlord to the whole congregation, he keeps them in very good order, and will suffer nobody to sleep in it [the church] besides himself; for if by chance he has been surprised into a short nap at sermon, upon recovering out of it, he stands up, and looks about him; and if he sees anybody else nodding, either wakes them himself, or sends his servant to them.

Joseph Addison 1672–1719: *The Spectator* 9 July 1711

3 *a rhyming marriage licence, said to have been composed for an al fresco ceremony outside Lichfield:*
Under an oak in stormy weather
I joined this rogue and whore together;
And none but he who rules the thunder
Can put this rogue and whore asunder.

Anonymous: has been attributed to Swift, but of doubtful authenticity; C. H. Wilson *Swiftiana* (1804)

4 Bernard always had a few prayers in the hall and some whiskey afterwards as he was rarther pious but Mr Salteena was not very addicted to prayers so he marched up to bed.

Daisy Ashford 1881–1972: *The Young Visiters* (1919)

5 I've a definite sense of spirituality. I want Brooklyn to be christened, but don't know into what religion yet.

David Beckham 1975– : in *Daily Mail* 5 September 2002

6 Gentlemen, I am a Catholic . . . If you reject me on account of my religion, I shall thank God that He has spared me the indignity of being your representative.

Hilaire Belloc 1870–1953: speech to voters of South Salford, 1906

7 FOSTER: I'm still a bit hazy about the Trinity, sir.
SCHOOLMASTER: Three in one, one in three, perfectly straightforward. Any doubts about that see your maths master.

Alan Bennett 1934– : *Forty Years On* (1969)

8 The attitude that regards entanglement with religion as something akin to entanglement with an infectious disease must be confronted broadly and directly.

William J. Bennett 1943– : in *New York Times* 8 August 1985

9 Broad of Church and 'broad of Mind',
Broad before and broad behind,
A keen ecclesiologist,
A rather dirty Wykehamist.

John Betjeman 1906–84: 'The Wykehamist' (1931)

10 The Church's Restoration
In eighteen-eighty-three
Has left for contemplation
Not what there used to be.

John Betjeman 1906–84: 'Hymn' (1931)

11 *of Bede Griffiths's visiting India with the intention of*
reconciling the Roman Catholic and Hindu faiths:
I suppose he's trying to combine Mumbo with Jumbo in
roughly equal proportions.

John Betjeman 1906–84: Bevis Hillier
Betjeman: the Bonus of Laughter
(2004)

12 If Jesus had been killed 20 years ago, Catholic school
children would be wearing little electric chairs around
their necks instead of crosses.

Lenny Bruce 1925–66: attributed

13 An atheist is a man who has no invisible means of
support.

John Buchan 1875–1940: H. E.
Fosdick *On Being a Real Person* (1943)

14 Thanks to God, I am still an atheist.

Luis Buñuel 1900–83: *Le Monde* 16
December 1959

15 Christians have burnt each other, quite persuaded
That all the Apostles would have done as they did.

Lord Byron 1788–1824: *Don Juan*
(1819–24)

16 I am always most religious upon a sunshiny day.

Lord Byron 1788–1824: 'Detached
Thoughts' 15 October 1821

17 The two dangers which beset the Church of England are
good music and bad preaching.

Lord Hugh Cecil 1869–1956: K. Rose
The Later Cecils (1975)

18 Blessed are the cheesemakers.
a misheard beatitude

Graham Chapman 1941–89, **John
Cleese** 1939– , et al.: *Monty Python's
Life of Brian* (1979 film)

19 Is man an ape or an angel? Now I am on the side of the
angels.

Benjamin Disraeli 1804–81: speech
at Oxford, 25 November 1864

20 A Protestant, if he wants aid or advice on any matter, can
only go to his solicitor.

Benjamin Disraeli 1804–81: *Lothair*
(1870)

21 Said Waldershare, 'Sensible men are all of the same
religion.' 'And pray what is that?' . . . 'Sensible men never
tell.'

Benjamin Disraeli 1804–81:
Endymion (1880)

22 A lady, if undressed at Church, looks silly,
One cannot be devout in dishabilly.

George Farquhar 1678–1707: *The
Stage Coach* (1704)

23 'I know of no joy,' she airily began, 'greater than a cool
white dress after the sweetness of confession.'

Ronald Firbank 1886–1926:
Valmouth (1919)

24 *Lady Carina Fitzalan-Howard was asked if her future husband
David Frost were religious:*
Yes, he thinks he's God Almighty.

Carina Frost 1952– : in *Sunday Times*
28 July 1985

25   What after all
Is a halo? It's only one more thing to keep clean.

Christopher Fry 1907–2005: *The
Lady's not for Burning* (1949)

26 A Consumer's Guide to Religion—The Best Buy—Church
of England. It's a jolly friendly faith. If you are one, there's
no onus to make everyone else join. In fact no one need
ever know.

Robert Gillespie and **Charles
Lewson**: *That Was The Week That
Was* BBC television 1962

27 *at Oxford, to an angry crowd who thought she was Charles II's
French Catholic mistress the Duchess of Portsmouth:*
Pray, good people, be civil. I am the Protestant whore.

Nell Gwyn 1650–87: B. Bevan *Nell
Gwyn* (1969)

28 No matter how I probe and prod
I cannot quite believe in God.
But oh! I hope to God that he
Unswervingly believes in me.

E. Y. Harburg 1898–1981: 'The
Agnostic' (1965)

29 For a halo up in heaven
I have never been too keen.
Who needs another gadget
That a fellow has to clean?

E. Y. Harburg 1898–1981: 'The Man who has Everything' (1965)

30 When Messiah comes,
He will say to us
'I apologise that I took so long,
But I had a little trouble finding you.
Over here a few and over there a few—
You were hard to reunite,
But everything is going to be all right.
Up in heaven there
How I wrang my hands
When they exiled you from the Promised Land.
In Babylon you went like castaways
On the first of many, many moving days.
What a day and what a blow,
How terrible I felt you'll never know!'

Sheldon Harnick 1924– : 'When Messiah Comes' (1964)

31 The Revised Prayer Book: a sort of attempt to suppress burglary by legalizing petty larceny.

Dean Inge 1860–1954: J. A. Gere and John Sparrow (eds.) *Geoffrey Madan's Notebooks* (1981)

32 *imagining how a Church of England Inquisition might have worked*
'Cake or death?' 'Cake, please.'

Eddie Izzard 1962– : *Dress to Kill* (stage show, San Francisco, 1998)

33 All moanday, tearsday, wailsday, thumpsday, frightday, shatterday till the fear of the Law.

James Joyce 1882–1941: *Finnegans Wake* (1939)

34 When suave politeness, tempering bigot zeal,
Corrected *I believe* to *One does feel.*

Ronald Knox 1888–1957: 'Absolute and Abitofhell' (1913)

35 'Oh, a cheque, I think,' said the rector; 'one can do so much more with it, after all.' 'Precisely,' said his father; he was well aware of many things that can be done with a cheque that cannot possibly be done with a font.

Stephen Leacock 1869–1944: *Arcadian Adventures with the Idle Rich* (1914)

36 Food was a very big factor in Christianity. What would the miracle of the loaves and fishes have been without it? And the Last Supper—how effective would that have been?

Fran Lebowitz 1946– : *Metropolitan Life* (1978)

37 Redemption does, on the whole, play a rather important part in the Christian religion, and . . . the Founder of it was particularly taken with the idea.

Bernard Levin 1928– : *If You Want My Opinion* (1992)

38 That the Almighty would send down His wisdom on the Queen's Ministers, who sorely need it.
prayer delivered in Crathie church, to Queen Victoria's amusement

Dr Macgregor: Arthur Ponsonby *Henry Ponsonby* (1942)

39 *Mahaffy had been asked 'Are you saved?' by 'a zealot who cornered him in a railway carriage':*
To tell you the truth, my good fellow, I am; but it was such a narrow squeak it does not bear talking about.

John Pentland Mahaffy 1839–1919: Oliver St John Gogarty *It Isn't This Time of Year at All* (1954)

40 The spirituality of man is most apparent when he is eating a hearty dinner.

W. Somerset Maugham 1874–1965: *A Writer's Notebook* (1949) written in 1897

41 Things have come to a pretty pass when religion is
allowed to invade the sphere of private life.

Lord Melbourne 1779–1848: on
hearing an evangelical sermon; G. W.
E. Russell *Collections and
Recollections* (1898)

42 Puritanism. The haunting fear that someone, somewhere,
may be happy.

H. L. Mencken 1880–1956:
Chrestomathy (1949)

43 It is now quite lawful for a Catholic woman to avoid
pregnancy by a resort to mathematics, though she is still
forbidden to resort to physics and chemistry.

H. L. Mencken 1880–1956:
Notebooks (1956) 'Minority Report'

44 The orgasm has replaced the Cross as the focus of longing
and the image of fulfilment.

Malcolm Muggeridge 1903–90:
Tread Softly (1966)

45 King David and King Solomon
Led merry, merry lives,
With many, many lady friends,
And many, many wives;
But when old age crept over them—
With many, many qualms!—
King Solomon wrote the Proverbs
And King David wrote the Psalms.

James Ball Naylor 1860–1945: 'King
David and King Solomon' (1935)

46 God is a man, so it must be all rot.
just before her marriage to Robert Graves in 1917

Nancy Nicholson d. 1977: R. Graves
Goodbye to All That (1929)

47 You are not an agnostic . . . You are just a fat slob who is
too lazy to go to Mass.

Conor Cruise O'Brien 1917– :
attributed

48 There's no reason to bring religion into it. I think we
ought to have as great a regard for religion as we can, so
as to keep it out of as many things as possible.

Sean O'Casey 1880–1964: *The
Plough and the Stars* (1926)

49 Good manners can replace religious beliefs. In the
Anglican Church they already have. Etiquette (and quiet,
well-cut clothes) are devoutly worshipped by Anglicans.

P. J. O'Rourke 1947– : *Modern
Manners* (1984)

50 He was an embittered atheist (the sort of atheist who does
not so much disbelieve in God as personally dislike Him),
and took a sort of pleasure in thinking that human affairs
would never improve.

George Orwell 1903–50: *Down and
Out in Paris and London* (1933)

51 No praying, it spoils business.

Thomas Otway 1652–85: *Venice
Preserved* (1682)

52 God and the doctor we alike adore
But only when in danger, not before;
The danger o'er, both are alike requited,
God is forgotten, and the Doctor slighted.

John Owen c.1563–1622: *Epigrams*

53 I've been a sinner, I've been a scamp,
But now I'm willin' to trim my lamp,
So blow, Gabriel, blow!

Cole Porter 1891–1964: 'Blow,
Gabriel, Blow' (1934)

54 How can you expect to convert England if you use a cope
like that?

Augustus Welby Pugin 1812–52: to
an unidentified Catholic priest;
Bernard Ward *The Sequel to Catholic
Emancipation* (1915)

55 Prove to me that you're no fool
Walk across my swimming pool.

Tim Rice 1944– : 'Herod's Song'
(1970)

56 I always claim the mission workers came out too early to catch any sinners on this part of Broadway. At such an hour the sinners are still in bed resting up from their sinning of the night before, so they will be in good shape for more sinning a little later on.

Damon Runyon 1884–1946: in *Collier's* 28 January 1933, 'The Idyll of Miss Sarah Brown'

57 I was told that the Chinese said they would bury me by the Western Lake and build a shrine to my memory. I have some slight regret that this did not happen as I might have become a god, which would have been very *chic* for an atheist.

Bertrand Russell 1872–1970: *Autobiography* (1968)

58 People may say what they like about the decay of Christianity; the religious system that produced green Chartreuse can never really die.

Saki 1870–1916: *Reginald* (1904)

59 Every reformation must have its victims. You can't expect the fatted calf to share the enthusiasm of the angels over the prodigal's return.

Saki 1870–1916: *Reginald* (1904)

60 Didn't some cynical critic say the Church of England is the only barrier between England and Christianity?

Saki 1870–1916: *Mrs Elmsley* (1911, published as by Hector Munro)

61 The conversion of England was thus effected by the landing of St Augustine in Thanet and other places, which resulted in the country being overrun by a Wave of Saints. Among these were St Ive, St Pancra, the great St Bernard (originator of the clerical collar), St Bee, St Ebb, St Neot (who invented whisky), St Kit and St Kin, and the Venomous Bead (author of *The Rosary*).

W. C. Sellar 1898–1951 and **R. J. Yeatman** 1898–1968: *1066 and All That* (1930)

62 There is only one religion, though there are a hundred versions of it.

George Bernard Shaw 1856–1950: preface to *Plays Pleasant and Unpleasant* (1898) vol. 2

63 Christianity never got any grip of the world until it virtually reduced its claims on the ordinary citizen's attention to a couple of hours every seventh day, and let him alone on week-days.

George Bernard Shaw 1856–1950: preface to *Getting Married* (1911)

64 How can what an Englishman believes be heresy? It is a contradiction in terms.

George Bernard Shaw 1856–1950: *Saint Joan* (1924)

65 I have not the smallest influence over Lord Byron, in this particular, and if I had, I certainly should employ it to eradicate from his great mind the delusions of Christianity, which, in spite of his reason, seem perpetually to recur.

Percy Bysshe Shelley 1792–1822: letter 11 April 1822

66 Baptists are only funny underwater.

Neil Simon 1927– : *Laughter on the 23rd Floor* (1994)

67 Deserves to be preached to death by wild curates.

Sydney Smith 1771–1845: Lady Holland *Memoir* (1855)

68 His followers threw a Rosary and a Bible at me, which I felt was at least an ecumenical gesture, and there was a near riot.
of Ian Paisley

Donald Soper 1903–98: speech in the House of Lords, 3 December 1968

69 I was going to be a nun, but they wouldn't have me because I didn't believe . . . not about him being the son of God, for instance, that's the part that put paid to my ambition, that's where we didn't see eye to eye.

Tom Stoppard 1937– : *If You're Glad I'll Be Frank* (1973)

70 Protestant women may take the pill. Roman Catholic women must keep taking The Tablet.

Irene Thomas 1919–2001: in *Guardian* 28 December 1990

71 Dr Gwynne himself, though a religious man, was also a thoroughly practical man of the world, and he regarded with no favourable eye the tenets of anyone who looked on the two things as incompatible.

Anthony Trollope 1815–82: *Barchester Towers* (1857)

72 When the missionaries came to Africa, they had the Bible and we had the land. They said: 'Let us pray'. We closed our eyes. When we opened them we had the Bible and they had the land.

Desmond Tutu 1931– : attributed; in *Mail on Sunday* 14 March 2004

73 Why did the Catholics invent the confessional? What is that but a phone box?

Peter Ustinov 1921–2004: *Monsieur René* (1999)

74 THE ARCHDEACON: Her deafness is a great privation to her. She can't even hear my sermons now.

Oscar Wilde 1854–1900: *A Woman of No Importance* (1893)

75 'God knows how you Protestants can be expected to have any sense of direction,' she said. 'It's different with us, I haven't been to mass for years, I've got every mortal sin on my conscience, but I know when I'm doing wrong. I'm still a Catholic, it's there, nothing can take it away from me.' 'Of course, duckie,' said Jeremy . . . 'once a Catholic always a Catholic.'

Angus Wilson 1913–91: *The Wrong Set* (1949)

Retirement

66 The transition from Who's Who to Who's He. 99
Eddie George

1 The transition from Who's Who to Who's He.
view of the former Governor of the Bank of England

Eddie George 1938– : in *Independent* 29 December 2003

2 I contemplate retirement every evening, and then I forget about it in the morning.

Peter Ustinov 1921–2004: in *The Times* 30 March 2004

Royalty

66 Ah'm sorry your Queen has to pay taxes. She's not a wealthy woman. 99
John Paul Getty

1 She is only 5ft 4in, and to make someone that height look regal is difficult. Fortunately she holds herself very well.
of Queen Elizabeth II

Hardy Amies 1909–2003: interview in *Sunday Telegraph* 9 February 1997

2 When I appear in public people expect me to neigh, grind my teeth, paw the ground and swish my tail—none of which is easy.

Anne, Princess Royal 1950– : in *Observer* 22 May 1977

3 *notice affixed to the gates of St James's Palace during one of*
George II's absences in Hanover:
Lost or strayed out of this house a man who has left a wife
and six children on the parish . . . [A reward of four
shillings and sixpence is offered] Nobody judging him to
deserve a crown.

Anonymous: Duke of Windsor 'My
Hanoverian Ancestors' (unpublished
reminiscences); Elizabeth Longford
(ed.) *The Oxford Book of Royal
Anecdotes* (1989)

4 King's Moll Reno'd in Wolsey's Home Town.

Anonymous: US newspaper headline
on Wallis Simpson's divorce
proceedings in Ipswich

5 *it was said that during a cruise Caroline of Brunswick would*
sleep in a tent on deck with her majordomo, and take a bath in
her cabin either with him or in his presence:
The Grand Master of St Caroline has found promotion's
path;
He is made both Knight Companion and Commander of
the Bath.

Anonymous: Roger Fulford *The Trial
of Queen Caroline* (1967)

6 *Caroline of Brunswick, estranged wife of George IV, while*
attending the debate in the House of Lords on the Bills of Pains
and Penalties whereby George IV was attempting to divorce
her, habitually fell asleep:
Her conduct at present no censure affords,
She sins not with courtiers but sleeps with the Lords.

Anonymous: Roger Fulford *The Trial
of Queen Caroline* (1967)

7 Most Gracious Queen, we thee implore
To go away and sin no more,
But if that effort be too great,
To go away at any rate.

Anonymous: epigram on Queen
Caroline, quoted in a letter from
Francis Burton to Lord Colchester, 15
November 1820

8 As Jordan's high and mighty squire
Her playhouse profits deigns to skim,
Some folks audaciously enquire:
If *he* keeps *her*, or *she* keeps *him*?
of the Duke of Clarence (later William IV) and his mistress,
the actress Mrs Jordan

Anonymous: Philip Ziegler *King
William IV* (1971)

9 Lousy but loyal.

Anonymous: London East End slogan
at George V's Jubilee, 1935

10 How different, how very different from the home life of our
own dear Queen!

Anonymous: comment overheard at a
performance of Cleopatra by Sarah
Bernhardt (probably apocryphal)

11 Which King did you say?

Anonymous: BBC receptionist to King
Haakon of Norway; in *Ned Sherrin in
his Anecdotage* (1993)

12 *comment made to Cecil Beaton by a lady-in-waiting to the*
exiled Queen Geraldine of Albania:
Of course, we'll go back there one day. Meanwhile, we
have to make a new life for ourselves at the Ritz.

Anonymous: Cecil Beaton diary 1940

13 One of Edward's Mistresses was Jane Shore, who has had a
play written about her, but it is a tragedy and therefore
not worth reading.

Jane Austen 1775–1817: *The History
of England* (written 1791)

14 Fate wrote her a most tremendous tragedy, and she played
it in tights.

Max Beerbohm 1872–1956: of
Caroline of Brunswick, wife of George
IV; *The Yellow Book* (1894)

15 Spirits of well-shot woodcock, partridge, snipe
Flutter and bear him up the Norfolk sky.

John Betjeman 1906–84: 'Death of King George V' (1937)

16 Green with lust and sick with shyness
Let me lick your lacquered toes,
Gosh, oh gosh, your Royal Highness,
Put your finger up my nose.
parodic poem on John Betjeman's being presented with the Duff Cooper Memorial Prize by Princess Margaret

Maurice Bowra 1898–1971: attributed; in *Daily Telegraph* 10 February 2002 (online edition)

17 *William IV, on his way to dissolve Parliament, with uproar growing in both Houses over the Reform Bill and a cannon heralding his approach, asked his Lord Chancellor what the noise could be:*
If you please, Your Majesty, it is the Lords debating.

Lord Brougham 1778–1868: *Works of Henry Lord Brougham* (1872)

18 'Where shall I begin, please your Majesty?' he asked.
'Begin at the beginning,' the King said, gravely, 'and go on till you come to the end: then stop.'

Lewis Carroll 1832–98: *Alice's Adventures in Wonderland* (1865)

19 I shall be an autocrat: that's my trade. And the good Lord will forgive me: that's his.

Catherine the Great 1729–96: attributed

20 We saw Queen Mary looking like the Jungfrau, white and sparkling in the sun.

Chips Channon 1897–1958: diary, 22 June 1937

21 He had been, he said, an unconscionable time dying; but he hoped that they would excuse it.

Charles II 1630–85: Lord Macaulay *History of England* (1849)

22 I've tried him drunk and I've tried him sober but there's nothing in him.

Charles II 1630–85: of his niece Anne's husband George of Denmark; Gila Curtis *The Life and Times of Queen Anne* (1972)

23 This is very true: for my words are my own, and my actions are my ministers'.

Charles II 1630–85: reply to 'The King's Epitaph'; *Thomas Hearne: Remarks and Collections* (1885–1921) 17 November 1706

24 Ma'am or Sir,
Sir or Ma'am
Makes every royal personage as happy as a clam.

Noël Coward 1899–1973: 'Sir or Ma'am' (1962)

25 *on being asked the identity of the small man sharing an open carriage with the large Queen Salote of Tonga in the British Coronation procession:*
Her lunch.

Noël Coward 1899–1973: attributed, but denied by Coward as offensive to Queen Salote; Dick Richards *The Wit and Wisdom of Noël Coward* (1968)

26 Everyone likes flattery; and when you come to Royalty you should lay it on with a trowel.

Benjamin Disraeli 1804–81: G. W. E. Russell *Collections and Recollections* (1898)

27 I never deny; I never contradict; I sometimes forget.

Benjamin Disraeli 1804–81: of his dealings as Prime Minister with Queen Victoria; Elizabeth Longford *Victoria R. I.* (1964)

28 I had three concubines, who in three diverse properties diversely excelled. One, the merriest; another the wiliest; the third, the holiest harlot in my realm, as one whom no man could get out of the church lightly to any place but it were to his bed.

Edward IV 1442–83: Thomas More *The History of Richard III*, composed about 1513

29 *to the Archbishop of Canterbury after the service of celebration at St Paul's for Queen Victoria's Diamond Jubilee in 1897:*
I have no objection whatsoever to the notion of the Eternal Father, but every objection to the concept of an eternal mother.

Edward VII 1841–1910: attributed, perhaps apocryphal

30 *on being asked if Queen Victoria would be happy in heaven:*
She will have to walk behind the angels—and she won't like that.

Edward VII 1841–1910: attributed, perhaps apocryphal

31 I think everybody really will concede that on this, of all days, I should begin my speech with the words 'My husband and I'.

Elizabeth II 1926– : speech at Guildhall, London, on her 25th wedding anniversary

32 *on being asked, just after George VI's accession, if she had seen Chips Channon's new gold dinner service in his Belgravia home:*
Oh no, we're not nearly grand enough to be asked there.

Queen Elizabeth, the Queen Mother 1900–2002: attributed, perhaps apocryphal

33 His Weariness the Prince entered the room in all his tinted orders.

Ronald Firbank 1886–1926: *The Flower Beneath the Foot* (1923)

34 I hate all Boets and Bainters.

George I 1660–1727: John Campbell *Lives of the Chief Justices* (1849) 'Lord Mansfield'

35 *when Queen Caroline, on her deathbed, urged him to marry again:*
No, I shall have mistresses.
     the Queen replied, 'Oh, my God! That won't make any difference'

George II 1683–1760: John Hervey *Memoirs of the Reign of George II* (1848)

36 *the Duke of Clarence had told his father that he made his mistress Mrs Jordan an allowance of £1000 per year:*
A thousand, a thousand; too much; too much! Five hundred quite enough! Quite enough!

George III 1738–1820: Brian Fothergill *Dorothy Jordan* (1965)

37 *on first seeing Caroline of Brunswick, his future wife:*
Harris, I am not well; pray get me a glass of brandy.

George IV 1762–1830: Earl of Malmesbury *Diaries and Correspondence* (1844), 5 April 1795

38 *in conversation with Anthony Eden, 23 December 1935, following Samuel Hoare's resignation as Foreign Secretary:*
I said to your predecessor: 'You know what they're all saying, no more coals to Newcastle, no more Hoares to Paris.' The fellow didn't even laugh.

George V 1865–1936: Earl of Avon *Facing the Dictators* (1962)

39 *on H. G. Wells's comment on 'an alien and uninspiring court':*
I may be uninspiring, but I'll be damned if I'm an alien!

George V 1865–1936: Sarah Bradford *George VI* (1989); attributed

40 *to Brigadier Hinde, who had replied to the question, 'Have we met before?' with 'I don't think so':*
You should bl-bloody well know.

George VI 1895–1952: Lord Carver *Out of Step* (1989)

41 Ah'm sorry your Queen has to pay taxes. She's not a wealthy woman.

John Paul Getty 1892–1976: in *Ned Sherrin in his Anecdotage* (1993); attributed

42 *of the Emperor Gordian:*
Twenty-two acknowledged concubines, and a library of sixty-two thousand volumes, attested the variety of his inclinations, and from the productions which he left behind him, it appears that the former as well as the latter

Edward Gibbon 1737–94: *The Decline and Fall of the Roman Empire* (1776–88)

were designed for use rather than ostentation. [Footnote]
By each of his concubines the younger Gordian left three
or four children. His literary productions were by no
means contemptible.

43 Another damned, thick, square book! Always scribble,
scribble, scribble! Eh! Mr Gibbon?

Duke of Gloucester 1743–1805:
Henry Best *Personal and Literary
Memorials* (1829); also attributed to
the Duke of Cumberland and King
George III

44 I left England when I was four because I found out I could
never be King.

Bob Hope 1903–2003: from the Bob
Hope Joke Files stored in two vaults of
his Toluca Lake estate office; William
Robert Faith *Bob Hope* (1983)

45 *notice on a playbill sent to her former lover, the Duke of
Clarence, refusing repayment of her allowance:*
Positively no money refunded after the curtain has risen.

Mrs Jordan 1762–1816: Duke of
Windsor 'My Hanoverian Ancestors'
(unpublished reminiscences);
Elizabeth Longford (ed.) *The Oxford
Book of Royal Anecdotes* (1989)

46 Not a fatter fish than he
Flounders round the polar sea.
See his blubber—at his gills
What a world of drink he swills . . .
By his bulk and by his size
By his oily qualities
This (or else my eyesight fails)
This should be the Prince of Wales.

Charles Lamb 1775–1834:
anonymously written in 1812;
Elizabeth Longford (ed.) *Oxford Book
of Royal Anecdotes* (1989)

47 What do the simple folk do?
. . . I have been informed
By those who know them well,
They find relief in quite a clever way.
When they're sorely pressed
They whistle for a spell:
And whistling seems to brighten up their day.
And that's what simple folk do;
So they say.

Alan Jay Lerner 1918–86: 'What Do
the Simple Folk Do?' (1960)

48 *England had declared war on France two weeks after the
accession of Queen Anne:*
It means I'm growing old when ladies declare war on me.

Louis XIV 1638–1715: Gila Curtis *The
Life and Times of Queen Anne* (1972)

49 My children are not royal, they just happen to have the
Queen as their aunt.

Princess Margaret 1930–2002:
Elizabeth Longford (ed.) *The Oxford
Book of Royal Anecdotes* (1989)

50 *on being told that one of the Royal paintings was a Mercier,
not by Nollekens:*
We prefer the picture to remain as by Nollekens.

Queen Mary 1867–1953: Michael Hill
(ed.) *Right Royal Remarks* (2003)

51 *on the abdication:*
Really, this might be Rumania.

Queen Mary 1867–1953: Michael Hill
(ed.) *Right Royal Remarks* (2003)

52 Superior to her waiting nymphs,
As lobster to attendant shrimps.
of Queen Caroline of Ansbach when dressed in pink

Lady Mary Wortley Montagu
1689–1762: 'Epistle to Lord Hervey
on the King's Birthday'

53 It used to occur to me when I lived in London . . . that it can't be easy being a queen. The poor old dear has had one *annus horribilis* after another. The kids are splitting up, the palace is falling down, the mother is on the gin. It is all like a particularly atrocious episode of *Eastenders*.

Joseph O'Connor 1963– : *The Secret World of the Irish Male* (1995)

54 She's head of a dysfunctional family—if she lived on a council estate in Sheffield, she'd probably be in council care.
on the Queen

Michael Parkinson 1935– : in *Mail on Sunday* 17 January 1999 'Quotes of the Week'

55 *after the death in childbirth of the Prince Regent's daughter Charlotte, four of the Regent's brothers married in an attempt to provide an heir to the throne:*
Yoics! the Royal sport's begun!
I'faith but it is glorious fun,
For hot and hard each Royal pair
Are at it hunting for an heir.

Peter Pindar 1738–1819: Elizabeth Longford (ed.) *The Oxford Book of Royal Anecdotes* (1989)

56 Here thou, great Anna! whom three realms obey,
Dost sometimes counsel take—and sometimes tea.

Alexander Pope 1688–1744: *The Rape of the Lock* (1714)

57 The Right Divine of Kings to govern wrong.

Alexander Pope 1688–1744: *The Dunciad* (1742)

58 I am his Highness' dog at Kew;
Pray, tell me sir, whose dog are you?

Alexander Pope 1688–1744: 'Epigram Engraved on the Collar of a Dog which I gave to his Royal Highness' (1738)

59 Here lies a great and mighty king
Whose promise none relies on;
He never said a foolish thing,
Nor ever did a wise one.

Lord Rochester 1647–80: 'The King's Epitaph' (an alternative first line reads: 'Here lies our sovereign lord the King')

60 *at the funeral of Edward VII the Kaiser asked Roosevelt to call on him the next day 'at two o'clock sharp—for I can give you only 45 minutes':*
I will be there at two, but unfortunately I have just 20 minutes to give you.

Theodore Roosevelt 1858–1919: attributed, perhaps apocryphal

61 The *éminence cerise*, the bolster behind the throne.
of Queen Elizabeth the Queen Mother

Will Self 1961– : in *Independent on Sunday* 8 August 1999

62 *questionnaire for would-be Kings in the Wars of the Roses:*
Are you Edmund Mortimer? If not, have you got him?

W. C. Sellar 1898–1951 and **R. J. Yeatman** 1898–1968: *1066 and All That* (1930)

63 The cruel Queen died and a post-mortem examination revealed the word 'CALLOUS' engraved on her heart.

W. C. Sellar 1898–1951 and **R. J. Yeatman** 1898–1968: of Mary Tudor; *1066 and All That* (1930)

64 Charles II was always very merry and was therefore not so much a king as a Monarch.

W. C. Sellar 1898–1951 and **R. J. Yeatman** 1898–1968: *1066 and All That* (1930)

65 *when preaching before Charles II and his court:*
My lord, you snore so loud you will wake the king.

Dr South 1634–1716: to Lord Lauderdale; Arthur Bryant *King Charles II* (rev. ed. 1964)

66 *to Harold Nicolson on the Abdication crisis:*
And now 'ere we 'ave this obstinate little man with 'is Mrs Simpson. Hit won't do, 'arold, I tell you that straight.

J. H. Thomas 1874–1949: Harold Nicolson letter, 26 February 1936

67 *of the British people:*
They 'ate 'aving no family life at Court.

J. H. Thomas 1874–1949: Harold Nicolson letter, 26 February 1936

68 Sire, your majesty seems to have won the race.
after the Battle of the Boyne to James II, who had complained that Lady Tyrconnel's countrymen had run away

Lady Tyrconnel d. 1731: Elizabeth Longford (ed.) *The Oxford Book of Royal Anecdotes* (1989)

69 He speaks to Me as if I was a public meeting.
of Gladstone

Queen Victoria 1819–1901: G. W. E. Russell *Collections and Recollections* (1898)

70 *When forced by a mob to cheer George IV's wife Caroline of Brunswick:*
God Save the Queen, and may all your wives be like her!

Duke of Wellington 1769–1852: Elizabeth Longford *Wellington: Pillar of State* (1972); also attributed to Lord Anglesey and others

71 *having been wakened with the news of his accession, William IV returned to bed:*
To enjoy the novelty of sleeping with a queen.

William IV 1765–1837: Duke of Windsor 'My Hanoverian Ancestors' (unpublished reminiscences); Elizabeth Longford (ed.) *The Oxford Book of Royal Anecdotes* (1989)

Russia

66 Miles of cornfields, and ballet in the evening. 99
Alan Hackney

1 I gather it has now been decided not to embrace the Russian bear, but to hold out a hand and accept its paw gingerly. No more. The worst of both worlds.

Chips Channon 1897–1958: diary, 16 May 1939

2 Miles of cornfields, and ballet in the evening.

Alan Hackney: *Private Life* (1958) (later filmed as *I'm All Right Jack*, 1959)

3 I was born under a squandering Tsar.

Dick Vosburgh and **Denis King**: *Beauty and the Beards* (2001)

Satisfaction and Discontent ····> Happiness, Hope and Despair

66 I can tolerate without discomfort being waited on hand and foot. 99
Osbert Lancaster

1 *Mr Bennet dissuading his daughter Mary from continuing to sing:*
You have delighted us long enough.

Jane Austen 1775–1817: *Pride and Prejudice* (1813)

2 *when asked what was the best day of her life:*
It was a night.

Brigitte Bardot 1934– : in *Independent on Sunday* 3 October 2004

3 *asked if he had any regrets:*
Yes, I haven't had enough sex.

John Betjeman 1906–84: on *Time With Betjeman* (BBC TV), February 1983; Nigel Rees (ed.) *Cassell Dictionary of Humorous Quotations* (1999)

4 There was a jolly miller once,
Lived on the river Dee;
He worked and sang from morn till night;
No lark more blithe than he . . .
And this the burthen of his song,
For ever used to be,
I care for nobody, not I,
If no one cares for me.

Isaac Bickerstaffe 1733–c.1808: *Love in a Village* (1762)

5 Does he paint? He would fain write a poem.
Does he write? He would fain paint a picture.

Robert Browning 1812–89: 'One Word More' (1855)

6 I ask very little. Some fragments of Pamphilides, a Choctaw blood-mask, the prose of Scaliger the Elder, a painting by Fuseli, an occasional visit to the all-in wrestling, or to my meretrix; a cook who can produce a passable 'poulet à la Khmer', a Pong vase. Simple tastes, you will agree, and it is my simple habit to indulge them.

Cyril Connolly 1903–74: *The Condemned Playground* 'Told in Gath', a parody of Aldous Huxley

7 If, of all words of tongue and pen,
The saddest are, 'It might have been,'
More sad are these we daily see:
'It is, but hadn't ought to be!'

Bret Harte 1836–1902: 'Mrs Judge Jenkins' (1867)

8 Frankly, my dear, I don't give a damn.

Sidney Howard 1891–1939: *Gone with the Wind* (1939 film, based on the novel by Margaret Mitchell); spoken by Clark Gable as Rhett Butler

9 You were only supposed to blow the bloody doors off!

Troy Kennedy-Martin 1932– : *The Italian Job* (1969 film); spoken by Michael Caine as Charlie Croker

10 I can tolerate without discomfort being waited on hand and foot.

Osbert Lancaster 1908–80: *All Done From Memory* (1953)

11 When fortune empties her chamberpot on your head, smile—and say 'we are going to have a summer shower'.

John A. Macdonald 1851–91: spoken c. 1875

12 It's no go the Yogi-Man, it's no go Blavatsky,
All we want is a bank balance and a bit of skirt in a taxi.

Louis MacNeice 1907–63: 'Bagpipe Music' (1938)

13 I test my bath before I sit,
And I'm always moved to wonderment
That what chills the finger not a bit
Is so frigid upon the fundament.

Ogden Nash 1902–71: 'Samson Agonistes' (1942)

14 My life was simply hellish
I didn't stand a chance
I thought that I would relish
A tomb like General Grant's
But now I feel so swellish
So Elsa Maxwellish
That I'm giving a dance.

Cole Porter 1891–1964: 'I'm Throwing a Ball Tonight' (1940)

15 'I must be going,' said Mrs Eggelby, in a tone which had been thoroughly sterilised of even perfunctory regret.

Saki 1870–1916: *Beasts and Super-Beasts* (1914)

16 My birthday. No adequate fuss made.

Barbara Skelton 1916–96: diary, 26 June 1952

17 His strongest tastes were negative. He abhorred plastics, Picasso, sunbathing and jazz—everything in fact that had happened in his own lifetime.

Evelyn Waugh 1903–66: *The Ordeal of Gilbert Pinfold* (1957)

18 It's better to be looked over than overlooked.

Mae West 1892–1980: *Belle of the Nineties* (1934 film)

19 Ice formed on the butler's upper slopes.

P. G. Wodehouse 1881–1975: *Pigs Have Wings* (1952)

20 He spoke with a certain what-is-it in his voice, and I could see that, if not actually disgruntled, he was far from being gruntled.

P. G. Wodehouse 1881–1975: *The Code of the Woosters* (1938)

Science ····> Progress, Technology

&&If I could remember the names of all these particles I'd be a botanist. 99
Enrico Fermi

1 All I know about the becquerel is that, like the Italian lira, you need an awful lot to amount to very much.

Arnold Allen 1924– : in *Financial Times* 19 September 1986

2 Multiplication is vexation,
Division is as bad;
The Rule of Three doth puzzle me,
And Practice drives me mad.

Anonymous: in *Lean's Collectanea* (1904), possibly 16th-century

3 When I find myself in the company of scientists, I feel like a shabby curate who has strayed by mistake into a drawing room full of dukes.

W. H. Auden 1907–73: *The Dyer's Hand* (1963)

4 The Microbe is so very small
You cannot make him out at all.
But many sanguine people hope
To see him through a microscope.

Hilaire Belloc 1870–1953: 'The Microbe' (1897)

5 Sir Humphrey Davy
Abominated gravy.
He lived in the odium
Of having discovered Sodium.

Edmund Clerihew Bentley 1875–1956: 'Sir Humphrey Davy' (1905)

6 Basic research is what I am doing when I don't know what I am doing.

Werner von Braun 1912–77: R. L. Weber *A Random Walk in Science* (1973)

7 Let's be frank, the Italians' technological contribution to humankind stopped with the pizza oven.

Bill Bryson 1951– : *Neither Here Nor There* (1991)

8 There was a young lady named Bright,
Whose speed was far faster than light;
She set out one day
In a relative way
And returned on the previous night.

Arthur Buller 1874–1944: 'Relativity' (1923)

9 If they are worthy of the name, they are indeed about
God's path and about his bed and spying out all his ways.
of scientists

Samuel Butler 1835–1902:
Notebooks (1912)

10 The Scylla's cave which men of science are preparing for
themselves to be able to pounce out upon us from it, and
into which we cannot penetrate.

Samuel Butler 1835–1902: of
scientific terminology; *Notebooks*
(1912)

11 *to an elderly scientist who had bored her by talking
interminably about the social organization of ants, which have
'their own police force and their own army':*
No navy, I suppose?'

Mrs Patrick Campbell 1865–1940:
James Agate diary, 11 February 1944

12 If an elderly but distinguished scientist says that
something is possible he is almost certainly right, but if he
says that it is impossible he is very probably wrong.

Arthur C. Clarke 1917–2008: in *New
Yorker* 9 August 1969

13 I have no more faith in men of science being infallible than
I have in men of God being infallible, principally on
account of them being men.

Noël Coward 1899–1973: diary, 1
July 1946

14 Equations are more important to me, because politics is for
the present, but an equation is something for eternity.

Albert Einstein 1879–1955: Stephen
Hawking *A Brief History of Time*
(1988)

15 If I could remember the names of all these particles I'd be a
botanist.

Enrico Fermi 1901–54: R. L. Weber
More Random Walks in Science
(1973)

16 Someone told me that each equation I included in the
book would halve the sales.

Stephen Hawking 1942– : *A Brief
History of Time* (1988)

17 It was Einstein who made the real trouble. He announced
in 1905 that there was no such thing as absolute rest.
After that there never was.

Stephen Leacock 1869–1944: *The
Boy I Left Behind Me* (1947)

18 When Rutherford was done with the atom all the solidity
was pretty well knocked out of it.

Stephen Leacock 1869–1944: *The
Boy I Left Behind Me* (1947)

19 Scientists are rarely to be counted among the fun people.
Awkward at parties, shy with strangers, deficient in
irony—they have had no choice but to turn their attention
to the close study of everyday objects.

Fran Lebowitz 1946– : *Metropolitan
Life* (1978)

20 My theory [is] that modern science was largely conceived
of as an answer to the servant problem and that it is
generally practised by those who lack a flair for
conversation.

Fran Lebowitz 1946– : *Metropolitan
Life* (1978)

21 It is a good morning exercise for a research scientist to
discard a pet hypothesis every day before breakfast.

Konrad Lorenz 1903–89: *On
Aggression* (1966)

22 The scientist who yields anything to theology, however
slight, is yielding to ignorance and false pretences, and as
certainly as if he granted that a horse-hair put into a bottle
of water will turn into a snake.

H. L. Mencken 1880–1956: *Minority
Report* (1956)

23 To mistrust science and deny the validity of the scientific
method is to resign your job as a human. You'd better go
look for work as a plant or wild animal.

P. J. O'Rourke 1947– : *Parliament of
Whores* (1991)

24 Realistically, the argument saying that you won't find a
good scientist without industry connections is almost
certainly right.

Doug Parr: in *Independent* 12 June
1999

25 Aristotle maintained that women have fewer teeth than men; although he was twice married, it never occurred to him to verify this statement by examining his wives' mouths.

Bertrand Russell 1872–1970: *Impact of Science on Society* (1952)

26 Science becomes dangerous only when it imagines that it has reached its goal.

George Bernard Shaw 1856–1950: preface to *The Doctor's Dilemma* (1911)

27 He had been eight years upon a project for extracting sunbeams out of cucumbers, which were to be put into vials hermetically sealed, and let out to warm the air in raw inclement summers.

Jonathan Swift 1667–1745: *Gulliver's Travels* (1726)

28 Her own mother lived the latter years of her life in the horrible suspicion that electricity was dripping invisibly all over the house.

James Thurber 1894–1961: *My Life and Hard Times* (1933)

29 There is something fascinating about science. One gets such wholesale returns of conjecture out of such a trifling investment of fact.

Mark Twain 1835–1910: *Life on the Mississippi* (1883)

30 It was absolutely marvellous working for Pauli. You could ask him anything. There was no worry that he would think a particular question was stupid, since he thought *all* questions were stupid.

Victor Weisskopf 1908–2002: in *American Journal of Physics* 1977

Scotland ····▸ Countries and Peoples, Places

❝ That state of mind which cartographers seek to define as Scotland. **❞**
Claud Cockburn

1 There are few more impressive sights in the world than a Scotsman on the make.

J. M. Barrie 1860–1937: *What Every Woman Knows* (performed 1908)

2 A young Scotsman of your ability let loose upon the world with £300, what could he not do? It's almost appalling to think of; especially if he went among the English.

J. M. Barrie 1860–1937: *What Every Woman Knows* (1918)

3 I had occasion, not for the first time, to thank heaven for that state of mind which cartographers seek to define as Scotland.

Claud Cockburn 1904–81: *Crossing the Line* (1958)

4 They christened their game golf because they were Scottish and revelled in meaningless Celtic noises in the back of the throat.

Stephen Fry 1957– : *Paperweight* (1992)

5 Norway, too, has noble wild prospects; and Lapland is remarkable for prodigious noble wild prospects. But, Sir, let me tell you, the noblest prospect which a Scotchman ever sees, is the high road that leads him to England!

Samuel Johnson 1709–84: James Boswell *Life of Samuel Johnson* (1791) 6 July 1763

6 *Oats.* A grain, which in England is generally given to horses, but in Scotland supports the people.

Samuel Johnson 1709–84: *A Dictionary of the English Language* (1755)

7 Can the United States ever become genuinely civilized? Certainly it is possible. Even Scotland has made enormous progress since the Eighteenth Century, when, according to Macaulay, most of it was on the cultural level of Albania.

H. L. Mencken 1880–1956: *Minority Report* (1956)

8 No McTavish
Was ever lavish.

Ogden Nash 1902–71: 'Genealogical Reflection' (1931)

9 Scotland has too many ninety-minute patriots whose nationalist outpourings are expressed only at major sporting events.

Jim Sillars 1937– : television interview following the 1992 general election; in *The Herald* 24 April 1992

10 That knuckle-end of England—that land of Calvin, oatcakes, and sulphur.

Sydney Smith 1771–1845: Lady Holland *Memoir* (1855)

11 It requires a surgical operation to get a joke well into a Scotch understanding. Their only idea of wit . . . is laughing immoderately at stated intervals.

Sydney Smith 1771–1845: Lady Holland *Memoir* (1855)

12 It is never difficult to distinguish between a Scotsman with a grievance and a ray of sunshine.

P. G. Wodehouse 1881–1975: *Blandings Castle and Elsewhere* (1935)

Secrecy ····> Security

❝ We never knows wot's hidden in each other's hearts. **❞**
Charles Dickens

1 *of the 19th-century diarist Charles Greville:*
For fifty years he listened at the door
He heard some secrets and invented more.

Charles M. Andrews 1863–1943: 'These Forty Years', annual address of the President of the American Historical Association, 27 December 1924

2 A Company for carrying on an undertaking of Great Advantage, but no one to know what it is.

Anonymous: Company Prospectus at the time of the South Sea Bubble (1711)

3 Everyone has a skeleton in their closet. The difference between Bill Clinton and myself is that he has a walk-in closet.

Pat Buchanan 1938– : in *Sunday Times* 21 November 1999

4 Secrets with girls, like loaded guns with boys,
Are never valued till they make a noise.

George Crabbe 1754–1832: *Tales of the Hall* (1819) 'The Maid's Story'

5 We never knows wot's hidden in each other's hearts; and if we had glass winders there, we'd need keep the shutters up, some on us, I do assure you!

Charles Dickens 1812–70: *Martin Chuzzlewit* (1844)

6 Anonymous, unseen—
You're dealing with the all-time king or queen
Of undercover loves.
The author of this valentine wore gloves.

Sophie Hannah 1971– : 'Poem for a Valentine Card' (1995)

7 That's another of those irregular verbs, isn't it? I give confidential briefings; you leak; he has been charged under Section 2a of the Official Secrets Act.

Jonathan Lynn 1943– and **Antony Jay** 1930– : *Yes Prime Minister* (1987) vol. 2 'Man Overboard'

Security

❝ The best leaks always take place in the urinal. **❞**
John Cole

---

1 I came to the conclusion that a man who could give such pleasure with his pen couldn't be much of a secret agent. I may well be wrong.
   view of the IRA army council's head of civilian intelligence on John Betjeman's role as a press attaché in wartime Dublin

Diarmuid Brennan: report, c.1941; in *Guardian* 22 April 2000

2 Is that man crazy? He thinks there's a bug behind all the pictures.
   as Director of the CIA, having visited Harold Wilson during Wilson's last premiership

George Bush 1924– :Peter Hennessy *The Prime Minister: the Office and its Holders since 1945* (2000)

3 The best leaks always take place in the urinal.

John Cole 1927– : in *Independent* 3 June 1996

4 The spy who came in for a cardie.
   on 85-year-old Melita Nelson, exposed in 1999 as having spied for Russia in the Cold War

Mike Coleman 1946– : on *Loose Ends* (BBC Radio 4) 18 September 1999

5 If a man cannot keep a measly affair secret, what is he doing in charge of the Intelligence Service?
   on the break-up of the marriage of Foreign Secretary Robin Cook

Frederick Forsyth 1938– : in *Guardian* 14 January 1998

6 Truth is suppressed, not to protect the country from enemy agents but to protect the Government of the day against the people.

Roy Hattersley 1932– : in *Independent* 18 February 1995

7 BLAIR: Everybody knows their safe house. Red Square we call it.
   HOGBIN: We call it Dunkremlin.

Tom Stoppard 1937– : *The Dog It Was That Died* (1983)

Self-Knowledge and Self-Deception ····▷ Character

❝ Most people who have dealt with me think that I am a pretty straight sort of guy. **❞**
Tony Blair

---

1 Lady Kill-Chairman, who is one of the greatest gossips in the kingdom, and knows everybody but herself.

Anonymous: in *The Female Tatler* December 1709

2 A person of low taste, more interested in himself than in me.

Ambrose Bierce 1842–c.1914: definition of an egotist; *Cynic's Word Book* (1906)

3 Our polite recognition of another's resemblance to ourselves.

Ambrose Bierce 1842–c.1914: definition of admiration; *Cynic's Word Book* (1906)

4 I think that most people who have dealt with me think that I am a pretty straight sort of guy.
on the handling of the decision to exempt Formula One motor racing from a proposed ban on tobacco advertising

Tony Blair 1953– : 'On the Record' interview with John Humphrys, 16 November 1997

5 They misunderestimated me.

George W. Bush 1946– : speech in Bentonville, Arkansas, November 2000

6 It exactly resembles a superannuated Jesuit . . . though my mind misgives me that it is hideously like. If it is—I can not be long for this world—for it overlooks seventy.

Lord Byron 1788–1824: of a bust of himself by Bartolini; letter 23 September 1822

7 The Crown Prince Umberto is charm itself, but has no great intelligence. He reminds me of myself.

Chips Channon 1897–1958: diary (undated entry); introduction to *Chips: the Diaries of Sir Henry Channon* (1993)

8 I wouldn't say I was the best manager, but I was in the top one.

Brian Clough 1935–2004: attributed; in *Scotsman* 21 September 2004 (online edition)

9 Long experience has taught me that to be criticized is not always to be wrong.

Anthony Eden 1897–1977: speech at Lord Mayor's Guildhall banquet during the Suez crisis; in *Daily Herald* 10 November 1956

10 *to a footman who had accidentally spilt cream over him:*
My good man, I'm not a strawberry!

Edward VII 1841–1910: William Lanceley *From Hall-Boy to House-Steward* (1925)

11   I tell you,
Miss, I knows an undesirable character
When I see one; I've been one myself for years.

Christopher Fry 1907–2005: *Venus Observed* (1950)

12 *having (unlike the Prime Minister in 2000) given a well-received address to the Women's Institute:*
My advice to Tony Blair would be to get in touch with his inner grandmother.

Bob Geldof 1954– : in *The Times* 30 June 2004

13 All my shows are great. Some of them are bad. But they are all great.

Lew Grade 1906–98: in *Observer* 14 September 1975

14 The photograph is not quite true to my own notion of my gentleness and sweetness of nature, but neither perhaps is my external appearance.

A. E. Housman 1859–1936: letter, 12 June 1922

15 Early in our relationship he told me he had a confession to make. I got quite excited and thought something wonderfully saucy was going to come out. But it was just that he couldn't put up shelves.
of her husband Michael Howard

Sandra Howard: in *Sunday Times* 18 April 2004

16 Without exactly *telling* them that I felt like a man swimming towards a raft in a sea of circling fins, I constructed a cry for help masterfully disguised as a manifesto.

Clive James 1939– : *The Dreaming Swimmer* (1992)

17 For self-revelation, whether it be a Tudor villa on the by-pass or a bomb-proof chalet at Berchtesgaden, there's no place like home.

Osbert Lancaster 1908–80: *Homes Sweet Homes* (1939)

18 I am not the type who wants to go back to the land; I am the type who wants to go back to the hotel.

Fran Lebowitz 1946– : *Social Studies* (1981)

19 Underneath this flabby exterior is an enormous lack of character.

Oscar Levant 1906–72: *Memoirs of an Amnesiac* (1965)

20 I believe that Sir Isaiah Berlin is the only man in Britain who talks more rapidly than I do, and even that is a close-run thing.

Bernard Levin 1928– : *In These Times* (1986)

21 I have low self-esteem, but I express it the healthy way . . . by eating a box of Double-Stuf Oreos.

Terri Minsky: *Sex and the City* 'The Baby Shower (1998), spoken by Miranda (Cynthia Nixon)

22 [I am] a doormat in a world of boots.

Jean Rhys c.1890–1979: in *Guardian* 6 December 1990

23 You're so vain
You probably think this song is about you.

Carly Simon 1945– : 'You're So Vain' (1972 song)

24 I can put two and two together, you know. Do not think you are dealing with a man who has lost his grapes.

Tom Stoppard 1937– : *Another Moon Called Earth* (1983)

25 The kind of person who embarks on an endless leap-frog down to the great moral issues. I put a position, rebut it, refute it, refute the rebuttal and rebut the refutation. Endlessly.
   on himself

Tom Stoppard 1937– : Mel Gussow *Conversations with Stoppard* (1995)

26 Satire is a sort of glass, wherein beholders do generally discover everybody's face but their own.

Jonathan Swift 1667–1745: *The Battle of the Books* (1704) preface

27 'He has a profound contempt for human nature.'
'Of course, he is much given to introspection.'
   of Fouché

Charles-Maurice de Talleyrand 1754–1838: Leon Harris *The Fine Art of Political Wit* (1965)

28 I am extraordinarily patient, provided I get my own way in the end.

Margaret Thatcher 1925– : in *Observer* 4 April 1989

29 Pavarotti is not vain, but conscious of being unique.

Peter Ustinov 1921–2004: in *Independent on Sunday* 12 September 1993

30 I'm the girl who lost her reputation and never missed it.

Mae West 1892–1980: P. F. Boller and R. L. Davis *Hollywood Anecdotes* (1988)

31 I don't at all like knowing what people say of me behind my back. It makes me far too conceited.

Oscar Wilde 1854–1900: *An Ideal Husband* (1895)

Sex ····▶ Love, Marriage

❝Sexual intercourse began In nineteen sixty-three.❞
Philip Larkin

1 Don't knock masturbation. It's sex with someone I love.

Woody Allen 1935– : *Annie Hall* (1977 film, with Marshall Brickman)

2 A fast word about oral contraception. I asked a girl to go to bed with me and she said 'no'.

Woody Allen 1935– : at a night-club in Washington, April 1965

3 On bisexuality: It immediately doubles your chances for a date on Saturday night.

Woody Allen 1935– : in *New York Times* 1 December 1975

4 That [sex] was the most fun I ever had without laughing.

Woody Allen 1935– : *Annie Hall* (1977 film, with Marshall Brickman)

5 I think people should mate for life. Like pigeons, or Catholics.

Woody Allen 1935– and **Marshall Brickman** 1941– : in *Manhattan* (1979 film), spoken by Woody Allen

6 My love life is terrible. The last time I was inside a woman was when I visited the Statue of Liberty.

Woody Allen 1935– : *Crimes and Misdemeanors* (1989 film)

7 *a former girlfriend's description of being made love to by Nicholas Soames:*
Like having a large wardrobe fall on top of you with the key still in the lock.

Anonymous: Gyles Brandreth *Breaking the Code* (1999)

8 You should make a point of trying every experience once, excepting incest and folk-dancing.

Anonymous: Arnold Bax *Farewell My Youth* (1943), quoting 'a sympathetic Scot'

9 Would you like to sin
With Elinor Glyn
On a tigerskin?
Or would you prefer
To err
With her
On some other fur?

Anonymous: verse alluding to Elinor Glyn's romantic novel *Three Weeks* (1907); A. Glyn *Elinor Glyn* (1955)

10 You're the burning heat of a bridal suite in use.
You're the breasts of Venus,
You're King Kong's penis,
You're self abuse.
You're an arch
In the Rome collection
You're the starch
In a groom's erection.

Anonymous: parody version of Cole Porter's 'You're the Top' (1934), possibly by Porter

11 'My mother made me a homosexual.'
'If I send her the wool will she make me one?'

Anonymous: New York graffito of the 1970s

12 Let us honour if we can
The vertical man
Though we value none
But the horizontal one.

W. H. Auden 1907–73: 'To Christopher Isherwood' (1930)

13 Give me chastity and continency—but not yet!

St Augustine of Hippo AD 354–430: *Confessions* (AD 397–8)

14 Norman doesn't bother with secret signals. It was just wham, thump and there we both were on the rug.

Alan Ayckbourn 1939– : *Table Manners* (1975)

15 My mother used to say, Delia, if S-E-X ever rears its ugly head, close your eyes before you see the rest of it.

Alan Ayckbourn 1939– : *Bedroom Farce* (1978)

16 I'll come and make love to you at five o'clock. If I'm late start without me.

Tallulah Bankhead 1903–68: Ted Morgan *Somerset Maugham* (1980)

17 I've no feeling in this arm and I can hardly see. Which knocks out at least three erogenous zones for a kick-off.

Alan Bennett 1934– : *Enjoy* (1980)

18 *on being told by her son that lesbians are women who sleep together:*
MRS HOPKINS: Well, that's nothing. I slept with your Auntie Phyllis all during the air raids.

Alan Bennett 1934– : *Me! I'm Afraid of Virginia Woolf* (1978)

19 I'm a trisexual. I'll try anything once.

Jenny Bicks: *Sex and the City* 'Boy, Girl, Boy, Girl . . . ' (2000), spoken by Samantha (Kim Cattrall)

20 *at the age of ninety-seven, Blake was asked at what age the sex drive goes:*
You'll have to ask somebody older than me.

Eubie Blake 1883–1983: in *Ned Sherrin in his Anecdotage* (1993)

21 *on being told he should not marry anyone as plain as his fiancée:*
My dear fellow, buggers can't be choosers.

Maurice Bowra 1898–1971: Hugh Lloyd-Jones *Maurice Bowra: a Celebration* (1974)

22 Genitals are a great distraction to scholarship.

Malcolm Bradbury 1932– : *Cuts* (1987)

23 If homosexuality were the normal way, God would have made Adam and Bruce.

Anita Bryant 1940– : in *New York Times* 5 June 1977

24 I'm afraid, you know, there isn't as much of this about as you seem to think.
on Julian Barnes's suggestion, c.1970, that 'blow-job' should be included in the Supplement to the Oxford English Dictionary

Robert Burchfield 1923–2004: quoted by Julian Barnes in *Imagine* (BBC2, 18 December 2003)

25 He said it was artificial respiration, but now I find I am to have his child.

Anthony Burgess 1917–93: *Inside Mr Enderby* (1963)

26 It was the afternoon of my eighty-first birthday, and I was in bed with my catamite when Ali announced that the archbishop had come to see me.

Anthony Burgess 1917–93: *Earthly Powers* (1980); opening sentence

27 What men call gallantry, and gods adultery,
Is much more common where the climate's sultry.

Lord Byron 1788–1824: *Don Juan* (1819–24)

28 A little still she strove, and much repented,
And whispering 'I will ne'er consent'—consented.

Lord Byron 1788–1824: *Don Juan* (1819–24)

29 *on homosexuality:*
It doesn't matter what you do in the bedroom as long as you don't do it in the street and frighten the horses.

Mrs Patrick Campbell 1865–1940: Daphne Fielding *The Duchess of Jermyn Street* (1964)

30 Do not adultery commit;
Advantage rarely comes of it.

Arthur Hugh Clough 1819–61: 'The Latest Decalogue' (1862)

31 The House of Commons en bloc do it,
Civil Servants by the clock do it.

Noël Coward 1899–1973: 'Let's Do It' (with acknowledgements to Cole Porter) (1940s)

32 I became one of the stately homos of England.

Quentin Crisp 1908–99: *The Naked Civil Servant* (1968)

33 For flavour, Instant Sex will never supersede the stuff you had to peel and cook.

Quentin Crisp 1908–99: in *Sunday Telegraph* 28 September 1999

34 *in 1951 the homosexual Labour politician Tom Driberg married a widow; he later complained:*
She broke her marriage vows; she tried to sleep with me.

Tom Driberg 1905–76: in *Ned Sherrin in his Anecdotage* (1993)

35 Seduction is often difficult to distinguish from rape. In seduction, the rapist bothers to buy a bottle of wine.

Andrea Dworkin 1946–2005: *Letters from a War Zone* (1988)

36 He in a few minutes ravished this fair creature, or at least would have ravished her, if she had not, by a timely compliance, prevented him.

Henry Fielding 1707–54: *Jonathan Wild* (1743)

37 My dad told me, 'Anything worth having is worth waiting for.' I waited until I was fifteen.

Zsa Zsa Gabor 1919– : attributed; Bob Chieger *Was It Good For You?* (1983)

38 Sex was a competitive event in those days and the only thing you could take as a certainty was that everyone else was lying, just as you were.

Bob Geldof 1954– : *Is That It?* (1986)

39 Only the Lion and the Cock;
As Galen says, withstand Love's shock.
So, dearest, do not think me rude
If I yield now to lassitude,
But sympathize with me. I know
You would not have me roar or crow.

Oliver St John Gogarty 1878–1957: 'After Galen' (1957)

40 'Ye'es, ye'es,' he finally observed with a certain dry relish, 'ye'es, I think I see some adulterers down there.'
   in the Press Gallery of the House of Commons during the Profumo scandal

Maurice Green 1906–87: recorded by Colin Welch; Ned Sherrin *Cutting Edge* (1984)

41 Masturbation is the thinking man's television.

Christopher Hampton 1946– : *The Philanthropist* (1970)

42 The trouble with a virgin is
She's always on the verge.
A virgin is the worst
Her method is reversed
She'll lead a horse to water
And then let him die of thirst.

E. Y. Harburg 1898–1981: 'Never Trust a Virgin' (1961)

43 I regret to say that we of the FBI are powerless to act in cases of oral-genital intimacy, unless it has in some way obstructed interstate commerce.

J. Edgar Hoover 1895–1972: Irving Wallace et al. *Intimate Sex Lives of Famous People* (1981)

44 My father told me all about the birds and the bees, the liar—I went steady with a woodpecker until I was 21.

Bob Hope 1903–2003: attributed; in *The Times* 29 July 2003

45 I am trisexual. The Army, the Navy, and the Household Cavalry.

Brian Desmond Hurst 1895–1986: Christopher Robbins *The Empress of Ireland* (2004)

46 The sexophones wailed like melodious cats under the moon.

Aldous Huxley 1894–1963: *Brave New World* (1932)

47 I can't get no satisfaction
I can't get no girl reaction.

Mick Jagger 1943– and **Keith Richard** 1943– : '(I Can't Get No) Satisfaction' (1965)

48 There is no unhappier creature on earth than a fetishist who yearns to embrace a woman's shoe and has to embrace the whole woman.

Karl Kraus 1874–1936: *Aphorisms and More Aphorisms* (1909)

49 Sexual intercourse began
In nineteen sixty-three
(Which was rather late for me)—
Between the end of the *Chatterley* ban
And the Beatles' first L.P.

Philip Larkin 1922–85: 'Annus Mirabilis' (1974)

50 Surely the sex business isn't worth all this damned fuss? I've met only a handful of people who cared a biscuit for it.
   on reading Lady Chatterley's Lover

T. E. Lawrence 1888–1935: Christopher Hassall *Edward Marsh* (1959)

51 He was into animal husbandry—until they caught him at it.

Tom Lehrer 1928– : in *An Evening Wasted with Tom Lehrer* (record album, 1953); Nigel Rees (ed.) *Cassell Dictionary of Humorous Quotations* (1999)

52 *on lesbianism:*
I can understand two men. There is something to get hold of. But how do two insides make love?

Lydia Lopokova 1892–1981: A. J. P. Taylor letter 5 November 1973

53 BARNARDINE: Thou hast committed—
BARABAS: Fornication? But that was in another country: and besides, the wench is dead.

Christopher Marlowe 1564–93: *The Jew of Malta* (c.1592)

54 Many years ago I chased a woman for almost two years, only to discover that her tastes were exactly like mine: we both were crazy about girls.

Groucho Marx 1895–1977: letter 28 March 1955

55 I've been around so long, I knew Doris Day before she was a virgin.

Groucho Marx 1895–1977: Max Wilk *The Wit and Wisdom of Hollywood* (1972)

56 I always thought music was more important than sex— then I thought if I don't hear a concert for a year-and-a-half it doesn't bother me.

Jackie Mason 1931– : in *Guardian* 17 February 1989

57 Continental people have sex life; the English have hot-water bottles.

George Mikes 1912–87: *How to be an Alien* (1946)

58 *on tantric sex:*
I prefer the plumber position. You stay in all day and nobody comes.

John Mortimer 1923– : in *The Times* 24 February 2003

59 An orgy looks particularly alluring seen through the mists of righteous indignation.

Malcolm Muggeridge 1903–90: *The Most of Malcolm Muggeridge* (1966) 'Dolce Vita in a Cold Climate'

60 Not tonight, Josephine.

Napoleon I 1769–1821: attributed, but probably apocryphal; R. H. Horne *The History of Napoleon* (1841) describes the circumstances in which the affront might have occurred

61 I toiled on a farm tilling soybeans,
In a struggle to chasten my brain,
But the girl beans got in with the boy beans,
And I never struggled again.

Ogden Nash 1902–71: in *One Touch of Venus* (1943 musical film)

62 She was as happy as the dey was long.
of the relationship between Caroline of Brunswick, estranged wife of George IV, and the dey (or governor) of Algiers

Lord Norbury 1745–1831: attributed; Nigel Rees *Cassell Dictionary of Humorous Quotations* (1998)

63 GARY: She put me right on a few technical details, yes.
DERMOT: She said it was like sleeping with a badly-informed labrador.

Simon Nye 1958– : *Men Behaving Badly* (ITV, series 1, 1992) 'Intruders'

64 You were born with your legs apart. They'll send you to the grave in a Y-shaped coffin.

Joe Orton 1933–67: *What the Butler Saw* (1969)

65 MIKE: There's no word in the Irish language for what you were doing.
WILSON: In Lapland they have no word for snow.

Joe Orton 1933–67: *The Ruffian on the Stair* (rev. ed. 1967)

66 His second question was, 'How queer are you?' If I myself had small talent to amuse, I could at least make an effort to please. 'Oh, about twenty per cent.' 'Really! Are you? I'm ninety-five.'

John Osborne 1929– : recollection of a conversation with Noël Coward in 1966; *Almost a Gentleman* (1991)

67 Thank God we're normal,
Yes, this is our finest shower!

John Osborne 1929– : *The Entertainer* (1957)

68 *on her abortion:*
It serves me right for putting all my eggs in one bastard.

Dorothy Parker 1893–1967: John Keats *You Might as well Live* (1970)

69 On a sofa upholstered in panther skin
Mona did researches in original sin.

William Plomer 1903–73: 'Mews Flat Mona' (1960)

70 Birds do it, bees do it,
Even educated fleas do it.
Let's do it, let's fall in love.

Cole Porter 1891–1964: 'Let's Do It' (1954; words added to the 1928 original)

71 Mister Harris, Plutocrat,
Wants to give my cheek a pat.
If a Harris pat
Means a Paris hat,
Bébé!

Cole Porter 1891–1964: 'Always True to You in my Fashion' (*Kiss Me Kate* 1949 musical)

72 No, no; for my virginity,
When I lose that, says Rose, I'll die:
Behind the elms last night, cried Dick,
Rose, were you not extremely sick?

Matthew Prior 1664–1721: 'A True Maid' (1718)

73 Your idea of fidelity is not having more than one man in bed at the same time.

Frederic Raphael 1931– : *Darling* (1965)

74 Sex is something I really don't understand too hot. You never know *where* the hell you are. I keep making up these sex rules for myself, and then I break them right away.

J. D. Salinger 1919– : *The Catcher in the Rye* (1951)

75 *the practice in a New York bath house was for someone wanting a partner to leave the cubicle door open. A young man, entering John Schlesinger's cubicle, recoiled on seeing 'this mound of flesh':*
ANONYMOUS: Oh, please. I couldn't. You've got to be kidding.
JOHN SCHLESINGER: A simple *No* will suffice.

John Schlesinger 1926–2003: Alan Bennett diary 2003, in *London Review of Books* 8 January 2004; a similar story was quoted to the Editor in the 1960s by the American writer Burt Shevelove as happening to him

76 Is it not strange that desire should so many years outlive performance?

William Shakespeare 1564–1616: *Henry IV, Part 2* (1597)

77 *of Marina, a beautiful virgin:*
She would serve after a long voyage at sea.

William Shakespeare 1564–1616: *Pericles* (1606–8)

78 How long do you want to wait until you start enjoying life? When you're sixty-five you get social security, not girls.

Neil Simon 1927– : *Come Blow Your Horn* (1961)

79 Where is she at the moment? Alone with probably the most attractive man she's ever met. Don't tell me *that* doesn't beat hell out of hair curlers and the *Late Late Show*.

Neil Simon 1927– : *Barefoot in the Park* (1964)

80 Fancy meeting someone and forgetting you've slept with them. It's not good, is it?

Arthur Smith 1954– : *The Live Bed Show* (1995)

81 How can a bishop marry? How can he flirt? The most he can say is, 'I will see you in the vestry after service.'

Sydney Smith 1771–1845: Lady Holland *Memoir* (1855)

82 BONES: A consummate artist, sir. I felt it deeply when she retired.
GEORGE: Unfortunately she retired from consummation about the same time as she retired from artistry.

Tom Stoppard 1937– : *Jumpers* (rev. ed. 1986)

83 [CHAIRMAN OF MILITARY TRIBUNAL:] What would you do if you saw a German soldier trying to violate your sister?
[STRACHEY:] I would try to get between them.

Lytton Strachey 1880–1932: in Robert Graves *Good-bye to All That* (1929); otherwise rendered as, 'I should interpose my body'

84 Masturbation: the primary sexual activity of mankind. In the nineteenth century, it was a disease; in the twentieth, it's a cure.

Thomas Szasz 1920– : *The Second Sin* (1973)

85 Gomer Owen who kissed her once by the pig-sty when she wasn't looking and never kissed her again although she was looking all the time.

Dylan Thomas 1914–53: *Under Milk Wood* (1954)

86 Chasing the naughty couples down the grassgreen gooseberried double bed of the wood.

Dylan Thomas 1914–53: *Under Milk Wood* (1954)

87 Dip me in chocolate and throw me to the lesbians.

Richard Thomas and **Stewart Lee**: *Jerry Springer—the Opera* (2003)

88 Enjoy your supper, Mr Percy, the port is on the chim-a-ney piece, and it's *still* adultery!
on finding her husband Herbert Beerbohm Tree dining à deux with the young and handsome actor Esmé Percy

Lady Tree 1863–1937: attributed, perhaps apocryphal

89 Enter the strumpet voluntary.

Kenneth Tynan 1927–80: of a guest at an Oxford party; attributed

90 I'm all for bringing back the birch, but only between consenting adults.

Gore Vidal 1925– : in *Sunday Times Magazine* 16 September 1973

91 All this fuss about sleeping together. For physical pleasure I'd sooner go to my dentist any day.

Evelyn Waugh 1903–66: *Vile Bodies* (1930)

92 In my day, I would only have sex with a man if I found him extremely attractive. These days, girls seem to choose them in much the same way as they might choose to suck on a boiled sweet.

Mary Wesley 1912– : in *Independent* 18 October 1997 'Quote Unquote'

93 Why don't you come up sometime, and see me?
usually quoted as, 'Why don't you come up and see me sometime?'

Mae West 1892–1980: in *She Done Him Wrong* (1933 film)

94 It's not the men in my life that counts—it's the life in my men.

Mae West 1892–1980: in *I'm No Angel* (1933 film)

Shopping

66 If it's shiny, I buy it. 99
Graham Norton

1 We used to build civilizations. Now we build shopping malls.

Bill Bryson 1951– : *Neither Here Nor There* (1991)

2 Always buy a good pair of shoes and a good bed—if you're not in one you're in the other.
   advice from her mother

Gloria Hunniford 1941– : in *Mail on Sunday* 16 June 2002

3 If it's shiny, I buy it.
   on buying clothes

Graham Norton 1963– : in *Observer* 13 June 2004

4 When in doubt buy shoes.

Marcelle D'Argy Smith: attributed; in *Independent* 20 August 1997

Sickness ····▸ Health, Medicine

66 A person . . . can develop a cold. 99
Frank Loesser

---

1 *Christopher Isherwood, apologising for his bad cold, had said that he should probably have cancelled his dinner invitation to Axelrod and Frederic Raphael:*
My dear Christopher, any cold of yours is a cold of mine.

George Axelrod 1922– : quoted by Frederic Raphael in *Times Literary Supplement* 4 February 2000

2 He was a very fine doctor. Very little he couldn't put right when he set his mind to it. Rita's knee got the better of him, though.

Alan Ayckbourn 1939– : *Sisterly Feelings* (1981)

3 What's happened to the galloping consumption you had last Thursday? Slowed down to a trot I suppose.

Alan Bennett 1934– : *Habeas Corpus* (1973)

4 I'm not unwell. I'm fucking dying.

Jeffrey Bernard 1932–97: in conversation with Dominic Lawson; in *The Spectator* 19 February 1994

5 A cough so robust that I tapped into two new seams of phlegm.

Bill Bryson 1951– : *Neither Here Nor There* (1991)

6 What fun—dear little Sidney
Produced a spectacular stone in his kidney,
He's had eleven
So God's in His heaven
And that is the end of the news.

Noël Coward 1899–1973: 'That is the End of the News' (1945)

7 The nurse sleeps sweetly, hired to watch the sick,
Whom, snoring, she disturbs.

William Cowper 1731–1800: *The Task* (1785)

8 This cough I've got is hacking,
The pain in my head is wracking,
I hardly need to mention my flu.
The Board of Health has seen me
They want to quarantine me,
I might as well be miserable with you.

Howard Dietz 1896–1983: 'Miserable with You' (1931)

9 I wish I had the voice of Homer
To sing of rectal carcinoma,
Which kills a lot more chaps, in fact,
Than were bumped off when Troy was sacked.

J. B. S. Haldane 1892–1964: 'Cancer's a Funny Thing'; Ronald Clark *J. B. S.* (1968)

10 My final word, before I'm done,
Is 'Cancer can be rather fun'.
Thanks to the nurses and Nye Bevan

J. B. S. Haldane 1892–1964: 'Cancer's a Funny Thing'; Ronald Clark *J. B. S.* (1968)

The NHS is quite like heaven
Provided one confronts the tumour
With a sufficient sense of humour.

11 *on reticent British acting:*
I am well, except for a slight cold caught watching Sir
Gerald du Maurier making love.

George S. Kaufman 1889–1961: Ilka
Chase *Past Imperfect* (1942)

12 You can feed her all day with the vitamin A and the
   Bromo fizz,
But the medicine never gets anywhere near where the
   trouble is,
If she's getting a kind of a name for herself, and the name
   ain't his—
A person . . . can develop a cough.

Frank Loesser 1910–69: 'Adelaide's
Lament', reprise (1950)

13 In other words just from waiting around
For that plain little band of gold
A person . . . can develop a cold.
You can spray her wherever you figure the streptococci
   lurk.
You can give her a shot for whatever she's got but it just
   won't work.
If she's tired of getting the fish-eye from the hotel clerk,
A person . . . can develop a cold.

Frank Loesser 1910–69: 'Adelaide's
Lament' (1950)

14 Besides death, constipation is the big fear in hospitals.

Robert McCrum 1953– : *My Year Off*
(1998)

15 *on hearing of the illness of Traill, who in 1904 had beaten him*
for the Provostship of Trinity Dublin:
Nothing trivial, I hope.

John Pentland Mahaffy 1839–1919:
Ulick O'Connor *Oliver St John
Gogarty* (1964)

16 To talk of diseases is a sort of *Arabian Nights*
entertainment.

William Osler 1849–1919: Oliver
Sacks *The Man Who Mistook his Wife
for a Hat* (1985)

17 Hypochondria is the one disease I haven't got.

David Renwick 1951– and **Andrew
Marshall**: *The Burkiss Way* (BBC
Radio, 1978); Nigel Rees *Cassell
Dictionary of Humorous Quotations*
(1999)

18 In rural cottage life not to have rheumatism is as glaring
an omission as not to have been presented at Court would
be in more ambitious circumstances.

Saki 1870–1916: *The Toys of Peace*
(1919)

19 When men die of disease they are said to die from natural
causes. When they recover (and they mostly do) the doctor
gets the credit of curing them.

George Bernard Shaw 1856–1950:
preface to *The Doctor's Dilemma*
(1911)

20 My aunt died of influenza: so they said. But it's my belief
they done the old woman in.

George Bernard Shaw 1856–1950:
Pygmalion (1916)

21 BUDDY: . . . Do you feel any better?
MOTHER: How do I know? I feel too sick to tell.

Neil Simon 1927– : *Come Blow Your
Horn* (1961)

Singing ····➤ Songs and Singing

Sleep and Dreams

66 And so to bed. 99
Samuel Pepys

1 'It would make anyone go to sleep, that bedstead would, whether they wanted to or not.' 'I should think,' said Sam . . . 'poppies was nothing to it.'

Charles Dickens 1812–70: *Pickwick Papers* (1837)

2 Try thinking of love, or something.
Amor vincit insomnia.

Christopher Fry 1907–2005: *A Sleep of Prisoners* (1951)

3 Sleep is when all the unsorted stuff comes flying out as from a dustbin upset in a high wind.

William Golding 1911–93: *Pincher Martin* (1956)

4 I want something that will keep me awake thinking it was the food I ate and not the show I saw.
after a disastrous preview

George S. Kaufman 1889–1961: Howard Teichmann *George S. Kaufman* (1973)

5 I love sleep because it is both pleasant and safe to use.

Fran Lebowitz 1946– : *Metropolitan Life* (1978)

6 And so to bed.

Samuel Pepys 1633–1703: diary 20 April 1660

7 Men who are unhappy, like men who sleep badly, are always proud of the fact.

Bertrand Russell 1872–1970: *The Conquest of Happiness* (1930)

8 I have had a dream, past the wit of man to say what dream it was.

William Shakespeare 1564–1616: *A Midsummer Night's Dream* (1595–6)

9 Many's the long night I've dreamed of cheese—toasted, mostly.

Robert Louis Stevenson 1850–94: *Treasure Island* (1883)

10 There ain't no way to find out why a snorer can't hear himself snore.

Mark Twain 1835–1910: *Tom Sawyer Abroad* (1894)

11 I haven't been to sleep for over a year. That's why I go to bed early. One needs more rest if one doesn't sleep.

Evelyn Waugh 1903–66: *Decline and Fall* (1928)

Smoking

66 A custom . . . hateful to the nose. 99
James I

1 I have to smoke more [cigarettes] than most people—because the ones I smoke are very small and full of holes.

Beryl Bainbridge 1933– : in *Daily Telegraph* 28 February 1998

2 It has been said that cigarettes are the only product that, if used according to the manufacturer's instructions, have a very high chance of killing you.

Michael Buerk 1946– : in *Sunday Times* 11 July 1999

3 The pipe with solemn interposing puff,
Makes half a sentence at a time enough;
The dozing sages drop the drowsy strain,
Then pause, and puff—and speak, and pause again.

William Cowper 1731–1800: 'Conversation' (1782)

4 A custom loathsome to the eye, hateful to the nose, harmful to the brain, dangerous to the lungs, and in the black, stinking fume thereof, nearest resembling the horrible Stygian smoke of the pit that is bottomless.

James I 1566–1625: *A Counterblast to Tobacco* (1604)

5 This very night I am going to leave off tobacco! Surely there must be some other world in which this unconquerable purpose shall be realized.

Charles Lamb 1775–1834: letter to Thomas Manning, 26 December 1815

6 I smoked my first cigarette and kissed my first woman on the same day. I have never had time for tobacco since.

Arturo Toscanini 1867–1957: in *Observer* 30 June 1946

Snobbery ····> Class

66 Vulgarity often cuts ice which refinement scrapes at vainly. 99
Max Beerbohm

1 I am not quite a gentleman but you would hardly notice it but can't be helped anyhow.

Daisy Ashford 1881–1972: *The Young Visiters* (1919)

2 Sir Walter Elliot, of Kellynch-hall, in Somersetshire, was a man who, for his own amusement, never took up any book but the Baronetage; there he found occupation for an idle hour, and consolation in a distressed one.

Jane Austen 1775–1817: *Persuasion* (1818)

3 Vulgarity has its uses. Vulgarity often cuts ice which refinement scrapes at vainly.

Max Beerbohm 1872–1956: letter, 21 May 1921

4 Sapper, Buchan, Dornford Yates, practitioners in that school of Snobbery with Violence that runs like a thread of good-class tweed through twentieth-century literature.

Alan Bennett 1934– : *Forty Years On* (1969)

5 From Poland to polo in one generation.

Arthur Caesar d. 1953: of Darryl Zanuck; Max Wilk *The Wit and Wisdom of Hollywood* (1972)

6 Just because I have made a point of never losing my accent it doesn't mean I am an eel-and-pie yob.

Michael Caine 1933– : in *The Times* 15 April 2000 'Quotes of the Week'

7 Why cannot you go down to Bristol and see some of the third and fourth class people there, and they'll do just as well?
to Charles Dickens, who had told her of his proposed trip to America

Lady Holland 1770–1845: U. Pope-Hennessy *Charles Dickens* (1947)

8 The trouble with Michael is that he had to buy all his furniture.

Michael Jopling 1930– : of Michael Heseltine; Alan Clark diary 17 June 1987

9 *as an undergraduate Curzon requested permission to be allowed to attend a ball in London in honour of the Empress Augusta of Germany:*
I don't think much of Empresses. Good morning.

Benjamin Jowett 1817–93: Kenneth Rose *Superior Person* (1969)

10 These are the same old fogies who doffed their lids and tugged the forelock to the British establishment.

Paul Keating 1944– : of Australian Conservative supporters of Great Britain, House of Representatives, 27 February 1992

11 *the Duchess of Devonshire had called on Queen Mary to apologize for her son's marrying the dancer Adele Astaire:*
Don't worry. I have a niece called Smith.

Queen Mary 1867–1953: in *The Times* 1 June 1994; obituary of Lady May Abel Smith

12 *on being told that Clare Boothe Luce was always kind to her inferiors:*
And where does she find them?

Dorothy Parker 1893–1967: Marion Meade *What Fresh Hell is This?* (1988)

13 Whenever he met a great man he grovelled before him, and my-lorded him as only a free-born Briton can do.

William Makepeace Thackeray 1811–63: *Vanity Fair* (1847–8)

Society and Social Life ····> Parties

66 I'm a man more dined against than dining. **99**
Maurice Bowra

1 CECIL BEATON: What on earth can I become?
FRIEND: I shouldn't bother too much. Just become a friend of the Sitwells and see what happens.

Anonymous: at the outset of Cecil Beaton's career; Laurence Whistler *The Laughter and the Urn* (1985)

2 Though you would often in the fifteenth century have heard the snobbish Roman say, in a would-be off-hand tone, 'I am dining with the Borgias tonight,' no Roman ever was able to say, 'I dined last night with the Borgias.'

Max Beerbohm 1872–1956: *And Even Now* (1920)

3 Phone for the fish-knives, Norman
As Cook is a little unnerved;
You kiddies have crumpled the serviettes
And I must have things daintily served.

John Betjeman 1906–84: 'How to get on in Society' (1954)

4 Gaily into Ruislip Gardens
Runs the red electric train,
With a thousand Ta's and Pardon's
Daintily alights Elaine;
Hurries down the concrete station
With a frown of concentration,
Out into the outskirt's edges
Where a few surviving hedges
Keep alive our lost Elysium—rural Middlesex again.

John Betjeman 1906–84: 'Middlesex' (1954)

5 I'm a man more dined against than dining.

Maurice Bowra 1898–1971: John Betjeman *Summoned by Bells* (1960)

6 NINOTCHKA: Why should you carry other people's bags?
PORTER: Well, that's my business, Madame.
NINOTCHKA: That's no business. That's social injustice.
PORTER: That depends on the tip.

Charles Brackett 1892–1969 and **Billy Wilder** 1906–2002: *Ninotchka* (1939 film, with Walter Reisch)

7 Children of the Ritz,
Mentally congealed
Lilies of the Field

Noël Coward 1899–1973: 'Children of the Ritz' (1932)

We say just how we want our quails done,
And then we go and have our nails done.

8 In London, at the Café de Paris, I sang to café society; in
Las Vegas, at the Desert Inn, I sang to Nescafé society.

Noël Coward 1899–1973: Sheridan
Morley *The Quotable Noël Coward*
(1999)

9 I notice she likes lights and commotion, which goes to
show she has social instincts.

Ronald Firbank 1886–1926:
Valmouth (1919)

10 The very pink of perfection.

Oliver Goldsmith 1730–74: *She
Stoops to Conquer* (1773)

11 I'm Burlington Bertie
I rise at ten thirty and saunter along like a toff,
I walk down the Strand with my gloves on my hand,
Then I walk down again with them off.

W. F. Hargreaves 1846–1919:
'Burlington Bertie from Bow' (1915)

12 I do wish we could chat longer, but I'm having an old
friend for dinner.

Thomas Harris 1940– and **Ted Tally**
1952– : *The Silence of the Lambs*
(1991 film)

13 Already at four years of age I had begun to apprehend that
refinement was very often an extenuating virtue; one that
excused and eclipsed almost every other unappetizing trait.

Barry Humphries 1934– : *More
Please* (1992)

14 Hail him like Etonians, without a single word,
Absolutely silent and indefinitely bored.

Ronald Knox 1888–1957: 'Magister
Reformator' (1906)

15 PLEASE ACCEPT MY RESIGNATION. I DON'T WANT TO BELONG TO
ANY CLUB THAT WILL ACCEPT ME AS A MEMBER.

Groucho Marx 1895–1977: telegram;
Groucho and Me (1959)

16 You can be in the Horseguards and still be common, dear.

Terence Rattigan 1911–77: *Separate
Tables* (1954) 'Table Number Seven'

17 All decent people live beyond their incomes nowadays,
and those who aren't respectable live beyond other
peoples'.

Saki 1870–1916: *Chronicles of Clovis*
(1911)

18 MENDOZA: I am a brigand: I live by robbing the rich.
TANNER: I am a gentleman: I live by robbing the poor.

George Bernard Shaw 1856–1950:
Man and Superman (1903)

19 MRS CANDOUR: I'll swear her colour is natural—I have seen
it come and go—
LADY TEAZLE: I dare swear you have, ma'am; it goes of a
night and comes again in the morning.

Richard Brinsley Sheridan
1751–1816: *The School for Scandal*
(1777)

20 I must say I take off my hat to you, coming home with
Rembrandt place mats for your mother. It's those little
touches that lift adultery out of the moral arena and make
it a matter of style.

Tom Stoppard 1937– : *The Real
Thing* (1988 rev. ed.)

21 GERALD: I suppose society is wonderfully delightful!
LORD ILLINGWORTH: To be in it is merely a bore. But to be
out of it simply a tragedy.

Oscar Wilde 1854–1900: *A Woman
of No Importance* (1893)

22 Never speak disrespectfully of Society, Algernon. Only
people who can't get into it do that.

Oscar Wilde 1854–1900: *The
Importance of Being Earnest* (1895)

23 Yes, dear Frank [Harris], we believe you: you have dined
in every house in London, *once*.

Oscar Wilde 1854–1900: William
Rothenstein *Men and Memories*
(1931)

24 Radical Chic . . . is only radical in Style; in its heart it is
part of Society and its tradition—Politics, like Rock, Pop,
and Camp, has its uses.

Tom Wolfe 1931– : in *New York* 8
June 1970

Songs and Singing ····> Opera

66 If something is not worth saying, people sing it. **99**
Pierre-Augustin Caron de Beaumarchais

---

1 A town-and-country soprano of the kind often used for augmenting grief at a funeral.

George Ade 1866–1944: Nat Shapiro (ed.) *An Encyclopedia of Quotations about Music* (1978)

2 It is a pity that the composer did not leave directions as to how flat he really did want it sung.

Anonymous: review in *West Wilts Herald* 1893; Ned Sherrin *Cutting Edge* (1984)

3 In saloons and drab hallways
You are what I'll grab, always
Our love will be as grand
As Paul Whiteman's band
And will weigh as much as Paul weighs.
See how I dispense
Rhymes which are immense;
But do they make sense?
Not
Always.

Anonymous: a 1930s parody of Irving Berlin's 'Always' in Lorenz Hart's rhyming style; Ned Sherrin *Cutting Edge* (1984)

4 A gender bender I
A creature of illusion,
Of genital confusion,
A gorgeous butterfly.
My list of hits is long
Through every passion ranging,
To every fashion changing,
I tune my latent song.

Alistair Beaton and **Ned Sherrin** 1931–2007: a parody of Gilbert and Sullivan's 'A Wandering Minstrel I' in *The Metropolitan Mikado* (1985)

5 Today if something is not worth saying, people sing it.

Pierre-Augustin Caron de Beaumarchais 1732–99: *Le Barbier de Séville* (1775)

6 'Mr Nash, I can't hear you. Sing up!'
'How do you expect me to sing my best in this position, Sir Thomas?'
'In that position, my dear fellow, I have given some of my best performances.'

Thomas Beecham 1879–1961: to a tenor in rehearsals for *La Bohème* while lying on Mimi's bed; Ned Sherrin *Cutting Edge* (1984)

7 I was just wondering, is this the place where I'm supposed to be drowned by the waves or by the orchestra?
the tenor in The Wreckers *explaining to Sir Thomas Beecham why he had stopped*

John Coates 1865–1941: ; C. Reid *Sir Thomas Beecham* (1961)

8 In writing songs I've learned as much from Cézanne as I have from Woody Guthrie.

Bob Dylan 1941– : Clinton Heylin *Dylan: Behind the Shades* (1991)

9 Maybe the most that you can expect from a relationship that goes bad is to come out of it with a few good songs.

Marianne Faithfull 1946– : *Faithfull* (1994)

10 LEW FIELDS: Ladies don't write lyrics.
DOROTHY FIELDS: I'm no lady, I'm your daughter.
to her father

Dorothy Fields 1905–74: Caryl Brahms and Ned Sherrin *Song by Song* (1984)

11 Jerry Kern didn't write 'Ol' Man River', *my* husband did! What Kern wrote was dum-dum-*dee*-dum.

Dorothy Hammerstein: attributed, but probably apocryphal (and specifically denied in conversation with Editor)

12 *refusing to accept further changes to lyrics:*
Call me Miss Birdseye. This show is frozen!

Ethel Merman 1909–84: in *The Times* 13 July 1985

13 Clichés make the best songs. I put down every one I can find.

Bob Merrill 1921–98: in *New York Times* 19 February 1998

14 'Who wrote that song?'
'Rodgers and Hammerstein. If you can imagine it taking *two* men to write one song.'
of 'Some Enchanted Evening' (1949)

Cole Porter 1891–1964: G. Eells *The Life that Late He Led* (1967)

15 I lift up my finger and I say 'tweet tweet'.

Leslie Sarony 1897–1985: title of song (1929)

16 Tenors are usually short, stout men (except when they are Wagnerian tenors, in which case they are large, stout men) made up predominantly of lungs, rope-sized vocal chords, large frontal sinuses, thick necks, thick heads, tantrums and *amour propre* . . . It is certain that they are a race apart, a race that tends to operate reflexively rather than with due process of thought.

Harold Schonberg 1915– : in *Show* December 1961

17 All the grittiness of *The Fantastics*.

Stephen Sondheim 1930– : of one of his own lyrics; in conversation

18 By the Great Wobbly top note of Jeanette Macdonald!

Dick Vosburgh: *A Saint She Ain't* (1999)

Speeches

66 Whales only get killed when they spout. 99
Denis Thatcher

1 I do not object to people looking at their watches when I am speaking. But I strongly object when they start shaking them to make certain they are still going.

Lord Birkett 1883–1962: in *Observer* 30 October 1960

2 Ah yes, the foreign affairs debate. Dear Anthony will make the speech which dear Anthony always makes so well.
on Anthony Eden

R. A. Butler 1902–82: attributed; in *Spectator* 14 June 2003

3 ALEXANDER SMYTH: You, sir, speak for the present generation, but I speak for posterity.
HENRY CLAY: Yes, and you seem resolved to speak until the arrival of *your* audience.

Henry Clay 1777–1852: in the US Senate; Robert V. Remini *Henry Clay* (1991)

4 *opening a Red Cross bazaar at Oxford:*
Desperately accustomed as I am to public speaking.

Noël Coward 1899–1973: Dick Richards *The Wit of Noël Coward* (1968)

5 Hubert Humphrey talks so fast that listening to him is like trying to read *Playboy* magazine with your wife turning the pages.

Barry Goldwater 1909–98: attributed; Ned Sherrin *Cutting Edge* (1984)

6 Lisp: to call a spade a thpade.

Oliver Herford 1863–1935: attributed; Evan Esar and Nicolas Bentley (eds.) *The Treasury of Humorous Quotations* (1951)

7 *a 'close second' to Robert Benchley's choice of the most disagreeable combination of words in English:*
Would you care to say a few words?

Richard Ingrams 1937– : in *Observer* 29 August 2004 (see also **Words** 7)

8 I may not know much, but I know chicken shit from a chicken salad.

Lyndon Baines Johnson 1908–73: on a speech by Richard Nixon; Merle Miller *Lyndon* (1980)

9 Did you ever think that making a speech on economics is a lot like pissing down your leg? It seems hot to you, but it never does to anyone else.
to J. K. Galbraith

Lyndon Baines Johnson 1908–73: J. K. Galbraith *A Life in Our Times* (1981)

10 *on Winston Churchill at a dinner at the London School of Economics:*
He searched always to end a sentence with a climax. He looked for antithesis like a monkey looking for fleas.

Harold Laski 1893–1950: letter to Oliver Wendell Holmes, 7 May 1927

11 The most popular speaker is the one who sits down before he stands up.

John Pentland Mahaffy 1839–1919: W. B. Stanford and R. B. McDowell *Mahaffy* (1971)

12 I speak with more passion on a full bladder.
refusing an invitation to use the Gents before a broadcast

Enoch Powell 1912–98: in *The Times* 21 January 2004

13 When someone asks a question about sex in Hyde Park you double the crowd and halve the argument.

Donald Soper 1903–98: attributed, in *The Times* 23 December 1998

14 I fear I cannot make an amusing speech. I have just been reading a book which says that 'all geniuses are devoid of humour'.

Stephen Spender 1909– : speech in a debate at the Cambridge Union, January 1938

15 Nixon's farm policy is vague, but he is going a long way towards slowing the corn surplus by his speeches.

Adlai Stevenson 1900–65: Bill Adler *The Stevenson Wit* (1966)

16 Someone must fill the gap between platitudes and bayonets.

Adlai Stevenson 1900–65: Leon Harris *The Fine Art of Political Wit* (1965)

17 Whales only get killed when they spout.
declining a request to be interviewed

Denis Thatcher 1915–2003: in *The Times* 8 July 2003

18 Reading a speech with his usual sense of discovery.
of ex-President Eisenhower at the Republican convention of 1964

Gore Vidal 1925– : in *New York Review of Books* 29 September 1983

Sports and Games ····▶ Baseball, Boxing, Cricket, Football, Golf, Tennis

66 Swearing is very much part of it. 99
Jimmy Greaves

1 Well rowed, Balliol!
shouted by a member of the audience when the film Sanders of the River *was shown in Oxford in the 1930s*

Anonymous: traditional story

2 *on being asked why he did not hunt:*
I do not see why I should break my neck because a dog chooses to run after a nasty smell.

Arthur James Balfour 1848–1930: Ian Malcolm *Lord Balfour: A Memory* (1930)

3 Playing snooker gives you firm hands and helps to build up character. It is the ideal recreation for dedicated nuns.
view of the Pope's emissary, attending a sponsored snooker championship at Tyburn convent

Luigi Barbarito 1922– : in *Daily Telegraph* 15 November 1989

4 If you think squash is a competitive activity, try flower arrangement.

Alan Bennett 1934– : *Talking Heads* (1988)

5 Oh wasn't it naughty of Smudges?
Oh, Mummy, I'm sick with disgust.
She threw me in front of the Judges
And my silly old collarbone's bust.

John Betjeman 1906–84: 'Hunter Trials' (1954)

6 A man described as a 'sportsman' is generally a bookmaker who takes actresses to night clubs.

Jimmy Cannon 1910–73: in *New York Post* c.1951–54 'Nobody Asked Me, But . . . '

7 The trouble with referees is that they just don't care which side wins.
a US basketball player's view

Tom Canterbury: in *Guardian* 24 December 1980 'Sports Quotes of the Year'

8 His blade struck the water a full second before any other: the lad had started well. Nor did he flag as the race wore on . . . as the boats began to near the winning-post, his oar was dipping into the water nearly *twice* as often as any other.
often quoted as, 'All rowed fast, but none so fast as stroke'

Desmond Coke 1879–1931: *Sandford of Merton* (1903)

9 He just can't believe what isn't happening to him.

David Coleman: in *Guardian* 24 December 1980 'Sports Quotes of the Year'

10 That's the fastest time ever run—but it's not as fast as the world record.

David Coleman: Barry Fantoni (ed.) *Private Eye's Colemanballs 3* (1986)

11 Makes me want to yell from St Paul's steeple
The people I'd like to shoot are the shooting people.

Howard Dietz 1896–1983: 'By Myself' (1937)

12 The thing about sport, any sport, is that swearing is very much part of it.

Jimmy Greaves 1940– : in *Observer* 1 January 1989 'Sayings of the Year'

13 Vladimir, Vladimir, Vladimir Kuts
Nature's attempt at an engine in boots.
on the Russian runner Vladimir Kuts in 1956

A. P. Herbert 1890–1971: Ned Sherrin *Cutting Edge* (1984)

14 The only athletic sport I ever mastered was backgammon.

Douglas Jerrold 1803–57: Walter Jerrold *Douglas Jerrold* (1914)

15 We all get cut and we all get stitched up. We get stud marks down our bodies, we break bones and we lose teeth. We play rugby.

Martin Johnson 1970– : Martin Johnson *Autobiography* (2003)

16 It is very strange, and very melancholy, that the paucity of human pleasures should persuade us ever to call hunting one of them.

Samuel Johnson 1709–84: Hester Lynch Piozzi *Anecdotes of . . . Johnson* (1786)

17 I remain of the opinion that there is no game from bridge to cricket that is not improved by a little light conversation; a view which . . . is shared only by a small and unjustly despised minority.

Osbert Lancaster 1908–80: *All Done From Memory* (1953)

18 Sport is an inarticulate human expression and its
practitioners should not be blamed for being, a lot of the
time, pretty inarticulate.

Rod Liddle 1960– : in *The Times*
April 2004

19 Rodeoing is about the only sport you can't fix. You'd have
to talk to the bulls and the horses, and they wouldn't
understand you.

Bill Linderman 1922–61: in 1961;
Jonathon Green and Don Atyeo (eds.)
The Book of Sports Quotes (1979)

20 If you shout hooray for the Pennsylvania Dutchmen
Every team that they play will be carried away with a
crutch when
They're out on the field if they're wearing the shield of the
Dutchmen.

Hugh Martin and **Ralph Blane**:
'Buckle Down Winsocki' (1941)

21 I hate all sports as rabidly as a person who likes sports
hates common sense.

H. L. Mencken 1880–1956: Laurence
J. Peter (ed.) *Quotations for our Time*
(1977)

22 Sport, as I have discovered, fosters international hostility
and leads the audience, no doubt from boredom, to assault
and do grievous bodily harm while watching it.

John Mortimer 1923– : *Clinging to
the Wreckage* (1982)

23 There's been a colour clash: both teams are wearing
white.

John Motson: in 'Colemanballs'
column in *Private Eye*; Ned Sherrin
Cutting Edge (1984)

24 All winter long I am one for whom the bell is tolling
I can arouse no interest in basketball, indoor fly casting or
bowling.
The sports pages are strictly no soap
And until the cry of 'Play Ball', I mope!

Ogden Nash 1902–71: in *Sports
Illustrated* 1957

25 The sport of ski-ing consists of wearing three thousand
dollars' worth of clothes and equipment and driving two
hundred miles in the snow in order to stand around at a
bar and get drunk.

P. J. O'Rourke 1947– : *Modern
Manners* (1984)

26 Most of their discourse was about hunting, in a dialect I
understand very little.

Samuel Pepys 1633–1703: diary, 22
November 1663

27 *Goering's excuse for being late was a shooting party:*
Animals, I hope.

Eric Phipps 1875–1945: Ned Sherrin
Cutting Edge (1984); attributed

28 SHE: Are you fond of riding, dear?
Kindly tell me, if so.
HE: Yes, I'm fond of riding, dear,
But in the morning, no.

Cole Porter 1891–1964: 'But in the
Morning, No' (1939)

29 *preparing to play rugby:*
All you need to do to warm up, is sit on the bog, have a
crap and read the match programme.

Dean Richards 1963– : Martin
Johnson *Autobiography* (2003)

30 A handicapper being a character who can dope out from
the form what horses ought to win the races, and as long
as his figures turn out all right, a handicapper is spoken of
most respectfully by one and all, although of course when
he begins missing out for any length of time as
handicappers are bound to do, he is no longer spoken of
respectfully, or even as a handicapper. He is spoken of as a
bum.

Damon Runyon 1884–1946: *Take it
Easy* (1938); 'All Horse Players Die
Broke'

31 You do not keep accounts and tell everybody that you think you are all square at the end of the year. You lie and you know it.

S. J. Simon 1904–48: *Why You Lose at Bridge* (1945)

32 I can't see who's in the lead but it's either Oxford or Cambridge.

John Snagge 1904– : C. Dodd *Oxford and Cambridge Boat Race* (1983)

33 It ar'n't that I loves the fox less, but that I loves the 'ound more.

R. S. Surtees 1805–64: *Handley Cross* (1843)

34 'Unting is all that's worth living for—all time is lost wot is not spent in 'unting—it is like the hair we breathe—if we have it not we die—it's the sport of kings, the image of war without its guilt, and only five-and-twenty per cent of its danger.

R. S. Surtees 1805–64: *Handley Cross* (1843)

35 I am here to propose a toast to the sports writers. It's up to you whether you stand or not.

Freddie Trueman 1931– : Michael Parkinson *Sporting Lives* (1993)

36 I have observed in women of her type a tendency to regard all athletics as inferior forms of foxhunting.

Evelyn Waugh 1903–66: *Decline and Fall* (1928)

37 I used to think the only use for it [sport] was to give small boys something else to kick besides me.

Katharine Whitehorn 1926– : *Observations* (1970)

38 The English country gentleman galloping after a fox—the unspeakable in full pursuit of the uneatable.

Oscar Wilde 1854–1900: *A Woman of No Importance* (1893); see **The Law** 42

39 The fascination of shooting as a sport depends almost wholly on whether you are at the right or wrong end of a gun.

P. G. Wodehouse 1881–1975: attributed

40 Jogging is for people who aren't intelligent enough to watch television.

Victoria Wood 1953– : *Mens Sana in Thingummy Doodah* (1990)

Stupidity

❝ Seriousness is stupidity sent to college. **❞**
P. J. O'Rourke

1 *shouting at his whist partner:*
Ye stupid auld bitch—I beg yer pardon, mem. I mistook ye for my wife.

Lord Braxfield 1722–99: attributed; quoted in *Literary Review* November 2003

2 *to a subordinate:*
You couldn't pour piss out of a boot if the instructions were printed on the heel.

Lyndon Baines Johnson 1908–73: Robert Caro *The Years of Lyndon Johnson: Master of the Senate*

3 Seriousness is stupidity sent to college.

P. J. O'Rourke 1947– : *Give War a Chance* (1992)

4 Better to keep your mouth shut and appear stupid than to open it and remove all doubt.

Mark Twain 1835–1910: James Munson (ed.) *The Sayings of Mark Twain* (1992); attributed, perhaps apocryphal

Success ····▶ Failure

66 Whom the gods wish to destroy they first call promising. 99
Cyril Connolly

---

1 Success is the one unpardonable sin against our fellows.

Ambrose Bierce 1842–c.1914: *The Enlarged Devil's Dictionary* (1967)

2 In the end, the golden goose will be cooked.
debate on antisocial behaviour

David Blunkett 1947– : in House of Commons, 19 January 2004

3 Where did we go right?
of an unexpected success

Mel Brooks 1926– : *The Producers* (1967 film), spoken by Zero Mostel

4 Not for Clan Campbell the loser's mentality that participation is as important as winning.

Alastair Campbell 1957– : in *The Times* 24 January 2004

5 I am that twentieth-century failure, a happy undersexed celibate.

Denise Coffey: Ned Sherrin *Cutting Edge* (1984)

6 Whom the gods wish to destroy they first call promising.

Cyril Connolly 1903–74: *Enemies of Promise* (1938)

7 The trouble with fulfilling your ambitions is you think you will be transformed into some sort of archangel and you're not. You still have to wash your socks.

Louis de Bernières 1954– : in *Independent* 14 February 1999

8 I think that's just another word for a washed-up has-been.
on being an 'icon'

Bob Dylan 1941– : in *Mail on Sunday* 18 January 1998 'Quotes of the Week'

9 All the rudiments of success in life can be found in ironing a pair of trousers.

Chris Eubank 1966– : in *Independent* 6 September 2003

10 *of David Steel, Leader of the Liberal Party:*
He's passed from rising hope to elder statesman without any intervening period whatsoever.

Michael Foot 1913– : in the House of Commons, 28 March 1979

11 *formula for success:*
Rise early. Work late. Strike oil.

John Paul Getty 1892–1976: attributed

12 My son, the world is your lobster.

Leon Griffiths 1928–92: *Minder* (TV series); Nigel Rees (ed.) *Cassell Dictionary of Humorous Quotations* (1999)

13 Well, we knocked the bastard off!
on conquering Mount Everest, 1953

Edmund Hillary 1919– : *Nothing Venture, Nothing Win* (1975)

14 It is sobering to consider that when Mozart was my age he had already been dead for a year.

Tom Lehrer 1928– : N. Shapiro (ed.) *An Encyclopedia of Quotations about Music* (1978)

15 How to succeed in business without really trying.

Shepherd Mead 1914– : title of book (1952)

16 The theory seems to be that as long as a man is a failure he is one of God's children, but that as soon as he succeeds he is taken over by the Devil.

H. L. Mencken 1880–1956: *Minority Report* (1956)

17 Be nice to people on your way up because you'll meet 'em on your way down.

Wilson Mizner 1876–1933: Alva Johnston *The Legendary Mizners* (1953)

18 The world is divided into people who do things and people who get the credit. Try, if you can, to belong to the first class. There's far less competition.

Dwight Morrow 1873–1931: letter to his son; Harold Nicolson *Dwight Morrow* (1935)

19 David Frost has risen without trace.

Kitty Muggeridge 1903–94: said c.1965 to Malcolm Muggeridge

20 It is difficult to soar like an eagle when you are surrounded by turkeys.
  words embroidered on a cushion for her husband John Osborne

Helen Osborne 1939–2004: in *Daily Telegraph* 14 January 2004

21 She regretted that Fate had not seen its way to reserve for her some of the ampler successes for which she felt herself well qualified.

Saki 1870–1916: *The Toys of Peace* (1919)

22 I never climbed any ladder: I have achieved eminence by sheer gravitation.

George Bernard Shaw 1856–1950: preface to *The Irrational Knot* (1905)

23 People who reach the top of the tree are only those who haven't got the qualifications to detain them at the bottom.

Peter Ustinov 1921–2004: interview with David Frost in 1969

24 Whenever a friend succeeds, a little something in me dies.

Gore Vidal 1925– : in *Sunday Times Magazine* 16 September 1973

25 Moderation is a fatal thing, Lady Hunstanton. Nothing succeeds like excess.

Oscar Wilde 1854–1900: *A Woman of No Importance* (1893)

26 Success is a science; if you have the conditions, you get the result.

Oscar Wilde 1854–1900: letter ?March–April 1883

27 *to the actor Victor Spinetti:*
Ah, Victor, still struggling to keep your head below water.

Emlyn Williams 1905–87: attributed; Ned Sherrin *Cutting Edge* (1984)

Taxes

66 Logic and taxation are not always the best of friends. **99**
James C. McReynolds

1 Tax collectors who'll never know the invigorating joys of treading water in the deep end without a life belt.

Jeffrey Bernard 1932–97: in *The Spectator* 3 March 1984

2 It was as true . . . as taxes is. And nothing's truer than them.

Charles Dickens 1812–70: *David Copperfield* (1850)

3 The collection of a lunatic and inequitable tax, however few the victims, must tend to breed an un-English dislike of taxation in general.

A. P. Herbert 1890–1971: *Misleading Cases* (1935)

4 *Excise.* A hateful tax levied upon commodities.

Samuel Johnson 1709–84: *A Dictionary of the English Language* (1755)

5 Logic and taxation are not always the best of friends.

James C. McReynolds 1862–1946: concurring in *Sonneborn Bros. v. Cureton* 1923

6 I'm up to my neck in the real world, every day. Just you try doing your VAT return with a head full of goblins.

Terry Pratchett 1948– : in *Sunday Times* 27 February 2000 'Talking Heads'

7 Income Tax has made more Liars out of the American people than Golf.

Will Rogers 1879–1935: *The Illiterate Digest* (1924) 'Helping the Girls with their Income Taxes'

8 What is the difference between a taxidermist and a tax collector? The taxidermist takes only your skin.

Mark Twain 1835–1910: *Notebook* 30 December 1902

Technology ····> Progress, Science

66 The first rule of intelligent tinkering is to save all the parts. 99
Paul Ralph Ehrlich

1 When man wanted to make a machine that would walk he created the wheel, which does not resemble a leg,

Guillaume Apollinaire 1880–1918: *Les Mamelles de Tirésias* (1918)

2 Inanimate objects are classified scientifically into three major categories—those that don't work, those that break down, and those that get lost.

Russell Baker 1925– : in *New York Times* 18 June 1968

3 Electric typewriters keep going 'mmmmmmm—what are you waiting for?'

Anthony Burgess 1917–93: Clare Boylan (ed.) *The Agony and the Ego* (1993)

4 The first rule of intelligent tinkering is to save all the parts.

Paul Ralph Ehrlich 1932– : in *Saturday Review* 5 June 1971

5 Why sir, there is every possibility that you will soon be able to tax it!
to Gladstone, when asked about the usefulness of electricity

Michael Faraday 1791–1867: W. E. H. Lecky *Democracy and Liberty* (1899 ed.)

6 For a successful technology, reality must take precedence over public relations, for nature cannot be fooled.

Richard Phillips Feynman 1918–88: Appendix to the *Rogers Commission Report on the Space Shuttle Challenger Accident* 6 June 1986

7 Technology . . . the knack of so arranging the world that we need not experience it.

Max Frisch 1911–91: *Homo Faber* (1957)

8 The itemised phone bill ranks up there with suspender belts, Sky Sports Channels and Loaded magazine as inventions women could do without.

Maeve Haran 1932– : in *Mail on Sunday* 25 April 1999

9 The thing with high-tech is that you always end up using scissors.

David Hockney 1937– : in *Observer* 10 July 1994 'Sayings of the Week'

10 Take up car maintenance and find the class is full of other thirty-something women like me, looking for a fella.

Marian Keyes: 'Late Opening at the Last Chance Saloon' (1997)

11 When the inventor of the drawing board messed things up, what did he go back to?

Bob Monkhouse 1928–2003: attributed; in *Guardian* 29 December 2003 (online edition)

12 Dr Strabismus (Whom God Preserve) of Utrecht has patented a new invention. It is an illuminated trouser-clip for bicyclists who are using main roads at night.

J. B. Morton 1893–1975: *Morton's Folly* (1933)

13 Father had a secret of making inanimate objects appear to possess malevolent life of their own, and sometimes it was hard to believe that his tools and materials were not really in a conspiracy against him.

Frank O'Connor 1903–66: *An Only Child* (1961)

14 The photographer is like the cod which produces a million eggs in order that one may reach maturity.

George Bernard Shaw 1856–1950: introduction to the catalogue for Alvin Langdon Coburn's exhibition at the Royal Photographic Society, 1906

15 He put this engine [a watch] to our ears, which made an incessant noise like that of a water-mill; and we conjecture it is either some unknown animal, or the god that he worships; but we are more inclined to the latter opinion.

Jonathan Swift 1667–1745: *Gulliver's Travels* (1726)

16 JACKIE: (*very slowly*) Take Tube A and apply to Bracket D.
VICTORIA: Reading it slower does not make it any easier to do.

Victoria Wood 1953– : *Mens Sana in Thingummy Doodah* (1990)

Telegrams

66 Am in Market Harborough. Where ought I to be? **99**
G. K. Chesterton

1 Along the electric wire the message came:
He is not better—he is much the same.

Anonymous: parodic poem on the illness of the Prince of Wales, later King Edward VII, in F. H. Gribble *Romance of the Cambridge Colleges* (1913); sometimes attributed to Alfred Austin (1835–1913), Poet Laureate

2 *as a young* Times *correspondent in America, Claud Cockburn received a telegram authorizing him to report a murder in Al Capone's Chicago:*
BY ALL MEANS COCKBURN CHICAGOWARDS. WELCOME STORIES EX-CHICAGO NOT UNDULY EMPHASISING CRIME.

Anonymous: Claud Cockburn *In Time of Trouble* (1956)

3 *telegraph message on arriving in Venice:*
STREETS FLOODED. PLEASE ADVISE.

Robert Benchley 1889–1945: R. E. Drennan *Wit's End* (1973)

4 HOW DARE YOU BECOME PRIME MINISTER WHEN I'M AWAY GREAT LOVE CONSTANT THOUGHT VIOLET.
to her father, H. H. Asquith, 7 April 1908

Violet Bonham Carter 1887–1969: Mark Bonham Carter and Mark Pottle (eds.) *Lantern Slides* (1996)

5 *to Irving Thalberg on the birth of his son:*
CONGRATULATIONS ON YOUR LATEST PRODUCTION. AM SURE IT WILL LOOK BETTER AFTER IT'S BEEN CUT.

Eddie Cantor 1892–1964: Max Wilk *The Wit and Wisdom of Hollywood* (1972)

6 *appeal to his wife:*
AM IN MARKET HARBOROUGH. WHERE OUGHT I TO BE?

G. K. Chesterton 1874–1936: *Autobiography* (1936)

7 Dear Mrs A.,
Hooray, hooray,
At last you are deflowered.
On this as every other day
I love you—Noel Coward.

Noël Coward 1899–1973: telegram to Gertrude Lawrence, 5 July 1940 (the day after her wedding)

8 HAVE MOVED HOTEL EXCELSIOR COUGHING MYSELF INTO A FIRENZE.

Noël Coward 1899–1973: telegram from Florence; Angus McGill and Kenneth Thomson *Live Wires* (1982)

9 LEGITIMATE AT LAST WONT MOTHER BE PLEASED.
on Gertrude Lawrence's first straight role

Noël Coward 1899–1973: Sheridan Morley *A Talent to Amuse* (1969)

10 *sent to his partner Jack Wilson in New York in 1938 as the threat of war increased:*
GRAVE POSSIBILITY WAR WITHIN FEW WEEKS OR DAYS MORE IF THIS HAPPENS POSTPONEMENT REVUE INEVITABLE AND ANNIHILATION ALL OF US PROBABLE.

Noël Coward 1899–1973: Sheridan Morley *A Talent to Amuse* (1969)

11 *despite the threat of war, arrangements for the revue* Set to Music *went ahead:*
SUGGEST YOU ENGAGE EIGHT REALLY BEAUTIFUL SHOWGIRLS MORE OR LESS SAME HEIGHT NO REAL TALENT REQUIRED.

Noël Coward 1899–1973: telegram to Jack Wilson; Sheridan Morley *A Talent to Amuse* (1969)

12 *in 1916 Norman Douglas had slipped bail on a charge of an indecent offence with a young man. He returned twenty-five years later, sending this telegram to a friend:*
FEEL LIKE A BOY AGAIN.

Norman Douglas 1868–1952: Angus McGill and Kenneth Thomson *Live Wires* (1982)

13 *sent by a cricket-playing coroner, W. G. Grace's elder brother, to postpone an inquest:*
PUT CORPSE ON ICE TILL CLOSE OF PLAY.

E. M. Grace d. 1911: A. A. Thomson *The Great Cricketer* (1957); perhaps apocryphal

14 *response to a telegraphic enquiry,* HOW OLD CARY GRANT?:
OLD CARY GRANT FINE. HOW YOU?

Cary Grant 1904–86: R. Schickel *Cary Grant* (1983)

15 LAST SUPPER AND ORIGINAL CAST COULDN'T DRAW IN THIS HOUSE.
telegram to his father during a bad week with a stock company

George S. Kaufman 1889–1961: Angus McGill and Kenneth Thomson *Live Wires* (1982)

16 *Carl Laemmle Jr. had sent a telegram to his father,* PLEASE WIRE MORE MONEY AM TALKING TO FRENCH COUNT RE MOVIE: NO MONEY TILL YOU LEARN TO SPELL.

Carl Laemmle 1867–1939: Angus McGill and Kenneth Thomson *Live Wires* (1982)

17 *an estate agent in Bermuda told her that the house she was considering came with a maid, a secretary, and a chauffeur:*
AIRMAIL PHOTOGRAPH OF CHAUFFEUR.

Beatrice Lillie 1894–1989: Angus McGill and Kenneth Thomson *Live Wires* (1982)

18 *telegram to Mrs Sherwood on the arrival of her baby:*
GOOD WORK, MARY. WE ALL KNEW YOU HAD IT IN YOU.

Dorothy Parker 1893–1967: Alexander Woollcott *While Rome Burns* (1934)

19 *to a couple who had married after living together:*
WHAT'S NEW?

Dorothy Parker 1893–1967: S. T. Brownlow (ed.) *The Sayings of Dorothy Parker* (1992)

20 *cables were soon arriving . . . 'Require earliest name life story photograph American nurse upblown Adowa.' We replied:*
NURSE UNUPBLOWN.

Evelyn Waugh 1903–66: *Waugh in Abyssinia* (1936)

21 FEAR I MAY NOT BE ABLE TO REACH YOU IN TIME FOR THE CEREMONY. DON'T WAIT.
telegram of apology for missing Oscar Wilde's wedding

James McNeill Whistler 1834–1903: E. J. and R. Pennell *The Life of James McNeill Whistler* (1908)

22 *his wife had requested him, when in Paris, to buy and send her a bidet:*
UNABLE OBTAIN BIDET. SUGGEST HANDSTAND IN SHOWER.

Billy Wilder 1906–2002: Leslie Halliwell *Filmgoer's Book of Quotes* (1973)

23 At this point in the proceedings there was another ring at the front door. Jeeves shimmered out and came back with a telegram.

P. G. Wodehouse 1881–1975: *Carry On, Jeeves!* (1925)

24 I HAVE BEEN LOOKING AROUND FOR AN APPROPRIATE WOODEN GIFT AND AM PLEASED HEREBY TO PRESENT YOU WITH ELSIE FERGUSON'S PERFORMANCE IN HER NEW PLAY.

Alexander Woollcott 1887–1943: congratulatory telegram for George S. Kaufman's fifth wedding anniversary; Howard Teichmann *George S. Kaufman* (1973)

Television ····➤ Broadcasting

ff The word is half Greek, half Latin. No good can come of it. 🟊🟊
C. P. Scott

1 TV—a clever contraction derived from the words Terrible Vaudeville . . . we call it a medium because nothing's well done.

Goodman Ace 1899–1982: letter to Groucho Marx, *c.*1953

2 The best that can be said for Norwegian television is that it gives you the sensation of a coma without the worry and inconvenience.

Bill Bryson 1951– : *Neither Here Nor There* (1991)

3 Television is more interesting than people. If it were not, we should have people standing in the corners of our rooms.

Alan Coren 1938–2007: attributed; in *The Penguin Dictionary of Twentieth-Century Quotations* (1993)

4 Television is for appearing on, not looking at.

Noël Coward 1899–1973: Dick Richards *The Wit of Noël Coward* (1968)

5 There was never sex in Ireland before television.

Oliver J. Flanagan 1920–87: *c.*1965, attributed

6 *returning to a Saturday-night slot with* Come Dancing:
I've always felt that on Saturday nights there is a kinder audience. That's probably because they're drunk.

Bruce Forsyth 1928– : in *BBC News* (online edition) 21 April 2004

7 Being taken no notice of in 10 million homes.
   of appearing on television

David Hare 1947– : *Amy's View* (1997)

8 It's television, you see. If you are not on the thing every week, the public think you are either dead or deported.

Frankie Howerd 1922–92: attributed

9 Television is simultaneously blamed, often by the same people, for worsening the world and for being powerless to change it.

Clive James 1939– : *Glued to the Box* (1981); introduction

10 *Television?* The word is half Greek, half Latin. No good can come of it.

C. P. Scott 1846–1932: view of the editor of the *Manchester Guardian*; Asa Briggs *The BBC: the First Fifty Years* (1985)

11 I didn't create Alf Garnett. Society did. I just grassed on him.

Johnny Speight 1920–1998: in *Mail on Sunday* 27 December 1998 'Quotes of the Year'

12 My show is the stupidest show on TV. If you are watching it, get a life.

Jerry Springer 1944– : in *Independent on Sunday* 7 March 1999

13 It always makes me laugh when people ask why anyone would want to do a sitcom in America. If it runs five years, you never have to work again.

Twiggy 1949– : in *Independent* 4 October 1997 'Quote Unquote'

14 Never miss a chance to have sex or appear on television.

Gore Vidal 1925– : attributed; Bob Chieger *Was It Good For You Too?* (1983)

15 *of television:*
It used to be that we in films were the lowest form of art. Now we have something to look down on.

Billy Wilder 1906–2002: A. Madsen *Billy Wilder* (1968)

16 You know daytime television? You know what it's supposed to be for? It's to keep unemployed people happy. It's supposed to stop them running to the social security demanding mad luxuries like cookers and windows.

Victoria Wood 1953– : *Mens Sana in Thingummy Doodah* (1990)

Tennis

66 You cannot be serious! 99
John McEnroe

1 In other sports, the lateral euphemism is still in its infancy (at Wimbledon, for example, they have only just realized that 'perfectionist' can be used to represent 'extremely bad-tempered'). In soccer, the form of the encoded adjective is well developed. 'Tenacious', for example, always means 'small'.

Julian Barnes 1946– : in *Observer* 4 July 1982

2 Miss J. Hunter Dunn, Miss J. Hunter Dunn,
Furnish'd and burnish'd by Aldershot sun,
What strenuous singles we played after tea,
We in the tournament—you against me.
Love-thirty, love-forty, oh! weakness of joy,
The speed of a swallow, the grace of a boy,
With carefullest carelessness, gaily you won,
I am weak from your loveliness, Joan Hunter Dunn.

John Betjeman 1906–84: 'A Subaltern's Love-Song' (1945)

3 No one is more sensitive about his game than a weekend tennis player.

Jimmy Cannon 1910–73: in *New York Post* c.1955 'Nobody Asked Me, But . . . '

4 I call tennis the McDonald's of sport—you go in, they make a quick buck out of you, and you're out.

Pat Cash 1965– : in *Independent on Sunday* 4 July 1999

5 New Yorkers love it when you spill your guts out there. Spill your guts at Wimbledon and they make you stop and clean it up.

Jimmy Connors 1952– : at Flushing Meadow; in *Guardian* 24 December 1984 'Sports Quotes of the Year'

6 You cannot be serious!

John McEnroe 1959– : said to tennis umpire at Wimbledon, early 1980s

7 I threw the kitchen sink at him, but he went to the bathroom and got his tub.
defeated by Roger Federer in the Wimbledon Final, 2004

Andy Roddick 1982: interview (BBC1), 4 July 2004

8 All gong and no dinner . . . we just wish Anna would finally win something aside from hearts.
of the Russian tennis star Anna Kournikova at Wimbledon 2000

Tim Sheridan: 'The Word from Wimbledon' (online report) 10 July 2000

The Theatre ····▸ Acting, Actors

❝ A play wot I wrote. ❞
Eddie Braben

1 Welcome to the Theatre,
To the magic, to the fun!
Where painted trees and flowers grow,
And laughter rings fortissimo,
And treachery's sweetly done.

Lee Adams: 'Welcome to the Theatre' (1970)

2 Shaw's plays are the price we pay for Shaw's prefaces.

James Agate 1877–1947: diary 10 March 1933

3 Why don't actors look out of the window in the morning? Because then they'd have nothing to do in the afternoon.
old theatre joke

Anonymous: Michael Simkins *What's My Motivation?* (2004)

4 STUDENT: Did Hamlet actually have an affair with Ophelia?
ACTOR-MANAGER: In our company, always.

Anonymous: Cedric Hardwicke *A Victorian in Orbit* (1961)

5 There is less in this than meets the eye.

Tallulah Bankhead 1903–68: of a revival of Maeterlinck's play 'Aglavaine and Selysette'; Alexander Woollcott *Shouts and Murmurs* (1922)

6 This [*Oh, Calcutta!*] is the kind of show to give pornography a dirty name.

Clive Barnes 1927– : in *New York Times* 18 June 1969

7 God, send me some good actors. Cheap

Lilian Baylis 1874–1937: Sybil Thorndike *Lilian Baylis* (1938)

8 Enter Michael Angelo. Andrea del Sarto appears for a moment at a window. Pippa passes.

Max Beerbohm 1872–1956: *Seven Men* (1919)

9 *on being asked 'What was the message of your play' after a performance of* The Hostage:
Message? Message? What the hell do you think I am, a bloody postman?

Brendan Behan 1923–64: Dominic Behan *My Brother Brendan* (1965)

10 ANONYMOUS: Why did you go on stage?
MICHAEL BLAKEMORE: To get out of the audience.

Michael Blakemore 1928– : attributed; in *The Times* 29 December 2003

11 A play wot I wrote.

Eddie Braben: spoken by Ernie Wise; Gary Morecambe and Martin Stirling *Behind the Sunshine* (1994)

12 *on hearing the Cockney playwright Henry Arthur Jones reading his play* Michael and his Lost Angel (*1896*):
But it's so *long*, Mr. Jones—even *without* the *h*'s.

Mrs Patrick Campbell 1865–1940: Margot Peters *Mrs Pat* (1984)

13 *of Lionel Bart's musical* Blitz:
Just as long as the real thing and twice as noisy.

Noël Coward 1899–1973: Sheridan Morley *The Quotable Noël Coward* (1999)

14 Stop being gallant
And don't be such a bore,
Pack up your talent,
There's always plenty more
And if you lose hope
Take dope
And lock yourself in the John,
Why must the show go on?

Noël Coward 1899–1973: 'Why Must the Show Go On?' (1955)

15 It's about as long as *Parsifal*, and not as funny.

Noël Coward 1899–1973. on *Camelot*; Dick Richards *The Wit of Noël Coward* (1968)

16 Shut up, Arnold, or I'll direct this play the way you wrote it!

John Dexter: to the playwright Arnold Wesker; in *Ned Sherrin in his Anecdotage* (1993)

17 The plot can be hot—simply teeming with sex,
A gay divorcee who is after her ex.
It could be Oedipus Rex,
Where a chap kills his father
And causes a lot of bother.
The clerk
Who is thrown out of work
By the boss
Who is thrown for a loss
By the skirt
Who is doing him dirt.
The world is a stage
The stage is a world of entertainment.

Howard Dietz 1896–1983: 'That's Entertainment' (1953)

18 Ridiculous farces worthy of Canadian savages.
of Shakespeare's plays

Frederick the Great 1712–86: Giles MacDonogh *Frederick the Great* (1999)

19 Prologues precede the piece—in mournful verse;
As undertakers—walk before the hearse.

David Garrick 1717–79: prologue to Arthur Murphy's *The Apprentice* (1756)

20 Applause, applause!
Vociferous applause
From orchestra to gallery
Could mean a raise in salary.
Give out, give in!—
Be noisy, make a din!
(The manager, he audits our plaudits.)

Ira Gershwin 1896–1983: 'Applause, Applause' (1953)

21 *a Broadway producer after a play about Napoleon had failed:* Never, never, will I do another play where a guy writes with a feather.

Max Gordon: attributed by Arthur Miller; in *Ned Sherrin's Theatrical Anecdotes* (1991)

22 I have knocked everything but the knees of the chorus girls, and nature has anticipated me there.

Percy Hammond: Ned Sherrin *Cutting Edge* (1984)

23 If any play has been produced only twice in three hundred years, there must be some good reason for it.

Rupert Hart-Davis 1907–99: letter to George Lyttelton, 7 July 1957

24 The difficulty about a theatre job is that it interferes with party-going.

Barry Humphries 1934– : *More Please* (1992)

25 I'll come no more behind your scenes, David; for the silk stockings and white bosoms of your actresses excite my amorous propensities.

Samuel Johnson 1709–84: James Boswell *Life of Samuel Johnson* (1791) 1750; John Wilkes recalls the remark [to Garrick] in the form: 'the silk stockings and white bosoms of your actresses do make my genitals to quiver'

26 For so many people, going to the theatre is just a little bit of a nuisance. When going out to have a good old laugh gets worthy, the writing is on the wall.

Griff Rhys Jones 1953– : in *Daily Telegraph* 22 January 1994

27 Mixed notices—they were good and rotten.
after sharing a flop, The Channel Road *(1929), with Alexander Woollcott*

George S. Kaufman 1889–1961: Howard Teichmann *George S. Kaufman* (1973)

28 I thought I heard one of the original lines of the show.
of the Marx Brothers' ad-libbing

George S. Kaufman 1889–1961: Howard Teichmann *George S. Kaufman* (1973)

29 There was laughter in the back of the theatre, leading to the belief that someone was telling jokes back there.

George S. Kaufman 1889–1961: Howard Teichmann *George S. Kaufman* (1973)

30 Well, Marc, there's only one thing we can do. We've got to call the audience in tomorrow morning for a ten o'clock rehearsal.
to convince Marc Connelly that a line would not work

George S. Kaufman 1889–1961: Howard Teichmann *George S. Kaufman* (1973)

31 Satire is what closes Saturday night.

George S. Kaufman 1889–1961: Scott Meredith *George S. Kaufman and his Friends* (1974)

32 Murder was one thing Hamlet sure did enjoy.
He was, how shall I say, quite a mischievious boy;
And the moral of this story was very, very plain;
You'd better get a mussle if you've got a great Dane!

Frank Loesser 1910–69: 'Hamlet' (1949)

33 I didn't like the play, but then I saw it under adverse conditions—the curtain was up.

Groucho Marx 1895–1977: ad-lib, attributed in an interview by Marx to George S. Kaufman; Peter Hay *Broadway Anecdotes* (1989)

34 Don't clap too hard—it's a very old building.

John Osborne 1929– : *The Entertainer* (1957)

35 In fact, now that you've got me right down to it, the only thing I didn't like about *The Barretts of Wimpole Street* was the play.

Dorothy Parker 1893–1967: review in *New Yorker* 21 February 1931

36 *House Beautiful* is play lousy.

Dorothy Parker 1893–1967: review in *New Yorker* 1933

37 'Ah,' I said to myself, for I love a responsive audience, 'so it's one of those plays.'

Dorothy Parker 1893–1967: review of A. A. Milne's *Give Me Yesterday* in *New Yorker* 14 March 1931

38 There still remains, to mortify a wit,
The many-headed monster of the pit.

Alexander Pope 1688–1744: *Imitations of Horace* (1737)

39 Another pain where the ulcers grow,
Another op'nin' of another show.

Cole Porter 1891–1964: 'Another Op'nin', Another Show' (1948)

40 We open in Venice,
We next play Verona,
Then on to Cremona,
Lotsa laughs in Cremona.

Cole Porter 1891–1964: 'We Open in Venice' (1948)

41 Brush up your Shakespeare,
Start quoting him now.
Brush up your Shakespeare
And the women you will wow . . .
If she says your behaviour is heinous
Kick her right in the 'Coriolanus'.
Brush up your Shakespeare
And they'll all kowtow.

Cole Porter 1891–1964: 'Brush Up your Shakespeare' (1948)

42 It is better to have written a damned play, than no play at all—it snatches a man from obscurity.

Frederic Reynolds 1764–1841: *The Dramatist* (1789)

43 You've got to perform in a role hundreds of times. In keeping it fresh one can become a large, madly humming, demented refrigerator.

Ralph Richardson 1902–83: in *Time* 21 August 1978

44 The most lamentable comedy, and most cruel death of Pyramus and Thisby.

William Shakespeare 1564–1616: *A Midsummer Night's Dream* (1595–6)

45 *Exit, pursued by a bear.*

William Shakespeare 1564–1616: stage direction in *The Winter's Tale* (1610–11)

46 You don't expect me to know what to say about a play when I don't know who the author is, do you?

George Bernard Shaw 1856–1950: *Fanny's First Play* (1914)

47 My intention is to do to the play what Hamlet himself longed to do to his mother.

Arthur Smith 1954– : *Arthur Smith's Hamlet*

48 Something appealing,
Something appalling,
Something for everyone:
A comedy tonight!

Stephen Sondheim 1930– : 'Comedy Tonight' (1962)

49 It's pure theatrical Viagra.
on The Blue Room, *starring Nicole Kidman*

Charles Spencer 1955– : in *Daily Telegraph* 24 September 1999

50 I can do you blood and love without the rhetoric, and I can do you blood and rhetoric without the love, and I can do you all three concurrent or consecutive, but I can't do you love and rhetoric without the blood. Blood is compulsory—they're all blood, you see.

Tom Stoppard 1937– : *Rosencrantz and Guildenstern are Dead* (1967)

51 To sum up: your father, whom you love, dies, you are his heir, you come back to find that hardly was the corpse cold before his young brother popped onto his throne and into his sheets, thereby offending both legal and natural practice. Now why exactly are you behaving in this extraordinary manner?

Tom Stoppard 1937– : *Rosencrantz and Guildenstern Are Dead* (1967)

52 *Moby Dick* nearly became the tragedy of a man who could not make up his nose.
on Welles's production of Moby Dick *in 1955, when his false nose fell off on the first night, alluding to the publicity for Olivier's* Hamlet *as 'the tragedy of a man who could not make up his mind'*

Kenneth Tynan 1927–80: *A View of the English Stage* (1975)

53 I've never much enjoyed going to plays . . . The unreality of painted people standing on a platform saying things they've said to each other for months is more than I can overlook.

John Updike 1932– : George Plimpton (ed.) *Writers at Work* 4th Series (1977)

54 In the old days, you went from ingenue to old bag with a long stretch of unemployment in between.

Julie Walters 1950– : in *Sunday Times* 26 May 2002

55 When you think about it, what other playwrights are there besides O'Neill, Tennessee and me?

Mae West 1892–1980: G. Eells and S. Musgrove *Mae West* (1989)

56 The play was a great success, but the audience was a total failure.

Oscar Wilde 1854–1900: after the first performance of *Lady Windermere's Fan*; Peter Hay *Theatrical Anecdotes* (1987)

57 *on Irving's revival of* Macbeth *at the Lyceum, with Ellen Terry as Lady Macbeth:*
Judging from the banquet, Lady Macbeth seems an economical housekeeper and evidently patronises local industries for her husband's clothes and the servants' liveries, but she takes care to do all her shopping in Byzantium.

Oscar Wilde 1854–1900: Rupert Hart-Davis (ed.) *The Letters of Oscar Wilde* (1962)

58 *the impresario Binkie Beaumont had been greatly impressed by* The Wind of Heaven *(1945):*
BEAUMONT: I've read your new play, Emlyn, and I like it twice as much as your last.
WILLIAMS: Does that mean you're going to pay me twice my usual royalties?

Emlyn Williams 1905–87: James Harding *Emlyn Williams* (1987)

59 *on the Company of Four's poorly attended revival of his play* Spring 1600 *in 1945:*
The Lyric housed the Company of Four and the Audience of Two.

Emlyn Williams 1905–87: James Harding *Emlyn Williams* (1987)

Time

❝Life is too short to stuff a mushroom.❞
Shirley Conran

1 *on receiving an invitation for 9 a.m.:*
Oh, are there two nine o'clocks in the day?

Tallulah Bankhead 1903–68: attributed, perhaps apocryphal

2 *to an effusive greeting 'I haven't seen you for 41 years':*
I thought I told you to wait in the car.

Tallulah Bankhead 1903–68: attributed; Nigel Rees *Cassell Dictionary of Humorous Quotations* (1999)

3 VLADIMIR: That passed the time.
ESTRAGON: It would have passed in any case.
VLADIMIR: Yes, but not so rapidly.

Samuel Beckett 1906–89: *Waiting for Godot* (1955)

4 I am a sundial, and I make a botch
Of what is done much better by a watch.

Hilaire Belloc 1870–1953: 'On a Sundial' (1938)

5 *arriving at Dublin Castle for the handover by British forces on 16 January 1922, and being told that he was seven minutes late:*
We've been waiting 700 years, you can have the seven minutes.

Michael Collins 1880–1922: Tim Pat Coogan *Michael Collins* (1990); attributed, perhaps apocryphal

6 Life is too short to stuff a mushroom.

Shirley Conran 1932– : *Superwoman* (1975)

7 There was a pause—just long enough for an angel to pass, flying slowly.

Ronald Firbank 1886–1926: *Vainglory* (1915)

8 I'll be with you in the squeezing of a lemon.

Oliver Goldsmith 1730–74: *She Stoops to Conquer* (1773)

9 We have passed a lot of water since then.

Sam Goldwyn 1882–1974: E. Goodman *The Fifty Year Decline of Hollywood* (1961); attributed, possibly apocryphal

10 Time spent on any item of the agenda will be in inverse proportion to the sum involved.

C. Northcote Parkinson 1909–93: *Parkinson's Law* (1958)

11 Wherever I travel I'm too late. The orgy has moved elsewhere.

Mordecai Richler 1931–2001: *Shovelling Trouble* (1972) 'A Sense of the Ridiculous'

12 Perpetual sunset
Is rather an unsettling thing.

Stephen Sondheim 1930– : 'The Sun Won't Set' in *A Little Night Music* (1973)

13 Eternity's a terrible thought. I mean, where's it all going to end?

Tom Stoppard 1937– : *Rosencrantz and Guildenstern are Dead* (1967)

14 *to a man in the street, carrying a grandfather clock:*
My poor fellow, why not carry a watch?

Herbert Beerbohm Tree 1852–1917: Hesketh Pearson *Beerbohm Tree* (1956)

Titles

66 No stronger craving in the world than that of the rich for titles. 99
Hesketh Pearson

1 Your official signature 'Archibald the Arctic' is the most romantic signature in the world and just one point ahead of 'William of Argyll and the Isles'.
to first Bishop of the Arctic, 1937

John Buchan 1875–1940: Archibald Lang Fleming *Archibald the Arctic* (1957)

2 Hit me with your Rhythm Stick.

Ian Dury 1942–2000: song title (1978)

3 *leading title on the autumn list of 'a new publishing house that would be sure to fail':*
Canada, Our Good Neighbour to the North.

Robert Gottlieb: in *Ned Sherrin in his Anecdotage* (1993)

4 *alleged response to being addressed as 'Mr Kingsley' rather than 'Sir Ben' on the set of his new film:*
It's a small word. It's not long. And it's not difficult to remember.

Ben Kingsley 1943– : attributed; in *The Times* 17 June 2003

5 Rum, Bum and Concertina.

George Melly 1926–2007: title of autobiography (1977)

6 There is no stronger craving in the world than that of the rich for titles, except perhaps that of the titled for riches.

Hesketh Pearson 1887–1964: *The Pilgrim Daughters* (1961)

7 If you are called Wayne or you say 'serviette' instead of 'napkin', it's unlikely you've got a title.

Meera Syal 1963– : in *Independent* 21 July 2001

8 *bestseller on punctuation named from the story of a panda which took exception to a badly punctuated dictionary entry:*
Eats, shoots and leaves.

Lynne Truss: book title, 2003

9 *title for a language-monitoring organization:*
Association for the Annihilation of the Aberrant Apostrophe.

Keith Waterhouse 1929– : in *Daily Mail* 22 February 1988

Tolerance ····▸ Prejudice and Tolerance

Towns and Cities ····▸ New York

❝ I went to Philadelphia, but it was closed. ❞
W. C. Fields

1 God made the harbour, and that's all right, but Satan made Sydney.

Anonymous: unnamed Sydney citizen; Mark Twain *More Tramps Abroad* (1897)

2 New York is big but this is Biggar.

Anonymous: slogan for the town of Biggar in Saskatchewan

3 Toronto the Good.
ironic nickname used by 'hilarious drunks'

Anonymous: Robert Thomas Allen *When Toronto was for Kids* (1961)

4 One has no great hopes from Birmingham. I always say there is something direful in the sound.

Jane Austen 1775–1817: *Emma* (1816)

5 Come, friendly bombs, and fall on Slough!
It isn't fit for humans now.

John Betjeman 1906–84: 'Slough' (1937)

6 And this is good old Boston,
The home of the bean and the cod,
Where the Lowells talk to the Cabots
And the Cabots talk only to God.

John Collins Bossidy 1860–1928: verse spoken at Holy Cross College alumni dinner in Boston, Massachusetts, 1910

7 A big hard-boiled city with no more personality than a paper cup.

Raymond Chandler 1888–1959: *The Little Sister* (1949)

8 People don't talk in Paris; they just look lovely . . . and eat.

Chips Channon 1897–1958: diary 22 May 1951

9 For some guys
The dream is Paris,
But I found a shrine
Where Hollywood Boulevard crosses Vine.

Ervin Drake: 'My Hometown' (1964)

10 Last week, I went to Philadelphia, but it was closed.

W. C. Fields 1880–1946: Richard J. Anobile *Godfrey Daniels* (1975); attributed

11 The people of Berlin are doing very exciting things with their city at the moment. Basically they had this idea of just knocking it through.

Stephen Fry 1957– and **Hugh Laurie**: *A Bit More Fry and Laurie* (1991)

12 Cities are above
The quarrels that were hapless.
Look who's making love:
St Paul and Minneap'lis!

Ira Gershwin 1896–1983: 'Love is Sweeping the Country' (1931)

13 I met him in Boston
In the native quarter.
He was from Harvard
Just across the border.

Sheldon Harnick 1924– : 'The Boston Beguine' (1952)

14 Try Manchester after midnight and you'll think you've walked into the Book of Revelations.

Howard Jacobson: *The Mighty Waltzer* (1999)

15 When a man is tired of London, he is tired of life; for there is in London all that life can afford.

Samuel Johnson 1709–84: James Boswell *Life of Samuel Johnson* (1791) 20 September 1777

16 Fleet-street has a very animated appearance; but I think the full tide of human existence is at Charing-Cross.

Samuel Johnson 1709–84: James Boswell *Life of Samuel Johnson* (1791) 2 April 1775

17 You're from Big D,
My, oh yes, I mean Big D, little a, double l-a-s
And that spells Dallas, my darlin' darlin' Dallas,
Don't it give you pleasure to confess
That you're from Big D?
My, oh yes!

Frank Loesser 1910–69: 'Big D' (1956)

18 *Ogden Nash had had his car broken into in Boston:*
I'd expect to be robbed in Chicago
But not in the land of the cod,
So I hope that the Cabots and Lowells
Will mention the matter to God.

Ogden Nash 1902–71: David Frost and Michael Shea *The Mid-Atlantic Companion* (1986)

19 Saigon is like all the other great modern cities of the world. It's the mess left over from people getting rich.

P. J. O'Rourke 1947– : *Give War a Chance* (1992)

20 Last Sunday afternoon
I took a trip to Hackensack
But after I gave Hackensack the once-over
I took the next train back.
I happen to like New York.

Cole Porter 1891–1964: 'I Happen to Like New York' (1931)

21 City of perspiring dreams.
  of Cambridge

Frederic Raphael 1931– : *The Glittering Prizes* (1976)

22 He took offence at my description of Edinburgh as the Reykjavik of the South.

Tom Stoppard 1937– : *Jumpers* (1972)

23 Toronto is a kind of New York operated by the Swiss.

Peter Ustinov 1921–2004: in *Globe & Mail* 1 August 1987; attributed

24 Brighton looks like a town that is constantly helping the police with their enquiries.

Keith Waterhouse 1929– : quoted by the author in conversation with the Editor

Transport

66 The only way of catching a train . . . is to miss the train before. 99
G. K. Chesterton

1 *of Annie's parking:*
That's OK, we can walk to the kerb from here.

Woody Allen 1935– : *Annie Hall* (1977 film)

2 Railways and the Church have their critics, but both are the best ways of getting a man to his ultimate destination.

Revd W. Awdry 1911–97: in *Daily Telegraph* 22 March 1997; obituary

3 The freeway is . . . the place where they [Angelenos] spend the two calmest and most rewarding hours of their daily lives.

Reynar Banham 1922–88: *Los Angeles: the Architecture of Four Ecologies* (1971)

4 We're gonna need a bigger boat!

Peter Benchley 1940– : *Jaws* (1975 film); spoken by Roy Schneider as Chief Brody

5 He [Benchley] came out of a night club one evening and, tapping a uniformed figure on the shoulder, said, 'Get me a cab.' The uniformed figure turned around furiously and informed him that he was not a doorman but a rear admiral. 'O.K.,' said Benchley, 'Get me a battleship.'

Robert Benchley 1889–1945: in *New Yorker* 5 January 1946

6 Q: If Mrs Thatcher were run over by a bus . . . ?
LORD CARRINGTON: It wouldn't dare.

Lord Carrington 1919– : during the Falklands War; Russell Lewis *Margaret Thatcher* (1984)

7 The only way of catching a train I ever discovered is to miss the train before.

G. K. Chesterton 1874–1936: attributed; Evan Esar and Nicolas Bentley (eds.) *Treasury of Humorous Quotations* (1951)

8 The ski are the most capricious things upon the earth.

Arthur Conan Doyle 1859–1930: 'Crossing an Alpine Pass' (1894)

9 That monarch of the road,
Observer of the Highway Code,
That big six-wheeler
Scarlet-painted
London Transport
Diesel-engined
Ninety-seven horse power
Omnibus!

Michael Flanders 1922–75 and **Donald Swann** 1923–94: 'A Transport of Delight' (c.1956)

10 Sir, Saturday morning, although recurring at regular and well-foreseen intervals, always seems to take this railway by surprise.

W. S. Gilbert 1836–1911: letter to the station-master at Baker Street, on the Metropolitan line; John Julius Norwich *Christmas Crackers* (1980)

11 For you dream you are crossing the Channel, and tossing
   about in a steamer from Harwich—
   Which is something between a large bathing machine and
   a very small second class carriage.

W. S. Gilbert 1836–1911: *Iolanthe* (1882)

12 What is this that roareth thus?
   Can it be a Motor Bus?
   Yes, the smell and hideous hum
   Indicat Motorem Bum! . . .
   How shall wretches live like us
   Cincti Bis Motoribus?
   Domine, defende nos
   Contra hos Motores Bos!

A. D. Godley 1856–1925: letter to C. R. L. Fletcher, 10 January 1914

13 Aunt Jane observed, the second time
   She tumbled off a bus,
   'The step is short from the Sublime
   To the Ridiculous.'

Harry Graham 1874–1936: 'Equanimity' (1899)

14 'Glorious, stirring sight!' murmured Toad, never offering
   to move. 'The poetry of motion! The *real* way to travel!
   The *only* way to travel! Here today—in next week
   tomorrow! Villages skipped, towns and cities jumped—
   always somebody else's horizon! O bliss! O poop-poop! O
   my! O my!'

Kenneth Grahame 1859–1932: *The Wind in the Willows* (1908)

15 *of Bishop Patrick's fatal error in crossing the street:*
   The light of God was with him,
   But the traffic light was not.

E. Y. Harburg 1898–1981: 'Lead Kindly Light' (1965)

16 There once was an old man who said, 'Damn!
   It is borne in upon me I am
   An engine that moves
   In determinate grooves,
   I'm not even a bus, I'm a tram.'

Maurice Evan Hare 1886–1967: 'Limerick' (1905)

17 The defendant is clearly one who insufficiently appreciates
   the value of the motor car to the human race. But we
   must not allow our natural detestation for such an
   individual to cloud our judgment.

A. P. Herbert 1890–1971: *Misleading Cases* (1935)

18 Home James, and don't spare the horses.

Fred Hillebrand 1893– : title of song (1934)

19 Cyclists see motorists as tyrannical and uncaring.
   Motorists believe cyclists are afflicted by a perversion.

Boris Johnson 1964– : in *Observer* 28 December 2003

20 The automobile changed our dress, manners, social
   customs, vacation habits, the shape of our cities,
   consumer purchasing patterns, common tastes and
   positions in intercourse.

John Keats 1920– : *The Insolent Chariots* (1958)

21 FATHER STACK: While you were out, I got the keys to your
   car. And drove it into a big wall. And if you don't like it,
   tough. I've had my fun, and that's all that matters.

Graham Linehan and **Arthur Mathews**: 'New Jack City' (1996), episode from *Father Ted* (Channel 4 TV, 1994–8)

22 'Take my camel, dear,' said my aunt Dot, as she climbed
   down from this animal on her return from High Mass.

Rose Macaulay 1881–1958: *The Towers of Trebizond* (1956)

23 *on a car called by Macmillan 'Mrs Thatcher':*
This car makes a noise if you don't fasten your seat belt, and a light starts flashing if you don't close the door. It's a *very bossy* car.

Harold Macmillan 1894–1986: Ludovic Kennedy *On My Way to the Club* (1989)

24 In Milan, traffic lights are instructions. In Rome, they are suggestions. In Naples, they are Christmas decorations.

Antonio Martino 1942– : in *Sunday Times* 24 February 2002

25 I've tried walking sideways, and walking to the front, But people laughed, and said, 'It's a publicity stunt.'

Spike Milligan 1918–2002: 'I'm Walking Backwards for Christmas' (1956)

26 *seeing the Morris Minor prototype in 1945:*
It looks like a poached egg—we can't make that.

Lord Nuffield 1877–1963: attributed

27 People who spend most of their natural lives riding iron bicycles over the rocky roadsteads of this parish get their personalities mixed up with the personalities of their bicycles as a result of the interchanging of the atoms of each of them and you would be surprised at the number of people in these parts who nearly are half people and half bicycles.

Flann O'Brien 1911–66: *The Third Policeman* (1967)

28 Why is it no one ever sent me yet
One perfect limousine, do you suppose?
Ah no, it's always just my luck to get
One perfect rose.

Dorothy Parker 1893–1967: 'One Perfect Rose' (1937)

29 Back in the house, I felt someone had put planks in my legs and turned my buttocks into wooden boxes.
his first experience of riding

V. S. Pritchett 1900–97: *Midnight Oil* (1971)

30 Sure, the next train has gone ten minutes ago.

Punch 1841–1992: vol. 60 (1871)

31 What is better than presence of mind in a railway accident? Absence of body.

Punch 1841–1992: vol. 16 (1849)

32 Denis Norden thought that Johann Strauss's car would have been registered as—123 123.

Steve Race 1921– : in *The Bibliophile* September 2000; attributed

33 Take most people, they're crazy about cars. They worry if they get a little scratch on them, and they're always talking about how many miles they get to a gallon . . . I don't even like *old* cars. I mean they don't even interest me. I'd rather have a goddam horse. A horse is at least *human*, for God's sake.

J. D. Salinger 1919– : *The Catcher in the Rye* (1951)

34 Walk! Not bloody likely. I am going in a taxi.

George Bernard Shaw 1856–1950: *Pygmalion* (1916)

35 I wonder if there are enough traffic cones for every student to have one in their bedroom.

Arthur Smith 1954– and **Chris England**: *An Evening with Gary Lineker* (1990)

36 BOATMAN: I 'ad that Christopher Marlowe in the back of my boat.

Tom Stoppard 1937– : *Shakespeare in Love* (1999 film, screenplay by Tom Stoppard and Mark Norman)

37 MAGNUS: How long have you been a pedestrian?
SIMON: Ever since I could walk.

Tom Stoppard 1937– : *The Real Inspector Hound* (1968)

38 *on the construction of the Canadian Pacific Railway across Canada:*
Building that railroad would have made a Canadian out of the German Emperor.

William Cornelius Van Horne 1843–1915: in *Canadian Encyclopedia* (1988) vol. 1

Travel and Exploration

66 If it's Tuesday, this must be Belgium. 99
David Shaw

1 In America there are two classes of travel—first class, and with children.

Robert Benchley 1889–1945: *Pluck and Luck* (1925)

2 I encountered Mr. Hackman, an Englishman, who has been walking the length and breadth of Europe for several years. I enquired of him what were his chief observations. He replied gruffly, 'I never look up', and went on his way.

N. Brooke: in 1796; Duncan Minshull *The Vintage Book of Walking* (2000)

3 But the principal failing occurred in the sailing,
And the Bellman, perplexed and distressed,
Said he *had* hoped, at least, when the wind blew due East,
That the ship would *not* travel due West!

Lewis Carroll 1832–98: *The Hunting of the Snark* (1876) 'Fit the Second: The Bellman's Speech'

4 They say travel broadens the mind; but you must have the mind.

G. K. Chesterton 1874–1936: 'The Shadow of the Shark' (1921)

5 *on travelling to the US:*
I'm often unlucky enough to be picked out for those 'special searches' due to my obvious resemblance to Mr bin Laden

Joan Collins 1933– : in *Sunday Times* 29 February 2004

6 Why do the wrong people travel, travel, travel,
When the right people stay back home?
What compulsion compels them
And who the hell tells them
To drag their cans to Zanzibar
Instead of staying quietly in Omaha?

Noël Coward 1899–1973: 'Why do the Wrong People Travel?' (1961)

7 *on his arrival in Turkey:*
I am of course known here as English Delight.

Noël Coward 1899–1973: Sheridan Morley *The Quotable Noël Coward* (1999)

8 Luggage left alone unloaded
Will be immediately exploded.

April De Angelis 1955– : Jonathan Dove and April De Angelis *Flight* (1998 opera)

9 A person can be stranded and get by, even though she will be imperilled; two people with a German shepherd and no money are in a mess.

Andrea Dworkin 1946–2005: *Letters from a War Zone* (1988)

10 At my age travel broadens the behind.

Stephen Fry 1957– : *The Liar* (1991)

11 Abroad is bloody.

George VI 1895–1952: W. H. Auden *A Certain World* (1970)

12 So think twice my friends, before you doubt Columbus,
Just imagine what happens to Posterity without Columbus.
No New York, and no skyscrapers,
No funnies in the papers,
No automat nickels,
No Heinz and his pickles,
No land of the Brave and the Free.

Ira Gershwin 1896–1983: 'The Nina, the Pinta, the Santa Maria' (1945)

13 And bound on that journey you find your attorney (who
started that morning from Devon);
He's a bit undersized, and you don't feel surprised when he
tells you he's only eleven.

W. S. Gilbert 1836–1911: *Iolanthe*
(1882)

14 In your shirt and your socks (the black silk with gold
clocks), crossing Salisbury Plain on a bicycle.

W. S. Gilbert 1836–1911: *Iolanthe*
(1882)

15 *on the Giant's Causeway:*
Worth seeing, yes; but not worth going to see.

Samuel Johnson 1709–84: James
Boswell *Life of Samuel Johnson*
(1791) 12 October 1779

16 What good is speed if the brain has oozed out on the way?

Karl Kraus 1874–1936: 'The
Discovery of the North Pole'

17 Thanks to the interstate highway system, it is now possible
to travel from coast to coast without seeing anything.

Charles Kuralt 1934–97: *On the
Road* (1980)

18 I wouldn't mind seeing China if I could come back the
same day.

Philip Larkin 1922–85: *Required
Writing* (1983), interview with
Observer, 1979

19 A sure cure for seasickness is to sit under a tree.

Spike Milligan 1918–2002:
attributed; in *Daily Telegraph* 28
February 2002

20 *filling in an embarkation form on a channel crossing:*
HAROLD NICOLSON: What age are you going to put, Osbert?
OSBERT SITWELL: What sex are you going to put, Harold?

Harold Nicolson 1886–1968:
attributed, perhaps apocryphal

21 Everybody in fifteenth-century Spain was wrong about
where China was and as a result, Columbus discovered
Caribbean vacations.

P. J. O'Rourke 1947– : *Parliament of
Whores* (1991)

22 If only I could get down to Sidcup! I've been waiting for
the weather to break. He's got my papers, this man I left
them with, it's got it all down there, I could prove
everything.

Harold Pinter 1930– : *The Caretaker*
(1960)

23 In these days of rapid and convenient travel . . . to come
from Leighton Buzzard does not necessarily denote any
great strength of character. It might only mean mere
restlessness.

Saki 1870–1916: *The Chronicles of
Clovis* (1911)

24 If it's Tuesday, this must be Belgium.

David Shaw: film title (1969)

25 *on airline food:*
The shiny stuff is tomatoes.
The salad lies in a group.
The curly stuff is potatoes,
The stuff that moves is soup.
Anything that is white is sweet,
Anything that is brown is meat.
Anything that is grey—don't eat.

Stephen Sondheim 1930– : 'Do I
Hear a Waltz?' (1965)

26 In Turkey it was always 1952, in Malaysia 1937;
Afghanistan was 1910 and Bolivia 1949. It is twenty
years ago in the Soviet Union, ten in Norway, five in
France. It is always last year in Australia and next week in
Japan.

Paul Theroux 1941– : *The Kingdom
by the Sea* (1983)

27 *asked why he had come to America:*
In pursuit of my life-long quest for naked women in wet
mackintoshes.

Dylan Thomas 1914–53: Constantine
Fitzgibbon *Dylan Thomas* (1965);
attributed

28 It is not worthwhile to go around the world to count the cats in Zanzibar.

Henry David Thoreau 1817–62: *Walden* (1854) 'Conclusion'

29 Done the elephants, done the poverty.
after a cricket tour of India

Phil Tufnell 1961– : attributed; in *Times Literary Supplement* 28 July 2000

30 Commuter—one who spends his life
In riding to and from his wife;
A man who shaves and takes a train,
And then rides back to shave again.

E. B. White 1899–1985: 'The Commuter' (1982)

Trust and Treachery ····▸ Security

❝ Defectors are like grapes. The first pressings from them are the best. **❞**
Maurice Oldfield

1 Outside Shakespeare the word treason to me means nothing. Only, you pissed in our soup and we drank it.
Coral Browne to Guy Burgess

Alan Bennett 1934– : *An Englishman Abroad* (1989)

2 The only recorded instance in history of a rat swimming *towards* a sinking ship.

Winston Churchill 1874–1965: of a former Conservative who proposed to stand as a Liberal; Leon Harris *The Fine Art of Political Wit* (1965)

3 You're . . . turning into a kind of serial monogamist.

Richard Curtis 1956– : *Four Weddings and a Funeral* (1994 film)

4 Frankly speaking it is difficult to trust the Chinese. Once bitten by a snake you feel suspicious even when you see a piece of rope.

Dalai Lama 1935 : attributed, 1981

5 *discussing a friend with Robert Lajeunesse:*
LAJEUNESSE: He deserves to be betrayed.
FEYDEAU: And even so, his wife has to help him.

Georges Feydeau 1862–1921: Caryl Brahms and Ned Sherrin *Ooh! La-La!* (1973)

6 When I was at Cambridge it was, naturally enough I felt, my ambition to be approached in some way by an elderly homosexual don and asked to spy for or against my country.

Stephen Fry 1957– : *Paperweight* (1992)

7 It is rather like sending your opening batsmen to the crease only for them to find the moment that the first balls are bowled that their bats have been broken before the game by the team captain.

Geoffrey Howe 1926– : resignation speech as Deputy Prime Minister, House of Commons 13 November 1990

8 *Pension.* Pay given to a state hireling for treason to his country.

Samuel Johnson 1709–84: *A Dictionary of the English Language* (1755)

9 He that hath a Gospel
Whereby Heaven is won
(Carpenter, or Cameleer,
Or Maya's dreaming son),
Many swords shall pierce Him,
Mingling blood with gall;

Rudyard Kipling 1865–1936: *Limits and Renewals* (1932)

But His Own Disciple
Shall wound Him worst of all!

10 Never trust a man who combs his hair straight from his left armpit.
of the careful distribution of hair on General MacArthur's balding head

Alice Roosevelt Longworth
1884–1980: Michael Teague *Mrs L* (1981)

11 Defectors are like grapes. The first pressings from them are the best. The third and fourth lack body.

Maurice Oldfield 1915–81: Chapman Pincher in *Mail on Sunday* 19 September 1982; attributed

12 Never take a reference from a clergyman. They always want to give someone a second chance.

Lady Selborne 1858–1950: K. Rose *The Later Cecils* (1975)

13 [Treason], Sire, is a question of dates.

Charles-Maurice de Talleyrand 1754–1838: Duff Cooper *Talleyrand* (1932)

14 He trusted neither of them as far as he could spit, and he was a poor spitter, lacking both distance and control.

P. G. Wodehouse 1881–1975: *Money in the Bank* (1946)

Truth ····▶ Lies

❝ Stranger than fiction. ❞
Lord Byron

1 The pursuit of truth is chimerical . . . What we should pursue is the most convenient arrangement of our ideas.

Samuel Butler 1835–1902: *Notebooks* (1912)

2 'Tis strange—but true; for truth is always strange; Stranger than fiction.

Lord Byron 1788–1824: *Don Juan* (1819–24)

3 He occasionally stumbled over the truth, but hastily picked himself up and hurried on as if nothing had happened.
of Stanley Baldwin

Winston Churchill 1874–1965: J. L. Lane (ed.) *The Sayings of Winston Churchill* (1992)

4 Our old friend . . . economical with the *actualité*.

Alan Clark 1928–99: under cross-examination at the Old Bailey during the Matrix Churchill case; in *Independent* 10 November 1992

5 Something unpleasant is coming when men are anxious to tell the truth.

Benjamin Disraeli 1804–81: *The Young Duke* (1831)

6 It is always the best policy to speak the truth—unless, of course, you are an exceptionally good liar.

Jerome K. Jerome 1859–1927: in *The Idler* February 1892

7 Never tell a story because it is true: tell it because it is a good story.

John Pentland Mahaffy 1839–1919: W. B. Stanford and R. B. McDowell *Mahaffy* (1971)

8 I never give them [the public] hell. I just tell the truth, and they think it is hell.

Harry S. Truman 1884–1972: in *Look* 3 April 1956

9 'The Adventures of Tom Sawyer' . . . was made by Mr Mark Twain, and he told the truth, mainly. There was things which he stretched, but mainly he told the truth.

Mark Twain 1835–1910: *The Adventures of Huckleberry Finn* (1884)

10 Get your facts first, and then you can distort 'em as much as you please.

Mark Twain 1835–1910: Rudyard Kipling *From Sea to Sea* (1899)

11 The truth is rarely pure, and never simple.

Oscar Wilde 1854–1900: *The Importance of Being Earnest* (1895)

Unhappiness ····> Happiness

The Universe

66 The universe is . . . queerer than we suppose. **99**

J. B. S. Haldane

---

1 Had I been present at the Creation, I would have given some useful hints for the better ordering of the universe.

Alfonso, King of Castile 1221–84: on studying the Ptolemaic system (attributed)

2 'I quite realized,' said Columbus,
'That the Earth was not a rhombus,
But I *am* a little annoyed
To find it an oblate spheroid.'

Edmund Clerihew Bentley 1875–1956: 'Columbus' (1929)

3 This is the first convention of the Space Age—when a candidate can promise the moon and mean it.

David Brinkley: Laurence J. Peter (ed.) *Quotations for our Time* (1977)

4 *on hearing that Margaret Fuller 'accepted the universe':*
Gad! she'd better!

Thomas Carlyle 1795–1881: William James *Varieties of Religious Experience* (1902)

5 Twinkle, twinkle, little bat!
How I wonder what you're at!
Up above the world you fly!
Like a teatray in the sky.

Lewis Carroll 1832–98: *Alice's Adventures in Wonderland* (1865)

6 The world has treated me very well, but then I haven't treated it so badly either.

Noël Coward 1899–1973: Sheridan Morley *The Quotable Noël Coward* (1999)

7   Listen: there's a hell
Of a good universe next door; let's go.

e. e. cummings 1894–1962: *1 x 1* (1944)

8 The world is disgracefully managed, one hardly knows to whom to complain.

Ronald Firbank 1886–1926: *Vainglory* (1915)

9 Now, my own suspicion is that the universe is not only queerer than we suppose, but queerer than we *can* suppose.

J. B. S. Haldane 1892–1964: *Possible Worlds* (1927)

10 If this planet is a sample,
Or a preview if you will,
Or a model demonstration
Of the great designer's stall,
I say without hesitation,
'Thank you, no reincarnation.'

E. Y. Harburg 1898–1981: 'Letter to my Gaza' (1976)

11 To make the longest story terse,
Be it blessing, be it curse
The Lord designed the Universe
With built in obsolescence . . .

E. Y. Harburg 1898–1981: 'The Odds on Favourite' (1976)

12 The only lyric writer on the Broadway treadmill to get comic with the cosmic.
  of E. Y. Harburg

John Lahr 1941– : Ned Sherrin *Cutting Edge* (1984)

13 I don't think there's intelligent life on other planets. Why should other planets be any different from this one?

Bob Monkhouse 1928–2003: attributed; in *BBC News* 29 December 2003 (online edition)

14 The Greeks said God was always doing geometry, modern physicists say he's playing roulette, everything depends on the observer, the universe is a totality of observations, it's a work of art created by us.

Iris Murdoch 1919–99: *The Good Apprentice* (1985)

15 Space is almost infinite. As a matter of fact, we think it is infinite.

Dan Quayle 1947– : in *Daily Telegraph* 8 March 1989

Virtue and Vice ····▸ Morality

❝The louder he talked of his honour, the faster we counted our spoons.❞
Ralph Waldo Emerson

1 I'm as pure as the driven slush.

Tallulah Bankhead 1903–68: in *Saturday Evening Post* 12 April 1947

2 All things are capable of excess. Absence of morbid moisture is a Whig virtue. But morbid dryness is a Whig vice.

Max Beerbohm 1872–1956: letter July 1928

3 A dead sinner revised and edited.

Ambrose Bierce 1842–c.1914: definition of a saint; *The Devil's Dictionary* (1911)

4 The rain, it raineth on the just
And also on the unjust fella:
But chiefly on the just, because
The unjust steals the just's umbrella.

Lord Bowen 1835–94: Walter Sichel *Sands of Time* (1923)

5 An original something, fair maid, you would win me
To write—but how shall I begin?
For I fear I have nothing original in me—
Excepting Original Sin.

Thomas Campbell 1777–1844: 'To a Young Lady, Who Asked Me to Write Something Original for Her Album' (1843)

6 In former days, everyone found the assumption of innocence so easy; today we find fatally easy the assumption of guilt.

Amanda Cross 1926– : *Poetic Justice* (1970)

7 Lydia was tired of being good. She felt it didn't altogether suit her. It made her feel a little dowdy, as though she had taken up residence in the suburbs of morality.

Alice Thomas Ellis 1932–2005: *Unexplained Laughter* (1985)

8 The louder he talked of his honour, the faster we counted our spoons.

Ralph Waldo Emerson 1803–82: *The Conduct of Life* (1860)

9 But if he does really think that there is no distinction between virtue and vice, why, Sir, when he leaves our houses, let us count our spoons.

Samuel Johnson 1709–84: James Boswell *Life of Samuel Johnson* (1791) 14 July 1763

10 He that but looketh on a plate of ham and eggs to lust after it, hath already committed breakfast with it in his heart.

C. S. Lewis 1898–1963: letter, 10 March 1954

11 honesty is a good
thing but
it is not profitable to
its possessor
unless it is
kept under control.

Don Marquis 1878–1937: *archys life of mehitabel* (1933) 'archygrams'

12 *on being discovered by his wife with a chorus girl:*
I wasn't kissing her, I was just whispering in her mouth.

Chico Marx 1891–1961: Groucho Marx and Richard J. Anobile *Marx Brothers Scrapbook* (1973)

13 If only the good were a little less heavy-footed!

W. Somerset Maugham 1874–1965: *A Writer's Notebook* (1949) written in 1896

14 Decency is Indecency's conspiracy of silence.

George Bernard Shaw 1856–1950: *Man and Superman* (1903) 'Maxims: Decency'

15 Self-denial is not a virtue: it is only the effect of prudence on rascality.

George Bernard Shaw 1856–1950: *Man and Superman* (1903)

16 There is nothing in this world constant, but inconstancy.

Jonathan Swift 1667–1745: *A Critical Essay upon the Faculties of the Mind* (1709)

17 I think I could be a good woman if I had five thousand a year.

William Makepeace Thackeray 1811–63: *Vanity Fair* (1847–8)

18 Barring that natural expression of villainy which we all have, the man looked honest enough.

Mark Twain 1835–1910: *A Curious Dream* (1872) 'A Mysterious Visit'

19 Her virtue was that she said what she thought, her vice that what she thought didn't amount to much.

Peter Ustinov 1921–2004: attributed; in *Daily Telegraph* 30 March 2004

20 When I'm good, I'm very, very good, but when I'm bad, I'm better.

Mae West 1892–1980: in *I'm No Angel* (1933 film)

21 I've been things and seen places.

Mae West 1892–1980: in *I'm No Angel* (1933 film)

22 I used to be Snow White . . . but I drifted.

Mae West 1892–1980: Joseph Weintraub *Peel Me a Grape* (1975)

23 Between two evils, I always pick the one I never tried before.

Mae West 1892–1980: in *Klondike Annie* (1936 film)

24 To err is human—but it feels divine.

Mae West 1892–1980: attributed; Fred Metcalf (ed.) *Penguin Dictionary of Modern Humorous Quotations* (1987)

25 I can resist everything except temptation.

Oscar Wilde 1854–1900: *Lady Windermere's Fan* (1892)

26 A little sincerity is a dangerous thing, and a great deal of it is absolutely fatal.

Oscar Wilde 1854–1900: 'The Critic as Artist' (1891)

Wales ·····➤ Countries and Peoples, Places

66 Now I perceive the devil understands Welsh. 99
William Shakespeare

1 *the cover of the Eurostat Yearbook 2004 showed the coastline of the British Isles beginning at the Welsh Border:*
Peter Mandelson has hardly been in Brussels two weeks and already Wales has fallen into the Irish Sea.

Michael Ancram 1945– : in *Independent* 7 October 2004

2 *a Board Member objecting to Richard Burton's candidature for leading a Welsh National Theatre Company, after hearing of Burton's international triumphs:*
Yes, but what has he done for Wales?

Anonymous: in *Ned Sherrin's Theatrical Anecdotes* (1992)

3 It profits a man nothing to give his soul for the whole world . . . But for Wales—!

Robert Bolt 1924–95: *A Man for All Seasons* (1960)

4 Now I perceive the devil understands Welsh.

William Shakespeare 1564–1616: *Henry IV, Part 1* (1597)

5 Not for Cadwallader and all his goats.

William Shakespeare 1564–1616: *Henry V* (1599)

6 The land of my fathers. My fathers can have it.

Dylan Thomas 1914–53: *Adam* December 1953

7 There are still parts of Wales where the only concession to gaiety is a striped shroud.

Gwyn Thomas 1913– : in *Punch* 18 June 1958

8 'I often think,' he continued, 'that we can trace almost all the disasters of English history to the influence of Wales!'

Evelyn Waugh 1903–66: *Decline and Fall* (1928)

9 The Welsh remain the only race whom you can vilify without being called a racist.

A. N. Wilson 1950– : in *Sunday Times* 23 April 2000 'Talking Heads'

War ·····➤ The Armed Forces

66 There never was a good war, or a bad peace. 99
Benjamin Franklin

1 *of the retreat from Dunkirk, May 1940:*
The noise, my dear! And the people!

Anonymous: Anthony Rhodes *Sword of Bone* (1942)

2 Kitchener is a great poster.

Margot Asquith 1864–1945: *More Memories* (1933)

3 After each war there is a little less democracy to save.

Brooks Atkinson 1894–1984: *Once Around the Sun* (1951) 7 January

4 Well, if you knows of a better 'ole, go to it.

Bruce Bairnsfather 1888–1959: *Fragments from France* (1915)

5 *on becoming aware of the Nazi threat:*
I shall put warmonger on my passport.

Robert Byron 1905–41: *The Road to Oxiana* (1980 ed.); introduction

6 *of Viscount Montgomery:*
In defeat unbeatable: in victory unbearable.

Winston Churchill 1874–1965:
Edward Marsh *Ambrosia and Small Beer* (1964)

7 Though Waterloo was won upon the playing fields of Eton,
The next war will be photographed, and lost, by Cecil Beaton.

Noël Coward 1899–1973: 'Bright Young People' (1931)

8 *when Park Lane was bombed:*
I was under the table with the telephone and Shakespeare.

Emerald Cunard 1872–1948: Chips Channon diary, 20 March 1945

9 A war hasn't been fought this badly since Olaf the Hairy,
High Chief of all the Vikings, ordered 80,000 battle helmets with the horns on the inside.

Richard Curtis 1956– and **Ben Elton** 1959– : *Blackadder Goes Forth* (1989) 'Major Star'

10 I gave my life for freedom—This I know:
For those who bade me fight had told me so.

William Norman Ewer 1885–1976: 'Five Souls' (1917)

11 There never was a good war, or a bad peace.

Benjamin Franklin 1706–90: letter to Josiah Quincy, 11 September 1783

12 Fortunately, just when things were blackest, the war broke out.

Joseph Heller 1923–99: *Catch-22* (1961)

13 I'd like to see the government get out of war altogether and leave the whole field to private industry.

Joseph Heller 1923–99: *Catch-22* (1961)

14 All the same, sir, I would put some of the colonies in your wife's name.
the Chief Rabbi to George VI, summer 1940

Joseph Herman Hertz 1872–1946: Chips Channon diary, 3 June 1943

15 *of war in Iraq:*
Vietnam without the mosquitoes.

Carl Hiaasen 1953– : attributed; in *Guardian* 23 October 2004

16 TRENTINO (Louis Calhern): I am willing to do anything to prevent this war.
FIREFLY (Groucho Marx): It's too late. I've already paid a month's rent on the battlefield.

Bert Kalmar 1884–1947 et al.: *Duck Soup* (1933 film)

17 I think from now on they're shooting without a script.
comment on the German invasion of Russia

George S. Kaufman 1889–1961: Howard Teichmann *George S. Kaufman* (1973)

18 Gentlemen, you can't fight in here. This is the war room.

Stanley Kubrick 1928–99, **Terry Southern**, and **Peter George**: *Dr Strangelove* (1963 film)

19 If we'd had as many soldiers as that, we'd have won the war!
on seeing the number of Confederate troops in Gone with the Wind *at the 1939 premiere*

Margaret Mitchell 1900–49: W. G. Harris *Gable and Lombard* (1976)

20 Like many men of my generation, I had an opportunity to give war a chance, and I promptly chickened out.

P. J. O'Rourke 1947– : *Give War a Chance* (1992)

21 The quickest way of ending a war is to lose it.

George Orwell 1903–50: in *Polemic* May 1946 'Second Thoughts on James Burnham'

22 Little girl . . . Sometime they'll give a war and nobody will come.

Carl Sandburg 1878–1967: *The People, Yes* (1936); 'Suppose They Gave a War and Nobody Came?' was the title of a 1970 film

23 'Our armies swore terribly in Flanders,' cried my uncle Toby,—'but nothing to this.'

Laurence Sterne 1713–68: *Tristram Shandy* (1759–67)

24 War is capitalism with the gloves off and many who go to war know it but they go to war because they don't want to be a hero.

Tom Stoppard 1937– : *Travesties* (1975)

25 The First World War had begun—imposed on the statesmen of Europe by railway timetables. It was an unexpected climax to the railway age.

A. J. P. Taylor 1906–90: *The First World War* (1963)

26 *Evelyn Waugh, returning from Crete in 1941, was asked his impression of his first battle:*
Like German opera, too long and too loud.

Evelyn Waugh 1903–66: Christopher Sykes *Evelyn Waugh* (1975)

27 I am in consultation with my editors on the subject. We think it a very promising little war. A microcosm you might say, of world drama.

Evelyn Waugh 1903–66: *Scoop* (1938)

28 As Lord Chesterfield said of the generals of his day, 'I only hope that when the enemy reads the list of their names, he trembles as I do.'

Duke of Wellington 1769–1852: letter, 29 August 1810, usually quoted 'I don't know what effect these men will have upon the enemy, but, by God, they frighten me'

29 *of an early attempt to write about Waterloo:*
Write the history of a battle? As well write the history of a ball!

Duke of Wellington 1769–1852: Richard Holmes *Firing Line* (1986)

30 Good-bye-ee! — Good-bye-ee!
Wipe the tear, baby dear, from your eye-ee.
Tho' it's hard to part, I know,
I'll be tickled to death to go.
Don't cry-ee — don't sigh-ee!
There's a silver lining in the sky-ee!
Bonsoir, old thing! cheerio! chin-chin!
Nahpoo! Toodle-oo! Good-bye-ee!

R. P. Weston 1878–1936 and **Bert Lee** 1880–1936: 'Good-bye-ee!' (*c.*1915)

31 The day war broke out.

Robb Wilton 1881–1957: customary preamble to radio monologues in the role of a Home Guard, from *c.*1940

32 *of Sir Charles Napier's conquest of Sindh:*
Peccavi—I have Sindh.
   reworking Latin peccavi *I have sinned*

Catherine Winkworth 1827–78: in *Punch* 18 May 1844, supposedly sent by Napier to Lord Ellenborough

33 'Anything in the papers, Jeeves?' 'Some slight friction threatening in the Balkans, sir.'

P. G. Wodehouse 1881–1975: *The Inimitable Jeeves* (1923)

Wealth ····> Money, Poverty

❝ A sumpshous spot all done up in gold with plenty of looking glasses. ❞
Daisy Ashford

1 *Ali G interviewing David and Victoria Beckham*
So they is some people who suddenly get loads of money who become very tasteless. How has you two managed to avoid that?

Ali G (Sacha Baron Cohen) 1970– : in *Sunday Times* 11 February 2001

2 It was a sumpshous spot all done up in gold with plenty of looking glasses.

Daisy Ashford 1881–1972: *The Young Visiters* (1919)

3 If you would know what the Lord God thinks of money, you have only to look at those to whom he gives it.

Maurice Baring 1874–1945: Malcolm Cowley (ed.) *Writers at Work* (1958) 1st series

4 I can walk. It's just that I'm so rich I don't need to.

Alan Bennett 1934– : *Forty Years On* (1969)

5 People say I wasted my money. I say 90 per cent went on women, fast cars and booze. The rest I wasted.

George Best 1946–2005: in *Daily Telegraph* 29 December 1990

6 Mrs Budge Bulkeley, worth £32,000,000, has arrived here [Isfahan] accompanied by some lesser millionairesses. They are in great misery because the caviare is running out.
   on fellow travellers in Persia

Robert Byron 1905–41: *The Road to Oxiana* (1937)

7 When I hear a rich man described as a colourful character I figure he's a bum with money.

Jimmy Cannon 1910–73: in *New York Post* c.1955 'Nobody Asked Me, But . . . '

8 The Rich aren't like us—they pay less taxes.

Peter de Vries 1910–93: in *Washington Post* 30 July 1989

9 £40,000 a year [is] a moderate income—such a one as a man might jog on with.

Lord Durham 1792–1840: Herbert Maxwell *The Creevey Papers* (1903); letter from Mr Creevey to Miss Elizabeth Ord, 13 September 1821

10 I used to walk in the shade,
   With those blues on parade,
   But I'm not afraid.
   This Rover crossed over.
   If I never have a cent
   I'll be rich as Rockefeller,
   Gold dust on my feet,
   On the sunny side of the street.

Dorothy Fields 1905–74: 'On the Sunny Side of the Street' (1930)

11 A rich man is nothing but a poor man with money.

W. C. Fields 1880–1946: attributed

12 To trust people is a luxury in which only the wealthy can indulge; the poor cannot afford it.

E. M. Forster 1879–1970: *Howards End* (1910)

13 The meek shall inherit the earth, but not the mineral rights.

John Paul Getty 1892–1976: Robert Lenzner *The Great Getty*; attributed

14 What a night—the furs, the jewels, the glamour . . . I haven't seen so much expensive jewellery go by since I watched Sammy Davis Jr.'s home sliding down Coldwater Canyon.
   hosting the Oscars, 1978

Bob Hope 1903–2003: attributed; in *Lansing State Journal* 28 July 2003

15 Poor Harold, he can live on his income all right, but he no longer can live on the income from his income.
   of Harold Vanderbilt

George S. Kaufman 1889–1961: Howard Teichmann *George S. Kaufman* (1973)

16 Wealth and power are much more likely to be the result of breeding than they are of reading.

Fran Lebowitz 1946– : on self-help books; *Social Studies* (1981)

17 When I want a peerage, I shall buy it like an honest man.

Lord Northcliffe 1865–1922: Tom Driberg *Swaff* (1974)

18 Where would the Rockefellers be today if sainted old John D. had gone on selling short-weight kerosene (paraffin to you) to widows and orphans instead of wisely deciding to mulct the whole country?

S. J. Perelman 1904–79: letter 25 October 1976

19 I've a shooting box in Scotland,
I've a chateau in Touraine,
I've a silly little chalet
In the Interlaken Valley,
I've a hacienda in Spain,
I've a private fjord in Norway,
I've a villa close to Rome,
And in travelling
It's really quite a comfort to know
That you're never far from home!

Cole Porter 1891–1964: 'I've a Shooting Box in Scotland' (1916)

20 HE: Who wants to be a millionaire?
SHE: I don't.
HE: Have flashy flunkeys ev'rywhere?
SHE: I don't . . .
HE: Who wants a marble swimming pool too?
SHE: I don't.
HE: And I don't,
BOTH: 'Cause all I want is you.

Cole Porter 1891–1964: 'Who Wants to be a Millionaire?' (1956)

21 A kiss on the hand may be quite continental,
But diamonds are a girl's best friend . . .

Men grow cold as girls grow old
And we all lose our charms in the end.
But square cut or pear shape,
These rocks won't lose their shape,
Diamonds are a girl's best friend.

Leo Robin 1900–84: 'Diamonds are a Girl's Best Friend' (1949)

22 I am a Millionaire. That is my religion.

George Bernard Shaw 1856–1950: *Major Barbara* (1907)

23 It is the wretchedness of being rich that you have to live with rich people.

Logan Pearsall Smith 1865–1946: *Afterthoughts* (1931)

24 To suppose, as we all suppose, that we could be rich and not behave as the rich behave, is like supposing that we could drink all day and keep absolutely sober.

Logan Pearsall Smith 1865–1946: *Afterthoughts* (1931)

25 It was very prettily said, that we may learn the little value of fortune by the persons on whom heaven is pleased to bestow it.

Richard Steele 1672–1729: *The Tatler* 27 July 1710

26 I've been poor and I've been rich—rich is better.

Sophie Tucker 1884–1966: attributed

27 I sometimes wished he would realize that he was poor instead of being that most nerve-racking of phenomena, a rich man without money.

Peter Ustinov 1921–2004: *Dear Me* (1977)

The Weather

❝ Summer has set in with its usual severity. ❞
Samuel Taylor Coleridge

1 When the foal and broodmare hinny,
And in every cut-down spinney
Ladysmocks grow mauve and mauver,

Alfred Austin 1835–1913: *Fortunatus the Pessimist* (1892)

Then the winter days are over.
   *Sometimes misquoted as, 'Spring is here, winter is over; the
   cuckoo-flower gets mauver and mauver'*

2 *on being asked why he never sunbathed in California instead of
sitting under a sun-lamp:*
And get hit by a meteor?

Robert Benchley 1889–1945: R. E.
Drennan *Wit's End* (1973)

3 Springtime for Hitler and Germany . . .
Winter for Poland and France.

Mel Brooks 1926– : 'Springtime for
Hitler', lyric from Mel Brooks and
Thomas Meehan *The Producers* (2001
musical)

4 The English winter—ending in July,
To recommence in August.

Lord Byron 1788–1824: *Don Juan*
(1819–24)

5 Summer has set in with its usual severity.

Samuel Taylor Coleridge
1772–1834: letter to Vincent Novello,
9 May 1826

6 It ain't a fit night out for man or beast.

W. C. Fields 1880–1946: adopted by
Fields but claimed by him not to be
original; letter 8 February 1944

7 A woman rang to say she heard there was a hurricane on
the way. Well don't worry, there isn't.
   *weather forecast on the night before serious gales in
   southern England*

Michael Fish 1944– : BBC TV, 15
October 1987

8 Some are weather wise, some are otherwise.

Benjamin Franklin 1706–90: *Poor
Richard's Almanac* (1735) February

9 I said, 'It is most extraordinary weather for this time of
year.' He replied, 'Ah, it isn't this time of year at all.'

Oliver St John Gogarty 1878–1957:
It Isn't This Time of Year At All (1954)

10 April in Fairbanks
There's nothing more appealing
You feel your blood congealing
In April in Fairbanks.

Murray Grand: 'April in Fairbanks'
(1952)

11 When two Englishmen meet, their first talk is of the
weather.

Samuel Johnson 1709–84: *The Idler*
24 June 1758

12 The most serious charge which can be brought against
New England is not Puritanism but February.

Joseph Wood Krutch 1893–1970:
The Twelve Seasons (1949) 'February'

13 SHE: I really can't stay
HE: But baby it's cold outside.

Frank Loesser 1910–69: 'Baby, It's
Cold Outside' (1949)

14 The rain drove us into the church—our refuge, our
strength, our only dry place . . . Limerick gained a
reputation for piety, but we knew it was only the rain.

Frank McCourt 1930– : *Angela's
Ashes* (1996)

15 It was such a lovely day I thought it was a pity to get up.

W. Somerset Maugham 1874–1965:
Our Betters (1923)

16 Winter is icummen in,
Lhude sing Goddamm,
Raineth drop and staineth slop,
And how the wind doth ramm!
Sing: Goddamm.

Ezra Pound 1885–1972: 'Ancient
Music' (1917)

17 'Anyhow,' Mme de Cambremer went on, 'I have a horror
of sunsets, they're so romantic, so operatic.'

Marcel Proust 1871–1922: *Sodome
et Gomorrhe* (Cities of the Plain,
1922)

18 Come December, people always say, 'Isn't it cold?' Well, of course it's cold. It's the middle of winter. You don't wander around at midnight saying, 'Isn't it dark?'

Arthur Smith 1954– : *Arthur Smith's Hamlet*

19 Thank heavens, the sun has gone in, and I don't have to go out and enjoy it.

Logan Pearsall Smith 1865–1946: *Afterthoughts* (1931)

20 Let no man boast himself that he has got through the perils of winter till at least the seventh of May.

Anthony Trollope 1815–82: *Doctor Thorne* (1858)

21 The way to ensure summer in England is to have it framed and glazed in a comfortable room.

Horace Walpole 1717–97: letter to Revd William Cole, 28 May 1774

22 It was the wrong kind of snow.

Terry Worrall: explaining disruption on British Rail; as quoted in *Evening Standard* 12 February 1991

Wine

66 A naïve domestic Burgundy without any breeding, but I think you'll be amused by its presumption. **99**
James Thurber

1 The teacher I most wanted to emulate, however, was single, drank wine and had been gassed in World War I. Of his three admirable traits, there was only one I wanted to copy, and sure enough, to this day, I love the sound of a popping cork.

Russell Baker 1925– : column in *New York Times*; Ned Sherrin *Cutting Edge* (1984)

2 *of claret:*
It would be port if it could.

Richard Bentley 1662–1742: R. C. Jebb *Bentley* (1902)

3 And Noah he often said to his wife when he sat down to dine,
'I don't care where the water goes if it doesn't get into the wine.'

G. K. Chesterton 1874–1936: 'Wine and Water' (1914)

4 'I rather like bad wine,' said Mr Mountchesney; 'one gets so bored with good wine.'

Benjamin Disraeli 1804–81: *Sybil* (1845)

5 *when the Queen accepted a second glass of wine at lunch:*
Do you think it's wise, darling? You know you've got to rule this afternoon.

Queen Elizabeth, the Queen Mother 1900–2002: Compton Miller *Who's Really Who* (1983)

6 When at dinner and supper, I drank, I know not how, of my own accord, so much wine, that I was even almost foxed and my head ached all night. So home.

Samuel Pepys 1633–1703: diary 29 September 1661

7 Was 1 a good year?

Michael Pertwee 1916– : *A Funny Thing Happened on the Way to the Forum* (film, 1966)

8 A good general rule is to state that the bouquet is better than the taste, and vice versa.
on wine-tasting

Stephen Potter 1900–69: *One-Upmanship* (1952)

9 I'm only a beer teetotaller, not a champagne teetotaller.

George Bernard Shaw 1856–1950: *Candida* (1898)

10 Good God! I've never drunk a vintage that starts with the number two before.

Nicholas Soames 1948– : in *Daily Mail* 5 June 2003

11 BRINDLEY: It does say Burgundy on the bottle.
MARKS: It's the old wine ramp, vicar! Cheapish, reddish and Spanish.

Tom Stoppard 1937– : *Where Are They Now?* (1973)

12 Champagne certainly gives one werry gentlemanly ideas, but for a continuance, I don't know but I should prefer mild hale.

R. S. Surtees 1805–64: *Jorrocks's Jaunts and Jollities* (1838)

13 It's a naïve domestic Burgundy without any breeding, but I think you'll be amused by its presumption.

James Thurber 1894–1961: cartoon caption in *New Yorker* 27 March 1937

Wit and Wordplay ····> Humour

66 'Curiouser and curiouser!' cried Alice. 99
Lewis Carroll

1 An ill-favoured thing, but Minoan.
supposedly a comment by the archaeologist Sir Arthur Evans on finding a fragment of Cretan pottery

Anonymous: in 'Quote . . . Unquote' Newsletter, April 1995

2 Wild horses on their bended knees would not get me out there.

Alan Bennett 1934– : *Forty Years On* (1969)

3 There's an element of mockery here I don't like. I don't mind your tongue being in your cheek, but I suspect your heart is there with it.

Alan Bennett 1934– : *Forty Years On* (1969)

4 'That's the reason they're called lessons,' the Gryphon remarked: 'because they lessen from day to day.'

Lewis Carroll 1832–98: *Alice's Adventures in Wonderland* (1865)

5 'Curiouser and curiouser!' cried Alice.

Lewis Carroll 1832–98: *Alice's Adventures in Wonderland* (1865)

6 A wit should be no more sincere than a woman constant; one argues a decay of parts, as t'other of beauty.

William Congreve 1670–1729: *The Way of the World* (1700)

7 His wit invites you by his looks to come,
But when you knock it never is at home.

William Cowper 1731–1800: 'Conversation' (1782)

8 Staircase wit.

Denis Diderot 1713–84: the witty riposte one thinks of only when one has left the drawing-room and is already on the way downstairs, in *Paradoxe sur le Comédien* (written 1773–8, published 1830)

9 O lovely O most charming pug
Thy graceful air and heavenly mug . . .
His noses cast is of the roman
He is a very pretty weoman
I could not get a rhyme for roman
And was oblidged to call it weoman.

Marjory Fleming 1803–11: 'Sonnet'

10 You've got to take the bull between your teeth.

Sam Goldwyn 1882–1974: N. Zierold *Hollywood Tycoons* (1969)

11 I can answer you in two words, im-possible.

Sam Goldwyn 1882–1974: Alva Johnston *The Great Goldwyn* (1937); apocryphal

12 Those who cannot miss an opportunity of saying a good thing . . . are not to be trusted with the management of any great question.

William Hazlitt 1778–1830: *Characteristics* (1823)

13 Dentist fills wrong cavity.
report of a dentist convicted of interfering with a patient

Ben Hecht 1894–1964: attributed

14 *on being told that the publisher of* Bentley's Miscellany *had thought of calling it* The Wits' Miscellany:
You need not have gone to the other extremity.

Douglas Jerrold 1803–57: Charles Cowden Clarke *Recollections of Writers* (1878)

15 It's hard not to write satire.

Juvenal AD c.60–c.130: *Satires*

16 *Ira Gershwin had noticed two aged men entering the theatre:*
GERSHWIN: That must be Gilbert and Sullivan coming to fix the show.
KAUFMAN: Why don't you put jokes like that into your lyrics?

George S. Kaufman 1889–1961: Howard Teichmann *George S. Kaufman* (1973)

17 '*Succès d'estime*' translates as 'a success that ran out of steam'.

George S. Kaufman 1889–1961: Philip Furia *Ira Gershwin* (1996)

18 The greatest thing since they reinvented unsliced bread.

William Keegan 1938– : in *Observer* 13 December 1987

19 [*Shogun* ended with] almost everybody except Richard Chamberlain being killed in the city of Osaka. *Moral*—Never give Osaka an even break.

Herbert Kretzmer: review of the miniseries *Shogun*; Ned Sherrin *Cutting Edge* (1984)

20 Many of us can still remember the social nuisance of the inveterate punster. This man followed conversation as a shark follows a ship.

Stephen Leacock 1869–1944: *The Boy I Left Behind Me* (1947)

21 Epigram: a wisecrack that played Carnegie Hall.

Oscar Levant 1906–72: in *Coronet* September 1958

22 *on being asked how to make an epigram by a young man in the flying corps:*
You merely loop the loop on a commonplace and come down between the lines.

W. Somerset Maugham 1874–1965: *A Writer's Notebook* (1949) written in 1933

23 Satire is a lesson, parody is a game.

Vladimir Nabokov 1899–1977: *Strong Opinions* (1974)

24 The dusk was performing its customary intransitive operation of 'gathering'.

Flann O'Brien 1911–66: *The Best of Myles* (1968)

25 *to the British actor Herbert Marshall who annoyed her by repeated references to his busy* '*shedule*':
I think you're full of skit.

Dorothy Parker 1893–1967: Marion Meade *What Fresh Hell Is This?* (1988)

26 The pellet with the poison's in the vessel with the pestle. The chalice from the palace has the brew that is true.

Norman Panama 1914– and **Melvin Frank** 1913–88: *The Court Jester* (1955 film); spoken by Danny Kaye

27 You beat your pate, and fancy wit will come:
Knock as you please, there's nobody at home.

Alexander Pope 1688–1744: 'Epigram: You beat your pate' (1732)

28 ADVERTISEMENT: Rice is nice, but ricicles are twicicles as nicicles.
CEDRIC PRICE: But testicles is besticles
in a Cambridge cinema watching the advertments

Cedric Price 1934–2003: Alan Bennett diary 2003, in *London Review of Books* 8 January 2004

29 I see a voice: now will I to the chink,
To spy an I can hear my Thisby's face.

William Shakespeare 1564–1616: *A Midsummer Night's Dream* (1595–6)

30 Most forcible Feeble.

William Shakespeare 1564–1616: *Henry IV, Part 2* (1597)

31 Comparisons are odorous.

William Shakespeare 1564–1616: *Much Ado About Nothing* (1598–9)

32 An aspersion upon my parts of speech!

Richard Brinsley Sheridan 1751–1816: *The Rivals* (1775)

33 He is the very pineapple of politeness!

Richard Brinsley Sheridan 1751–1816: *The Rivals* (1775)

34 If I reprehend any thing in this world, it is the use of my oracular tongue, and a nice derangement of epitaphs!

Richard Brinsley Sheridan 1751–1816: *The Rivals* (1775)

35 No caparisons, Miss, if you please!—Caparisons don't become a young woman.

Richard Brinsley Sheridan 1751–1816: *The Rivals* (1775)

36 She's as headstrong as an allegory on the banks of the Nile.

Richard Brinsley Sheridan 1751–1816: *The Rivals* (1775)

37 'I can't see the Speaker,
Pray, Hal, do you?'
'Not see the Speaker, Bill?
Why I see *two*.'

Richard Brinsley Sheridan 1751–1816: recalling an epigram commemorating the drunkenness of Pitt and Henry Dundas in the House of Commons; Walter Jerrold *Bon-Mots* (1893)

38 LADY SNEERWELL: There's no possibility of being witty without a little ill-nature; the malice of a good thing is the barb that makes it stick.

Richard Brinsley Sheridan 1751–1816: *The School for Scandal* (1777)

39 A man might sit down as systematically, and successfully, to the study of wit as he might to the study of mathematics . . . By giving up only six hours a day to being witty, he should come on prodigiously before midsummer.

Sydney Smith 1771–1845: *Sketches of Moral Philosophy* (1849)

40 *on seeing Mrs Grote in a huge rose-coloured turban:*
Now I know the meaning of the word 'grotesque'.

Sydney Smith 1771–1845: Peter Virgin *Sydney Smith* (1994)

41 You will find as you grow older that the weight of rages will press harder and harder upon the employer.

William Archibald Spooner 1844–1930: William Hayter *Spooner* (1977)

42 To our queer old dean.

William Archibald Spooner 1844–1930: a toast; *Oxford University What's What* (1948); attributed, perhaps apocryphal

43 You have tasted your worm, you have hissed my mystery lectures, and you must leave by the first town drain.

William Archibald Spooner 1844–1930: to an undergraduate; *Oxford University What's What* (1948); attributed, perhaps apocryphal

44 My parents bought a lavatory from a travelling circus, under the fond delusion that a Chipperfield commode was a desirable thing to have about the house.
at a British Antique Dealers' Association dinner in the 1970s

Tom Stoppard 1937– : attributed; in *Spectator* 19 December 1998

45 Do you think Diaghilev was the kind of person about whom you could say, 'Hail, Fellatio, well met?'

Peter Ustinov 1921–2004: John Drummond *Tainted by Experience* (2000); attributed

46 I'm aghast! If there ever was one.

Dick Vosburgh: *A Saint She Ain't* (1999)

47 I'm on the horns of a Dalai Lama.

Dick Vosburgh: *A Saint She Ain't* (1999)

48 *the American lexicographer Noah Webster was said to have been found by his wife embracing a chambermaid:*
MRS WEBSTER: Noah, I'm surprised.
NOAH WEBSTER: No, my dear. You are amazed. It is we who are surprised.

Noah Webster 1758–1843: apocryphal; William Safire in *New York Times* 15 October 1973

49 'Sesquippledan,' he would say. 'Sesquippledan verboojuice.'

H. G. Wells 1866–1946: *The History of Mr Polly* (1909)

50 OSCAR WILDE: How I wish I had said that.
WHISTLER: You will, Oscar, you will.

James McNeill Whistler 1834–1903: in R. Ellman *Oscar Wilde* (1987)

51 Oscar . . . picks from our platters the plums for the puddings he peddles in the provinces.

James McNeill Whistler 1834–1903: in *World* November 1886

52 I summed up all systems in a phrase, and all existence in an epigram.

Oscar Wilde 1854–1900: letter, from Reading Prison, to Lord Alfred Douglas, January–March 1897

Women and Woman's Role ····> Men and Women

❝A blonde to make a bishop kick a hole in a stained glass window.❞
Raymond Chandler

1 The only options open for girls then were of course mother, secretary or teacher . . . Now, I must say how lucky we are, as women, to live in an age where 'Dental Hygienist' has been added to the list.

Roseanne Arnold 1953– : *Roseanne* (1990)

2 The trouble with women in an orchestra is that if they are attractive it will upset my players and if they're not it will upset me.

Thomas Beecham 1879–1961: Harold Atkins and Archie Newman *Beecham Stories* (1978)

3 Zuleika, on a desert island, would have spent most of her time in looking for a man's footprint.

Max Beerbohm 1872–1956: *Zuleika Dobson* (1911)

4 The suffragettes were triumphant. Woman's place was in the gaol.

Caryl Brahms 1901–82 and **S. J. Simon** 1904–48: *No Nightingales* (1944)

5 I heard a man say that brigands demand your money *or* your life, whereas women require both.

Samuel Butler 1835–1902: *Further Extracts from Notebooks* (1934)

6 It was a blonde. A blonde to make a bishop kick a hole in a stained glass window.

Raymond Chandler 1888–1959: *Farewell, My Lovely* (1940)

7 I let go of her wrists, closed the door with my elbow and slid past her. It was like the first time. 'You ought to carry insurance on those,' I said.

Raymond Chandler 1888–1959: *The Little Sister* (1949)

8 Ful weel she soong the service dyvyne,
Entuned in hir nose ful semely;
And Frenssh she spak ful faire and fetisly,
After the scole of Stratford atte Bowe,
For Frenssh of Parys was to hire unknowe.

Geoffrey Chaucer c.1343–1400: of the Prioress; *The Canterbury Tales* 'The General Prologue'

9 When a woman isn't beautiful, people always say, 'You have lovely eyes, you have lovely hair.'

Anton Chekhov 1860–1904: *Uncle Vanya* (1897)

10 A woman can become a man's friend only in the following stages—first an acquaintance, next a mistress, and only then a friend.

Anton Chekhov 1860–1904: *Uncle Vanya* (1897)

11 Why do you rush through the fields in trains,
Guessing so much and so much.
Why do you flash through the flowery meads,
Fat-head poet that nobody reads;
And why do you know such a frightful lot
About people in gloves and such?

G. K. Chesterton 1874–1936: 'The Fat White Woman Speaks' (1933); an answer to Frances Cornford

12 O'erjoy'd was he to find
That, though on pleasure she was bent,
She had a frugal mind.

William Cowper 1731–1800: 'John Gilpin' (1785)

13 I'd have opened a knitting shop in Carlisle and been a part of life.
on his regret at not being born female

Quentin Crisp 1908–99: in *Spectator* 20 November 1999

14 A good uniform must work its way with the women, sooner or later.

Charles Dickens 1812–70: *Pickwick Papers* (1837)

15 She's the sort of woman . . . one would almost feel disposed to bury for nothing: and do it neatly, too!

Charles Dickens 1812–70: *Martin Chuzzlewit* (1844)

16 Plain women he regarded as he did the other severe facts of life, to be faced with philosophy and investigated by science.

George Eliot 1819–80: *Middlemarch* (1871–2)

17 When lovely woman stoops to folly and
Paces about her room again, alone,
She smoothes her hair with automatic hand,
And puts a record on the gramophone.

T. S. Eliot 1888–1965: *The Waste Land* (1922)

18 No woman can be a beauty without a fortune.

George Farquhar 1678–1707: *The Beaux' Stratagem* (1707)

19 'O! help me, heaven,' she prayed, 'to be decorative and to do right!'

Ronald Firbank 1886–1926: *The Flower Beneath the Foot* (1923)

20 The more underdeveloped the country, the more overdeveloped the women.

J. K. Galbraith 1908–2006: in *Time* 17 October 1969

21 I must have women. There is nothing unbends the mind like them.

John Gay 1685–1732: *The Beggar's Opera* (1728)

22 She may very well pass for forty-three
In the dusk with a light behind her!

W. S. Gilbert 1836–1911: *Trial by Jury* (1875)

23 I'm called Little Buttercup—dear Little Buttercup,
Though I could never tell why.

W. S. Gilbert 1836–1911: *HMS Pinafore* (1878)

24 To everybody's prejudice I know a thing or two;
I can tell a woman's age in half a minute—and I do!

W. S. Gilbert 1836–1911: *Princess Ida* (1884)

25 When lovely woman stoops to folly
And finds too late that men betray,
What charm can soothe her melancholy,
What art can wash her guilt away?

Oliver Goldsmith 1730–74: *The Vicar of Wakefield* (1766)

26 I didn't fight to get women out from behind the vacuum cleaner to get them onto the board of Hoover.

Germaine Greer 1939– : in *Guardian* 27 October 1986

27 She who must be obeyed.

Rider Haggard 1856–1925: *She* (1887)

28 Other girls are coy and hard to catch,
But other girls ain't havin' any fun.
Ev'ry time I lose a wrestlin' match
I have a funny feelin' that I won.

Oscar Hammerstein II 1895–1960: 'I Cain't Say No' (1943)

29 When she's narrow, she's narrow as an arrow
And she's broad, where a broad, should be broad.

Oscar Hammerstein II 1895–1960: 'Honey Bun' (1949)

30 I'm just a fool when lights are low,
I cain't be prissy and quaint.
I ain't the type thet c'n faint,
How c'n I be whut I ain't,
I cain't say no!

Oscar Hammerstein II 1895–1960: 'I Cain't Say No' (1943)

31 When Grandma was a lassie
That tyrant known as man
Thought a woman's place
Was just the space
Around a fryin' pan.
It was good enough for Grandma
But it ain't good enough for us!

E. Y. Harburg 1898–1981: 'It was Good Enough for Grandma' (1944)

32 Starlet is the name for any woman under thirty not actively employed in a brothel.

Ben Hecht 1894–1964: E. Goodman *The Fifty-Year Decline and Fall of Hollywood* (1961)

33 Other people's babies—
That's my life!
Mother to dozens,
And nobody's wife.
 of a nanny

A. P. Herbert 1890–1971: 'Other People's Babies' (1930)

34 A woman's preaching is like a dog's walking on his hinder legs. It is not done well; but you are surprised to find it done at all.

Samuel Johnson 1709–84: James Boswell *Life of Samuel Johnson* (1791) 31 July 1763

35 Remember, you're fighting for this woman's honour . . . which is probably more than she ever did.

Bert Kalmar 1884–1947 et al.: *Duck Soup* (1933 film); spoken by Groucho Marx

36 When you get to a man in the case,
They're like as a row of pins—
For the Colonel's Lady an' Judy O'Grady
Are sisters under their skins!

Rudyard Kipling 1865–1936: 'The Ladies' (1896)

37 I can stretch a greenback dollar from here to Kingdom Come.
I can play the numbers, pay my bills, an' still end up with some
I got a twenty dollar piece says
There ain't nothin' I can't do.

Jerry Leiber 1933– : 'I'm a Woman' (1962)

I can make a dress out of a feed bag an' I can make a man
   out of you.
'Cause I'm a woman
W-O-M-A-N
I'll say it again.

38 Thank heaven for little girls!
   For little girls get bigger every day.

Alan Jay Lerner 1918–86: 'Thank Heaven for Little Girls' (1958)

39 Women do not find it difficult nowadays to behave like men, but they often find it extremely difficult to behave like gentlemen.

Compton Mackenzie 1883–1972: *Literature in My Time* (1933)

40 When women kiss it always reminds one of prize-fighters shaking hands.

H. L. Mencken 1880–1956: *Chrestomathy* (1949)

41 'Always be civil to the girls, you never know who they may marry' is an aphorism which has saved many an English spinster from being treated like an Indian widow.

Nancy Mitford 1904–73: *Love in a Cold Climate* (1949)

42 I have never had any great esteem for the generality of the fair sex, and my only consolation for being of that gender has been the assurance it gave me of never being married to anyone amongst them.

Lady Mary Wortley Montagu 1689–1762: letter to Mrs Calthorpe, 7 December 1723

43 Be plain in dress and sober in your diet;
   In short my deary, kiss me, and be quiet.

Lady Mary Wortley Montagu 1689–1762: 'A Summary of Lord Lyttelton's Advice'

44 My only books
   Were woman's looks,
And folly's all they've taught me.

Thomas Moore 1779–1852: *Irish Melodies* (1807) 'The time I've lost in wooing'

45 The thinking man's crumpet.
   of Joan Bakewell

Frank Muir 1920–98: attributed

46 There was a young belle of old Natchez
   Whose garments were always in patchez.
When comment arose
On the state of her clothes,
She drawled, When Ah itchez, Ah scratchez.

Ogden Nash 1902–71: 'Requiem' (1938)

47 Feminism is the result of a few ignorant and literal-minded women letting the cat out of the bag about which is the superior sex.

P. J. O'Rourke 1947– : *Modern Manners* (1984)

48 I'd the upbringing a nun would envy . . . Until I was fifteen I was more familiar with Africa than my own body.

Joe Orton 1933–67: *Entertaining Mr Sloane* (1964)

49 She's like the old line about justice—not only must be done, but must be seen to be done.

John Osborne 1929– : *Time Present* (1968)

50 That woman speaks eighteen languages, and can't say No in any of them.

Dorothy Parker 1893–1967: Alexander Woollcott *While Rome Burns* (1934)

51 And there was that wholesale libel on a Yale prom. If all the girls attending it were laid end to end, Mrs Parker said, she wouldn't be at all surprised.

Dorothy Parker 1893–1967: Alexander Woollcott *While Rome Burns* (1934)

52 You can lead a horticulture, but you can't make her think.

Dorothy Parker 1893–1967: John Keats *You Might as well Live* (1970)

53 A busted, disgusted cocotte am I,
   Undesired on my tired little bottom, I,
While those fat femmes du monde

Cole Porter 1891–1964: 'The Cocotte' (1933)

With the men whom once I owned
Splash around like hell-bound hippopotami.

54 It's not 'cause I wouldn't,
It's not 'cause I shouldn't,
And, Lord knows, it's not 'cause I couldn't,
It's simply because I'm the laziest gal in town.

Cole Porter 1891–1964: 'The Laziest Girl in Town' (1927)

55 I do see her in tough joints more than somewhat.

Damon Runyon 1884–1946: in *Collier's* 22 May 1930 'Social Error'

56 O! when she's angry she is keen and shrewd.
She was a vixen when she went to school:
And though she be but little, she is fierce.

William Shakespeare 1564–1616: *A Midsummer Night's Dream* (1595–6)

57 The lady doth protest too much, methinks.

William Shakespeare 1564–1616: *Hamlet* (1601)

58 The fickleness of the women I love is only equalled by the infernal constancy of the women who love me.

George Bernard Shaw 1856–1950: *The Philanderer* (1898)

59 Here's to the ladies who lunch—
Everybody laugh—
Lounging in their caftans and planning a brunch
On their own behalf . . .
Off to the gym
Then to a fitting
Claiming they're fat,
And looking grim
'Cause they've been sitting
Choosing a hat—
Does anyone still wear a hat?
I'll drink to that . . .

. . . Another long exhausting day,
Another thousand dollars
A Matinée, a Pinter play,
Perhaps a piece of Mahler's—
I'll drink to that.
And one for Mahler . . .

. . . A toast to that invincible bunch
The dinosaurs surviving the crunch
Let's hear it for the ladies who lunch.

Stephen Sondheim 1930– : 'The Ladies who Lunch' (1970)

60 A woman seldom writes her mind but in her postscript.

Richard Steele 1672–1729: *The Spectator* 31 May 1711

61 A woman without a man is like a fish without a bicycle.

Gloria Steinem 1934– : attributed

62 We are becoming the men we wanted to marry.

Gloria Steinem 1934– : in *Ms* July/August 1982

63 There are worse occupations in this world than feeling a woman's pulse.

Laurence Sterne 1713–68: *A Sentimental Journey* (1768)

64 I had never seen a naked woman, and the way things were going I was never likely to. My family owned land.

Tom Stoppard 1937– : *Artist Descending a Staircase* (1973)

65 It's the last thing one would have expected of a woman who runs a donkey sanctuary—concubine to an opium addict.

Tom Stoppard 1937– : *The Dog It Was That Died* (1983)

66 Women never look so well as when one comes in wet and dirty from hunting.

R. S. Surtees 1805–64: *Mr Sponge's Sporting Tour* (1853)

67 I blame the women's movement for 10 years in a boiler suit.

Jill Tweedie 1936–93: attributed

68 When once a woman has given you her heart, you can never get rid of the rest of her body.

John Vanbrugh 1664–1726: *The Relapse* (1696)

69 The Queen is most anxious to enlist every one who can speak or write to join in checking this mad, wicked folly of 'Woman's Rights', with all its attendant horrors, on which her poor feeble sex is bent, forgetting every sense of womanly feeling and propriety.

Queen Victoria 1819–1901: letter to Theodore Martin, 29 May 1870

70 The world is full of care, much like unto a bubble; Woman and care, and care and women, and women and care and trouble.

Nathaniel Ward 1578–1652: epigram, attributed by Ward to a lady at the Court of the Queen of Bohemia; *The Simple Cobbler of Aggawam in America* (1647)

71 I will not stand for being called a woman in my own house.

Evelyn Waugh 1903–66: *Scoop* (1938)

72 I myself have never been able to find out precisely what feminism is: I only know that people call me a feminist whenever I express sentiments that differentiate me from a doormat or a prostitute.

Rebecca West 1892–1983: in 1913; *The Young Rebecca* (1982)

73 Glitter and be gay, That's the part I play. Here I am, unhappy chance. Forced to bend my soul To a sordid role, Victimized by bitter, bitter circumstance.

Richard Wilbur 1921– : 'Glitter and be Gay' (1956)

74 One should never trust a woman who tells one her real age. A woman who would tell one that, would tell one anything.

Oscar Wilde 1854–1900: *A Woman of No Importance* (1893)

75 Many a woman has a past, but I am told that she has at least a dozen, and that they all fit.

Oscar Wilde 1854–1900: *Lady Windermere's Fan* (1892)

Wordplay ····> Wit and Wordplay

Words ····> Language

66 It depends on what the meaning of 'is' is. 99
Bill Clinton

1 HONEY: I wonder if you could show me where the . . . I want to . . . put some powder on my nose.
GEORGE: Martha, won't you show her where we keep the . . . euphemism?

Edward Albee 1928– : *Who's Afraid of Virginia Woolf* (1964)

2 The most beautiful words in the English language are not 'I love you' but 'It's benign'.

Woody Allen 1935– : *Deconstructing Harry* (1997 film)

3 *after reports that cafeterias in Washington had changed the name of 'french fries' to 'freedom fries' in response to French criticism of American policy in Iraq:*

Woody Allen 1935– : in *Independent* 7 June 2003

I don't want to have to refer to my French fry potatoes as freedom fries, and I don't want to have to freedom kiss my wife.

4 *version of an old joke:*
VICTOR LEWIS SMITH: You clearly don't know the difference between a Joist and a Girder.
IRISH BUILDER: Yes I do. Joist wrote Ulysses and Girder wrote Faust.

Anonymous: in *Evening Standard* 12 September 2003

5 *as a young serviceman Dennis Potter was summoned for help with spelling by an elderly Major:*
How you do spell 'accelerator'? I've been all through the blasted 'Ex's' in this bloody dictionary.

Anonymous: related by Dennis Potter during the launch of his television show *Lipstick on Your Collar*; in *Ned Sherrin in his Anecdotage* (1993)

6 Serendipity means searching for a needle in a haystack and instead finding a farmer's daughter.

Anonymous: in 'Quote . . . Unquote' Newsletter, July 1995, as quoted by Sir Herman Bondi

7 The English language may hold a more disagreeable combination of words than 'The doctor will see you now.' I am willing to concede something to the phrase 'Have you anything to say before the current is turned on'.

Robert Benchley 1889–1945: *Love Conquers All* (1923); (see also **Speeches** 7)

8 You see it's like a portmanteau—there are two meanings packed up into one word.

Lewis Carroll 1832–98: *Through the Looking-Glass* (1872)

9 'There's glory for you!' 'I don't know what you mean by "glory",' Alice said. 'I meant, "there's a nice knock-down argument for you!" ' ' But "glory" doesn't mean "a nice knock-down argument",' Alice objected. 'When *I* use a word,' Humpty Dumpty said in a rather scornful tone, 'it means just what I choose it to mean—neither more nor less.'

Lewis Carroll 1832–98: *Through the Looking-Glass* (1872)

10 It depends on what the meaning of 'is' is.
videotaped evidence to the grand jury; tapes broadcast 21 September 1998

Bill Clinton 1946– : in *Guardian* 22 September 1998

11 'Do you spell it with a "V" or a "W"?' inquired the judge. 'That depends upon the taste and fancy of the speller, my Lord,' replied Sam [Weller].

Charles Dickens 1812–70: *Pickwick Papers* (1837)

12 Two such wonderful phrases—'I understand perfectly' and 'That is a lie'—a précis of life, aren't they?

Brian Friel 1929– : *The Communication Cord* (1983)

13 Excluding two-letter prepositions and 'an', I imagine *me* is the most used two-letter word in Songdom. 'I' (leaving out indefinite article 'a') is doubtless the most used one-letter word (and everywhere else, for that matter). 'You' (if definite article 'the' bows out) is the most frequent three-letter word. 'Love' probably gets the four-letter nod (referring strictly to songs that can be heard in the home). In the five-letter stakes I would wager that 'heart' and 'dream' photo-finish in a dead heat. As for words of more than five letters, you're on your own.

Ira Gershwin 1896–1983: *Lyrics on Several Occasions: A Brief Concordance* (1977)

14 Some word that teems with hidden meaning—like Basingstoke.

W. S. Gilbert 1836–1911: *Ruddigore* (1887)

15 It's exactly where a thought is lacking
That, just in time, a word shows up instead.

Goethe 1749–1832: *Faust* (1808) pt 1

16 Words are chameleons, which reflect the colour of their environment.

Learned Hand 1872–1961: in *Commissioner v. National Carbide Corp.* (1948)

17 Together they go places . . . Words make you think a thought. Music makes you feel a feeling. A song makes you feel a thought . . . The greatest romance in the life of a lyricist is when the right word meets the right note; often however, a Park Avenue phrase elopes with a Bleeker Street chord resulting in a shotgun wedding and a quickie divorce.

E. Y. Harburg 1898–1981: lecture given at the New York YMCA in 1970

18 Is there, can there be, such a word as *purposive?* There is: it was invented by a surgeon in 1855; and instead of being kept on the top shelf of an anatomical museum it is exhibited in both these volumes.

A. E. Housman 1859–1936: in *Cambridge Review* 1917

19 I understand your new play is full of single entendre.

George S. Kaufman 1889–1961: to Howard Dietz on *Between the Devil*; Howard Teichmann *George S. Kaufman* (1973)

20 I can't do splat . . . It doesn't translate.
the British Consul when asked to translate a description of the effect of a dum-dum bullet on the human skull

John le Carré 1931– : *Single & Single* (1999)

21 In my youth there were words you couldn't say in front of a girl; now you can't say 'girl'.

Tom Lehrer 1928– ; in *Sunday Telegraph* 10 March 1996 'Spirits of the Age'

22 Hypochondria is Greek for 'men'.

Kathy Lette 1958– : in *Mail on Sunday* 4 April 2004

23 I know
That's she's sweeter 'n sugar—
But oh!
You can't rhyme 'sugar'!

Frank Loesser 1910–69: 'I'm Ridin' for a Fall' in *Thank Your Lucky Stars* (1943 musical film)

24 They say the definition of ambivalence is watching your mother-in-law drive over a cliff in your new Cadillac.

David Mamet 1947– : in *Guardian* 19 February 2000

25 I often think how much easier life would have been for me and how much time I should have saved if I had known the alphabet. I can never tell where I and J stand without saying G, H to myself first.

W. Somerset Maugham 1874–1965: *A Writer's Notebook* (1949) written in 1941

26 He respects Owl, because you can't help respecting anybody who can spell TUESDAY, even if he doesn't spell it right; but spelling isn't everything. There are days when spelling Tuesday simply doesn't count.

A. A. Milne 1882–1956: *The House at Pooh Corner* (1928)

27 Words are like leaves; and where they most abound, Much fruit of sense beneath is rarely found.

Alexander Pope 1688–1744: *An Essay on Criticism* (1711)

28 Good authors too, who once knew better words
Now only use four-letter words
Writing prose
Anything goes.

Cole Porter 1891–1964: 'Anything Goes' (1934)

29 The trouble with words is that you never know whose mouth they've been in.

Dennis Potter 1935–94: attributed

30 Make me a beautiful word for doing things tomorrow; for that surely is a great and blessed invention.

George Bernard Shaw 1856–1950: *Back to Methuselah* (1921)

31 I asked my teacher what an oxymoron was and he said, 'I don't know what an "oxy" is, bastard.

Arthur Smith 1954– and **Chris England**: *An Evening with Gary Lineker* (1990)

32 *prescription when J. H. Thomas complained of 'an 'ell of an 'eadache':*
A couple of aspirates.

F. E. Smith 1872–1930: in *Ned Sherrin in his Anecdotage* (1993)

33 Man does not live by words alone, despite the fact that he sometimes has to eat them.

Adlai Stevenson 1900–65: *The Wit and Wisdom of Adlai Stevenson* (1965)

34 REPORTER: Can we have a quick word please?
GORDON STRACHAN: Velocity [walks off].

Gordon Strachan 1957– : Leo Moynihan *Gordon Strachan* (2004)

35 By hard, honest labour I've dug all the large words out of my vocabulary . . . I never write metropolis for seven cents because I can get the same money for city. I never write policeman, because I can get the same money for *Cop*.

Mark Twain 1835–1910: *Mark Twain's Speeches* (1923)

36 *defining 'narcissistic':*
An adjective currently used to describe anyone better-looking than oneself.

Gore Vidal 1925– : attributed; in *Mail on Sunday* 2 June 2002

37 It is a pity that Chawcer, who had geneyus, was so unedicated. He's the wuss speller I know of.

Artemus Ward 1834–67: *Artemus Ward in London* (1867)

38 In modern life nothing produces such an effect as a good platitude. It makes the whole world kin.

Oscar Wilde 1854–1900: *An Ideal Husband* (1895)

Work and Leisure

66 A professional is a man who can do his job when he doesn't feel like it. **99**
James Agate

1 I will undoubtedly have to seek what is happily known as gainful employment, which I am glad to say does not describe holding public office.

Dean Acheson 1893–1971: in *Time* 22 December 1952

2 A professional is a man who can do his job when he doesn't feel like it. An amateur is a man who can't do his job when he does feel like it.

James Agate 1877–1947: diary, 19 July 1945

3 It has more strings than a philharmonic orchestra.
the Communication Workers' Union rejecting a pay deal

Anonymous: in *Mail on Sunday* 31 August 2003

4 If I am doing nothing, I like to be doing nothing to some purpose. That is what leisure means.

Alan Bennett 1934– : *A Question of Attribution* (1989)

5 I realized I could have written two songs and made myself some money in that time.

Irving Berlin 1888–1989: after taking two days of piano lessons; Caryl Brahms and Ned Sherrin *Song by Song* (1984)

6 I suspect guys who say, 'I just send out for a sandwich for lunch,' as lazy men trying to impress me.

Jimmy Cannon 1910–73: in *New York Post* c.1955 'Nobody Asked Me, But . . . '

7 *when criticized for continually arriving late for work:*
But think how early I go.

Lord Castlerosse 1891–1943: while
working in the City in 1919 for his
uncle Lord Revelstoke; Leonard
Mosley *Castlerosse* (1956); remark
also claimed by Howard Dietz at
MGM

8 I do nothing, granted. But I see the hours pass—which is
better than trying to fill them.

E. M. Cioran 1911– : in *Guardian* 11
May 1993

9 Work is always so much more fun than fun.

Noël Coward 1899–1973: Sheridan
Morley *The Quotable Noël Coward*
(1999)

10 I never work. Work does age you so.

Quentin Crisp 1908–99: in *Observer*
10 January 1999 'Sayings of the
Week'

11 People who are lonely are those who do not know what to
do with the time when they are alone.

Quentin Crisp 1908–99: in *Sunday
Telegraph* 28 September 1999

12 My life is one demd horrid grind!

Charles Dickens 1812–70: *Nicholas
Nickleby* (1839)

13 Anythin' for a quiet life, as the man said wen he took the
sitivation at the lighthouse.

Charles Dickens 1812–70: *Pickwick
Papers* (1837)

14 I have long been of the opinion that if work were such a
splendid thing the rich would have kept more of it for
themselves.

Bruce Grocott 1940– : in *Observer*
22 May 1988 'Sayings of the Week'

15 I think some of the union rules are a little strict. I used to
sing in the bath tub at home, now I've got to have another
guy in there with me as a stand-by.
on trade unions

Bob Hope 1903–2003: attributed; in
The Times 29 July 2003

16 It is impossible to enjoy idling thoroughly unless one has
plenty of work to do.

Jerome K. Jerome 1859–1927: *Idle
Thoughts of an Idle Fellow* (1886) 'On
Being Idle'

17 Being a specialist is one thing, getting a job is another.

Stephen Leacock 1869–1944: *The
Boy I Left Behind Me* (1947)

18 A secretary is not a toy.

Frank Loesser 1910–69: song title
(1961)

19 I can think of few nobler callings for elderly persons with
leisure than to provide unindexed books with indexes.

E. V. Lucas 1868–1938: *365 Days and
One More* (1926)

20 Why do men delight in work? Fundamentally, I suppose,
because there is a sense of relief and pleasure in getting
something done—a kind of satisfaction not unlike that
which a hen enjoys on laying an egg.

H. L. Mencken 1880–1956: *Minority
Report* (1956)

21 Work expands so as to fill the time available for its
completion.

C. Northcote Parkinson 1909–93:
Parkinson's Law (1958)

22 It's true hard work never killed anybody, but I figure why
take the chance?

Ronald Reagan 1911– : interview; in
Guardian 31 March 1987

23 I understand. You work very hard two days a week and
you need a five-day weekend. That's normal.

Neil Simon 1927– : *Come Blow Your
Horn* (1961)

24 It's dogged as does it. It ain't thinking about it.

Anthony Trollope 1815–82: *The Last
Chronicle of Barset* (1867)

25 How to be an effective secretary is to develop the kind of lonely self-abnegating sacrificial instincts usually possessed only by the early saints on their way to martyrdom.

Jill Tweedie 1936–93: *It's Only Me* (1980)

26 Work is the curse of the drinking classes.

Oscar Wilde 1854–1900: Hesketh Pearson *Life of Oscar Wilde* (1946)

Writers ····▸ Books, Literature, Poetry, Poets, Reading, Writing

66 He's a writer for the ages—for the ages of four to eight. 99
Dorothy Parker

1 *of the Bloomsbury Group:*
They lived in squares and loved in triangles.

Anonymous: unattributed saying

2 *of Dr Johnson and her husband James Boswell:*
I have seen many a bear led by a man: but I never before saw a man led by a bear.

Margaret Boswell 1738?–89: James Boswell *Life of Samuel Johnson* (1791) 27 November 1773

3 In general I do not draw well with literary men—not that I dislike them but—I never know what to say to them after I have praised their last publication.

Lord Byron 1788–1824: 'Detached Thoughts' 15 October 1821

4 *his Intourist guide had protested that Shakespeare's plays could never have been written by a grocer from Stratford-upon-Avon:*
They are exactly the sort of plays I would expect a grocer to write.

Robert Byron 1905–41: *The Road to Oxiana* (1980 ed.); introduction

5 The compulsion to make rhymes was born in me. For those sated readers of my work who wish ardently that I would stop, the future looks dark indeed.

Noël Coward 1899–1973: foreword to the *The Lyrics of Noel Coward* (1965)

6 HANNEN SWAFFER: I have always said that you act much better than you write.
NOËL COWARD: How odd, I'm always saying the same about you.

Noël Coward 1899–1973: Sheridan Morley *A Talent to Amuse* (1969)

7 There are three reasons for becoming a writer. The first is that you need the money; the second, that you have something to say that you think the world should know; and the third is that you can't think what to do with the long winter evenings.

Quentin Crisp 1908–99: *The Naked Civil Servant* (1968)

8 Most people are vain, so I try to ensure that any author who comes to stay will find at least one of their books in their room.

Duke of Devonshire 1920– : in *The Spectator* 22 January 1994

9 I love being a writer. What I can't stand is the paperwork.

Peter de Vries 1910–93: Laurence J. Peter (ed.) *Quotations for our Time* (1977)

10 An author who speaks about his own books is almost as bad as a mother who talks about her own children.

Benjamin Disraeli 1804–81: at a banquet given in Glasgow on his installation as Lord Rector, 19 November 1873

11 The nicest old lady I ever met.
of Henry James

William Faulkner 1897–1962:
Edward Stone *The Battle and the Books* (1964)

12 A New Jersey Nero who mistakes his pinafore for a toga.
of Alexander Woollcott

Edna Ferber 1887–1968: R. E. Drennan *Wit's End* (1973)

13 It is splendid to be a great writer, to put men into the frying pan of your words and make them pop like chestnuts.

Gustave Flaubert 1821–80: letter to Louise Colet, 3 November 1851

14 The defendant, Mr. Haddock, is, among other things, an author, which fact should alone dispose you in the plaintiff's favour.

A. P. Herbert 1890–1971: *Misleading Cases* (1935)

15 The book of my enemy has been remaindered
And I rejoice . . .
What avail him now his awards and prizes,
The praise expended upon his meticulous technique,
His individual new voice?

Clive James 1939– : 'The Book of My Enemy has been Remaindered' (1986)

16 *a young admirer had asked if he might kiss the hand that wrote Ulysses:*
No, it did lots of other things too.

James Joyce 1882–1941: Richard Ellmann *James Joyce* (1959)

17 Tell them the author giveth and the author taketh away.
to a playwright afraid to tell the cast of cuts he had made

George S. Kaufman 1889–1961: Howard Teichmann *George S. Kaufman* (1972)

18 *objecting to having been appointed a Companion of Honour without his consent:*
How would you like it if you woke up and found yourself Archbishop of Canterbury?

Rudyard Kipling 1865–1936: letter to Bonar Law, 1917; Charles Carrington *Rudyard Kipling* (1978)

19 Mr. Ruskin, whose distinction it was to express in prose of incomparable grandeur thought of an unparalleled confusion.

Osbert Lancaster 1908–80: *Pillar to Post* (1938)

20 The writer is to the real world what Esperanto is to the language world—funny, maybe, but not *that* funny.

Fran Lebowitz 1946– : *Metropolitan Life* (1978)

21 E. M. Forster never gets any further than warming the teapot. He's a rare fine hand at that. Feel this teapot. Is it not beautifully warm? Yes, but there ain't going to be no tea.

Katherine Mansfield 1888–1923: diary, May 1917

22 Dear Willie, you may well be right in thinking you write like Shakespeare. Certainly I have noticed during these last few months an adulation of your name in the more vulgar portions of the popular press. And one word of brotherly advice. *Do Not Attempt the Sonnets.*

Viscount Maugham d. 1958: letter to his brother Somerset Maugham, in *Ned Sherrin in his Anecdotage* (1993)

23 The humour of Dostoievsky is the humour of a bar-loafer who ties a kettle to a dog's tail.

W. Somerset Maugham 1874–1965: *A Writer's Notebook* (1949) written in 1917

24 There is no need for the writer to eat a whole sheep to be able to tell you what mutton tastes like. It is enough if he eats a cutlet. But he should do that.

W. Somerset Maugham 1874–1965: *A Writer's Notebook* (1949) written in 1941

25 Poor Henry [James], he's spending eternity wandering round and round a stately park and the fence is just too high for him to peep over and they're having tea just too far away for him to hear what the countess is saying.

W. Somerset Maugham 1874–1965: *Cakes and Ale* (1930)

26 What obsesses a writer starting out on a lifetime's work is the panic-stricken search for a voice of his own.

John Mortimer 1923– : *Clinging to the Wreckage* (1982)

27 I am the kind of writer that people think other people are reading.

V. S. Naipaul 1932– : in *Radio Times* 14 March 1979

28 THE EDITOR: We can't have much more of this, space must also be found for my stuff.
MYSELF: All right, never hesitate to say so. I can turn off the tap at will.

Flann O'Brien 1911–66: *The Best of Myles* (1968)

29 [David Merrick] liked writers in the way that a snake likes live rabbits.

John Osborne 1929– : *Almost a Gentleman* (1991)

30 He's a writer for the ages—for the ages of four to eight.

Dorothy Parker 1893–1967: R. E. Drennan *Wit's End* (1973)

31 Authors are judged by strange capricious rules
The great ones are thought mad, the small ones fools.

Alexander Pope 1688–1744: prologue to *Three Hours after Marriage* (1717)

32 No, on the whole I think all writers should be in prison.

Ralph Richardson 1902–83: on being asked to appear in a charity programme in support of imprisoned writers; in *Ned Sherrin in his Anecdotage* (1993)

33 A confessional passage has probably never been written that didn't stink a little bit of the writer's pride in having given up his pride.

J. D. Salinger 1919– : *Catcher in the Rye* (1951)

34 Virginia Woolf, I enjoyed talking to her, but thought *nothing* of her writing. I considered her 'a beautiful little knitter'.

Edith Sitwell 1887–1964: letter to Geoffrey Singleton, 11 July 1955

35 *the critic Moon's assessment of a dramatist:*
An uncanny ear that might have belonged to a Van Gogh.

Tom Stoppard 1937– : *The Real Inspector Hound* (1968)

36 The shelf life of the modern hardback writer is somewhere between the milk and the yoghurt.

Calvin Trillin 1935– : in *Sunday Times* 9 June 1991; attributed

37 He never leaves off . . . and he always has two packages of manuscript in his desk, besides the one he's working on, and the one that's being published.
on her husband Anthony Trollope

Rose Trollope 1820–1917: Julian Hawthorne *Shapes that Pass: Memories of Old Days* (1928)

38 What other culture could have produced someone like Hemingway and *not* seen the joke?

Gore Vidal 1925– : *Pink Triangle and Yellow Star* (1982)

39 To see him [Stephen Spender] fumbling with our rich and delicate language is to experience all the horror of seeing a Sèvres vase in the hands of a chimpanzee.

Evelyn Waugh 1903–66: in *The Tablet* 5 May 1951

40 Let Shakespeare do it his way, I'll do it mine. We'll see who comes out better.

Mae West 1892–1980: G. Eells and S. Musgrove *Mae West* (1989)

41 Just as Voltaire attributed everything good to a China he had never seen, so La Fayette idealised an America he had forgotten.

Edmund White 1940– : *Fanny, a fiction* (2003)

42 Mr. [Henry] James writes fiction as if it were a painful duty.

Oscar Wilde 1854–1900: 'The Decay of Lying' (1891)

43 Meredith! Who can define him? His style is chaos illuminated by flashes of lightning. As a writer he has mastered everything except language: as a novelist he can

Oscar Wilde 1854–1900: 'The Decay of Lying' (1891)

do everything except tell a story. As an artist he is
everything, except articulate.

44 I know no person so perfectly disagreeable and even
dangerous as an author.

William IV 1765–1837: Philip Ziegler
King William IV (1971)

45 Every author really wants to have letters printed in the
papers. Unable to make the grade, he drops down a rung
of the ladder and writes novels.

P. G. Wodehouse 1881–1975: *Louder
and Funnier* (1932)

46 *A. A. Milne had written a hostile letter to the* Daily Telegraph
on the report of Wodehouse's broadcasting from Germany:
My personal animosity against a writer never affects my
opinion of what he writes. Nobody could be more anxious
than myself, for instance, that Alan Alexander Milne
should trip over a loose bootlace and break his bloody
neck, yet I re-read his early stuff at regular intervals with
all the old enjoyment.

P. G. Wodehouse 1881–1975: letter
27 November 1945

Writing ····> Books, Literature, Poetry, Poets, Reading, Writers

66 Authors with a mortgage never get writer's block. 99
Mavis Cheek

1 If you can't annoy somebody with what you write, I think
there's little point in writing.

Kingsley Amis 1922–95: in *Radio
Times* 1 May 1971

2 The biggest obstacle to professional writing is the necessity
for changing a typewriter ribbon.

Robert Benchley 1889–1945: *Chips
off the old Benchley* (1949)

3 The only thing that goes missing in Nature is a pencil.

Robert Benchley 1889–1945:
attributed, perhaps apocryphal

4 In the mind, as in the body, there is the necessity of
getting rid of waste, and a man of active literary habits
will write for the fire as well as for the press.

Jerome Cardan 1501–76: William
Osler *Aequanimites* (1904); epigraph

5 Authors with a mortgage never get writer's block.

Mavis Cheek 1948– : in *Bookseller*
19 September 2003

6 Writing, I explained, was mainly an attempt to out-argue
one's past; to present events in such a light that battles
lost in life were either won on paper or held to a draw.

Jules Feiffer 1929– : *Ackroyd* (1977)

7 You just have to work with what God sends, and if God
doesn't seem to understand the concept of commercial
success, then that's your bad luck.

Michael Frayn 1933– : in *Sunday
Times* 3 February 2002

8 No plagiarist can excuse the wrong by showing how much
of his work he did not pirate.

Learned Hand 1872–1961: *Sheldon v.
Metro-Goldwyn Pictures Corp.* 1936

9 I had my fill of this dreamy abstract thing called business
and I decided to face reality by writing lyrics . . . the
capitalists saved me in 1929 . . . I was left with a pencil
and finally had to write for a living.

E. Y. Harburg 1898–1981: lecture
given at the New York YMCA in 1970

10 *explaining why he wrote opinions while standing:*
Nothing conduces to brevity like a caving in of the knees.

Oliver Wendell Holmes Jr.
1841–1935: Catherine Drinker Bowen
Yankee from Olympus (1944);
attributed

11 Whence came the intrusive comma on p. 4? It did not fall
from the sky.

A. E. Housman 1859–1936: letter to
the Richards Press, 3 July 1930

12 Read over your compositions, and where ever you meet
with a passage which you think is particularly fine, strike
it out.

Samuel Johnson 1709–84: quoting a
college tutor; James Boswell *Life of
Samuel Johnson* (1791) 30 April 1773

13 No man but a blockhead ever wrote, except for money.

Samuel Johnson 1709–84: James
Boswell *Life of Samuel Johnson*
(1791) 5 April 1776

14 If you want to get rich from writing, write the sort of thing
that's read by persons who move their lips when reading.

Don Marquis 1878–1937: attributed;
Peter Kemp (ed.) *Oxford Dictionary of
Literary Quotations* (1997)

15 The art of writing, like the art of love, runs all the way
from a kind of routine hard to distinguish from piling
bricks to a kind of frenzy closely related to delirium
tremens.

H. L. Mencken 1880–1956: *Minority
Report* (1956)

16 If you steal from one author, it's plagiarism; if you steal
from many, it's research.

Wilson Mizner 1876–1933: Alva
Johnston *The Legendary Mizners*
(1953)

17   I'm glad you'll write,
You'll furnish paper when I shite.

Lady Mary Wortley Montagu
1689–1762: 'Reasons that Induced Dr
S— to write a Poem called the Lady's
Dressing Room'

18 It is our national joy to mistake for the first-rate, the
fecund rate.

Dorothy Parker 1893–1967: review
of Sinclair Lewis *Dodsworth*; in *New
Yorker* 16 March 1929

19 As to the Adjective: when in doubt, strike it out.

Mark Twain 1835–1910: *Pudd'nhead
Wilson* (1894)

20 Anyone could write a novel given six weeks, pen, paper,
and no telephone or wife.

Evelyn Waugh 1903–66: Chips
Channon diary 16 December 1934

Youth ····▸ Children, Middle Age, Old Age

❝ The only way to stay young is to avoid old people. ❞
James D. Watson

1 It is better to waste one's youth than to do nothing with it
at all.

Georges Courteline 1858–1929: *La
Philosophie de Georges Courteline*
(1948)

2 I am just an ingénue
And shall be till I'm eighty-two.

Noël Coward 1899–1973: 'Little
Women' (1928)

3 She's shy—of the Violet persuasion, but that's not a bad
thing in a young girl.

Ronald Firbank 1886–1926: *The
Flower Beneath the Foot* (1923)

4 Remember that as a teenager you are at the last stage in your life when you will be happy to hear that the phone is for you.

Fran Lebowitz 1946– : *Social Studies* (1981)

5 If you had seen me in my teens you would have bolted for the door without picking up your coat.

Joanna Lumley 1946– : in *Sunday Times* 24 February 2002

6 Youth is wasted on the young. I'm 52 now and I just can't stay up all night like I did.

Camille Paglia 1947– : interview in *Sunday Times* 6 June 1999

7 It's all that the young can do for the old, to shock them and keep them up to date.

George Bernard Shaw 1856–1950: *Fanny's First Play* (1914) 'Induction'

8 What music is more enchanting than the voices of young people, when you can't hear what they say?

Logan Pearsall Smith 1865–1946: *Afterthoughts* (1931)

9 Give me a girl at an impressionable age, and she is mine for life.

Muriel Spark 1918–2006: *The Prime of Miss Jean Brodie* (1961)

10 One's prime is elusive. You little girls, when you grow up, must be on the alert to recognize your prime at whatever time of your life it may occur.

Muriel Spark 1918–2006: *The Prime of Miss Jean Brodie* (1961)

11 The only way to stay young is to avoid old people.

James D. Watson 1928– : in *The Times* 9 March 2002

12 Being young is not having any money; being young is not minding not having any money.

Katharine Whitehorn 1926– : *Observations* (1970)

13 I have been in a youth hostel. I know what they're like. You are put in a kitchen with seventeen venture scouts with behavioural difficulties and made to wash swedes.

Victoria Wood 1953– : *Mens Sana in Thingummy Doodah* (1990)

Author Index

Beerbohm, Max *(cont.)*:
Art 6
Class 3
Cricket 5
Critics 3, 4
Education 4
Intelligence 2
Literature 2, 3
Love 3
Men 3
Morality 1
People 7
Royalty 14
Snobbery 3
Society 2
Theatre 8
Virtue 2
Women 3
Beethoven, Ludwig van
(1770–1827)
Cookery 1
Behan, Brendan (1923–64)
Behaviour 2
Critics 5
Death 10
Drink 5, 6
England 4
Ireland 1
Theatre 9
Behan, Dominic (1928–)
Publishing 3
Behn, Aphra (1640–89)
Poverty 3
Belasco, David
Boxing 2
Belloc, Hilaire (1870–1953)
Animals 5, 6, 7
Birds 1
Certainty 4
Children 3, 4
Class 4
Cookery 2
Death 11, 12
Languages 5
Lies 3, 4
Literature 4
Medicine 5
Money 3
Politicians 6
Power 1
Religion 6
Science 4
Time 4
Bellow, Saul (1915–2005)
Biography 3

Mind 1
New York 1
Benchley, Peter (1940–)
Transport 4
Benchley, Robert (1889–1945)
Architecture 2
Baseball 1
Countries 2
Critics 6
Drink 7, 8
Epitaphs 6
Health 1
Humour 3
Mistakes 3
Telegrams 3
Transport 5
Travel 1
Weather 2
Words 7
Writing 2, 3
Benn, Tony (1925–)
Libraries 2
Newspapers 6
Benner, Richard
Canada 1
Bennett, Alan (1934–)
America 4
Body 4
Bureaucracy 2
Censorship 3
Choice 2
Countries 3
Drink 9
Education 5, 6, 7
Family 4
Gardens 3
Generation Gap 1
History 2
Humour 4
Language 1
Life 4
Literature 5
Marriage 14
Medicine 6
Men and Women 4
Middle Age 3
Mind 2
Names 3
Old Age 4, 5
Past 3
Progress 1
Religion 7
Sex 17, 18
Sickness 3
Snobbery 4

Sports 4
Trust 1
Wealth 4
Wit 2, 3
Work 4
Bennett, Arnold (1867–1931)
Literature 6
Love 4
Marriage 15
Pride 1
Bennett, Jill (1931–90)
Marriage 16
Bennett, William J. (1943–)
Religion 8
Benny, Jack (1894–1974)
Money 4
Benson, A. C. (1862–1925)
Description 5
England 5
Benson, E. F. (1867–1940)
Character 2
Conversation 2
Home 1
Hospitality 2
Bentley, Edmund Clerihew
(1875–1956)
Architecture 3
Behaviour 3
Biography 4
Crime 3
Death 13
Economics 3
Mistakes 4, 5
Science 5
Universe 2
Bentley, Richard (1662–1742)
Wine 2
Bergman, Andrew (1945–) and
Brooks, Mel (1926–)
Body 5
Berlin, Irving (1888–1989)
Acting 3
Armed Forces 3
Debt 1
Work 5
Berlin, Irving (1888–1989) and
Whiting, George
Marriage 17
Bernard, Jeffrey (1932–97)
Betting 1
Fame 7
Friends 3
Happiness 4
Mistakes 6
Places 1

Sickness 4
Taxes 1
Berners, Lord (1883–1950)
People 8
Berra, Yogi (1925–)
Baseball 2, 3
Berton, Pierre (1920–2004)
Canada 2
Best, George (1946–2005)
Medicine 7
Wealth 5
Bethell, Richard (1800–73)
Judges 2
Betjeman, John (1906–84)
Animals 8
Architecture 4
Christmas 3
England 6
Food 4
Hope 1
Love 5
Men and Women 5
Religion 9, 10, 11
Royalty 15
Satisfaction 3
Society 3, 4
Sports 5
Tennis 2
Towns 5
Bevan, Aneurin (1897–1960)
Bureaucracy 3
Democracy 4
Future 1
Newspapers 7
Politicians 7, 8
Politics 11, 12
Prime Ministers 5
Bevin, Ernest (1881–1951)
Diplomacy 2
Politicians 9
Bible
Books 1
Bickerstaffe, Isaac (1733–c.1808)
Satisfaction 4
Bicks, Jenny
Sex 19
Bierce, Ambrose (1842–c.1914)
Bores 2
Fame 8
Food 5, 6
Friends 4
Future 2
History 3
Hope 2
Marriage 18

Mind 3
Mistakes 7
Music 9
Politics 13
Self-Knowledge 2, 3
Success 1
Virtue 3
Binchy, Maeve (1940–)
Body 6
Christmas 4
Cookery 3
Past 4
Birch, Nigel (1906–81)
Politics 14
Birkett, Lord (1883–1962)
Judges 3
Speeches 1
Birrell, Augustine (1850–1933)
God 11, 12
Blackburn, Tony (1943–)
Death 14
Blair, Lionel (1936–)
Middle Age 4
Blair, Tony (1953–)
Prime Ministers 6
Self-Knowledge 4
Blake, Eubie (1883–1983)
Old Age 6
Sex 20
Blake, William (1757–1827)
Anger 2
Blakemore, Michael (1928–)
Theatre 10
Blane, Ralph see **Martin, Hugh**
and **Blane, Ralph**
Blessington, Countess of
(1789–1849)
Marriage 19
Blix, Hans (1928–)
Certainty 5
Bloom, Marty see **Rose, Billy** and
Bloom, Marty
Blunkett, David (1947–)
Success 2
Blythe, Ronald (1922–)
Clergy 2
Bogart, John B. (1848–1921)
Journalism 3
Bohr, Niels (1885–1962)
Certainty 6
Future 3
Bolt, Robert (1924–95)
Morality 2
Wales 3

Bonaparte, Elizabeth
Patterson (1785–1879)
Marriage 20
Bone, James
Journalism 4
Bonfiglioli, Kyril (1928–85)
Birds 2
Bonham, Violet Carter
(1887–1969)
Housework 1
Telegrams 4
Bono (1960–)
Ireland 2
Booth, Connie see **Cleese, John**
and **Booth, Connie**
Boothroyd, Basil (1910–88)
Description 6
Gardens 4, 5
Bossidy, John Collins (1860–1928)
Towns 6
Boswell, James (1740–95)
Diaries 2
God 13
Boswell, Margaret (1738?–89)
Writers 2
Botham, Ian (1955–)
Holidays 1
Bottomley, Horatio (1860–1933)
Education 8
Punishment 1
Bowen, Elizabeth (1899–1973)
Description 7
Ireland 3
Bowen, Lord (1835–94)
Virtue 4
Bowra, Maurice (1898–1971)
Anger 3
Clergy 3
Honours 2
People 9
Royalty 16
Sex 21
Society 5
Braben, Eddie
Theatre 11
Brackett, Charles (1892–1969) and
Wilder, Billy (1906–2002)
Film Stars 3
Society 6
Bradbury, Malcolm (1932–)
Sex 22
Brahms, Caryl (1901–82)
Dance 2

Disraeli, Benjamin (*cont.*):
  Last Words 1, 2
  Lies 6
  Literature 15
  Love 14
  Marriage 51, 52
  Mistakes 13
  Newspapers 10
  Old Age 16
  Political Parties 5, 6
  Politics 27, 28
  Praise 1, 2
  Pride 3
  Prime Ministers 14, 15
  Reading 6
  Religion 19, 20, 21
  Royalty 26, 27
  Truth 5
  Wine 4
  Writers 10
Disraeli, Mary Anne (d. 1872)
  Body 15
Dobbs, Michael (1948–)
  Comedy 55
Docherty, Tommy (1928–)
  Football 10
Dodd, Ken (1931–)
  Humour 11
Donleavy, J. P. (1926–)
  Death 22
  Human Race 3
  Money 8
Donne, John (1572–1631)
  Family 13
Dorsey, Tommy (1905–56)
  Music 14
Douglas, Norman (1868–1952)
  Class 11
  Friends 7
  Government 9
  Progress 5
  Telegrams 12
Douglas, O. (1877–1948)
  Letters 8
  Quotations 5
  Reading 7
Douglas, Stephen A. (1813–61)
  Presidents 5
Douglas-Home, Caroline
  (1937–)
  Class 12
Doyle, Arthur Conan (1859–1930)
  Crime 12, 13
  Mind 5
  Transport 8

Drake, Ervin
  Towns 9
Driberg, Tom (1905–76)
  Country 3
  Sex 34
Drury, Reg (1928–2003)
  Football 11
Dryden, John (1631–1700)
  England 11
  Marriage 53
  Poetry 9
Dunne, Finley Peter (1867–1936)
  Drink 20
  Libraries 5
  New York 3
Durante, Jimmy (1893–1980)
  Music 15
Durham, Lord (1792–1840)
  Wealth 9
Dury, Ian (1942–2000)
  Titles 2
Dworkin, Andrea (1946–2005)
  Sex 35
  Travel 9
Dylan, Bob (1941–)
  Songs 8
  Success 8
Dyson, Hugo (1896–1975)
  Literature 16

Eban, Abba (1915–)
  History 6
Ebb, Fred
  Life 9
Edelman, Maurice (1911–75)
  Censorship 6
Eden, Anthony (1897–1977)
  Self-Knowledge 9
Edgar, Marriott (1880–1951)
  Places 9
Edgeworth, Maria (1767–1849)
  Prejudice 2
Edison, Thomas Alva (1847–1931)
  Intelligence 4
Edward IV (1442–83)
  Royalty 28
Edward VII (1841–1910)
  Dress 4, 5
  Royalty 29, 30
  Self-Knowledge 10
Edward VIII (1894–1972)
  America 12
Edwards, Oliver (1711–91)
  Philosophy 2

Edwards, Sherman
  America 13
Ehrenreich, Barbara (1941–)
  Health 4
Ehrlich, Paul Ralph (1932–)
  Technology 4
Einstein, Albert (1879–1955)
  Future 5
  Lifestyle 3
  Science 14
Ejogo, Carmen
  Names 10
Eliot, George (1819–80)
  Humour 12
  Women 16
Eliot, T. S. (1888–1965)
  Poetry 10
  Poets 3
  Women 17
Elizabeth I (1533–1603)
  Body 16
  Clergy 7
Elizabeth II (1926–)
  Football 12
  Honours 4
  Praise 3
  Progress 6
  Royalty 31
**Elizabeth, Queen, the Queen
Mother** (1900–2002)
  Animals 12
  Countries 16
  Poets 4
  Royalty 32
  Wine 5
Ellington, Duke (1899–1974)
  Music 16
Elliott, Ted see **Rossio, Terry** and
  Elliott, Ted
Ellis, Alice Thomas (1932–2005)
  Behaviour 12
  Character 5
  God 23
  Virtue 7
Ellson, Andy
  Failure 4
Elton, Ben (1959–)
  Fashion 7
  Political Parties 7
Elton, Ben (1959–) see **Curtis,
  Richard** and **Elton, Ben**
Elyot, Thomas (1499–1546)
  Football 13
Emerson, Ralph Waldo (1803–82)
  Children 15

Hughes, Simon (1951–)
Health 6
Humphries, Barry (1934–)
Armed Forces 18
Art 16
Bores 7
Comedy 20
Dress 9
Drink 31
Food 30
Prejudice 9
Society 13
Theatre 24
Hunniford, Gloria (1941–)
Shopping 2
Hunt, Leigh (1784–1859)
Conversation 12
Music 25
Hurley, Jack
Boxing 7
Death 35
Hurst, Brian Desmond
(1895–1986)
Sex 45
Huxley, Aldous (1894–1963)
Advertising 6
Argument 10
Bureaucracy 7
Countries 23
Men and Women 21
Power 4
Sex 46
Hyland, Richard (1949–)
Law 15

Ibsen, Henrik (1828–1906)
Dress 10
Ice Cube (1970–)
Parents 7
Ice-T (1958–)
Prejudice 10
Iles, Francis (1893–1970)
Murder 7
Inge, Charles (1868–1957)
Future 7
Inge, Dean (1860–1954)
Religion 31
Ingrams, Richard (1937–)
Appearance 10
Speeches 7
Ingrams, Richard (1937–) and
Wells, John (1936–)
Gardens 8
Ionesco, Eugène (1912–94)
Civil Servants 5

Future 8
Irvine, Derry (1940–)
Hospitality 7
Isaacson, Walter
Reading 9
Issigonis, Alec (1906–88)
Bureaucracy 8
Ivins, Molly (1944–2007)
Generation Gap 6
Izzard, Eddie (1962–)
Murder 8
Religion 32

Jackson, Donald L.
Acting 17
Jackson, Robert H. (1892–1954)
Books 5
Judges 10, 11
Money 17
Jacobs, Jim and **Casey, Warren**
Education 19
Jacobs, Joe (1896–1940)
Baseball 8
Boxing 8
Jacobson, Howard
Towns 14
Jagger, Mick (1943–) and
Richard, Keith (1943–)
Sex 47
James I (1566–1625)
Poets 8
Smoking 4
James, Clive (1939–)
Anger 5
Broadcasting 5
Business 5
Clergy 11
Description 18
Food 31
Self-Knowledge 16
Television 9
Writers 15
James, Henry (1843–1916)
Actors 22
America 19
Biography 8
Literature 22
Praise 4
James, P. D. (1920–)
Architecture 8
James, William (1842–1910)
Marriage 75
Jane, Duchess of Buccleuch and
Queensberry
Hospitality 3

Jarrell, Randall (1914–65)
America 20
Ideas 5
Jay, Antony (1930–) see **Lynn,
Jonathan** and **Jay, Antony**
Jefferson, Thomas (1743–1826)
Censorship 8
Politics 37
Jellinek, Roger (1938–)
Autobiography 12
Jenkins, Roy (1920–2003)
People 20
Prime Ministers 17
Jerome, Jerome K. (1859–1927)
Death 36
Drink 32
Home 13
Truth 6
Work 16
Jerrold, Douglas (1803–57)
Countries 24, 25
Love 27
Sports 14
Wit 14
John, Augustus (1878–1961)
Parents 8, 9
John, Elton (1947–)
Musicians 9
Johnson, Boris (1964–)
Transport 19
Johnson, Brian
Names 15
Johnson, Lyndon Baines
(1908–73)
Insults 19
Power 5, 6
Speeches 8, 9
Stupidity 2
Johnson, Martin (1970–)
Men 10
Sports 15
Johnson, Nunnally (1897–1977)
Film Stars 9
Johnson, Philander Chase
(1866–1939)
Future 9
Johnson, Samuel (1709–84)
Armed Forces 19
Autobiography 13
Bores 8
Choice 10
Clergy 12
Cookery 9, 10
Critics 14
Death 37

Parker, Dorothy (*cont.*):
Friends 10
Hollywood 17, 18, 19
Home 15
Insults 28, 29
Lies 8
Literature 28, 29
Love 36, 37
Marriage 92
Men and Women 38, 39
Names 23
Sex 68
Snobbery 12
Telegrams 18, 19
Theatre 35, 36, 37
Transport 28
Wit 25
Women 50, 51, 52
Writers 30
Writing 18
Parkinson, C. Northcote
(1909–93)
Bureaucracy 11
Economics 12
Management 5
Politics 56
Time 10
Work 21
Parkinson, Michael (1935–)
Royalty 54
Parr, Doug
Science 24
Parris, Matthew (1949–)
Animals 34
Character 7
People 28, 29
Politics 57
Parton, Dolly (1946–)
Body 31
Family 30
Insults 30
Pascal, Blaise (1623–62)
Letters 11
Pasternak, Joe (1901–91)
Film Stars 12
Paterson, Craig
Presidents 14
Paterson, Jennifer (1928–99)
Body 32
Health 11
Patten, Chris (1944–)
Political Parties 16
Paxman, Jeremy (1950–)
Diplomacy 12
Dress 18

Ideas 8
Journalism 17
Payn, James (1830–98)
Food 52
Peacock, Thomas Love
(1785–1866)
Food 53, 54
Gardens 10
Gossip 9
Humour 30
Marriage 93
Quotations 15
Pearson, Hesketh (1887–1964)
Quotations 16
Titles 6
Pearson, Lester Bowles
(1897–1972)
Diplomacy 13
Penn, Sean (1960–)
Acting 26
Pepys, Samuel (1633–1703)
Marriage 94, 95
Sleep 6
Sports 26
Wine 6
Perelman, S. J. (1904–79)
Country 15
Description 28
Food 55
God 39
Letters 12
Medicine 26
Middle Age 12
Places 13
Publishing 15
Wealth 18
Perelman, S. J. (1904–79), **Will B.
Johnstone,** and **Sheekman,
Arthur**
Poverty 13
Perelman, S. J. (1904–79) **et al.**
Behaviour 25
Perry, Grayson (1960–)
Awards 6
Perry, Jimmy (1923–) and **Croft,
David** (1922–)
Comedy 43, 57
Pertwee, Michael (1916–)
Wine 7
Pétain, Henri Philippe
(1856–1951)
Autobiography 20
Peter, Laurence J. (1919–)
Censorship 18
Countries 32

**Philip, Prince, Duke of
Edinburgh** (1921–)
Marriage 96
Phipps, Eric (1875–1945)
Sports 27
Phocion (c.402–317 BC)
Politicians 21
Pindar, Peter (1738–1819)
Royalty 55
Pinter, Harold (1930–)
Philosophy 5
Travel 22
Piron, Armand J.
Dance 12
Plautus (c.250–184 BC)
Poverty 14
Plomer, William (1903–73)
Art 23
Conversation 20
Description 29
Sex 69
Pollitt, Harry (1890–1960)
Poets 11
Pope, Alexander (1688–1744)
Children 29
Cookery 14
Critics 21
Death 55, 56, 57
England 25
Hope 9
Insults 31, 32, 33
Marriage 97
Old Age 31
Poetry 20
Poets 12, 13
Royalty 56, 57, 58
Theatre 38
Wit 27
Words 27
Writers 31
Porter, Cole (1891–1964)
Art 24
Behaviour 26, 27
Birds 8
Countries 33, 34
Country 16
Dance 13
Drink 48
Food 56, 57
Golf 8
Hope 10
Love 38, 39
Marriage 98, 99, 100
Medicine 27

address lost my A.   BOOKS 21
addresses A. are given to us to conceal
                                                          PLACES 14
adjective a. currently used   WORDS 36
  A.: when in doubt   WRITING 19
  than one German a.   LANGUAGES 25
administrative a. won't   ARGUMENT 13
admiral not a doorman but a rear a.
                                                          TRANSPORT 5
admirals A. extolled for standing   ARMED FORCES 9
admire cannot possibly a. them   POVERTY 22
admired more a. she was   POLITICIANS 10
admit Whenever you're wrong, a. it
                                                          MARRIAGE 88
adorable a. pancreas   APPEARANCE 12
  nauseatingly a.   PEOPLE 32
adore a. those sort of people   BEHAVIOUR 31
  need to a. me   FAME 18
adored I was a. once too   LOVE 41
ads watched the a.   EPITAPHS 20
adulterers I see some a. down there   SEX 40
adulterous would be a.   ARCHITECTURE 2
adultery a. out of the moral arena   SOCIETY 20
  common as a.   AUTOBIOGRAPHY 10
  Do not a. commit   SEX 30
  gallantry, and gods a.   SEX 27
  henceforward to the strictest a.   MORALITY 3
  it's still a.   SEX 88
adults how I regarded a.   GENERATION GAP 7
  only between consenting a.   SEX 90
advanced a. state of nudity   BODY 30
advancement useful for political a.   POLITICS 40
advantage A. rarely comes of it   SEX 30
  take a mean a.   BEHAVIOUR 39
  undertaking of Great A.   SECRECY 2
adversary mine a. had written   BOOKS 1
advertise eat what I a.   DRINK 17
advertisement one effective a.   ADVERTISING 6
  same as that of a.   ADVERTISING 9
advertisements column of a. by heart
                                                       QUOTATIONS 9
  real estate a.   AUTOBIOGRAPHY 11
advertisers a. don't object to   NEWSPAPERS 31
advertising A. is the most   ADVERTISING 4
  A. is the rattling   ADVERTISING 13
  A. may be described   ADVERTISING 8
  calls it a.   ADVERTISING 7
advise STREETS FLOODED. PLEASE A.   TELEGRAMS 3
advises It's my old girl that a.   MARRIAGE 49
advocate art of the a.   ARGUMENT 16
aesthete perfect a.   ART 22
aesthetic letting one's a. sense override
                                                        MORALITY 11

affair a. between Margot Asquith   INSULTS 29
  a. with Ophelia   THEATRE 4
  keep a measly a. secret   SECURITY 5
afford Can't a. them, Governor   MORALITY 14
afraid a. to die   DEATH 1
Africa more familiar with A.   WOMEN 48
African A. Primates Meeting   NAMES 29
after A. you, Claude   COMEDY 1
afternoon make love in the a.   FRANCE 1
  nothing to do in the a.   THEATRE 3
against always vote *a.*   DEMOCRACY 6
  life is 6 to 5 a.   GAMBLING 3
  most people vote a.   DEMOCRACY 1
agapanthus Beware of the a.   COUNTRY 12
age A. before Beauty   INSULTS 28
  can tell a woman's a.   WOMEN 24
  in an a. group   MONEY 19
  lie about his a.   HUMOUR 20
  Mozart was my a.   SUCCESS 14
  reached the a. to write   AUTOBIOGRAPHY 23
  slam the door in the face of a.   OLD AGE 12
  talk turns to a.   MIDDLE AGE 4
  Thirty-five is a very attractive a.   MIDDLE AGE 18
  What a. are you going to put   TRAVEL 20
  whatever a. she is   FAME 5
  when the a. is in   OLD AGE 34
  when you've the a.   ACTING 23
  woman who tells her real a.   WOMEN 74
  Work does a. you so   WORK 10
aged I saw an a., aged man   OLD AGE 8
agenda a. will be in inverse proportion   TIME 10
agent a. to a publisher   PUBLISHING 13
  good estate a.   HOME 10
  much of a secret a.   SECURITY 1
agents and west by a.   HOLLYWOOD 4
ages He's a writer for the a.   WRITERS 30
agglomerated your a. lucubrations   PRAISE 4
aghast I'm a.   WIT 46
AGM address the A.   BUSINESS 17
agnostic I have been an a.   GOD 12
  You are not an a.   RELIGION 47
agnosticism that a. means   CERTAINTY 11
agnostics fans and a.   BASEBALL 4
agony a. is abated   BEHAVIOUR 22
  it was a., Ivy   COMEDY 9
  someone's screaming in a.   LANGUAGES 17
agreeable idea of an a. person   ARGUMENT 4
agreement public a. among doctors   MEDICINE 30
  Too much a.   CONVERSATION 8
agrees person who a. with me   ARGUMENT 4
ahead a. in this world   LAW 18
ain't a. a fit night out for man   WEATHER 6
air apple-scented a. freshener   DESCRIPTION 26
  during the a. raids   SEX 18
airplanes feel about a.   DIETS 4

airport observing a. layouts   HEAVEN 4
airs give himself a.   MUSICIANS 2
Albanian A. . . . a language that sounded
    LANGUAGES 4
Albert A. must have married   ACTING 9
   take a message to A.   LAST WORDS 2
   Went there with young A.   PLACES 9
albino a. curate   FRIENDS 16
alcohol A. . . . enables Parliament   DRINK 53
   a. was a food   DRINK 62
   Mere a. doesn't thrill me at all   LOVE 39
   pleasant effects of a.   DRINK 31
   taken more out of a.   DRINK 13
ale no more cakes and a.   MORALITY 12
Alec Dull A. versus   CHOICE 6
alert I'll a. the media   FAME 13
Alf didn't create A. Garnett   TELEVISION 11
algebra no such thing as a.   EDUCATION 24
Alice may call me A.   INSULTS 23
   or control A.   PRESIDENTS 17
   Pass the sick bag, A.   COMEDY 41
alien I'll be damned if I'm an a.   ROYALTY 39
alike do everything a.   FAMILY 12
alive if I am a.   DEATH 32
   lucky if he gets out of it a.   LIFE 7
   no longer a.   DEATH 13
   not dead but a.   GOD 5
   Not while I'm a. he ain't   POLITICIANS 9
   To keep my love a.   MARRIAGE 69
all a. go together   COUNTRIES 26
   A. my shows are great   SELF-KNOWLEDGE 13
allegory headstrong as an a.   WIT 36
allergies provide the a.   GOD 26
all-round a.-round man   ART 6
almighty Even the A. took seven   POLITICS 18
   relieves the A.   ENGLAND 2
   thinks he's God A.   RELIGION 24
alone A. with probably the most   SEX 79
   sleeps a. at last   EPITAPHS 6
   that he is a.   ENGLAND 16
alphabet if I had known the a.   WORDS 25
altar high a. on the move   DESCRIPTION 7
alternative a. were immortality   DEATH 65
always Not A.   SONGS 3
amateur a. is a man who can't   WORK 2
amateurs Hell is full of musical a.   MUSIC 48
   that afflicts a.   ART 7
amazed You are a.   WIT 48
ambassador a. is an honest man   DIPLOMACY 17
ambassadors A. cropped up   GOVERNMENT 11
amber a. foam   FOOD 23
ambiguity is its a.   HUMOUR 15
ambition nice girl's a.   HOPE 1
ambitions their loyalties and a.   MONEY 17
ambitious less a. project   GOD 5

ambivalence definition of a.   WORDS 24
America A. is a model   AMERICA 5
   A. is a vast conspiracy   AMERICA 27
   A. was thus   HISTORY 9
   arts in A.   ART 5
   come back to A.   AMERICA 19
   do a sitcom in A.   TELEVISION 13
   England and A.   COUNTRIES 40
   I like A.   AMERICA 10
   like to be in A.   AMERICA 24
   most about A.   AMERICA 2
   what makes A.   AMERICA 25
   youth of A.   AMERICA 31
American A. *diplomacy*   DIPLOMACY 4
   A. girls turn   AMERICA 16
   A. joke   HUMOUR 37
   A. names as Cathcart   NAMES 14
   A. president   GOVERNMENT 40
   bad news to the A. people   PRESIDENTS 9
   Every A. woman   AMERICA 1
   living the A. dream   GENERATION GAP 8
   nod from an A.   AMERICA 6
   pay for my A. Express   ADVERTISING 15
   play A. music   COUNTRIES 9
Americans All A.   FILM STARS 14
   always liked A.   AMERICA 8
   A. have a perfect right   AMERICA 3
   A. will show up   DIPLOMACY 10
   bad A. are slobs   COUNTRIES 38
   bad A. die   AMERICA 30
   Canadians are A.   CANADA 4
   is concerned, the A.   AMERICA 4
   Never criticize A.   AMERICA 21
   To A., English manners   AMERICA 20
amoebae a. getting married   MARRIAGE 80
amor A. vincit insomnia   SLEEP 2
amount awful lot to a. to much   SCIENCE 1
amphibian no a. is harmed   FOOD 34
amused a. by its presumption   WINE 13
   One is not a. at that   FOOTBALL 12
Anantanarayanan Ah, A.   POETRY 22
anarchism A. is a game   POLITICS 63
anatomist bad a.   LAST WORDS 10
anatomy before he has studied a.   MARRIAGE 12
   portions of the human a.   DANCE 8
ancestor I am an a.   ARISTOCRACY 12
ancestry trace my a. back   ARISTOCRACY 5
angel a. to pass, flying slowly   TIME 7
   a. travelling incognito   PEOPLE 30
   Is man an ape or an a.   RELIGION 19
   to the recording a.   MURDER 5
   wrote like an a.   EPITAPHS 14
angels walk behind the a.   ROYALTY 30
anger A. makes dull men witty   ANGER 1

Having a b. CHILDREN 24
they have a b. MEN AND WOMEN 55
Bach Now B. is decomposing MUSICIANS 7
bachelors b. love dogs CHILDREN 27
back b. of my boat TRANSPORT 36
b. to the hotel SELF-KNOWLEDGE 18
come b. the same day TRAVEL 18
Don't look b. BASEBALL 11
saying things behind one's b. GOSSIP 13
say of me behind my b. SELF-KNOWLEDGE 31
Shoulders b. COMEDY 43
small of the b. DESCRIPTION 33
what did he go b. to TECHNOLOGY 11
backbone b. than a chocolate éclair

PRESIDENTS 16
backgammon I ever mastered was b. SPORTS 14
backing b. into the limelight PEOPLE 8
backward B. ran sentences LANGUAGE 5
backwards knew these lines b. ACTING 8
walking b. for Christmas CHRISTMAS 10
bacon heard of a saying by B. JUDGES 15
lordships asked B. CRIME 3
bad Aren't things b. enough already JUDGES 1
babies can't be all b. PEOPLE 31
b. anatomist LAST WORDS 10
b. as the play was ACTORS 27
b. aunts FAMILY 51
B. luck OLD AGE 13
b. poetry springs from POETRY 23
b. times just around HOPE 4
b. unhappily BOOKS 24
dearth of b. pictures CINEMA 10
entitled his album B. NAMES 2
how b. the picture is FILM 9
in for a b. time BIOGRAPHY 19
like b. wine WINE 4
relationship that goes b. SONGS 9
so many shocking b. hats POLITICIANS 27
Some of them are b. SELF-KNOWLEDGE 13
when I'm b., I'm better VIRTUE 20
badger not to b. buggers ANIMALS 2
bagging sagging, dragging or b. BODY 31
bags carry other people's b. SOCIETY 6
bainters I hate all Boets and B. ROYALTY 34
baked resembled a B. Alaska DESCRIPTION 19
balancing B. the budget ECONOMICS 8
bald Slightly b. FILM STARS 1
baldness far side of b. GENERATION GAP 11
Balham Lies B. PLACES 12
Balkans in the B. WAR 33
ball b. rolled out of her reach PEOPLE 1
business of a b. BEHAVIOUR 30
eye for the b. CRICKET 11
give the b. to George FOOTBALL 7
history of a b. WAR 29

man throwing the b. BASEBALL 6
only one b. FOOTBALL 2
Take me out to the b. game BASEBALL 10
until the cry of 'Play B. ' SPORTS 24
ballet at the Russian b. HANDWRITING 1
b. in the evening RUSSIA 7
Balliol Well rowed, B.! SPORTS 1
ball-point gave her a b. DIPLOMACY 15
balls b. look like FACES 5
three brass b. CLASS 8
Bambi B.—see the movie COOKERY 11
ban recommend they b. it CENSORSHIP 7
banana I am a b. LAW 14
bananas expect someone to produce b.

NAMES 29
band b. is always playing CHARACTER 3
prison b. was there CRIME 16
Silver B. so nonplussed DESCRIPTION 32
bands pursue Culture in b. ART 35
bang standing there, going 'B.' MURDER 8
banger more like an old b. CIVIL SERVANTS 1
bank All we want is a b. balance SATISFACTION 12
b. is a place MONEY 16
robbing a b. CRIME 5
banker as a Scotch b. CANADA 3
bankruptcy on the edge of b. ECONOMICS 11
banks b. went bust ECONOMICS 9
banquet Judging from the b. THEATRE 57
Banquo as B.'s ghost POLITICAL PARTIES 1
unnerved by B.'s valet ACTING 5
baptismal water b. DEATH 26
Baptists B. are only funny underwater

RELIGION 66
bar b. on the Piccola Marina COUNTRIES 11
Did a stunt at the b. PARTIES 1
wrong b. or bed MISTAKES 6
Barabbas B. was a much misunderstood

PUBLISHING 11
B. was a publisher PUBLISHING 8
barb b. that makes it stick WIT 38
barbecue Sue wants a b. FOOD 46
barbed like a b. wire fence FASHION 10
Barbie Ken and B. PARTIES 6
Ken and B.'s romance MEN AND WOMEN 2
talk like B. LIFESTYLE 6
Barbirolli wrath of Sir John B. MUSICIANS 3
bards Phoney-rustic b. BIRDS 9
barged b. down the Nile ACTORS 5
bark heard a seal b. CERTAINTY 23
barking b. up the wrong tree CRITICS 10
Barkis B. is willin' LOVE 12
bar-mitzvah idea for a b. HOLLYWOOD 12
baronet half mad b. PEOPLE 12
lily-handed b. ENGLAND 39
Baronetage any book but the B. SNOBBERY 2

baronetcy b. a b.   HONOURS 9
barracuda Man he eat the b.   NATURE 3
barrels slurp into the b.   MONEY 9
barrenness In b., at any rate   POETS 7
Barrie Sir James B.'s cans   LITERATURE 20
barring B. that natural expression   VIRTUE 18
bars parallel b.   HEALTH 13
   research in b.   JOURNALISM 16
barter finding b. cumbersome   BUSINESS 6
baseball b. fans   BASEBALL 4
   b. goes for pay   BASEBALL 5
   b. in Italian   OPERA 5
   B. is very big   BASEBALL 7
   b. on valium   CRICKET 19
   Hague has got a b. cap   POLITICAL PARTIES 7
bashful b. young potato   ART 11
bashfulness In England a particular b.
                                                               RELIGION 1
Basingstoke hidden meaning—like B.   WORDS 14
basket eggs in one b.   BUSINESS 20
Basque more difficult to master than B.
                                                            LANGUAGES 3
bass Slap that b.   MUSIC 18
basta 'B.!' his master replied   LANGUAGES 12
bastard all my eggs in one b.   SEX 68
   alternatives to 'b.'   CENSORSHIP 2
   b.! He doesn't exist   GOD 10
   Happy as a b.   HAPPINESS 2
   we knocked the b. off   SUCCESS 13
bat b. for the length of time   CRICKET 9
   gentleman holding the b.   BASEBALL 6
   Neither from owl or b.   ANIMALS 37
   see Dr Grace b.   CRICKET 4
   shake a b. at a white man   BASEBALL 7
   Twinkle, twinkle, little b.   UNIVERSE 5
bath b. every year   BEHAVIOUR 2
   coal in the b.   CLASS 23
   cold b. and a religious exercise   NEWSPAPERS 12
   Commander of the B.   ROYALTY 5
   Dizzy in his b.   BODY 15
   every morning, like a hot b.   NEWSPAPERS 17
   I'll take a b.   FAME 13
   in the b. overnight   FILM STARS 11
   I test my b. before I sit   SATISFACTION 13
   soaking in a hot b.   BUSINESS 1
   stepping from his b.   PRIDE 2
   used to sing in the b. tub   WORK 15
bathing caught the Whigs b.   POLITICAL PARTIES 6
   From the b. machine   DRINK 28
   surprised when b.   DESCRIPTION 9
bathroom as he goes to the b.   CLERGY 2
bathtub in bed and in the b.   NAMES 24
bats their b. have been broken   TRUST 7
batsman b.'s Holding   NAMES 15

battle b. for the mind   PRESIDENTS 13
   history of a b.   WAR 29
battlefield rent on the b.   WAR 16
baying b. for broken glass   ENGLAND 41
bayonets platitudes and b.   SPEECHES 16
BBC goad the B.   BROADCASTING 5
beak takes in his b.   BIRDS 7
bean Boston, the home of the b.   TOWNS 6
   not too French French b.   ART 11
beans in with the boy b.   SEX 61
bear b. led by a man   WRITERS 2
   B. of Very Little Brain   ANIMALS 28
   embrace the Russian b.   RUSSIA 1
   Exit, pursued by a b.   THEATRE 45
beard thin vague b.   APPEARANCE 2
beast B. stands for   NEWSPAPERS 34
   fit night out for man or b.   WEATHER 6
beastly b. to the Germans   COUNTRIES 12
beat guys I'd like to b. up   BODY 28
Beatles B.' first L.P.   SEX 49
beaut it's a b.   MISTAKES 19
beautiful better to be b.   APPEARANCE 24
   When a woman isn't b.   WOMEN 9
beauty Age before B.   INSULTS 28
   b. am faded   APPEARANCE 16
   b. being only skin-deep   APPEARANCE 12
   b. is only sin deep   APPEARANCE 18
   B. school report   EDUCATION 19
   If b. is truth   APPEARANCE 21
   No woman can be a b.   WOMEN 18
Beaverbrook B. is so pleased   POLITICIANS 3
   existence of Lord B.   PEOPLE 40
becquerel All I know about the b.   SCIENCE 1
bed about his b.   SCIENCE 9
   and a good b.   SHOPPING 2
   And so to b.   SLEEP 6
   any place but it were to his b.   ROYALTY 28
   b. fell on my father   FAMILY 46
   b. people   CLASS 5
   fell out of b.   PRESIDENTS 2
   gooseberried double b.   SEX 86
   I go to b. early   SLEEP 11
   in b. and in the bathtub   NAMES 24
   in b. at the same time   SEX 73
   in b. with my catamite   SEX 26
   never good in b.   APPEARANCE 5
   obliged to go to b.   PARENTS 6
   quick dip in b.   HEALTH 14
   should of stood in b.   BASEBALL 8
   sinners are still in b.   RELIGION 56
   stay in b. all day   MISTAKES 5
   what she wore in b.   DRESS 15
   Who goes to b. with whom   OLD AGE 33
   wrong bar or b.   MISTAKES 6
bedfellows strange b.   MISTAKES 24

blade bloody, blameful b. — ANGER 8
His b. struck the water — SPORTS 8
blaggard God's a b. — POETS 16
Blair if her B. was quite — LOVE 49
Mr B. is not the Archangel — PRIME MINISTERS 13
blame It's the poor wot gets the b. — POVERTY 1
manager gets the b. — FOOTBALL 18
pass the b. — BUREAUCRACY 12
blamed mothers go on getting b. — PARENTS 20
blameless led b. lives — LAW 2
blamelessness B. runs riot — BIOGRAPHY 16
Blavatsky no go B. — SATISFACTION 12
blazer make them wear a b. — MEN AND WOMEN 3
bleeding instead of b., he sings — OPERA 4
bleeper I do not wear a b. — PEOPLE 15
blessed B. are the cheesemakers — RELIGION 18
blind b. composer — FILM 13
deaf man to a b. woman — MARRIAGE 34
dust on a Venetian b. — CRITICS 7
Shakespeare Sonnets to the b. — ACTORS 11
blitz b. of a boy — CHILDREN 9
block never get writer's b. — WRITING 5
old b. itself — PRIME MINISTERS 8
blockhead No man but a b. — WRITING 13
blond He's b., he's quick — FOOTBALL 5
blonde b. to make a bishop kick — WOMEN 6
know I'm not b. — INSULTS 30
blood B., as all men know — COUNTRIES 23
b. and thirsty — FILM 6
b. to appear in the water — POLITICS 20
Fats Waller's b. — DRINK 15
I can do you b. and love — THEATRE 50
one drop of Negro b. — PREJUDICE 8
Scotch b. in her veins — PREJUDICE 2
show-business with b. — BOXING 2
bloody Abroad is b. — TRAVEL 11
b., blameful blade — ANGER 8
blow the b. doors off — SATISFACTION 9
Walk! Not b. likely — TRANSPORT 34
wipe a b. nose — ARGUMENT 6
bloom destined to b. late — APPEARANCE 13
blooming b. well dead — DEATH 62
blow 'b.-job' be included — SEX 24
b. the bloody doors off — SATISFACTION 9
otherwise you b. up — DIETS 5
So b., Gabriel, blow — RELIGION 53
bludgeoning b. of the people — DEMOCRACY 17
blue Blue Danube is really b. — OLD AGE 15
brilliant b. garment — COLOURS 6
invented b. jeans — FASHION 14
there isn't much b. — LITERATURE 32
blues future of the b. — FILM 11
blunder wonder At so grotesque a b. — MISTAKES 4
blurbs B. that appear on the back — ADVERTISING 3

blush b. into the cheek — ENGLAND 10
let other people b. — FOOLISHNESS 2
such large letters I b. — PRIDE 9
blushes B.. Or needs to — HUMAN RACE 12
blushing I always take b. — BEHAVIOUR 7
board b. of gods — GOD 35
wasn't any B. — GOVERNMENT 16
boasting B. about modesty — ENGLAND 1
boat back of my b. — TRANSPORT 36
need a bigger b. — TRANSPORT 4
boats sink my b. — MARRIAGE 3
bodega home is the b. — DRINK 42
Bodley losing a book from B. — LIBRARIES 9
body approaching the age when your b.
— MIDDLE AGE 3
borrow his b. — BODY 28
get rid of the rest of her b. — WOMEN 68
I should interpose my b. — SEX 83
looking for a b. — FILM PRODUCERS 7
my b. and your brains — MEN AND WOMEN 47
use of my b. — BODY 3
with Africa than my own b. — WOMEN 48
boets I hate all B. and Bainters — ROYALTY 34
bog sit on the b. — SPORTS 29
Bognor Bugger B. — LAST WORDS 3
bogus b. for some time — HEALTH 8
persons whom I knew to be b. — PEOPLE 25
Bohemian B. and artistic quarter — ART 41
boil vulgar b. — COOKERY 14
boiled bag of b. sweets — POLITICS 24
cold b. veal — ENEMIES 4
no politics in b. and roast — POLITICAL PARTIES 17
suck on a b. sweet — SEX 92
boiler 10 years in a b. suit — WOMEN 67
boiling b. oil — PUNISHMENT 7
Bolshevism this sort of madness [B.] — POLITICS 64
bolster b. behind the throne — ROYALTY 61
bomb atomic b. — IGNORANCE 4
b. the country — DIPLOMACY 10
bombazine B. would have shown — DEATH 24
bombs Come, friendly b. — TOWNS 5
bond B. James Bond. — NAMES 21
handle a b. offering — LAW 3
boneless see the b. wonder — PRIME MINISTERS 11
bones tongs and the b. — MUSIC 47
we break b. — SPORTS 15
bonhomie natural *b.* — ECONOMICS 3
bon-mots plucking b. from their places
— QUOTATIONS 14
bonnet b. in Germany — COUNTRIES 39
bonus that's a b. — BODY 45
book Another damned, thick, square b.
— ROYALTY 43
Arrival of B. of the Month — READING 5
because a b. is humorous — PUBLISHING 15

book (*cont.*):

b. flying a bullet	CRIME 4
b. in breeches	PEOPLE 33
B. of Life begins	BIBLE 8
b. of my enemy	WRITERS 15
b. publication	BOOKS 9
b. which people praise	READING 17
b. would have been finished	FAMILY 52
enjoy your b.	AUTOBIOGRAPHY 3
finishes his b.	READING 9
get a lawyer—not a b.	LAW 18
had written a b.	BOOKS 1
He's *got* a b.	BOOKS 4
knocks me out is a b.	READING 15
knows this out of the b.	EDUCATION 13
large b. is depicted	DRESS 16
losing a b. from Bodley	LIBRARIES 9
moment I picked up your b.	LITERATURE 24
no b.—it's a plaything	QUOTATIONS 15
only ever read one b. in my life	LITERATURE 27
rather read a b.	DANCE 5
read the b.	CRITICS 17
read the b. of Job	BIBLE 9
sent a new b.	INDEXES 2
What is the use of a b.	LITERATURE 12
with a good b.	HOLIDAYS 9
without mentioning a single b.	LITERATURE 31
written a b.	BOOKS 6
bookmaker b. who takes actresses	SPORTS 6
bookmaking tax on b.	BETTING 8
books any good b. lately	COMEDY 17
b. about homos	READING 13
b. about living men	BIOGRAPHY 7
B. are well written	BOOKS 23
B. from Boots'	ENGLAND 6
b. were read	DEATH 12
cream of other's b.	QUOTATIONS 14
do *you* read b. *through*	READING 10
had a lot of b.	BOOKS 13
If my b. had been any worse	LITERATURE 13
I hate b.	BOOKS 15
learned from b.	MORALITY 2
My only b.	WOMEN 44
oddity of Oxford b.	PUBLISHING 4
one of their b. in their room	WRITERS 8
provided with no b.	BOOKS 5
regular supply of b.	LIFESTYLE 7
respected b.	LIBRARIES 11
showed me his b.	LIBRARIES 7
so charming as b.	BOOKS 17
unindexed b. with indexes	WORK 19
world doesn't read its b.	READING 11
wrote a few b.	MARRIAGE 40
bookseller he once shot a b.	PUBLISHING 7
boot pour piss out of a b.	STUPIDITY 2

bootboy b. at Claridges	BOOKS 25
bootlace trip over a loose b.	WRITERS 46
boots doormat in a world of b.	
	SELF-KNOWLEDGE 22
engine in b.	SPORTS 13
look at his b.	CLASS 26
school without any b.	PRIME MINISTERS 7
top of his b.	ARMED FORCES 24
when I take my b. off	BODY 13
booze fool with b.	DRINK 21
bop 'B.' is like scrabble	MUSIC 16
bordello doorkeeper of a b.	MUSICIANS 17
bore b. is a man	BORES 14
b. is simply a nonentity	BORES 10
God is a b.	GOD 34
is an old b.	BORES 16
merely a b.	SOCIETY 21
not only a b.	BORES 12
not to b. yourself	BORES 11
Thou shalt not b.	FILM PRODUCERS 18
bored b. with good wine	WINE 4
I'd get b.	CRICKET 9
indefinitely b.	SOCIETY 14
man is b.	MEN AND WOMEN 39
boredom b. occasioned	BORES 9
b. threshold	BORES 17
bores destiny of b.	BORES 7
Borgias I dined last night with the B.	SOCIETY 2
boring b. kind of guy	BORES 3
b. old Swede	HOUSEWORK 3
b. you fall asleep	NAMES 3
not b. you	BORES 5
Somebody's b. me	BORES 15
born b. an Englishman	ENGLAND 4
b. in a manger	CHILDREN 1
b. with your legs apart	SEX 64
I was b. under	RUSSIA 3
man is b. in a stable	IRELAND 3
Never was b.	FAMILY 39
person b. who is so unlucky	MISTAKES 21
refusing to be b.	FUTURE 1
some men are b. great	PRIDE 5
That's b. into the world alive	POLITICAL PARTIES 9
borrow b. his body	BODY 28
b. the money	HAPPINESS 17
b. the words	DICTIONARIES 9
well enough to b. from	FRIENDS 4
borrowers to catch out b.	BOOKS 12
borrows b. a detective story	READING 11
Borstal it may have been B.	EDUCATION 7
bosom no b. and no behind	ENGLAND 33
boss funny man or a great b.	MANAGEMENT 3
bossy It's a *very* b. car	TRANSPORT 23

Boston B., the home of the bean — TOWNS 6
  B. social zones — CLASS 15
  I met him in B. — TOWNS 13
botanist I'd be a b. — SCIENCE 15
botch I make a b. — TIME 4
both friends in b. places — HEAVEN 6
bother B. it — LANGUAGE 7
  no time to b. — LETTERS 1
bothered Bewitched, b. and bewildered
  — MEN AND WOMEN 17
Botticelli B.'s a *cheese* — FOOD 60
  If B. were alive — FASHION 17
bottle b. just going to sit — HOME 19
  b. of hay — FOOD 65
  b. on the chimley-piece — DRINK 19
  catsup b. — FOOD 2
  little for the b. — LOVE 11
bottles English have hot-water b. — SEX 57
bottom baby, I'm the b. — MEN AND WOMEN 43
  my b. and thighs — BODY 22
  reach the b. first — CHILDREN 16
  Undesired on my tired little b. — WOMEN 53
  your b. will follow — DIETS 6
Boule Little sticks of B. — ART 18
bounded b. on the north — HOLLYWOOD 4
bouquet b. is better — WINE 8
Bourbon Wheaties with B. — DRINK 17
Bovril does her hair with B. — FRIENDS 5
bow b., ye tradesmen — CLASS 17
bowel lower b. of music — MUSIC 11
bowl not to see you b. — CRICKET 4
bowler b.'s Willey — NAMES 15
bow-wows gone to the demnition b. — MISTAKES 12
box pianoforte is a harp in a b. — MUSIC 25
boxes buttocks into wooden b. — TRANSPORT 29
boxing B. is show-business — BOXING 2
boy any b. ever had — HOLLYWOOD 21
  b. as he really is — CHILDREN 21
  Can befall a b. — FAMILY 25
  FEEL LIKE A B. AGAIN — TELEGRAMS 12
  fifteen-year-old b. — PARENTS 15
  He's a very naughty b.! — GOD 18
  I used to be a good b. — PAST 12
  mad about the b. — FILM STARS 4
  quite a little b. — CONVERSATION 4
  to your little b. — CHILDREN 8
  You stupid b. — COMEDY 57
boyfriend having no b. — MEN AND WOMEN 11
boys b. something else to kick — SPORTS 37
  By office boys for office b. — NEWSPAPERS 27
  Faded b., jaded boys — MEN 5
  Hello b. — BODY 5
  liked little b. too little — EDUCATION 44
  loaded guns with b. — SECRECY 4
  two sorts of b. — CHILDREN 14

brain b. and his expression — HUMOUR 6
  b. has oozed out — TRAVEL 16
  b.? It's my second favourite — BODY 1
  b. like Swiss cheese — FILM STARS 18
  certain to b. — ART 41
  definition of the b. — MIND 3
  if his b. was on fire — ENEMIES 1
  If I only had a b. — INTELLIGENCE 5
  leave that b. outside — POLITICS 31
  Very Little B. — ANIMALS 28
  with b. surgeons — JOURNALISM 6
brains b. are in the right place — DESCRIPTION 2
  b. of a Minerva — ACTORS 2
  feet instead of their b. — MUSIC 52
  his b. go to his head — INSULTS 1
  husbands having b. — MARRIAGE 133
  intelligence and no b. — CHARACTER 6
  my body and your b. — MEN AND WOMEN 47
  one minister with any b. — GOVERNMENT 2
brandy music is the b. of the damned — MUSIC 48
  must drink b. — DRINK 33
  pray get me a glass of b. — ROYALTY 37
braw b. bricht moonlicht nicht' — DRINK 41
Bray I will be the Vicar of B.; sir — POLITICIANS 1
Brazil aunt from B. — FAMILY 45
bread piece of b. and butter — FOOD 38
  reinvented unsliced b. — WIT 18
  She was cutting b. and butter
  — MEN AND WOMEN 54
break day will b. — FOOD 13
  give Osaka an even b. — WIT 19
  one-year b. — HOLIDAYS 2
  sucker an even b. — GAMBLING 3
  those that b. down — TECHNOLOGY 2
breakages B., Limited — BUSINESS 16
breakfast b. every five minutes — OLD AGE 18
  B. on our terrace — FOOD 10
  b. three times — FOOD 44
  brilliant at b. — BORES 18
  hath already committed b. — VIRTUE 10
  spoil your b. — CRITICS 1
  touch my b. — FOOD 83
breakfast-time period in matrimony is b.
  — MARRIAGE 71
breaking b. it in for a friend — NAMES 22
  b. my heart — HAPPINESS 4
breast boiling bloody b. — ANGER 8
breasts Big b. — BODY 40
  b. like granite — FILM STARS 18
  You're the b. of Venus — SEX 10
breath use your b. — DRINK 25
breathe like the hair we b. — SPORTS 34
breathing stopped b. — DEATH 48
bred B. en bawn — ANIMALS 18

breeches book in b. — PEOPLE 33
in my riding b. — DRESS 19
breeding b. our own team — FOOTBALL 30
or of ill b. — BEHAVIOUR 7
result of b. — WEALTH 16
brevity Nothing conduces to b. — WRITING 10
bribe b. or twist — JOURNALISM 25
Marriage is a b. — MARRIAGE 132
bribed b. by their loyalties — MONEY 17
bribes b. he had taken — CRIME 3
bricht braw b. moonlicht nicht' — DRINK 41
brick b. in his pocket — HOME 21
threw it a b. at a time — ACTING 15
bricks pile of b. — ARCHITECTURE 14
bride Including the b. and groom — MARRIAGE 92
It feels so fine to be a b. — MARRIAGE 99
bridegroom close as a b. — GARDENS 5
bridge Beautiful Railway B. — DEATH 43
b. to the future — FUTURE 10
brief B., to the point — MARRIAGE 46
briefing off-the-record b. — GOD 31
brier in a b.-patch — ANIMALS 18
brigade B. of Guards — POLITICS 47
brigand I am a b. — SOCIETY 18
brigands b. demand your money — WOMEN 5
bright He's not very b. — PRIME MINISTERS 18
quit looking on the b. side — GOVERNMENT 31
Brighton B. looks like a town — TOWNS 24
brilliant b. at breakfast — BORES 18
b. on paper — FOOTBALL 27
b.—to the top — ARMED FORCES 24
b. writer in the editor's chair — NEWSPAPERS 8
bring b. it to you, free — DEATH 4
do b. him — BEHAVIOUR 31
Britain B. and Spain — COUNTRIES 42
B. was no part of Europe — COUNTRIES 1
further you got from B. — POLITICIANS 10
Britannia Beer and B. — ENGLAND 34
British B. are not given — ENGLAND 40
B. history — ECONOMICS 11
Commander of the B. Empire — HONOURS 7
rules of B. conduct — BEHAVIOUR 11
too poor to be B. — ENGLAND 17
we're B. — COMEDY 37
Briton only a free-born B. can — SNOBBERY 13
Britons brave b. — ENGLAND 25
B. were only natives — ENGLAND 29
we B. alone — ENGLAND 42
Brits bad B. are snobs — COUNTRIES 38
Britten written By Benjamin B. — MUSICIANS 2
broad b., where a broad should be — WOMEN 29
b. mind — MIDDLE AGE 6
B. of Church — RELIGION 9
phone, a horse or a b. — PEOPLE 24
She's the B. and I'm the High — PRIDE 7

broadens travel b. the behind — TRAVEL 10
travel b. the mind — TRAVEL 4
Broadstairs Good old B. — HOLIDAYS 7
Broadway B.'s turning into Coney — NEW YORK 4
sinners on this part of B. — RELIGION 56
broccoli eat any more b. — FOOD 11
It's b. — FOOD 81
broken baying for b. glass — ENGLAND 41
b. my bloody leg — CRICKET 1
Sound of B. Glass — CLASS 4
their bats have been b. — TRUST 7
bronchial my b. tubes were entrancing — MEDICINE 27
broom extra b. for dear old mother — NATURE 2
brothel actively employed in a b. — WOMEN 32
male b. in Norway — BIOGRAPHY 5
brother B., can you spare — AMERICA 17
had a younger b. — ACTING 2
let my b. take over — BOXING 1
brow b. lifts are getting scary — MEDICINE 19
brown b. condom full of walnuts — DESCRIPTION 18
in a b. envelope — MONEY 13
never wear b. — COLOURS 3
Browning B.'s translation — CRITICS 33
browning Meredith's a prose B. — LITERATURE 37
browns sorry for the poor b. — COLOURS 2
browsing b. and sluicing — FOOD 85
Bruce made Adam and B. — SEX 23
brush B. up your Shakespeare — THEATRE 41
Brussels in B. two weeks — WALES 1
brute Feed the b. — MARRIAGE 101
bubble like unto a b. — WOMEN 70
bucket kicked the b. — DEATH 5
buckets behind with the buckets — HISTORY 2
budget Balancing the b. — ECONOMICS 8
bug As a b. — EPITAPHS 13
thinks there's a b. — SECURITY 2
bugger B. Bognor — LAST WORDS 3
not to b. badgers — ANIMALS 2
buggers b. can't be choosers — SEX 21
little b. hop — DANCE 1
build b. shopping malls — SHOPPING 1
building it's a very old b. — THEATRE 34
something like a public b. — MARRIAGE 129
built b. it to last — BODY 37
b. on large lines — BODY 44
bulimia yuppie version of b. — HEALTH 4
bull Beware of the b. — COUNTRY 12
bullslinging, and b.— — INSULTS 13
Cock and a B. — CONVERSATION 2
take the b. between your teeth — WIT 10
up a b.'s ass — LOVE 35
bullet book flying a b. — CRIME 4
bullfighting b., bullslinging — INSULTS 13

calf c. to share the enthusiasm   RELIGION 59
  lion and the c.   ANIMALS 1
California C. is a fine place to live   AMERICA 2
Californication C. of Ireland   CENSORSHIP 15
call c. the whole thing off   FOOD 26
  May I c. you 338   LETTERS 6
called Harry is c. Arthur   NAMES 12
callous 'c.' engraved on her heart   ROYALTY 63
calls her curtain c.   ACTORS 12
calmest c. and most rewarding hours
                                                                        TRANSPORT 3
calves susceptible to c.   MEN AND WOMEN 21
Calvin C., oat-cakes, and sulphur   SCOTLAND 10
Cambridge C. people rarely smile   PLACES 2
  C. was the first stopping place   PLACES 10
  it's either Oxford or C.   SPORTS 32
  When I was at C.   TRUST 6
camel c. is a horse designed   BUREAUCRACY 8
  come on a c.   COUNTRIES 34
  Take my c., dear   TRANSPORT 22
camelopardalis c. or giraffe   ANIMALS 14
camels none but she-c.   ANIMALS 20
campaigning two years organizing and c.
                                                                        POWER 2
Campbell breaks the C.'s back   NAMES 6
can C. I do you now   COMEDY 2
  He who c., does   EDUCATION 36
  horse c. do   BETTING 4
  I c. do that   AMERICA 22
  think you c.   FUTURE 7
Canada all over C.   CANADA 5
  C., Our Good Neighbour   TITLES 3
  C. is a country   CANADA 1
  Drink C. Dry   DRINK 5
  see C. as a country   CANADA 3
Canadian C. out of the German Emperor
                                                                        TRANSPORT 38
  C. savages   THEATRE 18
  little time left to be C.   COUNTRIES 32
Canadians C. are Americans   CANADA 4
Canaletto stare at C.   ART 34
Canalettos Then the C. go   POLITICS 44
canaries C., caged   BIRDS 8
can-can you can c. too   DANCE 13
cancer C. can be rather fun   SICKNESS 10
candidate c. can promise the moon   UNIVERSE 3
  c. talking to a rich person   POLITICS 15
candidates when c. appeal   POLITICS 2
candle I care not a farthing c.   MUSICIANS 10
candy C. is dandy   DRINK 43
cannabis import c.   CRIME 17
canned c. food came in   FOOD 35
cannibal c., but one   QUOTATIONS 8
  Said the c.   FOOD 28
cannibalism C. went right out   FOOD 35

cannibals formidable body of c.   PRESIDENTS 12
cannon c.-ball took off his legs   ARMED FORCES 16
canoe make love in a c.   CANADA 2
cant c. of criticism   HYPOCRISY 9
canting this c. world   HYPOCRISY 9
cap Housman's c.   DESCRIPTION 5
capable c. of reigning   POWER 10
caparisons No c., Miss   WIT 35
cape Risorgimento c.   APPEARANCE 7
capital c. is always timid   NEWSPAPERS 19
capitalism c. with the gloves off   WAR 24
  definition of c.   AMERICA 16
Capra rather be Frank C.   PEOPLE 21
capricious most c. things   TRANSPORT 8
captain by the team c.   TRUST 7
  nobody like the C.   JOURNALISM 20
car It's a *very bossy* c.   TRANSPORT 23
  keys to your c.   TRANSPORT 21
  motor c. to the human race   TRANSPORT 17
  Strauss's c.   TRANSPORT 32
  Take up c. maintenance   TECHNOLOGY 10
  wait in the c.   TIME 2
carbuncle monstrous c.   ARCHITECTURE 6
carcases c., which are to rise   BODY 7
carcinoma sing of rectal c.   SICKNESS 9
card c. to play for Honours   LITERATURE 6
  insulting Christmas c.   CHRISTMAS 7
cardie spy who came in for a c.   SECURITY 4
cardigan c. over his pyjamas   MEN AND WOMEN 27
care I c. for nobody   SATISFACTION 4
  I c. less and less   OLD AGE 33
  Take c. of him   MARRIAGE 113
  taken better c. of myself   OLD AGE 6
  women and c. and trouble   WOMEN 70
career c. must be slipping   AWARDS 2
  Good c. move   DEATH 70
  loyal to his own c.   PEOPLE 17
careful cannot be too c.   ENEMIES 8
  C. now   CENSORSHIP 11
carelessness looks like c.   FAMILY 49
Caribbean Columbus discovered C. vacations
                                                                        TRAVEL 21
caricature With a c. of a face   OLD AGE 20
Carlyle good of God to let C.   MARRIAGE 23
Carmen glanced at her C. rollers   NAMES 10
carnation We all wear a green c.   MEN 5
Carnegie wisecrack that played C. Hall   WIT 21
Carnera C. hadn't stunted   BODY 44
car park We sat in the c.   MEN AND WOMEN 5
carpenter being the c.   ACTING 26
carrier c. who carried his can   EPITAPHS 7
carrots naked, raw c.   FOOD 36
cars crazy about c.   TRANSPORT 33
  motor-', golf-caddies   HOSPITALITY 2
cartographers c. seek to define   SCOTLAND 3

Chanel C. No. 5 — DRESS 15
change c. from talking — CONVERSATION 7
  c. my plan — FASHION 6
  First you c. me schmall scheque — MONEY 5
  one thing to do with loose c. — MONEY 20
changed If voting c. anything — POLITICS 41
changes c. it more often — MEN AND WOMEN 20
  I make c. — FOOTBALL 24
changing c. a typewriter ribbon — WRITING 2
  not c. one's mind — CERTAINTY 18
channel you are crossing the C. — TRANSPORT 11
chaos emotional c. — HUMOUR 36
  His style is c. — WRITERS 43
  primordial c. — BODY 41
chaps Biography is about C. — BIOGRAPHY 4
chapters no Previous C. — BOOKS 8
character about a fellow's c. — CHARACTER 9
  any great strength of c. — TRAVEL 23
  c. dead — GOSSIP 12
  c. is to be abused — FAMILY 42
  enormous lack of c. — SELF-KNOWLEDGE 19
  have the strength of c. — HONOURS 5
  I knows an undesirable c. — SELF-KNOWLEDGE 11
  leave my c. behind — GOSSIP 11
characters too many c. — CINEMA 21
charge in c. of others — ARMED FORCES 1
  in c. of the Intelligence — SECURITY 5
charged asked me what I c. — MISTAKES 16
  c. straight through — ART 34
  he has been c. — SECRECY 7
charging c. like the Light Brigade — FOOD 75
Charing Cross human existence is at C.

  — TOWNS 16
charity C., dear Miss Prism — HUMILITY 5
Charles C. II was always very merry — ROYALTY 64
  In good King C.'s golden days — POLITICIANS 1
  used by C. the First — HOME 6
Charlotte Werther had a love for C.

  — MEN AND WOMEN 54
charm By my c. — BEHAVIOUR 10
  know what c. is — BEHAVIOUR 4
  Prince Umberto is c. itself — SELF-KNOWLEDGE 7
charmer Were t'other dear c. away — LOVE 17
charming c. face — ANIMALS 3
  Farming is so c. — COUNTRY 16
Chartreuse C. can never really die — RELIGION 58
chasing always c. Rimbauds — LITERATURE 28
  nobody's c. me — MEN AND WOMEN 42
chaste c. whore — HUMOUR 26
chastity c. and continency — SEX 13
chat kills a c. — CONVERSATION 8
chateau I've a c. in Touraine — WEALTH 19
Chatterley end of the C. ban — SEX 49
Chaucer C., who had geneyus — WORDS 37

chauffeur AIRMAIL PHOTOGRAPH OF C.

  — TELEGRAMS 17
cheap good actors—c. — THEATRE 7
  handy and c. — FAMILY 1
  how c. potent music — MUSIC 57
  how potent c. music is — MUSIC 10
  in c. shoes — FASHION 1
cheaper c. to lower the Atlantic — FILM 7
cheapish C., reddish — WINE 11
cheat lucrative to c. — CRIME 7
  trying to c. you — MIDDLE AGE 8
cheek blush into the c. — ENGLAND 10
  C. to Cheek — DANCE 9
  tongue being in your c. — WIT 3
cheekbones high c. — ACTORS 1
cheerful being so c. — COMEDY 29
cheerfulness c. was always breaking in

  — PHILOSOPHY 2
cheerio c. my deario — HOPE 6
cheese Botticelli's a c. — FOOD 60
  c.-eating surrender monkeys — FRANCE 5
  C. it is a peevish elf — FOOD 62
  chinks with c. — FOOD 74
  dreamed of c. — SLEEP 9
  soft c. will kill you — FOOD 42
  varieties of c. — FRANCE 3
  very new c. — FOOD 68
cheesed humanity soon had me c. off

  — LITERATURE 5
cheesemakers Blessed are the c. — RELIGION 18
cheetah like a c. — HUMOUR 10
chef c. and a cook — COOKERY 8
chefs c. screaming risotto recipes — OPERA 6
chemotherapy sessions of c. — MEDICINE 29
cheque be done with a c. — RELIGION 35
  mail that c. to the Judge — JUDGES 6
  schange me schmall c. — MONEY 5
  written a bad c. — DEBT 6
cheques publisher has to do is write c.

  — PUBLISHING 17
cherries c., hops, and women — PLACES 8
cherry c. blossom is quite nice — POETS 16
cherub c.'s face, a reptile all — INSULTS 32
chest c. to slip down — FOOD 84
Chesterton dared attack my C. — LITERATURE 4
chestnuts pop like c. — WRITERS 13
chew fart and c. gum — INSULTS 19
chewing drops c. gum — PUNISHMENT 8
chianti bottles of C. — COUNTRIES 37
  nice c. — FOOD 29
chic Radical C. — SOCIETY 24
  very c. for an atheist — RELIGION 57
Chicago I'd expect to be robbed in C. — TOWNS 18

church (*cont.*):

Churchill never was a C.   ARISTOCRACY 8

churchman British c.   CLERGY 2

chutzpah C. is that quality   FAMILY 34

cigarette c. into the lake   COUNTRIES 19

cigarettes c. are the only product   SMOKING 2

Cinderella If I made C.   FILM PRODUCERS 7

cinemas screens at c.   CINEMA 5

circumcision breast-feeding, c.   CHILDREN 28

circumlocution C. Office   BUREAUCRACY 4

circumstance bitter, bitter c.   WOMEN 73

circumstantial c. evidence is very strong   LAW 33

circus celebrated Barnum's c.   PRIME MINISTERS 11

cistern loud the c.   OLD AGE 5

cities c. on the hill   AMERICA 29

city big hard-boiled c.   TOWNS 7

civil Always be c. to the girls   WOMEN 41

civilisation collapse of c.   NEW YORK 1

civilities groundless c.   BEHAVIOUR 15

civilization can't say c. don't advance

civilizations build c.   SHOPPING 1

civilized become genuinely c.   SCOTLAND 7

civil servant c. doesn't make jokes

civil servants c. are human beings

civil service c. has finished   CIVIL SERVANTS 7

claiming each c. to be   ARGUMENT 23

clam personage as happy as a c.   ROYALTY 24

clan Not for C. Campbell   SUCCESS 4

clap Don't c. too hard   THEATRE 34

claret C. is the liquor for boys   DRINK 33

class c. distinctions   CLASS 22

classes Clashing of C.   POLITICS 23

classic 'C.' A book   READING 17

classics great homicidal c.   LITERATURE 34

classroom in every c.   COMPUTERS 4

clatter c. of Sir James Barrie's cans   LITERATURE 20

Claude After you, C.   COMEDY 1

Claus ain't no Sanity C.   CHRISTMAS 8

claws panes of glass with its c.   MUSIC 4

clay Feet of c. everywhere   BIOGRAPHY 1

clean c., verb active   EDUCATION 13

cleaner c. than a man's   MEN AND WOMEN 20

cleanliness c. everywhere   COUNTRIES 19

Cleopatra C.—and sank   ACTORS 5

clergyman beneficed c.   CLERGY 20

clergymen men, women, and c.   CLERGY 17

clever c. men at Oxford   EDUCATION 16

cliché c. and an indiscretion   DIPLOMACY 7

clichés C. make the best songs   SONGS 13

client c. moans and sighs   ADVERTISING 14

climax end a sentence with a c.   SPEECHES 10

climb c. every Mountie   CANADA 6

clinic Betty Fjord C.   DRINK 59

Clive like about C.   DEATH 13

close c. your eyes   SEX 15

cones enough traffic c.   TRANSPORT 35
confession after the sweetness of c.   RELIGION 23
    had a c. to make   SELF-KNOWLEDGE 15
confessional c. passage has probably   WRITERS 33
    invent the c.   RELIGION 73
confidential I give c. briefings   SECRECY 7
conflict C. and Art   FOOTBALL 22
confused but a bit c.   BODY 33
confusion of an unparalleled c.   WRITERS 19
congealing You feel your blood c.   WEATHER 10
congeals When love c.   LOVE 26
congratulation matter for c.   IDEAS 6
congregation landlord to the whole c.
     RELIGION 2
conjecture wholesale returns of c.   SCIENCE 29
conked c. out on November 15th   EPITAPHS 15
connect Only c.   BOXING 9
connections scientist without industry c.
     SCIENCE 24
conquer urge to c. Poland   MUSIC 1
conscience cut my c.   POLITICS 35
    live with a good c.   HYPOCRISY 8
    your c. well under control   POLITICS 42
consent I will ne'er c.   SEX 28
consenting only between c. adults   SEX 90
conservation make a speech on c.   NATURE 6
conservative c. when old   POLITICAL PARTIES 8
    nothing if not c.   FOOD 12
    Or else a little C.   POLITICAL PARTIES 9
    sound C. government   POLITICAL PARTIES 5
    which makes a man more c.   PAST 7
conservatives C. do not believe
     POLITICAL PARTIES 10
consolation c. in a distressed one   SNOBBERY 2
    that's one c.   PUNISHMENT 2
conspiracy c. to make you happy   AMERICA 27
    Indecency's c. of silence   VIRTUE 14
    really in a c. against him   TECHNOLOGY 13
constable C. had taken   ART 34
constabulary c. duty's to be done   HAPPINESS 7
constancy c. of the women who love me
     WOMEN 58
constant nothing in this world c.   VIRTUE 16
    Such a c. lover   LOVE 44
    than a woman c.   WIT 6
constipation c. is the big fear   SICKNESS 14
constitution C. for Iraq   GOVERNMENT 24
    holy resignation and an iron c.   MEDICINE 24
    left out of the C.   GOD 44
consume can c. locally   COUNTRIES 36
    c. like soup   POETRY 3
consumer c. isn't a moron   ADVERTISING 12
consumerism first rule of c.   BUSINESS 2
consummation retired from c.   SEX 82
consumption galloping c. you had   SICKNESS 3

contagious afraid it's c.   HOLLYWOOD 7
contemplation Has left for c.   RELIGION 10
contempt c. for human nature
     SELF-KNOWLEDGE 27
    Familiarity breeds c.   FAMILY 48
contest end a c. quicker   DRINK 55
continency chastity and c.   SEX 13
continental C. people have sex life   SEX 57
    may be quite c.   WEALTH 21
contraception word about oral c.   SEX 2
contraceptive bent her c. coil   LAW 9
contract c. is so one-sided   LAW 8
    verbal c.   CINEMA 15
contractions cheap c.   ADVERTISING 2
    uterine c.   HEALTH 8
contradict I never c.   ROYALTY 27
contradiction c. in terms   RELIGION 64
contraption TV —a clever c.   TELEVISION 1
contribution valuable c.   DEATH 48
control conscience well under c.   POLITICS 42
    kept rigidly under c.   CENSORSHIP 3
    or c. Alice   PRESIDENTS 17
    unless it is kept under c.   VIRTUE 11
conversation art of c.   CONVERSATION 9
    elegant c.   CONVERSATION 3
    flagging c.   CONVERSATION 12
    followed c. as a shark   WIT 20
    go on with the c.   CONVERSATION 32
    improved by a little light c.   SPORTS 17
    lack a flair for c.   SCIENCE 20
    lady's c.   COUNTRY 13
    make his c.   CONVERSATION 25
    ordinary c.   CONVERSATION 15
    pause in c.   MARRIAGE 47
conversations without pictures or c.
     LITERATURE 12
convert expect to c. England   RELIGION 54
convictions c. for drunken driving   DRINK 9
    man of no c.   CERTAINTY 14
convincing less c. than one   ARGUMENT 10
cook chef and a c.   COOKERY 8
    c. in the kitchen   MARRIAGE 68
    C. is a little unnerved   SOCIETY 3
    uncommon c.   COOKERY 17
cooked c. a few meals   MARRIAGE 40
    goose will be c.   SUCCESS 2
cookery Football and c.   FOOTBALL 28
    Kissing don't last: c. do   MARRIAGE 84
cooking missionary position of c.   COOKERY 15
cooks as c. go   COOKERY 16
    count the c.   COOKERY 18
    Devil sends c.   COOKERY 7
    'plain' c.   COOKERY 12
    Synod of C.   COOKERY 9
    those literary c.   QUOTATIONS 14

cope if you use a c. like that RELIGION 54
Copperfield C. kind of crap AUTOBIOGRAPHY 21
copy down for an early c. AUTOBIOGRAPHY 15
  make a c. of everything BUREAUCRACY 6
copying mode of c. HANDWRITING 8
copyright c. law is to be made LAW 35
  sense in any c. law GOD 43
cork I don't pop my c. MEN AND WOMEN 12
  sound of a popping c. WINE 1
  weasel took the c. DRINK 22
corn slowing the c. surplus SPEECHES 15
corner just around the c. HOPE 4
  standing on the c. MEN AND WOMEN 28
cornered cuddly as a c. ferret DESCRIPTION 4
corners people standing in c. TELEVISION 3
cornerstone c. of a public building PRESIDENTS 19
cornfields Miles of c. RUSSIA 2
Cornwall do you know *Tudor C.* BOOKS 18
corny c. as Kansas AMERICA 15
coroner we had our own c. EDUCATION 9
corporation industrial c. BUSINESS 16
corpse Another c. in the library LIBRARIES 10
  make a lovely c. DEATH 20
  makes a very handsome c. DEATH 25
  produce a c. CRIME 4
  PUT C. ON ICE TELEGRAMS 13
correct perfectly c. thing BEHAVIOUR 29
correspondence calls and c. LETTERS 14
corset Try wearing a c. FASHION 13
corsets thirty-shilling c. DRESS 11
Corsican In a coarse, rather C. way MARRIAGE 45
cosmic comic with the c. UNIVERSE 12
cosmopolitan true c. COUNTRIES 32
cost C. a million ARCHITECTURE 7
  c. me much MONEY 6
  [Gandhi] knew the c. POVERTY 12
costs curbed at all c. EDUCATION 1
  she's worth all she c. you LOVE 33
costume sung in the c. of the period MUSIC 36
  thirty-guinea c. DRESS 11
cottage Love and a c. HOME 5
couch psychiatrist's c. MIND 9
couches waste of good c. MIND 7
cough c. I've got is hacking SICKNESS 8
  c. so robust that I tapped SICKNESS 5
  person . . . can develop a c. SICKNESS 12
coughing birds c. in the trees HOLLYWOOD 6
  C. MYSELF INTO A FIRENZE TELEGRAMS 8
  group of people from c. ACTING 27
  one c., and one not coughing MUSIC 45
couldn't it's not 'cause I c. WOMEN 54
council she'd probably be in c. care ROYALTY 54
counsel Dost sometimes c. take ROYALTY 56

count c. four ANGER 10
  c. to five ANGER 4
  C. to ten, and man is bored MEN AND WOMEN 39
  let us c. our spoons VIRTUE 9
counted faster we c. our spoons VIRTUE 8
countenance disinheriting c. CHARACTER 11
counter I have left my side of the c.
   PRESIDENTS 11
counterfeit c. $20 bill BODY 9
countess hear what the c. is saying WRITERS 25
counting It's the c. DEMOCRACY 15
country another c. SEX 53
  c. retreat near the town MEN AND WOMEN 65
  English c. life COUNTRY 3
  every c. but his own FOOLISHNESS 6
  God made the c. COUNTRY 2
  good in the c. COUNTRY 19
  govern a c. FRANCE 3
  lawsuit C. ENGLAND 7
  leave the c. NEWSPAPERS 5
  likes the c. COUNTRY 1
  living in the c. CONVERSATION 9
  Love is sweeping the c. LOVE 20
  mulct the whole c. WEALTH 18
  My wife's gone to the c. MARRIAGE 17
  named a c. FILM 3
  no relish for the c. COUNTRY 18
  pray for the c. GOVERNMENT 14
  something of his own c. ENGLAND 38
  spy for or against my c. TRUST 6
  to be had in the c. COUNTRY 8
  weekend in the c. HOLIDAYS 10
countryman simple c. BUSINESS 6
countryside c. to be laughing DANCE 6
courage have enough c. MORALITY 7
court movies are the only c. CINEMA 6
  no family life at C. ROYALTY 67
courtesy professional c. INSULTS 24
courtiers She sins not with c. ROYALTY 6
courtmartialled c. in my absence DEATH 10
courtship C. is to marriage MARRIAGE 36
  They dream in c. MARRIAGE 97
cousins sisters and his c. FAMILY 17
Coutts banks with C. CLASS 16
Coventry In our C. homes FOOTBALL 4
cow c. and calf ART 2
  c. is of the bovine ilk ANIMALS 32
  Don't have a c., man COMEDY 6
  it was an open c. LAW 13
  like a c. in a milk bar PUBLISHING 14
  pet is a c. ANIMALS 9
cows till the c. come home CERTAINTY 8
coy Other girls are c. WOMEN 28
crab grimly playful c. CRICKET 14
cradle hand that rocked the c. DEATH 5

crap Copperfield kind of c.   AUTOBIOGRAPHY 21
  floating c. game   BETTING 5
  have a c.   SPORTS 29
crash C.! BANG! BLURP   MISTAKES 17
  c. is coming   DRINK 46
craving no stronger c.   TITLES 6
crawl c. in or kick your way in   POLITICS 12
crazy football c.   FOOTBALL 19
  Is that man c.   SECURITY 2
  should they go c.   POLITICIANS 21
creation exception in the case of *The C.*
     MUSIC 36
  Had I been present at the C.   UNIVERSE 1
creative C. writers are two a penny
     JOURNALISM 2
creator C. made Italy   COUNTRIES 44
creatures animated c.   HUMAN RACE 7
credit greatly to his c.   ENGLAND 13
  I never seek to take the c.   LITERATURE 29
  people who get the c.   SUCCESS 18
  very much to his c.   EXAMINATIONS 1
creep Almost any c.'ll   GOVERNMENT 15
crème c. de la crème   EDUCATION 40
Crete people of C.   COUNTRIES 36
crew haircut will be c.   FAMILY 16
cricket England did for c.   CRICKET 8
  It's not c. to picket   POLITICS 60
  looked upon c.   CRICKET 16
  not in support of c.   CRICKET 5
  to dare in c.   CRICKET 13
cricketer modern professional c.   CRICKET 7
crime c. you haven't committed   OLD AGE 32
  newspaper prints a sex c.   NEWSPAPERS 25
  UNDULY EMPHASISING C.   TELEGRAMS 2
  We like c.   CRIME 9
crimes respect of those c.   PUNISHMENT 9
  worst of c. is poverty   POVERTY 16
criminal c. investigation   CRIME 19
  ends I think c.   GOVERNMENT 21
crinolines top hats and C.   BUSINESS 11
cripple cannot meet a c.   CONVERSATION 3
crisis cannot be a c.   DIPLOMACY 6
  only panics in a c.   POLITICAL PARTIES 13
  real c. on your hands   NATURE 7
critic c. is a man   CRITICS 32
  c. spits on what is done   POETS 5
  in honour of a c.   CRITICS 27
critical c. period in matrimony   MARRIAGE 71
criticism cant of c.   HYPOCRISY 9
  C. is a study   CRITICS 14
  c. is ever inhibited by ignorance   POLITICS 48
  C. is not only   CRITICS 26
criticize Never c. Americans   AMERICA 21
criticized c. is not always to be wrong
     SELF-KNOWLEDGE 9

critics C. are like eunuchs   CRITICS 5
  C. search for ages   CRITICS 34
  know who the c. are   CRITICS 9
  lot of c.   CRITICS 19
  murderers or c.   ART 16
  of Music Among C.   CRITICS 25
crochet c. week in Rhyl   HOLIDAYS 12
crocodile it's c. land   APPEARANCE 17
crooning c. like a bilious pigeon   LANGUAGES 22
cross adjective 'c.'   ANGER 11
  attempt to c. it   FACES 4
  having a c. word   ARGUMENT 9
  orgasm has replaced the C.   RELIGION 44
  un-nailed from the c.   ACTORS 12
cross-dressing about c.   DRESS 17
crossed Was the cow c.   LAW 13
crosses instead of c.   RELIGION 12
crossing double c. of a pair of heels   LOVE 26
crossroads faces a c.   CHOICE 1
crow arse of a c.   FOOTBALL 3
  had the old c. over   POETS 10
crown c. of thorns *and* the thirty   POLITICS 11
  deserve a c.   ROYALTY 3
crucifixion after the C.   FILM 15
cruel Such c. glasses   INSULTS 18
crumpet thinking man's c.   WOMEN 45
crushed c. life is what I lead   MARRIAGE 90
crustaceans c. died in vain   POLITICS 36
crutch kick in the c.   ANGER 3
  Reality is a c.   DRUGS 8
cry babe with a c.   DEATH 126
  c. into your beer   DRINK 39
cryptogram charm of a c.   AUTOBIOGRAPHY 18
crystals Rose Geranium bath c.   BUSINESS 1
cuckoo c. clock   COUNTRIES 46
  sudden c.   COUNTRIES 47
cucumber c. should be well sliced   COOKERY 10
  when c. is added   FOOD 38
cucumbers extracting sun-beams out of c.
     SCIENCE 27
cuddlesome seeing nature as c.   NATURE 5
cuddly c. as a cornered ferret   DESCRIPTION 4
  c. in a frightening   DOGS 1
  kissable, c., and smelling good
     MEN AND WOMEN 10
culture c. could have produced   WRITERS 38
  political c.   POLITICS 49
  pursue C. in bands   ART 35
cultured real or c.   FAME 15
cunning I have a c. plan   COMEDY 27
cup nice c. of cocoa   HOLLYWOOD 2
curable Love's a disease. But c.   LOVE 32
curate albino c.   FRIENDS 16
  bland country c.   FACES 2
  I feel like a shabby c.   SCIENCE 3

curate (*cont.*):

like a Protestant c.	DANCE 10
pale young c.	CLERGY 9
remember the average c.	CLERGY 8
very name of a C.	CLERGY 19

curates preached to death by wild c. — RELIGION 67

curbed must be c. — EDUCATION 1

cure c. for sea sickness — TRAVEL 19

in the twentieth, it's a c.	SEX 84
no C. for this Disease	MEDICINE 5
once-bitten there is no c.	FISHING 3
you have a c.	MEDICINE 34

cured C. yesterday of my disease — MEDICINE 28

curiosity lost all c. — AUTOBIOGRAPHY 23

Love, c., freckles, and doubt — LOVE 37

curious like c. clothes — DRESS 19

curiouser C. and curiouser — WIT 5

current c. is turned on — WORDS 7

curry lampshade in a c. house — FASHION 11

curse c. of the drinking classes — WORK 26

Fathers don't c.	PARENTS 10
journalistic c. of Eve	JOURNALISM 23

curtain after the c. has risen — ROYALTY 45

c. was up	THEATRE 33
her c. calls	ACTORS 12
remove the c. rings	DRESS 9

curtains c. looked like duvets — HOTELS 2

sew rings on the new c. — INSULTS 7

curtsey C. while you're thinking — BEHAVIOUR 6

Curzon second Lady C. — DEATH 19

cushions c. had cushions — HOTELS 2

custard bathed us like warm c. — DESCRIPTION 6

custom aid of prejudice and c. — PREJUDICE 7

cut BETTER AFTER IT'S BEEN C. — TELEGRAMS 5

c. my conscience to fit	POLITICS 35
c. you down to my size	MEN AND WOMEN 19
right of final c.	FILM PRODUCERS 18

cuter When I was c. — MIDDLE AGE 13

cutlet enough if he eats a c. — WRITERS 24

cutting damned c. and slashing — PUBLISHING 6

cuttings press c. to prove it — ACTORS 24

cyclists C. see motorists — TRANSPORT 19

cymbal like an ill-tuned c. — JUDGES 15

cynic What is a c. — CHARACTER 18

cynical c. about politicians — POLITICS 71

cynics composed of c. — GOVERNMENT 27

d I mean Big D. — TOWNS 17

I never use a big, big D. — LANGUAGE 7

dad They fuck you up, your mum and d. — PARENTS 12

dada art belongs to D. — ART 24

mama of d. — LITERATURE 17

daddy D. sat up very late — DRINK 8

English teacher D.-o	EDUCATION 25
keep D. off her	FAMILY 30

dagger d. in one hand — POLITICAL PARTIES 20

daintily must have things d. served — SOCIETY 3

Dalai horns of a D. Lama — WIT 47

Dallas that spells D. — TOWNS 17

damage compensate people for the d.
— LITERATURE 36

dammed saved by being d. — COUNTRIES 22

damn don't give a d. — SATISFACTION 8

no general idea is worth a d.	IDEAS 4
old man who said 'D. '	TRANSPORT 16

damnations Twenty-nine distinct d. — BIBLE 1

damned lies, d. lies and statistics — LIES 6

Life is just one d. thing	LIFE 10
music is the brandy of the d.	MUSIC 48
public be d.	BUSINESS 21
those d. dots	ECONOMICS 5
written a d. play	THEATRE 42

damp like a d. mackintosh — DESCRIPTION 12

dance d. on pinheads — CERTAINTY 8

I'm giving a d.	SATISFACTION 14
join the d.	DANCE 4
no d. on Sunday	DANCE 15

dances Also d. — FILM STARS 1

dancing mature women, d. — DANCE 6

dandy Candy is d. — DRINK 43

Dane if you've got a great D. — THEATRE 32

play a D. — ACTING 4

danger be in less d. — FAMILY 26

But only when in d. — RELIGION 52

dangerous d. as an author — WRITERS 44

D. Dan McGrew	MEN AND WOMEN 45
d. when active	CENSORSHIP 6
Science becomes d.	SCIENCE 26

Daniel lionized was D. — HUMAN RACE 11

Daniels den of D. — FRIENDS 18

dank d. rock pools — FOOD 39

dare It wouldn't d. — TRANSPORT 6

dark those d. glasses — FILM STARS 10

too d. to read — ANIMALS 25

darken Never d. my Dior — FASHION 9

darling oh, he's a d. man — MEN 13

date keep them up to date — YOUTH 7

dates broken d. — LOVE 25

question of d. — TRUST 13

daughter Don't put your d. — ACTING 7

Elderly ugly d.	LOVE 21
happens to my d.	PARENTS 4
I'm your d.	SONGS 10
I trust Bush with my d.	PRESIDENTS 14

daughter-in-law her own d. — FAMILY 20

daughters D. are best — FAMILY 4

David D. wrote the Psalms — RELIGION 45

diary keep a d.   DIARIES 7
   living for one's d.   DIARIES 1
   more dull than a discreet d.   DIARIES 3
   without my d.   DIARIES 8
   write a d. every day   DIARIES 5
DiCanio You've got D.   FOOTBALL 1
Dick Any Tom, D. or Harry   MARRIAGE 100
   At Dirty D.'s   DRINK 4
Dickens put to D. as children   LITERATURE 5
dictation told at d. speed what he knew   LIFE 1
dictionaries Big d.   DICTIONARIES 2
   opening d.   DICTIONARIES 10
   Short d.   DICTIONARIES 7
   will publish d.   DICTIONARIES 11
dictionary D. has not attempted DICTIONARIES 6
   d. out of order   DICTIONARIES 5
   ever made the d.   DICTIONARIES 13
   'Ex's' in this bloody d.   WORDS 5
   Like Webster's D.   DICTIONARIES 4
   Oxford D. of Quotations   NEWSPAPERS 14
die afraid to d.   DEATH 1
   all must d.   EPITAPHS 24
   back to America . . . to d.   AMERICA 19
   choose to d.   MEDICINE 11
   D., and endow   DEATH 57
   D., my dear Doctor   LAST WORDS 6
   d. before they sing   DEATH 16
   d. beyond my means   DEATH 73
   d. in *The Times,*   FAME 2
   done my best to d.   BIOGRAPHY 11
   had to d. in my week   DEATH 38
   I'll d. young   DRUGS 3
   I shall some day d.   DEATH 40
   remain so until *they d.*   PARENTS 15
   shall d. ere he thrive   MARRIAGE 74
   tomorrow we shall d.   DEATH 52
   unfit to d.   DEATH 30
   You d. thin   DIETS 3
died crustaceans d. in vain   POLITICS 36
   d. last night of my physician MEDICINE 28
   nearly d. laughing   HUMOUR 3
dies little something in me d.   SUCCESS 24
   One d. only once   DEATH 49
diets feel about d.   DIETS 4
difference d. of taste   HUMOUR 12
different arguing from d. premises ARGUMENT 19
   d. from the home life   ROYALTY 10
   d. kinds of herring   FOOD 10
   d. sense of morality   MORALITY 4
   on d. subjects   IGNORANCE 6
difficult can be very d.   FUTURE 3
   D. do you call it   MUSIC 26
   Luckily, this is not d.   MEN AND WOMEN 61
   That would be d.   POLITICAL PARTIES 11
difficulties little local d.   POLITICS 45

digest wholesome to d.   FOOD 5
digesting D. it   BEHAVIOUR 18
digests It d. all things   FOOD 62
dignity I left the room with silent d. MISTAKES 15
   Official d.   BUREAUCRACY 7
digressions D., incontestably   BOOKS 19
dildos wooden d. are made   BUSINESS 14
dilly Don't d.-dally   HOME 4
dime Of a shiny new d.   POVERTY 15
dine d. with some men   ARCHITECTURE 3
dined d. in every house   SOCIETY 23
   I d. last night with the Borgias SOCIETY 2
   I have d. today   FOOD 69
   more d. against than dining   SOCIETY 5
diner without hitting a d.   BUSINESS 9
dining more dined against than d. SOCIETY 5
dinner All gong and no d.   TENNIS 8
   better than the d.   MARRIAGE 35
   doing for d.   BEHAVIOUR 18
   eating a hearty d.   RELIGION 40
   had a better d.   COOKERY 9
   having an old friend for d.   SOCIETY 12
   hungry for d.   BEHAVIOUR 16
   inviting us to d.   HANDWRITING 4
   number for a d.   FOOD 27
   served the sort of d.   HOTELS 5
   sherry before d.   DRINK 45
Dior Christian D. me   FAME 18
   Never darken my D.   FASHION 9
dip quick d. in bed   HEALTH 14
diplomacy D.—lying in state DIPLOMACY 5
diplomat D. these days   DIPLOMACY 16
   distinction of a d.   DIPLOMACY 13
diplomats D. tell lies   GOVERNMENT 22
direct d. this play the way you THEATRE 16
director being a d.   ACTING 26
direful something d. in the sound TOWNS 4
dirt d. doesn't get any worse HOUSEWORK 4
   not a d. gardener   GARDENS 1
dirty At D. Dick's   DRINK 4
   d. minds   CENSORSHIP 20
   d. or not   BEHAVIOUR 2
   give pornography a d. name THEATRE 6
   in a d. glass   FOOD 51
   wet and d. from hunting APPEARANCE 20
   You d. old man   COMEDY 54
disagreeable no person so perfectly d.
                  WRITERS 44
disappointed been d. as often as I have
            MEN AND WOMEN 10
   d. in human nature   HUMAN RACE 3
   never be d.   HOPE 9
   Sir! you have d. us   POLITICIANS 6
disappointment are a bitter d. CHILDREN 38
   bitter d.   FOOTBALL 16

dream d. you are crossing the Channel

TRANSPORT 11

living the American d.　　GENERATION GAP 8
say what d. it was　　SLEEP 8
They d. in courtship　　MARRIAGE 97
dreamed d. of cheese　　SLEEP 9
dreams City of perspiring d.　　TOWNS 21
dreary morals make you d.　　MORALITY 15
dredger sharp end of a d.　　ARGUMENT 22
dress All women d. like their mothers

MEN AND WOMEN 4

automobile changed our d.　　TRANSPORT 20
cool, white d.　　RELIGION 23
like to d. egos　　FASHION 18
plain in d.　　WOMEN 43
woman's d. should be　　FASHION 10
dressed d. with pepper　　COOKERY 10
drier Or come up d.　　IGNORANCE 3
drifted Snow White . . . but I d.　　VIRTUE 22
drink buy a d. from both　　HEALTH 13
don't d. liquor　　DRINK 36
D., sir, is a great provoker　　DRINK 52
D. and debauchery　　GOLF 2
d. and women　　EDUCATION 38
D. Canada Dry　　DRINK 5
D.! Drink　　COMEDY 7
d. it himself　　FOOD 83
d. one another's healths　　DRINK 32
gave up d.　　DIETS 1
has taken to d.　　DRINK 57
in favour iv d.　　DRINK 20
meat, d. and cigarettes　　HEALTH 11
One more d.　　DRINK 47
vanity and sometimes d.　　APPEARANCE 1
we could d. all day　　WEALTH 24
What a world of d. he swills　　ROYALTY 46
woman drove me to d.　　DRINK 24
your husband I would d. it　　INSULTS 4
drinking curse of the d. classes　　WORK 26
no d. after death　　DRINK 25
drinks d. as much as you do　　DRINK 58
dripping electricity was d. invisibly　　SCIENCE 28
drive can't d. the car　　CRITICS 32
d. has gone to pieces　　GOLF 1
driven pure as the d. slush　　VIRTUE 1
driver in the d.'s seat　　PRIME MINISTERS 4
drop don't d. players　　FOOTBALL 24
one d. of Negro blood　　PREJUDICE 8
drops d. chewing gum　　PUNISHMENT 8
drove d. it into a big wall　　TRANSPORT 21
woman d. me to drink　　DRINK 24
drowned d. by the waves　　SONGS 7
drowning death by d.　　OLD AGE 17

drudge harmless d.　　DICTIONARIES 8
drug depends what miracle d.　　MEDICINE 2
d. is neither　　DRUGS 9
drugs both on d.　　GENERATION GAP 2
can't cope with d.　　DRUGS 8
D. have taught　　DRUGS 6
had their d. and booze　　LIFESTYLE 8
quality of his d.　　DRUGS 5
drum d. out of the skin　　PRIME MINISTERS 20
Dumb as a d.　　MUSIC 12
drunk because they're d.　　TELEVISION 6
d. as a lord　　DRINK 29
d. for about a week　　LIBRARIES 6
Guinness makes you d.　　DRINK 6
I've tried him d.　　ROYALTY 22
not get d. at Lord's　　CRICKET 7
not so think as you d.　　DRINK 56
stand around at a bar and get d.　　SPORTS 25
Winston, you're d.　　INSULTS 10
You're not d.　　DRINK 40
drunken convictions for d. driving　　DRINK 9
d. porter　　GOVERNMENT 29
drunks two miniature d.　　CHILDREN 12
dry Drink Canada D.　　DRINK 5
d. she ain't　　FILM STARS 12
into a d. Martini　　DRINK 2
Those d. Martinis　　DRINK 1
dryness morbid d. is a Whig vice　　VIRTUE 2
Dubliners real D. lead　　IRELAND 9
duchess every D. in London　　PRIME MINISTERS 23
married to a d.　　PUBLISHING 18
duchesses four bereaved D.　　ARISTOCRACY 2
ducking like d. questions　　PEOPLE 11
ducks stick to d.　　BIRDS 4
duke avoided either d.　　BIRDS 6
D. of Fife　　BEHAVIOUR 3
enough who knows a d.　　CLERGY 5
palace of the D. of Ferrara　　ARISTOCRACY 17
dukes drawing room full of d.　　SCIENCE 3
d. were three a penny　　GOVERNMENT 11
dull always d.　　ENGLAND 43
Anger makes d. men witty　　ANGER 1
d. in a new way　　BORES 8
d. in himself　　BORES 6
land of the d.　　AMERICA 28
more d. than a discreet diary　　DIARIES 3
Only d. people　　BORES 18
paper appears d.　　BORES 13
quotations should be d.　　QUOTATIONS 12
that he be d.　　GOVERNMENT 1
dullness cardinal sin is d.　　CINEMA 2
cause of d.　　BORES 6
D. is so much stronger　　BORES 4
dum wrote d.-dum-*dee*-dum　　SONGS 11

educated Cabinet ministers are e.   LITERATURE 6
education branch of e.   EDUCATION 32
  e., taste   BEHAVIOUR 24
  e. and catastrophe   HISTORY 15
  E. in those elementary   EDUCATION 18
  e. is what is left   EDUCATION 5
  E. with socialists   EDUCATION 6
  liberal e.   EDUCATION 2
  poor e. I have received   EDUCATION 8
  Soap and e.   EDUCATION 41
  what I call e.   EDUCATION 39
educator overpaid as an e.   EDUCATION 30
Edwardians E., on the contrary   HOLIDAYS 11
eel e.-and-pie yob   SNOBBERY 6
  pick an e. out   HUMOUR 14
Eeyore E., the old grey Donkey   ANIMALS 27
effect get the full e.   APPEARANCE 9
efficient E. hacks are very rare   JOURNALISM 2
effort if that e. be too great   ROYALTY 7
effusive don't be too e.   PRAISE 3
egg demnition e.   FOOD 18
  e. on our face   MISTAKES 8
  e.'s way of making   BIRDS 3
  It looks like a poached e.   TRANSPORT 26
  learned roast, an e.   COOKERY 14
  like eating an e. without salt

      MEN AND WOMEN 23
  never see an e.   FOOD 17
  still eat a boiled e.   OLD AGE 4
  you've got a bad e.   FOOD 61
egghead E. weds hourglass   MARRIAGE 5
eggs all my e. in one bastard   SEX 68
  e. in one basket   BUSINESS 20
  hardboiled e.   CHARACTER 20
  Lays her e.   ANIMALS 26
  ways to dress e.   FRANCE 7
egos like to dress e.   FASHION 18
Egypt Remember you're in E.   ACTING 33
eiderdown flurry of e.   BIRDS 5
eight We met at e.   OLD AGE 26
eighth I'm Henery the E., I am   MARRIAGE 87
eighty After the age of e.   OLD AGE 18
  At e. life has clipped my claws   OLD AGE 21
eighty-two And shall be till I'm e.   YOUTH 2
Einstein E. who made the real trouble

      SCIENCE 17
either How happy I could be with e.   LOVE 17
élan with admirable é.   POETRY 22
elbow e. has a fascination   BODY 20
elder to e. statesman   SUCCESS 10
elderly e. fellow   GOD 38
  Judges commonly are e. men   JUDGES 9
  Mr Salteena was an e. man of 42   OLD AGE 2
  writing for an e. lady   JOURNALISM 15
eldest not the e. son   FAMILY 14

elected e. a President, not a Pope   PRESIDENTS 20
elections E. are won   DEMOCRACY 1
electric biggest e. train set   HOLLYWOOD 21
  e. typewriters keep going   TECHNOLOGY 3
  little e. chairs   RELIGION 12
  mend the E. Light   DEATH 11
electricity e. was dripping invisibly   SCIENCE 28
  paying the e. bill   MEDICINE 1
  usefulness of e.   TECHNOLOGY 5
elegant Economy was always 'e.'   MONEY 10
  e. simplicity   MONEY 23
elementary E., my dear Watson   CRIME 13
elephant e. seal   ANIMALS 34
  life an e.'s   BODY 8
  saw an E.   ANIMALS 10
  They couldn't hit an e.   LAST WORDS 8
elephantiasis e. and other dread diseases

      PLACES 11
elephants done the e.   TRAVEL 29
eleven e. at night   DRINK 53
elf Cheese it is a peevish e.   FOOD 62
  Oh fuck, not another e.!   LITERATURE 16
Elginbrodde Martin E.   EPITAPHS 18
Eliot I'd not read E.   POETS 14
élitist well-known é.   ARISTOCRACY 9
elms Behind the e. last night   SEX 72
elopement e. would be preferable   MARRIAGE 1
else does it to somebody e.   GOVERNMENT 30
  happening to Somebody E.   HUMOUR 31
elsewhere something that happens e.   LIFE 4
elusive One's prime is e.   YOUTH 10
emasculated has not been e.   AUTOBIOGRAPHY 17
embalm get some fluid and e. each other

      PARTIES 5
embalmer triumph of the e.'s art   PEOPLE 39
embarrass begins to e. other people

      MIDDLE AGE 3
embarrassing e. pause   MARRIAGE 47
emblem e. of mortality   DEATH 21
embody e. the Law   LAW 11
embrace e. your Lordship's principles   INSULTS 46
eminence e. by sheer gravitation   SUCCESS 22
éminence cerise é. cerise   ROYALTY 61
emotion poetry is an e.   POETRY 7
emotions gamut of the e.   ACTORS 26
emperor Canadian out of the German E.

      TRANSPORT 38
  snuff-box from an E.   AMERICA 6
employer press harder upon the e.   WIT 41
employment known as gainful e.   WORK 1
empresses I don't think much of E.   SNOBBERY 9
emptiness posed e.   FILM STARS 13
empty Bring on the e. horses   CINEMA 3
emulate most wanted to e.   WINE 1
encoded e. adjective   TENNIS 1

entrepeneur word for e.   LANGUAGES 6
envelope in a brown e.   MONEY 13
environment humdrum issues like the e.
     NATURE 7
envy thing I e. you for   GENERATION GAP 1
epic person of very *e.* appearance   PEOPLE 13
epicure e. would say   FOOD 69
epiglottis My e. filled him with glee   MEDICINE 27
epigram all existence in an e.   WIT 52
  E.: a wisecrack that played   WIT 21
  Impelled to try an e.   LITERATURE 29
  until it purrs like an e.   NEWSPAPERS 18
epitaph No e.   EPITAPHS 27
epitaphs nice derangement of e.   WIT 34
Epstein never forgive Mr E.   ART 3
equal all shall e. be   CLASS 16
  more e. than others   DEMOCRACY 13
equality e. in the servants' hall   CLASS 2
  true sexual e.   MEN AND WOMEN 33
equanimity No man can face with e.   POLITICS 30
equation each e. I included   SCIENCE 16
  e. is something for eternity   SCIENCE 14
equipment only item of essential e.   MARRIAGE 89
equity E. does not demand   LAW 2
erections Friends who give you e.
     MEN AND WOMEN 64
erogenous e. zones for a kick-off   SEX 17
  We retain our zones e.   OLD AGE 22
erotic you're an erratic e.   MEN AND WOMEN 16
err e. is human   COMPUTERS 1
     VIRTUE 24
errands run on little e.   GOVERNMENT 12
erratic For I'm a neurotic e.   MEN AND WOMEN 16
erroneous e. opinion   HUMAN RACE 6
error confessions of e.   BEHAVIOUR 40
errors factual e.   BIOGRAPHY 13
escape few e. that distinction   HONOURS 10
Eskimo proud to be an E.   ARCHITECTURE 11
Esperanto E. is to the language world
     WRITERS 20
  speak E.   LANGUAGES 18
essays used to write e.   EDUCATION 9
essential e. ingredient   MARRIAGE 96
  only item of e. equipment   MARRIAGE 89
esses so many e. in it   NAMES 13
establishment forelock to the British e.
     SNOBBERY 10
estate dealing with e. workers   CLASS 12
  good e. agent   HOME 10
eternal concept of an e. mother   ROYALTY 29
eternity equation is something for e.   SCIENCE 14
  E.'s a terrible thought   TIME 13
  some conception of e.   CRICKET 12
ethics yob e.   FOOTBALL 29

etiquette E., sacred subject   BEHAVIOUR 23
  E. (and quiet, well-cut clothes)   RELIGION 49
  It isn't e.   BEHAVIOUR 5
Eton hoidays from E.   EDUCATION 37
Etonians Hail him like E.   SOCIETY 14
eunuch e. and a snigger   CLERGY 8
eunuchs Critics are like e.   CRITICS 5
  seraglio of e.   POLITICS 29
euphemism keep the . . . e.   WORDS 1
  lateral e.   TENNIS 1
Euripides Mr E. was guilty   PREJUDICE 4
Europe Britain was no part of E.   COUNTRIES 1
  In E., when a rich woman   MEN AND WOMEN 55
  length and breadth of E.   TRAVEL 2
evacuated e. children   CHRISTMAS 2
even e. terror of their lives   PREJUDICE 13
evenings do with the long winter e.   WRITERS 7
  exciting e.   HOLIDAYS 9
  Shouting in the e.   ACTING 35
eventide perfect e. home   OLD AGE 36
ever Well, did you e.   MARRIAGE 98
every Climb e. Mountie   CANADA 6
  E. thinking man   POLITICS 2
everybody e. is ignorant   IGNORANCE 6
everyone e. else has   ACTORS 13
everything get e.   MARRIAGE 122
  Macaulay is of e.   CERTAINTY 19
evidence circumstantial e. is very strong
     LAW 33
  e. of life after death   POLITICS 66
  it's not e.   LAW 5
evil don't think that he's e.   GOD 1
  we must return good for e.   MORALITY 16
evils Between two e.   VIRTUE 23
  greatest of e.   POVERTY 16
exaggerated greatly e.   DEATH 68
examination like an e.   BIBLE 7
examiners than my e.   EXAMINATIONS 3
example annoyance of a good e.   CHARACTER 16
  don't set a good e.   CLASS 32
  pretty e.   EDUCATION 47
  vivid e.   GENERATION GAP 13
exams rigorous judging e.   JUDGES 7
exception glad to make an e.   INSULTS 25
excess Nothing succeeds like e.   SUCCESS 25
excise *e..* A hateful tax   TAXES 4
exclusive not mutually e.   MANAGEMENT 3
  put e. on the weather   NEWSPAPERS 21
excuse E. My Dust   EPITAPHS 21
excuses Several e.   ARGUMENT 10
execution e. of a senior colleague   POLITICS 21
exercise E. is the yuppie version   HEALTH 4
  who took e.   HEALTH 9
exercises two best e.   HEALTH 2
exertion e. is too much   HUMOUR 30

feather writes with a f.   THEATRE 21
feather-footed F. through the plashy fen
  LANGUAGE 10
feathers three white f.   CLASS 8
February not Puritanism but F.   WEATHER 12
fecund first-rate, the f. rate   WRITING 18
fee small f. in America   AMERICA 24
feeble Most forcible F.   WIT 30
feed F. the brute   MARRIAGE 101
feel f. a thought   WORDS 17
  F. LIKE A BOY AGAIN   TELEGRAMS 12
  how the Taj Mahal must f.   MARRIAGE 14
  I don't f. worse   MORALITY 5
  One does f.   RELIGION 34
  tragedy to those that f.   HUMAN RACE 14
feeling springs from genuine f.   POETRY 23
fees as they took their F.   MEDICINE 5
  My f. are sufficient punishment   LAW 1
  Whatever f. we earn   LAW 19
feet difficult f.   BODY 8
  F. of clay everywhere   BIOGRAPHY 1
  hear it through their f.   MUSIC 52
  Kandinsky had f. of Klee   ART 33
  lost the use of his f.   PROGRESS 7
  step on Lego with bare f.   PARENTS 19
  talking about f.   CONVERSATION 3
  talk under their f.   PRESIDENTS 18
felicity more f.   GENERATION GAP 11
fell F. half so flat   CRITICS 2
  f. in love with a rich   LOVE 21
  not love thee, Dr F.   ENEMIES 2
fellatio Hail, F.   WIT 45
fellow women like me, looking for a f.
  TECHNOLOGY 10
female f. equivalent   BODY 9
  f. llama   DESCRIPTION 9
  God has become f.   GOD 45
females eighty mile o' f.   MEN AND WOMEN 8
feminism F. is the result   WOMEN 47
feminist anti-f. books to review   JOURNALISM 23
  people call me a f.   WOMEN 72
fen through the plashy f.   LANGUAGE 10
fence colours to the f.   CERTAINTY 12
  f. is just too high for him   WRITERS 25
fermented drink f. liquids   DRINK 61
ferocious f. disbelief   DESCRIPTION 23
ferret cuddly as a cornered f.   DESCRIPTION 4
fertile to be so f.   ANIMALS 31
fetish as a savage approaches his f.   JUDGES 4
fetishist f. who years   SEX 48
fetlocks f. blowing   ANIMALS 22
fettle I'm in fine f.   HEALTH 11
few say a f. words   SPEECHES 7
fickleness f. of the women I love   WOMEN 58

fiction all forms of f.   AUTOBIOGRAPHY 22
  being decidedly for f.   NEWSPAPERS 10
  best thing in f.   ENGLAND 44
  f. as if it were a painful duty   WRITERS 42
  one form of continuous f.   NEWSPAPERS 7
  Stranger than f.   TRUTH 2
  what f. means   BOOKS 24
  work of f.   AUTOBIOGRAPHY 18
fiddle I the second f.   PRIDE 7
fidelity f. is a very good idea   MORALITY 8
  f. is not having more than one   SEX 73
field loaf with a f. in it   FOOD 82
fielder bad f.   BASEBALL 9
fields lies W. C. F.   EPITAPHS 12
fife practised on a f.   ANIMALS 10
fifteen always f. years older than I am
  OLD AGE 3
  until I was f.   SEX 37
fifth came f. and lost the job   FAILURE 6
fifty At f. I lost my hair   OLD AGE 21
  by the time you hit f.   APPEARANCE 27
  f. million Frenchmen   FOOD 57
  until he's f.   DRINK 21
fight before the f. begins   POLITICAL PARTIES 4
  Can't f. In here   WAR 18
  f. for freedom   DRESS 10
  If I don't f.   BOXING 6
  strength of character to f.   HONOURS 5
  those who bade me f.   WAR 10
  will f.   ARMED FORCES 6
fighter f. in the business world   BOXING 7
fighting f. for this woman's honour   WOMEN 35
  stop f. for it   FOOTBALL 2
figment like it to say 'f.'   EPITAPHS 27
figure f. is unbelievable   MARRIAGE 40
  losing her f. or her face   MIDDLE AGE 5
figurehead you're just a f.   ARGUMENT 22
file f. your waste-paper basket   LIBRARIES 2
files splash your f.   BIOGRAPHY 3
filibusterers Fat f. begat   POLITICS 33
filing mental capacities of a f. cabinet   LAW 3
fill better than trying to f. them   WORK 8
  f. hup the chinks   FOOD 74
  stuff to f. the space   NEWSPAPERS 15
fillet f. steak of life   MIDDLE AGE 9
fills f. wrong cavity   WIT 13
film and that is f.   HOLLYWOOD 20
  deal with the f. lab   FILM STARS 11
filmmaking no rules in f.   CINEMA 2
films f. were the lowest form   TELEVISION 15
financial seek f. succour   BETTING 1
Finchley Lord F. tried   DEATH 11
find f. a friend   FRIENDS 7
  f. God by tomorrow   GOD 29
  f. it in the index   INDEXES 1

find (*cont.*):

f. out what everyone is doing	LAW 12
f. out why a snorer	SLEEP 10
where does she f. them	SNOBBERY 12
finding I had a little trouble f. you	RELIGION 30
fine f., strike it out	WRITING 12
f. romance with no kisses	MEN AND WOMEN 13
OLD CARY GRANT F.	TELEGRAMS 14
finer for the f. folk	CLASS 20
finest this is our f. shower	SEX 67
finger I lift up my f.	SONGS 15
looking at your f.	FAME 22
what chills the f. not a bit	SATISFACTION 13
fingernails biting your f.	MISTAKES 22
finished the f.	FILM 10
finish draw right to the f.	DEATH 35
start together and f. together	MUSIC 8
until I f. talking	MANAGEMENT 7
finished f. in half the time	FAMILY 52
Then he's f.	MARRIAGE 59
fire f., a little food	HOSPITALITY 4
f. has gone out	OLD AGE 14
shouted 'F.'	LIES 4
supplied the f. themselves	MARRIAGE 18
write for the f.	WRITING 4
fired just got f. for it	APPEARANCE 11
Firenze COUGHING MYSELF INTO A F.	TELEGRAMS 8
fireside by his own f.	HOME 18
firing faced the f. squad	CHARACTER 15
first f. class, and with children	TRAVEL 1
f. ten million years	PAST 1
to mistake for the f.-rate	WRITING 18
fish came up with the f.	FOOD 40
f. are having their revenge	ANIMALS 12
f. without a bicycle	WOMEN 61
He eats a lot of f.	INTELLIGENCE 13
no self-respecting f.	NEWSPAPERS 26
Not a fatter f. than he	ROYALTY 46
surrounded by f.	BUREAUCRACY 3
throw her a f.	ACTORS 30
fishing 'angling' is the name given to f.	FISHING 5
angling or float f.	FISHING 4
F. is a form of madness	FISHING 3
f. is a religion	FISHING 1
fish-knives Phone for the f., Norman	SOCIETY 3
sling out the f.	BEHAVIOUR 12
fishy f. about the French	FRANCE 2
fit It isn't f. for humans now	TOWNS 5
five breakfast every f. minutes	OLD AGE 18
count to f.	ANGER 4
f.-day weekend	WORK 23
God in a f.-button suit	GOD 4
I have wedded f.	MARRIAGE 31
fiver No woman is worth more than a f.	LOVE 33

fix coming to f. the show	WIT 16
only sport you can't f.	SPORTS 19
fjord Betty F. Clinic	DRINK 59
flag High as a f.	AMERICA 15
flair You have f.	HAPPINESS 3
flamingo very large f.	DEBT 7
flap I can't f.	ACTORS 9
flappers London wants f.	ACTORS 9
flared copiously f.	DRESS 1
flashes f. of silence	CONVERSATION 25
flat Fell half so f.	CRITICS 2
how f. he really did want it	SONGS 2
just how f. and empty	PLACES 3
Very f., Norfolk	PLACES 6
flats can't walk in f.	FASHION 8
flatter they'd be rather f.	COUNTRIES 43
flattered f. by the censorship	CENSORSHIP 16
flattering you think him worth f.	PRAISE 8
flattery Everyone likes f.	ROYALTY 26
f. hurts no one	PRAISE 10
give them f.	ART 28
objects of f.	GOSSIP 8
what your f. is worth	PRAISE 5
flaunt f. it	COMEDY 25
flavour spearmint lose its f.	FOOD 63
flaw f. in any argument	ARGUMENT 16
no fault or f.	LAW 11
flea between a louse and a f.	POETS 9
fleas Even educated f. do it	SEX 70
reasonable amount o' f.	DOGS 7
smaller f. to bite 'em	ANIMALS 40
fleet F.'s lit up	DRINK 63
Fleet-street F. has a very animated appearance	TOWNS 16
flesh delicate white human f.	LOVE 15
have more f.	BODY 36
makes man and wife one f.	MARRIAGE 38
flood f. could not wash away	CLASS 6
flooded STREETS F. PLEASE ADVISE	TELEGRAMS 3
floor lie on the f.	DRINK 40
put diamonds on the f.	HEALTH 12
table near the f.	FOOD 41
floozie f. in the jacuzzi	ARCHITECTURE 1
flopping f. yourself down	FAMILY 9
floppy weak, f. thing in the chair	PRIME MINISTERS 25
flower damned f.-pots	GARDENS 6
try f. arrangement	SPORTS 4
flowers Beware of men bearing f.	MEN AND WOMEN 51
silk suit who sends f.	FILM PRODUCERS 6
smelling f.	HEALTH 6
wild f., and Prime Ministers	POLITICS 9
fluid get some f. and embalm each other	PARTIES 5

flutter F. and bear him up ROYALTY 15
fly f. to attempt to cross it FACES 4
f. which had been trained HANDWRITING 1
made the f. ANIMALS 30
show the f. the way out PHILOSOPHY 9
with an open f. FILM PRODUCERS 17
foal f. and broodmare WEATHER 1
foam amber f. FOOD 23
focus f. on my salad COOKERY 19
foe angry with my f. ANGER 2
find a f. FRIENDS 10
fogs insular country subject to f. POLITICS 28
foible omniscience is his f. INSULTS 40
Folies-Bergère goes to the F. MEDICINE 33
folk All music is f. music MUSIC 2
incest and f.-dancing SEX 8
folks W'en f. git ole OLD AGE 23
follies author's f. AUTOBIOGRAPHY 6
f. which a man regrets most MEN 14
My f. are intact OLD AGE 21
follow F. the van HOME 4
follower f. of fashion FASHION 5
follows lie f. BEHAVIOUR 28
folly f. of 'Woman's Rights' WOMEN 69
f.'s all they've taught me WOMEN 44
woman stoops to f. WOMEN 10
WOMEN 25
Fondas Henry F. lay on the evening
DESCRIPTION 12
font be done with a f. RELIGION 35
portable, second-hand f. CLERGY 13
food aftertaste of foreign f. DRINK 14
alcohol was a f. DRINK 62
f. a tragedy FOOD 59
f. enough for a week BIRDS 7
f. I ate and not the show SLEEP 4
f. is more dangerous FOOD 42
f. was a very big factor RELIGION 36
It was the f. DEATH 29
problem is f. MONEY 8
fool every f. is not a poet POETS 13
f. and his money GAMBLING 5
f. and his wife COUNTRY 15
f. at the other FISHING 4
f.'s paradise FOOLISHNESS 9
f. with booze DRINK 21
I'm just a f. WOMEN 30
let a kiss f. you FOOLISHNESS 7
Prove to me that you're no f. RELIGION 55
that does not marry a f. MARRIAGE 135
without being a f. FOOLISHNESS 16
foolish He never said a f. thing ROYALTY 59
most f. people NEW YORK 3
saying a f. thing FOOLISHNESS 15
foolproof f. items FOOLISHNESS 3

fools all the f. in town FOOLISHNESS 18
f. of gardeners GARDENS 9
house for f. and mad EPITAPHS 23
leaves 'em still two f. MARRIAGE 38
see these poor f. decoyed MARRIAGE 94
the small ones f. WRITERS 31
tolerate f. FOOLISHNESS 1
foot caught my f. in the mat MISTAKES 15
F.-in-the-grave MEN 8
Forty-second F. ARMED FORCES 17
One square f. less ARCHITECTURE 2
silver f. in his mouth PRESIDENTS 15
football become a f. referee FOOTBALL 15
F., wherein is FOOTBALL 13
F. and cookery FOOTBALL 28
f. crazy FOOTBALL 19
F.'s football FOOTBALL 9
go to the f. MEN 6
like he does a f. FOOTBALL 11
music and f. LITERATURE 35
no longer be a f. FOOTBALL 10
Queen Mother of f. FOOTBALL 26
state of the f. fan FOOTBALL 16
talking about f. FOOTBALL 6
think f. is a matter FOOTBALL 25
when I played f. FOOTBALL 17
footballers professional f. FOOTBALL 29
footnotes f. to Plato PHILOSOPHY 8
footprint looking for a man's f. WOMEN 3
forbids if the law f. it LAW 21
force fasteners do not respond to f. POWER 11
Other nations use f. ENGLAND 42
forcible Most f. Feeble WIT 30
ford Could Henry F. BUSINESS 10
I mean John F. FILM PRODUCERS 13
fore shout 'F.' when GOLF 5
foreign aftertaste of f. food DRINK 14
contempt for every thing f. COUNTRIES 5
f. conductors MUSIC 6
f. picture award FILM PRODUCERS 14
in a f. language PARENTS 13
foreigner lost on the f. HUMOUR 37
foreigners f. always spell better LANGUAGES 24
f. are fiends COUNTRIES 31
forelock tugged the f. SNOBBERY 10
foreseen no doubt have f. FUTURE 12
forest f. laments PRIME MINISTERS 10
foretell f. what is going to happen POLITICIANS 12
forever safire bracelet lasts f. AMERICA 23
forget Don't f. the diver COMEDY 5
f. about it in the morning RETIREMENT 2
I never f. a face INSULTS 25
I sometimes f. ROYALTY 27
forgetting f. you've slept with SEX 80

Freudian F. nightmare	FAMILY 29
friction f. threatening	WAR 33
fridge in the f.	AWARDS 4
fried in which their fat was f.	MARRIAGE 18
friend angry with my f.	ANGER 2
become a man's f.	WOMEN 10
breaking it in for a f.	NAMES 22
Diamonds are a girl's best f.	WEALTH 21
find a f.	FRIENDS 7
f. is not standing	DEMOCRACY 18
f. of the Sitwells	SOCIETY 1
goodnatured f.	FRIENDS 11
having an old f. for dinner	SOCIETY 12
man's best f.	ANIMALS 25
my f. Evelyn Waugh	FRIENDS 6
Reagan for his best f.	FILM STARS 15
terrific f. of yours	READING 15
Whenever a f. succeeds	SUCCESS 24
your enemey and your f.	FRIENDS 15
friends at all her f.	GOSSIP 7
Champagne for my real f.	FRIENDS 2
couldn't buy f.	FRIENDS 9
deserting one's f.	FRIENDS 1
f. are true	FUTURE 2
f. except two	CHRISTMAS 6
f. he loved	EPITAPHS 28
f. in both places	HEAVEN 6
f. of the author	ADVERTISING 3
F. who give you erections	MEN AND WOMEN 64
f. who took exercise	HEALTH 9
lay down his f.	FRIENDS 14
make f. fall out	MARRIAGE 107
make new f.	FRIENDS 3
nearly deceiving your f.	LIES 5
none of his f.	FRIENDS 17
not always the best of f.	TAXES 5
no true f. in politics	POLITICS 20
only two f.	FRIENDS 13
Seek younger f.	OLD AGE 35
two real f.	LIFESTYLE 7
friendship sort of f.	MARRIAGE 118
fries as freedom f.	WORDS 3
frighten by God, they f. me	WAR 28
f. the horses	SEX 29
frightening f. sort of way	DOGS 1
Frigidaire popped him in the F.	CHILDREN 17
frivolity how precious is f.	LITERATURE 18
frivolous Memoirs of the f.	AUTOBIOGRAPHY 5
frivolously ability to make love f.	LOVE 6
frock history of that f.	DRESS 9
frocks f. are built	FASHION 16
Frodo Let Bingo = F.	NAMES 28
frogs nothing to do with f.' legs	FOOD 34
frown Say that she f.	MEN AND WOMEN 46
frozen show is f.	SONGS 12

frugal She had a f. mind	WOMEN 12
fruit delicate exotic f.	IGNORANCE 8
Old Trafford f. machine	FOOTBALL 10
frying f. pan of your words	WRITERS 13
fuck couldn't write 'f.'	CRITICS 7
Everyone wants to f. you	FAME 21
Oh f., not another elf!	LITERATURE 16
They f. you up, your mum and dad	PARENTS 12
fugues Of masses and f.	MUSIC 19
fule As any f. kno	FOOLISHNESS 20
fulfilment image of f.	RELIGION 44
full f. tide of human existence	TOWNS 16
on a f. bladder	SPEECHES 16
fuller's earth Money, wife, is the true f.	
	MONEY 11
fume black, stinking f. thereof	SMOKING 4
fun Cancer can be rather f.	SICKNESS 10
counted among the f. people	SCIENCE 19
damps the f.	HOME 7
got to be a f. activity	POLITICS 22
Have f.	LIFESTYLE 1
Have some f.	HAPPINESS 16
I've had my f.	TRANSPORT 21
more f. than fun	WORK 9
most f. I ever had	SEX 4
most f. you can have	ADVERTISING 4
no concept of f.	COUNTRIES 4
no reference to f.	GOVERNMENT 17
Other girls ain't havin' any f.	WOMEN 28
function can't f. well	ART 1
fundament frigid on the f.	SATISFACTION 13
fundamentally He is f. unsound	PHILOSOPHY 10
funeral next day there's a f.	MEDICINE 32
nothing like a morning f.	DEATH 44
refused to attend his f.	DEATH 69
singing at my f.	FUNERALS 2
upon him for the f.	DEATH 36
funky f. pub pianist	MUSICIANS 9
funny but not *that* f.	WRITERS 20
Everything is f.	HUMOUR 31
f. man or a great boss	MANAGEMENT 3
F.-peculiar	HUMOUR 19
hard to be f.	HUMOUR 40
It's a f. old world	LIFE 7
Life is the f. thing	LIFE 6
saw anything so f.	ACTORS 19
fur bred for food or f.	MEN 9
F. is a subject	DRESS 18
Three kinds of f.	CLASS 13
furnace gone out in the f.	OLD AGE 14
furniture all that nice f.	POLITICS 44
buy all his f.	SNOBBERY 8
cumbersome f.	HOME 23
mere church f.	CLERGY 6
No f. so charming	BOOKS 17

furniture (*cont.*):

rearrange the f. POLITICS 51

twice as much f. HOME 20

furs f. the jewels, the glamour WEALTH 14

further explored the f. reaches MARRIAGE 8

f. they have to fall BOXING 5

f. you got from Britain POLITICIANS 10

fury beastly f. FOOTBALL 13

fuss insufficient f. SATISFACTION 16

fustian whose f.'s so sublimely bad POETRY 20

future about the f. AUTOBIOGRAPHY 23

bridge to the f. FUTURE 10

especially about the f. FUTURE 3

f. looks dark indeed WRITERS 5

f. refusing FUTURE 1

never think of the f. FUTURE 5

Gabriel Archangel G. DEMOCRACY 2

enough for the Archangel G. PRIME MINISTERS 13

So blow, G., blow RELIGION 53

gaffe terrible social g. PARTIES 6

gaiety g. is a striped shroud WALES 7

gaily G. into Ruislip Gardens SOCIETY 4

gainful happily known as g. employment

WORK 1

gaining Something may be g. BASEBALL 11

Galatians text in G. BIBLE 1

galaxy smart alecksy, With the g. PROGRESS 10

gallant Stop being g. THEATRE 14

gallantry What men call g. SEX 27

galleon Stately as a g. DANCE 7

galloping g. consumption you had SICKNESS 3

gallows upon the g. or of the pox INSULTS 46

galoshes vest and g. CHARACTER 13

gamble Life is a g. LIFE 16

gamblers g. are as happy GAMBLING 1

game always played the g. POLITICIANS 25

Anarchism is a g. POLITICS 63

g. at which only one EDUCATION 28

g. which takes less BASEBALL 13

latest popular g. FAMILY 19

no g. from bridge to cricket SPORTS 17

only a g. BASEBALL 14

parody is a g. WIT 23

Take me out to the ball g. BASEBALL 10

wouldn't be the g. it is FOOTBALL 9

gamut g. of the emotions ACTORS 26

Gandhi [G.] knew the cost POVERTY 12

ganged my parents and his mother g. up

PARENTS 3

gap g. between Dorothy and Chopin MUSICIANS 1

g. between platitudes SPEECHES 16

garbage week of the g. strike APPEARANCE 19

garbled Rather g. MARRIAGE 44

Garbo unwelcoming Greta G. MEN AND WOMEN 32

garden g., however small GARDENS 2

g. is a loathsome thing GARDENS 12

led up the g. path DIPLOMACY 1

man and a woman in a g. BIBLE 8

gardener not a dirt g. GARDENS 1

gardeners fools of g. GARDENS 9

grim g. GARDENS 11

garlic clove of g. round my neck POLITICIANS 20

gas G. smells awful DEATH 54

Had silicon been a g. EXAMINATIONS 6

gate A-sitting on a g. OLD AGE 8

gathering intransitive operation of g. WIT 24

gauze shoot her through g. FILM STARS 2

gay g. or not FOOTBALL 21

Glitter and be g. WOMEN 73

I think that g. marriage MARRIAGE 106

gazelle love a dear g. MONEY 6

geisha Get yourself a G. COUNTRIES 14

gender get My g. right GOD 8

general g. called Anthea MEN AND WOMEN 33

G. was essentially ARMED FORCES 33

host is like a g. HOSPITALITY 6

generals my other g. ARMED FORCES 11

we're all G. ARMED FORCES 32

generation g. of English DRUGS 6

Poland to polo in one g. SNOBBERY 5

generations g. of inbreeding BEHAVIOUR 19

geniality g. of the politician POLITICIANS 19

genitals actresses do make my g. quiver

THEATRE 25

breaking my g. HAPPINESS 4

G. are a great distraction SEX 22

genius G. is one percent inspiration

INTELLIGENCE 4

g. with the IQ of a moron ART 32

Men of g. are so few INTELLIGENCE 2

nothing to declare except my g. INTELLIGENCE 12

stronger than g. BORES 4

talent and g. INTELLIGENCE 1

geniuses g. are devoid of humour SPEECHES 14

gentle book is rather g. AUTOBIOGRAPHY 7

gentleman being a g. CLASS 29

English g. DRUGS 5

Every other inch a g. INSULTS 44

g. falls in love COUNTRY 13

g. never eats CLASS 1

He's a g. CLASS 26

He was a g. POVERTY 20

I am a g. SOCIETY 18

More like a g. JOURNALISM 18

Most g. don't like love LOVE 38

not quite a g. SNOBBERY 1

teach you to be a g. EDUCATION 35

gentlemanly werry g. ideas WINE 12

gentlemen behave like g.	WOMEN 39
first division are g.	CLASS 11
G. do not take soup	CLASS 10
G. never wear	COLOURS 3
most of the g. does	CLASS 31
stableboy among g.	CLASS 27
genuine springs from g. feeling	POETRY 23
genuineness doubtful of T. E. Lawrence's g.	
	PEOPLE 25
geography G. is about Maps	BIOGRAPHY 4
George G.—don't do that	COMEDY 12
G. the Third	MISTAKES 4
give the ball to G.	FOOTBALL 7
Georgian G. silver goes	POLITICS 44
geriatric g. home	HAPPINESS 1
g. set	DEATH 58
What's a g.	FOOTBALL 20
German G. footballer	FOOTBALL 20
G. soldier trying to violate	SEX 83
G. spoken underwater	LANGUAGES 1
Like G. opera, too long	WAR 26
than one G. adjective	LANGUAGES 25
Waiting for the G. verb	LANGUAGES 19
Germans beastly to the G.	COUNTRIES 12
G. went in	COUNTRIES 29
They're G.	COUNTRIES 8
Germany G. doesn't want	PAST 3
gerund Save the g.	GRAMMAR 5
gesture ecumenical g.	RELIGION 68
Morality's a g.	MORALITY 2
get Don't g. mad	MARRIAGE 122
g. a life	TELEVISION 12
g. anywhere in a marriage	MARRIAGE 86
g. everything	MARRIAGE 122
g. where I am today	COMEDY 23
Norwich didn't g.	FOOTBALL 14
Gettysburg where G. lived	READING 4
ghastly G. good taste	ARCHITECTURE 4
ghost as Banquo's g.	POLITICAL PARTIES 1
I can't give up the g.	OLD AGE 21
never mind Banquo's g.	ACTING 5
gibbon Eh! Mr G.	ROYALTY 43
giblet thick g. soup	FOOD 32
gifts most minor of g.	ACTING 16
gigantic Dome g.	ARCHITECTURE 8
giggles girls got the g.	POETS 4
Gilbert That must be G.	WIT 16
gin definite flavour of g.	DRINK 28
flavour of g.	DRINK 14
get out the g.	DRINK 50
G. was mother's milk	DRINK 54
g. will make them run	DRESS 6
such as g.	DRINK 61
two g.-and-limes	FOOD 55
gingerbread gilt Off the g.	HOME 7

giraffe camelopardalis or g.	ANIMALS 14
girder Joist and a G.	WORDS 4
girdle helps you with your g.	MEN AND WOMEN 34
girl come on a young g.	MARRIAGE 128
Diamonds are a g.'s best friend	WEALTH 21
first rock at a g. like I	MEN AND WOMEN 31
g. at an impressionable age	YOUTH 9
g. beans	SEX 61
g. needs good parent	MIDDLE AGE 17
I can't get no g. reaction	SEX 47
nice g.'s ambition	HOPE 1
Now you can't say 'g.'	WORDS 21
When I'm not near the g. I love	LOVE 24
girls American g. turn	AMERICA 16
At g. who wear glasses	MEN AND WOMEN 38
both were crazy about g.	SEX 54
G. are just friends	MEN AND WOMEN 64
g. I liked	FASHION 3
g. in slacks remember	CHRISTMAS 3
In Little G.	CHILDREN 3
options open for g.	WOMEN 1
Other g. are coy	WOMEN 28
secrets with g.	SECRECY 4
social security, not g.	SEX 78
Watching all the g. go by	MEN AND WOMEN 28
we like g.	MEN 6
give g. a war and nobody will come	WAR 22
g. them ours	GOVERNMENT 24
g. the public something	DEATH 64
given g. to government	FAMILY 10
giveth Tell them the author g.	WRITERS 17
GKC poor G.	EPITAPHS 16
glad are you just g. to see me	MEN AND WOMEN 58
I'm so g. I'm not young	OLD AGE 27
Gladstone G. may perspire	PRIME MINISTERS 10
G. . . . spent his declining years	IRELAND 10
If G. fell into the Thames	MISTAKES 13
glamour G. is on a life-support	APPEARANCE 6
Glasgow play the old G. Empire	HUMOUR 11
glasheen for a modest g.	DRINK 44
glass baying for broken g.	ENGLAND 41
g.-bottomed boat	HOLLYWOOD 14
g. so antique	HOME 1
in a dirty g.	FOOD 51
looked into the g.	PRIDE 3
panes of g. with its claws	MUSIC 4
Satire is a sort of g.	SELF-KNOWLEDGE 26
Sound of Broken G.	CLASS 4
take a g. of wine	HOME 18
glasses At girls who wear g.	MEN AND WOMEN 38
Such cruel g.	INSULTS 18
those dark g.	FILM STARS 10
wears dark g.	FAME 1
glitter G. and be gay	WOMEN 73
gloat Call Uncle Teddy and g.	FAMILY 23

glory *School for Scandal* in its g.   OLD AGE 25
There's g. for you   WORDS 9
Glossop Sir Roderick G. is always called
                                        MEDICINE 36
glove Par'n my g.   BEHAVIOUR 13
gloves valentine wore g.   SECRECY 6
white kid g.   FOOD 64
with my g. on my hand   SOCIETY 11
glued g. to Soho   PLACES 1
Glyn sin with Elinor G.   SEX 9
gnu look his g. in the face   ENGLAND 45
go all g. together   COUNTRIES 26
as cooks g.   COOKERY 16
better 'ole, g. to it   WAR 4
g. away at any rate   ROYALTY 7
g. in long enough after   MUSIC 50
g. on with the show   ACTING 3
I g.   COMEDY 26
I have a g.   ACTING 24
Let my people g.   CRITICS 24
One of us must g.   DEATH 74
goad g. the BBC   BROADCASTING 5
goal g. they finally got   FOOTBALL 14
it has reached its g.   SCIENCE 26
Woman's place was in the g.   WOMEN 4
goals scoring three g.   FOOTBALL 20
goats Cadwallader and all his g.   WALES 5
goblins head full of g.   TAXES 6
God about G.'s path   SCIENCE 9
argument for the being of G.   GOD 13
believe in G.   GOD 21
choose A Jewish G.   GOD 14
decides he is not G.   GOD 28
do I believe in G.   GOD 22
don't do G.   GOD 17
don't think G. comes well   BIBLE 9
find G. by tomorrow   GOD 29
Frank Capra than G.   PEOPLE 21
G., whom you doubtless   GOD 39
G. Almighty was satisfied   PRESIDENTS 3
G. also is   GOD 11
G. and Mammon   GOD 41
G. and the doctor we alike adore   RELIGION 52
G. Calls me God   GOVERNMENT 34
G. caught his eye   EPITAPHS 17
G. did nothing   GOD 12
G. does exist   GOD 23
G. does have a sense   FACES 3
G. has become female   GOD 45
G. has written all the books   GOD 15
G. in a five-button suit   GOD 4
G. is a bore   GOD 34
G. is a man   RELIGION 46
G. is a Republican   POLITICAL PARTIES 15

G. is my judge   JUDGES 3
G. is not dead   GOD 5
G. is silent   GOD 3
G. made the country   COUNTRY 2
G. Must think it   GOD 32
G. of wine   GOD 30
G.'s a blaggard   POETS 16
g. that he worships   TECHNOLOGY 15
G. . . . the bastard   GOD 10
G. was certainly not orthodox   PEOPLE 36
G. was left out   GOD 44
G. was very merciful   ARISTOCRACY 1
G. will know   EPITAPHS 16
G. will not always   GOD 16
G. will pardon me   GOD 27
G. would give me   GOD 2
G. would have made Adam   SEX 23
good of G.   MARRIAGE 23
grace of God, goes G.   POLITICIANS 13
I cannot quite believe in G.   RELIGION 28
if G. had been his wife   GOD 37
If G. had wanted us to   HEALTH 12
I might have become a g.   RELIGION 57
Isn't G. a shit   GOD 19
know you're G.   GOD 9
like kissing G.   DRUGS 3
odd of G.   GOD 24
one G. only   GOD 20
one of G.'s children   SUCCESS 16
only G. is watching him   GOLF 13
Thanks to G., I am still   RELIGION 14
there is a G.   GOD 1
thinks he's G. Almighty   RELIGION 24
what the Lord G. thinks of money   WEALTH 3
Where it will all end, knows G.   NEWSPAPERS 11
work with what G. sends   WRITING 7
Yours faithfully, G.   GOD 6
goddamm Lhude sing G.   WEATHER 16
Godot waiting for G.   CERTAINTY 3
gods board of g.   GOD 35
Whom the g. wish to destroy   SUCCESS 6
Goering G.'s excuse for being late SPORTS 27
goes Anything g.   BEHAVIOUR 27
It g. of a night   SOCIETY 19
going I must be g.   SATISFACTION 15
keeps me g.   COMEDY 29
gold all done up in g.   WEALTH 2
G. Cup week   GOVERNMENT 8
G. dust on my feet   WEALTH 10
half as g. as green   PLACES 12
golden g. goose will be cooked   SUCCESS 2
In good King Charles's g. days   POLITICIANS 1
lays the g. egg   FILM PRODUCERS 5
Goldwyn paved with G.   CINEMA 23

guns G. aren't lawful — DEATH 54
g. don't kill people — MURDER 8
loaded g. with boys — SECRECY 4
Guthrie as I have from Woody G. — SONGS 8
guts Spill your g. at Wimbledon — TENNIS 5
guy g.'s only doing it — MEN AND WOMEN 30
straight sort of g. — SELF-KNOWLEDGE 4

h even *without* the h.'s — THEATRE 12
ha funny h.-ha — HUMOUR 19
habit-forming Cocaine h. — DRUGS 2
habits Inhibit their h. — ANIMALS 16
hack some government h. — GOVERNMENT 20
Hackensack I took a trip to H. — TOWNS 20
hacks Efficient h. are very rare — JOURNALISM 2
had been h. by all — CHARACTER 17
WE ALL KNEW YOU H. IT IN YOU — TELEGRAMS 18
haddock *Quotations* and a very large h. — NEWSPAPERS 14
sausage and h. — COOKERY 21
Hague H. has got a baseball cap — POLITICAL PARTIES 7
hail H., Fellatio — WIT 45
H. him like Etonians — SOCIETY 14
hair At fifty I lost my h. — OLD AGE 21
beat hell out of h. curlers — SEX 79
does her h. with Bovril — FRIENDS 5
h. of the horse — HYPOCRISY 7
h. straight from his left armpit — TRUST 10
have their h. done — APPEARANCE 21
like the h. we breathe — SPORTS 34
pin up my h. with prose — LETTERS 4
Presbyterian h. — BODY 26
pubic h. factory — DESCRIPTION 22
rich mouse h. — APPEARANCE 8
smoothes her hair — WOMEN 17
You have lovely h. — WOMEN 9
your h. has become very white — OLD AGE 7
haircut h. will be crew — FAMILY 16
hairpiece not his own h. — APPEARANCE 23
hairpieces reliable as his h. — AUTOBIOGRAPHY 19
hairs h. weakly curled — APPEARANCE 2
half are cut in h. — ART 2
h. mad baronet — PEOPLE 12
hallelujah H.! Was the only — LAST WORDS 4
halo For a h. up in heaven — RELIGION 29
jealousy with a h. — MORALITY 17
What after all Is a h. — RELIGION 25
ham when there's h. — MEDICINE 10
Hamlet Did H. actually — THEATRE 4
H. himself longed — THEATRE 47
H. sure did enjoy — THEATRE 32
I'm doing H. — ACTING 32

hand h. of history on his collar — HISTORY 1
h. that lays — FILM PRODUCERS 5
H. that rocked the cradle — DEATH 5
kiss on the h. — WEALTH 21
'Tes the h. of Nature — NATURE 1
with automatic h. — WOMEN 17
handbag bred in a h. — FAMILY 50
hitting it with her h. — POWER 3
Handel For either of them, or for H. — MUSICIANS 10
handicap terrible a h. — ENGLAND 18
What is your h. — GOLF 2
What's your h. — GOLF 3
handicapper h. is spoken of most respectfully — SPORTS 30
handkerchief like a damp h. — FOOD 38
scent on a pocket h. — PRIME MINISTERS 19
handle doesn't h. very well — HUMAN RACE 13
hands has the most beautiful h. — ART 13
Holding h. at midnight — LOVE 18
ice on your h. — DRESS 3
Into the wrong h. — CENSORSHIP 7
prize-fighters shaking h. — WOMEN 40
handstand H. IN SHOWER — TELEGRAMS 77
handwriting exquisite h. — HANDWRITING 1
in his h. — HANDWRITING 3
your own h. — HANDWRITING 8
handy h. and cheap — FAMILY 1
hang Better to h. somebody — PUNISHMENT 10
they. h. a man first — LAW 23
hanged h. in a fortnight — DEATH 37
hanging H. is too good — PUNISHMENT 4
h. prevents a bad marriage — MARRIAGE 109
happen accidents which started to h. — MISTAKES 21
foretell what is going to h. — POLITICIANS 12
to whom things h. — MISTAKES 20
happened after they have h. — FUTURE 8
what h. to him — ARMED FORCES 7
happening believe what isn't h. — SPORTS 9
happens there when it h. — DEATH 1
happily h. a woman may be married — MARRIAGE 83
happiness h. is assured — FUTURE 2
Last Chance Gulch for h. — CHILDREN 35
lifetime of h. — HAPPINESS 12
man in pursuit of h. — MARRIAGE 25
Money won't buy h. — MONEY 24
result h. — MONEY 7
happy conspiracy to make you h. — AMERICA 27
H. as a bastard — HAPPINESS 2
h. as most people — GAMBLING 1
h. as the dey — SEX 62
h. families — FAMILY 47
h. New Year — INSULTS 43

happy (*cont.*):

sake of my h.	HEALTH 5
ways of mending a broken h.	LOVE 40
What they call 'h.'	BODY 25
woman has given you her h.	WOMEN 68
your h. is there with it	WIT 3
hearts H. just as pure	ARISTOCRACY 6
hidden in each other's h.	CHARACTER 4
	SECRECY 5
jining of h. and house-keeping	LOVE 13
heaven between H. and Hell	HEAVEN 7
h. is pleased to bestow it	WEALTH 25
H. will protect a working-girl	POVERTY 17
H. would be too dull	EPITAPHS 22
it's the Hebrew in H.	LANGUAGES 11
journey to h.	HEAVEN 1
leave to h.	CHOICE 10
leaving mercy to h.	PUNISHMENT 3
like going to h.	ECONOMICS 8
live in fear of H.	ENGLAND 28
my idea of h.	HEAVEN 5
NHS is quite like h.	SICKNESS 10
to h. might have gone	EPITAPHS 29
heavier seven stones h.	HEALTH 5
heavy less h.-footed	VIRTUE 13
heavyweight anything but a h.	BOXING 12
Hebrew I hear it's the H. in Heaven	
	LANGUAGES 11
Hebrews H. 13.8	CRITICS 6
heel instructions printed on the h.	STUPIDITY 2
heels double crossing of a pair of h.	LOVE 26
shoes with high h.	DRESS 12
height down to my h.	BOXING 4
MORE OR LESS THE SAME H.	TELEGRAMS 11
Heineken H. refreshes the parts	DRINK 37
heir at it hunting for an h.	ROYALTY 55
hell Acting is h.	ACTING 12
between Heaven and H.	HEAVEN 7
h. is a very large party	PARTIES 2
H. is full of musical amateurs	MUSIC 48
H. would not be Hell	EPITAPHS 22
I say the h. with it	FOOD 81
my idea of h.	FOOTBALL 6
probably re-designed H.	HEAVEN 4
they think it is h.	TRUTH 8
want to go to H.	HEAVEN 3
would be h. on earth	HAPPINESS 12
hellhound h. is always a hellhound	
	CHARACTER 21
hellish My life was simply h.	SATISFACTION 14
hello H. boys	BODY 5
H. possums	COMEDY 20
helluva New York,—a h. town	NEW YORK 2
helmets 80,000 battle h.	WAR 9

help his wife has to h. him	TRUST 5
I constructed a cry for h.	SELF-KNOWLEDGE 16
I will h. them there	HEAVEN 3
'O! h. me, heaven,' she prayed	WOMEN 19
sick enough to call for h.	MEDICINE 21
very present h.	LIES 1
you can't h. it	INSULTS 38
helped can't be h.	PUNISHMENT 2
Hemingway H. and *not* seen the joke	WRITERS 38
hen gentle useful h.	FOOD 17
h. is only an egg's way	BIRDS 3
h. you ran over the other day	MARRIAGE 90
this is Mr C. O. H.	NAMES 1
Henery I'm H. the Eighth, I am	MARRIAGE 87
hen-pecked have they not h. you all	
	INTELLIGENCE 3
herald Hark! the h. angels sing	MEDICINE 4
herbaceous h. border	LIES 7
herbs intolerance to h.	DRINK 61
herds H. of wildebeeste	PLACES 5
here H. at last is Asia	PLACES 4
H. lies Spike Milligan	EPITAPHS 19
H.'s . . . Johnny	COMEDY 18
I'm still h.	MISTAKES 18
want you to be h. and sexy	MARRIAGE 114
hereditary Insanity is h.	MIND 8
heresy Englishman believes be h.	RELIGION 64
hero aspires to be a h.	DRINK 33
h. is a bee	ANIMALS 15
h. is the author	BOOKS 22
they don't want to be a h.	WAR 24
Herod character of H.	CHILDREN 6
hour of H.	CHILDREN 18
heroes h. were good	BOOKS 11
heroine when a h. goes mad	MIND 11
heron h.'s eggs	FOOD 23
herring different kinds of h.	FOOD 10
these pickle h.	FOOD 66
Herveys men, women, and H.	ARISTOCRACY 15
Herzog thought Moses H.	MIND 1
heterodox It would have been less h.	LETTERS 2
heterodoxy another man's h.	BEHAVIOUR 33
hick Sticks nix h. pix	NEWSPAPERS 2
hidden h. in each other's hearts	CHARACTER 4
	SECRECY 5
teems with h. meaning	WORDS 14
hide Minister has nothing to h.	PRIDE 2
hideous horrid, h. notes of woe	MISTAKES 9
high fly fishing is h. church	FISHING 1
her h. days and low days	MEDICINE 2
h. altar on the move	DESCRIPTION 7
h. cheekbones	ACTORS 1
h. road that leads	SCOTLAND 5
h.-water mark	FAMILY 46
I'm getting h.	DRINK 15

high (*cont.*):

j. as a serious thing | HUMOUR 28
j.'s a very serious thing | HUMOUR 9
j. turns life inside out | HUMOUR 21
j. well into a Scotch | SCOTLAND 11
j. with a double meaning | HUMOUR 2
tell an Iowan a j. | HUMOUR 6
jokes and no j. | HUMOUR 27
doesn't make j. | CIVIL SERVANTS 5
every ten j. | HUMOUR 34
J. are fast running out | HUMOUR 5
little j. on thee | GOD 25
one of his own j. | HUMOUR 3
someone was telling j. | THEATRE 29
taste in j. | HUMOUR 12
jolly Awfully j. of you | LAST WORDS 5
Jones Lord J. Dead | JOURNALISM 9
Joneses keep up with the J. | LIFESTYLE 2
Josephine Not tonight, J. | SEX 60
journal keep a full j. | DIARIES 6
page of my J. | DIARIES 2
journalism first law of j. | JOURNALISM 11
J. is unreadable | JOURNALISM 24
J. largely consists | JOURNALISM 9
journalist British j. | JOURNALISM 25
than a j. | JOURNALISM 18
Journalists lies to j. | GOVERNMENT 22
Jovelike his J. side | FAMILY 24
J. wrath | ANGER 11
Judas J. who writes | BIOGRAPHY 18
judge best j. of a run | CRICKET 18
God is my j. | JUDGES 3
j. goes to the lawyer | CINEMA 6
j. had slept through his play | JUDGES 13
know who the j. is | JUDGES 5
mail that cheque to the J. | JUDGES 6
talking J. is like | JUDGES 15
they j. them | CHILDREN 41
judgement not give his j. rashly | ARGUMENT 1
judges j. are a mine of instruction | QUOTATIONS 3
J. commonly are elderly men | JUDGES 9
She threw me in front of the j. | SPORTS 5
judging never had the Latin for the j. | JUDGES 7
Judy O'Grady Colonel's Lady an' J. | WOMEN 36
jug loose fum de j. | DRINK 30
juice j. of two quarts | DRINK 16
Julian I'm J. | COMEDY 19
Julius here comes J. | CINEMA 1
July fourth of J. | AMERICA 15
Jumbo combine Mumbo with J. | RELIGION 11
June J. is bustin' out | COUNTRY 6
Jungfrau looking like the J. | ROYALTY 20
just J. like that | COMEDY 32
rain, it raineth on the j. | VIRTUE 4

justice doing j. | PUNISHMENT 3
If this is j., I am a banana | LAW 14
inquiring J. is not asleep | JUDGES 11
old line about j. | WOMEN 49
what stings is j. | LAW 22
juvenile Three j. delinquents | CRIME 9

Kandinsky K. had feet of Klee | ART 33
Kansas corny as K. | AMERICA 15
Keats K. or Ketch or whatever | POETS 1
keener k. than little Nina | DANCE 5
keep K. off the grass | EPITAPHS 26
k. up with the Joneses | LIFESTYLE 2
some day it'll k. you | DIARIES 7
keeps gave it us for k. | MEDICINE 3
If *he* k. *her* | ROYALTY 8
k. me going | COMEDY 29
Kells produce the Book of K. | BUSINESS 10
ken K. and Barbie | PARTIES 6
K. would still have won | DEMOCRACY 2
look like K. | LIFESTYLE 6
Kennedys like the K. | BOXING 1
Kensal Green go to K. | BUSINESS 15
Kensington leafy K. | COUNTRY 17
only seen in K. | ACTING 33
Kent everybody knows K. | PLACES 8
kerb walk to the k. | TRANSPORT 1
kerosene selling short-weight k. | WEALTH 18
kettle k. to a dog's tail | WRITERS 23
key k. still in the lock | SEX 7
keys half that's got my k. | DEATH 27
operated by depressing the k. | MUSIC 9
kick boys something else to k. | SPORTS 37
crawl in or k. your way in | POLITICS 12
I get a k. out of you | LOVE 39
k. in the crutch | ANGER 3
Yet I get a k. out of you | MEN AND WOMEN 40
kicked She k. it away | PEOPLE 1
kid white k. gloves | FOOD 64
kidding You've got to be k. | SEX 75
kidnapped I'm k. | FAMILY 2
kidney spectacular stone in his k. | SICKNESS 6
kidneys grilled mutton k. | FOOD 32
kids k. when they got married | PARENTS 5
wife and my k. | CRICKET 2
kill Athenians will k. thee | POLITICIANS 21
I'll k. you if you quote it | QUOTATIONS 2
k. you in a new way | PROGRESS 12
Lady K.-Chairman | SELF-KNOWLEDGE 1
let's k. all the lawyers | LAW 31
nervous to k. himself | CHARACTER 12
not going to k. too many | MURDER 8
Thou shalt not k. | DEATH 15

law *defeat a l. of God*   FOOLISHNESS 19
  fear of the L.   RELIGION 33
  if the l. forbids it   LAW 21
  know what the l. is   JUDGES 5
  l., however, is not   PUNISHMENT 9
  l. at the end of a nightstick   LAW 36
  l. is an ass   LAW 6
  L. is the true embodiment   LAW 11
  moral l.   HANDWRITING 7
  No brilliance is needed in the l.   LAW 25
  no l. or government   GOVERNMENT 3
  principle of the English l.   LAW 7
lawn Laid to l.   GARDENS 4
  want to be a l.   GARDENS 13
Lawrence By god, D. H. L. was right
     MARRIAGE 65
laws government of l.   GOVERNMENT 20
lawyer get a l.—not a book   LAW 18
  l.'s tongue   ART 9
  l. to tell me what I cannot do   LAW 24
  without bringing his l.   LAW 29
lawyers let's kill all the l.   LAW 31
lay l. a hat and a few friends   HOME 15
layout Perfection of planned l.   BUREAUCRACY 11
layouts observing airport l.   HEAVEN 4
Lazarus Come forth, L.   FAILURE 6
laziest I'm the l. girl in town   WOMEN 54
lazy l. men trying to impress me   WORK 6
lead back on his l.   FAMILY 3
  I can't see who's in the l.   SPORTS 32
  l. a horticulture   WOMEN 52
  ounce of l. in it   ENGLAND 45
leading have a l. lady   CINEMA 18
  than l. ladies   ACTORS 25
leaf Falls with the l.   DRINK 26
leafy l. Kensington   COUNTRY 17
leak you l.   SECRECY 7
leaks l. always take place   SECURITY 3
leap milk's l.   FOOD 21
leaping l.-before-you-look   LANGUAGES 9
leaps It moves in mighty l.   MEDICINE 3
learn don't want to l.   EDUCATION 34
learned all you have ever l.   EDUCATION 5
  going to a l. conference   LOVE 40
  l. as much from Cézanne   SONGS 8
  l. in seven years   GENERATION GAP 12
  Quote L.   JUDGES 10
lease Imagine signing a l. together   MARRIAGE 64
least man who promises l.   POLITICS 10
leather dress up in chamois l.   HAPPINESS 10
  in their l. shoes   DRESS 18
leave just who would have to l.   LAW 30
  l. off tobacco   SMOKING 5
  L. out the cherry   DRINK 48

leaves man who l. the room   POLITICAL PARTIES 4
  shoots and l.   TITLES 8
  Words are like l.   WORDS 27
leaving by l. it   PEOPLE 2
lecture tire of a l.   EDUCATION 22
leeks cabbages and l.   CENSORSHIP 12
left l. all my money   DEATH 14
  shelves of them l.   HONOURS 6
leftovers nothing but l.   COOKERY 20
leg anthologist lifts his l.   QUOTATIONS 1
  broken my bloody l.   CRICKET 1
  leave my second l.   ARMED FORCES 17
  which does not resemble a l.   TECHNOLOGY 1
  would break its l.   FACES 4
legacy l. from a rich relative   POLITICS 64
legal l. writing is one of those   LAW 15
  some l. experience   FAMILY 22
legality taint of l.   LAW 17
legalizing l. petty larceny   RELIGION 31
legend Being a l.   FAME 6
  l. in his own lunchtime   FAME 9
  She's not a l.   FAME 5
legibility dawn of l.   HANDWRITING 3
legible is to be l.   ARGUMENT 14
legion L. of Honour has been conferred
     HONOURS 10
  Ravel refuses the L. of Honour   MUSICIANS 13
legitimate L. AT LAST   TELEGRAMS 9
legs born with your l. apart   SEX 64
  chop off her l. and read the rings   MARRIAGE 82
  not for your bad l.   BODY 16
  nothing to do with frog's l.   FOOD 34
  planks in my l.   TRANSPORT 29
  recuvver the use of his l.   LETTERS 7
  see my l.   BODY 13
  took off his l.   ARMED FORCES 16
  two l. bad   ANIMALS 33
  uglier a man's l. are   GOLF 11
  walking on his hinder l.   WOMEN 34
Leighton Buzzard to come from L.   TRAVEL 23
leisure At l. married   MARRIAGE 39
  elderly persons with l.   WORK 19
  That is what l. means   WORK 4
lemon in the squeezing of a l.   TIME 8
lemonade I'll take a l.   FOOD 51
lend not well enough to l. to   FRIENDS 4
length exactly the same l.   AUTOBIOGRAPHY 9
lent In L. she ate onion soup   DIETS 1
Leonardo left at the L.   HOSPITALITY 3
Léonie Weep not for little L.   LANGUAGES 13
lepers Shakepeare to the l.   ACTORS 11
lesbian l. mud-wrestling   DESCRIPTION 31
  politest l.   BEHAVIOUR 1
lesbians dealt with l.   CINEMA 9
  throw me to the l.   SEX 87

life (*cont.*):

malevolent l. of their own	TECHNOLOGY 13
matter of l. and death	FOOTBALL 25
My l. was simply hellish	SATISFACTION 14
new terror to l.	INSULTS 42
no quality of l.	COUNTRIES 7
Not too much of l.	LIFE 13
on a l.-support machine	APPEARANCE 6
précis of l.	WORDS 12
read the l.	BIOGRAPHY 10
real l. escapes	BIOGRAPHY 12
sech is l.	LIFE 8
some problems with my l.	LIFE 15
stretch your l. out	MEDICINE 20
think there's intelligent l.	UNIVERSE 13
third of my l.	MIDDLE AGE 2
tired of l.	TOWNS 15
University of L.	EDUCATION 8
What a queer thing L. is	LIFE 19
write *A L.*	AUTOBIOGRAPHY 13
your money *or* your l.	WOMEN 5
life belt deep end without a l.	TAXES 1
lifelong l. romance	LOVE 48
lifetime knowledge of a l.	ART 37
l. of happiness	HAPPINESS 12
lift can't even l. them	GOVERNMENT 32
lifting do the heavy l.	AMERICA 29
light charging like the L. Brigade	FOOD 75
dusk with a l. behind	WOMEN 22
l. at the end of the tunnel	GAMBLING 2
l. of God was with him	TRANSPORT 15
speed was faster than l.	SCIENCE 8
travel l.	BODY 18
lighten l. a room	PEOPLE 2
lighthouse sitivation at the l.	WORK 13
lightly take stupid questions l.	WORDS 34
lightning illuminated by flashes of l.	WRITERS 43
not struck by l.	MARRIAGE 126
lights all-the-l.-on man	PRIDE 4
fool when l. are low	WOMEN 30
she likes l. and commotion	SOCIETY 9
switch off the l.	NEWSPAPERS 5
like finding a sickness you l.	HEALTH 7
I didn't l. the play	THEATRE 33
I l. America	AMERICA 10
l. it twice as much	THEATRE 58
made me l. him less	MARRIAGE 37
man you don't l.	DRINK 58
of his friends l. him	FRIENDS 17
only thing I didn't l.	THEATRE 35
liked always l. Americans	AMERICA 8
likely A mighty l. speech	MARRIAGE 63
Walk! Not bloody l.	TRANSPORT 34
Lillabullero bars of L.	ARGUMENT 21
limbo l. which divides	DRINK 3

limbs Yours are the l.	APPEARANCE 15
limelight backing into the l.	PEOPLE 8
Limerick L. gained a reputation	WEATHER 14
limericks l. stopped	POETRY 2
limes two gin-and-l.	FOOD 55
limousine One perfect l.	TRANSPORT 28
Lincoln I could be another L.	INTELLIGENCE 5
line along the l.	BUREAUCRACY 12
l. I take	PEOPLE 29
stopped at l. two	POETRY 2
lines come down between the l.	WIT 22
knew these l. backwards	ACTING 8
l. having similar sounds	POETRY 15
on their own l.	CHARACTER 2
original l. of the show	THEATRE 28
lingering Something l.	PUNISHMENT 7
linoleum shoot me through l.	FILM STARS 2
lion achieve a l. by hearsay	DESCRIPTION 20
l. and the calf	ANIMALS 1
l. in a den	FRIENDS 18
lionized spoilt by being l.	HUMAN RACE 11
lip Stiff upper l.	ENGLAND 12
lips Lombard's l.	ACTORS 15
move their l.	WRITING 14
put my l. to it	DRINK 19
lipstick too much l.	MEN AND WOMEN 34
liquor bumper of good l.	DRINK 55
don't drink l.	DRINK 36
drank our l. straight	DRINK 4
l. Is quicker	DRINK 43
L. talks mighty loud	DRINK 30
Lord above made l.	DRINK 35
lira like the Italian l.	SCIENCE 1
lisp L.: call a spade	SPEECHES 6
lisped l. in numbers	CHILDREN 29
list I've got a little l.	PUNISHMENT 6
listen people don't l.	CONVERSATION 30
women who l. to it	MUSIC 21
you wish him to l.	BORES 2
listened l. at the door	SECRECY 1
listener was a good l.	CONVERSATION 23
listening ain't l.	ACTORS 20
listens l. to both sides	ARGUMENT 12
lit Fleet's l. up	DRINK 63
literal home of the l.	AMERICA 28
ignorant and l.-minded	WOMEN 47
literary British l. critics	CRITICS 15
draw well with l. men	WRITERS 3
head of the l. profession	PRAISE 2
l. censorship	CENSORSHIP 17
l. gift is a mere accident	LITERATURE 3
l. man—*with* a wooden leg	LITERATURE 14
Of all the l. scenes	POETRY 21
those l. cooks	QUOTATIONS 14

literate If, with the l., I am impelled
LITERATURE 29

literature failed in l.
CRITICS 9

great Cham of l.
PEOPLE 35

He knew everything about l.
LITERATURE 21

history to produce a little l.
LITERATURE 22

ideas of their own about l.
PUBLISHING 5

life had been ruined by l.
LITERATURE 7

l. is not read
JOURNALISM 24

L.'s always a good card to play
LITERATURE 6

locks of l.
CRITICS 30

litigant l. drawn to the United States
LAW 4

littered come down and l.
ARCHITECTURE 13

little I ask very l.
SATISFACTION 6

l. local difficulties
POLITICS 45

Thank heaven for l. girls
WOMEN 38

though she be but l.
WOMEN 56

very l. one
CHILDREN 25

live didn't l. there all the time
POLITICIANS 17

gonna l. this long
OLD AGE 6

l. in *Who's Who*
FAME 2

l. to be over ninety
OLD AGE 1

l. well on nothing a year
POVERTY 21

never to l.
AMERICA 19

you have to l. with rich people
WEALTH 23

You might as well l.
DEATH 54

lived where Gettysburg l.
READING 4

liver ate his l.
FOOD 29

l. is on the right
MEDICINE 22

l.-wing of a fowl
HONOURS 8

living books about l. men
BIOGRAPHY 7

But who calls dat l.
OLD AGE 19

Dogs who earn their l.
DOGS 2

had to write for a l.
WRITING 9

I *love* l.
LIFE 15

Lady Disdain, are you yet l.
INSULTS 35

l. for one's diary
DIARIES 1

work for a l.
ACTING 22

Lizzie Borden L. took an axe
MURDER 1

llama female l.
DESCRIPTION 9

Lloyd George L. did not seem to care
PRIME MINISTERS 4

loaded I practise when I'm l.
MUSICIANS 14

loafing organized l.
CRICKET 16

loathsome l. thing
GARDENS 12

lobster l. to attendant shrimps
ROYALTY 52

small l.
FOOD 54

world is your l.
SUCCESS 12

local little l. difficulties
POLITICS 45

lock key still in the l.
SEX 7

locks louse in the l.
CRITICS 30

lodging count l. houses
EDUCATION 3

lodgings pent up in a frowzy l.
POVERTY 19

log hut piano gets into a l.
MUSIC 17

logic L. and taxation
TAXES 5

[L.] is neither
ARGUMENT 11

Professor of L.
PHILOSOPHY 1

logical l. positivists
LOVE 2

Well, that's l.
PHILOSOPHY 7

logo l. twice the size
ADVERTISING 14

London in L. only is a trade
POETRY 9

L. at night
CRIME 8

L. Transport Diesel-engined
TRANSPORT 9

tired of L.
TOWNS 15

wear brown in L.
COLOURS 3

lonely People who are l.
WORK 11

troubled with her l. life
MARRIAGE 95

long As l. as I could walk
TRANSPORT 37

as the dey was l.
SEX 62

But it's so l.
THEATRE 12

gonna live this l.
OLD AGE 6

It often lasts too l.
LIFE 13

Like German opera, too l.
WAR 26

l., long time
BROADCASTING 2

l. as the real thing
THEATRE 13

longevity attribute my l.
OLD AGE 13

longing focus of l.
RELIGION 44

longitude l. with no platitude
LANGUAGE 4

look I never l. up
TRAVEL 2

l. another
BODY 24

l. at me that way
MORALITY 9

l. like the second week
APPEARANCE 19

looked better to be l. over
SATISFACTION 18

looking she was l. all the time
SEX 85

looking-glass cracked l.
ART 17

looks One of those l.
MARRIAGE 43

she needs good l.
MIDDLE AGE 17

looney-bin janitor to the l.
MEDICINE 36

loop l. on a commonplace
WIT 22

loose one thing to do with l. change
MONEY 20

lord L. above made liquor
DRINK 35

L. designed the Universe
UNIVERSE 11

L. says
DEBT 4

representation of Our L.
ART 3

to a point, L. Copper
JOURNALISM 21

lords it is the L. debating
ROYALTY 17

only a wit among L.
INSULTS 21

sleeps with the L.
ROYALTY 6

to be said for the L.
ARISTOCRACY 10

lordships good enough for their l.
POLITICS 4

Los Angeles Versailles of L.
HOLLYWOOD 16

lose l. no time
READING 6

l. one parent
FAMILY 49

l. one's mind
FOOLISHNESS 12

l. them
FRIENDS 3

way of ending a war is to l.
WAR 21

loser l.'s mentality
SUCCESS 4

loss sense of her l.
DEATH 24

stress of financial l.
BUSINESS 1

mouse except that damned M.   CHOICE 7
    invention of a m.   FAME 11
    rich m. hair   APPEARANCE 8
moustache bishop with a m.   PROGRESS 1
    chap with a small m.   DESCRIPTION 35
    man who *didn't* wax his m.   MEN AND WOMEN 23
moustaches men with waxed moustaches
    APPEARANCE 1
mouth I was just whispering in her m.   VIRTUE 12
    keep your m. shut   STUPIDITY 4
    m. you was born with   LANGUAGES 7
    silver foot in his m.   PRESIDENTS 15
    smacked in the m.   BOXING 10
    whose m. they've been in   WORDS 29
    z is keeping your m. shut   LIFESTYLE 3
move high altar on the m.   DESCRIPTION 7
    I daren't m.   CRICKET 1
moves stuff that m. is soup   TRAVEL 25
movie make a m. out of   BOOKS 10
    m. executive   INSULTS 15
    m. I want to make   FILM PRODUCERS 11
    m. so good   FILM 3
    wanted to be m. stars   FILM STARS 14
movies Life in the m.   CINEMA 20
    m. are the only court   CINEMA 6
    M. should have   CINEMA 8
    not to write for the m.   BIBLE 3
moving first of many, many m. days   RELIGION 30
    often m. in opposite directions   MARRIAGE 115
Mozart M. was my age   SUCCESS 14
    Some cry up Haydn, some M.   MUSICIANS 10
MP Being an M. feeds your vanity   POLITICS 57
    M. is the sort of job   POLITICS 1
MPs dull M. in close proximity   POLITICS 30
    more M. called John   NAMES 16
    When in that House M. divide   POLITICS 31
much Didn't do m.   PRESIDENTS 7
    guessing so much and so m.   WOMEN 11
    isn't as m. of this around   SEX 24
    seem m. for them to be   HUMAN RACE 1
muddle beginning, a m.   LITERATURE 23
muddy m. horsepond   MARRIAGE 93
muffin well-buttered m.   FOOD 54
mug heavenly m.   WIT 9
mulct m. the whole country   WEALTH 18
multiplication M. is vexation   SCIENCE 2
multipurpose master of the m. metaphor
    POLITICIANS 4
mum 'M.'s the word'   ADVERTISING 5
    They fuck you up, your m. and dad   PARENTS 12
Mumbo combine M. with Jumbo   RELIGION 11
mummy make one's m. just as nice   ART 36
murder brought back m. into the home
    MURDER 6
    I met M. on the way   MURDER 12

m. a tiger   ANIMALS 39
M. is a serious business   MURDER 7
m. often   MARRIAGE 73
M. was one thing   THEATRE 32
say 'm. is wrong'   MURDER 2
murdered m. reputations   GOSSIP 2
murderer common m.   COOKERY 17
    m. for a fancy prose style   MURDER 10
murderers mass m.   ART 16
    upset some m.   MURDER 2
murdering executed for m. his publisher
    PUBLISHING 2
Murdoch wrapped in a M. newspaper
    NEWSPAPERS 26
museum shelf of an anatomical m.   WORDS 18
mushroom too short to stuff a m.   TIME 6
music all his m. accepts it   MUSICIANS 13
    All m. is folk music   MUSIC 2
    all the better for m.   MUSICIANS 12
    Appreciation of M.   CRITICS 25
    But the m. that excels   MONEY 9
    Classic m. is th'kind   MUSIC 24
    good m. and bad preaching   RELIGION 17
    how potent cheap m. is   MUSIC 10
    I don't like my m.   MUSIC 33
    I hate m.   MUSIC 15
    It'll be good Jewish m.   MUSIC 28
    love best about m.   MUSIC 21
    may not like m.   ENGLAND 3
    measured malice of m.   MUSIC 29
    m. and football   LITERATURE 35
    m. had finished   DANCE 8
    M. helps not the toothache   MUSIC 23
    m. is the brandy of the damned   MUSIC 48
    M. makes you feel a feeling   WORDS 17
    m. of our own opinions   LAW 32
    m. one must hear several times   MUSIC 42
    m. was more important than sex   SEX 56
    play American m.   COUNTRIES 9
    plays good m.   CONVERSATION 30
    potent m. can be   MUSIC 57
    reasonable good ear in m.   MUSIC 47
    What m. is more enchanting   YOUTH 8
    with its own verbal m.   MUSIC 49
musical disclosing m. secrets   MUSICIANS 11
    M. people are so absurdly unreasonable
    MUSIC 56
    not unduly m.   MARRIAGE 46
music-hall m. singer attends a series   MUSIC 19
musicologist m. is a man who   MUSICIANS 5
mustard Pass the m.   HUMOUR 17
mutton make them into m.-pies   COOKERY 5
    what m. tastes like   WRITERS 24
mutual m. knowledge   FRIENDS 16
my M. arse   COMEDY 35

my-lorded m. him SNOBBERY 13
myopia all we got was Dev's m. IRELAND 4
myself He reminds me of m. SELF-KNOWLEDGE 7
mystery hissed my m. lectures WIT 43
wrap it up in m. MEDICINE 34

nailing n. his colours CERTAINTY 12
nails have our n. done SOCIETY 7
relatively clean finger n. LAW 25
naive n. domestic Burgundy WINE 13
naïve both a little n. FOOLISHNESS 8
naked I had never seen a n. woman WOMEN 64
n. and not be upstaged BODY 35
n. women TRAVEL 27
name alien, distasteful n. NAMES 14
colonies in your wife's n. WAR 14
halfway through her n. NAMES 3
has got a bad n. ARGUMENT 15
I don't wish to sign my n. LETTERS 15
If my n. had been Edmund NAMES 17
if my n. occurs AUTOBIOGRAPHY 1
I write my n. BOOKS 12
my n. in such large letters PRIDE 9
n. is Bond NAMES 21
n. is neither one thing NAMES 7
n. is not in the obits DEATH 18
n. *not* suggest COUNTRIES 2
n. we give the people DEMOCRACY 7
remember your n. NAMES 27
Under an assumed n. GAMBLING 6
named n. a country FILM 3
names American n. as Cathcart NAMES 14
n. of all these particles SCIENCE 15
new n. NAMES 5
Napoleon Jesus Christ and N. PRIME MINISTERS 22
N.'s armies ARMED FORCES 28
Napoleons worship the Caesars and N. POWER 4
narcissistic defining 'n.' WORDS 36
narcotic classic is a synonym for n. LITERATURE 1
narrow n. waist MIDDLE AGE 6
notions should be so n. CLERGY 7
nasty n., expensive MEDICINE 34
n. as himself HOPE 11
Something n. in the woodshed MISTAKES 14
when we turn n. CHARACTER 7
Natchez young belle of old N. WOMEN 46
nation let alone a n. HUMOUR 7
Our N. stands for ENGLAND 6
top n. HISTORY 9
national N. Debt DEBT 8
nations n. behave wisely HISTORY 6
Other n. use force ENGLAND 42
native Esperanto like a n. LANGUAGES 18

natural her colour is n. SOCIETY 19
I do it more n. FOOLISHNESS 13
n. animosity ACTORS 4
On the stage he was n. ACTORS 21
twice as n. LIFE 5
nature missing in N. is a pencil WRITING 3
n. has anticipated me THEATRE 22
N. has no cure POLITICS 64
N. is creeping up ART 38
N.'s way of telling you DEATH 6
phenomenon of n. FILM STARS 9
position in n. HUMAN RACE 6
seeing n. as cuddlesome NATURE 5
stuff that n. replaces it with NATURE 8
'Tes the hand of N. NATURE 1
natures terribly weak n. CHARACTER 19
naughty He's a very n. boy! GOD 18
Oh wasn't it n. of Smudges SPORTS 5
Navaho than Basque or N. LANGUAGES 3
naval n. tradition ARMED FORCES 5
navy joined the N. ARMED FORCES 3
n. blue of India COLOURS 8
No n., I suppose SCIENCE 11
of the Queen's N. ARMED FORCES 12
part played by the Irish N. ARMED FORCES 4
Ruler of the Queen's N. LAW 10
Nazi join the N. Party POLITICAL PARTIES 3
Neanderthal N. A glowering thug MEN 10
near When I'm not n. the girl I love LOVE 24
necessarily It ain't n. so BIBLE 5
necessity nasty old invention—N. POVERTY 7
n. invented HOME 8
neck break his bloody n. WRITERS 46
why I should break my n. SPORTS 2
need n. a bigger boat TRANSPORT 4
whenever we n. them DEMOCRACY 7
needle n. in a haystack WORDS 6
neglect die of n. IDEAS 8
perfectly understandable n. MEN AND WOMEN 29
Negro N. could never *hope* PREJUDICE 1
one drop of N. blood PREJUDICE 8
Negroes culture of the N. MUSIC 38
neigh people expect me to n. ROYALTY 2
neighbour Our Good N. TITLES 3
neighbourhood if you only lived in a better n.
MARRIAGE 131
neighbours N. you annoy together
MARRIAGE 116
neither N. am I BOOKS 3
Nell death of Little N. CRITICS 37
Little N. and Lady Macbeth PEOPLE 43
nephews erring n. FAMILY 54
Nero New Jersey N. WRITERS 12

peace deep p. of the double-bed — MARRIAGE 28
democracy and p. — COUNTRIES 46
essentially a man of p. — ARMED FORCES 33
good war, or a bad p. — WAR 11
like the p. of God — POETS 8
Now she's at p. — MARRIAGE 53
p. of mind — HOPE 3
peaceful p. solution — CHARACTER 1
peacock mornin' till night like a p.
— MEN AND WOMEN 37
pearls having a string of p. — FAME 15
P. at Random Strung — POETRY 8
P. before swine — INSULTS 28
pears no need for Peter P. — MUSICIANS 2
peasant *For* Pheasant *read* P. — MISTAKES 23
peccavi P.—I have Sindh — WAR 32
pecker I want his p. in my pocket — POWER 5
peculiar Funny-p. — HUMOUR 19
pedagogue Ev'ry p. — EDUCATION 15
pedantry smells of p. — BOOKS 2
pedestal Mommy on a p. — FAMILY 30
place my wife under a p. — MARRIAGE 2
pedestrian have you been a p. — TRANSPORT 37
peel p. me a grape — FOOD 80
plums and orange p. — QUOTATIONS 17
stuff you had to p. — SEX 33
peerage study the P. — ENGLAND 44
When I want a p. — WEALTH 17
peers do not create p. — GOVERNMENT 8
House of P. — GOVERNMENT 13
peke supply of books, and a P. — LIFESTYLE 7
pelican wondrous bird is the p. — BIRDS 7
pellet p. with the poison — WIT 26
pen every stroke of the p. — HANDWRITING 7
pleasure with his p. — SECURITY 1
prevents his holding a p. — LETTERS 7
penchant p. for something romantic
— LITERATURE 32
pencil I was left with a p. — WRITING 9
missing in Nature is a p. — WRITING 3
penetrate into which we cannot p. — SCIENCE 10
penis non compos p. — CRITICS 18
You're King Kong's p. — SEX 10
pension P. Pay given to a state — TRUST 8
pentagon P., that immense monument
— BUREAUCRACY 5
pentameter 'Twas his rhythm—Iambic P.
— POETRY 1
people betting on p. — BETTING 2
bludgeoning of the p. — DEMOCRACY 17
half p. and half bicycles — TRANSPORT 24
Let my p. go — CRITICS 24
noise, my dear! And the p. — WAR 1
opposite of p. — ACTORS 28
p. are only human — HUMAN RACE 1

P. he don't like — HUMAN RACE 10
p. is first what it eats — ENGLAND 9
p. know what they want — DEMOCRACY 10
p. standing in corners — TELEVISION 3
p. who do things — SUCCESS 18
protect the p. from the press — NEWSPAPERS 33
supports the p. — SCOTLAND 6
peppered Shepherd's pie p. — FOOD 71
perennials P. are the ones — GARDENS 14
perfect everyone has p. teeth — APPEARANCE 17
It's not p. — PAST 4
None of us are p. — HUMILITY 5
Well, nobody's p. — MARRIAGE 130
perfection P. of planned layout — BUREAUCRACY 11
very pink of p. — SOCIETY 10
perform p. in a role hundreds of times
— THEATRE 43
performance ELSIE FERGUSON'S P. — TELEGRAMS 24
so many years outlive p. — SEX 76
takes away the p. — DRINK 52
performances some of my best p. — SONGS 6
performed p. for twelve presidents — PRESIDENTS 8
performing faint aroma of p. seals — LOVE 26
thing wrong with p. — ACTING 21
Peron Eva P. as either a saint — PEOPLE 23
perpendicular out of the p. — HANDWRITING 5
p. expression — DANCE 14
perpetual p. middle age — MIDDLE AGE 10
P. sunset — TIME 12
Perrier P. or Malvern water — CHOICE 2
persecuted generally p. when living — OLD AGE 16
persecuting p. civil servants — CIVIL SERVANTS 2
persistence p. of public officials — BUREAUCRACY 9
person I am a most superior p. — PEOPLE 3
not to be the kind of p. — CHARACTER 3
one p. at a time — GOSSIP 3
p. . . . can develop a cold — SICKNESS 13
p. . . . can develop a cough — SICKNESS 12
p. you and I took me for — MARRIAGE 30
personality From 35 to 55, good p.
— MIDDLE AGE 17
no more p. than a paper cup — TOWNS 7
where p. is concerned — AMERICA 4
perspiration ninety-nine percent p.
— INTELLIGENCE 4
perspire Gladstone may p. — PRIME MINISTERS 10
perspiring City of p. dreams — TOWNS 21
persuasion of the Violet p. — YOUTH 3
Peru young man from P. — POETRY 2
pessimist what a p. is — HOPE 11
pet p. is a cow — ANIMALS 9
petal p. down the Grand Canyon — POETRY 16
Peter Pan wholly in P. ever since — PEOPLE 38
pews p. and steeples — HYPOCRISY 3
phagocytes stimulate the p. — MEDICINE 31

piss pitcher of warm p. — PRESIDENTS 6
  pour p. out of a boot — STUPIDITY 2
  wouldn't p. in his ear — ENEMIES 1
pissed you p. in our soup — TRUST 1
pissing inside the tent p. out — POWER 6
  like p. down your leg — SPEECHES 9
pistol Is that a p. in your pocket — MEN AND WOMEN 58
  p. misses fire — ARGUMENT 7
pit many-headed monster of the p. — THEATRE 38
pitchfork thrown on her with a p. — DRESS 20
pith p. is in the postscript — LETTERS 9
Pitt P. is to Addington — PRIME MINISTERS 9
Pittsburgh guy I knew in P. — MEN AND WOMEN 32
pity it was a p. to get up — WEATHER 15
pix Sticks nix hick p. — NEWSPAPERS 2
pizza stopped with the p. oven — SCIENCE 7
place good p. to have them — BEHAVIOUR 36
  know your p. — CLASS 21
  our only dry p. — WEATHER 14
  to keep in the same p. — PROGRESS 3
place mats coming home with Rembrandt p. — SOCIETY 20
places been things and seen p. — VIRTUE 21
  friends in both p. — HEAVEN 6
plagiarism gets in the way of their p. — MUSIC 13
  is p. — HOLLYWOOD 17
  steal from one author, it's p. — WRITING 16
plagiarist No p. can excuse the wrong — WRITING 8
plain I was very p. — APPEARANCE 8
  need of the p. — BEHAVIOUR 34
  'p.' cooking — COOKERY 12
  p. in dress — WOMEN 43
  P. women he regarded — WOMEN 16
plan by his p. of attack — ARMED FORCES 26
  change my p. — FASHION 6
  I have a cunning p. — COMEDY 27
planet If this p. is a sample — UNIVERSE 10
planets other p. be any different — UNIVERSE 13
planks p. in my legs — TRANSPORT 29
plants talking to p. — CONVERSATION 7
plashy through the p. fen — LANGUAGE 10
plastics He abhorred p. — SATISFACTION 17
platinum bullets made of p. — ANIMALS 5
platitude effect as a good p. — WORDS 38
  longitude with no p. — LANGUAGE 4
  stroke a p. until it purrs — NEWSPAPERS 18
platitudes p. and bayonets — SPEECHES 16
  sea of p. — CONVERSATION 18
Plato attachment à la P. — ART 11
  footnotes to P. — PHILOSOPHY 8
plausibility dreadful p. — GOVERNMENT 23
play bad as the p. was — ACTORS 27
  House Beautiful is p. lousy — THEATRE 36
  I didn't like the p. — THEATRE 33

know what to say about a p. — THEATRE 46
not the way I p. it — GAMBLING 4
p. Ercles rarely — ACTING 30
p. has been produced only twice — THEATRE 23
p. is full — THEATRE 27
p. it — GOLF 7
p. was a great success — THEATRE 56
p. wot I wrote — THEATRE 11
prick that can p. — MUSIC 14
read your p. — CRITICS 31
(the professor) can p. — EDUCATION 28
this p. the way you wrote it — THEATRE 16
Wimpole Street was the p. — THEATRE 35
witty prologue to a very dull p. — MARRIAGE 36
written a damned p. — THEATRE 42
y is p. — LIFESTYLE 3
playboy read *P.* magazine — SPEECHES 5
played always p. the game — POLITICIANS 25
  especially when it's p. — MUSIC 15
  p. the King — ACTORS 16
players don't drop p. — FOOTBALL 24
  for 22 p. — FOOTBALL 2
  p. who hate your guts — BASEBALL 12
playground laid to adventure p. — GARDENS 4
  three times round the p. — ACTING 14
playhouse Paper Mill P. — DESCRIPTION 28
playing P. around — CHARACTER 13
  p. in the other room — CHARACTER 3
  p. like Tarzan — GOLF 9
  terribly hard at p. — EDUCATION 27
  where it's p. — FILM 9
plays best critic of my p. — CRITICS 36
  never criticized your p. — CRITICS 36
  never much enjoyed going to p. — THEATRE 53
  p. I would expect a grocer — WRITERS 4
  Shaw's p. are the price — THEATRE 2
playschool pretend they are in p. — MIDDLE AGE 8
plaything no book—it's a p. — QUOTATIONS 15
playwrights what other p. are there — THEATRE 55
please No sex, p. — COMEDY 37
pleasure greater than the p. — PUBLISHING 18
  if this is p. — HOLIDAYS 4
  It becomes a p. — MORALITY 18
  Money gives me p. — MONEY 3
  my p., business — BUSINESS 23
  never attempt as a p. — MORALITY 10
  No p. is worth — HAPPINESS 1
  of a perfect p. — HAPPINESS 18
  p. with his pen — SECURITY 1
  though on p. she was bent — WOMEN 12
pleasures paucity of human p. — SPORTS 16
pleats witty little p. — FASHION 3
plonker You p. — COMEDY 56
plonking 'p.' tone — CONVERSATION 21

skin taxidermist takes only your s.   TAXES 8
   what a white s. was   BODY 15
skinhead s. big brother   DESCRIPTION 27
skins had such white s.   CLASS 9
   sisters under their s.   WOMEN 36
skit I think you're full of s.   WIT 25
Skugg S. Lies snug   EPITAPHS 13
skulk s. in broad daylight   PEOPLE 19
skunks I never sidestep s.   INSULTS 11
sky s. falls on my head   FILM PRODUCERS 11
slab Beneath this s.   EPITAPHS 20
slain swain getting s.   CINEMA 4
slam Don't s. the lid   MEDICINE 37
   s. the door in the face of age   OLD AGE 12
slamming s. Doors   CHILDREN 3
slap S. that bass   MUSIC 18
slapped s. my mother   APPEARANCE 25
slashed s.-wrist shot   FILM PRODUCERS 14
slashing damned cutting and s.   PUBLISHING 6
   s. article   JOURNALISM 20
slate thoughts upon a s.   POETS 5
slave most beautiful s.-quarters   HOLLYWOOD 8
slaves never will be s.   ENGLAND 32
   Rum to S.   AMERICA 13
   s. . . . are so cordial   FILM 11
sleep been to s. for over a year   SLEEP 11
   I love s.   SLEEP 5
   I s. easier now   MIDDLE AGE 13
   like men who s. badly   SLEEP 7
   make anyone go to s.   SLEEP 1
   she tried to s. with me   SEX 34
   s. is so deep   LIBRARIES 4
   suffer nobody to s. in it   RELIGION 2
   when you can't get to s.   LIFE 11
   won't get much s.   ANIMALS 1
sleeping s. with a queen   ROYALTY 71
sleepless S. themselves   POETS 12
sleeps Homer sometimes s.   LITERATURE 10
   s. alone at last   EPITAPHS 6
   s. with the enemy   MARRIAGE 6
   s. with the Lords   ROYALTY 6
sleeve lacy s. with a bottle of vitriol   PEOPLE 43
sleigh overtaken a s.   DESCRIPTION 32
slept forgetting you've s. with   SEX 80
   hearing that a judge had s.   JUDGES 13
   s. more than any other   GOVERNMENT 26
   s. with mice   FAME 10
   s. with your Auntie Phyllis   SEX 18
slice S. him where you like   CHARACTER 21
sliding home s. down Coldwater   WEALTH 14
slightly he was S. in *Peter Pan*   PEOPLE 38
slime doin' 'The S.'   DANCE 9
sling s. out the fish-knives   BEHAVIOUR 12
slipping career must be s.   AWARDS 2
slob You are just a fat s.   RELIGION 47

slogged s. up to Arras   ARMED FORCES 26
slopes butler's upper s.   SATISFACTION 19
Slough fall on S.   TOWNS 5
slow s. boat to China   COUNTRIES 28
   Talk s.   ACTING 36
   telling you to s. down   DEATH 6
   was s. poison   DRINK 7
slower Reading it s.   TECHNOLOGY 16
slowly angel to pass, flying s.   TIME 7
sluicing browsing and s.   FOOD 85
slum swear-word in a rustic s.   LITERATURE 2
slums intimacy of the s.   EDUCATION 43
slurp s., slurp, slurp into the barrels   MONEY 9
slush pure as the driven s.   VIRTUE 1
smacked s. in the mouth   BOXING 10
small as a s. whisky   DRINK 27
   desire s. beer   DRINK 51
   It's a s. word   TITLES 4
   Microbe is so very s.   SCIENCE 4
   pictures that got s.   FILM STARS 3
   schange me s. scheque   MONEY 5
   s. and full of holes   SMOKING 1
   s. of the back   DESCRIPTION 33
   s.-talking world   LANGUAGE 4
smaller s. fleas to bite 'em   ANIMALS 40
smallest s. room of my house   LETTERS 13
smart Don't get s. alecksy   PROGRESS 10
   versus S. Alec   CHOICE 6
smarter many who thought themselves s.   PRIME MINISTERS 3
smarty be a s.   POLITICAL PARTIES 3
smell run after a nasty s.   SPORTS 2
   s. too strong of the lamp   LITERATURE 33
smelt Are you s.   FOOD 4
smile Cambridge people rarely s.   PLACES 2
   Colman's s.   ACTORS 15
   faint fleeting s.   CHARACTER 15
   occasions for a s.   DICTIONARIES 6
   s. bathed us   DESCRIPTION 6
   s. on the face of the tiger   ANIMALS 4
   You're the s. on the Mona Lisa   MEN AND WOMEN 43
smirk serious and the s.   ART 8
smith Chuck it, S.   HYPOCRISY 3
   I have a niece called S.   SNOBBERY 11
smoke horrible Stygian s.   SMOKING 4
smoking famous s.-parlour   HOME 1
smut sex crime, it is s.   NEWSPAPERS 25
snake by a s. tenderiser   CHOICE 3
   in case I see a s.   DRINK 23
   Once bitten by a s.   TRUST 4
   S. is living yet   ANIMALS 7
   s. likes live rabbits   WRITERS 29
   s. of a poem   POETRY 4
snapper s.-up of unconsidered   CHARACTER 10

town country retreat near the t.

	MEN AND WOMEN 65
man made the t.	COUNTRY 2
studies it in t.	COUNTRY 1
toy secretary is not a t.	WORK 18
work in the t. department	JOURNALISM 7
toyshop verandah over the t.	BODY 2
trace Frost has risen without t.	SUCCESS 19
track good t. record	BIOGRAPHY 15
trade autocrat: that's my t.	ROYALTY 19
in London only is a t.	POETRY 9
isn't any T.	GOVERNMENT 16
it is His t.	GOD 27
tradesmen bow, ye t.	CLASS 17
tradition their oldest t.	AMERICA 31
traditionalist I was very much the t.	LOVE 16
traffic But the t. light was not	TRANSPORT 15
t. lights are instructions	TRANSPORT 24
tragedies two t. in life	HAPPINESS 13
with the t. of antiquity	LITERATURE 34

tragedy *Moby Dick* nearly became the t.

	THEATRE 52
most tremendous t.	ROYALTY 14
only Greek T. I know	PEOPLE 42
simply a t.	SOCIETY 21
That is their t.	MEN AND WOMEN 63
t. and therefore not worth	ROYALTY 13
tragic acted so t.	ACTING 15
tragical t.-comical-historical	ACTING 29
train biggest electric t. set	HOLLYWOOD 21
miss the t. before	TRANSPORT 7
moving t. needs	ART 29
next t. has gone	TRANSPORT 30
oncoming t.	GAMBLING 2
Runs the red electric t.	SOCIETY 4
shaves and takes a t.	TRAVEL 30
to read in the t.	DIARIES 8
t. going into a tunnel	HUMOUR 42
trained We t. hard	MANAGEMENT 2
trainers pair of t.	ARISTOCRACY 9
trains rush through the fields in t.	WOMEN 11
tram I'm a t.	TRANSPORT 16
tramp lady is a t.	BEHAVIOUR 16
tranquillity remembered in t.	HUMOUR 36

transcendental t. meditation with a punch-line

	FISHING 2

transformed t. into some sort of archangel

	SUCCESS 7
transition t. from Who's Who	RETIREMENT 1
translate It doesn't t.	WORDS 20
translated t. into Italian	LANGUAGES 26
translation Browning's t.	CRITICS 33
mistake in the t.	MORALITY 16
Perhaps we could have a t.	LANGUAGES 16
translations T. (like wives)	MARRIAGE 29

transplanted When our organs have been t.

	OLD AGE 22
transvestite t. potter won	AWARDS 6
trap t. in a trap	DANCE 11
trapped t. or shot	MEN 9
trashman t. and the policeman	INSULTS 23
travel award for t.-writing	AWARDS 7
Englishman does not t.	ENGLAND 37
never t. without	DIARIES 8
rapid and convenient t.	TRAVEL 23
real way to t.	TRANSPORT 14
ship would not t. due West	TRAVEL 3
thirty years of t. together	MARRIAGE 89
t. broadens the behind	TRAVEL 10
t. broadens the mind	TRAVEL 4
t. I'm too late	TIME 11
t. light	BODY 18
two classes of t.	TRAVEL 1
Why do the wrong people t.	TRAVEL 6
travelled which way he t.	PRIME MINISTERS 4
travelling T. Swede	COUNTRIES 10
trawler When seagulls follow a t.	JOURNALISM 8
tread t. most neatly	EPITAPHS 1
treason [T.], Sire, is a question	TRUST 13
t. to his country	TRUST 8
word t. to me means nothing	TRUST 1
treated t. me very well	UNIVERSE 6

treatment scientific t. for all diseases

	MEDICINE 31
tree barking up the wrong t.	CRITICS 10
billboard lovely as a t.	ADVERTISING 11
cut down a redwood t.	NATURE 6
sit under a t.	TRAVEL 19
when we chop a t.	NATURE 2
trees birds coughing in the t.	HOLLYWOOD 6
I think of the poor t.	NEWSPAPERS 20
naturally felled t.	BUSINESS 14
T. in the orchard	COUNTRY 5
trembles list of their names, he t.	WAR 28
trench like t. warfare	PRESIDENTS 13
triangle idea for a new t.	IDEAS 1
triangles loved in t.	WRITERS 1
trickle T.-down theory	ECONOMICS 6
tried pick the one I never t.	VIRTUE 23
trinity also is a T. man	GOD 11
hazy about the T.	RELIGION 7
trip t. through a sewer	HOLLYWOOD 14
trisexual I am t.	SEX 45
I'm a t.	SEX 19
triste jamais t.	HOPE 7
triumph t. of hope over experience	MARRIAGE 76
t. of modern science	MEDICINE 35
t. of the embalmer's art	PEOPLE 39
trivial diversion of t. men	POLITICS 52
Nothing t., I hope	SICKNESS 15

Oxford Paperback Reference

The Concise Oxford Dictionary of Quotations
Edited by Elizabeth Knowles

Based on the highly acclaimed *Oxford Dictionary of Quotations*, this
paperback edition maintains its extensive coverage of literary and
historical quotations, and contains completely up-to-date material. A
fascinating read and an essential reference tool.

The Oxford Dictionary of Humorous Quotations
Edited by Ned Sherrin

From the sharply witty to the downright hilarious, this sparkling
collection will appeal to all senses of humour.

Quotations by Subject
Edited by Susan Ratcliffe

A collection of over 7,000 quotations, arranged thematically for easy
look-up. Covers an enormous range of nearly 600 themes from 'The
Internet' to 'Parliament'.

The Concise Oxford Dictionary of Phrase and Fable
Edited by Elizabeth Knowles

Provides a wealth of fascinating and informative detail for over 10,000
phrases and allusions used in English today. Find out about anything
from the 'Trojan horse' to 'ground zero'.

OXFORD

Oxford Paperback Reference

The Concise Oxford Dictionary of English Etymology
T. F. Hoad

A wealth of information about our language and its history, this reference source provides over 17,000 entries on word origins.

'A model of its kind'

Daily Telegraph

A Dictionary of Euphemisms
R. W. Holder

This hugely entertaining collection draws together euphemisms from all aspects of life: work, sexuality, age, money, and politics.

Review of the previous edition
'This ingenious collection is not only very funny but extremely instructive too'

Iris Murdoch

The Oxford Dictionary of Slang
John Ayto

Containing over 10,000 words and phrases, this is the ideal reference for those interested in the more quirky and unofficial words used in the English language.

'hours of happy browsing for language lovers'

Observer

OXFORD

Oxford Paperback Reference

The Concise Oxford Companion to English Literature
Margaret Drabble and Jenny Stringer

Based on the best-selling *Oxford Companion to English Literature*, this is an indispensable guide to all aspects of English literature.

Review of the parent volume
'a magisterial and monumental achievement'

Literary Review

The Concise Oxford Companion to Irish Literature
Robert Welch

From the ogam alphabet developed in the 4th century to Roddy Doyle, this is a comprehensive guide to writers, works, topics, folklore, and historical and cultural events.

Review of the parent volume
'Heroic volume ... It surpasses previous exercises of similar nature in the richness of its detail and the ecumenism of its approach.'

Times Literary Supplement

A Dictionary of Shakespeare
Stanley Wells

Compiled by one of the best-known international authorities on the playwright's works, this dictionary offers up-to-date information on all aspects of Shakespeare, both in his own time and in later ages.

OXFORD